Oxford Primary French Dictionary

Editor Michael Janes
Consultants Danièle Bourdais
Sue Finnie

OXFORD
UNIVERSITY PRESS

Great Clarendon Street, Oxford OX2 6DP

Oxford University Press is a department of the University of Oxford.
It furthers the University's objective of excellence in research, scholarship,
and education by publishing worldwide in

Oxford New York

Auckland Cape Town Dar es Salaam Hong Kong Karachi
Kuala Lumpur Madrid Melbourne Mexico City Nairobi
New Delhi Shanghai Taipei Toronto

with offices in

Argentina Austria Brazil Chile Czech Republic France Greece
Guatemala Hungary Italy Japan Poland Portugal Singapore
South Korea Switzerland Thailand Turkey Ukraine Vietnam

Oxford is a registered trade mark of Oxford University Press
in the UK and in certain other countries

© Oxford University Press 2007

Database right Oxford University Press (maker)

First published 2007

This dictionary contains some words which have or are asserted to have
proprietary status as trademarks or otherwise. Their inclusion does not
imply that they have acquired for legal purposes a non-proprietary or
general significance, nor any other judgement concerning their legal
status. In cases where the editorial staff have some evidence that a word
has proprietary status this is indicated in the entry for that word by the
symbol® but no judgement concerning the legal status of such words is
made or implied thereby.

Contents

Introduction

The *Oxford Primary French Dictionary* is a completely new dictionary written for primary schoolchildren between the ages of 7 and 11.

This dictionary is much more than a basic resource for looking up translations: it also helps children to see patterns in the way French is used and structured and identify relationships between similar-looking French and English words. It provides an understanding of the basic concepts of grammar and also includes age-appropriate and interesting cultural information.

The layout is modern and clear with French picked out in green and English picked out in blue. Child-friendly example sentences and phrases illustrate common usage and constructions, and feature panels present information in a simple graphic way.

The illustrated thematic centre section of the dictionary is a further opportunity to develop key vocabulary skills with its topic-based phrases and sentences. The central verb table section provides a simple first step into using and understanding verb tenses.

The *Oxford Primary French Dictionary* makes learning another language enjoyable, fun, and easy. It is a vital and effective tool that will enable children to start using French confidently.

The publishers and editor are indebted to all the advisors, consultants, teachers, and readers who were involved in planning and compiling this dictionary. Special thanks go to Danièle Bourdais, Sue Finnie, and Isabelle Stables-Lemoine.

MJ

Get to know your dictionary

The dictionary is divided into two halves, the *French-English* side and the *English-French* side. These are separated by a picture section and verb tables in the middle.

French English

- **Where do I find the English translation of a French word?**
- Look in the *French-English* half which comes first.

English French

- **Where do I find the French translation of an English word?**
- Look in the *English-French* half towards the back of the book.

b
c
d

- **How do I find a word quickly?**
- Use the alphabet on the edge of each page to find the first letter of the word you need.

mais → maman

- Then use the guidewords highlighted on the top of the page. They are the first and last words on the page. Think of the order of letters in your word to make sure you are on the right page.

  For example, what does maison mean in English?

- Look in the *French-English* half.

- Find where m is highlighted in the alphabet on the edge of the page.

- Look at the two words at the top of a page. Find the words beginning with ma, then mai , then mais until you get to maison.

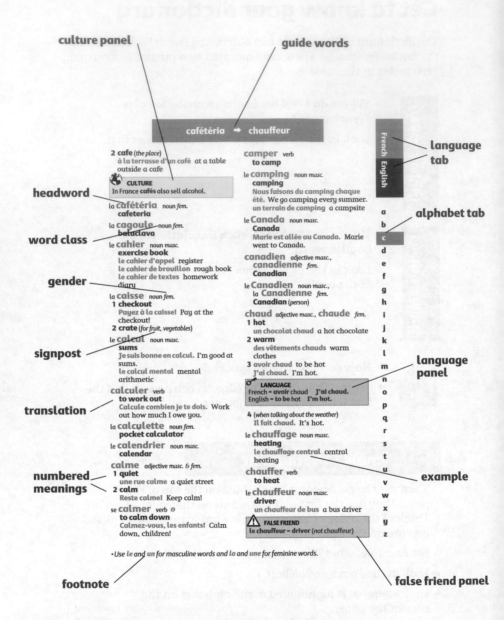

culture panel

guide words

cafétéria ➡ **chauffeur**

French English

language tab

headword

2 **cafe** (*the place*)
à la terrasse d'un café at a table outside a cafe

🌏 **CULTURE**
In France **cafés** also sell alcohol.

la **cafétéria** noun *fem.*
cafeteria

word class

la **cagoule** noun *fem.*
balaclava

gender

le **cahier** noun *masc.*
exercise book
le cahier d'appel register
le cahier de brouillon rough book
le cahier de textes homework diary

la **caisse** noun *fem.*
1 **checkout**
Payez à la caisse! Pay at the checkout!
2 **crate** (*for fruit, vegetables*)

signpost

le **calcul** noun *masc.*
sums
Je suis bonne en calcul. I'm good at sums.
le calcul mental mental arithmetic

translation

calculer verb
to work out
Calcule combien je te dois. Work out how much I owe you.

la **calculette** noun *fem.*
pocket calculator

le **calendrier** noun *masc.*
calendar

numbered meanings

calme adjective *masc. & fem.*
1 **quiet**
une rue calme a quiet street
2 **calm**
Reste calme! Keep calm!

se **calmer** verb ⊘
to calm down
Calmez-vous, les enfants! Calm down, children!

camper verb
to camp

le **camping** noun *masc.*
camping
Nous faisons du camping chaque été. We go camping every summer.
un terrain de camping a campsite

le **Canada** noun *masc.*
Canada
Marie est allée au Canada. Marie went to Canada.

canadien adjective *masc.,*
canadienne *fem.*
Canadian

le **Canadien** noun *masc.,*
la **Canadienne** *fem.*
Canadian (*person*)

chaud adjective *masc.,* **chaude** *fem.*
1 **hot**
un chocolat chaud a hot chocolate
2 **warm**
des vêtements chauds warm clothes
3 avoir chaud to be hot
J'ai chaud. I'm hot.

🔑 **LANGUAGE**
French = avoir chaud   J'ai chaud.
English = to be hot   I'm hot.

4 (*when talking about the weather*)
Il fait chaud. It's hot.

le **chauffage** noun *masc.*
heating
le chauffage central central heating

chauffer verb
to heat

le **chauffeur** noun *masc.*
driver
un chauffeur de bus a bus driver

⚠ **FALSE FRIEND**
le chauffeur = **driver** (*not chauffeur*)

alphabet tab

a
b
c
d
e
f
g
h
i
j
k
l
m
n
o
p
q
r
s
t
u
v
w
x
y
z

language panel

example

false friend panel

• Use le and un for masculine words and la and une for feminine words.

footnote

headwords

These are the words you look up. The French headwords are in green. The English headwords are in blue.

word classes

Most headwords in the dictionary are nouns, verbs, or adjectives. Sometimes a word can be more than one word class: for example, 'phone' can be a noun (He's on the phone) or a verb (Phone me tomorrow). For nouns, the dictionary gives the French word for 'the', e.g. le jardin, la maison, les spaghettis.

gender

French nouns and adjectives are either masculine (*masc.*) or feminine (*fem.*). Nouns and adjectives can be singular (just one) or plural (more than one).

translations

These are the headwords translated in English or French.

examples

Examples show you how to use the headword in a typical way.

numbered meanings

If a headword has more than one translation, numbers separate each translation.

signposts

These point you to the right translation, usually when there is more than one meaning of the word you are looking up, e.g. a 'picture' can be a *drawing*, and the French is dessin, or a picture you see (*in a book or on TV*) and then the French is image.

language panels

Vital information about how to use the headwords correctly is shown in the key language panels.

false friend panels

These are important warnings to stop you from using a French word which looks like an English one but which has a completely different meaning!

culture panels

Interesting facts about French culture are shown in these panels.

alphabet tab

To help you navigate your way through the dictionary, the letter you are on is highlighted on the alphabet strip on every page.

language tab

This shows which side of the dictionary you are on.

guide words

These help you to find the word you are looking for easily. They show you the first and last word on the page.

footnotes

These give you useful general language reminders.

Aa

a verb SEE **avoir**
1 (*in the present tense*) **has**
Aurélien a un ordinateur. Aurélien has a computer.
2 (*when used to form a past tense*)
Elle a fini ses devoirs. She has finished her homework.
3 (*when talking about somebody's age*) **is**
Il a 9 ans. He is 9 years old.

> 🔑 **LANGUAGE**
> French = **avoir** 10 ans J'ai 10 ans.
> English = to be 10 (years old) I am 10 (years old).

à preposition

> 🔑 **LANGUAGE**
> à + le = au
> à + les = aux

1 **at**
Nous sommes à l'école. We're at school.
On arrive à deux heures. We're coming at two.
2 **in**
Elle habite à Londres. She lives in London.
Il neige beaucoup au Canada. It snows a lot in Canada.
à l'hôpital in hospital
au printemps in the spring
3 **to**
Je vais à la poste. I'm going to the post office.
Nous allons à Londres. We're going to London.
Il part au Japon. He's off to Japan.
Envoie un courriel à tes parents. Send an email to your parents.
C'est facile à faire. It's easy to do.
4 (*to show that something belongs to somebody*)
C'est à moi. It's mine.
C'est à Emilie. It's Emilie's.

5 **on**
Il écrit au tableau. He's writing on the board.
aller à pied to go on foot
6 (*in the distance*) **away**
C'est à six kilomètres. It's six kilometres away.
C'est à cinq minutes d'ici. It's five minutes away from here.
7 À mardi! See you on Tuesday!
À demain! See you tomorrow!
À plus tard! See you later!

une **abeille** noun *fem.*
bee

abîmer verb
to ruin
Il abîme tous mes jouets! He's ruining all my toys!

d'**abord** adverb
first
Je vais manger d'abord. I'm going to eat first.
D'abord, il va en France, ensuite en Espagne. First, he's going to France, then Spain.

aboyer verb
to bark
Le chien aboie. The dog is barking.

un **abricot** noun *masc.*
apricot

absent adjective *masc.*,
absente *fem.*
absent

absolument adverb
absolutely

un **accent** noun *masc.*
accent
Il a un drôle d'accent! He has a funny accent!

*ⓔ means use **être** to make the past tense.*

a
b
c
d
e
f
g
h
i
j
k
l
m
n
o
p
q
r
s
t
u
v
w
x
y
z

accepter verb
to accept

un **accident** noun *masc.*
accident
un accident de voiture a car accident

d'**accord** adverb
1 (*answering 'yes'*) **all right**
Tu viens? – D'accord! Are you coming? – All right!
2 **être d'accord** to agree
Je suis d'accord avec toi. I agree with you.

accrocher verb
to hang
Je vais accrocher le tableau au mur. I'm going to hang the picture on the wall.

l'**accueil** noun *masc.*
1 **reception**
Elle travaille à l'accueil. She works at the reception desk.
2 (*on web page*) **home**
la page d'accueil the home page

accueillir verb
to welcome

acheter verb
to buy
Mes parents vont m'acheter un vélo. My parents are going to buy me a bike.
Je n'achète jamais de chips. I never buy crisps.
J'ai acheté un souvenir pour ma sœur. I bought a souvenir for my sister.

un **acteur** noun *masc.*
actor

une **activité** noun *fem.*
activity

une **actrice** noun *fem.*
actress

les **actualités** plural noun *fem.*
news

une **addition** noun *fem.*
1 (*in maths*) **sum**
faire des additions to do sums
2 (*in a restaurant*) **bill**
L'addition, s'il vous plaît! The bill, please!

additionner verb
to add up
J'ai additionné les deux nombres. I added up the two numbers.

un **adjectif** noun *masc.*
adjective

admettre verb
to admit

un or une **ado** noun *masc. & fem.*
teenager
C'est un magazine pour ados. It's a magazine for teenagers.

un **adolescent** noun *masc.*, une **adolescente** *fem.*
teenager

adorable adjective *masc. & fem.*
lovely

adorer verb
to love
Omar adore le sport. Omar loves sport.
Sophie adore jouer de la guitare. Sophie loves playing the guitar.

une **adresse** noun *fem.*
address
Écris ton adresse sur l'enveloppe. Write your address on the envelope.
Tu me donnes ton adresse électronique? Can you give me your email address?

LANGUAGE
French = adresse
English = address

un or une **adulte** noun *masc. & fem.*
grown-up, **adult**

•*Languages, nationalities, and religions do not take a capital letter in French.*

un **adverbe** noun *masc.*
adverb

un or une **adversaire** noun *masc. & fem.*
opponent

un **aéroport** noun *masc.*
airport

les **affaires** plural noun *fem.*
1 (*clothes and personal objects*) **things**
Range tes affaires! Put your things away!
J'ai oublié mes affaires de piscine. I forgot my swimming kit.
2 business
une femme d'affaires a business woman

une **affiche** noun *fem.*
poster

affreux adjective *masc.*, **affreuse** *fem.*
awful

africain adjective *masc.*, **africaine** *fem.*
African

un **Africain** noun *masc.*, une **Africaine** *fem.*
African (*person*)

l'**Afrique** noun *fem.*
Africa
l'Afrique du Nord North Africa
l'Afrique du Sud South Africa

agacer verb
to annoy
Tu m'agaces! You're getting on my nerves!

l'**âge** noun *masc.*
age
à l'âge de douze ans at twelve years of age
Quel âge as-tu? How old are you?

âgé adjective *masc.*, **âgée** *fem.*
old
les personnes âgées old people

ⓔ means use être to make the past tense.

une **agence de voyages** noun *fem.*
travel agent's

un **agenda** noun *masc.*
diary
Note la date sur ton agenda. Write the date in your diary.

⚠ **FALSE FRIEND**
un agenda = a diary (*not* an agenda)

un **agent de police** noun *masc.*, une **agente de police** *fem.*
police officer

agiter verb
1 to shake
Agite la bouteille. Shake the bottle.
2 to wave
Papy agite son mouchoir. Grandpa is waving his handkerchief.

un **agneau** noun *masc.* (plural les **agneaux**)
lamb

une **agrafe** noun *fem.*
staple

agréable adjective *masc. & fem.*
pleasant

un **agriculteur** noun *masc.*, une **agricultrice** *fem.*
farmer

ai verb SEE **avoir**
1 (*in the present tense*) **have**
J'ai un chien. I have a dog.
Je n'ai pas d'animal. I haven't got a pet.
2 (*when talking about somebody's age*) **am**
J'ai 11 ans. I am 11 years old.
3 (*when used to form a past tense*)
J'ai fini mes devoirs lundi. I finished my homework on Monday.
J'ai perdu ma clé. I've lost my key.

l'**aide** noun *fem.*
help

a
b
c
d
e
f
g
h
i
j
k
l
m
n
o
p
q
r
s
t
u
v
w
x
y
z

aider verb
to help
Tu m'aides? Can you help me?

aïe exclamation
ouch

un **aigle** noun masc.
eagle

aigre adjective masc. & fem.
sour

aigu adjective masc.
l'accent aigu the acute accent
Léa, ça s'écrit l, e accent aigu, a.
Léa is spelt l, e acute, a.

une **aiguille** noun fem.
1 needle
2 (on a clock or watch) **hand**
la grande et la petite aiguille
the big and the little hand

l'**ail** noun masc.
garlic

une **aile** noun fem.
wing

ailleurs adverb
somewhere else

aimable adjective masc. & fem.
kind, **nice**

un **aimant** noun masc.
magnet

aimer verb
1 to like
Tu aimes la musique? Do you like music?
Mon frère aime bien son prof.
My brother likes his teacher.
J'aimerais bien une glace au chocolat. I would like a chocolate ice cream.
J'aimerais bien visiter le musée.
I would like to visit the museum.

🔑 **LANGUAGE**
French = J'aimerais bien ...
English = I would like ...

2 to love
Elle aime Anthony. She loves Anthony.
3 aimer mieux to prefer
J'aime mieux rester chez moi.
I prefer to stay at home.

aîné adjective masc., **aînée** fem.
older
ma sœur aînée my older sister

l'**aîné** noun masc., l'**aînée** fem.
oldest child

l'**air** noun masc.
1 air
Sautez en l'air! Jump up in the air!
2 (of a song) **tune**
Chantez sur l'air de Frère Jacques!
Sing to the tune of Frère Jacques!
3 avoir l'air to look
Papa a l'air content. Dad looks pleased.
Maman a l'air contente. Mum looks pleased.

une **aire de jeux** noun fem.
(in the park) **playground**

ajouter verb
to add

l'**alcool** noun masc.
alcohol

l'**Algérie** noun fem.
Algeria

algérien adjective masc.,
algérienne fem.
Algerian

un **Algérien** noun masc.,
une **Algérienne** fem.
Algerian (person)

l'**alimentation** noun fem.
food
le rayon alimentation the food department

allé verb masc., **allée** fem. SEE **aller**

• The months of the year and days of the week do not take a capital letter in French.

une **allée** noun *fem.*
(*in the park*) **path**

l'**Allemagne** noun *fem.*
Germany

l'**allemand** noun *masc.*
German (*the language*)
Tu apprends l'allemand? Are you learning German?

allemand adjective *masc.*,
allemande *fem.*
German

un **Allemand** noun *masc.*,
une **Allemande** *fem.*
German (*person*)

aller verb *ø*
1 to go
Tu aimes aller à l'école? Do you like going to school?
Elle va en Espagne tous les ans. She goes to Spain every year.
Je ne vais pas à la piscine. I'm not going to the swimming pool.
2 (*used after* **être**)
Je suis allé chez Nadia. (*boy speaking*)
Je suis allée chez Nadia. (*girl speaking*) I went to Nadia's.
3 (*used with another verb in the infinitive to talk about the future*) **to be going**
On va manger du poisson ce soir. We're going to eat fish tonight.
4 (*when talking about how you feel*) **to be**
Comment allez-vous? How are you?
Je vais bien. I'm all right.
Ça va? – Ça va, merci. How are you? – Fine, thanks.
5 (*when talking about clothes etc.*) **to suit**
La jupe te va bien. The skirt suits you.

un **aller** noun *masc.*
single (ticket)
Je voudrais un aller pour Paris. Could I have a single to Paris?
un aller simple a single ticket
un aller retour a return ticket

ø means use **être** *to make the past tense.*

allergique adjective *masc. & fem.*
allergic
Je suis allergique au lait. I'm allergic to milk.

allez verb SEE **aller**
Allez tout droit! Go straight on!
Allez, viens! Come on!

allô exclamation
(*on the phone only*) **hello**

s'**allonger** verb *ø*
to lie down
Allongez-vous par terre! Lie down on the floor!

allons verb SEE **aller**
Nous allons voir un film. We're going to see a film.
Allons-y! Let's go!

allumer verb
to put on, to switch on
Allume la lumière! Put the light on!
Je peux allumer la télé? May I switch the TV on?

une **allumette** noun *fem.*
match

alors adverb
so
Alors, quelle heure est-il? So what time is it?
Et alors? So what?

les **Alpes** plural noun *fem.*
the Alps

l'**alphabet** noun *masc.*
alphabet

alphabétique adjective *masc. & fem.*
alphabetical
par ordre alphabétique in alphabetical order

une **amande** noun *fem.*
almond
la pâte d'amande marzipan

une **ambulance** noun *fem.*
ambulance

French English

a
b
c
d
e
f
g
h
i
j
k
l
m
n
o
p
q
r
s
t
u
v
w
x
y
z

améliorer verb
to improve

amener verb
to bring

amer adjective *masc.*, **amère** *fem.*
bitter

américain adjective *masc.*,
américaine *fem.*
American

un **Américain** noun *masc.*,
une **Américaine** *fem.*
American (*person*)

l'**Amérique** noun *fem.*
America
l'Amérique du Nord
North America
l'Amérique du Sud South America

un **ami** noun *masc.*, une **amie** *fem.*
friend
un petit ami a boyfriend
une petite amie a girlfriend
mon meilleur ami my best friend

amical adjective *masc.*, **amicale**
fem., **amicaux** *masc. plural*,
amicales *fem. plural*
friendly

l'**amitié** noun *fem.*
friendship

l'**amour** noun *masc.*
love

amoureux adjective *masc.*,
amoureuse *fem.*
in love
Elle est amoureuse de Tom. She's
in love with Tom.

une **ampoule** noun *fem.*
1 light bulb
2 blister

amusant adjective *masc.*,
amusante *fem.*
funny
Estelle est amusante. Estelle's
funny.

• *See the centre section for verb tables.*

s'**amuser** verb @
to have fun, **to play**
Amusez-vous bien! Have fun!

un **an** noun *masc.*
1 year
l'an dernier last year
l'an prochain next year
2 (*when saying how old somebody is*)
J'ai huit ans. I'm eight years
old., I'm eight.

🔑 **LANGUAGE**
French never leaves out the word **ans**.

3 le jour de l'an New Year's Day
le nouvel an New Year

un **ananas** noun *masc.*
pineapple

ancien adjective *masc.*,
ancienne *fem.*
1 (*before the noun*) **old**
C'est mon ancienne adresse.
That's my old address.
2 (*after the noun*) **old**
un bâtiment très ancien a very old
building

🔑 **LANGUAGE**
The first meaning of **ancien** is 'from your
past', and the second is 'made a long time
ago'.

un **âne** noun *masc.*
donkey

un **ange** noun *masc.*
angel

une **angine** noun *fem.*
throat infection

l'**anglais** noun *masc.*
English (*the language*)
Cyprien apprend l'anglais.
Cyprien is learning English.

🔑 **LANGUAGE**
French = Je parle anglais.
English = I speak English.

anglais adjective *masc.*,
anglaise *fem.*
English

un **Anglais** noun *masc.*,
une **Anglaise** *fem.*
Englishman, **Englishwoman**
les Anglais the English

> **LANGUAGE**
> **Anglais** and **Anglaise** can also mean an English boy or an girl, for example: **Il y a une Anglaise dans notre classe.** means 'There's an English girl in our class'.

l'**Angleterre** noun *fem.*
England

un **animal** noun *masc.* (plural les **animaux**)
animal
un animal de compagnie a pet

un **animateur** noun *masc.*,
une **animatrice** *fem.*
1 (*at a summer camp*) **group leader**
2 (*on a TV show*) **presenter**

animé adjective *masc.*,
animée *fem.*
1 **lively**
une rue animée a lively street
2 **un dessin animé** a cartoon

une **année** noun *fem.*
year
cette année this year
l'année dernière last year
l'année prochaine next year
l'année scolaire the school year
Bonne Année! Happy New Year!

un **anniversaire** noun *masc.*
1 **birthday**
Mon anniversaire est le cinq juin. My birthday is the fifth of June.
un cadeau d'anniversaire a birthday present
Joyeux anniversaire! Happy birthday!

2 **anniversary**
C'est l'anniversaire de mariage de mes parents. It's my parents' wedding anniversary.

> **LANGUAGE**
> **Anniversaire** comes from **an** (year) because it happens every year.

une **annonce** noun *fem.*
advert
les annonces dans le journal adverts in the newspaper

un **annuaire** noun *masc.*
phone book, **directory**

annuler verb
to cancel

un **anorak** noun *masc.*
anorak

un **antibiotique** noun *masc.*
antibiotic

antillais adjective *masc.*,
antillaise *fem.*
West Indian

un **Antillais** noun *masc.*,
une **Antillaise** *fem.*
West Indian (*person*)

les **Antilles** plural noun *fem.*
West Indies

août noun *masc.*
August
en août in August
le quinze août the fifteenth of August

apparaître verb ⊕
Un monstre venait d'apparaître. A monster had just appeared.

un **appareil** noun *masc.*
un appareil photo a camera
un appareil photo numérique a digital camera
un appareil dentaire a brace
Je porte un appareil dentaire. I wear a brace.

⊕ *means use* **être** *to make the past tense.*

7

un **appartement** noun *masc.*
flat

appartenir verb
to belong
Le chien appartient à Sophie. The dog belongs to Sophie.

un **appel** noun *masc.*
1 **phone call**
Il y a un appel pour toi. There's a call for you.
2 (*in school*) **registration**
La maîtresse fait l'appel. The teacher is taking the register.

appeler verb
to call
Maman t'appelle. Mum's calling you.

s'**appeler** verb ⊘
to be called
Comment tu t'appelles? What's your name?
Je m'appelle Pierre. My name's Pierre.
Comment ça s'appelle en français? What's this called in French?

l'**appétit** noun *masc.*
appetite
Bon appétit! Enjoy your meal!

applaudir verb
to clap
Applaudissez! Clap your hands!

apporter verb
to bring
J'apporte un gâteau pour ton anniversaire. I'm bringing a cake for your birthday.

apprendre verb
1 **to learn**
apprendre à faire quelque chose to learn to do something
J'apprends à faire du vélo. I'm learning to ride a bike.
2 **to teach**
Papa m'apprend à jouer au tennis. Dad's teaching me to play tennis.

appris verb SEE **apprendre**
J'ai appris le nom des couleurs. I learnt to say the colours.

s'**approcher** verb ⊘
to get closer
Approche-toi, un peu! Come a bit closer!

appuyer verb
to press
Appuyez ici! Press here!

après preposition, conjunction, adverb
after, **afterwards**
après cinq heures after five o'clock
Qu'est-ce que tu as fait après? What did you do afterwards?
Après avoir mangé il a dormi. After eating, he slept.

après-demain adverb
the day after tomorrow

un or une **après-midi** noun *masc. & fem.* (plural les **après-midi**)
afternoon
L'après-midi, je regarde la télé. In the afternoon, I watch TV.
à trois heures de l'après-midi at three o'clock in the afternoon
cet après-midi this afternoon
le samedi après-midi on Saturday afternoons
tous les après-midi every afternoon

une **aquarelle** noun *fem.*
watercolours (*method of painting*)

un **aquarium** noun
fish tank

l'**arabe** noun *masc.*
Arabic (*the language*)

arabe adjective *masc. & fem.*
Arab
les pays arabes the Arab countries

un or une **Arabe** noun *masc. & fem.*
Arab (*person*)

• *Use* **le** *and* **un** *for masculine words and* **la** *and* **une** *for feminine words.*

une **araignée** noun *fem.*
spider
une toile d'araignée a spider's web

un **arbitre** noun *masc.*
1 (*in football or rugby*) **referee**
2 (*in tennis or baseball*) **umpire**

un **arbre** noun *masc.*
tree
un arbre de Noël a Christmas tree

un **arc** noun *masc.*
bow
un arc et des flèches a bow and arrows

un **arc-en-ciel** noun *masc.*
rainbow

une **ardoise** noun *fem.*
slate

l'**argent** noun *masc.*
1 money
Combien as-tu d'argent de poche? How much pocket money do you get?
2 silver
un bracelet en argent a silver bracelet

une **arme** noun *fem.*
weapon

l'**armée** noun *fem.*
army

une **armoire** noun *fem.*
wardrobe

arranger verb
1 to sort out
Il a tout arrangé. He's sorted everything out.
2 to arrange
La maîtresse va arranger une visite au musée. The teacher will arrange a visit to the museum.
3 Ça m'arrange. That's OK for me.

un **arrêt** noun *masc.*
stop
l'arrêt de bus the bus stop

arrêter verb
Arrête! Stop it!
Arrête de pousser! Stop pushing!

s'**arrêter** verb ⓔ
to stop
Le bus s'arrête devant l'école. The bus stops in front of the school.

arrière adjective
back
le siège arrière the back seat

une **arrière-grand-mère** noun *fem.*
great-grandmother

un **arrière-grand-père** noun *masc.*
great-grandfather

une **arrivée** noun *fem.*
arrival
C'est l'arrivée du Tour de France. It's the finish of the Tour de France.

arriver verb ⓔ
1 to arrive
On arrive à quelle heure? What time do we arrive?
Il est arrivé en retard. He arrived late.
2 to happen
Qu'est-ce qui est arrivé à papa? What's happened to dad?
3 arriver à faire quelque chose to manage to do something
Je n'arrive pas à dormir. I can't sleep.

un **arrondissement** noun *masc.*
district

 CULTURE
Some big towns in France are divided into **arrondissements**. Paris has twenty of them.

arroser verb
to water

ⓔ *means use* être *to make the past tense.*

9

un **article** noun *masc.*
article

> 🔑 **LANGUAGE**
> In French grammar the articles are **le**, **la**, **l'**, **les**; **un**, **une**; **de**, **du**, **de la**, **d'**, **des**.

un or une **artiste** noun *masc. & fem.*
artist

as verb SEE **avoir**
1 (*in the present tense*) **have**
Tu as un animal? Do you have a pet?
2 (*when talking about somebody's age*) **are**
Quel âge as-tu? How old are you?
3 (*used to form a past tense*)
Tu as reçu mon courriel? Did you get my email?

un **as** noun *masc.*
ace
l'as de cœur the ace of hearts

un **ascenseur** noun *masc.*
lift
On prend l'ascenseur. Let's take the lift.

asiatique adjective *masc. & fem.*
Asian

un or une **Asiatique** noun *masc. & fem.*
Asian (*person*)

l'**Asie** noun *fem.*
Asia

un **aspirateur** noun *masc.*
vacuum cleaner
passer l'aspirateur to vacuum

s'**asseoir** verb ⊘
to sit down
On peut s'asseoir? Can we sit down?
Assieds-toi correctement! Sit down properly!
Asseyez-vous, les enfants! Sit down, children!

assez adverb
1 enough
Tu as assez mangé? Have you had enough to eat?
J'en ai assez! I've had enough!

2 assez de enough
Il n'a pas assez d'argent. He hasn't got enough money.

> 🔑 **LANGUAGE**
> French = **assez de** + noun
> English = **enough** + noun

3 quite
assez souvent quite often
Tes parents sont assez sympa. Your parents are quite nice.

asseyez, **asseyons** verb
SEE s'**asseoir**

assied, **assieds** verb SEE s'**asseoir**

une **assiette** noun *fem.*
plate

assis adjective *masc.*, **assise** *fem.*
sitting
Tristan est assis dans un fauteuil. Tristan is sitting in an armchair.

un **assistant** noun *masc.*, une **assistante** *fem.*
(*in a school*) **assistant**
Il est assistant de français. He's a French assistant.

l'**asthme** noun *masc.*
asthma
J'ai de l'asthme. I have asthma.

une **astuce** noun *fem.*
tip, **trick**

un **atelier** noun *masc.*
1 workshop
2 studio
3 (*an activity*) **class**
J'ai choisi l'atelier poterie. I chose the pottery class.

l'**Atlantique** noun *masc.*
Atlantic

un **atlas** noun *masc.*
atlas

• *Languages, nationalities, and religions do not take a capital letter in French.*

attacher verb
1 to tie
Elle attache ses cheveux. She ties her hair back.
2 to fasten
Attache ta ceinture! Fasten your seatbelt!

attaquer verb
to attack

attendre verb
1 to wait, **to wait for**
Attends une minute! Wait a minute!
J'attends papa. I'm waiting for dad.
2 to expect
Elle attend un bébé. She's expecting a baby.

⚠ **FALSE FRIEND**
attendre = to wait, to wait for, to expect (*not* to attend)

l'**attente** noun *fem.*
wait
une salle d'attente a waiting room

l'**attention** noun *fem.*
1 attention
Fais attention à ce que tu fais! Pay attention to what you're doing!
2 Attention! Careful!, Watch out!

attentivement adverb
Écoutez attentivement! Listen carefully!

atterrir verb
to land
L'avion atterrit à midi. The plane lands at midday.

attraper verb
to catch
Attrape la balle! Catch the ball!

au preposition SEE à

🔑 **LANGUAGE**
à + le = au

means use être to make the past tense.

On va au parc? Shall we go to the park?
au printemps in the spring

une **auberge de jeunesse** noun *fem.*
youth hostel

aucun adjective *masc.*, **aucune** *fem.*
no
Tu n'as aucun livre. You have no book.
Aucune idée! No idea!

aucun pronoun *masc.*, **aucune** *fem.*
none

au-dessous adverb
below, **underneath**
l'appartement au-dessous the flat below

au-dessous de preposition
below, **under**
les enfants au-dessous de 12 ans children under 12

au-dessus adverb
above
l'appartement au-dessus the flat above

au-dessus de preposition
above, **over**
au-dessus du tableau above the blackboard

aujourd'hui adverb
today
Aujourd'hui, c'est mardi. It's Tuesday today.

aura, aurai, auras verb
SEE avoir (avoir *in the future tense*)
J'aurai dix ans lundi. I'll be ten on Monday.
Il y aura du soleil. It'll be sunny.

au revoir exclamation
goodbye

aussi adverb
1 too
Tu viens aussi? Are you coming too?
Moi aussi! Me too!
2 (when comparing) **as**
Je suis aussi grand que toi. I'm as tall as you.

aussitôt adverb
immediately
Aussitôt dit, aussitôt fait. No sooner said than done.

l'**Australie** noun fem.
Australia

australien adjective masc.,
australienne fem.
Australian

un **Australien** noun masc.,
une **Australienne** fem.
Australian (person)

autant adverb
1 so much, so many
Ne mange pas autant de pain.
Don't eat so much bread.
Je n'ai jamais vu autant de livres.
I've never seen so many books.
2 as much, as many
J'ai autant de copains que toi.
I have as many friends as you.

un **auteur** noun masc.
author

une **auto** noun fem.
car

un **autobus** noun masc.
bus

un **autocar** noun masc.
coach

un **autocollant** noun masc.
sticker

une **auto-école** noun fem.
driving school

l'**automne** noun masc.
autumn
en automne in the autumn

une **automobile** noun fem.
car

un or une **automobiliste** noun masc. & fem.
motorist

une **autoroute** noun fem.
motorway

autour adverb, preposition
around
autour du lac around the lake

autre adjective masc. & fem.
1 other
l'autre jour the other day
une autre fois another time
Tu veux un autre bonbon? Do you want another sweet?
2 autre chose something else
On joue à autre chose? Shall we play something else?

l'**autre** pronoun masc. & fem.
1 other one
Je n'aime pas ce tee-shirt, je prends l'autre. I don't like this T-shirt, I'll have the other one.
Où sont les autres? Where are the others?
2 d'autre else
rien d'autre nothing else
quelqu'un d'autre somebody else
3 ni l'un ... ni l'autre neither of them
Je ne veux ni l'un ni l'autre. I want neither of them.

autrefois adverb
in days gone by

l'**Autriche** noun fem.
Austria

une **autruche** noun fem.
ostrich

• The months of the year and days of the week do not take a capital letter in French.

aux preposition SEE à

🔑 **LANGUAGE**
à + les = aux

Catherine habite aux États-Unis.
Catherine lives in the United States.
Il parle aux élèves. He's speaking
to the pupils.

avais, avait verb SEE **avoir** (avoir *in
the past tense*)
1 had
J'avais un chien avant. I had a dog
before.
2 il y avait there was, there were

avaler verb
to swallow

l'**avance** noun *fem.*
1 en avance early
2 à l'avance beforehand

avancer verb
to move forward

avant adverb
before
Tu habitais où avant? Where did
you live before?

avant preposition
before
avant les vacances before the
holidays
avant de commencer before we
start

avant adjective
front
le siège avant the front seat

en **avant** adverb
forward

l'**avant** noun *masc.*
front
Tu veux t'asseoir à l'avant? Do you
want to sit in the front?

un **avantage** noun *masc.*
advantage

ⓔ *means use* être *to make the past tense.*

avant-dernier adjective *masc.*,
avant-dernière *fem.*
last but one
Je suis arrivé avant-dernier. (*boy
speaking*) **Je suis arrivée
avant-dernière.** (*girl speaking*) I came
last but one.

avant-hier adverb
the day before yesterday

avec preposition
with
Tu viens avec moi? Are you coming
with me?

l'**avenir** noun *masc.*
future
À l'avenir, arrive à l'heure! In
future, arrive on time!

une **aventure** noun *fem.*
adventure

🔑 **LANGUAGE**
French = aventure
English = adventure

une **avenue** noun *fem.*
avenue

une **averse** noun *fem.*
shower

aveugle adjective *masc. & fem.*
blind

avez verb SEE **avoir**
1 (*in the present tense*) **have**
Vous avez un ordinateur? Do you
have a computer?
2 (*when used to form a past tense*)
Vous avez fini? Have you finished?

un **avion** noun *masc.*
plane
voyager en avion to travel by
plane
par avion (*on a letter*) by airmail

un **avis** noun *masc.*
opinion
à mon avis in my opinion
Luc a changé d'avis. Luc changed his mind.

un **avocat** noun *masc.*
avocado

un **avocat** noun *masc.*, une **avocate** *fem.*
lawyer

avoir verb
1 (*when used in the present tense*)
to have
J'ai un petit frère. I have a little brother.
Elle a les cheveux blonds. She has blond hair.
Nous avons une nouvelle prof. We have a new teacher.
2 (*when used to form a past tense*)
J'ai joué au foot lundi dernier. I played football last Monday.
Tu as eu des cadeaux? Did you get any presents?

Bb

le **baby-foot** noun *masc.*
table football

le or la **baby-sitter** noun *masc.* & *fem.*
babysitter

le **baby-sitting** noun *masc.*
faire du baby-sitting to babysit

le **baccalauréat** noun *masc.*
A levels

 CULTURE
Le baccalauréat is the examination that students take when they leave school. It is called **le bac** for short.

◯ **LANGUAGE**
Avoir is used with other verbs to speak about the past, for example: **j'ai joué**, **tu as eu une problem** etc. I played, you had a problem etc.

3 **to be**
Elle a de la chance. She's lucky.
Tu vas avoir peur. You'll be scared.
J'ai dix ans. I'm ten.
4 **Qu'est-ce que tu as?** What's the matter with you?
5 **il y a** there is SEE **il y a**

avons verb SEE **avoir**
1 (*in the present tense*) **have**
Nous avons un chien. We have a dog.
2 (*used to form a past tense*) **Nous avons dormi.** We slept.

avril noun *masc.*
April
en avril in April
Mon anniversaire, c'est le sept avril. My birthday's on the seventh of April.

les **bagages** plural noun *masc.*
luggage
Je vais faire mes bagages. I'm going to pack.

◯ **LANGUAGE**
French = **les bagages** is plural
English = **luggage** is singular

la **bagarre** noun *fem.*
fight

la **bague** noun *fem.*
ring
une bague en or a gold ring

• *See the centre section for verb tables.*

la baguette noun fem.
1 (*French bread*) **baguette**
2 wand
une baguette magique a magic wand
3 des baguettes (*for eating with*) chopsticks

les Bahamas plural noun fem.
les îles Bahamas the Bahamas, the Bahama Islands

se baigner verb *ê*
to go swimming
Tu veux te baigner? Do you want to go swimming?

la baignoire noun fem.
bath

bâiller verb
to yawn

le bain noun masc.
bath
prendre un bain to have a bath
un bain moussant a bubble bath

le baiser noun masc.
kiss

baisser verb
1 to put down
Baisse ta main, Jamal. Put your hand down, Jamal.
2 to turn down
Tu peux baisser un peu la télé? Can you turn the TV down a bit?
3 to pull down
Baisse les stores! Pull down the blinds!

se balader verb *ê*
to go for a walk

le baladeur noun masc.
personal stereo
le baladeur MP3 MP3 player

le balai noun masc.
broom

la balançoire noun fem.
swing

balayer verb
to sweep

le balcon noun masc.
balcony

la baleine noun fem.
whale

la balle noun fem.
(*for tennis, ping-pong, or golf*) **ball**

le ballon noun masc.
1 (*for football, rugby, or basketball*) **ball**
Ils jouent au ballon. They're playing with a ball.
un ballon de football a football
2 balloon
Pour la fête, il y a des ballons bleus, blancs et rouges. For the party there are blue, white, and red balloons.

la banane noun fem.
banana

le banc noun masc.
bench

la bande noun fem.
group
une bande d'amis a group of friends

la bande dessinée noun fem.
comic
Mon père adore les bandes dessinées. My father loves comics.

CULTURE
Comics are a lot more popular in France than in Britain. Grown-ups often read them too.

la banlieue noun fem.
suburbs
J'habite en banlieue. I live in the suburbs.

ê means use être to make the past tense.

French English

a
b
c
d
e
f
g
h
i
j
k
l
m
n
o
p
q
r
s
t
u
v
w
x
y
z

a
b
c
d
e
f
g
h
i
j
k
l
m
n
o
p
q
r
s
t
u
v
w
x
y
z

la **banque** noun *fem.*
bank

le **baptême** noun *masc.*
christening

le **bar** noun *masc.*
bar

la **Barbade** noun *fem.*
Barbados

barbadien adjective *masc.*,
barbadienne *fem.*
Barbadian

un **Barbadien** noun *masc.*,
une **Barbadienne** *fem.*
Barbadian (*person*)

la **barbe** noun *fem.*
beard

la **barbe à papa** noun *fem.*
candyfloss

> **LANGUAGE**
> Word for word this means 'dad's beard'.

le **barbecue** noun *masc.*
barbecue

la **barque** noun *fem.*
rowing boat

la **barre** noun *fem.*
bar
une **barre de chocolat** a chocolate
bar

barrer verb
to cross out

le **bar-tabac** noun *masc.*
cafe (*where stamps, newspapers, cigarettes
are sold*)

bas adjective *masc.*, **basse** *fem.*
low
des nuages bas low clouds

le **bas** noun *masc.*
bottom (*of a wall, hill, page, etc.*)
en bas de la page at the bottom of
the page

en **bas** adverb
1 downstairs
Je regarde la télé en bas. I'm
watching TV downstairs.
2 down
Ne regardez pas en bas, les
enfants! Don't look down,
children!

le **basket** noun *masc.*
basketball
Je joue au basket. I play
basketball.

les **baskets** plural noun *fem.*
trainers
J'ai des baskets neuves. I've got
new trainers.

> ⚠ **FALSE FRIEND**
> **baskets = trainers** (*not* baskets)

la **bataille** noun *fem.*
1 battle
2 On joue à la bataille? (*popular card
game*) Shall we play snap?
3 la bataille navale (*strategy game*)
battleships

le **bateau** noun *masc.* (plural les
bateaux)
boat
en bateau by boat

le **bâtiment** noun *masc.*
building
Ce grand bâtiment, c'est mon
école. That big building is my
school.

le **bâton** noun *masc.*
stick

la **batterie** noun *fem.*
drums
Manuel joue de la batterie.
Manuel plays the drums.

> **LANGUAGE**
> **la batterie = drums** (*not* battery)

• *Use* le *and* un *for masculine words and* la *and* une *for feminine words.*

16

battre verb
to beat
Les rouges ont battu les jaunes.
The reds have beaten the
yellows.

se **battre** verb ◉
to fight
Deux garçons se battent dans la
cour. Two boys are fighting in the
playground.

bavard adjective *masc.*,
bavarde *fem.*
talkative
Alice est très bavarde. Alice is very
talkative.
Quel bavard! What a chatterbox!

bavarder verb
to chat
Vous bavardez tout le temps.
You're always chatting.

le **bazar** noun *masc.*
mess
Quel bazar! What a mess!

la **BD** noun *fem.* (plural les **BD**)
(*short for* bande dessinée) **comic**
Tu aimes les BD? Do you like
comics?

beau adjective *masc.*, **bel** *masc.*,
belle *fem.*, **beaux** *masc. plural,*
belles *fem. plural*
1 beautiful
une belle fille comme toi
a beautiful girl like you
2 lovely
une belle promenade a lovely
walk
3 good-looking
Daniel est beau. Daniel is
good-looking.
4 handsome
un bel homme a handsome
man
5 (*when it's about the weather*)
Il fait beau. It's a nice day.

◉ *means use* être *to make the past tense.*

Vivement le beau temps! I can't
wait for the nice weather!

🔑 **LANGUAGE**
The form **bel** is used before a masculine
singular noun beginning with *a, e, i, o, u,* or
silent h, for example: **un bel exemple**.

beaucoup adverb
1 a lot
J'aime beaucoup le tennis. I like
tennis a lot.
30 euros, c'est beaucoup. 30 euros,
it's a lot.
2 beaucoup de a lot of
Tu as beaucoup de DVD. You have
a lot of DVDs.
3 (*with ne ... pas*) **not ... much**
Je n'aime pas beaucoup les
légumes. I don't like vegetables
much.
Je n'ai pas beaucoup d'argent.
I don't have much money.
4 beaucoup plus much more
beaucoup plus grand much bigger
beaucoup mieux much better

le **beau-fils** noun *masc.* (plural les
beaux-fils)
1 stepson
2 son-in-law

le **beau-frère** noun *masc.* (plural les
beaux-frères)
brother-in-law

le **beau-père** noun *masc.* (plural les
beaux-pères)
1 stepfather
2 father-in-law

le **bébé** noun *masc.*
baby

le **bec** noun *masc.*
beak

le **beignet** noun *masc.*
doughnut

bel adjective *masc.* SEE **beau**

belge adjective *masc. & fem.*
Belgian

French English

a
b
c
d
e
f
g
h
i
j
k
l
m
n
o
p
q
r
s
t
u
v
w
x
y
z

un or une **Belge** noun *masc. & fem.*
Belgian (*person*)

la **Belgique** noun *fem.*
Belgium

belle adjective *fem.* SEE **beau**
une **belle fleur** a beautiful flower

la **belle-fille** noun *fem.* (plural les **belles-filles**)
1 **stepdaughter**
2 **daughter-in-law**

la **belle-mère** noun *fem.* (plural les **belles-mères**)
1 **stepmother**
2 **mother-in-law**

la **belle-sœur** noun *fem.* (plural les **belles-sœurs**)
sister-in-law

le **berger** noun *masc.*
shepherd

le **bermuda** noun *masc.*
bermuda shorts

le **besoin** noun *masc.*
Tu as besoin de quelque chose? Do you need anything?
J'ai besoin de téléphoner. I need to phone.
J'ai besoin d'un mouchoir. I need a handkerchief.

bête adjective *masc. & fem.*
stupid, **silly**
Tu es bête! You're being silly!

la **bête** noun *fem.*
animal
une **bête sauvage** a wild animal

les **bêtises** plural noun *fem.*
1 **faire des bêtises** to mess about
Il fait des bêtises. He's messing about.
2 **dire des bêtises** to talk nonsense
Ne dis pas de bêtises! Don't talk nonsense!

la **betterave** noun *fem.*
beetroot

le **beurre** noun *masc.*
butter

le **biberon** noun *masc.*
baby's bottle

la **Bible** noun *fem.*
Bible

la **bibliothèque** noun *fem.*
1 **library**
2 **bookcase**

le **bic**® noun *masc.*
Biro®

la **bicyclette** noun *fem.*
bicycle
à **bicyclette** by bicycle

bien adverb
1 **well**
Dors bien! Sleep well!
bien cuit well cooked
2 **okay**
Tu vas bien? Are you okay?
Bien! On y va? Okay! Shall we go?
3 **properly**
La porte n'était pas bien fermée. The door wasn't closed properly.
4 **really**
Tu as bien changé! You've really changed!

bien adjective
1 **good**
Il est bien, ton livre? Is your book good?
2 **nice**
Ce sont des gens bien. They're nice people.
C'est bien ici. It's nice here.

> **⚷ LANGUAGE**
> **Bien** is the same in the masculine, feminine, or plural, for example: **un garçon bien, une fille bien, des gens bien**.

bien sûr adverb
of course
bien sûr que non of course not

• *Languages, nationalities, and religions do not take a capital letter in French.*

bientôt adverb
soon
À bientôt! See you soon!

la **bienvenue** noun *fem.*
welcome

la **bière** noun *fem.*
beer

le **bifteck** noun *masc.*
steak

LANGUAGE
Bifteck comes from the English word
'beefsteak'.

le **bijou** noun *masc.* (plural les **bijoux**)
jewel

la **bijouterie** noun *fem.*
jewellery shop

bilingue adjective *masc. & fem.*
bilingual

le **billard** noun *masc.*
billiards

la **bille** noun *fem.*
marble
Tu veux jouer aux billes? Do you
want to play marbles?

le **billet** noun *masc.*
1 ticket
un billet de train a train ticket
2 note
un billet de cinquante euros
a fifty-euro note

la **biscotte** noun *fem.*
continental toast

CULTURE
Les biscottes are sold in packets in France
and can be eaten for breakfast.

le **biscuit** noun *masc.*
biscuit

la **bise** noun *fem.*
kiss (*on the cheek*)
Fais-moi une bise! Give me a kiss!

Grosses bises (*at the end of a letter*) Love
and kisses

CULTURE
In France, girls usually say hello or
goodbye to each other with a kiss on each
cheek; it's the same between boys and
girls but between boys it's usual to shake
hands. The number of kisses may vary
according to where you are in France.

le **bisou** noun *masc.*
kiss
Fais un bisou à Mamie! Give
Grandma a kiss!

bizarre adjective *masc. & fem.*
strange

la **blague** noun *fem.*
joke
Elle m'a fait une blague. She
played a joke on me.

blanc adjective *masc.*, **blanche** *fem.*
white
des cheveux blancs white hair
une robe blanche a white dress

le **blanc** noun *masc.*
white
en blanc in white
J'aime bien le blanc. I like white.

le **blé** noun *masc.*
wheat

blessé adjective *masc.*,
blessée *fem.*
injured

la **blessure** noun *fem.*
injury

bleu adjective *masc.*, **bleue** *fem.*
blue
J'ai les yeux bleus. I've got blue
eyes.

le **bleu** noun *masc.*
1 blue
Ma couleur préférée, c'est le bleu.
Blue is my favourite colour.
2 bruise

ⓔ *means use* être *to make the past tense.*

French English

a
b
c
d
e
f
g
h
i
j
k
l
m
n
o
p
q
r
s
t
u
v
w
x
y
z

J'ai des bleus partout! I'm covered in bruises!

le **bloc-notes** noun *masc.* (plural les **blocs-notes**)
notepad

blond adjective *masc.*, **blonde** *fem.*
blond
Il a les cheveux blonds. He has blond hair.

le **blouson** noun *masc.*
jacket

le **bobo** noun *masc.*
un petit bobo a little scratch

le **bocal** noun *masc.* (plural les **bocaux**)
jar

le **bœuf** noun *masc.*
beef

bof exclamation
Ça va? – Bof! Are you okay? – So-so!
Tu aimes les maths? – Bof! Do you like maths? – Not much!

boire verb
to drink

le **bois** noun *masc.*
1 **wood**
un jouet en bois a wooden toy
2 (*little forest*) **wood**
dans les bois in the woods

la **boisson** noun *fem.*
drink
une boisson fraîche a cold drink

la **boîte** noun *fem.*
1 **box**
une boîte à outils a tool box
2 **tin**
une boîte de conserve a tin
3 **une boîte aux lettres** a postbox, a letterbox

le **bol** noun *masc.*
bowl
un bol de chocolat chaud a bowl of hot chocolate

la **bombe** noun *fem.*
1 **bomb**
2 **riding hat**

bon adjective *masc.*, **bonne** *fem.*
1 **good**
un bon film a good film
Amélie est bonne en anglais. Amélie is good at English.
2 **right**
le bon moment the right time
la bonne réponse the right answer
3 **Bon! Je m'en vais.** Right! I'm leaving.
Ah bon? (*for showing surprise*) Really?
4 (*when wishing somebody something*)
Bon anniversaire! Happy birthday!
Bonne année! Happy New Year!
Bonne chance! Good luck!
Bonne nuit! Good night!
Bonne journée! Have a nice day!
Bon week-end! Have a good weekend!
Bon voyage! Have a good trip!
Bon appétit! Enjoy your meal!
Bonnes vacances! Enjoy your holiday!
5 **bon marché** cheap
un ordinateur bon marché a cheap computer

🔑 **LANGUAGE**
Bon marché is the same in the masculine, feminine, or plural, for example: **des DVD bon marché**.

le **bonbon** noun *masc.*
sweet
un paquet de bonbons a bag of sweets

le **bonheur** noun *masc.*
1 **happiness**
2 **luck**
Ça porte bonheur. It brings you luck.

• *The months of the year and days of the week do not take a capital letter in French.*

le **bonhomme de neige** noun *masc.*
snowman

bonjour exclamation
1 **hello**
Bonjour, monsieur! Hello!
2 **good morning**
3 **good afternoon**

🔑 **LANGUAGE**
Use **bonjour** in the morning or afternoon and **bonsoir** in the evening or at night.

bonne adjective *fem.* SEE **bon**

le **bonnet** noun *masc.*
hat
un bonnet de laine a woolly hat

bonsoir exclamation
1 **hello**
2 **good evening**

🔑 **LANGUAGE**
Use **bonsoir** in the evening or at night, and **bonne nuit** (good night) before going to bed.

le **bord** noun *masc.*
edge
au bord de la mer at the seaside
au bord de la rivière on the river bank
le bord du trottoir the kerb

bordeaux adjective
burgundy

🔑 **LANGUAGE**
Bordeaux is the same in the masculine, feminine, or plural, for example: **des chaussures bordeaux**.

la **bosse** noun *fem.*
1 **bump**
J'ai une grosse bosse sur la tête. I've got a big bump on my head.
2 **hump**
Le chameau a deux bosses. The camel has two humps.

ⓔ *means use* être *to make the past tense.*

la **botte** noun *fem.*
boot
des bottes en caoutchouc wellingtons

la **bouche** noun *fem.*
mouth
Ouvre la bouche! Open your mouth!

le **boucher** noun *masc.*, la **bouchère** *fem.*
butcher
Il est boucher. He's a butcher.

la **boucherie** noun *fem.*
butcher's shop

le **bouchon** noun *masc.*
1 **bottle top**
Remets le bouchon! Put the top back on!
2 **cork**
le bouchon de champagne the champagne cork
3 **traffic jam**

la **boucle d'oreille** noun *fem.*
earring
des boucles d'oreille en argent silver earrings

bouclé adjective *masc.*, **bouclée** *fem.*
curly
avoir les cheveux bouclés to have curly hair

bouddhisme adjective
Buddhism

bouder verb
to sulk

le **boudoir** noun *masc.*
sponge finger (*biscuit*)

la **boue** noun *fem.*
mud

la **bouée** noun *fem.*
1 **rubber ring**
une bouée de sauvetage a lifebelt
2 **buoy**

a
b
c
d
e
f
g
h
i
j
k
l
m
n
o
p
q
r
s
t
u
v
w
x
y
z

bouger verb
to move
Ne bougez pas! Don't move!
Tu peux bouger ta jambe? Can you move your leg?

la **bougie** noun *fem.*
candle

bouillant adjective *masc.*,
bouillante *fem.*
boiling
L'eau est bouillante. The water is boiling hot.

bouillir verb
to boil
L'eau bout. The water is boiling.
Fais bouillir de l'eau! Boil some water!

la **bouilloire** noun *fem.*
kettle

le **boulanger** noun *masc.*,
la **boulangère** *fem.*
baker

la **boulangerie** noun *fem.*
baker's shop

la **boulangerie-pâtisserie**
noun *fem.*
bakery (*selling fresh bread, pastries, cakes, etc*)

la **boule de neige** noun *fem.*
snowball

la **boule de Noël** noun *fem.*
bauble

les **boules** plural noun *fem.*
bowls
Tes parents jouent aux boules? Do your parents play bowls?

CULTURE
People play **boules** in France with small metal balls on hard ground, not on grass, often in places like town squares. The game is also called **la pétanque**.

la **boum** noun *fem.*
party
Ma grande sœur va à une boum. My big sister's going to a party.

le **bouquet** noun *masc.*
un bouquet de fleurs a bunch of flowers

bousculer verb
to push

la **boussole** noun *fem.*
compass

le **bout** noun *masc.*
1 end
au bout de la rue at the end of the street
2 piece
un bout de pain a piece of bread

la **bouteille** noun *fem.*
bottle

la **boutique** noun *fem.*
shop
une boutique de souvenirs a souvenir shop

le **bouton** noun *masc.*
1 button
les boutons de mon manteau the buttons of my coat
Appuie sur le bouton! Press the button!
2 spot
Tu es couverte de boutons. You're covered in spots.

boutonner verb
to do up
Boutonne ton blouson! Do up your jacket!

le **bowling** noun *masc.*
1 bowling
Tu veux jouer au bowling? Do you want to go bowling?
2 bowling alley

• See the centre section for verb tables.

la **boxe** noun *fem.*
boxing

le **bracelet** noun *masc.*
bracelet
un bracelet en or a gold bracelet
un bracelet de montre
a watch strap

la **branche** noun *fem.*
branch

branché adjective *masc.*,
branchée *fem.*
(*fashionable*) **cool**
Elle est branchée. She's cool.

brancher verb
to plug in
L'ordinateur n'est pas branché.
The computer isn't plugged in.

le **bras** noun *masc.*
arm

le **brassard** noun *masc.*
armband

bravo exclamation
well done

la **Bretagne** noun *fem.*
Brittany

le **brevet des collèges** noun
masc.
certificate of general education

LANGUAGE
In France **le brevet des collèges** (word for word 'college certificate') is an exam students take at the age of fifteen when they leave the **collège**; its closest equivalent is the GCSE.

le **bricolage** noun *masc.*
DIY

bricoler verb
to do DIY

brillant adjective *masc.*, **brillante**
fem.
1 shiny
2 (*student, results, etc.*) **brilliant**

briller verb
to shine

la **brioche** noun *fem.*
brioche

la **brique** noun *fem.*
brick
un mur en briques a brick wall

britannique adjective *masc. & fem.*
British

le or la **Britannique** noun *masc. & fem.*
British person
les Britanniques the British

la **brochette** noun *fem.*
kebab

le **brocoli** noun *masc.*
broccoli

LANGUAGE
French = brocoli
English = broccoli

le **bronze** noun *masc.*
bronze
une médaille de bronze a bronze medal

bronzé adjective *masc.*,
bronzée *fem.*
tanned, **brown**

la **brosse** noun *fem.*
brush
une brosse à dents a toothbrush
une brosse à cheveux a hairbrush

brosser verb
to brush

se **brosser** verb ✪
to brush
Je me brosse les dents. I'm brushing my teeth.
Elle se brosse les cheveux. She's brushing her hair.

la **brouette** noun *fem.*
wheelbarrow

✪ *means use* **être** *to make the past tense.*

le **brouillard** noun *masc.*
fog
Il y a du brouillard. It's foggy.

le **brouillon** noun *masc.*
rough copy
D'abord, écrivez la phrase au brouillon! First, write the sentence out in rough!

le **bruit** noun *masc.*
noise
Les enfants font beaucoup de bruit. The children are making a lot of noise.

brûlant adjective *masc.*, **brûlante** *fem.*
boiling hot

brûler verb
to burn
La maison brûle. The house is on fire.
Ne te brûle pas les doigts! Don't burn your fingers!

la **brume** noun *fem.*
mist

brun adjective *masc.*, **brune** *fem.*
brown
Chloé a les cheveux bruns. Chloé has brown hair.
Je suis brune. I have brown hair.

brusquement adverb
suddenly

Bruxelles noun
Brussels

bruyant adjective *masc.*, **bruyante** *fem.*
noisy

bu verb SEE **boire**
J'ai bu deux verres d'eau. I've drunk two glasses of water.

la **bûche** noun *fem.*
log
la bûche de Noël the Yule log

CULTURE
In France **la bûche de Noël** is a sort of chocolate Swiss roll that people eat as part of the Christmas meal instead of Christmas pudding.

le **buffet** noun *masc.*
sideboard

le **buisson** noun *masc.*
bush

buissonnière adjective *fem.*
faire l'école buissonnière to play truant

la **bulle** noun *fem.*
1 bubble
2 (*in comics*) **speech bubble**

le **bulletin** noun *masc.*
report
un bulletin scolaire a school report

le **bureau** noun *masc.* (plural les **bureaux**)
1 office
Mon frère travaille dans un bureau. My brother works in an office.
2 desk
Papa est assis à son bureau. Dad's sitting at his desk.
3 study
Chez moi, il y a trois chambres et un bureau. In my house, there are three bedrooms and a study.
4 un bureau de poste a post office

le **bus** noun *masc.*
bus
en bus by bus

le **but** noun *masc.*
goal
marquer un but to score a goal

le **buteur** noun *masc.*
striker

• *Use* **le** *and* **un** *for masculine words and* **la** *and* **une** *for feminine words.*

Cc

c' pronoun SEE **ce**
  C'est facile. It's easy.

ça pronoun
1 that
  Donne-moi ça! Give me that!
  Ça, c'est vrai. That's very true.
  Ça y est! That's it!
  C'est ça! That's right!
2 this
  Il est grand comme ça. He's as tall as this.
3 it
  Ça ne marche pas. It doesn't work.
  Ça fait mal. It hurts.
4 (when talking about how you feel)
  Ça va? How are you?
  Ça va, merci! I'm fine, thanks!
5 (when talking about how things are)
  Ça va, à l'école? How are things at school?

> 🔑 **LANGUAGE**
> **Ça va? = Comment ça va?**

la cabane noun fem.
  hut

la cabine noun fem.
1 cabin (on a ferry)
2 une cabine téléphonique a phone box
3 une cabine d'essayage a changing room

le cabinet noun masc.
  surgery (doctor's)

les cabinets plural noun masc.
  toilet

le câble noun masc.
  cable

la cacahuète noun fem.
  peanut

le cacao noun masc.
  cocoa

cache-cache noun masc.
  jouer à cache-cache to play hide-and-seek

cacher verb
  to hide
  Il a caché mon stylo. He has hidden my pen.

se cacher verb ℮
  to hide
  Ils se cachent derrière le mur. They're hiding behind the wall.

le cachet noun masc.
  tablet
  un cachet d'aspirine an aspirin

la cachette noun fem.
  hiding place

le caddie® noun masc.
  trolley (in a supermarket)

le cadeau noun masc. (plural les **cadeaux**)
  present
  un cadeau d'anniversaire a birthday present

cadet adjective masc., **cadette** fem.
1 younger
2 youngest

le cadet noun masc., la **cadette** fem.
  youngest child

le café noun masc.
1 coffee
  un café au lait a white coffee
  un café crème an espresso with milk

> 🌍 **CULTURE**
> In France **un café** is usually a coffee without milk.

℮ *means use* **être** *to make the past tense.*

a
b
c
d
e
f
g
h
i
j
k
l
m
n
o
p
q
r
s
t
u
v
w
x
y
z

2 cafe (*the place*)
à la terrasse d'un café at a table outside a cafe

🌎 **CULTURE**
In France **cafés** also sell alcohol.

la **cafétéria** noun *fem.*
cafeteria

la **cage** noun *fem.*
cage
la cage à poules climbing frame

la **cagoule** noun *fem.*
balaclava

le **cahier** noun *masc.*
exercise book
le cahier d'appel register
le cahier de brouillon rough book
le cahier de textes homework diary

le **caillou** noun *masc.* (plural les **cailloux**)
stone

la **caisse** noun *fem.*
1 checkout
Payez à la caisse! Pay at the checkout!
2 crate (*for fruit, vegetables*)

le **caissier** noun *masc.*, la **caissière** *fem.*
cashier

le **calcul** noun *masc.*
sums
Je suis bonne en calcul. I'm good at sums.
le calcul mental mental arithmetic

la **calculatrice** noun *fem.*
calculator

calculer verb
to work out
Calcule combien je te dois. Work out how much I owe you.

la **calculette** noun *fem.*
pocket calculator

le **caleçon** noun *masc.*
boxer shorts

🔑 **LANGUAGE**
French = **le caleçon** is singular
English = **boxer shorts** is plural

le **calendrier** noun *masc.*
calendar

calme adjective *masc. & fem.*
1 quiet
une rue calme a quiet street
2 calm
Reste calme! Keep calm!

le **calme** noun *masc.*
peace and quiet
Nous avons besoin de calme.
We need peace and quiet.

se **calmer** verb ⊘
to calm down
Calmez-vous, les enfants! Calm down, children!

le or la **camarade** noun *masc. & fem.*
friend
un camarade d'école a school friend

le **cambrioleur** noun *masc.*
burglar

la **caméra** noun *fem.*
camera (*for film, TV*)

le **caméscope**® noun *masc.*
camcorder

le **camion** noun *masc.*
lorry

la **camionnette** noun *fem.*
van

le **camp** noun *masc.*
camp

la **campagne** noun *fem.*
country
Aurélie habite à la campagne.
Aurélie lives in the country.

• *Languages, nationalities, and religions do not take a capital letter in French.*

camper verb
to camp

le **camping** noun *masc.*
camping
Nous faisons du camping chaque été. We go camping every summer.
un terrain de camping a campsite

le **Canada** noun *masc.*
Canada
Marie est allée au Canada. Marie went to Canada.

canadien adjective *masc.*,
canadienne *fem.*
Canadian

le **Canadien** noun *masc.*,
la **Canadienne** *fem.*
Canadian (*person*)

le **canapé** noun *masc.*
sofa

le **canard** noun *masc.*
duck

le **canari** noun *masc.*
canary

le **cancer** noun *masc.*
cancer
Il a un cancer. He has cancer.

la **canette** noun *fem.*
can
une canette de coca a can of coke®

le **caniche** noun *masc.*
poodle

le **canif** noun *masc.*
penknife

la **canne** noun *fem.*
walking stick
une canne à pêche a fishing rod

le **canoë** noun *masc.*
canoe

*ⓔ means use **être** to make the past tense.*

la **cantine** noun *fem.*
canteen
Nous mangeons à la cantine. We eat in the canteen.

CULTURE
In French schools eating in the canteen is the same as having school dinners in British schools.

le **caoutchouc** noun *masc.*
rubber
des bottes en caoutchouc
wellington boots

capable adjective *masc. & fem.*
Tu es capable de grimper sur l'arbre? Can you climb up the tree?

le **capitaine** noun *masc.*
captain

la **capitale** noun *fem.*
capital
Bruxelles est la capitale de la Belgique. Brussels is the capital of Belgium.

car conjunction
because

le **car** noun *masc.*
coach
en car by coach

⚠ **FALSE FRIEND**
le car = the coach (*not the car*)

le **caractère** noun *masc.*
personality
Il a mauvais caractère. He's bad-tempered.
Elle a bon caractère. She's good-natured.

la **carafe** noun *fem.*
jug
une carafe d'eau a jug of water

les **Caraïbes** plural noun *fem.*
the Caribbean Islands

a
b
c
d
e
f
g
h
i
j
k
l
m
n
o
p
q
r
s
t
u
v
w
x
y
z

27

French English

a
b
c
d
e
f
g
h
i
j
k
l
m
n
o
p
q
r
s
t
u
v
w
x
y
z

le **caramel** noun masc.
  toffee

la **caravane** noun fem.
  caravan

caresser verb
  to stroke
  Chloé caresse le chat. Chloé is
  stroking the cat.

le **carnaval** noun masc.
  carnival

 CULTURE
In France **le carnaval** is the name given to
the celebrations on **Mardi gras** (Shrove
Tuesday). This is the last day before **le
Carême** (Lent) when French children put
on fancy dress, eat **crêpes** (pancakes),
and often take part in processions
through the streets.

le **carnet** noun masc.
1 notebook
  Note la date dans ton carnet.
  Write down the date in your
  notebook.
2 book
  un carnet de tickets a book of
  tickets
  un carnet de timbres a book of
  stamps
  un carnet d'adresses an address
  book
3 le carnet de notes the school
  report
  le carnet de correspondance the
  school diary

la **carotte** noun fem.
  carrot

 LANGUAGE
French = carotte
English = carrot

carré adjective masc., **carrée** fem.
  square
  une table carrée a square table

le **carré** noun masc.
  square

le **carreau** noun masc. (plural les
  carreaux)
1 window pane
2 (pattern)
  les carreaux check
  une chemise à carreaux a checked
  shirt
3 diamonds (in cards)

le **carrefour** noun masc.
  crossroads
  au carrefour at the crossroads

le **cartable** noun masc.
  schoolbag

 CULTURE
A **cartable** is made from a strong
material and is worn on the back. Many
French schoolchildren have to carry a lot
of books and some have schoolbags on
wheels.

la **carte** noun fem.
1 card
  une carte d'anniversaire
  a birthday card
  une carte de vœux a greetings
  card

 CULTURE
In France people send greetings cards in
January for the New Year instead of
Christmas. It is not at all common in
France to exchange cards with people you
see everyday.

  une arte postale a postcard
  une carte d'identité an identity
  card

CULTURE
All French people have an identity card.
They can use it instead of a passport to
travel around the European Union.

2 (for playing games) **card**
  un jeu de cartes a pack of cards
  jouer aux cartes to play cards
3 map
  une carte de l'Europe a map of
  Europe

• *The months of the year and days of the week do not take a capital letter in French.*

une **carte routière** a road map
4 menu

le **carton** noun *masc.*
cardboard box

le **cas** noun *masc.*
case
en tout cas anyway
au cas où just in case

la **case** noun *fem.*
1 (*in crosswords etc.*) **square**
2 (*on forms, worksheets, etc.*) **box**

la **caserne** noun *fem.*
une **caserne de pompiers** a fire station

le **casier** noun *masc.*
locker

le **casque** noun *masc.*
1 helmet
2 headphones

la **casquette** noun *fem.*
cap

le **casse-croûte** noun *masc.* (plural les **casse-croûte**)
snack

casse-pieds adjective *masc. & fem.*
Elle est casse-pieds. She's a pest.

casser verb
to break
Théo a cassé un verre. Théo has broken a glass.

se **casser** verb @
to break
Le vase est tombé et s'est cassé. The vase fell and broke.
Je me suis cassé la jambe. I've broken my leg.

la **casserole** noun *fem.*
saucepan

⚠️ **FALSE FRIEND**
la casserole = the saucepan (*not* the casserole)

la **cassette** noun *fem.*
tape
une **cassette vidéo** a video

la **catastrophe** noun *fem.*
disaster

la **cathédrale** noun *fem.*
cathedral

catholique adjective *masc. & fem.*
Catholic

le **cauchemar** noun *masc.*
nightmare
faire des cauchemars to have nightmares

la **cause** noun *fem.*
1 cause
2 à cause de because of
Je vais être en retard à cause de toi. I'm going to be late because of you.

le **cavalier** noun *masc.*,
la **cavalière** *fem.*
rider

la **cave** noun *fem.*
cellar

⚠️ **FALSE FRIEND**
la cave = the cellar (*not* the cave)

le **CD** noun *masc.* (plural les **CD**)
CD
J'ai deux CD. I have two CDs.

ce adjective *masc.*, **cet** *masc.*, **cette** *fem.*,
ces *masc. & fem. plural*
1 this
ce soir this evening
cette chaise this chair
cet homme this man

🔑 **LANGUAGE**
Use **cet** with masculine nouns beginning with *a, e, i, o, u,* or *silent h.*

2 (*when pointing to* **this one**, *not* **that one**)
ce livre-ci this book
cette photo-ci this photo
cet élève-ci this pupil
3 that

@ *means use* **être** *to make the past tense.*

a
b
c
d
e
f
g
h
i
j
k
l
m
n
o
p
q
r
s
t
u
v
w
x
y
z

ce vélo that bike
cette montagne that mountain
cet ordinateur that computer
4 (*when pointing to* **that one**, *not* **this one**)
ce village-là that village
cette rue-là that street
cet hôtel-là that hotel

ce pronoun
1 it
Qui est-ce? Who is it?
Ce sont Marie et Fabrice. It's Marie and Fabrice.
C'est lui. It's him.

⚷ **LANGUAGE**
Ce becomes **c'** before an 'e'.

2 (*when describing people*) **he**, **she**, **they**
C'est un garçon intelligent. He's a clever boy.
C'est une fille intelligente. She's a clever girl.
Ce sont des médecins. They are doctors.
3 ce que what
Dis-moi ce que tu sais. Tell me what you know.
4 ce qui what
Ce qui m'intéresse, c'est la lecture. What I'm interested in is reading.

le **CE1** noun *masc.*
Year 3

le **CE2** noun *masc.*
Year 4

⚷ **LANGUAGE**
CE is short for **cours élémentaire** (elementary class).

ceci pronoun
this
Ceci est la vérité. This is the truth.

la **cédille** noun *fem.*
cedilla

'ç' est un c cédille. 'ç' is a c cedilla.

⚷ **LANGUAGE**
The cedilla goes under the letter 'c' in French: it tells you that the 'c' sounds like an 's' and not a 'k', for example in **garçon**.

la **ceinture** noun *fem.*
belt
une ceinture noire a black belt
une ceinture de sécurité a seatbelt

cela pronoun
1 that
Cela dépend. That depends.
2 it
Cela vaut la peine. It's worth it.

célèbre adjective *masc. & fem.*
famous

le **céleri** noun *masc.*
celery

célibataire adjective *masc. & fem.*
not married
Ma sœur est célibataire. My sister isn't married.

celle pronoun *fem.* SEE **celui**

celles pronoun *fem. plural* SEE **ceux**

celui pronoun *masc.*, **celle** *fem.*
1 the one
Quel livre? – Celui qui est sur la table. Which book? – The one on the table.
Tu aimes cette chemise? – Je préfère celle de Clément. Do you like this shirt? – I prefer Clément's.
2 (*when pointing to the one that's here, not there*)
celui-ci this one, **celle-ci** this one
Quel cahier? – Celui-ci. Which exercise book? – This one.
Quelle robe? – Celle-ci. Which dress? – This one.
3 (*when pointing to the one that's there, not here*)
celui-là that one, **celle-là** that one
Quel ordinateur? – Celui-là. Which computer? – That one.

• *See the centre section for verb tables.*

Quelle maison? – Celle-là. Which house? – That one.

cent number
a hundred
cent personnes a hundred people
deux cents euros two hundred euros
deux cent trente two hundred and thirty

LANGUAGE
You put an **s** at the end of **cent** to make the plural, for example: **deux cents**, but not when **cent** is followed by another number, for example: **deux cent vingt** (220).

la **centaine** noun fem.
about a hundred
une centaine de touristes about a hundred tourists
des centaines de voitures hundreds of cars

centième adjective masc. & fem.
hundredth

le **centime** noun masc.
cent
Il y a cent centimes dans un euro. There are a hundred cents in a euro.

le **centimètre** noun masc.
centimetre

le **centre** noun masc.
centre
au centre de la classe in the centre of the classroom
un centre commercial a shopping centre

le **centre-ville** noun masc.
town centre

cependant adverb
yet
C'est incroyable, cependant c'est la vérité. It's hard to believe, yet it's the truth.

le **cercle** noun masc.
circle

les **céréales** plural noun fem.
cereal
Je mange des céréales au petit déjeuner. I eat cereal for breakfast.

LANGUAGE
French = **les céréales** is plural
English = **cereal** is singular

le **cerf-volant** noun masc. (plural les **cerfs-volants**)
kite
faire voler un cerf-volant to fly a kite

la **cerise** noun fem.
cherry

certain adjective masc.,
certaine fem.
1 **certain**, **sure**
C'est certain. It's certain.
J'en suis certaine. I'm sure.
2 **some**
Certains élèves ont fini. Some pupils have finished.
un certain temps some time

certain pronoun masc.,
certaine fem.
some
Certains sont petits, d'autres grands. Some are big and some small.

certainement adverb
1 **most probably**
Il va certainement neiger. It's most probably going to snow.
2 **certainly**
Tu viens? – Certainement pas! Are you coming? – Certainly not!

le **certificat** noun masc.
certificate

le **cerveau** noun masc. (plural les **cerveaux**)
brain

ces plural adjective masc. & fem.
1 **these**
ces garçons these boys

*means use **être** to make the past tense.*

a
b
c
d
e
f
g
h
i
j
k
l
m
n
o
p
q
r
s
t
u
v
w
x
y
z

a
b
c
d
e
f
g
h
i
j
k
l
m
n
o
p
q
r
s
t
u
v
w
x
y
z

ces tables these tables
2 (*when pointing to these here, not those there*)
ces maisons-ci these houses
3 those
ces vélos those bikes
ces chaises those chairs
4 (*when pointing to those there, not these here*)
ces gens-là those people

le **CES** noun *masc.*
secondary school

 CULTURE
From the ages of 11 to 15 French children go to the **CES** (collège d'enseignement secondaire) and then they go on to the **lycée** until they are 18.

c'est-à-dire conjunction
that is
C'est à 8 kilomètres, c'est-à-dire 5 miles. It's 8 km away, that's 5 miles.

cet adjective *masc.* SEE **ce**

cette adjective *fem.* SEE **ce**

ceux pronoun *masc. plural*,
celles *fem. plural*
1 the ones
Quels élèves? – Ceux qui sont dans la cour. Which pupils? – The ones who are in the playground.
Donne-moi mes chaussettes, pas celles de papa! Give me my socks, not dad's!
2 (*when pointing to the ones that are here, not there*)
ceux-ci these, **celles-ci** these
Quel ordinateurs? – Ceux-ci. Which computers? – These.
Quelles jupes? – Celles-ci. Which skirts? – These.
3 (*when pointing to the ones that are there, not here*)
ceux-là those, **celles-là** those
Quelles chaises? – Celles-là. Which chairs? – Those.

chacun pronoun *masc.*,
chacune *fem.*
1 each
Nous avons chacun cinq euros. We each have five euros.
chacun de vous each of you
2 everyone
Chacun peut décider. Everyone can decide.
3 Chacun son tour! Wait your turn!

la **chaîne** noun *fem.*
1 chain
une chaîne en or a gold chain
2 channel
une chaîne de télévision a TV channel
Je peux changer de chaîne? Can I change the channel?
3 une chaîne stéréo a stereo

la **chair** noun *fem.*
flesh
la chair de poule goose pimples

la **chaise** noun *fem.*
chair
une chaise longue a deckchair
une chaise roulante a wheelchair

la **chaleur** noun *fem.*
heat

la **chambre** noun *fem.*
bedroom
une chambre d'hôtel a hotel room
une chambre d'amis a guest room

le **chameau** noun *masc.* (plural les **chameaux**)
camel

le **champ** noun *masc.*
field

le **champignon** noun *masc.*
mushroom

le **champion** noun *masc.*,
la **championne** *fem.*
champion

le **championnat** noun *masc.*
championship

• *Use* **le** *and* **un** *for masculine words and* **la** *and* **une** *for feminine words.*

la chance noun *fem.*
 1 luck
   Bonne chance! Good luck!
   Pas de chance! Bad luck!
   J'ai de la chance. I am lucky.
 2 chance
   Ils n'ont aucune chance de gagner.
   They have no chance of winning.

le changement noun *masc.*
 change
   Il va y avoir des changements.
   There are going to be some
   changes.

changer verb
 1 to change
   Je peux changer la date? Can I
   change the date?
   Il n'a pas changé. He hasn't
   changed.
   **Nous devons changer à
   Montparnasse.** (*connection in the train
   or underground*) We have to change at
   Montparnasse.
 2 changer de to change
   Tu veux changer de place? Do you
   want to change places?

se changer verb ⊘
 1 (*to put on different clothes*) **to change**
   Va te changer! Go and change!
 2 se changer en to turn into
   **Le prince s'est changé en
   grenouille.** The prince turned into
   a frog.

la chanson noun *fem.*
 song

le chant noun
 singing
   des cours de chant singing lessons

chanter verb
 to sing
   Elle chante juste. She sings in tune.
   Il chante faux. He sings out of
   tune.

> ⚠ **FALSE FRIEND**
> **chanter = to sing** (*not* to chant)

le chanteur noun *masc.*,
 la chanteuse *fem.*
 singer

le chapeau noun *masc.* (plural **les
 chapeaux**)
 hat

le chapitre noun *masc.*
 chapter

chaque adjective *masc. & fem.*
 every
   chaque fois qu'il me voit every
   time he sees me
   chaque jour every day

le charbon noun *masc.*
 coal

la charcuterie noun *fem.*
 1 pork butcher's
 2 cooked pork meats

le chariot noun *masc.*
 trolley (*in a supermarket or airport*)

charmant adjective *masc.*,
 charmante *fem.*
 lovely
   le prince charmant Prince
   Charming

la chasse noun *fem.*
 hunting
   la chasse au trésor a treasure hunt

chasser verb
 1 to hunt
   Ils chassent le renard. They hunt
   foxes.
 2 chasser quelqu'un to throw
   somebody out

le chasseur noun *masc.*
 hunter

le chat noun *masc.*
 cat
   On joue à chat? Shall we play 'it'?

la châtaigne noun *fem.*
 chestnut

châtain adjective *masc.*
 brown

⊘ *means use* **être** *to make the past tense.*

a
b
c
d
e
f
g
h
i
j
k
l
m
n
o
p
q
r
s
t
u
v
w
x
y
z

le **château** noun masc. (plural les **châteaux**)
castle
un château de sable a sandcastle

le **chaton** noun masc.
kitten

chatouiller verb
to tickle

la **chatte** noun fem.
female cat

chaud adjective masc., **chaude** fem.
1 hot
un chocolat chaud a hot chocolate
2 warm
des vêtements chauds warm clothes
3 avoir chaud to be hot
J'ai chaud. I'm hot.

> 🔑 **LANGUAGE**
> French = **avoir** chaud   **J'ai chaud.**
> English = **to be** hot   **I'm hot.**

4 (when talking about the weather)
Il fait chaud. It's hot.

le **chauffage** noun masc.
heating
le chauffage central central heating

chauffer verb
to heat

le **chauffeur** noun masc.
driver
un chauffeur de bus a bus driver

> ⚠️ **FALSE FRIEND**
> le chauffeur = driver (not chauffeur)

la **chaussette** noun fem.
sock
une paire de chaussettes a pair of socks

le **chausson** noun masc.
slipper

la **chaussure** noun fem.
1 shoe

un magasin de chaussures a shoe shop
2 boot
des chaussures de football football boots

chauve adjective masc. & fem.
bald

la **chauve-souris** noun fem. (plural les **chauves-souris**)
bat

> 🔑 **LANGUAGE**
> Word for word **chauve-souris** means 'bald mouse'.

le **chef** noun masc.
1 leader
un chef de bande a gang leader
2 boss
C'est le chef. He's the boss.
3 chef
Il est chef dans un restaurant chinois. He's a chef in a Chinese restaurant.
4 Pierre est chef d'orchestre. Pierre's a conductor.

le **chemin** noun masc.
1 path
Prenons ce petit chemin! Let's go along this little path!
2 way
J'ai demandé le chemin pour aller au cinéma. I asked the way to the cinema.
en chemin on the way

le **chemin de fer** noun masc.
railway
une ligne de chemin de fer a railway line

la **cheminée** noun fem.
1 chimney
2 fireplace

la **chemise** noun fem.
1 shirt
une chemise de nuit a nightdress
2 folder

• Languages, nationalities, and religions do not take a capital letter in French.

le **chemisier** noun masc.
blouse

le **chêne** noun masc.
oak

la **chenille** noun fem.
caterpillar

le **chèque** noun masc.
cheque

cher adjective masc., **chère** fem.
1 **dear**
　Cher Julien ... Dear Julien ...
2 **expensive**
　trop cher too expensive
　pas cher cheap

cher adverb
　Ça coûte cher. It's expensive.

chercher verb
1 **to look for**
　Je cherche la poste. I'm looking for
　the post office.
　Qu'est-ce que tu cherches? What
　are you looking for?
2 **to look up**
　Je cherche 'tonnerre' dans le
　dictionnaire. I'm looking up
　'tonnerre' in the dictionary.
3 **aller chercher** to go and get
　Va chercher ton cahier. Go and get
　your exercise book.
4 **venir chercher quelqu'un** to pick
　somebody up
　Viens me chercher à l'école! Pick
　me up from school!

le **chercheur** noun masc.,
la **chercheuse** fem.
scientist

chère adjective fem. SEE **cher**

le **chéri** noun masc., la **chérie** fem.
darling
　Ma petite chérie! My little darling!

le **cheval** noun masc. (plural les
chevaux)
horse
　à cheval on horseback

faire du cheval to go horseriding
un cheval à bascule a rocking
horse

le **chevalier** noun masc.
knight

les **cheveux** plural noun masc.
hair
　J'ai les cheveux noirs. I've got
　black hair.

LANGUAGE
French = **les cheveux** is plural
English = **hair** is singular

la **cheville** noun fem.
ankle

la **chèvre** noun fem.
goat
　le fromage de chèvre goat cheese

chez preposition
1 **at**
　Je suis chez moi. I am at home.
　Lola est chez Jérémie. Lola's at
　Jérémie's.
　Il est chez le médecin. He's at the
　doctor's.
2 **to**
　Je vais chez Léo. I'm going to Léo's.
　Venez chez moi samedi! Come to
　my place on Saturday!
　Je vais chez le boulanger. I'm
　going to the baker's.
3 **home**
　chez moi at home
　Tu rentres chez toi? Are you going
　home?

chic adjective masc. & fem.
smart
　une veste chic a smart jacket

LANGUAGE
Chic is the same in the masculine,
feminine, and plural.

le **chien** noun masc.
dog

⊘ means use **être** to make the past tense.

35

French English

a
b
c
d
e
f
g
h
i
j
k
l
m
n
o
p
q
r
s
t
u
v
w
x
y
z

la **chienne** noun *fem.*
bitch

le **chiffon** noun *masc.*
rag, **cloth**

le **chiffre** noun *masc.*
figure
en chiffres in figures

la **Chine** noun *fem.*
China

le **chinois** noun *masc.*
Chinese (*the language*)

chinois adjective *masc.*,
chinoise *fem.*
Chinese

le **Chinois** noun *masc.*,
la **Chinoise** *fem.*
Chinese person

le **chiot** noun *masc.*
puppy

les **chips** plural noun *fem.*
crisps
un paquet de chips a bag of crisps

⚠️ **FALSE FRIEND**
les chips = crisps (*not* chips)

le **chirurgien** noun *masc.*,
la **chirurgienne** *fem.*
surgeon
un chirurgien-dentiste a dental surgeon

le **chocolat** noun *masc.*
chocolate
une boîte de chocolats a box of chocolates
un gâteau au chocolat a chocolate cake
le chocolat noir plain chocolate
le chocolat au lait milk chocolate
le chocolat en poudre drinking chocolate

choisir verb
to choose

le **choix** noun *masc.*
choice
Tu n'as pas le choix. You don't have a choice.

le **chômage** noun *masc.*
au chômage unemployed

la **chorale** noun *fem.*
choir
la chorale de l'école the school choir

la **chose** noun *fem.*
thing
J'ai des choses à faire. I've got things to do.

le **chou** noun *masc.* (plural les **choux**)
cabbage
les choux de Bruxelles Brussels sprouts
un chou à la crème a cream puff

le **chouchou** noun *masc.*,
la **chouchoute** *fem.*
teacher's pet

la **choucroute** noun *fem.*
sauerkraut

chouette adjective *masc. & fem.*
cool
Elle est chouette, ta sœur! Your sister's really cool!

la **chouette** noun *fem.*
owl

le **chou-fleur** noun *masc.* (plural les **choux-fleurs**)
cauliflower

chrétien adjective *masc.*,
chrétienne *fem.*
Christian

le **chronomètre** noun *masc.*
stopwatch

chuchoter verb
to whisper

chut exclamation
shh!

• *The months of the year and days of the week do not take a capital letter in French.*

-ci adverb
ce garçon-ci this boy
ces maisons-ci these houses
celle-ci this one
celui-ci this one
ceux-ci these
celles-ci these

la **cible** noun *fem.*
target

la **cicatrice** noun *fem.*
scar

le **cidre** noun *masc.*
cider

le **ciel** noun *masc.*
sky

la **cigale** noun *fem.*
cicada

CULTURE
La cigale is often a symbol of the south of France, especially the area of **Provence**.

la **cigogne** noun *fem.*
stork

CULTURE
La cigogne is often a symbol of the east of France, especially the area of **Alsace**.

le **cil** noun *masc.*
eyelash

la **cime** noun *fem.*
top, peak

le **cimetière** noun *masc.*
cemetery

le **cinéma** noun *masc.*
cinema

cinq number
five
Il est cinq heures. It's five o'clock.
J'ai cinq ans. I'm five.
le cinq juin the fifth of June

la **cinquantaine** noun *fem.*
une cinquantaine about fifty

une cinquantaine d'élèves about fifty pupils

cinquante number
fifty
Ma tante a cinquante ans. My aunt is fifty.

la **cinquième** noun *fem.*
Year 8 (*in a French collège*)

cinquième adjective *masc. & fem.*
fifth
au cinquième étage on the fifth floor

circonflexe adjective *masc.*
un accent circonflexe a circumflex accent (*as on* â, ê, î, ô, û)

la **circulation** noun *fem.*
traffic

le **cirque** noun *masc.*
circus

les **ciseaux** plural noun *masc.*
scissors
une paire de ciseaux a pair of scissors

la **cité** noun *fem.*
housing estate
J'habite dans une cité. I live on an estate.

le **citron** noun *masc.*
lemon
le citron vert lime
le citron pressé freshly squeezed lemon juice

LANGUAGE
The French word citron is related to 'citrus' in English; citrus fruits include lemons and oranges.

la **citrouille** noun *fem.*
pumpkin

clair adjective *masc.*, **claire** *fem.*
1 (*talking about daylight*) **light**
C'est une pièce très claire. It's a very light room.
2 (*describing colours*) **light**

 means use être *to make the past tense.*

a b c d e f g h i j k l m n o p q r s t u v w x y z

une couleur claire a light colour
des chemises bleu clair light blue shirts

3 clear
Cette explication est claire. This explanation is clear.

clairement adverb
clearly

la **claque** noun *fem.*
slap
Il m'a donné une claque. He slapped me.

claquer verb
to slam
Il a claqué la porte. He slammed the door.

la **clarinette** noun *fem.*
clarinet
Justin joue de la clarinette. Justin plays the clarinet.

la **classe** noun *fem.*
1 class
Cyril est dans ma classe. Cyril is in my class.
2 classroom
Rangez la classe! Tidy up the classroom!
3 lesson
la classe d'anglais the English lesson

classer verb
to sort out (*papers*)

le **classeur** noun *masc.*
ring binder

le **clavier** noun *masc.*
keyboard
un clavier d'ordinateur a computer keyboard

la **clé** noun *fem.*
key
Je ferme la porte à clé. I lock the door.

le **client** noun *masc.*, la **cliente** *fem.*
customer

le **climat** noun *masc.*
climate

climatisé adjective *masc.*, **climatisée** *fem.*
air-conditioned

le **clin d'œil** noun *masc.*
wink

le **clip** noun *masc.*
music video

cliquer verb
to click
Clique sur l'icône! Click on the icon!

la **cloche** noun *fem.*
bell

à **cloche-pied** adverb
sauter à cloche-pied to hop

le **clocher** noun *masc.*
church tower

le **clou** noun *masc.*
nail

le **clown** noun *masc.*
clown

LANGUAGE
The French word **clown** is pronounced 'cloon'.

le **club** noun *masc.*
club

le **CM1** noun *masc.*
Year 5

le **CM2** noun *masc.*
Year 6

LANGUAGE
CM is short for **cours moyen** (intermediate class).

le **coca** noun *masc.*
Coke®
Tu veux un coca? Do you want a Coke®?

la **coccinelle** noun *fem.*
ladybird

• The months of the year and days of the week do not take a capital letter in French.

cocher verb
to tick
Coche la bonne réponse. Tick the correct answer.

le **cochon** noun masc.
pig

le **cochon d'Inde** noun masc.
guinea pig

le **code** noun masc.
code
un code postal a postcode

le **cœur** noun masc.
1 **heart**
par cœur by heart
2 avoir mal au cœur to feel sick
3 **hearts** (in cards)

le **coffre** noun masc.
boot
C'est dans le coffre de la voiture. It's in the boot of the car.

se **cogner** verb ⊘
to bump
Il s'est cogné la tête. He bumped his head.

se **coiffer** verb ⊘
to do your hair
Ma sœur se coiffe. My sister is doing her hair.

le **coiffeur** noun masc.,
la **coiffeuse** fem.
hairdresser

la **coiffure** noun fem.
hairstyle

le **coin** noun masc.
1 **corner**
Il y a un restaurant au coin de la rue. There's a restaurant on the corner.
2 **spot**
un coin tranquille a quiet spot

coincé adjective masc.,
coincée fem.
stuck

⊘ means use être to make the past tense.

Le tiroir est coincé. The drawer is stuck.

le **col** noun masc.
collar

la **colère** noun fem.
anger
en colère angry

le **colis** noun masc.
parcel

le **collage** noun masc.
collage

le **collant** noun masc.
tights

LANGUAGE
French = le collant is singular
English = tights is plural

collant adjective masc.,
collante fem.
sticky

la **colle** noun fem.
1 **glue**
2 **detention**
On a une heure de colle. We have an hour's detention.

collectionner verb
to collect
Je collectionne les timbres. I collect stamps.

le **collège** noun masc.
secondary school

⚠ **FALSE FRIEND**
le collège = secondary school (not college)

🌍 **CULTURE**
French children go to the collège from the ages of 11 to 15, and then go on to the lycée until they are 18.

le **collégien** noun masc.,
la **collégienne** fem.
secondary school pupil

39

coller verb
1 to stick
Colle les timbres! Stick on the stamps!
2 to be sticky
J'ai les doigts qui collent. I've got sticky fingers.

le **collier** noun masc.
1 necklace
un collier en or a gold necklace
2 collar
Est-ce que ton chien porte un collier? Does your dog wear a collar?

la **colline** noun fem.
hill

la **colonie de vacances** noun fem.
summer camp
aller en colonie de vacances to go to summer camp

CULTURE
Schoolchildren in France often spend part of the summer at a **colonie de vacances** doing sports and other activities.

la **colonne** noun fem.
column

le **coloriage** noun masc.
colouring
J'aime faire du coloriage. I like colouring.

colorier verb
to colour in
un album à colorier a colouring book

combien adverb
1 how much
C'est combien? How much is it?
Tu pèses combien? How much do you weigh?
2 how many
Combien êtes-vous? How many of you are there?

• See the centre section for verb tables.

Il y a combien de filles? How many girls are there?
3 combien de temps how long
4 Tu chausses du combien? What size shoes do you take?
5 Le combien sommes-nous? What's today's date?

la **comédie** noun fem.
comedy

le **comédien** noun masc.,
la **comédienne** fem.
actor, actress

⚠ **FALSE FRIEND**
un comédien = an actor (not a comedian)

comique adjective masc. & fem.
funny

le or la **comique** noun masc. & fem.
comedian

commander verb
to order
On a commandé deux cocas®. We've ordered two Cokes®.

comme conjunction
1 like
C'est une maison comme les autres. It's a house like the others.
Ne mange pas comme ça! Don't eat like that!
2 as
Fais comme tu veux! Do as you like!
3 as a
J'ai M. Duc comme prof. I have Mr Duc as a teacher.
4 Qu'est-ce que tu veux comme glace? What sort of ice cream do you want?
Qu'est-ce que tu aimes comme musique? What sort of music do you like?
Qu'est-ce qu'on mange comme dessert? What are we having for dessert?

comme adverb
how
Comme c'est grand! It's so big!

comme ci, comme ça adverb
so-so

commencer verb
to start
Mon nom commence par un 's'.
My name starts with an 's'.
Ça commence à cinq heures.
It starts at five.
Daniel a commencé à jouer de la
guitare. Daniel has started playing
the guitar.

comment adverb
1 how
Comment vas-tu? How are you?
Comment est-ce qu'on dit 'bike' en
français? How do you say 'bike' in
French?
Comment tu t'appelles? What's
your name?
Comment ça s'écrit? How do you
spell it?
2 pardon
Comment? Tu peux répéter?
Pardon? Can you say that again?

le **commerçant** noun masc.,
la **commerçante** fem.
shopkeeper

le **commissariat** noun masc.
police station

LANGUAGE
Commissariat de police is also used.

les **commissions** plural noun fem.
shopping
faire les commissions to do the
shopping

commode adjective masc. & fem.
convenient

la **commode** noun fem.
chest of drawers

commun adjective masc.,
commune fem.
en commun in common
Nous avons beaucoup en commun.
We've got a lot in common.
les transports en commun public
transport

la **communion** noun fem.
communion
J'ai fait ma première communion.
I made my first communion.

la **compagnie** noun fem.
company
la compagnie aérienne airline

comparer verb
to compare

le **compas** noun masc.
compasses (mathematics)

LANGUAGE
French = le compas is singular
English = compasses is plural

la **compétition** noun fem.
(for sports) **competition**
s'inscrire à une compétition to go
in for a competition
une compétition de basket
a basket-ball competition

complet adjective masc.,
complète fem.
full
L'hôtel est complet. The hotel is
full.
la famille au grand complet the
entire family

complètement adverb
completely

compléter verb
to complete
Complétez cette phrase! Complete
this sentence!

compliqué adjective masc.,
compliquée fem.
complicated

a
b
c
d
e
f
g
h
i
j
k
l
m
n
o
p
q
r
s
t
u
v
w
x
y
z

means use être to make the past tense.

a
b
c
d
e
f
g
h
i
j
k
l
m
n
o
p
q
r
s
t
u
v
w
x
y
z

le **comportement** noun masc.
behaviour

le **compositeur** noun masc.,
la **compositrice** fem.
composer

composter verb
to punch
Il faut composter ton billet de
train. You must punch your train
ticket.

 CULTURE
In France you punch your train ticket at
the machine before you get on the train,
otherwise you could be fined.

la **compote** noun fem.
stewed fruit
la compote de pommes stewed
apples

comprendre verb
to understand
Je ne comprends pas l'anglais.
I don't understand English.
Tu comprends? Do you
understand?

le **comprimé** noun masc.
tablet
un comprimé d'aspirine an aspirin

compris verb masc., **comprise**
fem. SEE **comprendre**
Je n'ai pas compris. I didn't
understand.

compris adjective masc.,
comprise fem.
included
Les boissons sont comprises. The
drinks are included.

le or la **comptable** noun masc. & fem.
accountant

le **compte** noun masc.
account (in a bank)

compter verb
to count

Comptez jusqu'à vingt! Count to
twenty!

la **comptine** noun fem.
nursery rhyme

le **comptoir** noun masc.
1 counter
2 bar

se **concentrer** verb ⓔ
to concentrate

le **concert** noun masc.
concert

le or la **concierge** noun masc. & fem.
caretaker

le **concombre** noun masc.
cucumber

le **concours** noun masc.
competition
le concours hippique
showjumping

la **condition** noun fem.
en bonne condition in good
condition

le **conducteur** noun masc.,
la **conductrice** fem.
driver

conduire verb
to drive
conduire une voiture to drive a car
Mon père me conduit à l'école. My
dad drives me to school.

se **conduire** verb ⓔ
to behave
Théo se conduit bien. Théo is
behaving himself.

la **confiance** noun fem.
trust
J'ai confiance en toi. I trust you.

la **confiture** noun fem.
jam
la confiture de prunes plum jam

confortable adjective masc. & fem.
comfortable

• Use **le** and **un** for masculine words and **la** and **une** for feminine words.

un fauteuil **confortable**
a comfortable armchair

🔑 **LANGUAGE**
French = confortable
English = comfortable

le **congé** noun *masc.*
(*from work*) **holiday**
**Mon père est en congé cette
semaine.** My dad's on holiday this
week.
un jour de congé a day off

le **congélateur** noun *masc.*
freezer

congelé adjective *masc.*,
congelée *fem.*
frozen

la **conjugaison** noun *fem.*
conjugation

connaître verb
to know
Je connais ton frère. I know your
brother.

se **connecter** verb
to connect
se connecter à Internet to connect
to the Internet

connu adjective *masc.*, **connue** *fem.*
well-known

le **conseil** noun *masc.*
advice
un conseil a piece of advice
Je peux te donner un conseil? Can
I give you a piece of advice?

conseiller verb
1 to advise
**Je te conseille d'aller parler au
prof.** I advise you to go and talk to
the teacher.
2 to recommend
Je te conseille ce film.
I recommend this film.

le **conservatoire** noun *masc.*
music school

la **conserve** noun *fem.*
une boîte de conserve a tin
en conserve tinned

la **consigne** noun *fem.*
left-luggage office

la **console** noun *fem.*
une console de jeu a games
console

la **consonne** noun *fem.*
consonant

constamment adverb
constantly

construire verb
to build

🔑 **LANGUAGE**
In English 'construct' is another word for
'build'.

contacter verb
to contact

le **conte** noun *masc.*
tale
un conte de fées a fairy tale

content adjective *masc.*, **contente**
fem.
pleased

⚠️ **FALSE FRIEND**
content = pleased (*not* content)

le **continent** noun *masc.*
continent
le continent africain the African
continent

continuer verb
to carry on
Continuez votre travail! Carry on
with your work!
Je peux continuer à jouer? Can I
carry on playing?

le **contraire** noun *masc.*
opposite
'Grand' est le contraire de 'petit'.
'Big' is the opposite of 'small'.

ⓔ means use être to make the past tense.

a
b
c
d
e
f
g
h
i
j
k
l
m
n
o
p
q
r
s
t
u
v
w
x
y
z

contre preposition
against
contre le mur against the wall
Ils jouent contre Saint-Étienne.
They're playing against
Saint-Étienne.

le **contrôle** noun masc.
1 **test**
un contrôle d'anglais an English
test
2 (of tickets, passports, etc.) **check**
le contrôle d'identité an identity
check

contrôler verb
to check

cool adjective masc. & fem.
cool
Tu as l'air cool! You look cool!

le **copain** noun masc.
1 **friend**
un copain d'école a schoolfriend
2 **boyfriend**
son nouveau copain her new
boyfriend
Tu as un petit copain? Do you have
a boyfriend?

la **copie** noun fem.
copy
Fais une copie du fichier. Make a
copy of the file.

copier verb
to copy
Il a copié sur moi. He copied from
me.

copier-coller verb
to cut and paste

la **copine** noun fem.
1 **friend**
une copine d'école a schoolfriend
2 **girlfriend**
sa nouvelle copine his new
girlfriend
Tu as une petite copine? Do you
have a girlfriend?

le **coq** noun masc.
cockerel

🌍 **CULTURE**
The cockerel is a symbol of French
fighting spirit and pride. The sound it
makes is **cocorico** (cock-a-doodle-doo)
and people sometimes use this word to
show they are proud to be French.

la **coque** noun fem.
un œuf à la coque a boiled egg

le **coquetier** noun masc.
egg cup

le **coquelicot** noun masc.
poppy

le **coquillage** noun masc.
seashell

la **coquille** noun fem.
shell

le **corail** noun masc. (plural les
coraux)
coral

le **Coran** noun masc.
Koran

le **corbeau** noun masc. (plural les
corbeaux)
crow

la **corbeille** noun fem.
basket
une corbeille à papier
a wastepaper basket

la **corde** noun fem.
1 **rope**
une corde à sauter a skipping rope
2 **string**
une corde de guitare a guitar
string

le **cordonnier** noun masc.
shoe repairer

la **corne** noun fem.
horn

la **cornemuse** noun fem.
bagpipes

• Languages, nationalities, and religions do not take a capital letter in French.

Arthur joue de la cornemuse.
Arthur plays the bagpipes.

le **corner** noun *masc.*
corner (kick)

le **cornet** noun *masc.*
cone
un cornet de glace an ice-cream cone
un cornet de frites a bag of chips (shaped like a cone)

le **cornichon** noun *masc.*
gherkin

le **corps** noun *masc.*
body

correct adjective *masc.*,
correcte *fem.*
correct

correctement adverb
correctly

la **correspondance** noun *fem.*
(for trains or buses) **connection**
Où est la correspondance? Where do you change trains (or buses)?

le **correspondant** noun *masc.*,
la **correspondante** *fem.*
penfriend

correspondre verb
to correspond
Ça correspond à … It corresponds to …

corriger verb
1 **to correct**
corriger une faute to correct a mistake
2 **to mark**

corse adjective *masc. & fem.*
Corsican

le or la **Corse** noun *masc. & fem.*
Corsican *(person)*

la **Corse** noun *fem.*
Corsica

le **costume** noun *masc.*
1 **suit**
Mon père porte un costume chic.
My father is wearing a smart suit.
2 **costume** *(for dressing up)*
un costume de cowboy a cowboy costume

la **côte** noun *fem.*
1 **coast**
Calais est sur la côte. Calais is on the coast.
la Côte d'Azur the French Riviera
2 **rib**
François s'est cassé une côte.
François has broken a rib.
3 **chop**
une côte d'agneau a lamb chop
4 **hill**
grimper une côte to climb a hill

le **côté** noun *masc.*
1 **side**
Ils habitent de l'autre côté de la rue. They live on the other side of the road.
C'est de quel côté? Which way is it?
2 **à côté de** next to
Tu peux t'asseoir à côté de moi.
You can sit next to me.
3 **à côté** nearby

la **côtelette** noun *fem.*
chop
une côtelette d'agneau a lamb chop

le **coton** noun *masc.*
cotton
un tee-shirt en coton a cotton T-shirt
le coton hydrophile cotton wool

> 🔑 **LANGUAGE**
> French = coton
> English = cotton

le **cou** noun *masc.*
neck

◉ *means use* **être** *to make the past tense.*

French English

a b **c** d e f g h i j k l m n o p q r s t u v w x y z

la **couche** noun *fem.*
nappy

couché adjective *masc.*,
couchée *fem.*
1 **lying**
Philippe est couché sur le canapé.
Philippe is lying on the sofa.
2 **in bed**
Les enfants sont couchés. The
children are in bed.

le **coucher** noun *masc.*
le coucher du soleil the sunset

se **coucher** verb ⓔ
1 **to go to bed**
Je me couche à dix heures. I go to
bed at ten.
2 **to set**
Le soleil se couche. The sun is
setting.

la **couchette** noun *fem.*
berth

coucou exclamation
hello
Coucou! C'est moi! Hello! It's me!

le **coude** noun *masc.*
elbow

coudre verb
to sew

la **couette** noun *fem.*
duvet

les **couettes** plural noun *fem.*
bunches (*hairstyle*)

couler verb
1 **to flow**
L'eau coule. The water is flowing.
2 **to sink**
Le bateau a coulé. The boat sank.
3 **to run**
J'ai le nez qui coule. My nose is
running.

la **couleur** noun *fem.*
colour

Ma couleur préférée est le rouge.
My favourite colour is red.
C'est de quelle couleur? What
colour is it?
De quelle couleur est ton vélo?
What colour is your bike?

le **couloir** noun *masc.*
corridor
au bout du couloir at the end of the
corridor

le **coup** noun *masc.*
1 **knock**
Il a reçu un coup sur la tête. He got
a knock on his head.
2 un coup de pied a kick
donner un coup de pied à
quelqu'un to kick somebody
3 un coup de poing a punch
donner un coup de poing à
quelqu'un to punch somebody
4 un coup d'œil a look
jeter un coup d'œil to have a look
5 un coup de main a helping hand
donner un coup de main à
quelqu'un to give somebody a
hand
6 un coup de soleil sunburn
7 du premier coup first time
8 tout à coup suddenly

coupable adjective *masc. & fem.*
guilty

la **coupe** noun *fem.*
1 **cup**
la Coupe du Monde the World Cup
2 une coupe de cheveux a haircut
3 une coupe de glace an ice cream

couper verb
to cut
J'ai coupé le pain en tranches. I cut
the bread into slices.

se **couper** verb ⓔ
to cut
Ne te coupe pas les doigts! Don't
cut your fingers!
se faire couper les cheveux to have
your hair cut

• *The months of the year and days of the week do not take a capital letter in French.*

46

le couple noun *masc.*
  couple
  un jeune couple a young couple

la coupure noun *fem.*
  cut
  J'ai mis un pansement sur ma coupure. I put a plaster on my cut.
  une coupure d'électricité a power cut

la cour noun *fem.*
  1 la cour de récréation the school playground
  2 la cour de notre immeuble the courtyard of our block of flats

le courage noun *masc.*
  courage
  Bon courage! Good luck!

courageux adjective *masc.*,
  courageuse *fem.*
  brave

couramment adverb
  fluently
  Je parle couramment anglais. I speak English fluently.

courant adjective *masc.*,
  courante *fem.*
  common
  une faute très courante a very common mistake

le courant noun *masc.*
  1 current (*in sea, river*)
  2 un courant d'air a draught
  3 une panne de courant a power cut
  4 être au courant de quelque chose to know about something

le coureur noun *masc.*,
  la coureuse *fem.*
  runner
  les coureurs du marathon the marathon runners
  le coureur cycliste (racing) cyclist

courir verb
  to run
  Ne courez pas! Don't run!

❸ means use être to make the past tense.

J'ai couru chez moi. I ran home.
On va courir? Shall we go for a run?

la couronne noun *fem.*
  crown

le courriel noun *masc.*
  email
  J'ai reçu un courriel. I've got an email.

le courrier noun *masc.*
  1 mail
  Il y a du courrier pour toi. There's some mail for you.
  2 le courrier électronique email

cours verb SEE **courir**
  Je cours tous les matins. I run every morning.

le cours noun *masc.*
  1 class
  J'ai un cours de maths. I've got a maths class.
  2 course
  Mon frère prend des cours d'italien. My brother's doing an Italian course.

la course noun *fem.*
  1 race
  Je fais la course avec toi. I'll race you.
  une course de chevaux a horse race
  2 running
  la course à pied running race
  3 shopping
  J'ai une course à faire. I have one bit of shopping to do.

les courses plural noun *fem.*
  shopping
  faire les courses to go shopping
  une liste de courses a shopping list

le court de tennis noun *masc.*
  tennis court

court adjective *masc.*, **courte** *fem.*
  short
  les cheveux courts short hair

le **couscous** noun *masc.*
couscous

🌍 **CULTURE**
Le couscous is a North African dish, and is very popular in France.

le **cousin** noun *masc.*,
la **cousine** *fem.*
cousin

le **coussin** noun *masc.*
cushion

le **couteau** noun *masc.* (plural les **couteaux**)
knife

coûter verb
to cost
Ça coûte combien? How much does it cost?
Ça coûte cher. It's expensive.

la **couture** noun *fem.*
sewing

le **couvercle** noun *masc.*
lid

couvert adjective *masc.*, **couverte** *fem.*
1 covered
Tu es couvert de boue. You're covered in mud.
2 cloudy
un ciel couvert a cloudy sky
3 indoor
une piscine couverte an indoor swimming pool

le **couvert** noun *masc.*
mettre le couvert to lay the table

les **couverts** plural noun *masc.*
cutlery

la **couverture** noun *fem.*
blanket

couvrir verb
to cover
Nous devons couvrir nos livres. We have to cover our books.

• *See the centre section for verb tables.*

se **couvrir** verb ⓔ
to dress warmly
Couvre-toi bien, il fait froid! Dress warmly, it's cold!

le **CP** noun *masc.*
Year 2

🔑 **LANGUAGE**
CP is short for **cours préparatoire**.

le **crabe** noun *masc.*
crab

cracher verb
to spit

la **craie** noun *fem.*
chalk

le **crapaud** noun *masc.*
toad

la **cravate** noun *fem.*
tie

le **crayon** noun *masc.*
pencil
au crayon in pencil
un crayon de couleur a coloured pencil

⚠️ **FALSE FRIEND**
un crayon = a pencil (*not* a crayon)

la **crèche** noun *fem.*
nursery
Elle va à la crèche. She goes to a nursery.

la **crème** noun *fem.*
cream
un gâteau à la crème a cream cake
la crème Chantilly whipped cream
la crème solaire sun cream

la **crêpe** noun *fem.*
pancake

🌍 **CULTURE**
Children in France eat **crêpes** on **Mardi gras** (Shrove Tuesday).

la **crêperie** noun *fem.*
pancake restaurant

creuser verb
to dig

creux adjective *masc.*, **creuse** *fem.*
hollow

crevé adjective *masc.*, **crevée** *fem.*
1 **exhausted**
Je suis crevé! I'm exhausted!
2 un pneu crevé a flat tyre

crever verb
to burst
Il a crevé mon ballon. He's burst my balloon.
Ils ont crevé. They had a puncture.

la crevette noun *fem.*
prawn

le cri noun *masc.*
shout
pousser des cris to scream

crier verb
to shout

la crise noun *fem.*
attack
une crise d'asthme an asthma attack
une crise cardiaque a heart attack

critiquer verb
to criticize

le crocodile noun *masc.*
crocodile

croire verb
1 **to think**
Je crois qu'il s'appelle Jérôme. I think his name is Jérôme.
Tu crois? Do you think so?
Je ne crois pas. I don't think so.
2 **to believe**
Je ne te crois pas. I don't believe you.
Tu crois au père Noël? Do you believe in Father Christmas?

croiser verb
croiser les jambes to cross your legs
croiser les bras to fold your arms

la croix noun *fem.*
cross

le croque-monsieur noun *masc.*
(plural les **croque-monsieur**)
toasted ham and cheese sandwich

la crotte noun *fem.*
1 la crotte de chien dog mess
2 des crottes en chocolat chocolate drops

la croûte noun *fem.*
1 **crust**
la croûte du pain the crust of the bread
2 **rind**
la croûte du fromage the rind of the cheese

cru verb *masc.*, **crue** *fem.* SEE **croire**
Je t'ai cru. I believed you.

cru adjective *masc.*, **crue** *fem.*
raw
une carotte crue a raw carrot

les crudités plural noun *fem.*
raw vegetables

cruel adjective *masc.*, **cruelle** *fem.*
cruel

Cuba noun *fem.*
Cuba

le cube noun *masc.*
cube

cueillir verb
to pick

la cuillère, **la cuiller** noun *fem.*
spoon
une petite cuillère a teaspoon

la cuillerée noun *fem.*
spoonful

means use être to make the past tense.

le **cuir** noun *masc.*
leather
un blouson en cuir a leather jacket

cuire verb
to cook
C'est en train de cuire. It's cooking.
faire cuire to cook

la **cuisine** noun *fem.*
1 kitchen
Léa est dans la cuisine. Léa's in the kitchen.
2 cooking
faire la cuisine to do the cooking
un livre de cuisine a cookbook
3 food
la cuisine française French food

cuisiner verb
to cook
J'adore cuisiner. I love cooking.

le **cuisinier** noun *masc.*,
la **cuisinière** *fem.*
cook

la **cuisinière** noun *fem.*
cooker

la **cuisse** noun *fem.*
thigh
une cuisse de poulet a chicken leg

cuit adjective *masc.*, **cuite** *fem.*
cooked

bien cuit well cooked
trop cuit overcooked
un steak bien cuit a steak well done

la **culotte** noun *fem.*
knickers

le **cultivateur** noun *masc.*,
la **cultivatrice** *fem.*
farmer

cultiver verb
to grow

curieux adjective *masc.*,
curieuse *fem.*
curious, **nosy**

le **curseur** noun *masc.*
cursor

le **cybercafé** noun *masc.*
Internet cafe

cyclable adjective *masc & fem.*
une piste cyclable a cycle path

le **cyclisme** noun *masc.*
cycling

le or la **cycliste** noun *masc. & fem.*
cyclist

le **cygne** noun *masc.*
swan

Dd

d' preposition SEE **de**

> 🔑 **LANGUAGE**
> **d'** = **de** before *a, e, i, o, u, y,* or *silent h*

1 of
un verre d'eau a glass of water
le père d'Amélie Amélie's father
2 from
une carte postale d'Éric a postcard from Éric
pas loin d'ici not far from here

d' determiner SEE **de**

> 🔑 **LANGUAGE**
> **d'** = **de** before *a, e, i, o, u,* or *silent h*

any
Elle n'a pas d'amies. She doesn't have any friends.

d'abord adverb
first
Je vais manger d'abord. I'm going to eat first.

• *Use* **le** *and* **un** *for masculine words and* **la** *and* **une** *for feminine words.*

D'abord, il va en France, ensuite en Espagne. First, he's going to France, then Spain.

d'accord adverb

1 (*answering 'yes'*) **all right**
On part? – D'accord! Shall we leave? – All right!

2 être d'accord to agree
Je suis d'accord avec toi. I agree with you.

la **dame** noun *fem.*

1 lady
Tu vois la dame là-bas? Can you see the lady over there?
une vieille dame an old lady

2 les dames draughts
Tu veux jouer aux dames? Do you want to play draughts?

3 (*in cards*) **la dame de cœur** the queen of hearts

le **danger** noun *masc.*
danger

dangereux adjective *masc.*,
dangereuse *fem.*
dangerous

danois adjective *masc.*,
danoise *fem.*
Danish

le **danois** noun *masc.*
Danish (*the language*)

un **Danois** noun *masc.*,
une **Danoise** *fem.*
Dane (*person*)

dans preposition

1 in
C'est dans mon sac. It's in my bag.
Le film commence dans dix minutes. The film starts in ten minutes.

2 into
J'ai mis mes CD dans un carton. I put my CDs into a box.

la **danse** noun *fem.*
dance
Je fais de la danse. I go to dancing classes.
la danse classique ballet

danser verb
to dance

le **danseur** noun *masc.*,
la **danseuse** *fem.*
dancer
une danseuse étoile a principal dancer

la **date** noun *fem.*
date
Quelle est ta date de naissance? What's your date of birth?
Quelle est la date d'aujourd'hui? What's the date today?

la **datte** noun *fem.*
date (*fruit*)

le **dauphin** noun *masc.*
dolphin

davantage adverb
more

de preposition

> **⚡ LANGUAGE**
> **de + la = de la**
> **de + le = du**
> **de + les = des**
> **de + le** or **la** + *a, e, i, o, u,* or *silent h* = **de l'**
> **de** + *a, e, i, o, u, y,* or *silent h* = **d'**

1 of
une bouteille de lait a bottle of milk
un garçon de dix ans a boy of ten
la fin du mois the end of the month
la plupart des enfants most of the children

2 (*talking about who something belongs to*)
la maison de mes parents my parents' house
la porte de la classe the classroom door

3 from

❷ *means use **être** to make the past tense.*

a b c **d** e f g h i j k l m n o p q r s t u v w x y z

French English

a
b
c
d
e
f
g
h
i
j
k
l
m
n
o
p
q
r
s
t
u
v
w
x
y
z

Je viens de Glasgow. I come from Glasgow.

de dix heures à midi from ten o'clock till midday

4 by

un livre de J.K. Rowling a book by J.K. Rowling

5 to

Je suis content de te voir. I'm pleased to see you.

Il a décidé de partir. He has decided to leave.

de article

🔑 LANGUAGE

de +la = de la
de +le = du
de + les = des
de + le or la+ *a, e, i, o, u,* or *silent h* = de l'
de + *a, e, i, o, u, y,* or *silent h* = d'

---

1 some

Il boit du jus d'orange. He's drinking some orange juice.

Nous écoutons de la musique. We're listening to some music.

2 any

Je ne veux pas de gâteau. I don't want any cake.

Je n'ai pas d'amis. I don't have any friends.

Est-ce que tu as des amis? Do you have any friends?

3 (**de** *not translated*) **du pain et du fromage** bread and cheese

Je mange des pommes. I eat apples.

Je ne mange pas de pommes. I don't eat apples.

le **dé** noun *masc.*
dice
Jette les dés! Throw the dice!

débarrasser verb
to clear
Peux-tu débarrasser la table? Can you clear the table?

se **débarrasser** verb ∅
se débarrasser de quelque chose to get rid of something

déborder verb
Ça déborde! It's spilling over!

debout adverb
standing
Tout le monde debout! Everybody get up!
Debout, c'est l'heure! Time to get up!

se **débrouiller** verb ∅
to manage
Je me débrouille. I can manage.
Débrouille-toi! Get on with it!

le **début** noun *masc.*
1 beginning
au début de la semaine at the beginning of the week
début janvier at the beginning of January
2 au début at first

le **débutant** noun *masc.*,
la **débutante** *fem.*
beginner
Je suis débutant. I'm a beginner.

le **décalage horaire** noun *masc.*
time difference

 CULTURE
There's a time difference between France and Britain: France is one hour ahead.

---

décalquer verb
to trace

la **décapotable** noun *fem.*
convertible (*car*)

décédé adjective *masc.*,
décédée *fem.*
dead

décembre noun *masc.*
December
en décembre in December

• *Languages, nationalities, and religions do not take a capital letter in French.*

Je pars en vacances fin décembre. I'm going on holiday at the end of December.
J'ai dix ans le cinq décembre. I'll be ten on the fifth of December.

déchirer verb
to tear
Mon pantalon est déchiré. My trousers are torn.
Il a déchiré la lettre. He tore up the letter.

décider verb
to decide
J'ai décidé de venir te voir. I decided to come and see you.

la décision noun fem.
decision
prendre une décision to make a decision

décoller verb
to take off
L'avion décolle à six heures. The plane takes off at six.

décontracté adjective masc., décontractée fem.
relaxed
Il est toujours décontracté. He's always relaxed.

les décorations plural noun fem.
decorations
On va mettre les décorations de Noël. We'll put up the Christmas decorations.

décorer verb
to decorate
Les élèves ont décoré la classe avec des dessins. The pupils have decorated the classroom with pictures.

découper verb
to cut out
Découpez ces photos de magazine. Cut out these photos from the magazine.

se décourager verb ⓔ
to give up hope
Il ne faut pas te décourager. You mustn't give up.

la découverte noun fem.
discovery

découvrir verb
to discover

décrire verb
to describe
Décrivez votre famille. Describe your family.

déçu adjective masc., déçue fem.
disappointed

dedans adverb
inside
Il n'y a rien dedans. There's nothing inside.

défaire verb
1 to undo
défaire un nœud to undo a knot
Tes lacets sont défaits. Your laces are undone.
2 to unpack
Tu veux défaire ta valise? Do you want to unpack your case?

défendre verb
1 to defend
Il défend toujours sa petite sœur. He always defends his little sister.
2 to forbid
Papa me défend de sortir. Dad forbids me to go out.
C'est défendu! That's not allowed!

la défense noun fem.
1 (on signs)
'Défense de fumer' 'No smoking'
2 les défenses d'éléphant elephant tusks

le défi noun masc.
challenge

le défilé noun masc.
1 parade
2 un défilé de mode a fashion show

ⓔ means use être to make the past tense.

a
b
c
d
e
f
g
h
i
j
k
l
m
n
o
p
q
r
s
t
u
v
w
x
y
z

dégoûtant adjective *masc.*,
  dégoûtante *fem.*
1 disgusting
2 really dirty

le **degré** noun *masc.*
degree
Il fait vingt degrés à l'ombre.
It's twenty degrees in the shade.

déguisé adjective *masc.*, **déguisée**
fem.
dressed up
Elle est déguisée en sorcière.
She's dressed up as a witch.

le **déguisement** noun *masc.*
dressing up costume
un déguisement de pirate
a pirate's costume

se **déguiser** verb ℮
to dress up
Je vais me déguiser en fée.
I'm going to dress up as a fairy.

dehors adverb
outside
On va jouer dehors. Let's go and
play outside.

déjà adverb
1 already
Il est déjà trois heures. It's already
three o'clock.
2 before
Léo est déjà allé à Londres. Léo has
been to London before.

déjeuner verb
1 (*lunchtime*) **to have lunch**
2 (*morning*) **to have breakfast**

le **déjeuner** noun *masc.*
lunch
**Qu'est-ce que tu as mangé au
déjeuner?** What did you have for
lunch?
le petit déjeuner breakfast

délicieux adjective *masc.*,
  délicieuse *fem.*
delicious

demain adverb
tomorrow
À demain! See you tomorrow!
demain matin tomorrow morning
demain soir tomorrow night

demander verb
to ask, **to ask for**
Tu vas demander à tes parents?
Are you going to ask your parents?
J'ai demandé un MP3 à Noël.
I asked for an MP3 for Christmas.

se **demander** verb ℮
to wonder
Je me demande où il va. I wonder
where he's going.

déménager verb
to move house

demi adjective *masc.*, **demie** *fem.*
1 half
quatre et demi four and a half
trois kilos et demi three and a half
kilos
une heure et demie an hour and a
half
Il est huit heures et demie. It's half
past eight.
2 demi- half
un demi-litre half a litre
une demi-journée half a day
une demi-douzaine d'œufs half a
dozen eggs

le **demi-cercle** noun *masc.*
semicircle
en demi-cercle in a semicircle

la **demi-finale** noun *fem.*
semifinal

le **demi-frère** noun *masc.*
stepbrother, **half brother**

la **demi-heure** noun *fem.*
half an hour

la **demi-sœur** noun *fem.*
stepsister, **half sister**

le **demi-tour** noun *masc.*
faire demi-tour to turn back

• *The months of the year and days of the week do not take a capital letter in French.*

démodé adjective *masc.*,
démodée *fem.*
old-fashioned

la **demoiselle** noun *fem.*
young lady
une demoiselle d'honneur
a bridesmaid

démolir verb
to knock down
Ils vont démolir ce mur. They're
going to knock down this wall.

démonter verb
to take apart

la **dent** noun *fem.*
tooth
les dents de lait milk teeth
J'ai mal aux dents. I've got
toothache.

le **dentifrice** noun *masc.*
toothpaste

le or la **dentiste** noun *masc. & fem.*
dentist
Il est allé chez le dentiste. He went
to the dentist's.

le **départ** noun *masc.*
departure

le **département** noun *masc.*
department

> **CULTURE**
> France is divided into 96 **départements**.
> They are numbered up to 95. These
> numbers feature on car number plates as
> well as in postcodes.

se **dépêcher** verb ⊘
to hurry
Dépêche-toi! Hurry up!

dépendre verb
to depend
Ça dépend de tes parents!
It depends on your parents!

dépenser verb
to spend

Il a dépensé beaucoup d'argent.
He's spent a lot of money.

déposer verb
to drop
Tu me déposes à la gare? Will you
drop me at the station?

depuis preposition
1 since
J'apprends l'anglais depuis 2007.
I've been learning English since
2007.
depuis ce moment-là since then
depuis ce matin since this morning
2 for
J'apprends l'anglais depuis deux
ans. I've been learning English for
two years.
depuis deux heures for two hours
Tu attends depuis combien de
temps? How long have you been
waiting?
Tu attends depuis quand? How
long have you been waiting?

depuis conjunction
depuis que ever since
Il pleut depuis que je suis arrivé.
It's been raining ever since I
arrived.

déranger verb
1 to bother
Je ne veux pas vous déranger.
I don't want to bother you.
Ça ne me dérange pas. I don't
mind.
2 to mess up
Tu as dérangé mes affaires! You've
messed up my things!

dernier adjective *masc.*,
dernière *fem.*
1 last
les deux dernières semaines
the last two weeks
l'année dernière last year
mardi dernier last Tuesday
la dernière fois last time

a b c **d** e f g h i j k l m n o p q r s t u v w x y z

⊘ *means use être to make the past tense.*

French English

a
b
c
d
e
f
g
h
i
j
k
l
m
n
o
p
q
r
s
t
u
v
w
x
y
z

Romain est arrivé dernier. Romain came last.

2 latest
le dernier film de Disney Disney's latest film

le **dernier** noun *masc.*,
la **dernière** *fem.*

1 last one
Tu veux le dernier? Do you want the last one?

2 bottom
Tristan est le dernier de la classe. Tristan is bottom of the class.

derrière preposition
behind
Je vais m'asseoir derrière. I'm going to sit behind.

le **derrière** noun *masc.*

1 bottom
Il est tombé sur le derrière. He fell on his bottom.

2 back
la porte de derrière the back door

des determiner

> ⚷ **LANGUAGE**
> des = de + les

1 some
Je vais acheter des bonbons. I'm going to buy some sweets.

2 any
Est-ce que tu as des animaux? Do you have any pets?

des preposition

> ⚷ **LANGUAGE**
> des = de + les

1 of the
la moitié des pommes half of the apples
les devoirs des élèves the pupils' homework
la maison des voisins the neighbours' house

2 from the
Elle vient des États-Unis. She comes from the United States.

• *See the centre section for verb tables.*

dès preposition
from
dès l'âge de cinq ans from the age of five

dès conjunction
dès que as soon as
Téléphone dès que tu seras là! Phone as soon as you get there!

désagréable adjective *masc. & fem.*
unpleasant

le **désastre** noun *masc.*
disaster

descendre verb ℮

1 to go down
Je n'aime pas descendre à la cave. I don't like going down to the cellar.

2 to come down
Descends dire au revoir. Come down and say goodbye.

3 to get down
Descends de l'arbre! Get down from the tree!

4 to get off
On descend au prochain arrêt. We're getting off at the next stop.

le **désert** noun *masc.*
desert

se **déshabiller** verb ℮
to get undressed
Je me déshabille. I'm getting undressed.

désirer verb
to want
Vous désirez, monsieur? What would you like?

désobéissant adjective *masc.*,
désobéissante *fem.*
disobedient

désolé adjective *masc.*,
désolée *fem.*
sorry
Je suis désolé. (*boy speaking*) **Je suis désolée.** (*girl speaking*) I'm sorry.

le **désordre** noun *masc.*
mess
Quel désordre! Look at this mess!
en désordre in a mess

le **dessert** noun *masc.*
dessert
Qu'est-ce que tu veux comme dessert? What do you want for dessert?

le **dessin** noun *masc.*
1 drawing
un joli dessin a lovely drawing
2 un dessin animé a cartoon

dessiner verb
to draw
Dessinez un cheval. Draw a horse.

en **dessous** adverb
underneath

le **dessous** noun *masc.*
1 bottom
Le dessous de l'assiette est sale. The bottom of the plate is dirty.
2 les voisins du dessous the neighbours below

dessus adverb
1 on top
L'ordinateur est neuf. Ne mets rien dessus. The computer is new. Don't put anything on top.
2 on it
Voici mon cahier. Mon nom est dessus. Here's my exercise book. My name's on it.

le **dessus** noun *masc.*
1 top
le dessus du frigo the top of the fridge
2 les voisins du dessus the neighbours above

la **destination** noun *fem.*
destination
le train à destination de Paris the train for Paris

le **détail** noun *masc.*
detail
en détail in detail

le **détective** noun *masc.*
detective
un détective privé a private detective

se **détendre** verb *⊕*
to relax
Daniel joue de la guitare pour se détendre. Daniel plays the guitar to relax.

détendu adjective *masc.*, **détendue** *fem.*
relaxed

détester verb
to hate
Je déteste les maths. I hate maths.

détruire verb
to destroy

deux number
1 two
à deux heures at two o'clock
Elle a deux ans. She's two.
le deux mai the second of May
deux fois twice
2 tous les deux, toutes les deux both
Karim et Jo sont tous les deux malades. Karim and Jo are both ill.

deuxième adjective *masc. & fem.*
second
au deuxième étage on the second floor

devant preposition
1 in front of
devant la bibliothèque in front of the library
2 past
Le bus passe devant la maison. The bus goes past the house.

devant adverb
in front
Mets-toi devant! Go in front!

⊕ means use être to make the past tense.

a
b
c
d
e
f
g
h
i
j
k
l
m
n
o
p
q
r
s
t
u
v
w
x
y
z

développer verb
to develop

devenir verb
to become
Il veut devenir acteur. He wants to become an actor.

devez verb SEE **devoir**
Vous devez écouter. You've got to listen.

deviner verb
to guess
Devine ce qu'il a fait! Guess what he did!

la **devinette** noun *fem.*
riddle

devoir verb
1 to have to
Je dois aller chez le médecin. I have to go to the doctor's.
2 must
On ne doit pas mentir. You mustn't tell lies.
3 (*when guessing*) **must**
Tu dois avoir soif. You must be thirsty.
4 to owe
Je dois dix euros à ma sœur. I owe my sister ten euros.

les **devoirs** plural noun *masc.*
homework
Je fais toujours mes devoirs. I always do my homework.

devons verb SEE **devoir**
Nous devons faire un effort. We've got to make an effort.

le **diabète** noun *masc.*
diabetes
Clément a du diabète. Clément has diabetes.

le **diabolo** noun *masc.*
un diabolo citron a lemonade with lemon cordial

le **diagramme** noun *masc.*
chart

le **diamant** noun *masc.*
diamond
un collier de diamants a diamond necklace

la **diarrhée** noun *fem.*
diarrhoea

la **dictée** noun *fem.*
dictation
On va faire une dictée. We're going to do a dictation.

CULTURE
Dictations are very common to help pupils with their spelling. Lots of words in French are pronounced in the same way but have different spellings.

le **dictionnaire** noun *masc.*
dictionary
Regardez dans le dictionnaire! Look in the dictionary!

LANGUAGE
French = dictio**nn**aire
English = dictio**n**ary

le **dieu** noun *masc.* (plural les **dieux**)
god

la **différence** noun *fem.*
difference
Quelle est la différence entre ces deux mots? What's the difference between these two words?

différent adjective *masc.*,
différente *fem.*
different
Je suis très différente de ma sœur. I'm very different from my sister.

difficile adjective *masc. & fem.*
difficult
C'est difficile à faire. It's difficult to do.
Je ne suis pas difficile, je mange de tout. I'm not fussy, I eat everything.

• *Use* **le** *and* **un** *for masculine words and* **la** *and* **une** *for feminine words.*

le **dimanche** noun *masc.*
1 Sunday
C'est dimanche aujourd'hui. It's Sunday today.
dimanche prochain next Sunday
dimanche dernier last Sunday
tous les dimanches every Sunday
2 on Sunday
J'arrive dimanche matin. I'm coming on Sunday morning.
À dimanche! See you on Sunday!
3 on Sundays
C'est fermé le dimanche. It's closed on Sundays.

la **dinde** noun *fem.*
turkey

dîner verb
to have dinner
Nous dînons à six heures. We have dinner at six.

le **dîner** noun *masc.*
dinner
C'est l'heure du dîner. It's dinner time.

la **dînette** noun *fem.*
toy tea set

le **dinosaure** noun *masc.*
dinosaur

le **diplôme** noun *masc.*
1 certificate
2 (*from a university*) **degree**

dire verb
1 to say
Qu'est-ce que tu dis? What are you saying?
'C'est vrai,' dit-elle. 'It's true,' she said.
Comment dit-on 'maison' en anglais? How do you say 'maison' in English?
Dis bonjour! Say hello!
2 to tell
Elle dit la vérité. She's telling the truth.

Dis-moi ce que tu penses! Tell me what you think!
Tu peux me dire l'heure? Can you tell me the time?
Elle nous a dit de travailler. She told us to work.
3 dire une blague to tell a joke
dire des bêtises to talk nonsense

direct adjective *masc.*, **directe** *fem.*
1 direct
C'est un train direct. It's a fast train.
2 (*in broadcasting*) **en direct de ...** live from ...

directement adverb
straight
Il est rentré directement. He went straight home.

le **directeur** noun *masc.*
1 headmaster
2 manager

la **direction** noun *fem.*
direction
C'est la bonne ou la mauvaise direction? Is it the right or the wrong direction?

la **directrice** noun *fem.*
1 headmistress
2 manager

dis verb SEE **dire**
Tu me dis des bêtises! You're talking rubbish!

la **discothèque** noun *fem.*
disco
Tu es trop jeune pour aller en discothèque. You're too young to go clubbing.

discuter verb
to talk
Nous avons discuté de choses intéressantes. We talked about interesting things.

disent, **disons** verb SEE **dire**

❷ means use être to make the past tense.

disparaître verb
1 **to disappear**
Il a fait disparaître l'oiseau.
He made the bird disappear.
2 **to go missing**
Mon stylo a disparu. My pen is missing.

dispensé adjective *masc.*,
dispensée *fem.*
Elle est dispensée de piscine. She's excused from swimming.

la **dispute** noun *fem.*
argument

se **disputer** verb Ⓔ
to argue
Elle se dispute toujours avec son frère. She's always arguing with her brother.

le **disque** noun *masc.*
1 **disk**
sur disque on disk
2 **record**
C'est un vieux disque. It's an old record.

la **distance** noun *fem.*
distance
Quelle est la distance entre Nice et Toulon? What's the distance between Nice and Toulon?

distrait adjective *masc.*,
distraite *fem.*
absent-minded

distribuer verb
to hand out
Distribue les cahiers! Can you hand out the exercise books?

le **distributeur automatique** noun *masc.*
1 **cash machine**
2 **vending machine** (*for drinks, sweets, etc.*)

dit, **dites** verb SEE **dire**
Je n'entends pas ce qu'il dit. I can't hear what he's saying.
Dites-moi ce que vous voulez faire. Tell me what you want to do.

le **divan** noun *masc.*
sofa

diviser verb
to divide
Douze divisé par trois égale quatre. Twelve divided by three is four.

divorcé adjective *masc.*,
divorcée *fem.*
divorced
Mes parents sont divorcés. My parents are divorced.

divorcer verb
to get divorced

dix number
ten
dix jours ten days
Nous partons à dix heures. We're leaving at ten.
Il est une heure moins dix. It's ten to one.
Il est cinq heures dix. It's ten past five.
J'ai dix ans. I'm ten.
le dix juillet the tenth of July

dix-huit number
eighteen
Mon frère a dix-huit ans.
My brother is eighteen.
Le train arrive à dix-huit heures.
The train arrives at six o'clock.
le dix-huit septembre the eighteenth of September

dixième adjective *masc. & fem.*
tenth
au dixième étage on the tenth floor

dix-neuf number
nineteen

• Languages, nationalities, and religions do not take a capital letter in French.

French English

a
b
c
d
e
f
g
h
i
j
k
l
m
n
o
p
q
r
s
t
u
v
w
x
y
z

Mon cousin a dix-neuf ans.
My cousin is nineteen.
L'avion décolle à dix-neuf heures.
The plane takes off at seven o'clock.
le dix-neuf janvier the nineteenth
of January

dix-sept number
seventeen
Ma sœur a dix-sept ans. My sister
is seventeen.
Prends le bus à dix-sept heures.
Catch the bus at five o'clock.
le dix-sept juin the seventeenth of
June

la **dizaine** noun *fem.*
une dizaine about ten
une dizaine de personnes about
ten people

le **docteur** noun *masc.*
doctor
Elle doit aller chez le docteur. She
has to go to the doctor's.

le **documentaire** noun *masc.*
documentary

le **dodo** noun *masc.*
faire dodo (*baby language*) to sleep

le **doigt** noun *masc.*
finger
Je me suis coupé le doigt. I've cut
my finger.
mes doigts de pied my toes

dois, **doit**, **doivent** verb
SEE **devoir**
Tu dois avoir faim. You must be
hungry.
Lucas doit faire ses devoirs. Lucas
has got to do his homework.
Ils doivent partir ce soir. They
have to leave tonight.

le **domicile** noun *masc.*
address
livrer à domicile to deliver

les **dominos** plural noun *masc.*
dominoes

On joue aux dominos? Shall we
play dominoes?

le **dommage** noun *masc.*
C'est dommage. It's a pity.

donc adverb
so
Il pleut, donc il faut prendre un
parapluie. It's raining, so we must
take an umbrella.

donner verb
1 to give
Donne-moi ton adresse! Give me
your address!
J'ai donné le CD à mon frère. I gave
the CD to my brother.
2 Ça donne soif. It makes you thirsty.

dont pronoun
1 whose
Sara, dont la mère est médecin...
Sara, whose mother is a doctor...
2 of which
J'ai des DVD, dont un en anglais.
I've got some DVDs, one of which is
in English.
3 of whom
dix enfants, dont cinq sont des
filles ten children, five of whom
are girls

doré adjective *masc.*, **dorée** *fem.*
golden

dormir verb
to sleep
Elle dort. She's sleeping.
Vous avez bien dormi? Did you
sleep well?

le **dortoir** noun *masc.*
dormitory

le **dos** noun *masc.*
back
J'ai mal au dos. My back is aching.
derrière son dos behind his back

means use être to make the past tense.

le **dossier** noun masc.
1 project
Le dossier de Luc est le meilleur de la classe. Luc's project is the best in the class.
2 record
un dossier scolaire a school record
3 (on a computer) **folder**
Mes fichiers sont dans ce dossier. My files are in this folder.
4 le dossier de la chaise the back of the chair

la **douane** noun fem.
customs

le **double** noun masc.
1 twice as much
Il a payé le double. He paid twice as much.
Vingt est le double de dix. Twenty is twice as many as ten.
2 avoir quelque chose en double to have two of something
Tu veux ce timbre? Je l'ai en double. Do you want this stamp? I've got two of them.

doublé adjective masc.,
doublée fem.
(film) **dubbed**
Le film est doublé en anglais. The film is dubbed in English.

doubler verb
1 to overtake
Le bus double. The bus is overtaking.
2 to double

douce adjective fem. SEE **doux**
une peau douce a soft skin

doucement adverb
1 gently
Marie caresse doucement le chat. Marie is gently stroking the cat.
2 quietly
Parlez doucement! Talk quietly!
3 slowly
Maman roule très doucement. Mum's driving very slowly.

la **douche** noun fem.
shower
Tu veux prendre une douche? Do you want to have a shower?
Je suis sous la douche. I'm in the shower.

se **doucher** verb ⊘
to have a shower

doué adjective masc., **douée** fem.
Elle est très douée pour les langues. She's very good at languages.
doué en maths good at maths

le **doute** noun masc.
doubt
J'ai des doutes. I have doubts.
sans doute probably

se **douter** verb ⊘
se douter de quelque chose to suspect something
La maîtresse ne se doute de rien. The teacher has no idea.

Douvres noun
Dover

doux adjective masc., **douce** fem.
1 (hands, voice, etc.) **soft**
la peau douce soft skin
2 gentle
Il est très doux. He's very gentle.
3 mild
Il fait doux. The weather's mild.

la **douzaine** noun fem.
une douzaine a dozen
une douzaine d'œufs a dozen eggs

douze number
twelve
douze œufs twelve eggs
J'ai douze ans. I'm twelve.
le douze août the twelfth of August

douzième adjective masc. & fem.
twelfth
au douzième étage on the twelfth floor

• The months of the year and days of the week do not take a capital letter in French.

la **dragée** noun *fem.*
sugared almond

CULTURE
At French christenings, communions, and weddings, friends and family are given a small box of **dragées** as a souvenir.

le **dragon** noun *masc.*
dragon

le **drap** noun *masc.*
sheet

le **drapeau** noun *masc.* (plural les **drapeaux**)
flag
le drapeau tricolore the French flag

droit adverb
straight
Marchez droit devant vous. Walk straight ahead.
tout droit straight ahead

le **droit** noun *masc.*
J'ai le droit de sortir. I'm allowed to go out.

droit adjective *masc.*, **droite** *fem.*
1 **right**
Levez la main droite! Raise your right hand!
Marche sur le côté droit de la route! Walk on the right-hand side of the road!
2 **straight**
une ligne droite a straight line
Tiens-toi droit, Julien! Sit up straight, Julien!

la **droite** noun *fem.*
right
Tournez à droite! Turn right!
la première rue sur votre droite the first street on your right
En France, on roule à droite. In France, we drive on the right.

droitier adjective *masc.*, **droitière** *fem.*
right-handed

means use être to make the past tense.

drôle adjective *masc. & fem.*
1 **funny**
Ce film est très drôle. This film is very funny.
2 **weird**
C'est un drôle d'endroit. It's a weird place.

drôlement adverb
C'est drôlement bien. It's really good.

du determiner

LANGUAGE
de + le = du

1 **some**
Je mange du pain. I'm eating some bread.
2 **any**
Est-ce qu'il y a du fromage? Is there any cheese?

du preposition

LANGUAGE
de + le = du

1 **of the**
la voiture du voisin the neighbour's car
2 **from the**
Je rentre du bureau. I've come back from the office.

dû verb *masc.*, **due** *fem.* SEE **devoir**
J'ai dû attendre. I had to wait.

le **duo** noun *masc.*
duet

dur adverb
hard
Camille travaille dur. Camille works hard.

dur adjective *masc.*, **dure** *fem.*
hard
un matelas dur a hard mattress
Cet exercice est trop dur. This exercise is too hard.
un œuf dur a hard-boiled egg

a
b
c
d
e
f
g
h
i
j
k
l
m
n
o
p
q
r
s
t
u
v
w
x
y
z

durant preposition

1 for

Il a neigé durant trois jours.
It snowed for three days.

2 during

durant l'hiver during the winter

la **durée** noun *fem.*
length

durer verb
to last

Le voyage dure combien de temps?
How long is the journey?
Ça a duré longtemps. It lasted a
long time.
Ça dure depuis deux jours. It's
been going on for two days.

le **DVD** noun *masc.* (plural les **DVD**)
DVD
un lecteur DVD a DVD player

dyslexique adjective *masc. & fem.*
dyslexic
Je suis dyslexique. I am dyslexic.

Ee

l'**eau** noun *fem.*
water
Je bois de l'eau. I drink water.
Tu peux me donner de l'eau?
Can you give me some water?
l'eau gazeuse fizzy water
l'eau minérale mineral water

un **écart** noun *masc.*

1 distance

Il est toujours à l'écart. He's
always by himself.

2 le grand écart the splits

écarter verb
to open (*arms, legs*)

un **échange** noun *masc.*

1 faire un échange to swap
Je te donne un bonbon en échange.
I'll give you a sweet for it.

2 exchange
Je vais en échange à Londres.
I'm going to London on an
exchange trip.

échanger verb
to swap
J'échange mon livre contre ton CD.
I'll swap my book for your CD.

• *See the centre section for verb tables.*

s'**échapper** verb ℗
to escape
La perruche s'est échappée de sa
cage. The budgie has escaped from
its cage.

une **écharpe** noun *fem.*
scarf

les **échecs** plural noun *masc.*
chess
Tu joues aux échecs? Do you play
chess?

une **échelle** noun *fem.*
ladder

un **éclair** noun *masc.*

1 flash of lightning
J'ai peur des éclairs. I'm afraid of
lightning.

2 un éclair au chocolat a chocolate
eclair

éclairer verb
to light up
Cette lampe de poche éclaire toute
la pièce. This torch lights up the
whole room.

éclater verb
to burst
Mon ballon a éclaté. My balloon has burst.

une école noun fem.
school
Je vais à l'école le samedi matin. I go to school on Saturday mornings.
l'école maternelle nursery school
l'école primaire primary school

 CULTURE
Children go to l'école maternelle between the ages of 3 and 6, and then to l'école primaire from 6 to 11. Schooldays are Monday, Tuesday, Thursday, Friday, and Saturday morning. Wednesday is a day off. Some schools have a four-day week.

un écolier noun masc.,
une écolière fem.
schoolboy, **schoolgirl**
les écoliers schoolchildren

les **économies** plural noun fem.
savings
faire des économies to save up

écossais adjective masc.,
écossaise fem.
1 Scottish
2 tartan
une jupe écossaise a tartan skirt

un Écossais noun masc.,
une Écossaise fem.
Scot

l'**Écosse** noun fem.
Scotland

écouter verb
to listen, **to listen to**
Écoute, Clément! Listen, Clément!
Écoutez la cassette! Listen to the tape!
Tu dois écouter tes parents. You have to listen to your parents.

un écran noun masc.
screen

écraser verb
1 to crush
2 se faire écraser to get run over

s'**écrier** verb ⊘
to cry out
'Attention,' s'écrie-t-elle. 'Be careful,' she cried out.

écrire verb
1 to write
Écris la date au tableau. Write the date on the board.
C'est écrit dans mon cahier. It's written in my exercise book.
Écrivez votre nom! Write your name!
2 to spell
Comment ça s'écrit? How do you spell that?

l'**écriture** noun fem.
handwriting
Tu as une belle écriture. You have a lovely handwriting.

un écrivain noun masc.
writer

un écureuil noun masc.
squirrel

une écurie noun fem.
stable

Édimbourg noun
Edinburgh

éducatif adjective masc.,
éducative fem.
educational
un site éducatif an educational website

effacer verb
1 to rub out
Efface ce que tu as écrit. Rub out what you've written.
2 to delete
J'ai effacé mon fichier. I've deleted my file.

⊘ *means use être to make the past tense.*

en **effet** adverb
indeed

un **effort** noun *masc.*
effort
Il ne fait aucun effort. He makes no effort.

effrayant adjective *masc.*,
effrayante *fem.*
frightening

égal adjective *masc.*, **égale** *fem.*,
égaux *masc. plural*, **égales** *fem.*
plural
1 **equal**
un nombre égal de filles et de garçons an equal number of girls and boys
2 **Ça m'est égal.** I don't mind.

égaler verb
to equal
Trois plus sept égalent dix. Three plus seven equals ten.

égaliser verb
to equalize

l'**égalité** noun *fem.*
Les deux équipes sont à égalité. The two teams are even.

une **église** noun *fem.*
church

égoïste adjective *masc. & fem.*
selfish

eh bien exclamation
well!
Eh bien, tu as raison! Well, you're right!

un **élastique** noun *masc.*
elastic band

un **électricien** noun *masc.*,
une **électricienne** *fem.*
electrician

l'**électricité** noun *fem.*
electricity

électrique adjective *masc. & fem.*
electric

électronique adjective *masc. & fem.*
electronic

un **éléphant** noun *masc.*
elephant

un or une **élève** noun *masc. & fem.*
pupil

éliminé adjective *masc.*,
éliminée *fem.*
eliminated, **out**

elle pronoun *fem.*
1 **she**
Elle chante. She sings.
2 **it**
La clé? Elle est sur le frigo. The key? It's on top of the fridge.

> **LANGUAGE**
> When **elle** stands for a thing or animal that is feminine, translate as 'it'.

3 *(after a preposition etc.)* **her**
avec elle with her
Tu es plus intelligente qu'elle. You're smarter than her.
C'est elle. It's her.
4 **à elle** hers
Ce CD est à elle. This CD is hers.

elle-même pronoun
herself

elles pronoun

> **LANGUAGE**
> **Elles** stands for plural feminine words: people, things, or animals.

1 **they**
Elles jouent dans le jardin. They're playing in the garden.
Léa et Chloé? Elles sont dans la cuisine. Léa and Chloé? They're in the kitchen.
2 *(after a preposition etc.)* **them**
avec elles with them

• *Use **le** and **un** for masculine words and **la** and **une** for feminine words.*

Nicole et Marie? Je suis plus petite qu'elles. Nicole and Marie? I'm shorter than them.
Ce sont elles. It's them.
3 à elles theirs
Ces CD sont à elles. These CDs are theirs.

un **email** noun *masc.*
email
J'envoie un email? Shall I send an email?

l'**embarquement** noun *masc.*
boarding
une carte d'embarquement a boarding card

embêtant adjective *masc.*,
embêtante *fem.*
annoying

embêter verb
to annoy
Tu m'embêtes! You're annoying me!

s'**embêter** verb ⊘
to be bored
On s'embête ici. It's boring here.

un **embouteillage** noun *masc.*
traffic jam

embrasser verb
to kiss
Je t'embrasse. (*at the end of a letter*) Lots of love.

s'**embrasser** verb ⊘
to kiss each other
On s'embrasse? Shall we kiss each other?

CULTURE
Girls normally kiss each other on the cheek to say hello or goodbye; it's the same between boys and girls but between boys it's more usual to shake hands.

une **émission** noun *fem.*
programme

⊘ *means use* être *to make the past tense.*

Il y a une bonne émission à la télé. There's a good programme on TV.

empêcher verb
to stop
Ça m'empêche de dormir. It stops me from sleeping.

un **emploi** noun *masc.*
1 **job**
Mon père a trouvé un emploi. My dad has found a job.
2 **un emploi du temps** a timetable

un **employé** noun *masc.*,
une **employée** *fem.*
un employé de bureau an office worker
une employée de banque a bank clerk

employer verb
1 **to use**
2 **to employ**

emporter verb
1 **to take**
N'oublie pas d'emporter tes CD. Don't forget to take your CDs.
2 **to take away**
un repas chinois à emporter a Chinese meal to take away

emprunter verb
to borrow
J'ai emprunté cinq euros à mon frère. I borrowed five euros from my brother.

en preposition
1 **in**
en été in summer
en mars in March
en 2007 in 2007
en anglais in English
en Angleterre in England
2 **to**
On va en France. We're off to France.
3 **by**
en voiture by car

a b c d e f g h i j k l m n o p q r s t u v w x y z

a
b
c
d
e
f
g
h
i
j
k
l
m
n
o
p
q
r
s
t
u
v
w
x
y
z

4 into
Traduisez 'arbre' en anglais.
Translate 'arbre' into English.
Je vais en ville. I'm going into town.

5 (*talking about what something is made of*)
un lit en bois a wooden bed

6 (*before a verb*) **while**, **when**
Elle a pleuré en sortant. She cried when she was leaving.

en pronoun

1 of it, **of them**
Je n'aime pas le sucre. Tu m'en as donné trop. I don't like sugar. You've given me too much of it.
Des frères? J'en ai trois. Brothers? I have three of them.

2 about it, **about them**
Éric a vu le film. Il va nous en parler. Éric has seen the film. He's going to talk to us about it.
Tu veux en parler? Do you want to talk about it?

3 some
Il reste des pommes. Tu en veux? There are some apples left. Do you want some?
J'en ai. I have some.

4 any
Je n'en veux pas. I don't want any.
Il y a du chocolat? – Non, il n'y en a pas. Is there any chocolate? – No, there isn't any.

encore adverb

1 still
Tu regardes encore la télé? Are you still watching TV?

2 again
Elle a encore oublié son livre. She's forgotten her book again.
encore une fois once again

3 more
encore deux jours two more days
Tu veux encore du gâteau? Would you like some more cake?

4 even
encore mieux even better

5 pas encore not yet
Je n'ai pas encore fini. I haven't finished yet.

encourager verb
to encourage

l'**encre** noun *fem.*
ink

l'**endive** noun *fem.*
chicory

endormi adjective *masc.*,
endormie *fem.*
asleep

s'**endormir** verb ℮
to fall asleep
Je m'endors vite. I go to sleep quickly.

un **endroit** noun *masc.*

1 place
C'est mon endroit préféré. It's my favourite place.

2 à l'endroit the right way round

énervé adjective *masc.*,
énervée *fem.*
irritated, **annoyed**

énerver verb
to annoy
Tu m'énerves. You're annoying me.

s'**énerver** verb ℮
to get annoyed
Ne t'énerve pas! Calm down!

enfermer verb
to shut
J'enferme mon hamster dans sa cage. I shut my hamster in its cage.

s'**enfermer** verb ℮
to shut yourself
Je m'enferme dans ma chambre. I shut myself in my bedroom.

enfin adverb

1 at last
2 last of all

• Languages, nationalities, and religions do not take a capital letter in French.

3 well
Ici, il pleut toujours, enfin presque.
It's always raining here, well almost always.

enflé adjective *masc.*, **enflée** *fem.*
swollen

s'**enfuir** verb *◎*
to run away
Il s'est enfui. He ran away.

enlever verb
1 to take away
Enlève tes affaires de la table.
Take your things off the table.
2 to take off
Enlevez vos chaussures! Take your shoes off!

un **ennemi** noun *masc.*,
une **ennemie** *fem.*
enemy

⚷ LANGUAGE
French = ennemi
English = enemy

les **ennuis** plural noun *masc.*
problems
Papa a des ennuis. Dad has problems.

ennuyer verb
1 to bother
Ça m'ennuie beaucoup. That really bothers me.
2 to bore

s'**ennuyer** verb *◎*
to be bored
Je m'ennuie. I'm bored.

ennuyeux adjective *masc.*,
ennuyeuse *fem.*
boring
C'est ennuyeux. It's boring.

énorme adjective *masc. & fem.*
huge, enormous

une **enquête** noun *fem.*
investigation

◎ means use **être** *to make the past tense.*

enregistrer verb
1 to record
Fabien va enregistrer le film.
Fabien's going to record the film.
2 (*at an airport*) **to check in**

enrhumé adjective *masc.*,
enrhumée *fem.*
être enrhumé to have a cold

un **enseignant** noun *masc.*,
une **enseignante** *fem.*
teacher

enseigner verb
to teach
Mademoiselle Spooner enseigne l'anglais. Miss Spooner teaches English.

ensemble adverb
together
Répétez tous ensemble! Repeat all together!

un **ensemble** noun *masc.*
outfit

ensoleillé adjective *masc.*,
ensoleillée *fem.*
sunny

ensuite adverb
then
On va aller à la piscine et ensuite au parc. We're going swimming and then to the park.

entendre verb
to hear
Je t'entends. I can hear you.
Vous m'entendez bien? Can you hear me properly?

s'**entendre** verb *◎*
s'entendre avec quelqu'un to get on with somebody
Je m'entends bien avec mes parents. I get on well with my parents.

French English

entier adjective *masc.*, **entière** *fem.*
whole
la classe entière the whole class
Je n'ai pas vu le film en entier.
I haven't seen the whole film.

> 🔑 **LANGUAGE**
> **Tout** (all) is often put in front of **entier**, for example: **J'ai mangé le gâteau tout entier.** (I ate the whole cake.)

entièrement adverb
completely

entourer verb
to surround
La maison est entourée d'arbres.
The house is surrounded by trees.

un **entracte** noun *masc.*
interval
à l'entracte in the interval

l'**entraînement** noun *masc.*
training
Il y a un entraînement de foot samedi. We have football training on Saturday.

s'**entraîner** verb 🔘
to train
On s'entraîne tous les lundis.
We train every Monday.

entre preposition
between
L'école est entre la gare et le cinéma. The school is between the station and the cinema.

l'**entrée** noun *fem.*
1 entrance
à l'entrée de l'école at the school entrance
2 hall
Tes chaussures sont dans l'entrée.
Your shoes are in the hall.
3 starter
Qu'est-ce qu'il y a comme entrée?
What's for starter?

entrer verb 🔘
1 to go in
Sophie entre dans le magasin.
Sophie goes into the shop.
2 to come in
Entrez! Come in!

une **enveloppe** noun *fem.*
envelope

> 🔑 **LANGUAGE**
> French = enveloppe
> English = envelope

envelopper verb
to wrap

à l'**envers** adverb
1 inside out
Tes chaussettes sont à l'envers.
Your socks are inside out.
2 upside down
La photo est à l'envers. The photo is upside down.

l'**envie** noun *fem.*
J'ai envie d'une glace. I want an ice cream.
Tu as envie de dormir? Do you feel sleepy?
Je n'ai pas envie. I don't feel like it.

environ adverb
about
environ quinze élèves about fifteen pupils
à environ deux heures at about two o'clock

un **envoi** noun *masc.*
Clique sur Envoi! Click on Send!

envoyer verb
to send
Je vais t'envoyer des photos. I'm going to send you some photos.
Envoie-moi un courriel. Send me an email.

épais adjective *masc.*, **épaisse** *fem.*
thick
une tranche épaisse a thick slice

• *The months of the year and days of the week do not take a capital letter in French.*

une **épaule** noun *fem.*
shoulder

une **épée** noun *fem.*
sword

épeler verb
to spell
Tu peux épeler ton nom? Can you spell your name?

épicé adjective *masc.*, **épicée** *fem.*
spicy

une **épicerie** noun *fem.*
grocer's (shop)

les **épinards** plural noun *masc.*
spinach

> **LANGUAGE**
> French = **épinards** is plural
> English = **spinach** is singular

une **épingle** noun *fem.*
pin
une épingle de sûreté a safety pin

l'**Épiphanie** noun *fem.*
Epiphany

> **CULTURE**
> On the day of l'**Épiphanie**, people eat the **galette des Rois**. This is a kind of cake, with a small figurine or a bean hidden inside. The person who gets the piece of cake with the trinket becomes king (or queen) for the day and wears the paper crown that comes with the galette.

éplucher verb
to peel

une **éponge** noun *fem.*
sponge

une **époque** noun *fem.*
time
à cette époque at that time

épouser verb
to marry

Ⓔ *means use* **être** *to make the past tense.*

l'**EPS** noun *fem.*
PE

> **LANGUAGE**
> EPS is short for **éducation physique et sportive** (physical and sports education).

équestre adjective *masc. & fem.*
un centre équestre a riding school

l'**équilibre** noun *masc.*
balance
Elle a perdu l'équilibre. She lost her balance.

un **équipage** noun *masc.*
crew

une **équipe** noun *fem.*
team

l'**équitation** noun *fem.*
horse-riding
Tu fais de l'équitation? Do you go horse-riding?

une **erreur** noun *fem.*
mistake

es verb SEE **être**
 1 (*the present tense*)
  Tu es mon amie. You're my friend.
 2 (*when used to form a past tense*)
  Tu es arrivé en retard. You arrived late.

l'**escalade** noun *fem.*
climbing
un mur d'escalade a climbing wall

un **escalier** noun *masc.*
stairs
un escalier de secours a fire escape
un escalier roulant an escalator

un **escargot** noun *masc.*
snail

l'**escrime** noun *fem.*
fencing

l'**espace** noun *masc.*
space
un voyage dans l'espace a journey into space

l'**Espagne** noun *fem.*
Spain

l'**espagnol** noun *masc.*
Spanish (*the language*)

espagnol adjective *masc.*,
espagnole *fem.*
Spanish

un **Espagnol** noun *masc.*,
une **Espagnole** *fem.*
Spaniard

une **espèce** noun *fem.*
1 sort
C'est une espèce d'ordinateur.
It's a sort of computer.
2 species
une espèce en voie de disparition
an endangered species

espérer verb
to hope
J'espère bien! I hope so.
J'espère que non. I hope not.

espiègle adjective *masc. & fem.*
mischievous

un **espion** noun *masc.*,
une **espionne** *fem.*
spy

l'**espoir** noun *masc.*
hope

un **esquimau**® noun *masc.*
choc ice

un **essai** noun *masc.*
try (*in rugby*)

essayer verb
1 to try
Essaie de dormir. Try to sleep.
2 to try on
Je peux essayer ces chaussures?
Can I try these shoes on?

l'**essence** noun *fem.*
petrol

l'**essentiel** noun *masc.*
the main thing

Elle vient – c'est l'essentiel. She's
coming – that's the main thing.

l'**essuie-tout** noun *masc.*
kitchen towel

essuyer verb
1 to wipe
Tu peux essuyer la table? Can you
wipe the table?
2 to dry
Papa essuie la vaisselle. Dad's
drying the dishes.

est verb SEE **être**
1 (*the present tense*)
Il est triste. He's sad.
Il est huit heures. It's eight o'clock.
2 (*when used to form a past tense*)
Elle est partie ce matin. She left
this morning.

est adjective *masc. & fem.*
east
la côte est the east coast

l'**est** noun *masc.*
east
C'est dans l'est de la France. It's in
the east of France.
à l'est de Grenoble to the east of
Grenoble

> **LANGUAGE**
> **Est** is the same in the masculine,
> feminine, and plural.

est-ce que phrase
Est-ce que tu es fatigué? Are you
tired?
Est-ce qu'elle a fini? Has she
finished?

> **LANGUAGE**
> **Est-ce que** can be put in front of any
> normal statement (like **tu es fatigué**) to
> make it a question; word for word it
> means 'is it that'.

l'**estomac** noun *masc.*
stomach

et conjunction
and

• *See the centre section for verb tables.*

une pomme et une orange
an apple and an orange
Et alors? And so what?

un **étage** noun *masc.*
floor
au troisième étage on the third
floor

une **étagère** noun *fem.*
shelf

étais, **était** verb SEE **être**
(**être** *in the past tense*)
Hier, j'étais malade. Yesterday, I
was sick.
Tu étais où hier? Where were you
yesterday?
C'était génial! It was great!
C'était nul! It was rubbish!

étaler verb
to spread
Étale le beurre sur le pain. Spread
the butter on the bread.

l'**état** noun *masc.*
condition
en bon état in good condition

les **États-Unis** plural noun *masc.*
United States

etc adverb
etc, and so on

été verb SEE **être**
Léo a été grondé. Léo has been told
off.

l'**été** noun *masc.*
summer
en été in the summer
cet été this summer

éteindre verb
to switch off
J'ai éteint la lumière. I switched
the light off.

éternuer verb
to sneeze

❷ means use **être** *to make the past tense.*

CULTURE
In France people say **À tes souhaits!**,
meaning 'to your wishes', when
somebody sneezes.

êtes verb SEE **être**
1 (*in the present tense*)
Léa et Lisa, vous êtes les premières.
Léa and Lisa, you're the first.
Monsieur Clet, vous êtes prêt?
Monsieur Clet, are you ready?
2 (*when used to form a past tense*)
Vous êtes arrivés quand? When
did you arrive?

une **étiquette** noun *fem.*
label

s'**étirer** verb ❷
to stretch
Je m'étire. I'm stretching.

une **étoile** noun *fem.*
star
une étoile filante a shooting star
une étoile de mer a starfish

étonnant adjective *masc.*,
étonnante *fem.*
surprising

étonner verb
to surprise
Ça ne m'étonne pas. I'm not
surprised.
Ça m'étonnerait! I'd be surprised!

étourdi adjective *masc.*,
étourdie *fem.*
absent-minded

étrange adjective *masc. & fem.*
strange

LANGUAGE
The English word comes from the French:
sometimes a French word with an é has
the letter 's' instead in the English word. A
few words follow this pattern, for
example: **étrange** is 'strange' in English,
étudier is 'to study'.

a
b
c
d
e
f
g
h
i
j
k
l
m
n
o
p
q
r
s
t
u
v
w
x
y
z

a
b
c
d
e
f
g
h
i
j
k
l
m
n
o
p
q
r
s
t
u
v
w
x
y
z

étranger adjective *masc.*,
  étrangère *fem.*
  foreign

un **étranger** noun *masc.*,
  une **étrangère** *fem.*
  1 foreigner
  C'est une étrangère. She's a
  foreigner.
  2 à l'étranger abroad

être verb
  1 to be
  Je suis grand. I'm tall.
  Tu es sympa. You are nice.
  On est samedi. It's Saturday today.
  Ma mère est coiffeuse. My mum's
  a hairdresser.
  Mes parents sont stricts.
  My parents are strict.
  2 (*for making the past tense of some verbs*)
  Je suis allé. (*boy speaking.*) Je suis
  allée. (*girl speaking*) I went.
  Elle est partie. She has left.
  Vous êtes venus. You have come.
  Ils sont arrivés. They have arrived.

les **étrennes** plural noun *fem.*
  New Year's Day present

 CULTURE
In the New Year, some people give
étrennes to children, often little gifts of
money, or to people like their postman.

étroit adjective *masc.*, **étroite** *fem.*
  narrow

les **études** plural noun *fem.*
  studies
  faire des études to study

un **étudiant** noun *masc.*,
  une **étudiante** *fem.*
  student

étudier verb
  to study

eu verb *masc.*, **eue** *fem.* SEE **avoir**
  J'ai eu un problème. I had a
  problem.

euh exclamation
  er, **hmm** (*when you hesitate*)

un **euro** noun *masc.*
  euro
  Ça coûte huit euros. It costs eight
  euros.

l'**Europe** noun *fem.*
  Europe

européen adjective *masc.*,
  européenne *fem.*
  European

un **Européen** noun *masc.*,
  une **Européenne** *fem.*
  European (*person*)

eux pronoun
  1 (*after a preposition etc.*) **them**
  Tu connais Tom et Axel? On joue
  avec eux? Do you know Tom and
  Axel? Shall we play with them?
  Ce sont eux. It's them.
  2 à eux theirs
  C'est à eux. It's theirs.

s'**évader** verb ℮
  to escape

s'**évanouir** verb ℮
  to faint

un **événement** noun *masc.*
  event

évidemment adverb
  of course

évident adjective *masc.*,
  évidente *fem.*
  obvious

un **évier** noun *masc.*
  sink

éviter verb
  to avoid

exact adjective *masc.*, **exacte** *fem.*
  exact
  C'est exact. That's right.

exactement adverb
  exactly

• *Use le and un for masculine words and la and une for feminine words.*

ex æquo adverb
Ils sont premiers ex æquo. They're joint winners.

exagérer verb
to exaggerate
Tu exagères toujours. You always exaggerate.
Là, tu exagères! That's pushing it a bit!

⚷ **LANGUAGE**
French = exagérer
English = exaggerate

un **examen** noun masc.
exam
un examen d'anglais an English exam

excellent adjective masc.,
excellente fem.
excellent

excité adjective masc., **excitée** fem.
excited

l'**exclamation** noun fem.
exclamation
un point d'exclamation an exclamation mark

une **excursion** noun fem.
trip
Nous avons fait une excursion à Versailles. We went on a trip to Versailles.

une **excuse** noun fem.
Il faut un mot d'excuse des parents. You need a note from your parents.

excuser verb
1 (when asking a question)
Excusez-moi! Excuse me!
2 (when you mean you're sorry)
Excusez-moi! Sorry!
Excusez-moi de vous déranger! Sorry to bother you!

@ means use être to make the past tense.

s'**excuser** verb @
to apologize
Je m'excuse. I apologize.

les **excuses** plural noun fem.
faire des excuses à quelqu'un to apologize to somebody

un **exemple** noun masc.
example
par exemple for example

⚷ **LANGUAGE**
French = exemple
English = example

s'**exercer** verb @
to practise

un **exercice** noun masc.
exercise
un exercice de grammaire a grammar exercise
Tu fais de l'exercice? Do you exercise?

⚷ **LANGUAGE**
French = exercice
English = exercise

exister verb
to exist

une **expérience** noun fem.
1 **experiment**
faire une expérience to do an experiment
2 **experience**
avoir beaucoup d'expérience to have lots of experience

une **explication** noun fem.
explanation

expliquer verb
to explain
Explique-moi pourquoi tu es en retard. Explain to me why you're late.

exploser verb
to explode

un **exposé** noun *masc.*
talk
faire un exposé to give a talk (*to the class*)

une **exposition** noun *fem.*
exhibition

exprès adverb
1 on purpose
Tu le fais exprès? Do you do this on purpose?
2 specially
Il est venu exprès. He came specially.

l'**extérieur** noun *masc.*
1 outside
l'extérieur de la maison the outside of the house
2 à l'extérieur outside

extra adjective *masc. & fem.*
great
Ces gâteaux sont extra! These cakes are great!

> 🔑 **LANGUAGE**
> **Extra** is the same in the masculine, feminine, and plural.

extraordinaire adjective *masc. & fem.*
amazing

un or une **extra-terrestre** noun *masc. & fem.*
extraterrestrial

extrêmement adverb
extremely

l'**Extrême-Orient** noun *masc.*
Far East

Ff

la **fable** noun *fem.*
fable

fabriquer verb
to make
fabriqué en France made in France

la **face** noun *fem.*
1 en face opposite
Mes cousins habitent en face. My cousins live opposite.
C'est en face de la poste. It's opposite the post office.
2 (*when throwing a coin*) **heads**
Pile ou face? Heads or tails?

fâché adjective *masc.*, **fâchée** *fem.*
angry
Tu es fâché contre moi? Are you angry with me?
Ils sont fâchés. They've fallen out.

se **fâcher** verb 🔊
1 to get angry
Il va se fâcher. He'll get angry.

2 to have an argument
Je me suis fâché avec elle. I had an argument with her.

facile adjective *masc. & fem.*
easy
C'est facile à comprendre. It's easy to understand.

facilement adverb
easily

la **façon** noun *fem.*
way
On écrit ce mot de deux façons. You can spell this word in two ways.
de toute façon anyway

le **facteur** noun *masc.*, la **factrice** *fem.*
postman, **postwoman**

la **facture** noun *fem.*
bill

• *Languages, nationalities, and religions do not take a capital letter in French.*

la facture de gaz the gas bill

faible adjective *masc. & fem.*
weak
Je suis faible en musique. I'm weak
in music.

faillir verb
J'ai failli gagner. I almost won.
Il a failli tomber. He nearly fell.

la **faim** noun *fem.*
hunger
J'ai faim. I'm hungry.
Il n'a pas faim. He isn't hungry.

🔑 **LANGUAGE**
French = **avoir** faim   **J'ai faim.**
English = **to be** hungry   **I'm hungry.**
---

fainéant adjective *masc.*,
fainéante *fem.*
lazy

faire verb
1 to do
Je fais mes devoirs. I'm doing my
homework.
Je n'ai rien fait. I didn't do
anything.
2 to make
On fait des gaufres? Shall we make
waffles?
Tu fais beaucoup de bruit. You're
making a lot of noise.
3 to play
Nous faisons du foot. We play
football.
Léa fait de la guitare. Léa plays the
guitar.
4 to have
J'ai fait un cauchemar. I had a
nightmare.
Je vais me faire couper les
cheveux. I'm going to have a
haircut.
5 to go
Ils font du camping. They go
camping.
Je fais du cheval. I go riding.
6 to be

*ℯ means use **être** to make the past tense.*

Il fait froid. It's cold.
Il fait beau. It's a lovely day.
Ça fait combien? How much is it?
Ça fait vingt euros. It's twenty
euros.
Deux et sept font neuf. Two and
seven are nine.
7 Ça fait deux heures que j'attends.
I've been waiting for two hours.
Ça fait un mois qu'il est parti. He
left a month ago.
8 Ça ne fait rien. It doesn't matter.

fais verb SEE **faire**
Je fais des progrès. I'm making
progress.
Tu fais tes devoirs? Are you doing
your homework?

faisais, **faisait** verb SEE **faire**
(**faire** *in the past tense*)
Il faisait beau. The weather was
nice.

faisons verb SEE **faire**
Nous faisons la vaisselle. We're
doing the washing-up.

fait verb SEE **faire**
Il fait une erreur. He's making a
mistake.
Elle a fait ça toute seule. She did
that by herself.

fait adjective *masc.*, **faite** *fem.*
made
C'est fait en verre. It's made of
glass.

faites verb SEE **faire**
Qu'est-ce que vous faites? What
are you doing?
Faites ce que vous voulez. Do what
you like.

la **falaise** noun *fem.*
cliff

falloir verb
Il va falloir travailler. You're
going to have to work.
Il faut dire la vérité. You must tell
the truth.

a
b
c
d
e
f
g
h
i
j
k
l
m
n
o
p
q
r
s
t
u
v
w
x
y
z

familier adjective *masc.*,
familière *fem.*
un animal familier a pet

la **famille** noun *fem.*
1 family
une famille nombreuse a large
family
2 relatives
J'ai de la famille à Bordeaux. I've
got relatives in Bordeaux.

le **fan** noun *masc. & fem.*
fan
C'est un fan de Madonna. He's a
fan of Madonna.

fantastique adjective *masc. & fem.*
fantastic

le **fantôme** noun *masc.*
ghost

la **farce** noun *fem.*
trick
faire une farce à quelqu'un to play
a trick on somebody

⚠ **FALSE FRIEND**
une farce = a trick (*not* a farce)

farci adjective *masc.*, **farcie** *fem.*
stuffed
des poivrons farcis stuffed peppers

la **farine** noun *fem.*
flour

fatigant adjective *masc.*,
fatigante *fem.*
tiring

fatigué adjective *masc.*,
fatiguée *fem.*
tired

fausse adjective *fem.* SEE **faux**

faut verb SEE **falloir**
Il faut lire ce livre. You have to
read this book.
Il faut rester à la maison? Do we
have to stay at home?

la **faute** noun *fem.*
1 mistake
une faute d'orthographe a
spelling mistake
2 fault
C'est ta faute! It's your fault!

le **fauteuil** noun *masc.*
armchair
un fauteuil roulant a wheelchair

faux adjective *masc.*, **fausse** *fem.*
1 not true
Ce qu'elle dit est faux. What she
says isn't true.
2 wrong
Ta réponse est fausse. Your answer
is wrong.
3 false
une fausse barbe a false beard
Vrai ou faux? True or false?

favori adjective *masc.*,
favorite *fem.*
favourite

la **fée** noun *fem.*
fairy
un conte de fées a fairy tale

les **félicitations** plural noun *fem.*
congratulations

féliciter verb
to congratulate
Je te félicite! Congratulations!

femalle adjective *masc. & fem.*
female

la **femelle** noun *fem.*
female

féminin adjective *masc.*, **féminine**
fem.
feminine

la **femme** noun *fem.*
1 woman
les hommes et les femmes men
and women
2 wife
C'est la femme de mon cousin.
She's my cousin's wife.

• *The months of the year and days of the week do not take a capital letter in French.*

la **fenêtre** noun *fem.*
window

le **fer** noun *masc.*
1 iron
C'est en fer. It's made of iron.
2 (*for clothes*)
un fer à repasser an iron
3 un fer à cheval a horseshoe

fera, **ferai**, **feras**, **ferez** verb
SEE **faire** (faire *in the future tense*)
Il fera le ménage. He will do the housework.
Je ferai ce que tu veux. I'll do what you want.
Est-ce que tu feras la sieste? Will you have a nap?
J'espère que vous ne ferez pas de bruit. I hope you won't make any noise.

férié adjective *masc.*
un jour férié a public holiday

la **ferme** noun *fem.*
farm
à la ferme on the farm

fermé adjective *masc.*, **fermée** *fem.*
closed
La fenêtre est fermée. The window is closed.

fermer verb
1 to close
Fermez vos livres! Close your books!
Le supermarché ferme à neuf heures. The supermarket closes at nine o'clock.
2 to turn off
N'oublie pas de fermer le robinet! Don't forget to turn off the tap!
3 fermer à clé to lock

la **fermeture** noun *fem.*
les heures de fermeture the closing times
une fermeture éclair® a zip

ⓔ means use être to make the past tense.

le **fermier** noun *masc.*,
la **fermière** *fem.*
farmer

féroce adjective *masc. & fem.*
fierce

ferons, **feront** verb SEE **faire**
(faire *in the future tense*)
Nous ne ferons pas de bruit. We won't make any noise.
Qu'est-ce qu'elles feront? What will they do?

les **fesses** plural noun *fem.*
bottom

la **fête** noun *fem.*
1 party
une fête d'anniversaire a birthday party
2 holiday
les fêtes de fin d'année the Christmas holidays
3 la fête des Mères Mother's Day
la fête des Pères Father's Day
la Fête Nationale Bastille Day

4 (*Saint's*) **name day**
Bonne fête! Happy saint's day!

fêter verb
to celebrate

On fête les 40 ans de mon père.
We're celebrating my father's 40th
birthday.

le **feu** noun *masc.* (plural les **feux**)
1 **fire**
   faire du feu to make a fire
2 **traffic light**
   le feu orange the amber light
3 **le feu d'artifice** fireworks

la **feuille** noun *fem.*
1 **leaf**
   les feuilles mortes dead leaves
2 **une feuille de papier** a sheet of
   paper

le **feuilleton** noun *masc.*
   soap
   C'est mon feuilleton préféré à la
   télé. It's my favourite TV soap.

le **feutre** noun *masc.*
   felt-tip pen

la **fève** noun *fem.*
   broad bean

février noun *masc.*
   February
   en février in February
   Il a fait très froid au mois de
   février. It was very cold during
   February.
   le trois février the third of
   February

les **fiançailles** plural noun *fem.*
   engagement
   une bague de fiançailles an
   engagement ring

fiancé adjective *masc.*, **fiancée** *fem.*
   engaged
   Ils sont fiancés. They're engaged.

se **fiancer** verb ☺
   to get engaged

la **ficelle** noun *fem.*
   string

la **fiche** noun *fem.*
   card
   Remplis la fiche. Fill in the card.

le **fichier** noun *masc.*
   file
   J'ai sauvegardé mon fichier sur ce
   CD. I've saved my file onto this CD.

fier adjective *masc.*, **fière** *fem.*
   proud
   Je suis fier de toi. I'm proud of you.

la **fièvre** noun *fem.*
   temperature, **fever**
   Est-ce que tu as de la fièvre?
   Do you have a temperature?

la **figure** noun *fem.*
   face

le **fil** noun *masc.*
1 **thread**
2 **wire**
   un fil électrique an electric wire
   du fil de fer wire
3 **un coup de fil** a phone call

la **file** noun *fem.*
   line
   en file indienne in single file

le **filet** noun *masc.*
   net

la **fille** noun *fem.*
1 **girl**
   une petite fille a little girl
   une jeune fille a young girl
2 **daughter**
   Ils ont un fils et une fille. They
   have a son and a daughter.

la **fillette** noun *fem.*
   little girl

le **filleul** noun *masc.*,
la **filleule** *fem.*
   godson, **goddaughter**

le **film** noun *masc.*
   film
   un film d'aventures an adventure
   film
   un film en relief a 3-D film

• *See the centre section for verb tables.*

le **fils** noun masc.
son

la **fin** noun fem.
end
à la fin du livre at the end of the book
jusqu'à la fin till the end
Fin The End

fin adjective masc., **fine** fem.
thin
des jambes fines thin legs

la **finale** noun fem.
final
La France est en finale. France is in the final.

finalement adverb
in the end

finir verb
to finish
Je finis mes devoirs. I'm finishing my homework.
Le film finit à six heures. The film finishes at six.
Tu as fini? Have you finished?

finlandais adjective masc.,
finlandaise fem.
Finnish

un **Finlandais** noun masc.,
une **Finlandaise** fem.
Finn (person)

la **Finlande** noun fem.
Finland

le **finnois** noun masc.
Finnish (language)

le **flamand** noun masc.
Flemish (language)

🌍 **CULTURE**
Flemish is a language like Dutch that is spoken in Belgium as well as French.

flamand adjective masc.,
flamande fem.
Flemish

ⓔ *means use être to make the past tense.*

un **Flamand** noun masc.,
une **Flamande** fem.
Flemish man, Flemish woman

la **flamme** noun fem.
flame

🔑 **LANGUAGE**
French = flamme
English = flame

le **flan** noun masc
baked custard

la **flaque** noun fem.
puddle

la **flèche** noun fem.
arrow

les **fléchettes** plural noun fem.
darts

la **fleur** noun fem.
flower
cueillir des fleurs to pick flowers
Les arbres sont en fleurs. The trees are in bloom.
un bouquet de fleurs a bunch of flowers

le or la **fleuriste** noun masc. & fem.
florist

le **fleuve** noun masc.
river

le **flipper** noun masc.
pinball

les **flocons** plural noun masc.
des flocons d'avoine porridge oats
des flocons de neige snowflakes

flotter verb
to float

la **flûte** noun fem.
flute
Mélissa joue de la flûte. Mélissa plays the flute.
une flûte à bec a recorder

a
b
c
d
e
f
g
h
i
j
k
l
m
n
o
p
q
r
s
t
u
v
w
x
y
z

a
b
c
d
e
f
g
h
i
j
k
l
m
n
o
p
q
r
s
t
u
v
w
x
y
z

le **foie** noun *masc.*
liver

le **foin** noun *masc.*
hay
le rhume des foins hay fever

la **foire** noun *fem.*
fair

la **fois** noun *fem.*
time
une fois once
combien de fois? how many times?
encore une fois once again
deux fois par mois twice a month
la première fois the first time
cette fois-ci this time
Deux fois six égalent douze. Two times six is twelve.
Il était une fois ... Once upon a time there was ...

folle adjective *fem.* SEE **fou**

foncé adjective *masc.*, **foncée** *fem.*
(*describing colours*) **dark**
des chemises vert foncé dark green shirts
Elle a les cheveux foncés. She's got dark hair.

le **fond** noun *masc.*
1 bottom
au fond de la rivière at the bottom of the river
2 back
au fond de la classe at the back of the class

fondre verb
to melt
La glace fond. The ice is melting.

la **fondue** noun *fem.*
fondue
la fondue savoyarde cheese fondue
la fondue bourguignonne meat fondue

font verb SEE **faire**
Qu'est-ce qu'ils font? What are they doing?

la **fontaine** noun *fem.*
fountain

le **foot** noun *masc.*
football
On joue au foot? Shall we play football?

⚲ **LANGUAGE**
Le **foot** is short for 'football'.

le **football** noun *masc.*
football
Il fait du football tous les samedis. He plays football every Saturday.

le **footballeur** noun *masc.*,
la **footballeuse** *fem.*
footballer

le **footing** noun *masc.*
jogging
faire du footing to go jogging

foraine adjective *fem.*
une fête foraine a funfair

la **force** noun *fem.*
strength

la **forêt** noun *fem.*
forest

⚲ **LANGUAGE**
French = forê**t**
English = for**est**

la **forme** noun *fem.*
1 shape
un gâteau en forme de cœur a cake in the shape of a heart
2 être en forme to be feeling well
Tu es en forme? Are you well?

formidable adjective *masc. & fem.*
fantastic, **great**

le **formulaire** noun *masc.*
form
remplir un formulaire to fill in a form

• *Use* le *and* un *for masculine words and* la *and* une *for feminine words.*

la **formule** noun *fem.*
une formule magique a magic spell

fort adverb
1 hard
Ne tape pas fort! Don't hit hard!
2 loud
Parle plus fort! Speak louder!

fort adjective *masc.*, **forte** *fem.*
1 strong
Tu es très fort. You're very strong.
2 loud
Baissez le son, c'est trop fort. Turn the sound down, it's too loud.
3 good
fort en anglais good at English

fou adjective *masc.*, **folle** *fem.*
mad

la **foudre** noun *fem.*
lightning

le **foulard** noun *masc.*
scarf

> **LANGUAGE**
> A **foulard** is a thin square scarf, not a long warm one.

la **foule** noun *fem.*
crowd

le **four** noun *masc.*
oven
un four à micro-ondes a microwave oven

la **fourchette** noun *fem.*
fork

la **fourmi** noun *fem.*
1 ant
2 J'ai des fourmis. I've got pins and needles.

les **fournitures scolaires** plural noun *fem.*
school stationery

fourré adjective *masc.*, **fourrée** *fem.*
filled
des biscuits fourrés au chocolat chocolate-filled biscuits

la **fourrure** noun *fem.*
fur

frais adjective *masc.*, **fraîche** *fem.*
1 fresh
du poisson frais fresh fish
2 cool
une boisson fraîche a cool drink
Il fait frais. The weather's cool.

la **fraise** noun *fem.*
strawberry
une glace à la fraise a strawberry ice cream
la confiture de fraises strawberry jam

la **framboise** noun *fem.*
raspberry
un yaourt à la framboise a raspberry yoghurt
la gelée de framboises raspberry jelly

le **franc** noun *masc.*
franc
le franc suisse the Swiss franc

> **CULTURE**
> In 2002, the **franc** was replaced by the euro in France, Belgium, and Luxembourg. The **franc** is still in use in Switzerland and some African countries.

franc adjective *masc.*, **franche** *fem.*
honest

le **français** noun *masc.*
French (the language)
Il parle français. He speaks French.
un cours de français a French lesson

a
b
c
d
e
f
g
h
i
j
k
l
m
n
o
p
q
r
s
t
u
v
w
x
y
z

*℮ means use **être** to make the past tense.*

français adjective *masc.*,
française *fem.*
French

le **Français** noun *masc.*,
la **Française** *fem.*
Frenchman, **Frenchwoman**

🔑 **LANGUAGE**
Français and **Française** can also mean
'French boy' or 'French girl'.

la **France** noun *fem.*
France
J'habite en France. I live in
France.
Tu vas en France? Are you going
to France?

franche adjective *fem.* SEE **franc** adj.

franchement adverb
frankly

francophone adjective *masc. & fem.*
French-speaking

la **frange** noun *fem.*
fringe

frapper verb
1 to knock
On frappe à la porte. Somebody's
knocking at the door.
2 to clap
Frappez des mains! Clap your
hands!
3 to hit
Ne frappe pas ton petit frère.
Don't hit your little brother.

le **frère** noun *masc.*
brother
C'est mon grand frère. He's my big
brother.

le **frien** noun *masc.*
brake

le **frigidaire**® noun *masc.*
fridge

le **frigo** noun *masc.*
fridge

frimer verb
to show off
Il frime devant les filles. He shows
off in front of girls.

frisé adjective *masc.*, **frisée** *fem.*
curly

🔑 **LANGUAGE**
Frisé describes hair with small, tight curls.

le **frisson** noun *masc.*
shiver

frissonner verb
to shiver

la **frite** noun *fem.*
chip
J'adore les frites. I love chips.
un poulet frites chicken and
chips

froid adjective *masc.*, **froide** *fem.*
1 cold
Ton café est froid. Your coffee is
cold.
2 J'ai froid. I'm cold.

🔑 **LANGUAGE**
French = **avoir** froid   **J'ai froid.**
English = **to be** cold   **I'm cold.**

3 (*when talking about the weather*)
Il fait froid. It's cold.

le **fromage** noun *masc.*
cheese
une omelette au fromage a cheese
omelette

le **front** noun *masc.*
forehead

la **frontière** noun *fem.*
border

• *Languages, nationalities, and religions do not take a capital letter in French.*

le **fruit** noun *masc.*
fruit
Tu veux un fruit? Do you want a piece of fruit?
J'adore les fruits. I love fruit.

les **fruits de mer** plural noun *masc.*
seafood

fumé adjective *masc.*, **fumée** *fem.*
smoked

la **fumée** noun *fem.*
smoke

Gg

le **gage** noun *masc.*
forfeit (*in a game*)

le **gagnant** noun *masc.*,
la **gagnante** *fem.*
winner

gagner verb
1 to win
Qui a gagné? Who won?
2 to earn
Mon frère gagne beaucoup d'argent. My brother earns a lot of money.
3 to save
gagner du temps to save time

la **galère** noun *fem.*
C'est galère! It's a real pain!

la **galerie** noun *fem.*
une galerie marchande a shopping mall

le **galet** noun *masc.*
pebble

la **galette** noun *fem.*
1 round flat cake
2 biscuit
3 la galette des Rois Twelfth Night cake

furieux adjective *masc.*, **furieuse** *fem.*
furious

la **fusée** noun *fem.*
rocket

le **fusil** noun *masc.*
gun

le **futur** noun *masc.*
(*in grammar*) **future**
Mettez ce verbe au futur. Put this verb in the future.

CULTURE
La galette des Rois is a cake that French people eat on 6th January (Epiphany). Inside is a little figurine or a bean called a **fève**. The person who finds the **fève** is known as the king (or queen) for the day and wears the paper crown that usually comes with the **galette**.

Galles plural noun *fem.*
le pays de Galles Wales

le **gallois** noun *masc.*
Welsh (*the language*)

gallois adjective *masc.*, **galloise** *fem.*
Welsh

le **Gallois** noun *masc.*,
la **Galloise** *fem.*
Welshman, **Welshwoman**

le **gamin** noun *masc.*,
la **gamine** *fem.*
kid

le **gant** noun *masc.*
glove
un gant de toilette a flannel

LANGUAGE
Un gant de toilette is a flannel that is worn on the hand like a glove.

🗝 *means use* **être** *to make the past tense.*

a
b
c
d
e
f
g
h
i
j
k
l
m
n
o
p
q
r
s
t
u
v
w
x
y
z

le **garage** noun *masc.*
garage

le or la **garagiste** noun *masc. & fem.*
car mechanic

le **garçon** noun *masc.*
boy
un petit garçon a little boy
un garçon de café a waiter

garder verb
1 to keep
Garde-moi une place! Keep a seat
for me!
2 to look after
Qui va garder le bébé? Who will
look after the baby?

la **garderie** noun *fem.*
day nursery

le **gardien** noun *masc.*,
la **gardienne** *fem.*
1 caretaker
un gardien d'immeuble
a caretaker
un gardien de nuit a night
watchman
2 un gardien de but a goalkeeper

la **gare** noun *fem.*
station
la gare routière the bus station

garer verb
garer la voiture to park the car

le **gars** noun *masc.*
guy
Salut les gars! Hi guys!

gaspiller verb
to waste
Elle a gaspillé son argent. She has
wasted her money.

gâté adjective *masc.*, **gâtée** *fem.*
spoilt
C'est un enfant gâté. He's spoilt.

le **gâteau** noun *masc.* (plural les
gâteaux)
cake

un gâteau d'anniversaire
a birthday cake
un gâteau sec a biscuit

gauche adjective *masc. & fem.*
left
Daniel écrit de la main gauche.
Daniel writes with his left hand.
**Marche sur le côté gauche de la
route.** Walk on the left-hand side
of the road.

la **gauche** noun *fem.*
left
à gauche on the left
sur ta gauche on your left
**En Grande-Bretagne, on roule à
gauche.** In Britain, they drive on
the left.
Tournez à gauche! Turn left!
Regarde dans le tiroir de gauche.
Look in the left-hand drawer.

gaucher adjective *masc.*,
gauchère *fem.*
left-handed

la **gaufre** noun *fem.*
waffle

la **gaufrette** noun *fem.*
wafer

le **Gaulois** noun *masc.*, la **Gauloise**
fem.
Gaul

CULTURE
Long ago **les Gaulois** were the people
who lived in an area called **la Gaule**
(Gaul), which is where France and
Belgium are today. French people are
sometimes known as **Gaulois**, and the
comics of *Astérix le Gaulois* are very popular
in France.

le **gaz** noun *masc.*
gas

gazeux adjective *masc.*,
gazeuse *fem.*
fizzy
une boisson gazeuse a fizzy drink
de l'eau gazeuse fizzy water

• *The months of the year and days of the week do not take a capital letter in French.*

géant adjective *masc.*, **géante** *fem.*
huge

le **géant** noun *masc.*, la **géante** *fem.*
giant

la **gelée** noun *fem.*
jelly

geler verb
to freeze
Il gèle. It's freezing.
Je suis gelé. I'm frozen.

gêné adjective *masc.*, **gênée** *fem.*
embarrassed

le **gendarme** noun *masc.*
policeman

la **gendarmerie** noun *fem.*
police station

général adjective *masc.*, **générale**
fem., **généraux** *masc. plural*,
générales *fem. plural*
general
en général generally

généralement adverb
generally

généreux adjective *masc.*,
généreuse *fem.*
generous

génial adjective *masc.*, **géniale**
fem., **géniaux** *masc. plural*,
géniales *fem. plural*
great
C'est génial! That's great!

le **génie** noun *masc.*
genius
C'est un génie! He's a genius!

le **genou** noun *masc.* (plural les
genoux)
knee
Mets-toi à genoux! Kneel down!

le **genre** noun *masc.*
1 kind
**C'est le genre de livres que j'aime
lire.** It's the kind of book I like
reading.

2 gender
**C'est quel genre, masculin ou
féminin?** What gender is it,
masculine or feminine?

les **gens** plural noun *masc.*
people
la plupart des gens most people

gentil adjective *masc.*,
gentille *fem.*
nice, **kind**

gentiment adverb
nicely
Demande gentiment! Ask nicely!

la **géographie** noun *fem.*
geography

la **gerbille** noun *fem.*
gerbil

germain adjective *masc.*,
germaine *fem.*
un cousin germain a first cousin

gigantesque adjective *masc. & fem.*
gigantic

le **gigot** noun *masc.*
un gigot d'agneau a leg of lamb

le **gilet** noun *masc.*
1 cardigan
2 waistcoat

la **girafe** noun *fem.*
giraffe

> **LANGUAGE**
> French = girafe
> English = giraffe

le **gîte** noun *masc.*
**rented holiday house in the
country**

la **glace** noun *fem.*
1 ice
J'ai glissé sur la glace. I slipped on
the ice.
2 ice cream
une glace à la vanille a vanilla ice
cream

@ means use être to make the past tense.

a b c d e f g h i j k l m n o p q r s t u v w x y z

3 mirror
Regarde-toi dans la glace! Look at yourself in the mirror!

glacé adjective *masc.*, glacée *fem.*
frozen
J'ai les pieds glacés. My feet are frozen.

le glaçon noun *masc.*
ice cube

glisser verb
1 to slip
Ian a glissé sur des feuilles et il est tombé. Ian slipped on some leaves and fell.
2 to slide
Les garçons glissent sur la glace. The boys are sliding on the ice.
3 to be slippery
Ça glisse ici! It's slippery here!

le gobelet noun *masc.*
beaker

le golf noun *masc.*
golf
un terrain de golf a golf course

la gomme noun *fem.*
rubber

gommer verb
to rub out

gonflable adjective *masc. & fem.*
inflatable

gonfler verb
1 to blow up
On gonfle des ballons? Let's blow up some balloons!
2 to pump up
Gonfle les pneus de ton vélo. Pump up your bicycle tyres.

la gorge noun *fem.*
throat
Elle a mal à la gorge. She has a sore throat.

le gorille noun *masc.*
gorilla

gourmand adjective *masc.*, gourmande *fem.*
greedy
Je suis très gourmande. I've got a sweet tooth.

le goût noun *masc.*
taste
Ça n'a aucun goût. It has no taste.
Ça a un goût de poulet. It tastes like chicken.
Ce gâteau a très bon goût. This cake tastes very nice.

goûter verb
1 to taste
Goûte ça! Taste this!
2 to have an afternoon snack

le goûter noun *masc.*
children's afternoon snack
un goûter d'anniversaire a children's birthday party

la goutte noun *fem.*
drop

la goyave noun *fem.*
guava

le grain noun *masc.*
un grain de raisin a grape

la graine noun *fem.*
seed

la grammaire noun *fem.*
grammar
une faute de grammaire a grammatical mistake

le gramme noun *masc.*
gram

grand adjective *masc.*, grande *fem.*
1 big
une grande ville a big town
C'est mon grand frère. He's my big brother.
2 tall
Tu es plus grande que moi. You're taller than me.

• See the centre section for verb tables.

French English

a
b
c
d
e
f
g
h
i
j
k
l
m
n
o
p
q
r
s
t
u
v
w
x
y
z

3 un grand magasin a department store

une grande personne a grown-up

les grandes vacances the summer holidays

grand-chose pronoun
pas grand-chose not much
Je n'ai pas grand-chose à faire. I don't have much to do.

la **Grande-Bretagne** noun *fem.*
Great Britain

grandir verb
to grow

la **grand-mère** noun *fem.* (plural les **grands-mères**)
grandmother

le **grand-père** noun *masc.* (plural les **grands-pères**)
grandfather

les **grands-parents** plural noun *masc.*
grandparents

la **grappe** noun *fem.*
une grappe de raisin a bunch of grapes

le **gras** noun *masc.*
fat
le gras du jambon the fat of the ham

gras adjective *masc.*, **grasse** *fem.*
1 fatty
les aliments gras fatty foods
2 greasy
Tu as les cheveux gras. You've got greasy hair.

le **gratin** noun *masc.*
cheese-topped dish

le **gratte-ciel** noun *masc.* (plural les **gratte-ciel**)
skyscraper

gratter verb
1 to scratch
Ne te gratte pas! Don't scratch!

2 to be itchy
Ça me gratte. It's itchy.

gratuit adjective *masc.*, **gratuite** *fem.*
free
un billet gratuit a free ticket
L'entrée est gratuite. Entry is free of charge.

gratuitement adverb
free
Nous sommes entrés gratuitement. We got in free.

grave adjective *masc. & fem.*
1 serious
une maladie grave a serious illness
Pardon! – Ce n'est pas grave. Sorry! – It's all right.
2 un accent grave a grave accent

gravement adverb
seriously

le **grec** noun *masc.*
Greek (*the language*)

grec adjective *masc.*, **grecque** *fem.*
Greek

le **Grec** noun *masc.*, la **Grecque** *fem.*
Greek (*person*)

la **Grèce** noun *fem.*
Greece

la **grêle** noun *fem.*
hail

la **grenadine** noun *fem.*
grenadine

CULTURE
La grenadine is a sweet red drink made from pomegranates and other red fruits.

le **grenier** noun *masc.*
loft, attic

la **grenouille** noun *fem.*
frog

la **grève** noun *fem.*
strike
en grève on strike

means use **être** *to make the past tense.*

griffer verb
to scratch

grignoter verb
to nibble

la **grille** noun *fem.*
metal gate

le **grille-pain** noun *fem.* (plural les **grille-pain**)
toaster

griller verb
1 **faire griller** to grill
du poisson grillé grilled fish
2 **du pain grillé** toast

la **grimace** noun *fem.*
funny face

grimper verb
to climb

grincheux adjective *masc.*, **grincheuse** *fem.*
grumpy

la **grippe** noun *fem.*
flu

gris adjective *masc.*, **grise** *fem.*
grey
un ciel gris a grey sky

le **gris** noun *masc.*
grey
Elle porte du gris. She's wearing grey.

grogner verb
1 **to growl**
Le chien grogne. The dog is growling.
2 **to grunt**
Le cochon grogne. The pig is grunting.

gronder verb
to tell off
Ma mère va me gronder. My mum will tell me off.

gros adjective *masc.*, **grosse** *fem.*
1 **big**
un gros livre a big book
J'ai un gros rhume. I've got a bad cold.
2 **fat**
Le chat est trop gros. The cat's too fat.
3 **un gros mot** a rude word

> ⚠️ **FALSE FRIEND**
> **un gros mot** = a rude word (*not* a big word)

grossir verb
to put on weight

> 🔑 **LANGUAGE**
> **Grossir** comes from **gros** (fat).

la **grotte** noun *fem.*
cave

> 🔑 **LANGUAGE**
> **La grotte** is like the English word 'grotto', another word for a 'cave'.

le **groupe** noun *masc.*
group
un groupe de rock a rock band

le **guépard** noun *masc.*
cheetah

la **guêpe** noun *fem.*
wasp

guérir verb
1 **to cure**
Le médecin l'a guéri. The doctor cured him.
2 **to get better**
Hugo est guéri. Hugo is better.

la **guerre** noun *fem.*
war

le **guichet** noun *masc.*
1 **counter**
le guichet de la banque the bank counter
2 **ticket office**

• *Use le and un for masculine words and la and une for feminine words.*

90

le **guide** noun *masc.*
guide
Il est guide. He's a guide.
J'ai acheté un guide. (*a book*)
I bought a guide.

guider verb
to guide

le **guidon** noun *masc.*
handlebars

> **LANGUAGE**
> French = **le guidon** is singular
> English = **handlebars** is plural

le **guignol** noun *masc.*
puppet show

la **guimauve** noun *fem.*
marshmallow

les **guirlandes** plural noun *fem.*
tinsel

On décore le sapin de Noël avec des guirlandes. We decorate the Christmas tree with tinsel.

la **guitare** noun *fem.*
guitar
Léa joue de la guitare. Léa plays the guitar.

> **LANGUAGE**
> French = guitare
> English = guitar

la **gym** noun *fem.*
(*at school*) **PE**
On a gym. We have PE.

le **gymnase** noun *masc.*
gym

la **gymnastique** noun *fem.*
gymnastics, PE
Je fais de la gymnastique. I do gymnastics.

Hh

s'**habiller** verb @
to get dressed
Je m'habille. I'm getting dressed.

l'**habitant** noun *masc.*,
l'**habitante** *fem.*
inhabitant
les habitants du quartier the people living in the area

habiter verb
to live
J'habite en France. I live in France.
Tu habites à Paris. You live in Paris.
Où habites-tu? Where do you live?

les **habits** plural noun *masc.*
clothes

l'**habitude** noun *fem.*
1 habit
une mauvaise habitude a bad habit

2 J'ai l'habitude de boire du lait le matin. I'm used to drinking milk for breakfast.
J'ai l'habitude! I'm used to it!

d'**habitude** adverb
usually
D'habitude, je vais à l'école à pied.
I usually walk to school.
comme d'habitude as usual

haché adjective *masc.*, **hachée** *fem.*
minced
de la viande hachée minced meat

le **hachis Parmentier** noun *masc.*
shepherd's pie

les **halles** plural noun *fem.*
covered market

@ *means use* **être** *to make the past tense.*

a
b
c
d
e
f
g
h
i
j
k
l
m
n
o
p
q
r
s
t
u
v
w
x
y
z

le **handball** noun *masc.*
handball
Nous jouons au handball. We're playing handball.

CULTURE
Le handball is a game where two teams of seven players each (six players and a goalkeeper) pass and bounce a ball trying to throw it in the goal of the opposing team. Kicking the ball is not allowed. It's played on a smaller pitch than football, often indoors and is very popular in France.

handicapé adjective *masc.*,
handicapée *fem.*
disabled
les handicapés the disabled

le **haricot** noun *masc.*
bean
les haricots blancs haricot beans
les haricots verts green beans

l'**harmonica** noun *masc.*
mouth organ

la **harpe** noun *fem.*
harp

le **hasard** noun *masc.*
1 par hasard by chance
J'ai vu Sophie par hasard dans la rue. I bumped into Sophie by chance in the street.
2 au hasard at random

hausser verb
hausser les épaules to shrug your shoulders

haut adjective *masc.*, **haute** *fem.*
high
Cette montagne est très haute. This mountain is very high.
à haute voix aloud

le **haut** noun *masc.*
top
le haut de l'armoire the top of the wardrobe

en haut de la page at the top of the page
l'étagère du haut the top shelf

en **haut** adverb
upstairs, **up**
Olivier est en haut. Olivier is upstairs.

le **hautbois** noun *masc.*
oboe

la **hauteur** noun *fem.*
height

hein exclamation
eh
C'est grand, hein? It's big, eh?

l'**hélicoptère** noun *masc.*
helicopter

l'**herbe** noun *fem.*
grass
une mauvaise herbe a weed
des fines herbes herbs

le **hérisson** noun *masc.*
hedgehog

l'**héroïne** noun *fem.*
heroine

le **héros** noun *masc.*
hero

LANGUAGE
French = héros
English = hero

hésiter verb
to be unable to decide
J'hésite entre Rome et Paris. I can't decide between Rome and Paris.
Je ne sais pas, j'hésite. I don't know, I can't decide.

l'**heure** noun *fem.*
1 hour
La leçon dure une heure. The lesson lasts an hour.
un quart d'heure a quarter of an hour
une demi-heure half an hour

• *Languages, nationalities, and religions do not take a capital letter in French.*

une heure et demie an hour and a half

2 time
C'est l'heure d'aller au lit. It's time to go to bed.
On est à l'heure. We're on time.
Quelle heure est-il? What time is it?
Il est une heure. It's one o'clock.
à quelle heure? what time?
à six heures du soir at six o'clock in the evening

3 de bonne heure early

heureusement adverb
fortunately

heureux adjective *masc.*,
heureuse *fem.*
happy

l'Hexagone noun *masc.*
France

🌍 **CULTURE**
France is sometimes called **l'Hexagone** because of its shape on the map: it has six sides like a hexagon.

le hibou noun *masc.* (plural **les hiboux**)
owl

hier adverb
yesterday
hier matin yesterday morning
hier soir yesterday evening

hindou adjective *masc.*,
hindoue *fem.*
Hindu

hip hip hip hourra exclamation
hip hip hurrah

hippique adjective *masc. & fem.*
un centre hippique a riding school
le concours hippique show jumping

l'hippopotame noun *masc.*
hippopotamus

l'hirondelle noun *fem.*
swallow

l'histoire noun *fem.*
1 story
Maman m'a raconté une histoire. Mum told me a story.
une histoire vraie a true story
2 history
l'histoire de France French history

le hit-parade noun *masc.*
the charts
premier au hit-parade top of the charts

l'hiver noun *masc.*
winter
en hiver in the winter

le or la HLM noun *masc.* (plural **les HLM**)
council flat
J'habite en HLM. I live in a council flat.

le hockey noun *masc.*
hockey
le hockey sur glace ice hockey

le hollandais noun *masc.*
Dutch (*the language*)

hollandais adjective *masc.*,
hollandaise *fem.*
Dutch

le Hollandais noun *masc.*,
la Hollandaise *fem.*
Dutchman, **Dutchwoman**

la Hollande noun *fem.*
Holland

le homard noun *masc.*
lobster

l'homme noun *masc.*
man

la hongrie noun *fem.*
Hungary

honnête adjective *masc. & fem.*
honest

la honte noun *fem.*
shame

a
b
c
d
e
f
g
h
i
j
k
l
m
n
o
p
q
r
s
t
u
v
w
x
y
z

*❷ means use **être** to make the past tense.*

French English

a
b
c
d
e
f
g
h
i
j
k
l
m
n
o
p
q
r
s
t
u
v
w
x
y
z

avoir honte de quelque chose to be ashamed of something
Tu n'as pas honte? Aren't you ashamed?

hop exclamation
Allez, hop, dehors! Off you go, out of here!
Je clique et hop, c'est parti! I click and presto, it's gone!

l'**hôpital** noun masc. (plural les **hôpitaux**)
hospital

🔑 **LANGUAGE**
French = h**ô**pital
English = h**o**spital

le **hoquet** noun masc.
avoir le hoquet to have hiccups

l'**horaire** noun masc.
timetable
les horaires de bus the bus timetable

horizontalement adverb
horizontally

l'**horloge** noun fem.
clock
l'horloge de la gare the station clock

l'**horreur** noun fem.
1 J'ai horreur des épinards. I hate spinach.
2 un film d'horreur a horror film

le **hors-d'œuvre** noun masc. (plural les **hors-d'œuvre**)
starter

l'**hôtel** noun masc.
hotel
On va à l'hôtel. We're staying in a hotel.
l'hôtel de ville the town hall

l'**hôtesse de l'air** noun fem.
air stewardess

le **houx** noun masc.
holly

l'**huile** noun fem.
oil
l'huile d'olive olive oil

huit number
eight
Il part à huit heures. He leaves at eight.
J'ai huit ans. I'm eight.
le huit mai the eighth of May

huitième adjective masc. & fem.
eighth
au huitième étage on the eighth floor

l'**huître** noun fem.
oyster

humain adjective masc., **humaine** fem.
human
un être humain a human being

l'**humeur** noun fem.
mood
Est-ce que maman est de bonne ou de mauvaise humeur? Is mum in a good or bad mood?

humide adjective masc. & fem.
damp

l'**humour** noun masc.
avoir le sens de l'humour to have a sense of humour

hurler verb
1 to scream
2 to howl

l'**hymne** noun masc.
l'hymne national the national anthem

🌍 **CULTURE**
The French national anthem is called **la Marseillaise**.

l'**hypermarché** noun masc.
superstore

• The months of the year and days of the week do not take a capital letter in French.

Ii

ici adverb
1 here
   Qu'est-ce que tu fais ici? What are
   you doing here?
   C'est loin d'ici. It's a long way from
   here.
2 par ici this way
3 par ici around here
   Il y a un cinéma par ici? Is there a
   cinema around here?

une **icône** noun fem.
   icon
   Cliquez sur l'icône! Click on the
   icon!

idéal adjective masc., **idéale** fem.,
   idéaux masc. plural, **idéales**
   fem. plural
   ideal

une **idée** noun fem.
   idea
   J'ai une bonne idée. I have a good
   idea.
   Aucune idée! No idea!

identique adjective masc. & fem.
   identical

l'**identité** noun fem.
   identity
   une carte d'identité an identity
   card

CULTURE
All French people must have an identity
card. They can also use it instead of a
passport to travel around the European
Union.

idiot adjective masc., **idiote** fem.
   stupid

une **igname** noun fem.
   yam

il pronoun
1 he
   Il dort. He's sleeping.

2 it
   Regarde mon vélo, il est tout neuf!
   Look at my bike, it's brand new!
   Il pleut. It's raining.
   Il fait chaud. It's hot.
   Il est trois heures. It's three
   o'clock.

LANGUAGE
When **il** stands for a thing or animal that is
masculine singular in French, or when you
are talking about the weather or the time,
translate **il** as 'it'.

3 Il était une fois... Once upon a
   time...
4 il y a SEE **il y a**

une **île** noun fem.
   island
   les îles Anglo-Normandes
   the Channel Islands
   les îles Britanniques the British
   Isles

illustré adjective masc.,
   illustrée fem.
   illustrated

ils pronoun

LANGUAGE
Ils stands for plural masculine words in
French: people, things, or animals.

   they
   Ils jouent au foot. They're playing
   football.
   Paul et Lucy? Ils sont ici. Paul and
   Lucy? They're here.

il y a phrase
1 there is
   Il y a une école dans mon village.
   There's a school in my village.
   Est-ce qu'il y a un problème? Is
   there a problem?
   Qu'est-ce qu'il y a? What's the
   matter?

*means use **être** to make the past tense.*

French English

a
b
c
d
e
f
g
h
i
j
k
l
m
n
o
p
q
r
s
t
u
v
w
x
y
z

2 there are

Il y a deux bars dans ma rue. There are two bars in my street.

Il n'y a pas de bonbons. There aren't any sweets.

3 ago

Nous sommes arrivés il y a quatre jours. We arrived four days ago.

il y a longtemps a long time ago

une **image** noun *fem.*
picture

imaginaire adjective *masc. & fem.*
imaginary

l'**imagination** noun *fem.*
imagination

imaginer verb
to imagine
Imagine que tu habites une belle maison au bord de la mer. Imagine you live in a lovely house by the sea.

un or une **imbécile** noun *masc. & fem.*
idiot
faire l'imbécile to play around

imiter verb
to imitate

immédiatement adverb
immediately

immense adjective *masc. & fem.*
huge

un **immeuble** noun *masc.*
block of flats
Loïc habite dans un immeuble. Loïc lives in a block of flats.

impair adjective *masc.*
un nombre impair an odd number

une **impasse** noun *fem.*
dead end

impatient adjective *masc.*,
impatiente *fem.*
impatient, **keen**

un **imper** noun *masc.*
(= imperméable) **mac**

un **imperméable** noun *masc.*
raincoat

impoli adjective *masc.*,
impolie *fem.*
rude

l'**importance** noun *fem.*
importance
Ça n'a pas d'importance. It doesn't matter.

important adjective *masc.*,
importante *fem.*
important
un homme important an important man

impossible adjective *masc. & fem.*
impossible
Impossible n'est pas français. (*a saying*) There's no such word as 'can't'!

une **impression** noun *fem.*
feeling
J'ai l'impression qu'elle ne veut pas venir. I have a feeling she doesn't want to come.

impressionnant adjective *masc.*,
impressionnante *fem.*
awesome

une **imprimante** noun *fem.*
printer

imprimer verb
to print
Clique ici pour imprimer. Click here to print.

imprudent adjective *masc.*,
imprudente *fem.*
careless

• *The months of the year and days of the week do not take a capital letter in French.*

incapable adjective masc. & fem.
incapable de faire quelque chose
unable to do something

un **incendie** noun masc.
fire
L'incendie a détruit la forêt.
The fire burnt down the forest.

incollable adjective masc. & fem.
Il est incollable sur les dinosaures.
He knows everything about
dinosaurs.

un **inconnu** noun masc.,
une **inconnue** fem.
stranger
Il ne faut pas parler aux inconnus.
You must not talk to strangers.

incorrect adjective masc.,
incorrecte fem.
incorrect

incroyable adjective masc. & fem.
incredible

l'**Inde** noun fem.
India

indéfini adjective masc.
l'article indéfini the indefinite
article

> 🔑 **LANGUAGE**
> In French grammar the indefinite article is
> **un** or **une** ('a' or 'an'), or **des** (some).

Indépendant adjective masc.,
indépendante fem.
independent

> 🔑 **LANGUAGE**
> French = indépendant
> English = independent

l'**index** noun masc.
index finger

🔘 means use **être** to make the past tense.

les **indications** plural noun fem.
instructions

un **indice** noun masc.
clue

indien adjective masc.,
indienne fem.
Indian
un film indien an Indian film

un **Indien** noun masc.,
une **Indienne** fem.
Indian

indispensable adjective masc. & fem.
essential

inexcusable adjective masc. & fem.
unforgiveable

infect adjective masc., **infecte** fem.
disgusting, **revolting**

l'**infinitif** noun masc.
infinitive

une **infirmerie** noun fem.
medical room

un **infirmier** noun masc.,
une **infirmière** fem.
nurse

un **informaticien** masc.,
une **informaticienne** fem.
computer specialist

l'**information** noun fem.
1 les informations the news
2 **information**
demander des informations to ask
for information
une information utile a useful bit
of information

> 🔑 **LANGUAGE**
> **Information** is usually used in the plural
> but the singular can be used to mean one
> piece of news or information only.

a
b
c
d
e
f
g
h
i
j
k
l
m
n
o
p
q
r
s
t
u
v
w
x
y
z

l'**informatique** noun *fem.*
IT, **ICT**, **computing**
un cours d'informatique an IT course

les **infos** plural noun *fem.*
news

un **ingénieur** noun *masc.*
engineer

un **ingrédient** noun *masc.*
ingredient

les **initiales** plural noun *fem.*
initials

une **initiation** noun *fem.*
J'ai fait une initiation au japonais. I've done an introduction to Japanese.

injuste adjective *masc. & fem.*
unfair
C'est trop injuste! It's too unfair!

une **inondation** noun *fem.*
flood

inquiet adjective *masc.*,
inquiète *fem.*
worried
Tu as l'air inquiet. You look worried.

s'**inquiéter** verb ℮
to worry
Ne t'inquiète pas pour moi. Don't worry about me.

s'**inscrire** verb ℮
to join
Je me suis inscrit à un club de judo. I joined a judo club.

un **insecte** noun *masc.*
insect

insolent adjective *masc.*,
insolente *fem.*
cheeky

un **inspecteur** noun *masc.*,
une **inspectrice** *fem.*
inspector

installer verb
to install
Clique ici pour installer le programme. Click here to install the program.

s'**installer** verb ℮
to settle down
Installez-vous en silence! Settle down quietly!

un **instant** noun *masc.*
moment
Un instant, s'il vous plaît! One moment, please!

un **instituteur** noun *masc.*,
une **institutrice** *fem.*
primary school teacher

un **instrument** noun *masc.*
instrument
Est-ce que tu joues d'un instrument? Do you play an instrument?

insupportable adjective *masc. & fem.*
(*children, pupils, etc.*) **really annoying**

intelligent adjective *masc.*,
intelligente *fem.*
intelligent, **clever**

une **interdiction** noun *fem.*
'Interdiction de fumer' (*on sign*) 'No smoking'

interdire verb
to forbid
Mes parents m'ont interdit de sortir. My parents have forbidden me to go out.
C'est interdit! That's forbidden!

intéressant adjective *masc.*,
intéressante *fem.*
interesting
C'est intéressant. It's interesting.

• *See the centre section for verb tables.*

98

intéresser verb
to interest
Ça ne m'intéresse pas. I'm not interested.
Je m'intéresse aux sports. I'm interested in sport.

l'intérêt noun masc.
interest
Ça n'a pas d'intérêt. It is not at all interesting.
Tu as intérêt à travailler. You'd better start working.

l'intérieur noun masc.
à l'intérieur inside

un or une internaute noun masc. & fem.
Internet user

l'Internet noun masc.
Internet
sur Internet on the Internet

l'interrogation noun fem.
1 test
une interrogation écrite a written test
2 un point d'interrogation a question mark

Interrompre verb
to interrupt
Ne m'interromps pas! Don't interrupt me!

intime adjective masc. & fem.
le journal intime diary

inutile adjective masc. & fem.
useless

inventer verb
1 to invent
Qui a inventé le téléphone? Who invented the telephone?
2 to make up
Il a inventé une histoire. He made up a story.
Je n'invente rien. I'm not making anything up.

means use être to make the past tense.

un inventeur noun masc.,
une inventrice fem.
inventor

l'inverse noun masc.
opposite

un invité noun masc.,
une invitée fem.
guest

Inviter verb
to invite
Je voudrais t'inviter à ma fête. I would like to invite you to my party.

Ira, irai verb SEE **aller**
(aller in the future tense)
Un jour, elle ira en France. One day, she'll go to France.
J'irai à Paris. I will go to Paris.

l'Irak noun masc.
Iraq

l'Iran noun masc.
Iran

iras, irez verb SEE **aller**
(aller in the future tense)
J'espère que tu iras voir le médecin. I hope you'll go and see the doctor.
Vous irez où après? Where will you go afterwards?

irlandais adjective masc.,
irlandaise fem.
Irish

un Irlandais noun masc.,
une Irlandaise fem.
Irishman, Irishwoman

l'Irlande noun fem.
Ireland
la République d'Irlande the Irish Republic
l'Irlande du Nord Northern Ireland

French English

a b c d e f g h i j k l m n o p q r s t u v w x y z

French English

irons, **iront** verb SEE **aller**
(aller in the future tense)
Dans 50 ans, nous irons sur Mars en vacances. In 50 years, we will go to Mars on holiday.
Demain ils n'iront pas à l'école. Tomorrow they won't go to school.

isolé adjective masc., **isolée** fem.
remote
un village isolé a remote village

Israël noun masc.
Israel

israélien adjective masc., **israélienne** fem.
Israeli

un **Israélien** noun masc., une **Israélienne** fem.
Israeli (person)

l'**Italie** noun fem.
Italy

italien adjective masc., **italienne** fem.
Italian

l'**italien** noun masc.
Italian (the language)

un **Italien** noun masc., une **Italienne** fem.
Italian (person)

une **issue** noun fem.
une voie sans issue dead end

Jj

j' pronoun
I
J'ai onze ans. I'm eleven.
J'apprends le français. I'm learning French.
J'habite en France. I live in France.

> **LANGUAGE**
> **j'** = **je** before a, e, i, o, u, y, or silent h

Jacques a dit phrase
On joue à Jacques a dit? Shall we play Simon says?

jaloux adjective masc., **jalouse** fem.
jealous
Je ne suis pas jaloux de toi. I'm not jealous of you.

jamaïquain adjective masc., **jamaïquaine** fem.
Jamaican

le **Jamaïquain** noun masc., la **Jamaïquaine** fem.
Jamaican (person)

la **Jamaïque** noun fem.
Jamaica

jamais adverb
never
Tu vas à l'école à vélo? – Non, jamais. Do you ride your bike to school? – No, never.

la **jambe** noun fem.
leg

le **jambon** noun masc.
ham
Tu veux du jambon fumé? Would you like some smoked ham?

janvier noun masc.
January
en janvier in January
Je suis née le dix janvier. I was born on the tenth of January.

le **Japon** noun masc.
Japan

japonais adjective masc., **japonaise** fem.
Japanese

• Use **le** and **un** for masculine words and **la** and **une** for feminine words.

le **japonais** noun masc.
Japanese (*the language*)

le **Japonais** noun masc.,
la **Japonaise** fem.
Japanese man, **Japanese woman**

le **jardin** noun masc.
garden
un jardin public a park

le **jardinage** noun masc.
gardening
Il fait du jardinage. He's doing some gardening.

le **jardinier** noun masc.,
la **jardinière** fem.
gardener

jaune adjective masc. & fem.
yellow

le **jaune** noun masc.
1 yellow
Je n'aime pas le jaune. I don't like yellow.
2 un jaune d'œuf an egg yolk

je pronoun
I
Je vais à l'école. I'm going to school.

> 🔑 **LANGUAGE**
> **Je = j'** before *a, e, i, o, u, y,* or *silent h*

le **jean** noun masc.
1 jeans
Il porte un jean. He's wearing jeans.
2 denim
un blouson en jean a denim jacket

> 🔑 **LANGUAGE**
> French = **le jean** is singular
> English = **jeans** is plural

jeter verb
1 to throw
Jette l'emballage à la poubelle! Throw the packaging into the bin!

2 to throw away
Je jette mes vieux jouets. I'm throwing away my old toys.

le **jeton** noun masc.
counter
Donne un jeton à chaque joueur. Give a counter to each player.

le **jeu** noun masc. (plural les **jeux**)
game
On a joué à un jeu génial! We played a really great game!
les Jeux Olympiques the Olympic Games
un jeu électronique a computer game
un jeu vidéo a video game
un jeu de cartes a card game
un jeu télévisé a TV game show
un jeu de société a board game, a party game

le **jeudi** noun masc.
1 Thursday
On est jeudi. It's Thursday today.
2 on Thursday
Nous partons jeudi. We're leaving on Thursday.
On va au cinéma jeudi soir. We're going to the cinema on Thursday evening.
À jeudi! See you on Thursday!
3 on Thursdays
On va au marché le jeudi. We go to the market on Thursdays.

jeune adjective masc. & fem.
young
Tu es plus jeune que moi. You're younger than me.
un jeune homme a young man
une jeune fille de seize ans a girl of sixteen

les **jeunes** plural noun masc.
young people
la maison des jeunes youth club

la **jeunesse** noun fem.
youth

ℯ *means use* **être** *to make the past tense.*

French English

a b c d e f g h i **j** k l m n o p q r s t u v w x y z

le **jogging** noun *masc.*
1 jogging
 faire du jogging to go jogging
2 tracksuit
 porter un jogging to wear a tracksuit

la **joie** noun *fem.*
 joy

joli adjective *masc.*, **jolie** *fem.*
 pretty

jongler verb
 to juggle

la **jonquille** noun *fem.*
 daffodil

la **Jordanie** noun *fem.*
 Jordan

la **joue** noun *fem.*
 cheek

jouer verb
1 to play
 Tu veux jouer avec nous? Do you want to play with us?
 jouer un air to play a tune
2 jouer à to play
 Ils jouent au football. They're playing football.

> **LANGUAGE**
> Use **jouer à** with games and sports.

3 jouer de to play
 Daniel joue de la guitare. Daniel plays the guitar.
 Léa joue du piano. Léa plays the piano.

> **LANGUAGE**
> Use **jouer de** with musical instruments.

4 to act
 Il joue le rôle du méchant. He's acting the part of the baddie.

le **jouet** noun *masc.*
 toy
 Olivier joue avec ses jouets. Olivier is playing with his toys.

le **joueur** noun *masc.*, la **joueuse** *fem.*
 player
 un joueur de football a football player

le **jour** noun *masc.*
1 day
 les jours de la semaine the days of the week
 trois fois par jour three times a day
 tous les jours every day
 On est quel jour aujourd'hui? What day is it today?
 le jour de l'an New Year's Day
 le jour de Noël Christmas Day
 un jour férié a public holiday
 Il fait jour. It's light.
2 huit jours a week
 quinze jours two weeks, a fortnight
 C'est mon anniversaire dans quinze jours. It's my birthday in two weeks.

> **LANGUAGE**
> French has two words for 'day': **jour** and **journée**.
> **un jour** = a period of twenty-four hours
> **une journée** = from morning till evening (the daytime) when people are awake

le **journal** noun *masc.* (plural les **journaux**)
1 newspaper
2 news
 le journal télévisé the TV news
3 diary
 Je l'ai écrit dans mon journal. I wrote it in my diary.

le or la **journaliste** noun *masc. & fem.*
 journalist

la **journée** noun *fem.*
 day
 J'ai passé une bonne journée. I've had a good day.
 toute la journée all day long

• *Languages, nationalities, and religions do not take a capital letter in French.*

joyeux adjective *masc.*,
  joyeuse *fem.*
  happy
  Joyeux Noël! Happy Christmas!
  Joyeux anniversaire! Happy
  birthday!
  Joyeuses Pâques! Happy Easter!

le **judo** noun *masc.*
  judo
  Elle fait du judo. She does judo.

le **juge** noun *masc.*
  judge

juger verb
  to judge

juif adjective *masc.*, **juive** *fem.*
  Jewish

juillet noun *masc.*
  July
  en juillet in July
  au mois de juillet in July
  Elle arrive le deux juillet. She
  arrives on the second of July.

 CULTURE
On 14th July French people celebrate **la
Fête Nationale** (Bastille Day). On that
day in 1789 the Bastille prison was
attacked and captured, and the French
Revolution began. People celebrate with
fireworks and there is a big parade of
soldiers on the Champs-Élysées in Paris.

---

juin noun *masc.*
  June
  en juin in June
  On est le vendredi six juin. It's
  Friday the sixth of June.

jumeau adjective *masc.*,
  jumelle *fem.*, **jumeaux** *masc.*
  plural, **jumelles** *fem. plural*
  twin
  mon frère jumeau my twin brother
  ma sœur jumelle my twin sister
  Ils sont jumeaux. They're twins.

jumelé adjective *masc.*,
  jumelée *fem.*
  twinned
  **Notre ville est jumelée avec
  Liverpool.** Our town is twinned
  with Liverpool.

les **jumelles** plural noun *fem.*
  binoculars

la **jupe** noun *fem*
  skirt

jurer verb
  to swear
  Je jure que c'est la vérité. I swear
  it's the truth.

le **jus** noun *masc.*
  juice
  du jus d'orange orange juice

jusqu'à preposition
1 until
  Reste jusqu'à cinq heures. Stay
  until five o'clock.

2 as far as
  Vous allez jusqu'à la gare. Go as
  far as the station.

3 up to
  Comptez jusqu'à dix. Count up to
  ten.

juste adjective *masc. & fem.*
1 fair
  Ce n'est pas juste! That's not fair!
2 right
  la réponse juste the right answer

juste adverb
  just
  juste après le petit déjeuner just
  after breakfast
  juste à temps just in time

justement adverb
  exactly

---

*❸ means use **être** to make the past tense.*

Kk

kaki adjective *masc. & fem.*
khaki green
des sandales kaki khaki green sandals

🔑 **LANGUAGE**
Kaki is the same in the masculine, feminine, or plural.

le kangourou noun *masc.*
kangaroo

le karaté noun *masc.*
karate
Alicia fait du karaté. Alicia does karate.

la kermesse noun *fem.*
fête
la kermesse de l'école the school fête

le kilo noun *masc.*
kilo
deux euros le kilo two euros a kilo

le kilomètre noun *masc.*
kilometre
J'habite à cent kilomètres de Paris. I live a hundred kilometres from Paris.
Il roule à cent kilomètres à l'heure. He's driving at a hundred kilometres an hour.

le kiosque noun *masc.*
un kiosque à journaux a news-stand

le klaxon® noun *masc.*
horn
Maman a donné un coup de klaxon. Mum sounded her horn.

le kleenex® noun *masc.*
tissue

le koala noun *masc.*
koala bear

le K-way® noun *masc.*
windcheater

Ll

l' determiner *masc. & fem.*

🔑 **LANGUAGE**
l' = le or la before a, e, i, o, u, or silent h

1 the
l'assiette the plate
l'hôtel the hotel
2 (*no translation*)
l'eau minérale mineral water
L'Inde est très loin. India is very far away.

l' pronoun

🔑 **LANGUAGE**
l' = le or la before a, e, i, o, u, y, or silent h

1 him
Mon frère est dans le jardin, je vais l'aider. My brother's in the garden. I'm going to help him.
2 her
Elle m'a appelé mais je ne l'ai pas vue. She called me but I didn't see her.

• *The months of the year and days of the week do not take a capital letter in French.*

3 it
Je l'ai fait. I've done it.

la determiner *fem.*

> 🔑 **LANGUAGE**
> **la** = **l'** before *a, e, i, o, u,* or *silent h*

1 the
la gare the station
2 (*no translation*) J'aime la France.
I like France.

la pronoun *fem.*

> 🔑 **LANGUAGE**
> **la** = **l'** before *a, e, i, o, u, y,* or *silent h*

1 her
Je la connais. I know her.
2 it
Où est ma veste? Je ne la vois pas.
Where's my jacket? I can't see it.

là adverb
1 there
Qui est là? Who's there?
2 here
Je suis là. I'm here.

-là adverb
cette pomme-là that apple
ces enfants-là those children
celui-là that one
celle-là that one
ceux-là those
celles-là those

là-bas adverb
over there

le **labyrinthe** noun *masc.*
maze

le **lac** noun *masc.*
lake

le **lacet** noun *masc.*
lace
Attache tes lacets! Tie your laces!

lâcher verb
to let go of
Lâche-moi! Let go of me!

là-dedans adverb
in there

ⓔ means use être to make the past tense.

là-dessous adverb
under there

là-dessus adverb
on there

là-haut adverb
up there

laid adjective *masc.*, **laide** *fem.*
ugly

la **laine** noun *fem.*
wool
un pull en laine a woolly jumper

laïque adjective *masc. & fem.*
non-religious
(*in France*) l'école laïque the state
primary school system

> **CULTURE**
> French primary state schools are **laïques**,
> that is to say that no religion is taught.

laisser verb
1 to leave
J'ai laissé mon sac chez toi. I've left
my bag at your house.
Laisse-moi tranquille! Leave me
alone!
2 to let
Laisse-moi faire! Let me do it!

le **lait** noun *masc.*
milk
un café au lait a white coffee

la **laitue** noun *fem.*
lettuce

la **lampe** noun *fem.*
lamp
une lampe de poche a torch

lancer verb
to throw
Lance la balle! Throw the ball!

la **langue** noun *fem.*
1 tongue
Julie me tire la langue. Julie is
sticking her tongue out at me.

a b c d e f g h i j k l m n o p q r s t u v w x y z

Tu donnes ta langue au chat?
Do you give up?
2 language
J'apprends une langue étrangère.
I'm learning a foreign language.

le **lapin** noun *masc.*
rabbit

laquelle pronoun *fem.*
which one
Tu vois la fille là-bas? – Laquelle?
Can you see the girl over there? –
Which one?

le **lard** noun *masc.*
bacon

⚠ **FALSE FRIEND**
le lard = bacon (*not* lard)

large adjective *masc. & fem.*
wide
La rivière est large ici. The river is
wide here.

⚠ **FALSE FRIEND**
large = wide (*not* large)

la **largeur** noun *fem.*
width

la **larme** noun *fem.*
tear

le **lavabo** noun *masc.*
washbasin, **sink**

la **lavande** noun *fem.*
lavender

laver verb
to wash

se **laver** verb ℮
to wash
Je me lave. I'm washing.
Je me lave les cheveux. I'm
washing my hair.

le **lave-vaisselle** noun *masc.*
(plural les **lave-vaisselle**)
dishwasher

• *See the centre section for verb tables.*

Le determiner *masc.*

🔑 **LANGUAGE**
le = l' before *a, e, i, o, u,* or *silent h*

1 the
le dessin the drawing
2 (*no translation*)
J'adore le poisson.
I love fish.
Je ne connais pas le Portugal.
I don't know Portugal.

Le pronoun *masc.*

🔑 **LANGUAGE**
le = l' before *a, e, i, o, u, y,* or *silent h*

1 him
Où est Paul? Je ne le vois pas.
Where's Paul? I can't see him.
2 it
Ce magazine, tu peux le prendre.
This magazine, you can take it.

lécher verb
to lick

la **leçon** noun *fem.*
lesson
une leçon d'anglais an English
lesson

le **lecteur** noun *masc.*,
la **lectrice** *fem.*
1 reader
2 un lecteur DVD a DVD player

la **lecture** noun *fem.*
reading

⚠ **FALSE FRIEND**
la lecture = reading (*not* lecture)

la **légende** noun *fem.*
1 legend
2 key (*on a map*)
3 caption (*under a picture*)

léger adjective *masc.,* **légère** *fem.*
light
un repas léger a light meal

légèrement adverb
slightly

les **légumes** plural noun *masc.*
vegetables

le **lendemain** noun *masc.*
next day
Nous sommes arrivés le lendemain. We arrived the next day.
Le lendemain de mon anniversaire the day after my birthday

lent adjective *masc.*, **lente** *fem.*
slow

lentement adverb
slowly

les **lentilles** plural noun *fem.*
1 lentils
des saucisses aux lentilles sausages and lentils
2 les lentilles de contact contact lenses

le **léopard** noun *masc.*
leopard

lequel pronoun *masc.*,
laquelle *fem.*
which one
Voici deux livres. Lequel tu préfères? Here are two books. Which one do you prefer?

les plural determiner *masc. & fem.*
1 the
les cadeaux the presents
les étoiles the stars
2 (*no translation*)
J'aime les épinards. I like spinach.
les garçons et les filles boys and girls

les plural pronoun *masc. & fem.*
them
Pierre et Cécile? Je les connais. Pierre and Cécile? I know them.

*ⓔ means use **être** to make the past tense.*

lesquels plural pronoun *masc.*,
lesquelles *fem.*
which ones
Passez-moi les biscuits. – Lesquels? Pass me the biscuits. – Which ones?

la **lessive** noun *fem.*
1 washing
Elle fait la lessive. She's doing the washing.
2 washing powder

la **lettre** noun *fem.*
letter
La lettre D the letter D
Mon amie m'a écrit une lettre. My friend wrote me a letter.

leur adjective *masc. & fem.*
their
leur cahier their exercise book
leur maison their house

leur pronoun *masc. & fem.*
1 them
Je leur ai donné quelque chose à manger. I gave them something to eat.
2 to them
Maman veut leur parler. Mum wants to speak to them.

leurs plural adjective *masc. & fem.*
their
leurs enfants their children
leurs idées their ideas

lever verb
to put up
Levez le doigt! Put your hand up!

se **lever** verb ⓔ
1 to get up
Je me lève à sept heures. I get up at seven.
2 to stand up
Levez-vous! Stand up!
3 to rise
Le soleil se lève à l'est. The sun rises in the east.

la **lèvre** noun *fem.*
lip

le **lézard** noun *masc.*
lizard

la **liberté** noun *fem.*
freedom

la **librairie** noun *fem.*
bookshop

⚠ **FALSE FRIEND**
la librairie = bookshop (*not* library)

libre adjective *masc. & fem.*
free
La place est libre? Is this seat free?

le **lien** noun *masc.*
link
Cliquez sur le lien! Click on the link!

le **lieu** noun *masc.* (plural les **lieux**)
1 place
le lieu de naissance the place of birth
2 au lieu de instead of
Je peux avoir des frites au lieu des haricots verts? Can I have chips instead of green beans?

le **lièvre** noun *masc.*
hare

la **ligne** noun *fem.*
1 line
une ligne droite a straight line
2 en ligne online
des jeux en ligne online games

la **limonade** noun *fem.*
lemonade

le **linge** noun *masc.*
washing
Mets le linge sale dans la machine à laver. Put the dirty washing in the washing machine.

le **lion** noun *masc.*, la **lionnne** *fem.*
lion, lioness

le **lionceau** noun *masc.* (plural les **lionceaux**)
lion cub

lire verb
to read
Luc apprend à lire. Luc is learning to read.
Je lis tous les soirs. I read every night.
Tu as lu ce livre? Have you read this book?

lis, lisent, lisez, lisons verb
SEE **lire**

la **liste** noun *fem.*
list
la liste des courses the shopping list

le **lit** noun *masc.*
bed
Je vais au lit. I'm going to bed.
Je fais mon lit. I make my bed.
des lits superposés bunk beds
des lits jumeaux twin beds

le **litre** noun *masc.*
litre

la **littérature** noun *fem.*
literature

le **livre** noun *masc.*
book
un livre de cuisine a cookbook
un livre de lecture a reading book

la **livre** noun *fem.*
1 pound
Ça coûte dix livres. It costs ten pounds.
2 half a kilo
une livre de pommes half a kilo of apples

🔑 **LANGUAGE**
A pound in weight is just under half a kilo.

le **livret scolaire** noun *masc.*
school report book

• *Languages, nationalities, and religions do not take a capital letter in French.*

la **locomotive** noun *fem.*
engine

le **logiciel** noun *masc.*
software

logique adjective *masc. & fem.*
logical
Ce n'est pas logique. That doesn't make sense.

la **loi** noun *fem.*
law

loin adverb
far
C'est loin? Is it far?
pas loin d'ici not far from here
Nous sommes allés un peu plus loin. We went a bit further.

lointain adjective *masc.*,
lointaine *fem.*
distant
dans un pays lointain in a far and distant land

les **loisirs** plural noun *masc.*
1 spare time
Qu'est-ce que tu fais pendant tes loisirs? What do you do in your spare time?
2 spare-time activities

Londres noun
London

long adjective *masc.*, **longue** *fem.*
long
J'ai les cheveux longs. I have long hair.
une jupe longue a long skirt

longtemps adverb
a long time
Ça fait longtemps que tu es là. You've been here a long time.
J'ai vu ce film il y a longtemps. I saw this film a long time ago.
Tu peux rester plus longtemps. You can stay longer.

la **longueur** noun *fem.*
length

la **loterie** noun *fem.*
lottery

le **loto** noun *masc.*
bingo
jouer au loto to play bingo

louer verb
1 to rent
On loue une villa à Nice. We're renting a villa in Nice.
2 to hire
On va louer des vélos. We're going to hire bicycles.

le **loup** noun *masc.*
wolf

la **loupe** noun *fem.*
magnifying glass

le **loup-garou** noun *masc.* (plural les **loups-garous**)
werewolf

lourd adjective *masc.*, **lourde** *fem.*
heavy

la **louve** noun *fem.*
she-wolf

lu verb *masc.*, **lue** *fem.* SEE **lire**

la **luge** noun *fem.*
sledge

lui pronoun *masc. & fem.*
1 him
Appelle Éric et dis-lui de venir. Call Éric and tell him to come.
Va avec lui. Go with him.
Je suis plus jeune que lui. I'm younger than him.
C'est lui. It's him.
2 to him
Où est Théo? Je veux lui parler. Where's Théo? I want to speak to him.
3 à lui his
Ce livre est à lui. This book is his.

a
b
c
d
e
f
g
h
i
j
k
l
m
n
o
p
q
r
s
t
u
v
w
x
y
z

⊘ *means use* **être** *to make the past tense.*

French English

a
b
c
d
e
f
g
h
i
j
k
l
m
n
o
p
q
r
s
t
u
v
w
x
y
z

4 her
Appelle maman et dis-lui de venir.
Call mum and tell her to come.
5 to her
Où est Zoé? Je veux lui parler.
Where's Zoé? I want to speak to her.
6 it
Si le chien a faim, donne-lui un os.
If the dog's hungry, give it a bone.

lui-même pronoun *masc.*
1 himself
2 (*for masculine things*) **itself**

la **lumière** noun *fem.*
light
Allume la lumière! Turn on the light!
Éteins la lumière! Turn off the light!

le **lundi** noun *masc.*
1 Monday
lundi prochain next Monday
lundi dernier last Monday
On est lundi. Today's Monday.
2 on Monday
Viens me voir lundi. Come and see me on Monday.

Mm

M. abbreviation
Mr
M. Lançon Mr Lançon

> **LANGUAGE**
> M. is short for **Monsieur**.

m' pronoun

> **LANGUAGE**
> m' = me before *a, e, i, o, u, y,* or *silent h*

1 me
Tu m'entends? Can you hear me?
2 to me

Je viens lundi soir. I'm coming on Monday evening.
À lundi! See you on Monday!
3 on Mondays
Nous avons gym le lundi. We have gym on Mondays.

la **lune** noun *fem.*
moon
Il est toujours dans la lune. He's always daydreaming.

les **lunettes** plural noun *fem.*
glasses
Fabien porte des lunettes. Fabien wears glasses.
des lunettes de soleil sunglasses
des lunettes de plongée swimming goggles

le **lycée** noun *masc.*
secondary school

> **CULTURE**
> French children go to the **lycée** for the last three years before the baccalauréat (the equivalent of A levels).

le **lycéen** noun *masc.*,
la **lycéenne** *fem.*
secondary school student

Elle ne m'a rien dit. She said nothing to me.
3 (*no translation*)
Je m'habille. I'm getting dressed.

ma adjective *fem.* SEE **mon**
my
ma cousine my cousin

mâcher verb
to chew

le **machin** noun *masc.*
thing
C'est quoi, ce machin? What's that thing?

• *The months of the year and days of the week do not take a capital letter in French.*

la **machine** noun *fem.*
machine
une machine à laver a washing machine

le **maçon** noun *masc.*
builder

madame noun *fem.* (plural **mesdames**)
1 **Bonjour, madame!** Good morning!
2 **Madame** Mrs
Madame Duc Mrs Duc
3 (*in a letter*)
Madame ... Dear Madam ...

mademoiselle noun *fem.* (plural **mesdemoiselles**)
1 **Bonsoir, mademoiselle!** Good evening!

> 🔑 **LANGUAGE**
> Used when talking to a young woman in a polite way and not usually translated.

2 **Mademoiselle** Miss
Mademoiselle Patel Miss Patel

le **magasin** noun *masc.*
shop
un grand magasin a department store
faire les magasins to go shopping

le **magazine** noun *masc.*
magazine

le **magicien** noun *masc.*,
la **magicienne** *fem.*
magician

la **magie** noun *fem.*
magic
un tour de magie a magic trick
par magie by magic

magique adjective *masc. & fem.*
magic
une baguette magique a magic wand

le **magnétophone** noun *masc.*
tape recorder

le **magnétoscope** noun *masc.*
video recorder

magnifique adjective *masc. & fem.*
fantastic

mai noun *masc.*
May
en mai in May
au mois de mai in May
le trois mai on the third of May
le Premier Mai May Day

> 🌍 **CULTURE**
> In France the **Premier Mai** (first of May) is a holiday when people give each other small bunches of **muguet** (lily of the valley) for good luck.

maigre adjective *masc. & fem.*
thin

le **maillot** noun *masc.*
1 **shirt**
un maillot de football a football shirt
le maillot jaune the yellow jersey (*worn by the leader of the Tour de France*)
2 un maillot de bain (*for girls*) a swimming costume; (*for boys*) swimming trunks

la **main** noun *fem.*
hand
Levez la main! Put your hands up!
Donne-moi la main! Hold my hand!
Ils se serrent la main. They shake hands.
Mon frère m'a donné un coup de main. My brother gave me a hand.

maintenant adverb
now
pas maintenant not now
à partir de maintenant from now on

la **mairie** noun *fem.*
town hall

🔵 means use **être** to make the past tense.

French English

a
b
c
d
e
f
g
h
i
j
k
l
m
n
o
p
q
r
s
t
u
v
w
x
y
z

mais conjunction
but
Je mange du poisson mais je n'aime pas vraiment ça. I eat fish but I don't really like it.

le **maïs** noun *masc.*
sweetcorn

la **maison** noun *fem.*
1 house
J'habite dans une grande maison. I live in a big house.
2 à la maison at home, home
Reste à la maison! Stay at home!
Je veux rentrer à la maison. I want to go home.
3 une maison de poupée a doll's house

le **maître** noun *masc.*,
la **maîtresse** *fem.*
teacher (*in a primary school*)
Oui, maîtresse! Yes, miss!

le **maître-nageur** noun *masc.*
swimming instructor

la **majuscule** noun *fem.*
capital letter
en majuscules in capital letters

mal adverb
1 badly
Je chante très mal. I sing very badly.
Mon oncle va mal. My uncle's not well.
2 pas mal not bad
Ce livre n'est pas mal. This book isn't bad.
3 pas mal de quite a lot of
J'ai pas mal d'idées. I've got quite a lot of ideas.

le **mal** noun *masc.* (plural les **maux**)
1 ache
avoir mal aux dents to have toothache
avoir mal à la tête to have a headache
J'ai le mal de mer. I'm seasick.

2 faire mal à quelqu'un to hurt somebody
Je me suis fait mal. I hurt myself.
Ça fait mal. That hurts.
3 avoir du mal à faire quelque chose to have trouble doing something
J'ai du mal à m'endormir. I have trouble going to sleep.

malade adjective *masc. & fem.*
ill

le or la **malade** noun *masc. & fem.*
sick person

la **maladie** noun *fem.*
illness

maladroit adjective *masc.*,
maladroite *fem.*
clumsy

mâle adjective *masc. & fem.*
male

le **mâle** noun *masc.*
male

malgré preposition
in spite of
Papi fait du jogging malgré le froid. Granddad goes jogging in spite of the cold.

le **malheur** noun *masc.*
bad luck
Ça porte malheur! It's bad luck!

malheureusement adverb
unfortunately

malheureux adjective *masc.*,
malheureuse *fem.*
unhappy
Tu as l'air malheureuse, Léa! You look unhappy, Léa!

malin adjective *masc.*,
maligne *fem.*
smart
Ce n'est pas malin! That's not very clever!

la **maman** noun *fem.*
mum

• *See the centre section for verb tables.*

la **mamie** noun *fem.*
granny

la **manche** noun *fem.*
1 sleeve
une chemise à manches courtes
a shirt with short sleeves
2 la Manche the Channel

🗝 **LANGUAGE**
The shape of the Channel is similar to a sleeve.

le **manche** noun *masc.*
handle
le manche d'un couteau the
handle of a knife

la **mandarine** noun *fem.*
mandarin orange

le **manège** noun *masc.*
merry-go-round

la **manette de jeu** noun *fem.*
joystick

manger verb
to eat
Il n'y a rien à manger! There's
nothing to eat!
Donne à manger au chat! Feed the
cat!

la **mangue** noun *fem.*
mango

la **manière** noun *fem.*
1 way
Je n'aime pas sa manière de me
regarder. I don't like the way he
looks at me.
2 les manières manners
les bonnes manières good
manners

le **manioc** noun *masc.*
cassava

le **mannequin** noun *masc.*
model

manquer verb
1 to miss
Elle a manqué la balle. She missed
the ball.
2 to be missing
Il manque deux CD. Two CDs are
missing.
3 Tu me manques. I miss you.
Je te manque? Do you miss me?
Ma grand-mère me manque.
I miss my grandmother.

le **manteau** noun *masc.* (plural les
manteaux)
coat

la **maquette** noun *fem.*
model
une maquette d'avion a model
plane

le **maquillage** noun *masc.*
make-up

se **maquiller** verb ⊘
to put on make-up
Élise se maquille. Élise puts
make-up on.

le **marchand** noun *masc.*,
la **marchande** *fem.*
shopkeeper
un marchand de journaux
a newsagent
un marchand de légumes
a greengrocer
On joue à la marchande? Shall we
play 'shop'?

la **marche** noun *fem.*
step

le **marché** noun *masc.*
1 market
au marché at the market
le marché aux puces flea market
2 bon marché cheap
des ordinateurs bon marché cheap
computers

⊘ *means use* **être** *to make the past tense.*

a
b
c
d
e
f
g
h
i
j
k
l
m
n
o
p
q
r
s
t
u
v
w
x
y
z

a
b
c
d
e
f
g
h
i
j
k
l
m
n
o
p
q
r
s
t
u
v
w
x
y
z

marcher verb

1 to walk

Paul marche trop vite. Paul walks too fast.

2 (*talking about machines, radios, TVs, etc.*) **to work**

Le lave-vaisselle ne marche pas. The dishwasher isn't working.

3 Ça marche? How are things going? **Ça marche bien.** Things are going well.

le **mardi** noun *masc.*

1 Tuesday

C'est mardi aujourd'hui. It's Tuesday today.

mardi prochain next Tuesday

mardi dernier last Tuesday

tous les mardis every Tuesday

2 on Tuesday

Nous allons en Espagne mardi. We're going to Spain on Tuesday.

Ne viens pas avant mardi matin! Don't come before Tuesday morning!

À mardi! See you on Tuesday!

3 on Tuesdays

Nous jouons aux échecs le mardi. We play chess on Tuesdays.

le **Mardi gras** noun *masc.* **Shrove Tuesday**

CULTURE

Children in France and in Britain eat pancakes on this day (also called Pancake Day); **Mardi gras** means 'fat Tuesday' because it's the last day you can eat fat before the Christian Lent.

la **marée** noun *fem.* **tide**

la **marelle** noun *fem.* **hopscotch**

la **margarine** noun *fem.* **margarine**

la **marge** noun *fem.* **margin**

Écrivez dans la marge. Write in the margin.

le **mari** noun *masc.* **husband**

le **mariage** noun *masc.*

1 wedding

Ils sont invités à un mariage. They're invited to a wedding.

2 marriage

Mon beau-père a deux enfants de son premier mariage. My step-father has two children from his first marriage.

LANGUAGE

French = mariage
English = marriage

marié adjective *masc.*, **mariée** *fem.* **married**

le **marié** noun *masc.* **bridegroom**

les mariés the bride and groom

la **mariée** noun *fem.* **bride**

une robe de mariée a wedding dress

se **marier** verb *⊘* **to get married**

Jo et Zoé se marient. Jo and Zoé are getting married.

le **marin** noun *masc.* **sailor**

marine adjective *masc. & fem.* **bleu marine** navy blue

LANGUAGE

Bleu marine is the same in the masculine, feminine, and plural.

la **marionnette** noun *fem.* **puppet**

la **marmite** noun *fem.* **cooking pot**

• *Use* **le** *and* **un** *for masculine words and* **la** *and* **une** *for feminine words.*

le **Maroc** noun *masc.*
Morocco

marocain adjective *masc.*,
marocaine *fem.*
Moroccan

un **Marocain** noun *masc.*,
une **Marocaine** *fem.*
Moroccan (*person*)

la **marque** noun *fem.*
1 mark
des marques de doigts finger
marks
2 make
**De quelle marque est ton
caméscope?** What make is your
camcorder?
3 À vos marques, prêts, partez!
Ready, steady, go!

marquer verb
1 to mark
C'est marqué d'une croix. It's
marked with a cross.
2 to write down
**J'ai marqué la date dans ton
carnet.** I've written down the date
in your book.
3 to score
Benjamin a marqué un but.
Benjamin scored a goal.

la **marraine** noun *fem.*
godmother

marrant adjective *masc.*,
marrante *fem.*
1 funny
**Cette histoire est vraiment
marrante.** That story's really
funny.
2 fun
Il n'est pas marrant, ton frère!
He's not much fun, your brother!

marre adverb
J'en ai marre! I'm fed up!
On en a marre d'attendre! We're
fed up with waiting!

ⓔ *means use* **être** *to make the past tense.*

marron adjective *masc. & fem.*
brown

🔑 **LANGUAGE**
Marron is the same in the masculine,
feminine, and plural.

le **marron** noun *masc.*
1 brown
2 chestnut
la crème de marrons sweet
chestnut purée

mars noun *masc.*
March
en mars in March
au mois de mars in March
le douze mars on the twelfth of
March

la **Marseillaise** noun *fem.*
the French national anthem

Marseille noun
Marseilles

le **marteau** noun *masc.* (plural les
marteaux)
hammer

le **martien** noun *masc.*,
la **martienne** *fem.*
Martian

masculin adjective *masc.*,
masculine *fem.*
masculine

le **masque** noun *masc.*
mask

le **match** noun *masc.*
1 match
un match de football a football
match
2 Match nul! It's a draw!
**Les deux équipes ont fait match
nul.** The two teams drew.

le **matelas** noun *masc.*
mattress

maternelle adjective *fem.*
l'école maternelle nursery school

CULTURE
L'école maternelle (or **la maternelle** for short) is for children from 3 to 6.

les **mathématiques** plural noun *fem.*
mathematics

les **maths** plural noun *fem.*
(*short for mathématiques*) **maths**

la **matière** noun *fem.*
subject (*at school*)
Le français est ma matière préférée. French is my favourite subject.

le **matin** noun *masc.*
morning
Le matin, je me lève à sept heures. In the morning I get up at seven.
à neuf heures du matin at nine o'clock in the morning
ce matin this morning
demain matin tomorrow morning
hier matin yesterday morning
tous les matins every morning

la **matinée** noun *fem.*
morning
Je suis resté chez moi toute la matinée. I stayed at home all morning.

LANGUAGE
French has two words for 'morning': **matin** and **matinée**. Use **matinée** when you mean the whole time from when you get up until the afternoon.

mauvais adjective *masc.*,
mauvaise *fem.*
1 bad
Ce film est mauvais. This film is bad.
Je suis mauvaise en dessin. I'm bad at drawing.
Il fait mauvais. The weather's bad.
Ça sent mauvais. It smells.

2 wrong
la mauvaise réponse the wrong answer
la mauvaise direction the wrong way

me pronoun

LANGUAGE
me = **m'** before *a, e, i, o, u, y,* or *silent h*

1 me
Tu me vois? Can you see me?
2 to me
Tu veux me parler? Do you want to speak to me?
3 (*no translation*)
Je me lève. I'm getting up.
Je me lave. I'm having a wash.
4 myself
Je me suis fait mal. I've hurt myself.

le **mécanicien** noun *masc.*,
la **mécanicienne** *fem.*
mechanic

méchant adjective *masc.*,
méchante *fem.*
nasty
Il est méchant avec sa sœur. He's nasty to his sister.
Attention chien méchant! Beware of the dog!

la **médaille** noun *fem.*
medal
une médaille d'argent a silver medal

le **médecin** noun *masc.*
doctor
Ma mère est médecin. My mum's a doctor.
Je vais chez le médecin. I'm going to the doctor's.

LANGUAGE
The French word **médecin** is related to the English word 'medicine'.

le **médicament** noun *masc.*
medicine

• *Languages, nationalities, and religions do not take a capital letter in French.*

J'ai pris mes médicaments. I've taken my medicine.

la **Méditerranée** noun *fem.*
Mediterranean

la **méduse** noun *fem.*
jellyfish

meilleur adjective *masc.*,
meilleure *fem.*
1 better
Mon gâteau est meilleur que les autres. My cake is better than the others.
2 best
C'est ma meilleure amie. She's my best friend.
Meilleurs vœux! Best wishes!

le **meilleur** noun *masc.*,
la **meilleure** *fem.*
the best
C'est toi le meilleur en français. You're the best at French.

le **mélange** noun *masc.*
mixture

mélanger verb
1 to mix
Mélangez le beurre et la farine. Mix the butter and flour.
2 to mix up
Tu as mélangé tous mes CD! You've mixed up all my CDs!

la **mélodie** noun *fem.*
tune

le **melon** noun *masc.*
melon
un chapeau melon a bowler hat

le **membre** noun *masc.*
member

même adjective *masc. & fem.*
same
J'ai le même vélo que Luc. I have the same bike as Luc.
en même temps at the same time

même adverb
even
Je ne sais même pas nager. I can't even swim.
Nous jouons au foot même s'il neige. We play football even if it snows.

la **mémé** noun *fem.*
granny

la **mémoire** noun *fem.*
memory

menacer verb
to threaten

le **ménage** noun *masc.*
housework
faire le ménage to do the housework
une femme de ménage a cleaning lady

le **mendiant** noun *masc.*,
la **mendiante** *fem.*
beggar

mener verb
to lead
Leur équipe mène par deux buts à un. Their team is leading by two goals to one.
Où mène cette route? Where does this road lead?

le **mensonge** noun *masc.*
lie

le **mensuel** noun *masc.*
monthly magazine

le **menteur** noun *masc.*,
la **menteuse** *fem.*
liar
C'est une menteuse. She's a liar.

la **menthe** noun *fem.*
mint
un bonbon à la menthe a mint
le sirop de menthe mint cordial

mentir verb
to lie

*Ⓔ means use **être** to make the past tense.*

117

le **menton** noun *masc.*
chin

le **menu** noun *masc.*
menu
Qu'est-ce qu'il y a au menu?
What's on the menu?

le **menuisier** noun *masc.*
carpenter

la **mer** noun *fem.*
sea
la mer du Nord the North Sea
Dieppe est au bord de la mer.
Dieppe is by the sea.
Je vais au bord de la mer. I'm going
to the seaside.

merci exclamation
thank you
Merci beaucoup! Thank you very
much!
Merci d'être venu. Thank you for
coming.

le **mercredi** noun *masc.*
1 Wednesday
On est mercredi aujourd'hui. It's
Wednesday today.
mercredi prochain next
Wednesday
mercredi dernier last Wednesday
tous les mercredis every
Wednesday
2 on Wednesday
Je pars en vacances mercredi. I'm
going on holiday on Wednesday.
Nous avons des invités mercredi
soir. We have guests on
Wednesday evening.
À mercredi! See you on
Wednesday!
3 on Wednesdays
Je me lève tard le mercredi. I get
up late on Wednesdays.

le **mercurochrome**® noun *masc.*
red antiseptic lotion

la **mère** noun *fem.*
mother

la **merguez** noun *fem.*
spicy beef sausage

mériter verb
to deserve

merveilleux adjective *masc.*,
merveilleuse *fem.*
marvellous

mes plural adjective *mas. & fem.* SEE **mon**
my

mesdames plural noun *fem.*
Bonjour, mesdames! Good
morning ladies!
mesdames, mesdemoiselles,
messieurs ladies and gentlemen

mesdemoiselles plural noun *fem.*
Bonjour, mesdemoiselles! Good
morning ladies!

la **messe** noun *fem.*
mass
Ils vont à la messe. They go to
mass.
la messe de minuit midnight mass

messieurs plural noun *masc.*
Bonjour, messieurs! Good
morning!

mesurer verb
to mesure
Mesure cette ligne avec une règle!
Measure this line with a ruler!
Je mesure un mètre cinquante. I'm
1.5 metres tall., I'm five foot tall.

met, **mettent**, **mettez**,
mettons verb SEE **mettre**

le **métal** noun *masc.* (plural les
métaux)
metal

la **météo** noun *fem.*
weather forecast

le **métier** noun *masc.*
job
Qu'est-ce qu'il fait comme métier
ton père? What's your father's job?

• The months of the year and days of the week do not take a capital letter in French.

le **mètre** noun masc.
1 metre
2 metre rule
un mètre ruban a tape mesure

le **métro** noun masc.
underground
On y va en métro? Shall we go by underground?
On prend le métro pour aller à l'école. We're taking the underground to go to school

mets, **mettant**, **mettez**, **mettons** verb SEE **mettre**

mettre verb
1 to put
Je mets le livre sur l'étagère. I put the book on the shelf.
J'ai mis ta photo dans l'album.
I put your photo in the album.
2 to put on
Mets un CD! Put a CD on!
Je mets mon chapeau. I put my hat on.
3 to wear
Qu'est-ce que tu mets pour aller chez Lola? What will you wear to go to Lola's?
4 mettre le couvert to lay the table

se **mettre** verb ⊙
Mettez-vous en rang! Line up!
Je vais me mettre en short. I'm going to put shorts on.
Il se met en colère. He's getting angry.

le **meuble** noun masc.
les meubles furniture
un meuble a piece of furniture

miauler verb
to miaow

le **micro** noun masc.
microphone

le **micro-ondes** noun masc.
microwave

⊙ means use être to make the past tense.

le **midi** noun masc.
1 midday
à midi at midday
Il est midi. It's midday.
Il est midi moins le quart. It's quarter to twelve.
2 lunchtime
Qu'est-ce que tu manges à midi?
What do you eat at lunchtime?

le **Midi** noun masc.
the South of France

la **mie** noun fem.
the soft part of the bread

le **miel** noun masc.
honey

le **mien** pronoun masc., la **mienne** fem., les **miens** masc. plural, les **miennes** fem. plural
mine
Mélissa a un stylo comme le mien.
Mélissa has a pen like mine.
Cette règle, c'est la mienne? Is this ruler mine?
Les parents de Miguel sont espagnols et les miens aussi.
Miguel's parents are Spanish and so are mine.

les **miettes** plural noun fem.
crumbs

mieux adverb
1 better
Mohamed joue mieux que moi.
Mohamed plays better than me.
Elle va mieux aujourd'hui. She's better today.
2 best
C'est Martin qui me connaît le mieux. It's Martin who knows me best.

mieux adjective masc. & fem.
1 better
Oui, c'est mieux. Yes, that's better.
Tu es mieux avec les cheveux longs. You look better with long hair.

a
b
c
d
e
f
g
h
i
j
k
l
m
n
o
p
q
r
s
t
u
v
w
x
y
z

2 best

Ton dessin est le mieux de tous.
Your picture is the best out of all of them.

> **LANGUAGE**
> **Mieux** is the same in the masculine, feminine, and plural.

mignon adjective *masc.*,
mignonne *fem.*
sweet

Elle est mignonne, ta petite sœur!
Your little sister is really sweet!

le **milieu** noun *masc.*
middle

au milieu de in the middle of
l'étagère du milieu the middle shelf

mille number
a thousand

mille personnes a thousand people
deux mille euros two thousand euros

le **milliard** noun *masc.*
billion

le **millier** noun *masc.*
about a thousand

un millier d'euros about a thousand euros
des milliers de thousands of

le **millimètre** noun *masc.*
millimetre

le **million** noun *masc.*
million

deux millions two million
un million d'euros a million euros

> **LANGUAGE**
> French = **un million de** + noun
> English = **a million** + noun

le or la **millionnaire** noun *masc. & fem.*
millionaire

> **LANGUAGE**
> French = millionnaire
> English = millionaire

mince adjective *masc. & fem.*
1 slim

Tu es mince. You're slim.

2 thin

Il a les lèvres minces. He has thin lips.

la **mine** noun *fem.*
1 mine

une mine d'or a gold mine

2 une mine de crayon a pencil lead

3 Elle a bonne mine. She looks well.
Elle a mauvaise mine. She doesn't look well.

minérale adjective *fem.*
l'eau minérale mineral water

le **minimum** noun *masc.*
minimum

au minimum at the very least

le **Minitel®** noun *masc.*

> 🌐 **CULTURE**
> **Minitel** is an online service connected to the telephone. People use a special computer to get information such as transport timetables, phone numbers, or lists of films showing.

minuit noun *masc.*
midnight

à minuit at midnight
Il est minuit. It's midnight.

minuscule adjective *masc. & fem.*
1 tiny

une pièce minuscule a tiny room

2 small

un 's' minuscule a small 's'

la **minuscule** noun *fem.*
small letter

en minuscules in small letters

• *See the centre section for verb tables.*

la **minute** noun *fem.*
minute
Attends une minute! Wait a minute!

le **miroir** noun *masc.*
mirror
Raphaël se regarde dans le miroir. Raphaël is looking at himself in the mirror.

mis verb *masc.*, **mise** *fem.*
SEE **mettre**
J'ai mis mon livre dans le tiroir. I've put my book in the drawer.

la **mi-temps** noun *fem.*
half-time
à la mi-temps at half-time

Mlle abbreviation
(= **Mademoiselle**) **Miss**
Mlle Jourdain Miss Jourdain

Mme abbreviation
(= **Madame**) **Mrs**
Mme Picard Mrs Picard

la **mobylette**® noun *fem.*
moped

moche adjective *masc. & fem.*
1 ugly
Elle est vraiment moche. She's really ugly.
2 awful
Le temps est moche. The weather's awful.

la **mode** noun *fem.*
fashion
la dernière mode the latest fashion
à la mode fashionable
Ces baskets ne sont pas à la mode. These trainers aren't fashionable.

le **modèle** noun *masc.*
1 model
C'est un ancien modèle. It's an old model.
2 example
Il faut suivre le modèle. We have to follow the example.
3 un modèle réduit a model

*ⓔ means use **être** to make the past tense.*

moi pronoun
1 (*after a preposition etc.*) **me**
avec moi with me
Tu marches plus vite que moi. You walk faster than me.
C'est moi. It's me.
2 à moi mine
Ce CD est à moi. This CD is mine.
C'est à moi. It's my turn. (*in a game*)

moins adverb
1 less
Je lis moins que toi. I read less than you.
Je suis moins grand que toi. I'm not as tall as you.
Ton vélo est moins cher que le mien. Your bike is less expensive than mine.
2 moins de less, fewer
Il y a moins de gens qu'avant. There are fewer people than before.
Nous avons attendu moins de cinq minutes. We waited less than five minutes.
3 le moins, la moins, les moins the least
Maman a acheté le moins cher. Mum bought the least expensive one.
la fille la moins intelligente the least intelligent girl
les livres les moins intéressants the least interesting books
C'est Clara qui travaille le moins. It's Clara who works the least.
4 au moins at least
J'ai au moins trente jeux vidéo. I have at least thirty video games.

moins preposition
1 minus
Neuf moins cinq font quatre. Nine minus five is four.
2 to
Il est huit heures moins le quart. It's a quarter to eight.

le **mois** noun *masc.*
  month
  ce mois-ci this month
  le mois dernier last month
  le mois prochain next month
  au mois de mars in March

la **moitié** noun *fem.*
  1 half
  la moitié des élèves half the pupils
  2 à moitié half
  Ma tasse est à moitié vide. My cup is half empty.

molle adjective *fem.* SEE **mou**
  une balle molle a soft ball

le **moment** noun *masc.*
  1 moment
  Attends un moment! Wait a moment!
  en ce moment at the moment
  2 time
  Ce n'est le pas bon moment. It isn't the right time.
  à ce moment-là at that time

mon adjective *masc.*, **ma** *fem.*, **mes** *masc. & fem. plural*
  my
  mon père my father
  ma robe my dress
  mes copains my friends
  mes sœurs my sisters
  mon idée my idea

🔑 **LANGUAGE**
Use **mon** instead of **ma** before a feminine noun starting with *a, e, i, o, u,* or *silent h.*

le **monde** noun *masc.*
  1 world
  le monde entier the whole world
  2 people
  Il y a du monde ici. There are lots of people here.
  beaucoup de monde lots of people
  tout le monde everybody

le **moniteur** noun *masc.*
  monitor (*of a computer*)

le **moniteur** noun *masc.*, la **monitrice** *fem.*
  1 instructor
  un moniteur de natation a swimming instructor
  2 group leader (*in a holiday camp*)

la **monnaie** noun *fem.*
  1 change
  Tu as de la monnaie pour le métro? Do you have any change for the underground?
  une pièce de monnaie a coin
  2 currency
  En France, la monnaie c'est l'euro. In France the currency is the euro.

monsieur noun *masc.* (plural **messieurs**)
  1 man
  Demande à ce monsieur. Ask that man.
  2 Bonjour, monsieur! Good morning!

🔑 **LANGUAGE**
Used when talking to a man in a polite way and not usually translated, though 'sir' is sometimes used in English, especially at school, e.g. **Oui, monsieur** (Yes, sir).

  3 Monsieur Mr
  Monsieur Lebrun Mr Lebrun
  4 (*in a letter*)
  Monsieur ... Dear Sir ...

le **monstre** noun *masc.*
  monster

la **montagne** noun *fem.*
  1 mountain
  à la montagne in the mountains
  2 les montagnes russes the roller coaster

monter verb ☺
  1 to go up
  Monte dans ta chambre. Go up to your room.
  Elle monte l'escalier. She's going up the stairs.
  2 to come up

• *Use* **le** *and* **un** *for masculine words and* **la** *and* **une** *for feminine words.*

Tu montes ou tu attends en bas?
Are you coming up or are you waiting downstairs?

3 to get in
Les enfants sont montés dans la voiture. The children got into the car.

4 to get on
Montez dans le bus! Get on the bus!

5 to take up
Monte ma valise, s'il te plaît papa! Take up my suitcase, please, dad!

6 to put on
Les élèves vont monter un spectacle. The pupils are putting on a show.

7 monter à cheval to ride a horse

la **montre** noun *fem.*
watch

montrer verb
to show
Montre! Show me!
Montrez-moi! Show me!
Montre-moi comment tu fais! Show me how you do it!

le **monument** noun *masc.*
historic building

la **moquette** noun *fem.*
carpet

le **morceau** noun *masc.* (plural les **morceaux**)
piece
un morceau de pain a piece of bread

mordre verb
to bite

mort adjective *masc.*, **morte** *fem.*
dead

la **mosquée** noun *fem.*
mosque

le **mot** noun *masc.*
1 word
C'est un mot difficile. It's a difficult word.
un mot de passe a password
les mots cachés wordsearch
des mots croisés a crossword
2 note
Ton copain a laissé un mot.
Your friend has left a note.

le **moteur** noun *masc.*
engine

le **motif** noun *masc.*
pattern

la **moto** noun *fem.*
motorbike

mou adjective *masc.*, **molle** *fem.*
soft
Le beurre est mou. The butter is soft.

la **mouche** noun *fem.*
fly

se **moucher** verb ⊘
to blow your nose

le **mouchoir** noun *masc.*
1 handkerchief
2 tissue
un mouchoir en papier a tissue

la **mouette** noun *fem.*
seagull

mouillé adjective *masc.*, **mouillée** *fem.*
wet

les **moules** plural noun *fem.*
mussels

le **moulin à vent** noun *masc.*
windmill

mourir verb ⊘
1 to die
Il est mort hier. He died yesterday.
2 mourir de faim to starve
Je meurs de faim! I'm starving!

⊘ *means use* **être** *to make the past tense.*

la **moustache** noun fem.
1 **moustache**
2 **les moustaches** whiskers

le **moustique** noun masc.
mosquito

la **moutarde** noun fem.
mustard

le **mouton** noun masc.
1 **sheep**
2 (the meat) **mutton**

moyen adjective masc.,
moyenne fem.
1 **medium**
Je suis de taille moyenne. I'm of medium height.
2 **average**
un élève moyen an average pupil

le **Moyen-Orient** noun masc.
the Middle East

le **muguet** noun masc.
lily of the valley

> **CULTURE**
> In France people give each other small bunches of **muguet** for good luck on the May Day holiday (first of May).

multiplier verb
to multiply

municipal adjective masc.,
municipale fem.
une bibliothèque municipale a public library

le **mur** noun masc.
wall

mûr adjective masc., **mûre** fem.
1 **ripe**
La poire n'est pas mûre. The pear isn't ripe.
2 **grown-up**
Nathan est mûr pour son âge. Nathan is grown-up for his age.

la **mûre** noun fem.
blackberry

murmurer verb
to whisper

le **musée** noun masc.
1 **museum**
2 **art gallery**

le **musicien** noun masc.,
la **musicienne** fem.
musician

la **musique** noun fem.
music

musulman adjective masc.,
musulmane fem.
Muslim

myope adjective masc. & fem.
short-sighted

le **mystère** noun masc.
mystery

mystérieux adjective masc.,
mystérieuse fem.
mysterious

Nn

n' adverb

> **LANGUAGE**
> **n' = ne** before a, e, i, o, u, y, or silent h

Je n'aime pas le chocolat. I don't like chocolate.

Il n'habite pas en France. He doesn't live in France.

nager verb
to swim
Je ne sais pas nager. I can't swim.

• Languages, nationalities, and religions do not take a capital letter in French.

le **nain** noun *masc.*, la **naine** *fem.*
dwarf

la **naissance** noun *fem.*
birth
Quelle est ta date de naissance?
What's your date of birth?

naître verb *☉*
to be born
Je suis né le dix mai. (*boy speaking*)
Je suis née le dix mai. (*girl speaking*)
I was born on the tenth of May.

> **⚷ LANGUAGE**
> French = Je **suis** né (*masc.*)
>   Je **suis** née (*fem.*)
> English = I **was** born

la **nappe** noun *fem.*
tablecloth

la **natation** noun *fem.*
swimming

la **nationalité** noun *fem.*
nationality
Il est de quelle nationalité? What
nationality is he?

la **natte** noun *fem.*
plait
Noémie a des nattes. Noémie has
plaits.

nature adjective *masc. & fem.*
plain
une omelette nature a plain
omelette

> **⚷ LANGUAGE**
> **Nature** is the same in the plural, for
> example: **des yaourts nature**.

la **nature** noun *fem.*
nature

naturel adjective *masc.*,
naturelle *fem.*
natural

naturellement adverb
of course

nautique adjective *masc. & fem.*
le ski nautique water-skiing

*☉ means use **être** to make the past tense.*

le **navet** noun *masc.*
turnip

la **navette** noun *fem.*
shuttle
une navette spatiale a space
shuttle

le **navire** noun *masc.*
ship

ne adverb

> **⚷ LANGUAGE**
> **Ne** is used with other words (**pas, plus,
> rien**, etc.) usually to make sentences in
> the negative; **ne** becomes **n'** before *a, e, i,
> o, u, y*, or *silent h*.

1 ne … pas not
Je ne veux pas de fromage. I don't
want any cheese.

2 ne … plus not any more
Nous n'allons plus au bord de la
mer. We don't go to the seaside
any more.

3 ne … rien not anything
Bruno ne mange rien. Bruno
doesn't eat anything.

4 ne … personne not anybody
Je ne connais personne. I don't
know anybody.

5 ne … que only
Ibrahim n'a que cinq euros.
Ibrahim only has five euros.

6 ne … jamais never
Elle ne vient jamais chez moi. She
never comes to my house.

né verb *masc.*, **née** *fem.* SEE **naître**
born
Je suis né en 1998. (*boy speaking*)
Je suis née en 1998. (*girl speaking*) I
was born in 1998.

> **⚷ LANGUAGE**
> French = Je **suis** né (masc.)
>   Je **suis** née (fem.)
> English = I **was** born

nécessaire adjective *masc. & fem.*
necessary

a b c d e f g h i j k l m **n** o p q r s t u v w x y z

le **néerlandais** noun masc.
Dutch (language)

néerlandais adjective masc.,
néerlandaise fem.
Dutch

le **Néerlandais** noun masc.,
la **Néerlandaise** fem.
Dutchman, **Dutchwoman**

la **neige** noun fem.
snow
un bonhomme de neige
a snowman

neiger verb
to snow
Il neige. It's snowing.

néo-zélandais adjective masc.,
néo-zélandaise fem.
New Zealand
l'équipe néo-zélandaise the New
Zealand team

le **Néo-Zélandais** noun masc.,
la **Néo-Zélandaise** fem.
New Zealander

nerveux adjective masc.,
nerveuse fem.
nervous

le **Net** noun masc.
Net
surfer sur le Net to surf the Net

net adjective masc., **nette** fem.
clear
une photo très nette a very clear
photo

nettement adverb
1 much
**Il est nettement plus grand que
moi.** He's much taller than me.
2 clearly
On voit nettement que ... You can
clearly see that ...

nettoyer verb
to clean

neuf number
nine
à neuf heures at nine
Il a neuf ans. He's nine.
le neuf décembre the ninth of
December

neuf adjective masc., **neuve** fem.
new
Il est tout neuf, ton ordinateur?
Is your computer brand-new?
J'ai des chaussures neuves. I've got
new shoes.

neuvième adjective masc. & fem.
ninth
au neuvième étage on the ninth
floor

le **neveu** noun masc. (plural les
neveux)
nephew

le **nez** noun masc.
nose

ni conjunction
1 ni ... ni neither ... nor
ni Lizzy ni sa sœur neither Lizzy
nor her sister
2 ni l'un ni l'autre neither
**Tu veux le blanc ou le vert? – Ni
l'un ni l'autre.** Do you want the
white one or the green one? –
Neither.

la **niche** noun fem.
kennel

le **nid** noun masc.
nest

la **nièce** noun fem.
niece

le **niveau** noun masc. (plural les
niveaux)
level

Noël noun masc.
Christmas
Joyeux Noël! Happy Christmas!
un arbre de Noël a Christmas tree

• The months of the year and days of the week do not take a capital letter in French.

des cadeaux de Noël Christmas presents

 CULTURE
French children sometimes put their shoes by the fireplace on Christmas Eve so that Father Christmas (**le père Noël**) can fill them with presents.

le **nœud** noun masc.
knot
le nœud papillon bow tie

noir adjective masc., **noire** fem.
1 black
un costume noir a black suit
2 dark
des lunettes noires dark glasses

le **noir** noun masc.
1 black
Elle s'habille en noir. She wears black.
2 dark
Mathis a peur du noir. Mathis is afraid of the dark.

la **noisette** noun fem.
hazelnut

la **noix** noun fem. (plural les **noix**)
walnut
une noix de coco a coconut

le **nom** noun masc.
1 name
Quel est ton nom de famille? What's your surname?
2 noun
Le mot 'garçon' est un nom. The word 'boy' is a noun.

le **nombre** noun masc.
number

nombreux adjective masc., **nombreuse** fem.
1 many
Ils sont trop nombreux. There are too many of them.
2 big
une famille nombreuse a big family

ⓔ means use être to make the past tense.

nommer verb
to name
Nommez ces instruments. Name these instruments.

non adverb
1 no
Tu viens? – Non! Are you coming? – No!
2 not
Tu viens ou non? Are you coming or not?
3 Tu aimes lire, non? You like reading, don't you?

🔑 **LANGUAGE**
Non? is used for checking if the person you're speaking to thinks something is true.

4 non plus not … either
Matthieu n'aime pas le poisson et moi non plus. Matthieu doesn't like fish and I don't either.

nord adjective masc. & fem.
north
la côte nord the north coast

🔑 **LANGUAGE**
Nord is the same in the masculine, feminine, and plural.

le **nord** noun masc.
north
Nous vivons dans le nord. We live in the north.
au nord de Poitiers to the north of Poitiers
la mer du Nord the North Sea
nord-est northeast
nord-ouest northwest

normal adjective masc., **normale** fem., **normaux** masc. plural, **normales** fem. plural
normal
C'est normal. That's normal.

French English

Il n'a pas téléphoné, ce n'est pas **normal.** He hasn't phoned,that isn't right.

normalement adverb
normally

la **Normandie** noun fem.
Normandy

la **Norvège** noun fem.
Norway

norvégien adjective masc.,
norvégienne fem.
Norwegian

le **Norvégien** noun masc.,
la **Norvégienne** fem.
Norwegian (person)

nos plural adjective masc. & fem.
SEE **notre**
our
nos parents our parents
nos amies our friends

le **notaire** noun masc.
solicitor
Il est notaire. He's a solicitor.

la **note** noun fem.
1 mark
Léa a eu une bonne note. Léa got a good mark.
2 note
Les élèves prennent des notes. The pupils are taking notes.
3 note (in music)
4 bill
La note, s'il vous plaît! The bill, please!

noter verb
to write down
Note mon adresse dans ton carnet. Write down my address in your book.

notre adjective masc. & fem.,
nos masc. & fem. plural
our
notre vélo our bike

• See the centre section for verb tables.

notre école our school
nos parents our parents

🔑 **LANGUAGE**
Notre + masculine or feminine noun in the singular, and **nos** + plural noun.

le **nôtre** pronoun masc., la **nôtre** fem.,
les **nôtres** masc. & fem. plural
ours
Votre appartement est plus grand que le nôtre. Your flat is bigger than ours.
Votre école est grande, la nôtre est petite. Your school is big, ours is small.

nouer verb
to tie
J'ai noué mes lacets. I tied my shoelaces.

les **nouilles** plural noun fem.
pasta
les nouilles chinoises Chinese noodles

la **nounou** noun fem.
1 nanny
2 childminder

le **nounours** noun masc.
teddy bear

la **nourrice** noun fem.
childminder

la **nourriture** noun fem.
food

nous pronoun
1 we
Nous sommes en CM2. We are in Year 6.
2 us
Venez avec nous! Come with us!
3 to us
John nous parle toujours en anglais. John always speaks to us in English.
4 (no translation)
Nous nous levons à 7 heures. We get up at 7.

5 à nous ours
C'est à nous. It's ours.

> 🔑 **LANGUAGE**
> **Nous** is often replaced by **on** in the spoken language. For example: **On y va!** instead of **Nous y allons!**

nouveau adjective *masc.*,
nouvelle *fem.*,
nouveaux *masc. plural*,
nouvelles *fem. plural*
new
C'est le nouveau film de Disney.
It's the new Disney film.
Ma sœur a une nouvelle robe.
My sister has a new dress.
le nouvel an the New Year

> 🔑 **LANGUAGE**
> The form **nouvel** is used with a masculine singular noun beginning with *a, e, i, o, u,* or *silent h,* for example: **un nouvel ordinateur** is 'a new computer'.

le **nouveau** noun *masc.*,
la **nouvelle** *fem.* (plural les
nouveaux)
new boy, **new girl**
Il y a un nouveau dans la classe. There's a new boy in the class.

la **nouvelle** noun *fem.*
news
J'ai une mauvaise nouvelle. I have some bad news.
C'est une bonne nouvelle. That's good news.
des nouvelles news
les nouvelles de vingt heures the eight o'clock news

la **Nouvelle-Zélande** noun *fem.*
New Zealand

novembre noun *masc.*
November
en novembre in November
au mois de novembre in November

Julia est née le huit novembre.
Julia was born on the eighth of November.

> 🌍 **CULTURE**
> **Le 1er novembre** is 'la Toussaint' (All Saints' Day) and it's a bank holiday in France.

le **noyau** noun *masc.* (plural les
noyaux)
stone (*of a fruit*)

se **noyer** verb ⓔ
to drown

nu adjective *masc.*, **nue** *fem.*
naked

le **nuage** noun *masc.*
cloud

la **nuit** noun *fem.*
night
pendant la nuit during the night
toute la nuit all night
Il fait froid la nuit. It's cold at night.
Cette nuit, j'ai entendu du bruit.
Last night, I heard a noise.
Il va rentrer cette nuit. He'll be back tonight.
Il fait nuit. It's dark.
Bonne nuit! Good night!

nul adjective *masc.*, **nulle** *fem.*
1 rubbish
Ce CD est nul. This CD is rubbish.
2 useless
Je suis nul en anglais! I'm useless at English!
3 un match nul a draw
Son équipe a fait match nul. His team drew.

nulle part adverb
nowhere
Où vas-tu? – Nulle part. Where are you going? – Nowhere.

numérique adjective *masc. & fem.*
digital

ⓔ *means use* **être** *to make the past tense.*

un appareil photo numérique a digital camera

le **numéro** noun masc.
number

Donne-moi ton numéro de téléphone! Give me your phone number!
Elle habite au numéro douze. She lives at number twelve.

Oo

obéir verb
to obey
obéir à quelqu'un to obey somebody

obéissant adjective masc.,
obéissante fem.
obedient

un **objet** noun masc.
object
les objets trouvés lost property

obligé adjective masc.,
obligée fem.
être obligé de faire quelque chose to have to do something
Elle est obligée de ranger sa chambre. She has to tidy up her bedroom.
Tu n'es pas obligé de répondre. You don't have to answer.

obliger verb
obliger quelqu'un à faire quelque chose to make somebody do something
Papa m'oblige à faire la vaisselle. Dad makes me do the washing-up.

observer verb
to watch
J'observe les oiseaux avec des jumelles. I watch the birds with binoculars.

un **obstacle** noun masc.
une course d'obstacles an obstacle race

une **occasion** noun fem.
1 occasion
une occasion très spéciale a very special occasion
2 d'occasion used
J'ai acheté un vélo d'occasion. I bought a used bike.

l'**Occident** noun masc.
the West

occupé adjective masc.,
occupée fem.
1 busy
Maman est très occupée. Mum's very busy.
2 taken
Cette place est occupée. This seat is taken.
3 (talking about the toilet or phone)
engaged
C'est occupé. It's engaged.

s'**occuper** verb
s'occuper de to take care of
Tu t'occupes des enfants? Are you taking care of the children?

l'**océan** noun masc.
ocean

octobre noun masc.
October
en octobre in October
au mois d'octobre in October
le cinq octobre on the fifth of October

une **odeur** noun fem.
smell
une bonne odeur a nice smell

• Use **le** and **un** for masculine words and **la** and **une** for feminine words.

Quelle odeur! What a stink!

🔑 **LANGUAGE**
An **odeur** can be good or bad but in English an odour is a bad smell.

un **œil** noun *masc.* (plural les **yeux**)
eye
J'ai quelque chose dans l'œil. I've got something in my eye.
J'ai les yeux bleus. I have blue eyes.

un **œuf** noun *masc.*
egg
des œufs brouillés scrambled eggs
un œuf à la coque a boiled egg
un œuf dur a hard-boiled egg
un œuf sur le plat a fried egg

l'**office du tourisme** noun *masc.*
tourist office

offrir verb
1 to give
Tu lui offres quoi? What will you give her?
Il m'a offert un DVD. He gave me a DVD.
2 to buy
Je t'offre une glace. I'll buy you an ice cream.
3 to offer
Elle a offert de nous aider. She offered to help us.

une **oie** noun *fem.*
goose
le jeu de l'oie (*board game*) snakes and ladders

un **oignon** noun *masc.*
onion

un **oiseau** noun *masc.* (plural les **oiseaux**)
bird

une **olive** noun *fem.*
olive
l'huile d'olive olive oil

olympique adjective *masc. & fem.*
Olympic

les Jeux Olympiques the Olympic Games

l'**ombre** noun *fem.*
1 shade
Il fait trente degrés à l'ombre. It's thirty degrees in the shade.
2 shadow
Je vois ton ombre sur le mur. I can see your shadow on the wall.

une **omelette** noun *fem.*
omelette

on pronoun
1 we
On a français aujourd'hui. We have French today.
On va chez mamie ce soir. We're going to granny's house tonight.
2 you
On n'a pas le droit d'entrer. You're not allowed to come in.
3 somebody
On frappe à la porte. Somebody's knocking on the door.
4 people
En France, on roule à droite. In France people drive on the right.

un **oncle** noun *masc.*
uncle

un **ongle** noun *masc.*
nail (*on finger*)

ont verb SEE **avoir**
1 (*in the present tense*) **have**
Elles ont les yeux marron. They have brown eyes.
2 (*when used to form a past tense*)
Les enfants ont mal dormi. The children slept badly.

onze number
eleven
J'ai onze ans. I'm eleven.
à onze heures at eleven
le onze août the eleventh of August

a
b
c
d
e
f
g
h
i
j
k
l
m
n
o
p
q
r
s
t
u
v
w
x
y
z

ℯ *means use* **être** *to make the past tense.*

a
b
c
d
e
f
g
h
i
j
k
l
m
n
o
p
q
r
s
t
u
v
w
x
y
z

onzième adjective *masc. & fem.*
eleventh
au onzième étage on the eleventh floor

un opticien noun *masc.*,
une opticienne *fem.*
optician

optimiste adjective *masc. & fem.*
optimistic

l'or noun *masc.*
gold
des boucles d'oreille en or gold earrings

un orage noun *masc.*
storm

orageux adjective *masc.*,
orageuse *fem.*
stormy

orange adjective *masc. & fem.*
orange
des chaussettes orange orange socks

> **LANGUAGE**
> **Orange** is the same in the masculine, feminine, and plural.

une orange noun *fem.*
orange
Je bois du jus d'orange. I'm drinking some orange juice.

l'orange noun *masc.*
orange
Ma couleur préférée, c'est l'orange. My favourite colour is orange.

un orchestre noun *masc.*
1 orchestra
2 band

> **LANGUAGE**
> In French **un orchestre** can be a big orchestra or a small band.

ordinaire adjective *masc. & fem.*
ordinary

un ordinateur noun *masc.*
computer

une ordonnance noun *fem.*
prescription

l'ordre noun *masc.*
1 order
par ordre alphabétique in alphabetical order
dans le bon ordre in the right order
2 en ordre tidy

les ordures plural noun *fem.*
rubbish

une oreille noun *fem.*
ear
avoir mal aux oreilles to have an earache

un oreiller noun *masc.*
pillow

organiser verb
to organize

un orgue noun *masc.*
organ

l'Orient noun *masc.*
the East

un orphelin noun *masc.*,
une orpheline *fem.*
orphan

un orteil noun *masc.*
toe

l'orthographe noun *fem.*
spelling
une faute d'orthographe a spelling mistake

un os noun *masc.*
bone

oser verb
to dare
Je n'ose pas lui parler. I don't dare to speak to him.

ou conjunction
or

• *Languages, nationalities, and religions do not take a capital letter in French.*

Tu préfères l'anglais ou l'espagnol? Do you prefer English or Spanish?

où adverb
where
Où est Vincent? Where's Vincent?
Où vas-tu? Where are you going?
Où habites-tu? Where do you live?
Où se trouve l'office du tourisme? Where's the tourist office?
Dis-moi où c'est. Tell me where it is.

où pronoun
1 where
C'est la ville où j'habite. It's the town where I live.
2 when, that
le jour où Lucas est né the day when Lucas was born

oublier verb
1 to forget
oublier de to forget to
J'ai oublié de prendre mon livre. I forgot to take my book.
2 to leave
Papa a oublié ses clés à la maison. Dad left his keys at home.

ouest adjective
west
la côte ouest the west coast

l'**ouest** noun *masc.*
west
Nous vivons dans l'ouest. We live in the west.
à l'ouest d'Avignon to the west of Avignon

ouf exclamation
Phew
Ouf, j'ai fini mes devoirs! Phew, I've finished my homework!

@ means use être to make the past tense.

oui adverb
yes
Tu viens avec nous? – Oui! Are you coming with us? – Yes!

ouille exclamation
ouch

un **ours** noun *masc.*
bear
un ours brun a brown bear
un ours en peluche a teddy bear

🌍 **CULTURE**
There are a few brown bears in the Pyrenees.

les **outils** plural noun *masc.*
tools
une boîte à outils a tool box

ouvert adjective *masc.*,
ouverte *fem.*
open
La fenêtre est ouverte. The window is open.

l'**ouverture** noun *fem.*
les heures d'ouverture the opening hours

un **ouvre-boîtes** noun *masc.* (plural les **ouvre-boîtes**)
a can opener

un **ouvrier** noun *masc.*,
une **ouvrière** *fem.*
worker

ouvrir verb
1 to open
Ouvrez vos livres! Open your books!
2 to turn on
Je ne peux pas ouvrir le robinet. I can't turn on the tap.

un **OVNI** noun *masc.*
UFO

Pp

le **Pacifique** noun *masc.*
Pacific

la **page** noun *fem.*
page
la page d'accueil the home page

la **paille** noun *fem.*
straw

le **pain** noun *masc.*
bread
un morceau de pain a piece of bread
une tranche de pain a slice of bread
un pain a loaf of bread
un petit pain a roll
du pain grillé toast
le pain de mie sandwich loaf
le pain d'épices gingerbread

pair adjective *masc.*
1 un nombre pair an even number
2 une jeune fille au pair an au pair

la **paire** noun *fem.*
pair
une paire de chaussures a pair of shoes

la **paix** noun *fem.*
peace
Est-ce qu'on peut avoir la paix? Can we have some peace?

le **Pakistan** noun *masc.*
Pakistan

pakistanais adjective *masc.*,
pakistanaise *fem.*
Pakistani

le **Pakistanais** noun *masc.*,
la **Pakistanaise** *fem.*
Pakistani (*person*)

le **palais** noun *masc.*
palace

pâle adjective *masc. & fem.*
pale

le **palmier** noun *masc.*
palm tree

le **pamplemousse** noun *masc.*
grapefruit

pané adjective *masc.*, **panée** *fem.*
in breadcrumbs
Le poisson pané fish in breadcrumbs

le **panier** noun *masc.*
basket

la **panique** noun *fem.*
panic
Pas de panique! Don't panic!

la **panne** noun *fem.*
breakdown
La voiture est en panne. The car has broken down.

le **panneau** noun *masc.* (plural les **panneaux**)
sign
un panneau d'affichage a notice board

la **panoplie** noun *fem.*
dressing up outfit
une panoplie de cowboy a cowboy outfit

le **pansement** noun *masc.*
plaster
J'ai un pansement au doigt. I've got a plaster on my finger.

le **pantalon** noun *masc.*
trousers

⚷ **LANGUAGE**
French = un pantalon is singular
English = trousers is plural

la **panthère** noun *fem.*
panther

• *The months of the year and days of the week do not take a capital letter in French.*

la **pantoufle** noun *fem.*
slipper

le **papa** noun *masc.*
dad

la **papaye** noun *fem.*
pawpaw

le **pape** noun *masc.*
pope

la **papeterie** noun *fem.*
stationery shop

le **papi**, le **papy** noun *masc.*
granddad

le **papier** noun *masc.*
paper
une feuille de papier a sheet of paper
un sac en papier a paper bag
le papier alu tinfoil
le papier brouillon rough paper
le papier cadeau wrapping paper
le papier-calque tracing paper
le papier peint wallpaper
le papier toilette toilet paper

le **papillon** noun *masc.*
butterfly
un papillon de nuit a moth

Pâques noun
Easter
à Pâques at Easter
Joyeuses Pâques! Happy Easter!
un œuf de Pâques an Easter egg

> ### 🌍 CULTURE
> There's a tradition in France of children hunting for chocolate Easter eggs in the garden. Church bells, called **cloches de Pâques** (Easter bells), are supposed to fly away to Rome and fly back over the gardens of all children who have been good, dropping the eggs as gifts.

le **paquet** noun *masc.*
1 packet
un paquet de chips a packet of crisps

2 parcel
Tu as reçu mon paquet? Did you get my parcel?

par preposition
1 by
J'ai été piqué par une guêpe. I was stung by a wasp.
par erreur by mistake
2 through
Nous passons par le tunnel. We're going through the tunnel.
3 out of
Il est tombé par la fenêtre. He fell out of the window.
4 (when saying how many times) **a**
cinq fois par mois five times a month
5 par ici this way
Venez par ici! Come this way!
6 par ici around here
Il y a un café par ici? Is there a cafe around here?
7 par là that way
Passez par là! Go that way!
8 par là around there
Je l'ai vu par là. I saw him somewhere around there.

la **parabole** noun *fem.*
satellite dish

paraître verb
to seem

le **parapluie** noun *masc.*
umbrella

le **parasol** noun *masc.*
umbrella

le **parc** noun *masc.*
park
un parc d'attractions a theme park

parce que conjunction

> ### 🔑 LANGUAGE
> parce que = parce qu' before *a, e, i, o, u,* or silent *h*

because

 means use **être** *to make the past tense.*

J'aime les maths parce que c'est facile. I like maths because it's easy.
Elle va au lit parce qu'elle est fatiguée. She's going to bed because she's tired.

le **parcours** noun masc.
route, **course**
un parcours santé a fitness trail

par-dessous adverb
underneath
Passe par-dessous! Go underneath!

par-dessus adverb
over
Passe par-dessus! Go over it!

pardon exclamation
1 sorry
Oh, pardon! – Ce n'est pas grave! So sorry! – That's all right!
2 excuse me
Pardon, monsieur, où est la gare? Excuse me, where is the station?
3 Pardon? Je n'ai pas compris. Pardon? I didn't understand.

pardonner verb
to forgive

pareil adjective masc.,
pareille fem.
the same

la **parenthèse** noun fem.
bracket
entre parenthèses in brackets

les **parents** plural noun masc.
1 parents
2 relatives

paresseux adjective masc.,
paresseuse fem.
lazy

parfait adjective masc.,
parfaite fem.
perfect

parfois adverb
sometimes

le **parfum** noun masc.
1 perfume
un flacon de parfum a bottle of perfume
2 flavour
Qu'est-ce qu'il y a comme parfum? What flavours are there?

le **Parisien** noun masc.,
la **Parisienne** fem.
somebody from Paris

le **parking** noun masc.
car park

⚠ **FALSE FRIEND**
le parking = **car park** (not parking)

parler verb
1 to speak
Vous parlez anglais? Do you speak English?
2 to talk
Cléo ne me parle pas. Cléo doesn't talk to me.

parmi preposition
among

la **parole** noun fem.
1 Tu n'as pas la parole. It's not your turn to speak.
2 les paroles the words
J'ai oublié les paroles de la chanson. I've forgotten the words of the song.

le **parquet** noun masc.
wooden floor

le **parrain** noun masc.
godfather

pars, **part** verb SEE **partir**

la **part** noun fem.
1 piece
une part de gâteau a piece of cake
2 à part apart from
à part moi apart from me

• See the centre section for verb tables.

À part ça, ça va? Apart from that, how is it going?

partager verb

1 to share
On partage une chambre.
We share a room.

2 to divide
Maman partage la pizza en cinq.
Mum divides the pizza into five.

le or la **partenaire** noun masc. & fem.
partner

participer verb
participer à to take part in

particulier adjective masc.,
particulière fem.

1 private
Tu prends des cours particuliers?
Are you having private lessons?

2 special
rien de particulier nothing special

la **partie** noun fem.

1 part
la première partie du film the first part of the film

2 faire partie de quelque chose to be part of something
Il fait partie de notre équipe. He's in our team.

3 game
faire une partie d'échecs to play a game of chess

partir verb ⓔ

1 to go
Arthur part en vacances. Arthur is going on holiday.
Justine est partie à Paris. Justine has gone to Paris.

2 to leave
Le train part à quelle heure? What time does the train leave?

3 à partir de from
à partir de trois heures from three o'clock on

partout adverb
everywhere

ⓔ *means use* **être** *to make the past tense.*

pas adverb

1 ne ... pas not
Je ne suis pas son ami. I'm not his friend.
Elle n'a pas d'ordinateur. She doesn't have a computer.

2 not
Tu viens ou pas? Are you coming or not?
Ce n'est pas mal. That's not bad.
pas encore not yet
pas moi not me
pas du tout not at all

> **LANGUAGE**
> ne + *verb* + **pas**, for example: Je **ne** sais **pas**

le **pas** noun masc.
step
Un pas en avant, deux pas en arrière! One step forwards, two steps backwards!

le **passage** noun masc.

1 un passage pour piétons a pedestrian crossing

2 un passage souterrain a subway

le **passager** noun masc.,
la **passagère** fem.
passenger

le **passé** noun masc.

1 past
dans le passé in the past

2 past tense

le **passeport** noun masc.
passport

passer verb

1 to go
Passe chez le boucher! Go to the butcher's!
Passez par là! Go that way!

2 to go past
Le bus passe devant chez toi? Does the bus go past your house?

3 to go through
Il faut passer par le tunnel. You have to go through the tunnel.

a
b
c
d
e
f
g
h
i
j
k
l
m
n
o
p
q
r
s
t
u
v
w
x
y
z

4 to get through
Je ne peux pas passer, il y a trop de monde! I can't get through, there are too many people!

5 to come
Le facteur n'est pas encore passé. The postman hasn't come yet.

6 to spend (time)
J'ai passé une semaine à Tours. I spent a week in Tours.

7 to pass
Passe-moi le sucre! Pass me the sugar!

8 passer un examen to take an exam

⚠ **FALSE FRIEND**
passer un examen = to take an exam (not to pass an exam)

se **passer** verb ⓔ

1 to happen
Qu'est-ce qui se passe? What's happening?

2 to take place
L'histoire se passe il y a cent ans. The story takes place a hundred years ago.

3 to go
Ça s'est bien passé. It went well.

le **passe-temps** noun masc. (plural les **passe-temps**)
hobby
J'ai plusieurs passe-temps. I have several hobbies.

passionnant adjective masc., **passionnante** fem.
exciting

la **pastèque** noun fem.
watermelon

la **pastille** noun fem.
une pastille pour la toux a cough sweet

la **patate douce** noun fem.
sweet potato

la **pâte** noun fem.
1 (for bread) **dough**

2 (for pies) **pastry**

3 la pâte à modeler Plasticine®

le **pâté** noun masc.
1 pâté
2 un pâté de sable a sandcastle

les **pâtes** plural noun fem.
pasta

🔑 **LANGUAGE**
French = **les pâtes** is plural
English = **pasta** is singular

le **patin** noun masc.
1 skate
les patins à glace ice skates
les patins à roulettes roller skates

2 skating
Nous faisons du patin à glace. We go ice-skating.

la **patinoire** noun fem.
skating rink

la **pâtisserie** noun fem.
cake shop

la **patte** noun fem.
1 paw
les pattes du chat the cat's paws

2 leg
les pattes de l'araignée the spider's legs

pauvre adjective masc. & fem.
poor
Notre famille est pauvre. Our family is poor.
Pauvre Max! Poor Max!

payant adjective masc., **payante** fem.
C'est gratuit? – Non, c'est payant. Is it free? – No, you have to pay.

payer verb
1 to pay
C'est Pierre qui va payer. Pierre will pay.

2 to pay for
Mon cousin l'a payé trente euros. My cousin paid thirty euros for it.

• Use **le** and **un** for masculine words and **la** and **une** for feminine words.

le **pays** noun masc.
country

le **paysage** noun masc.
scenery

le **paysan** noun masc.,
la **paysanne** fem.
farmer

les **Pays-Bas** plural noun masc.
Netherlands

le **pays de Galles** noun masc.
Wales

le **PC** noun masc.
PC

la **peau** noun fem.
skin

la **pêche** noun fem.
1 **peach**
2 **fishing**
Nous allons à la pêche demain.
We're going fishing tomorrow.

le **pêcheur** noun masc.
fisherman

la **pédale** noun fem.
pedal

le **peigne** noun masc.
comb

se **peigner** verb @
to comb your hair

le **peignoir** noun masc.
dressing-gown

peindre verb
to paint
Il a peint la porte en vert.
He painted the door green.

la **peine** noun fem.
Ça vaut la peine. It's worth it.
Ce n'est pas la peine. It's not worth it.

le **peintre** noun masc.
painter

la **peinture** noun fem.
1 **paint**
un pot de peinture a tin of paint
2 **painting**
J'adore faire de la peinture. I love painting.

la **pelle** noun fem.
1 **shovel**
2 **spade**

la **pellicule** noun fem.
film

la **pelouse** noun fem.
lawn

la **peluche** noun fem.
soft toy
un ours en peluche a teddy bear

se **pencher** verb @
1 **to lean over**
se pencher par la fenêtre to lean out of the window
2 **to bend over**

pendant preposition
1 **during**
pendant la nuit during the night
2 **for**
Elle est restée pendant une semaine. She stayed for a week.
3 **pendant que** while
On joue pendant que papa fait la cuisine. We play while dad does the cooking.

pendre verb
to hang

le **pendu** noun masc.
hangman
On joue au pendu? Shall we play hangman?

la **pendule** noun fem.
clock

pénible adjective masc. & fem.
Elle est pénible. She's a pain.
C'est pénible. It's a nuisance.

a
b
c
d
e
f
g
h
i
j
k
l
m
n
o
p
q
r
s
t
u
v
w
x
y
z

@ means use être to make the past tense.

French English

a
b
c
d
e
f
g
h
i
j
k
l
m
n
o
p
q
r
s
t
u
v
w
x
y
z

la **pensée** noun *fem.*
thought

penser verb
to think
Je pense qu'il pleut. I think it's raining.
Oui, je pense. Yes, I think so.
Je pense à toi. I'm thinking of you.

la **pension** noun *fem.*
boarding school
Il est en pension. He's at boarding school.

la **pente** noun *fem.*
slope

la **Pentecôte** noun *fem.*
Whitsun

le **pépé** noun *masc.*
granddad

le **pépin** noun *masc.*
pip
sans pépins seedless

percé adjective *masc.*, **percée** *fem.*
pierced
Ma copine a les oreilles percées. My friend has her ears pierced.

le **perdant** noun *masc.*,
la **perdante** *fem.*
loser

perdre verb
1 to lose
J'ai perdu mes clés. I've lost my keys.
2 to waste
Tu perds ton temps! You're wasting your time!

perdu adjective *masc.*, **perdue** *fem.*
lost

le **père** noun *masc.*
father
le père Noël Father Christmas

la **perle** noun *fem.*
pearl

un collier de perles a pearl necklace

le **perroquet** noun *masc.*
parrot

la **perruche** noun *fem.*
budgie

le **persil** noun *masc.*
parsley

le **personnage** noun *masc.*
character
C'est mon personnage préféré. She's my favourite character.

la **personnalité** noun *fem.*
personality

personne pronoun
1 ne ... personne nobody
Il n'y a personne dans la cour. There's nobody in the playground.
Personne n'a téléphoné. Nobody phoned.
2 nobody
Tu as vu qui? – Personne. Who did you see? – Nobody.
3 not ... anybody
Je ne connais personne. I don't know anybody.

> **LANGUAGE**
> ne + *verb* + **personne**, for example: Je ne vois **personne**

la **personne** noun *fem.*
1 person
une autre personne another person
une grande personne a grown-up
2 les personnes people
les personnes âgées old people
cinq personnes five people

> **LANGUAGE**
> French = personne
> English = person

personnellement adverb
personally

• *Languages, nationalities, and religions do not take a capital letter in French.*

le **pèse-personne** noun *masc.*
(*bathroom*) **scales**

peser verb
to weigh
Je pèse trente kilos. I weigh thirty kilos.

pessimiste adjective *masc. & fem.*
pessimistic

la **pétanque** noun *fem.*
bowls

CULTURE
People play **pétanque** in France with small metal balls (called **boules**) on hard ground, not on grass, often in places like town squares.

le **pétard** noun *masc.*
banger

petit adjective *masc.*, **petite** *fem.*
1 small
Elle est petite. She's small.
2 little
mon petit frère my little brother
3 un petit ami a boyfriend
une petite amie a girlfriend
4 le petit déjeuner breakfast

la **petite-fille** noun *fem.* (plural les **petites-filles**)
granddaughter

le **petit-fils** noun *masc.* (plural les **petits-fils**)
grandson

les **petits-enfants** plural noun *masc.*
grandchildren

peu adverb
1 un peu a bit
C'est un peu triste. It's a bit sad.
Tu veux un peu de pain? Do you want a bit of bread?
2 à peu près about
Le film dure à peu près deux heures. The film is about two hours long.

la **peur** noun *fem.*
fear
avoir peur to be afraid
Il a peur des araignées. He's afraid of spiders.

LANGUAGE
French = **avoir** peur **J'ai peur**.
English = **to be** afraid **I'm afraid**.

peut verb SEE **pouvoir**
Elle peut venir. She can come.

peut-être adverb
maybe, perhaps
Tu as peut-être raison. Maybe you're right.
Peut-être pas! Maybe not!

peuvent, peux verb SEE **pouvoir**
Est-ce qu'ils peuvent attendre? Can they wait?
Je peux rester une heure. I can stay an hour.
Tu peux m'aider? Can you help me?

le **phare** noun *masc.*
lighthouse

le **pharaon** noun *masc.*
pharaoh

la **pharmacie** noun *fem.*
chemist's
Il est allé à la pharmacie. He went to the chemist's.

le **pharmacien** noun *masc.*, la **pharmacienne** *fem.*
chemist

le **phoque** noun *masc.*
seal

la **photo** noun *fem.*
photo
Je peux prendre une photo? Can I take a photo?

la **photocopie** noun *fem.*
photocopy

photocopier verb
to photocopy

@ *means use* **être** *to make the past tense.*

a b c d e f g h i j k l m n o **p** q r s t u v w x y z

la **photocopieuse** noun fem.
photocopier

le or la **photographe** noun masc. &
fem.
photographer

la **phrase** noun fem.
sentence

⚠ **FALSE FRIEND**
une phrase = a sentence (not a phrase)

le or la **pianiste** noun masc. & fem.
pianist

le **piano** noun masc.
piano
Yasmina joue du piano. Yasmina
plays the piano.

la **pièce** noun fem.
1 room
**Il y a trois pièces dans
l'appartement.** There are three
rooms in the flat. (excluding kitchen and
bathroom)
2 coin
une pièce d'un euro a euro coin
3 play
une pièce de théâtre a theatre play
4 piece
les pièces du puzzle the pieces of
the jigsaw

le **pied** noun masc.
foot
à pied on foot
Je vais à l'école à pied. I walk to
school.
un coup de pied a kick

le **piège** noun masc.
trap

la **pierre** noun fem.
stone

le **piéton** noun masc.,
la **piétonne** fem.
pedestrian

la **pile** noun fem.
1 battery
Les piles sont usées. The batteries
are used up.
2 pile
une pile de CD a pile of CDs
3 (when throwing a coin) **tails**
Pile ou face? Heads or tails?

le **pilote** noun masc.
pilot
un pilote de course a racing driver
un pilote de ligne an airline pilot

le **pion** noun masc.
counter (for board games)

le **pinceau** noun masc. (plural les
pinceaux)
paintbrush

le **pingouin** noun masc.
penguin

le **pipi** noun masc.
wee
J'ai envie de faire pipi. I need a
wee.

piquant adjective masc.,
piquante fem.
spicy
une sauce piquante a spicy sauce

le **pique** noun masc.
spades (in cards)
le valet de pique the jack of spades

le **pique-nique** noun masc.
picnic
faire un pique-nique to have a
picnic

pique-niquer verb
to have a picnic

piquer verb
1 to sting
Inès a été piquée par une abeille.
Inès was stung by a bee.
2 to bite
Un moustique m'a piqué au bras.
A mosquito has bitten me on the
arm.

• The months of the year and days of the week do not take a capital letter in French.

3 to pinch
Il m'a piqué mon crayon. He's pinched my pencil.

la **piqûre** noun *fem.*
1 injection
Le médecin m'a fait une piqûre. The doctor gave me an injection.
2 sting
une piqûre de guêpe a wasp sting
3 bite
une piqûre de moustique a mosquito bite

pire adjective *masc. & fem.*
1 worse
C'est pire qu'avant. It's worse than before.
2 worst
son pire ennemi his worst enemy

le or la **pire** noun *masc. & fem.*
worst
C'est elle la pire. She's the worst.

la **piscine** noun *fem.*
swimming pool
On va à la piscine? Shall we go swimming?

la **pistache** noun *fem.*
pistachio

la **piste** noun *fem.*
1 track
2 runway
3 une piste cyclable a cycle path
4 une piste de ski a ski slope

le **pistolet** noun *masc.*
gun

le **placard** noun *masc.*
cupboard

la **place** noun *fem.*
1 room
Il n'y a pas beaucoup de place. There isn't much room.
2 place
Garde ma place! Keep my place!
J'ai terminé à la quatrième place. I finished in fourth place.

3 seat
La place est libre? Is this seat free?
4 square
la place du village the village square
5 à la place instead
Il n'y a plus de limonade. Tu veux du coca à la place? There is no lemonade left. Do you want some Coke® instead?

le **plafond** noun *masc.*
ceiling

la **plage** noun *fem.*
beach
une plage de sable a sandy beach
une plage de galets a shingle beach

se **plaindre** verb ◎
to complain
Maman se plaint du bruit. Mum's complaining about the noise.

plaire verb
1 Ça me plaît. I like it.
Ça t'a plu? Did you like that?
Elle me plaît beaucoup. I like her a lot.
2 s'il vous plaît (to an adult or several people) please
s'il te plaît (to a person you know very well) please

plaisanter verb
to joke
Tu plaisantes? Are you joking?

la **plaisanterie** noun *fem.*
joke

le **plaisir** noun *masc.*
pleasure
faire plaisir à quelqu'un to make somebody happy
J'aime bien faire plaisir à mes parents. I like to make my parents happy.
Ça te ferait plaisir de venir me voir? Would you like to come and see me?

◎ *means use* être *to make the past tense.*

143

French English

a
b
c
d
e
f
g
h
i
j
k
l
m
n
o
p
q
r
s
t
u
v
w
x
y
z

plaît verb SEE **plaire**

le **plan** noun *masc.*
1 **map**
  un plan de Paris a map of Paris
  un plan du métro an underground
  map
2 **plan**
  le plan d'une maison the plan of a
  house

la **planche** noun *fem.*
1 **board**
  une planche à roulettes
  a skateboard
2 **plank**

la **planche à voile** noun *fem.*
  sailboard
  faire de la planche à voile to go
  windsurfing

le or la **planchiste** noun *masc. & fem.*
  windsurfer

la **planète** noun *fem.*
  planet

la **plante** noun *fem.*
  plant

planter verb
  to plant

la **plaquette** noun *fem.*
  une plaquette de chocolat a bar of
  chocolate

le **plastique** noun *masc.*
  plastic
  C'est en plastique. It's made of
  plastic.
  un sac en plastique a plastic bag

plat adjective *masc.*, **plate** *fem.*
  flat

le **plat** noun *masc.*
1 **dish**
  un plat à emporter a takeaway
  le plat du jour today's special
2 **course**
  le plat principal the main course

le **platane** noun *masc.*
  plane tree

le **plateau** noun *masc.* (plural les
  plateaux)
  tray

la **platine** noun *fem.*
  une platine laser a CD player

le **plâtre** noun *masc.*
  plaster
  Philippe a une jambe dans le
  plâtre. Philippe has his leg in
  plaster.

plein adjective *masc.*, **pleine** *fem.*
1 **full**
  une maison pleine d'enfants
  a house full of children
2 en plein jour in broad daylight
  en pleine nuit in the middle of the
  night
  en plein air out in the open
3 plein de loads of
  plein de ketchup loads of ketchup
  Il y a plein de gens. There are loads
  of people.

pleurer verb
  to cry
  Il pleure tout le temps.
  He's always crying.

pleuvoir verb
  to rain
  Il pleut. It's raining.
  Il va pleuvoir. It's going to rain.
  Il a plu. It rained.

plier verb
  to fold
  Plie le papier en deux. Fold the
  paper in half.

le **plombier** noun *masc.*
  plumber

la **plongée** noun *fem.*
  diving
  faire de la plongée to go diving

plonger verb
  to dive

• *The months of the year and days of the week do not take a capital letter in French.*

plouf exclamation
splash

plu verb
1 SEE **plaire**
Ça m'a beaucoup plu. I liked it very much.
2 SEE **pleuvoir**
Il a plu hier. It rained yesterday.

la **pluie** noun *fem.*
rain
sous la pluie in the rain

la **plume** noun *fem.*
feather

la **plupart** noun *fem.*
most
la plupart du temps most of the time
la plupart des gens most people

le **pluriel** noun *masc.*
plural

plus adverb
1 **more**
Il est plus grand que moi.
He's taller than me.
2 plus de more
Il y a plus de filles que de garçons.
There are more girls than boys.
3 le plus de the most
Notre équipe a le plus de points.
Our team has the most points.
4 de plus (with numbers) more
Il a deux ans de plus que moi.
He's two years older than me.
5 le plus, la plus, les plus the most
la robe la plus belle the most beautiful dress
le garçon le plus sympa the nicest boy
les livres les plus intéressants the most interesting books
C'est Élise qui lit le plus. It's Élise who reads the most.
6 de plus en plus more and more
Il fait de plus en plus froid.
It's getting colder and colder.

7 en plus also
Elle est sympa et, en plus, elle est intelligente. She's nice and also she's clever.
8 ne ... plus not ... any more
Il n'a plus de vélo. He doesn't have a bike any more.

plus preposition
plus
Trois plus six font neuf. Three plus six is nine.

plusieurs plural adjective *masc. & fem.*
several

plutôt adverb
1 **instead**
Bois plutôt de l'eau. Drink water instead.
2 **quite**, **rather**
Il est plutôt gentil. He's quite nice.
3 plutôt que rather than
Viens demain plutôt que samedi.
Come tomorrow rather than Saturday.

le **pneu** noun *masc.*
tyre

la **poche** noun *fem.*
pocket
de l'argent de poche pocket money
une lampe de poche a torch

la **poêle** noun *fem.*
frying pan

le **poème** noun *masc.*
poem

le **poète** noun *masc.*
poet

le **poids** noun *masc.*
weight

le **poids lourd** noun *masc.*
lorry

🔑 **LANGUAGE**
A **poids lourd** is a big heavy lorry: it's a 'heavy weight'.

🄔 *means use* être *to make the past tense.*

la poignée noun *fem.*
1 **la poignée de la porte** the door handle
2 **une poignée de main** a handshake

le poignet noun *masc.*
wrist

le poil noun *masc.*
1 **hair**
des poils de chat cat hairs
2 **fur**
Mon chat a le poil gris. My cat has grey fur.

poilu adjective *masc.*, **poilue** *fem.*
hairy

le poing noun *masc.*
fist
un coup de poing a punch

le point noun *masc.*
1 **full stop**
2 **point**
3 **un point d'exclamation** an exclamation mark
un point d'interrogation a question mark
4 (*talking about food*) **un bifteck cuit à point** a medium rare steak

la pointe noun *fem.*
sur la pointe des pieds on tiptoe

pointu adjective *masc.*, **pointue** *fem.*
pointed

la pointure noun *fem.*
shoe size

la poire noun *fem.*
pear

le poireau noun *masc.* (plural **les poireaux**)
leek

le pois noun *masc.*
1 **les petits pois** peas
2 **spot**
une jupe bleue à pois verts a blue skirt with green spots

• *See the centre section for verb tables.*

le poisson noun *masc.*
fish
un poisson rouge a goldfish
Poisson d'avril! April fool!

CULTURE
In France there's a tradition of sticking a paper fish on somebody's back as a joke on April Fools' Day.

la poissonnerie noun *fem.*
fish shop

le poissonnier noun *masc.*, **la poissonnière** *fem.*
fishmonger

la poitrine noun *fem.*
chest

le poivre noun *masc.*
pepper
le sel et le poivre salt and pepper

le poivron noun *masc.*
pepper
des poivrons rouges et verts red and green peppers

polaire adjective *masc. & fem.*
un ours polaire a polar bear
une veste polaire a fleece

le pôle noun *masc.*
le pôle Nord the North Pole
le pôle Sud the South Pole

poli adjective *masc.*, **polie** *fem.*
polite

la police noun *fem.*
police
La police est arrivée. The police have come.

LANGUAGE
la police + *singular verb*

policier adjective *masc.*
un roman policier a detective story

le **policier** noun *masc.*
policeman

poliment adverb
politely

la **Pologne** noun *fem.*
Poland

polonais adjective *masc.*,
polonaise *fem.*
Polish

le **polonais** adjective *masc.*,
la **polonaise** *fem.*
Polish (*language*)

le **Polonais** noun *masc.*,
la **Polonaise** *fem.*
Pole (*person*)

pollué adjective *masc.*,
polluée *fem.*
polluted

la **pollution** noun *fem.*
pollution

la **pomme** noun *fem.*
1 apple
du jus de pomme apple juice
2 une pomme de terre a potato
des pommes de terre cuites au four
baked potatoes
des pommes frites chips

le **pommier** noun *masc.*
apple tree

la **pompe** noun *fem.*
pump
une pompe à vélo a bicycle
pump

le **pompier** noun *masc.*
fireman
une voiture de pompiers a fire
engine

> **LANGUAGE**
> **Pompier** comes from the **pompe** (pump)
> for pumping water on to fires.

ⓔ means use **être** to make the past tense.

le **poney** noun *masc.*
pony
Je fais du poney le week-end. I go
pony-riding at the weekend.

> **LANGUAGE**
> French = poney
> English = pony

le **pont** noun *masc.*
bridge

pop adjective *masc. & fem.*
pop
la musique pop pop music

le **porc** noun *masc.*
1 pork
une côtelette de porc a pork
chop
2 pig

le **port** noun *masc.*
harbour

le **portable** noun *masc.*
1 mobile
Appelle-moi sur mon portable!
Call me on my mobile!
2 laptop

le **portail** noun *masc.*
gate

la **porte** noun *fem.*
door

le **porte-clés** noun *masc.*
keyring

le **portefeuille** noun *masc.*
wallet

le **portemanteau** noun *masc.*
(plural les **portemanteaux**)
1 peg
2 coat hanger

le **porte-monnaie** noun *masc.*
(plural les **porte-monnaie**)
purse

a
b
c
d
e
f
g
h
i
j
k
l
m
n
o
p
q
r
s
t
u
v
w
x
y
z

porter verb
1 to carry
Je porte mon cartable sur le dos. I carry my schoolbag on my back.
2 to wear
Je porte un jean et une chemise. I'm wearing jeans and a shirt.
Je porte un uniforme à l'école. I wear a uniform at school.

portoricain adjective *masc.*, portoricaine *fem.*
Puerto Rican

le Portoricain noun *masc.*, la Portoricaine *fem.*
Puerto Rican (*person*)

Porto Rico noun *masc.*
Puerto Rico

portugais adjective *masc.*, portugaise *fem.*
Portuguese

le portugais noun *masc.*, la portugaise *fem.*
Portuguese (*language*)

le Portugais noun *masc.*, la Portugaise *fem.*
Portuguese (*person*)

le Portugal noun *masc.*
Portugal

poser verb
1 to put down
Posez les crayons! Put down your pencils!
2 to put
Pose le vase sur la table! Put the vase on the table!
3 to ask
Tu veux poser une question? Do you want to ask a question?

possible adjective *masc. & fem.*
possible
le plus vite possible as quickly as possible

postal adjective *masc.*, postale *fem.*, postaux *masc. plural*, postales *fem. plural*
une carte postale a postcard
un code postal a postcode

la poste noun *fem.*
1 post office
2 mettre quelque chose à la poste to post something

poster verb
to post
Mélissa a posté sa lettre. Mélissa has posted her letter.

le poster noun *masc.*
poster

le pot noun *masc.*
1 jar
un pot de confiture a jar of jam
2 pot
un pot de fleurs a flowerpot
3 tin
un pot de peinture a tin of paint

le potage noun *masc.*
soup

le pou noun *masc.* (plural les **poux**)
louse
Elle a des poux. She's got lice.

la poubelle noun *fem.*
dustbin

le pouce noun *masc.*
thumb

la poudre noun *fem.*
powder

la poule noun *fem.*
hen

le poulet noun *masc.*
chicken

la poupée noun *fem.*
doll
Élodie joue à la poupée. Élodie is playing with her dolls.
une maison de poupée a doll's house

• *Use* le *and* un *for masculine words and* la *and* une *for feminine words.*

pour preposition
1 for
C'est pour moi? Is this for me?
pour la première fois for the first time
2 to
J'ai un euro pour acheter des bonbons. I have one euro to buy sweets.
le train pour Bruxelles the train to Brussels

pourquoi adverb
why
Pourquoi tu me dis ça? Why are you telling me this?
Pourquoi pas? Why not?

pourra, pourrai, pourras, pourrez, pourrons, pourront verb SEE **pouvoir**
(pouvoir in the future tense) Éric ne pourra pas venir. Eric won't be able to come.
Je pourrai te voir ce soir. I can see you this evening.
Tu pourras regarder la télé jusqu'à dix heures. You can watch TV until ten.
Vous ne pourrez pas rester. You won't be able to stay.
Est-ce que nous pourrons jouer au foot? Will we be able to play football?
Elles pourront aller à la plage. They'll be able to go to the beach.

pourvu que conjunction
let's hope that
Pourvu que tu viennes! Let's hope you can come!

pousser verb
1 to push
Poussez la porte! Push the door!
Elle m'a poussé. She pushed me.
2 to grow
Ces plantes poussent bien. These plants are growing well.

se **pousser** verb ⓔ
to move over
Pousse-toi, je n'ai pas de place! Move over, I've got no room!

la **poussette** noun fem.
pushchair

la **poussière** noun fem.
dust

le **poussin** noun masc.
chick

pouvoir verb
1 can
Je fais ce que je peux. I'm doing what I can.
Tu peux partir maintenant. You can go now.
Elle ne peut pas marcher. She can't walk.
Oui, ils peuvent rester. Yes, they can stay.
2 could
Tu peux fermer la porte, s'il te plaît? Could you close the door, please?
Je ne pouvais pas dormir. I couldn't sleep.

le **praliné** noun masc.
praline (praline is a sweet made of almonds and caramelized sugar)

pratique adjective masc. & fem.
1 handy
Mon portable est très pratique. My mobile is very handy.
2 practical
Ce sac à dos est très pratique. This backsack is very practical.

précieux adjective masc., **précieuse** fem.
precious

précis adjective masc., **précise** fem.
1 definite
une date précise a definite date
2 exact
à cet instant précis at that exact moment

ⓔ means use être to make the past tense.

préféré adjective *masc.*,
préférée *fem.*
favourite
Ma couleur préférée, c'est le bleu.
My favourite colour is blue.

préférer verb
to prefer
Je préfère le poisson à la viande.
I prefer fish to meat.
Clara préfère lire des BD. Clara
prefers to read comics.

premier adjective *masc.*,
première *fem.*
1 **first**
la première fois the first time
le premier février the first of
February
2 le premier ministre the Prime
Minister

le **premier** noun *masc.*,
la **première** *fem.*
1 **first one**
Tu n'es pas le premier. You're not
the first one.
2 **top**
Marc est premier en français.
Marc is top in French.

la **première** noun *fem.*
Year 12

prendre verb
1 **to take**
Prenez vos livres! Take your books!
J'ai pris le bus. I took the bus.
2 **to have**
Je prends mon petit déjeuner à huit
heures. I have breakfast at eight.
Tu vas prendre un dessert? Are you
going to have dessert?

le **prénom** noun *masc.*
first name
un deuxième prénom a middle
name

préparer verb
1 **to prepare**

Papa prépare un bon repas. Dad is
preparing a nice meal.
2 **to get ready**
As-tu préparé tes affaires? Have
you got your things ready?

se **préparer** verb @
to get ready
Je me prépare à partir en vacances.
I'm getting ready to go on holiday.
Prépare-toi, il est l'heure! Get
ready, it's time to go!

près adverb
1 **près de** near
J'habite près de l'école. I live near
the school.
près d'ici near here
2 **tout près** nearby
3 **à peu près** about
à peu près une heure about an
hour

présent adjective *masc.*,
présente *fem.*
present
Tous les élèves sont présents.
All the pupils are present.

le **présent** noun *masc.*
1 **present tense**
au présent in the present tense
2 **present**
le passé et le présent the past and
the present

présenter verb
to present

le **président** noun *masc.*,
la **présidente** *fem.*
president

presque adverb
nearly, **almost**
J'ai presque dix ans. I'm nearly
ten.

pressé adjective *masc.*, **pressée** *fem.*
1 **in a hurry**
Vite, je suis pressé! Quick, I'm in a
hurry!

• *Languages, nationalities, and religions do not take a capital letter in French.*

a b c d e f g h i j k l m n o p q r s t u v w x y z

2 un citron pressé a freshly squeezed lemon juice

prêt adjective *masc.*, **prête** *fem.*
ready
Je suis prête. I'm ready.
Ils sont prêts à nous aider. They're ready to help us.

prêter verb
to lend
Tu peux me prêter ton stylo? Can you lend me your pen?

prévenir verb
to warn
Je te préviens! I'm warning you!

prier verb
to pray

primaire adjective *masc. & fem.*
l'école primaire primary school

CULTURE
L'école primaire is for children from 6 to 11.

le prince noun *masc.*
prince
le prince charmant Prince Charming

la princesse noun *fem.*
princess

principal adjective *masc.*, **principale** *fem.*, **principaux** *masc. plural*, **principales** *fem. plural*
main
le personnage principal the main character

le printemps noun *masc.*
spring
au printemps in the spring

pris verb *masc.*, **prise** *fem.*
SEE **prendre**
J'ai pris une photo. I've taken a photo.

pris adjective *masc.*, **prise** *fem.*
taken
Cette place est prise. This seat is taken.

la prison noun *fem.*
prison
Il est en prison. He's in prison.

le prisonnier noun *masc.*, **la prisonnière** *fem.*
prisoner

privé adjective *masc.*, **privée** *fem.*
private

le prix noun *masc.*
1 price
Quel est le prix de ce vélo? What's the price of this bike?
2 prize
J'ai gagné le premier prix. I've won first prize.

probablement adverb
probably

le problème noun *masc.*
problem
Pas de problème! No problem!

prochain adjective *masc.*, **prochaine** *fem.*
next
l'année prochaine next year
la prochaine fois next time
À la semaine prochaine! See you next week!

proche adjective *masc. & fem.*
near
Où est le café le plus proche? Where is the nearest café?

produire verb
to produce

le produit noun *masc.*
product

means use être to make the past tense.

le or la **prof** noun *masc. & fem.*
teacher

🔑 **LANGUAGE**
Prof is short for **professeur**.

le **professeur** noun *masc.*
teacher
Elle est professeur d'anglais. She's an English teacher.
le professeur des écoles primary school teacher
le professeur d'université university lecturer

profond adjective *masc.*,
profonde *fem.*
deep
C'est profond. It's deep.
Ce n'est pas profond. It's shallow.

le **programme** noun *masc.*
1 program
un programme informatique a computer program
2 programme
Quel est le programme aujourd'hui? What's on today?

les **progrès** plural noun *masc.*
progress
Alicia fait des progrès. Alicia is making progress.

🔑 **LANGUAGE**
French = **les progrès** is plural
English = **progress** is singular

progresser verb
to make progress

le **projet** noun *masc.*
plan
Quels sont tes projets pour les vacances? What are your plans for the holidays?

la **promenade** noun *fem.*
1 walk
On fait une petite promenade? Shall we go for a little walk?

2 ride
Hakim a fait une promenade à vélo. Hakim went for a ride on his bike.
une promenade en voiture a ride in the car

⚠ **FALSE FRIEND**
une promenade = **a walk** *or* **a ride** (*not* a promenade)

promener verb
to take for a walk
Je promène le chien tous les jours. I take the dog for a walk every day.

se **promener** verb ⊘
to go for a walk
On va se promener sur la plage. We're going for a walk on the beach.

la **promesse** noun *fem.*
promise

promettre verb
to promise
Je te promets de dire la vérité. I promise to tell you the truth.
C'est promis. That's a promise.

prononcer verb
to pronounce
Comment ça se prononce? How is that pronounced?

propre adjective *masc. & fem.*
1 clean
un tee-shirt propre a clean T-shirt
2 own
J'ai ma propre chambre. I have my own room.

le or la **propriétaire** noun *masc. & fem.*
owner

protéger verb
to protect

protestant adjective *masc.*,
protestante *fem.*
Protestant

• *The months of the year and days of the week do not take a capital letter in French.*

152

prouver verb
to prove

le **proverbe** noun *masc.*
proverb

les **provisions** plural noun *fem.*
shopping
faire les provisions to go shopping

prudent adjective *masc.*,
prudente *fem.*
1 careful
Sois prudent! Be careful!
2 sensible, wise
Prends un pull, c'est plus prudent.
Take a jumper, it's wiser.

la **prune** noun *fem.*
plum

⚠ **FALSE FRIEND**
une prune = a plum (*not* a prune)

le **pruneau** noun *masc.* (plural les
pruneaux)
prune

pu verb SEE **pouvoir**
Je n'ai pas pu. I couldn't.

la **pub** noun *fem.*
advert

⚠ **FALSE FRIEND**
une pub = an ad (*not* a pub)

public adjective *masc.*,
publique *fem.*
public
un jardin public a park
une école publique a state school

le **public** noun *masc.*
public
ouvert au public open to the public

la **publicité** noun *fem.*
advert
J'ai vu une publicité pour ce jeu.
I've seen an advert for that game.

la **puce** noun *fem.*
flea
le marché aux puces flea market

puer verb
to stink
Ça pue le poisson. It stinks of fish.

puis adverb
then
Je vais à Lille puis à Bruxelles.
I'm going to Lille then to Brussels.

puisque conjunction
since
Je finis le gâteau puisque tu n'en
veux pas. I'll finish the cake since
you don't want any.

puissant adjective *masc.*,
puissante *fem.*
powerful

le **puits** noun *masc.*
well

le **pull** noun *masc.*
jumper

🔑 **LANGUAGE**
pull is short for pullover

la **punaise** noun *fem.*
drawing pin

punir verb
to punish
Il est puni. He's punished.

la **punition** noun *fem.*
punishment

la **purée** noun *fem.*
mashed potatoes

le **puzzle** noun *masc.*
jigsaw puzzle

le **pyjama** noun *masc.*
pyjamas
Je suis en pyjama. I'm in my
pyjamas.

🔑 **LANGUAGE**
French = le pyjama is singular
English = pyjamas is plural

les **Pyrénées** plural noun *fem.*
the Pyrenees

❸ means use être to make the past tense.

a
b
c
d
e
f
g
h
i
j
k
l
m
n
o
p
q
r
s
t
u
v
w
x
y
z

Qq

qu' conjunction SEE **que, qu'est-ce que**

> 🔑 **LANGUAGE**
> qu' = que before *a, e, i, o, u*, and *silent h*

J'espère qu'elle a raison. I hope that she's right.

le **quai** noun *masc.*
platform
Le train arrive au quai numéro deux. The train gets in at platform two.

quand conjunction
when
Quand est-ce que tu reviens? When are you coming back?
Je mange quand j'ai faim. I eat when I'm hungry.

la **quantité** noun *fem.*
quantity

la **quarantaine** noun *fem.*
une quarantaine about forty
une quarantaine de personnes about forty people

quarante number
forty
Ma tante a quarante ans. My aunt is forty.

le **quart** noun *masc.*
quarter
un quart d'heure a quarter of an hour
Il a attendu une heure et quart. He waited an hour and a quarter.
Il est six heures et quart. It's a quarter past six.
à six heures moins le quart at a quarter to six

le **quartier** noun *masc.*
area (*of a town*)
On visite le quartier? Shall we visit the area?

quatorze number
fourteen
quatorze enfants fourteen children
Mon frère a quatorze ans. My brother is fourteen.
Le train part à quatorze heures. The train leaves at two o'clock.
le quatorze mars the fourteenth of March

quatre number
four
quatre saisons four seasons
Je regarde la télé à quatre heures. I watch TV at four.
Amélie a quatre ans. Amélie is four.
le quatre novembre the fourth of November

quatre-vingt-dix number
ninety

quatre-vingts number
eighty

quatrième adjective *masc. & fem.*
fourth
au quatrième étage on the fourth floor

que conjunction
1 that
Je crois que tu as raison. I think that you're right.
2 than
Je suis plus petite que toi. I'm shorter than you.
3 as
Je suis aussi sportif que lui. I'm as sporty as he is.
4 ne ... que only

• *See the centre section for verb tables.*

Il ne parle que français. He only speaks French.

> 🔑 **LANGUAGE**
> **Que** becomes **qu'** before *a, e, i, o, u,* and *silent h.* When **que** means 'that' it is often not translated.

que pronoun
1 that
C'est le film que je préfère. It's the film I like best.
2 what
Que fait-elle? What is she doing?
3 ce que what
Fais ce que tu veux. Do what you want.

quel adjective *masc.*, **quelle** *fem.*
1 what, **which**
Quel jour sommes-nous? What day is it today?
Quel CD tu veux écouter? Which CD do you want to listen to?
Quelle heure est-il? What time is it?
2 what (*in exclamation*)
Quelle jolie robe! What a pretty dress!

quelque chose pronoun
1 something
J'ai quelque chose pour toi. I've got something for you.
2 anything
Tu veux quelque chose à boire? Would you like anything to drink?

quelquefois adverb
sometimes

quelque part adverb
somewhere

quelques plural adjective *masc. & fem.*
a few
Je vais passer quelques jours à Paris. I'm going to spend a few days in Paris.

ℯ *means use* être *to make the past tense.*

quelqu'un pronoun
1 somebody
Il y a quelqu'un à la porte. There's somebody at the door.
2 anybody
Il y a quelqu'un? Is there anybody there?

quels plural adjective *masc.*,
quelles *fem.* SEE **quel**
Quels sont tes films préférés? What are your favourite films?

qu'est-ce que pronoun

> 🔑 **LANGUAGE**
> **qu'est-ce que** = **qu'est-ce qu'** before *a, e, i, o, u,* or *silent h*

what
Qu'est-ce que c'est? What is it?
Qu'est-ce que tu veux? What do you want?
Qu'est-ce qu'il y a? What's the matter?

qu'est-ce qui pronoun
what
Qu'est-ce qui se passe? What's happening?
Qu'est-ce qui s'est passé? What happened?

la **question** noun *fem.*
question
Je peux vous poser une question? Can I ask you a question?

la **queue** noun *fem.*
1 tail
une queue de cheval a ponytail
2 queue
faire la queue to queue up

qui pronoun
1 who
Qui est-ce? Who is it?
Toc, toc, toc, qui est là? Knock, knock, who's there?
Tu sais qui sera là? Do you know who will be there?

French English

a b c d e f g h i j k l m n o p q r s t u v w x y z

2 that
J'adore les photos qui sont sur ton site. I love the photos that are on your site.

3 qui est-ce que who
Qui est-ce que tu admires le plus? Who do you admire the most?

4 qui est-ce qui who
Qui est-ce qui veut jouer? Who wants to play?

5 à qui whose
À qui le tour? Whose turn is it?

6 ce qui what
Je ne sais pas ce qui se passe. I don't know what's happening.

la **quinzaine** noun fem.
une quinzaine about fifteen
une quinzaine de jours a fortnight

Rr

le **raccourci** noun masc.
short cut

la **race** noun fem.
1 race
la race humaine the human race
2 breed
une race de chats a breed of cats

raconter verb
1 to tell
Raconte-nous une histoire! Tell us a story!
2 to tell about
Il nous raconte son voyage. He's telling us about his trip.

la **radio** noun fem.
1 radio
à la radio on the radio
2 X-ray
Elle a passé une radio du bras. She had an X-ray of her arm.

le **radis** noun masc.
radish

quinze number
fifteen
quinze joueurs fifteen players
quinze jours two weeks
Il a quinze ans. He is fifteen.
le quinze juin the fifteenth of June
à quinze heures at three p.m.

quitter verb
to leave
Tu quittes la maison à huit heures. You leave the house at eight am.

quoi pronoun
what
C'est quoi? What is it?
De quoi tu parles? What are you talking about?

raide adjective masc. & fem.
1 straight
J'ai les cheveux raides. I have straight hair.
2 steep
une côte raide a steep hill

le **raisin** noun masc.
grapes
Je mange du raisin. I'm eating grapes.
une grappe de raisin a bunch of grapes
un grain de raisin a grape
le raisin blanc green grapes
le raisin noir red grapes
les raisins secs raisins

 LANGUAGE
French = **le raisin** is singular
English = **grapes** is plural

⚠ **FALSE FRIEND**
le raisin = **grapes** (not raisins)

• Use le and un for masculine words and la and une for feminine words.

la raison noun *fem.*
1 reason
2 Tu as raison. You're right.

> 🔑 **LANGUAGE**
> French = **avoir** raison   **J'ai raison**.
> English = **to be right**   **I'm right.**

raisonnable adjective *masc. & fem.*
1 sensible
C'est un enfant raisonnable. He's a sensible child.
2 reasonable
Ce n'est pas un prix raisonnable. It's not a reasonable price.

le rallye noun *masc.*
car rally

ramasser verb
1 to pick up
J'ai ramassé les papiers dans la cour. I picked up the papers in the playground.
2 to collect
Ramasse les cahiers! Collect the exercise books!

ramener verb
1 to take back
Maman va te ramener. Mum's going to take you back.
2 to bring back
J'ai ramené un souvenir de Paris. I brought a souvenir back from Paris.

la randonnée noun *fem.*
hike
une randonnée à vélo a long bike ride

le rang noun *masc.*
row
Je suis assise au dernier rang. I'm sitting in the back row.
En rang! Line up!

rangé adjective *masc.*, **rangée** *fem.*
tidy

la rangée noun *fem.*
row

ranger verb
1 to put away
Range ton livre! Put your book away!
2 to tidy
Olivier doit ranger sa chambre. Olivier has to tidy his room.

râpé adjective *masc.*, **râpée** *fem.*
du fromage râpé grated cheese
les carottes râpées grated carrots

rapide adjective *masc. & fem.*
1 quick
Prends le bus, c'est plus rapide! Take the bus, it's quicker!
2 fast
Le guépard est l'animal le plus rapide. The cheetah is the fastest animal.

rapidement adverb
quickly

rappeler verb
1 to remind
Rappelle-moi d'appeler ma mère. Remind me to call my mum.
Ça me rappelle l'école. It reminds me of school.
2 to call back
Tu peux rappeler demain? Can you call back tomorrow?

se rappeler verb ⓔ
to remember
Je ne me rappelle pas. I don't remember.

rapporter verb
to bring back

la raquette noun *fem.*
1 racket
une raquette de tennis a tennis racket
2 bat
une raquette de ping-pong a table tennis bat

a
b
c
d
e
f
g
h
i
j
k
l
m
n
o
p
q
r
s
t
u
v
w
x
y
z

ⓔ *means use **être** to make the past tense.*

a
b
c
d
e
f
g
h
i
j
k
l
m
n
o
p
q
r
s
t
u
v
w
x
y
z

rarement adverb
rarely

se **raser** verb ℮
to shave
Il se rase. He's shaving.

le **rasoir** noun *masc.*
razor

le **rat** noun *masc.*
rat

la **ratatouille** noun *fem.*
vegetable dish (with onions, tomatoes, courgettes, aubergines)

le **rateau** noun *masc.* (plural les **rateaux**)
rake

rater verb
1 to miss
J'ai raté le bus. I missed the bus.
2 to fail
Arthur a raté son examen. Arthur failed his exam.
3 to mess up
Papa rate toujours ses photos. Dad always messes up his photos.

la **rature** noun *fem.*
crossing-out

rayé adjective *masc.*, **rayée** *fem.*
striped

le **rayon** noun *masc.*
1 ray
les rayons du soleil the sun's rays
2 department
Où est le rayon des jouets? Where is the toy department?

la **rayure** noun *fem.*
stripe
une jupe à rayures vertes et grises a skirt with green and grey stripes

re- verb part

🔑 **LANGUAGE**
In French there are lots of verbs beginning **re** that mean you're doing something again, for example: **redemander** (to ask again), **redescendre** (to go back down), **remonter** (to go back up).

rebondir verb
to bounce

récemment adverb
recently

le or la **réceptionniste** noun *masc. & fem.*
receptionist

la **recette** noun *fem.*
recipe

recevoir verb
to get
Je ne reçois pas tes courriels. I'm not getting your emails.

se **réchauffer** verb ℮
to get warm
Tu te réchauffes, Antoine? Are you getting warm, Antoine?

la **récitation** noun *fem.*
J'ai appris ma récitation. I learnt my poem off by heart.

🌍 **CULTURE**
Une récitation is a text, often a poem, that pupils learn off by heart and then say to the class.

réciter verb
to recite
Paul va réciter un poème. Paul will recite a poem.

reçois, **reçoit**, **reçoivent** verb
SEE **recevoir**
Je reçois une lettre de maman tous les vendredis. I get a letter from mum every Friday.

• Languages, nationalities, and religions do not take a capital letter in French.

Léo reçoit toujours des cadeaux super à Noël. Léo always gets great presents for Christmas.
Ils ne reçoivent jamais de lettres. They never get any mail.

recommander verb
to recommend

recommencer verb
to start again

la **récompense** noun *fem.*
reward

reconnaître verb
to recognize
Tu ne vas pas me reconnaître. You're not going to recognize me.
Je t'ai reconnu tout de suite. I recognized you straight away.

recopier verb
to copy out
Recopiez votre texte au propre! Copy out your text on a new sheet!

le **record** noun *masc.*
record
Elle a battu le record du monde. She broke the world record.

la **récré** noun *fem.*
(*short for récréation*) **break, playtime**
On joue ensemble à la récré. We play together at break.

la **récréation** noun *fem.*
break, playtime
la récréation du matin the morning break
la cour de récréation the playground

reçu verb *masc.*, **reçue** *fem.*
SEE **recevoir**
1 **J'ai reçu ta lettre.** I got your letter.
2 **être reçu à un examen** to pass an exam
Il n'est pas reçu. He hasn't passed.

reculer verb
1 **to move back**

Reculez de trois cases! Move back three spaces!
2 **to reverse**
Attention, le camion recule! Careful, the lorry is reversing!

redoubler verb
to repeat a year

CULTURE
Children who don't do very well sometimes have to repeat the whole year.

refaire verb
1 **to do again**
J'ai refait cet exercice. I've done that exercise again.
2 **to make again**
Il a refait la même faute. He's made the same mistake again.
3 **to redo**

réfléchir verb
to think
Je vais réfléchir. I'm going to think about it.

le **refrain** noun *masc.*
chorus

le **réfrigérateur** noun *masc.*
refrigerator

refroidir verb
1 **to cool down**
Laissez refroidir avant de servir. Let it cool down before serving.
2 **to get cold**
Mange vite ou ça va refroidir! Eat up quickly or it will get cold!

refuser verb
to refuse

regarder verb
1 **to look at, to look**
Regarde-moi! Look at me!
Regardez au tableau! Look at the blackboard!
Je regarde par la fenêtre. I'm looking out of the window.
2 **to watch**

@ means use être to make the past tense.

159

J'ai regardé le film à la télé.
I watched the film on TV.

le **régime** noun masc.
diet
Emily est au régime. Emily's on a
diet.

la **région** noun fem.
region

le **registre** noun masc.
class register

la **règle** noun fem.
1 ruler
2 rule
les règles du jeu the rules of the
game

le **règlement** noun masc.
rules

regretter verb
to be sorry
Je regrette, je ne peux pas venir.
I'm sorry, I can't come.
Je regrette ce que j'ai dit. I'm sorry
about what I said.

la **reine** noun fem.
queen

le **relief** noun masc.
en relief 3D

la **religieuse** noun fem.
1 nun
2 une religieuse au chocolat
a round chocolate éclair

🌐 **CULTURE**
Une religieuse is a popular éclair-style
cake with two choux buns on top of
each other, filled with chocolate- or
coffee-flavoured cream and covered with
chocolate or coffee icing.

remarquable adjective masc. & fem.
outstanding

la **remarque** noun fem.
comment

remarquer verb
to notice
As-tu remarqué quelque chose?
Did you notice anything?

rembourser verb
to pay back

remercier verb
to thank
Je te remercie pour ta carte. Thank
you for your card.

remettre verb
1 to put back
Remets ce CD à sa place! Put this
CD back in its place!
2 to put back on
J'ai remis mes chaussures. I put
my shoes back on.

se **remettre** verb ⓐ
to get better
Remets-toi vite! Get better soon!

le **remplaçant** noun masc.,
la **remplaçante** fem.
1 (in a football match etc.) **reserve**
2 supply teacher

remplacer verb
1 to replace
Je vais remplacer les piles.
I'm going to replace the batteries.
2 to stand in for
Qui va remplacer Madame
Laffitte? Who's going to stand in
for Madame Laffitte?

remplir verb
1 to fill
J'ai rempli mon verre de lait.
I filled my glass with milk.
2 to fill in
remplir un formulaire to fill in a
form

le **renard** noun masc.
fox

rencontrer verb
to meet

• The months of the year and days of the week do not take a capital letter in French.

J'ai rencontré Cathy en ville. I met Cathy in town.
J'aimerais rencontrer J. K. Rowling. I would like to meet J. K. Rowling.

se **rencontrer** verb ⊘
to meet
Nous nous sommes rencontrés par hasard. We met by chance.

le **rendez-vous** noun *masc.*
appointment
J'ai rendez-vous chez le dentiste. I have an appointment at the dentist's.
Maman a rendez-vous avec mon institutrice. Mum's arranged to meet my teacher.

rendre verb
1 to give back
Rends-moi ma balle! Give me back my ball!
2 to return
J'ai rendu le livre à la bibliothèque. I returned the book to the library.

renifler verb
to sniff

le **renne** noun *masc.*
reindeer

le **renseignement** noun *masc.*
information
Je peux avoir un renseignement, s'il vous plaît? Could I have some information, please?
Je cherche des renseignements sur la Bretagne. I'm looking for information about Brittany.

la **rentrée** noun *fem.*
la rentrée des classes the start of the school year
le jour de la rentrée the first day back at school

rentrer verb ⊘
1 to get back

Maman rentre à quelle heure? What time does mum get back?
2 to go home
Je veux rentrer chez moi. I want to go home.
3 to come back in
Rentre, papa t'appelle! Come back in, dad's calling you!
4 to bring in
Rentre ton vélo! Bring your bike in!

renverser verb
1 to spill
J'ai renversé de la sauce. I spilt some sauce.
2 to knock over
Ne renverse rien! Don't knock anything over!

réparer verb
to fix

le **repas** noun *masc.*
meal

le **repassage** noun *masc.*
ironing
Nathan fait le repassage. Nathan is doing the ironing.

repasser verb
to iron

répéter verb
to repeat
Répétez après moi! Repeat after me!

la **répétition** noun *fem.*
1 rehearsal
2 repetition

le **répondeur** noun *masc.*
answering machine
J'ai laissé un message sur ton répondeur. I left a message on your answering machine.

répondre verb
to answer
Elle ne répond pas. She's not answering.

⊘ *means use* **être** *to make the past tense.*

Réponds à ma question! Answer my question!

la **réponse** noun *fem.*
answer
la bonne réponse the right answer
la mauvaise réponse the wrong answer

se **reposer** verb ⊘
to have a rest
Je me repose un peu après l'école. I have a little rest after school.

représenter verb
to show
Mon dessin représente un garçon qui pleure. My drawing shows a boy crying.

la **république** noun *fem.*
republic
la République française the French Republic
la République d'Irlande Éire

> **CULTURE**
> France is a republic (**la République française**) and has a president, not a king or queen.

le **requin** noun *masc.*
shark

le **RER** noun *masc.*
(*short for Réseau express régional*)
highspeed branch of the Paris métro, serving mostly the suburbs

réserver verb
to book
Papa a réservé trois places pour le match de football. Dad booked three tickets for the football match.

respecter verb
to respect

respirer verb
to breathe

responsable adjective *masc. & fem.*
1 responsible

Qui est responsable de l'accident? Who's responsible for the accident?
2 in charge
Je suis responsable du registre. I'm in charge of the register.

> **LANGUAGE**
> French = responsable
> English = responsible

le or la **responsable** noun *masc. & fem.*
1 person responsible
2 person in charge

ressembler verb
ressembler à to look like
Noémie ressemble à sa cousine. Noémie looks like her cousin.

se **ressembler** verb ⊘
to look alike
Les deux frères se ressemblent. The two brothers look alike.

le **reste** noun *masc.*
rest
Dis-nous le reste de l'histoire! Tell us the rest of the story!
les restes the leftovers

rester verb ⊘
1 to stay
Je reste chez moi ce week-end. I'm staying at home this weekend.
2 to be left
Il reste du dessert. There's some pudding left.
Il ne me reste plus rien. I have nothing left.

le **résultat** noun *masc.*
result

le **résumé** noun *masc.*
summary

le **retard** noun *masc.*
delay
être en retard to be late
Je suis en retard. I'm late.
Le train a du retard. The train is late.

• *See the centre section for verb tables.*

retardé adjective *masc.*,
retardée *fem.*
Le vol est retardé. The flight is delayed.

la **retenue** noun *fem.*
detention
J'ai une demi-heure de retenue.
I've got a half hour's detention.

retirer verb
to take off
Retire ta veste! Take your jacket off!

⚠️ **FALSE FRIEND**
retirer = to take off (*not* to retire)

le **retour** noun *masc.*
1 return
le retour des hirondelles the return of the swallows
2 return journey
Le voyage du retour était long.
The return journey was long.
3 un billet aller-retour a return ticket

retourner verb
1 to turn over
Retournez une carte! Turn one card over!
2 to go back
Je veux retourner en Angleterre.
I'd like to go back to England.

se **retourner** verb @
to turn round
Ne te retourne pas! Don't turn round!

retraité adjective *masc.*, **retraitée** *fem.*
retired

retrouver verb
1 to find
J'ai retrouvé mon sac. I've found my bag.
2 to meet
Je vous retrouve ici. I'll meet you here.

@ *means use* **être** *to make the past tense.*

la **réunion** noun *fem.*
meeting

réussi adjective *masc.*, **réussie** *fem.*
successful

réussir verb
to be successful
Il a réussi à son examen. He passed his exam.

la **revanche** noun *fem.*
1 revenge
2 (*in sports, games*) **return game**

le **rêve** noun *masc.*
dream
J'ai fait un rêve. I had a dream.

le **réveil** noun *masc.*
alarm clock

réveiller verb
to wake up
Ne réveille pas ta petite sœur!
Don't wake up your little sister!

se **réveiller** verb @
to wake up
Je me réveille à six heures. I wake up at six.

le **réveillon** noun *masc.*
le réveillon de Noël late-night Christmas Eve celebrations
le réveillon de la Saint-Sylvestre New Year's Eve celebrations

 CULTURE
In France the **réveillons** are a big part of the Christmas and New Year celebrations. People like to have more unusual and fine food, for example, oysters, foie gras, caviar, lobster, lots of sweets.

réveillonner verb
1 to celebrate Christmas Eve
2 to see the New Year in

revenir verb @
to come back

rêver verb
to dream

réviser verb
to revise
Je dois réviser mes maths. I have to revise my maths.

les **révisions** plural noun *fem.*
revision
faire des révisions to do revision

🔑 **LANGUAGE**
French = **révisions** is plural
English = **revision** is singular

revoir verb
1 to see again
Je voudrais revoir ce film. I would like to see this film again.
2 Au revoir! Goodbye!

la **révolution** noun *fem.*
revolution
la Révolution française the French Revolution

le **rez-de-chaussée** noun *masc.*
ground floor

le **rhinocéros** noun *masc.*
rhinoceros

le **rhum** noun *masc.*
rum
le baba au rhum rum baba

le **rhume** noun *masc.*
cold
J'ai un gros rhume. I have a bad cold.
le rhume des foins hay fever

riche adjective *masc. & fem.*
rich

le **rideau** noun *masc.* (plural les **rideaux**)
curtain

ridicule adjective *masc. & fem.*
ridiculous

rien adverb
1 ne ... rien nothing
Ce n'est rien. It's nothing.
2 nothing

Rien n'a changé. Nothing has changed.
Qu'est-ce que tu fais? – Rien. What are you doing? – Nothing.
rien de bien nothing good
rien du tout nothing at all
3 not ... anything
Je n'entends rien. I can't hear anything.
4 Ça ne fait rien. It doesn't matter.
5 Merci! – De rien. Thank you! – You're welcome!

rigoler verb
to laugh, **to have fun**
On rigole bien avec elle. We have fun with her.

rigolo adjective *masc.*,
rigolote *fem.*
funny
Arrête de rire, ce n'est pas rigolo! Stop laughing, it's not funny!

la **rime** noun *fem.*
rhyme

rimer verb
to rhyme

rire verb
to laugh
Ça me fait rire. It makes me laugh.

le **risque** noun *masc.*
risk

la **rivière** noun *fem.*
river

🔑 **LANGUAGE**
A **rivière** is a river that flows into a bigger river (called **un fleuve**) or into a lake.

le **riz** noun *masc.*
rice
le riz au lait rice pudding

la **robe** noun *fem.*
1 dress
une robe d'été a summer dress
2 une robe de chambre a dressing gown

• *Use* le *and* un *for masculine words and* la *and* une *for feminine words.*

le **robinet** noun *masc.*
tap
l'eau du robinet tap water
Ouvre le robinet! Turn the tap on!
Ferme le robinet! Turn the tap off!

le **rocher** noun *masc.*
rock

le **rock** noun *masc.*
rock
un chanteur de rock a rock singer

le **roi** noun *masc.*
king
la fête des Rois Twelfth Night
les Rois mages the Three Wise Men

 CULTURE
La fête des Rois is named after **les Rois mages**, the Three Wise Men who came to see the baby Jesus. French people celebrate this on 6th January, the day of the **Épiphanie**, twelve days after Christmas. On this day they eat a special cake called **la galette des Rois**.

le **rôle** noun *masc.*
part
Il joue le rôle d'un prince. He plays the part of a prince.
le jeu de rôles role-play

les **rollers** plural noun *masc.*
rollerblades

romain adjective *masc.*,
romaine *fem.*
Roman

les **Romains** plural noun *masc.*
Romans

le **roman** noun *masc.*
novel

la **ronce** noun *fem.*
bramble

ronchon adjective *masc.*,
ronchonne *fem.*
grumpy

rond adjective *masc.*, **ronde** *fem.*
round
une table ronde a round table

le **rond** noun *masc.*
circle
Asseyez-vous en rond! Sit in a circle!

la **rondelle** noun *fem.*
slice (*of a sausage*)

le **rond-point** noun *masc.* (plural les **ronds-points**)
roundabout

ronfler verb
to snore

se **ronger** verb ⊚
Je me ronge les ongles. I bite my nails.

le **rosbif** noun *masc.*
roast beef

rose adjective *masc. & fem.*
pink
un sweatshirt rose a pink sweater

le **rose** noun *masc.*
pink
J'aime beaucoup le rose. I like pink a lot.

la **rose** noun *fem.*
rose
un bouquet de roses a bunch of roses

rôti adjective *masc.*, **rôtie** *fem.*
roast
un poulet rôti a roast chicken

le **rôti** noun *masc.*
roast
un rôti de bœuf roast beef

la **roue** noun *fem.*
1 wheel
la roue de secours the spare wheel
2 cartwheel
Je sais faire la roue. I can do cartwheels.

⊚ *means use* être *to make the past tense.*

a b c d e f g h i j k l m n o p q r s t u v w x y z

a
b
c
d
e
f
g
h
i
j
k
l
m
n
o
p
q
r
s
t
u
v
w
x
y
z

rouge adjective *masc. & fem.*
red

le **rouge** noun *masc.*
red
un rouge à lèvres a lipstick

rougir verb
to blush

le **rouleau** noun *masc.* (plural les
rouleaux)
roll
un rouleau de papier toilette
a toilet roll

rouler verb
1 to drive
**Nous avons roulé pendant trois
heures.** We drove for three hours.
Le camion roule trop vite. The
lorry is going too fast.
2 to roll
La pièce a roulé sous la chaise. The
coin rolled under the chair.

rousse adjective *fem.* SEE **roux**
Elle est rousse. She's a redhead.

la **route** noun *fem.*
1 road
une grande route a main road
au bord de la route at the side of
the road
un accident de la route a road
accident
2 way
Ce n'est pas sur ma route. It's not
on my way.
en route on the way
3 journey
Tu as fait la route à pied? Did you
do the journey on foot?
Bonne route! Have a safe journey!

le **routier** noun *masc.*
lorry driver

roux adjective *masc.*, **rousse** *fem.*
1 red
Charlotte a les cheveux roux.
Charlotte has red hair.

2 red-haired
une petite fille rousse a little
red-haired girl

le **royaume** noun *masc.*
kingdom

le **Royaume-Uni** noun *masc.*
the United Kingdom

le **ruban** noun *masc.*
1 ribbon
2 du ruban adhésif sticky tape

la **ruche** noun *fem.*
beehive

la **rue** noun *fem.*
street
dans la rue in the street
une rue piétonne a pedestrian
street

le **rugby** noun *masc.*
rugby
jouer au rugby to play rugby

la **ruine** noun *fem.*
ruin
les ruines du château the ruins of
the castle

le **ruisseau** noun *masc.* (plural les
ruisseaux)
stream

russe adjective *masc. & fem.*
Russian

le **russe** noun *masc.*
Russian (*language*)

le or la **Russe** noun *masc. & fem.*
Russian

la **Russie** noun *fem.*
Russia

le **rythme** noun *masc.*
rhythm

LANGUAGE
French = rythme
English = rhythm

• *Languages, nationalities, and religions do not take a capital letter in French.*

Ss

s' pronoun

> 🔑 **LANGUAGE**
> **s' = se** before *a, e, i, o, u, y* or *silent h*

1 himself
Il **s'**est amusé. He enjoyed himself.
2 herself
Elle **s'**est coupée. She cut herself.
3 itself
Le chien **s'**est brûlé. The dog burnt itself.
4 themselves
Ils **s'**enferment dans la cave. They're shutting themselves in the cellar.
5 each other
Ils **s'**aiment. They love each other.
6 (*no translation*)
Il **s'**habille. He's getting dressed.
Elles **s'**embêtent. They're getting bored.

s' conjunction

> 🔑 **LANGUAGE**
> **s' = si** before **il** or **ils**

if
Demande-lui **s'**il veut venir. Ask him if he wants to come.

sa adjective *fem.* SEE **son**
1 his
Bruno mange **sa** glace. Bruno is eating his ice cream.
2 her
Élodie mange **sa** glace. Élodie is eating her ice cream.
3 its
Le chien reste dans **sa** niche. The dog stays in its kennel.

> 🔑 **LANGUAGE**
> **Sa** is used before feminine nouns starting with a consonant.

❷ means use **être** to make the past tense.

le **sable** noun *masc.*
sand

le **sac** noun *masc.*
bag
un **sac** en plastique a plastic bag
un **sac** à dos a backpack
un **sac** à main a handbag
un **sac** de couchage a sleeping bag

le **sachet** noun *masc.*
bag
un **sachet** de thé a teabag

sage adjective *masc. & fem.*
good, well-behaved
Soyez sages! Be good!

saigner verb
to bleed
Ça saigne. It's bleeding.

saint adjective *masc.*, **sainte** *fem.*
holy
la Saint-Sylvestre New Year's Eve
la Saint-Valentin Valentine's Day
le vendredi saint Good Friday
C'est la Sainte Sophie. It's Saint Sophie's day.

> **CULTURE**
> In France every day of the year has its own special saint (for example: Saint Sophie's day is 25th May). If somebody has the same name as the saint whose day it is, you wish them a happy day (**Bonne fête**) and give them a little present.

sais verb SEE **savoir**
Oui, je sais. Yes, I know.
Tu sais où il est? Do you know where he is?

la **saison** noun *fem.*
season

sait verb SEE **savoir**
Elle sait tout. She knows everything.

la **salade** noun fem.
1 salad
une salade de fruits a fruit salad
2 lettuce
la salade verte lettuce

le **salaire** noun masc.
pay

sale adjective masc. & fem.
dirty
Tu as les mains sales. You've got
dirty hands.

salé adjective masc., **salée** fem.
1 salty
trop salé too salty
2 salted
des cacahuètes salées salted
peanuts

salir verb
salir quelque chose to get
something dirty

la **salle** noun fem.
1 room
la salle à manger the dining room
la salle d'attente the waiting
room
la salle de bains the bathroom
la salle de classe the classroom
2 hall
une salle de concert a concert hall

le **salon** noun masc.
living room
un salon de thé a tearoom
un salon de coiffure a hairdresser's
salon

la **salopette** noun fem.
dungarees

salut exclamation
1 hi
2 bye

⚷ **LANGUAGE**
You use **salut** as a friendly way to say
hello or goodbye.

---

le **samedi** noun masc.
1 Saturday
C'est samedi aujourd'hui. It's
Saturday today.
samedi prochain next Saturday
samedi dernier last Saturday
2 on Saturday
Je te revois samedi. I'll see you on
Saturday.
On fait du jogging samedi matin.
We're going jogging on Saturday
morning.
À samedi! See you on Saturday!
3 on Saturdays
Ils jouent au foot le samedi. They
play football on Saturdays.

la **sandale** noun fem.
sandal

le **sandwich** noun masc.
sandwich
un sandwich au fromage a cheese
sandwich

le **sang** noun masc.
blood

sans preposition
without
Ne va pas à l'école sans manger!
Don't go to school without eating
something!

la **santé** noun fem.
health
en bonne santé in good health

le **sapin** noun masc.
fir tree
un sapin de Noël a Christmas tree

le **satellite** noun masc.
satellite
la télévision par satellite satellite
television

la **sauce** noun fem.
1 sauce
des pâtes à la sauce tomate pasta
with tomato sauce
2 gravy

• *The months of the year and days of the week do not take a capital letter in French.*

la **saucisse** noun *fem.*
sausage

le **saucisson** noun *masc.*
sausage (*slicing sausage, similar to salami*)
le saucisson sec dry sausage
le saucisson à l'ail garlic sausage

sauf preposition
1 except
Ils savent tous nager sauf moi.
They can all swim except me.
2 sauf si unless
Je ne vais pas à la fête sauf si tu viens avec moi. I'm not going to the party unless you come with me.

le **saumon** noun *masc.*
salmon

le **saut** noun *masc.*
jump

sauter verb
to jump
sauter à la corde to skip

sauvage adjective *masc. & fem.*
wild
un animal sauvage a wild animal

sauvegarder verb
to save
sauvegarder un fichier sur un CD
to save a file onto a CD

sauver verb
to save

le **savant** noun *masc.*
scientist

savoir verb
1 to know
Je ne sais pas où elle est. I don't know where she is.
On sait pourquoi tu as fait ça.
We know why you did that.
Elles savent qu'elles ont raison.
They know they're right.
2 to know how to
Vous savez tous nager? Do you all know how to swim?

ⓔ *means use* être *to make the past tense.*

le **savon** noun *masc.*
soap

le **saxophone** noun *masc.*
saxophone

scandinave adjective *masc. & fem.*
Scandinavian

le or la **Scandinave** noun *masc. & fem.*
Scandinavian (*person*)

la **Scandinavie** noun *fem.*
Scandinavia

la **science** noun *fem.*
science
J'adore les sciences. I love science.
Mélissa est forte en sciences.
Mélissa is good at science.

🔑 **LANGUAGE**
The French word **sciences** is used in the plural for the school subject.

scolaire adjective *masc. & fem.*
school
l'année scolaire the school year
un bulletin scolaire a school report
le livret scolaire school report
les fournitures scolaires school stationery
les vacances scolaires school holidays

le **scotch**® noun *masc.*
Sellotape®

se pronoun

🔑 **LANGUAGE**
se = s' before *a, e, i, o, u, y,* or *silent h*

1 himself
Il se lave. He's washing himself.
2 herself
Elle se regarde. She's looking at herself.
3 itself
Le chat s'est brûlé. The cat burnt itself.

a
b
c
d
e
f
g
h
i
j
k
l
m
n
o
p
q
r
s
t
u
v
w
x
y
z

4 themselves
Ils se sont blessés. They hurt themselves.
5 each other
Ils se connaissent. They know each other.
6 (*no translation*)
Il se lève. He gets up.
Elles se préparent. They're getting ready.

le **seau** noun *masc.* (plural les **seaux**)
bucket

sec adjective *masc.*, **sèche** *fem.*
1 dry
Est-ce que tes cheveux sont secs? Is your hair dry?
2 dried
des fruits secs dried fruit

le **sèche-cheveux** noun *masc.* (plural les **sèche-cheveux**)
hairdrier

le **sèche-linge** noun *masc.* (plural les **sèche-linge**)
tumble-drier

sécher verb
to dry

second adjective *masc.*, **seconde** *fem.*
second

la **seconde** noun *fem.*
1 second
2 Year 11

secouer verb
to shake
Louis secoue la tête. Louis is shaking his head.

le **secours** noun *masc.*
help
Au secours! Help!
les premiers secours first aid
une sortie de secours an emergency exit

le **secret** noun *masc.*
secret

secret adjective *masc.*, **secrète** *fem.*
secret

le or la **secrétaire** noun *masc. & fem.*
secretary

la **sécurité** noun *fem.*
1 safety
en sécurité safe
2 une ceinture de sécurité a seatbelt

seize number
sixteen
Ibrahim a seize ans. Ibrahim is sixteen.
le seize janvier the sixteenth of January
Le train part à seize heures. The train leaves at four o'clock.

le **séjour** noun *masc.*
1 stay
Bon séjour! Enjoy your stay!
J'ai beaucoup aimé mon séjour chez vous. I very much enjoyed staying with you.
2 sitting-room
La télé est dans le séjour. The TV is in the sitting-room.

le **sel** noun *masc.*
salt

le **self** noun *masc.*
self-service restaurant

la **semaine** noun *fem.*
week
cette semaine this week
la semaine dernière last week
la semaine prochaine next week
en semaine during the week

semblable adjective *masc. & fem.*
similar

semblant noun *masc.*
faire semblant to pretend
Elle fait semblant d'être malade. She's pretending to be ill.

• *See the centre section for verb tables.*

sembler verb
to seem
Elle semble fatiguée. She seems tired.

le **sens** noun *masc.*
1 direction
dans le sens des aiguilles d'une montre clockwise
2 meaning
le sens d'une phrase the meaning of a sentence
3 avoir le sens de l'humour to have a sense of humour

sensible adjective *masc. & fem.*
sensitive

 FALSE FRIEND
sensible = sensitive (*not* sensible)

le **sentiment** noun *masc.*
feeling

sentir verb
1 to smell
Ça sent bon. It smells nice.
Ça sent mauvais. It smells bad.
2 to smell of
Ça sent le poulet. It smells of chicken.
3 sentir quelque chose to feel something
Je ne sens rien. I don't feel a thing.

se **sentir** verb ⓔ
to feel
Comment tu te sens? How do you feel?
Je me sens bien. I feel well.
Je me sens triste. I feel sad.

séparé adjective *masc.*,
séparée *fem.*
separated

séparer verb
to separate

sept number
seven
sept nains seven dwarfs

ⓔ *means use* **être** *to make the past tense.*

Nous dînons à sept heures. We have dinner at seven.
Luc a sept ans. Luc is seven.
le sept juin the seventh of June

septembre noun *masc.*
September
en septembre in September
La rentrée des classes, c'est le 3 septembre. School starts again on the third of September

septième adjective *masc. & fem.*
seventh

sera, serai, seras, serez verb
SEE **être** (**être** *in the future tense*)
Ça sera la dernière fois. This will be the last time.
Un jour, je serai docteur. One day I'll be a doctor.
Tu seras le seul garçon. You'll be the only boy
Vous serez chez Pierre jusqu'à six heures? Will you be at Pierre's until six?

la **série** noun *fem.*
series
une série télévisée a TV series

sérieusement adverb
seriously

sérieux adjective *masc.*,
sérieuse *fem.*
1 serious
Tu as l'air sérieux. You look serious.
2 responsible
C'est un garçon très sérieux. He's a very responsible boy.

serons, seront verb
SEE **être** (**être** *in the future tense*)
Nous serons en retard. We'll be late.
Papa et maman ne seront pas avec nous. Mum and dad won't be with us.

le **serpent** noun masc.
snake

serré adjective masc., **serrée** fem.
tight

serrer verb
serrer la main à quelqu'un
to shake hands with somebody
Il a serré la main au prof. He shook
hands with the teacher.

CULTURE
In France boys usually shake hands when
they say hello or goodbye to each other.
Between girls or between boys and girls
it's usual to kiss each other on the cheek.

la **serrure** noun fem.
lock
par le trou de la serrure through
the keyhole

le **serveur** noun masc., la **serveuse**
fem.
waiter, **waitress**

la **serviette** noun fem.
1 towel
2 napkin

servir verb
1 to be useful
Ça sert à quoi? What's it for?
Ça ne sert à rien. It's no use.
2 to serve
On sert le petit déjeuner à 8 heures.
Breakfast is served at 8.

se **servir** verb ℗
Sers-toi! Help yourself!
Servez-vous! Help yourselves!
**Je ne sais pas me servir de la
douche.** I don't know how to use
the shower.

ses plural adjective masc. & fem.
1 his
Il cherche ses lunettes. He's
looking for his glasses.
2 her
Elle cherche ses lunettes. She's
looking for her glasses.

3 its
La chatte cherche ses petits. The
cat's looking for its kittens.

seul adjective masc., **seule** fem.
1 only
Tu es mon seul ami. You're my
only friend.
une seule fois only once
2 alone
Tu es seul à la maison? Are you
alone in the house?
tout seul (boy) on your own, **toute
seule** (girl) on your own

seulement adverb
only
J'ai seulement cinq euros. I only
have five euros.

sévère adjective masc. & fem.
strict

le **shampooing** noun masc.
shampoo

le **short** noun masc.
shorts

LANGUAGE
French = **un short** is singular
English = **shorts** is plural

si conjunction

LANGUAGE
si = **s'** before **il** or **ils**, but not before **elle**
or **elles**

if
Chante si tu veux. Sing if you want.

si adverb
1 so
Ne parle pas si fort! Don't speak so
loud!
2 yes
Tu ne sors pas? – Si! You're not
going out? – Yes, I am!

LANGUAGE
Use **si** instead of **oui** when the question
has **ne … pas** (not) in it.

• Use **le** and **un** for masculine words and **la** and **une** for feminine words.

le **siècle** noun masc.
century
au vingt-et-unième siècle in the twenty-first century

le **sien** pronoun masc., la **sienne** fem.,
les **siens** masc. plural,
les **siennes** fem. plural
1 his
J'ai perdu mon parapluie mais Martin m'a prêté le sien. I lost my umbrella but Martin lent me his.
J'ai perdu mes clés. Rémy m'a prêté les siennes. I lost my keys. Rémy lent me his.
2 hers
Noémie est ma cousine. Ce vélo est le sien. Noémie is my cousin. This bicycle is hers.
Anne est ma copine. Ces CD sont les siens. Anne is my friend. These CDs are hers.

la **sieste** noun fem.
nap
faire la sieste to have a nap

siffler verb
to whistle

le **sifflet** noun masc.
whistle

le **signal** noun masc. (plural les signaux)
signal
un signal sonore a beep

le **signe** noun masc.
sign
le langage des signes sign language

signer verb
to sign

signifier verb
to mean

s'il te plaît exclamation
please
(to a friend or relative) Dépêche-toi, s'il te plaît! Hurry, please!

s'il vous plaît exclamation
please
(to an adult who isn't part of your family)
Vous avez l'heure, s'il vous plaît Monsieur? Could you tell me the time, please?
(to several people) Taisez-vous s'il vous plaît! Quiet, please!

silencieux adjective masc.,
silencieuse fem.
silent

simple adjective masc. & fem.
simple

simplement adverb
1 just
2 simply

le **singe** noun masc.
monkey
Arrête de faire le singe! Stop monkeying about!

le **singulier** noun masc.
singular

sinon conjunction
otherwise
Mange, sinon tu vas avoir faim! Eat, otherwise you'll be hungry!

la **sirène** noun fem.
mermaid

le **sirop** noun masc.
1 cordial
Tu veux du sirop de fraise? Would you like a strawberry cordial?
2 un sirop contre la toux a cough medicine

CULTURE
Le sirop is a thick sweet liquid which you dilute, as you would do with squash. Le sirop de grenadine is a very popular one, but there are lots of different flavours.

le **site** noun masc.
site
un site web a website

⊘ means use être to make the past tense.

a
b
c
d
e
f
g
h
i
j
k
l
m
n
o
p
q
r
s
t
u
v
w
x
y
z

French English

a
b
c
d
e
f
g
h
i
j
k
l
m
n
o
p
q
r
s
t
u
v
w
x
y
z

situé adjective *masc.*, **située** *fem.*
Notre maison est située à un kilomètre de l'école. Our house is a kilometre from the school.

six number
six
six oies six geese
J'ai six ans. I'm six.
à six heures at six
le six avril the sixth of April

sixième adjective *masc. & fem.*
sixth

la **sixième** noun *fem.*
Year 7

 CULTURE
In French secondary schools, the first year is called **la sixième**. This is the equivalent of Year 7.

le **ski** noun *masc.*
1 ski
une paire de skis a pair of skis
2 skiing
Nous faisons du ski. We go skiing.
3 le ski nautique water skiing

skier verb
to ski

le **slip** noun *masc.*
pants
un slip de bain swimming trunks

🔑 **LANGUAGE**
French = **le slip** is singular
English = **pants** is plural

la **sœur** noun *fem.*
sister
J'ai une sœur. I have a sister.
Je n'ai pas de sœur. I haven't got a sister.
C'est ma petite sœur. She's my little sister.

la **soie** noun *fem.*
silk

la **soif** noun *fem.*
thirst
J'ai soif. I'm thirsty.
Elle n'a pas soif. She isn't thirsty.

🔑 **LANGUAGE**
French = **avoir** soif **J'ai soif.**
English = **to be** thirsty **I'm thirsty.**

le **soin** noun *masc.*
1 care
avec soin carefully
2 Prends soin de tes affaires! Take care of your things!

le **soir** noun *masc.*
evening
Le soir, je me couche à neuf heures. In the evening, I go to bed at nine.
à six heures du soir at six o'clock in the evening
ce soir this evening
demain soir tomorrow evening
hier soir yesterday evening

🔑 **LANGUAGE**
French has two words for 'evening': **soir** and **soirée**.
le soir = the normal period between afternoon and night
la soirée = the whole time from the afternoon till you go to bed

la **soirée** noun *fem.*
evening
Il a dormi toute la soirée. He slept all evening.

sois verb SEE **être**
Sois gentil avec ta sœur! Be nice to your sister!
Il faut que tu sois ici à 9 heures. You must be here at 9.

la **soixantaine** noun *fem.*
une soixantaine de livres about sixty books

soixante number
sixty

• *Languages, nationalities, and religions do not take a capital letter in French.*

soixante-dix number
seventy

solaire adjective masc. & fem.
solar
la crème solaire sun cream

le **soldat** noun masc.
soldier

le **soleil** noun masc.
sun
au soleil in the sun
Il y a du soleil. It's sunny.

le **solfège** noun masc.
music theory

solide adjective masc. & fem.
strong

sombre adjective masc. & fem.
dark

le **sommeil** noun masc.
1 sleep
sept heures de sommeil seven
hours' sleep
2 avoir sommeil to be sleepy
Il a sommeil. He's sleepy.

> **LANGUAGE**
> French = avoir sommeil J'ai sommeil.
> English = to be sleepy I'm sleepy.

sommes verb SEE **être**
1 (in the present tense)
Nous sommes en juin. We are in
June.
Nous sommes en été. It's
summertime.
2 (when used to form a past tense)
Nous sommes allés en France. We
went to France.

le **sommet** noun masc.
top

le **son** noun masc.
sound
Baisse un peu le son de la télé!
Turn down the TV sound slightly!

@ means use **être** to make the past tense.

son adjective masc., **sa** fem.,
ses masc. & fem. plural
1 his
Olivier a dessiné son père, sa mère,
et ses frères. Olivier drew a picture
of his father, his mother, and his
brothers.
2 her
Lucie a dessiné son père, sa mère,
et ses frères. Lucie drew a picture
of her father, her mother, and her
brothers.
3 its
Le chien est dans sa niche. The
dog's in its kennel.

> **LANGUAGE**
> Use **son** instead of **sa** before a feminine
> noun starting with a, e, i, o, u, or silent h, for
> example **son idée**.

le **sondage** noun masc.
survey

sonner verb
to ring
Le téléphone sonne. The phone's
ringing.
On sonne à la porte. Somebody's
ringing at the door.

sont verb SEE **être**
1 (in the present tense)
Ils sont là. They're here.
2 (when used to form a past tense)
Elles sont allées à la piscine.
They've gone swimming.

le **sorcier** noun masc.
wizard

la **sorcière** noun fem.
witch

le **sort** noun masc.
1 spell
jeter un sort to cast a spell
2 tirer au sort to draw lots

a
b
c
d
e
f
g
h
i
j
k
l
m
n
o
p
q
r
s
t
u
v
w
x
y
z

la **sorte** noun *fem.*
sort
C'est une sorte de poisson. It's a sort of fish.
J'ai toutes sortes de bonbons. I've got all sorts of sweets.

la **sortie** noun *fem.*
1 way out
La sortie est par ici. This is the way out.
une sortie de secours an emergency exit
à la sortie de l'école when school is over
2 outing
On a fait une sortie avec l'école. We went on a school outing.

sortir verb ⊘
1 to go out
Je suis sorti hier soir. I went out last night.
2 to come out
Sors de là! Come out of there!
3 to take out
J'ai sorti tous mes jouets. I took all my toys out.

sot adjective *masc.*, **sotte** *fem.*
silly

les **sottises** plural noun *fem.*
Ne dis pas de sottises! Don't say such silly things!

la **soucoupe** noun *fem.*
saucer
une soucoupe volante a flying saucer

soudain adverb
suddenly

souffler verb
1 to blow
Le vent souffle. The wind blows.
2 to blow out
souffler une bougie to blow out a candle

le **souhait** noun *masc.*
wish

faire un souhait to make a wish
À tes souhaits! Bless you!

CULTURE
The French say **À tes souhaits!**, meaning 'To your wishes', when somebody sneezes.

souhaiter verb
to wish
Je te souhaite bonne chance. I wish you luck.

soulever verb
to lift

souligner verb
to underline

la **soupe** noun *fem.*
soup

le **sourcil** noun *masc.*
eyebrow

sourd adjective *masc.*, **sourde** *fem.*
deaf

souriant adjective *masc.*, **souriante** *fem.*
cheerful

sourire verb
to smile
Elle m'a souri. She smiled at me.

le **sourire** noun *masc.*
smile
Fais-moi un sourire! Give me a smile!

la **souris** noun *fem.*
mouse
un tapis de souris a mouse mat
la petite souris the tooth fairy

CULTURE
French children just like British ones leave their tooth under the pillow at bedtime and in the morning find some money there instead. The difference is it's not a fairy but a little mouse (**la petite souris**) that comes to take it away.

• *The months of the year and days of the week do not take a capital letter in French.*

sous preposition
under
Le chat est sous ton lit. The cat is under your bed.
Tu sais nager sous l'eau? Can you swim underwater?
Je ne veux pas sortir sous la pluie. I don't want to go out in the rain.

le **sous-marin** noun *masc.*
submarine

le **sous-sol** noun *masc.*
basement

les **sous-titres** plural noun *masc.*
subtitles

le **sous-vêtement** noun *masc.*
underwear

le **soutien-gorge** noun *masc.*
(plural les **soutiens-gorge**)
bra

souterrain adjective *masc.*,
souterraine *fem.*
underground

le **souvenir** noun *masc.*
1 **memory**
J'ai un bon souvenir de ces vacances. I have good memories of that holiday.
2 **souvenir**
J'ai rapporté un souvenir de Madrid. I brought back a souvenir of Madrid.

se **souvenir** verb ⊘
Tu te souviens de la chanson? Do you remember the song?
Je me souviens de Lily. I remember Lily.

souvent adverb
often

les **spaghettis** plural noun *masc.*
spaghetti

🔑 **LANGUAGE**
French = **spaghettis** is singular
English = **spaghetti** is plural

le **sparadrap** noun *masc.*
sticking plaster

spécial adjective *masc.*,
spéciale *fem.*, **spéciaux** *masc.*
plural, **spéciales** *fem. plural*
1 **special**
Ce sont des gants spéciaux. They are special gloves.
2 **odd**
Il est un peu spécial. He's a bit odd.

spécialement adverb
specially

le or la **spécialiste** noun *masc. & fem.*
expert

le **spectacle** noun *masc.*
show
Ils vont monter un spectacle. They're going to put on a show.

spectaculaire adjective *masc. & fem.*
spectacular

les **spectateurs** plural noun *masc.*
audience

le **sport** noun *masc.*
sport
Je fais du sport à l'école. I play a lot of sport in school.
Qu'est-ce que tu aimes comme sport? What sort of sport do you like?
un terrain de sport a sports ground
Nous allons aux sports d'hiver. We're going on a skiing holiday.

sportif adjective *masc.*,
sportive *fem.*
sports
un club sportif a sports club
Lucie est très sportive. Lucie plays a lot of sport.

le **sportif** noun *masc.*,
la **sportive** *fem.*
sportsman, sportswoman

le **squelette** noun *masc.*
skeleton

⊘ *means use* **être** *to make the past tense.*

a
b
c
d
e
f
g
h
i
j
k
l
m
n
o
p
q
r
s
t
u
v
w
x
y
z

le **stade** noun masc.
stadium

la **station** noun fem.
1 station
une station de métro
an underground station
une station-service a petrol
station
2 une station de ski a ski resort

le **steak** noun masc.
steak
un steak frites steak and chips
un steak haché a hamburger (with
no bun)

stéréo adjective masc. & fem.
une chaîne stéréo a stereo

le **store** noun masc.
roller blind

⚠ **FALSE FRIEND**
le store = roller blind (not a store)

stressé adjective masc.,
stressée fem.
stressed out

stupide adjective masc. & fem.
stupid

le **stylo** noun masc.
pen
un stylo à bille a ballpoint pen

le **succès** noun masc.
success
avoir du succès to be successful

sucer verb
to suck

la **sucette** noun fem.
lollipop

le **sucre** noun masc.
sugar
le sucre en poudre caster sugar
le sucre glace icing sugar
le sucre roux brown sugar
le sucre vanillé vanilla-flavoured
sugar

• See the centre section for verb tables.

sucré adjective masc., **sucrée** fem.
sweet
C'est trop sucré. It's too sweet.

les **sucreries** plural noun fem.
sweet things
Je n'ai pas le droit aux sucreries.
I'm not allowed sweet things.

sud adjective masc. & fem.
south
la côte sud the south coast

🔑 **LANGUAGE**
Sud is the same in the masculine,
feminine, and plural.

le **sud** noun masc.
south
au sud de Poitiers to the south of
Poitiers
le sud de la France the South of
France
sud-est southeast
sud-ouest southwest

la **Suède** noun fem.
Sweden

le **suédois** noun masc.
Swedish (language)

suédois adjective masc.,
suédoise fem.
Swedish

le **Suédois** noun masc.,
la **Suédoise** fem.
Swede

suffire verb
to be enough
Une heure, ça suffit? Is an hour
enough?
Tais-toi, ça suffit! Be quiet, that's
enough!

suis verb
1 SEE **être**
(in the present tense) Je suis ton copain.
I'm your friend.

2 (when used to form a past tense)
Je suis allé à l'école. (boy speaking)
Je suis allée à l'école. (girl speaking)
I went to school.
3 SEE **suivre**
Suis-moi! Follow me!

la **Suisse** noun fem.
Switzerland

suisse adjective masc. & fem.
Swiss

le or la **Suisse** noun masc. & fem.
Swiss man, **Swiss woman**

la **suite** noun fem.
1 rest
Dis-nous la suite de l'histoire! Tell us the rest of the story!
2 tout de suite straight away

suivant adjective masc.,
suivante fem.
next

suivre verb
1 to follow
Suis-moi, Éric! Follow me, Éric!
2 'À suivre' 'To be continued'

super adjective masc. & fem.
great
C'est super! It's great!

le **supermarché** noun masc.
supermarket

superposés plural adjective masc.
des lits superposés bunk beds

supplémentaire adjective masc. & fem.
extra
des cours supplémentaires extra classes

supporter verb
to stand
Je ne supporte pas ça. I can't stand this.

le **supporter** noun masc.
supporter
Je suis supporter de cette équipe. I support this team.

sur preposition
1 on
Mon verre est sur la table.
My glass is on the table.
sur DVD on DVD
2 about
un film sur les animaux a film about animals
3 out of
J'ai eu huit sur dix. I got eight out of ten.

sûr adjective masc., **sûre** fem.
1 sure
Je ne suis pas sûr. (boy speaking)
Je ne suis pas sûre. (girl speaking) I'm not sure.
2 safe
dans un endroit sûr in a safe place

sûrement adverb
very probably
Sûrement pas! Certainly not!

surfer verb
surfer sur Internet to surf the Internet

surgelé adjective masc.,
surgelée fem.
frozen

le **surnom** noun masc.
nickname

la **surprise** noun fem.
surprise

surtout adverb
1 mainly
Nous mangeons surtout du poisson. We mainly eat fish.
2 especially
Surtout pas toi! Especially not you!

means use **être** *to make the past tense.*

a
b
c
d
e
f
g
h
i
j
k
l
m
n
o
p
q
r
s
t
u
v
w
x
y
z

French English

a
b
c
d
e
f
g
h
i
j
k
l
m
n
o
p
q
r
s
t
u
v
w
x
y
z

3 above all
Surtout, ne dis rien à maman!
Above all, don't say anything to
mum!

surveiller verb
to watch
Jo surveille les sacs. Jo is watching
the bags.

le **survêtement** noun masc.
tracksuit

le **sweatshirt** noun,
le **sweat** masc.
sweatshirt

sympa adjective masc. & fem.
nice

Tt

t' pronoun

LANGUAGE
t' = **te** before before a, e, i, o, u, y, or silent h

1 you
Je t'attends. I'm waiting for you.
2 to you
Je t'ai déjà parlé de ça. I've already
spoken to you about that.
3 (no translation)
Tu t'habitues? Are you getting
used to it?
Tu t'ennuies. You're getting bored.
4 yourself
Ne t'enferme pas! Don't shut
yourself in!

LANGUAGE
Use **t'** when you're talking to a person you
know well, such as a friend or somebody
in your family, or somebody of your own
age or younger. In other cases, use **vous**.

ta adjective fem.
your

Il est très sympa, ton frère. Your
brother's very nice.
Tes copines sont sympa. Your
friends are nice.

LANGUAGE
Sympa is short for **sympathique** and is
the same in the masculine, feminine, and
plural.

sympathique adjective masc. & fem.
nice
Tes parents sont sympathiques.
Your parents are nice.

⚠ **FALSE FRIEND**
sympathique = **nice** (not sympathetic)

la **synagogue** noun fem.
synagogue

le **tabac** noun masc.
1 tobacconist's shop
2 tobacco

🌍 **CULTURE**
Un tabac sells stamps and lottery tickets
as well as cigarettes and tobacco. In
Britain newsagents usually sell these
things.

la **table** noun fem.
1 table
Mets la table! Lay the table!
Tu peux débarrasser la table?
Could you clear the table?
À table! Dinner's ready!
2 les tables de multiplication the
times tables

le **tableau** noun masc. (plural les
tableaux)
1 painting
2 blackboard
3 le tableau blanc the whiteboard

• Use **le** and **un** for masculine words and **la** and **une** for feminine words.

la **tablette** noun fem.
une tablette de chocolat a bar of chocolate

le **tablier** noun masc.
apron

le **tabouret** noun masc.
stool

la **tache** noun fem.
1 stain
des taches d'encre ink stains
2 des taches de rousseur freckles

la **taille** noun fem.
1 size
Tu fais quelle taille? What size are you?
2 height
3 waist
le tour de taille waist size

le **taille-crayon** noun masc. (plural les **taille-crayons**)
pencil sharpener

tailler verb
to sharpen
tailler un crayon to sharpen a pencil

se **taire** verb ☉
to stop talking, to be quiet
Tais-toi! Be quiet!
Taisez-vous! Be quiet!

le **talent** noun masc.
talent
Il a beaucoup de talent. He's very talented.

le **talon** noun masc.
heel

le **tambour** noun masc.
drum

tant mieux adverb
That's good!

tant pis adverb
Never mind!, Too bad!

la **tante** noun fem.
aunt

taper verb
1 to bang
2 to hit
3 taper des pieds to stamp your feet
taper des mains to clap your hands

le **tapis** noun masc.
rug
un tapis de souris a mouse mat

taquiner verb
to tease

tard adverb
late
Il est très tard. It's very late.
Tu es arrivé trop tard. You arrived too late.
À plus tard! See you later!

la **tarte** noun fem.
tart
une tarte aux pommes an apple tart

la **tartine** noun fem.
slice of bread
une tartine de pain beurré a slice of bread and butter

tartiner verb
to spread
du fromage à tartiner cheese spread

le **tas** noun masc.
1 pile
un tas de sable a pile of sand
2 un tas de loads of
J'ai appris un tas de choses. I've learnt loads of things.

la **tasse** noun fem.
cup

le **taureau** noun masc. (plural les **taureaux**)
bull

☉ means use **être** to make the past tense.

a
b
c
d
e
f
g
h
i
j
k
l
m
n
o
p
q
r
s
t
u
v
w
x
y
z

te pronoun

> 🔑 **LANGUAGE**
> te = **t'** before *a, e, i, o, u, y,* or *silent h*

1 you
Je te crois. I believe you.

2 to you
Je te le donne. I'm giving it to you.

3 yourself
Va te laver! Go and wash yourself!

4 (*no translation*)
Tu te souviens? Do you remember?
Tu te lèves toujours tard. You
always get up late.

> 🔑 **LANGUAGE**
> Use **te** when you're talking to a person
> you know well, such as a friend or
> somebody in your family, or somebody of
> your own age or younger. In other cases,
> use **vous**.

le **tee-shirt** noun *masc.*
T-shirt

la **télé** noun *fem.*
TV
à la télé on TV
J'aime bien regarder la télé. I like
watching TV.

télécharger verb
to download

la **télécommande** noun *fem.*
remote control

le **téléphone** noun *masc.*
phone
Samir est au téléphone. Samir's on
the phone.
un téléphone portable a mobile
phone

téléphoner verb
to phone
Je peux téléphoner à mes parents?
May I phone my parents?

la **télévision** noun *fem.*
television
à la télévision on television

tellement adverb
1 so
C'est tellement petit! It's so small!

2 so much
Il aime tellement les chiens qu'il
en a cinq. He likes dogs so much
that he's got five of them.

3 so many
Il n'a pas tellement de jouets.
He hasn't go so many toys.

la **température** noun *fem.*
temperature

la **tempête** noun *fem.*
storm
une tempête de neige a snowstorm

le **temps** noun *masc.*
1 time
Je n'ai pas le temps. I don't have
time.
Il est temps de rentrer. It's time to
go home.
en même temps at the same time
tout le temps all the time
de temps en temps from time to
time
Tu attends depuis combien de
temps? How long have you been
waiting?

2 weather
Quel temps fait-il? What's the
weather like?

tenir verb
1 to hold
Clara tient son petit frère par la
main. Clara is holding her little
brother by the hand.
Tiens, cette lettre est pour toi.
Here, this letter's for you.

2 to keep
Clément ne tient jamais ses
promesses. Clément never keeps
his promises.

3 Tiens-toi droit! Stand up straight!

le **tennis** noun *masc.*
tennis

• *Languages, nationalities, and religions do not take a capital letter in French.*

la **tente** noun fem.
tent

la **tenue** noun fem.
la tenue de sport sports kit

la **terminaison** noun fem.
ending

la **terminale** noun fem.
Year 13

terminer verb
to finish

se **terminer** verb ⊘
to end
L'histoire se termine bien. The story ends well.

le **terrain** noun masc.
1 land
Ses parents ont acheté un terrain. His parents bought some land.
2 un terrain de sport a playing field
un terrain de football a football pitch
un terrain de golf a golf course
un terrain de jeux a playground
un terrain de camping a campsite

la **terrasse** noun fem.
1 patio
On mange sur la terrasse? Shall we eat on the patio?
2 assis à la terrasse d'un café sitting at a table outside a café

la **terre** noun fem.
1 earth
2 par terre (inside) on the floor
par terre (outside) on the ground
3 land
sur la terre ferme on dry land

terrible adjective masc. & fem.
1 terrible
un orage terrible a terrible storm
2 pas terrible not too good
Le concert n'est pas terrible. The concert isn't too good.

tes plural adjective masc. & fem.
your

tes copains your friends

le **têtard** noun masc.
tadpole

la **tête** noun fem.
1 head
2 en tête in the lead
Le coureur anglais est en tête. The English runner is in the lead.

la **tétine** noun fem.
dummy

têtu adjective masc., **têtue** fem.
stubborn

le **texto**® noun masc.
text message
J'ai reçu ton texto. I received your text.

le **TGV** noun masc.
high-speed train

le **thé** noun masc.
tea
un thé au lait a tea with milk
un thé au citron a lemon tea

le **théâtre** noun masc.
1 theatre
2 drama
Nous faisons du théâtre à l'école. We do drama in school.

⊘ *means use être to make the past tense.*

la **théière** noun *fem.*
teapot

le or la **thermos®** noun *masc. & fem.*
thermos® flask

le **thon** noun *masc.*
tuna

le **ticket** noun *masc.*
ticket
un ticket de bus a bus ticket
un carnet de tickets de métro
a book of underground tickets

tiède adjective *masc. & fem.*
warm

le **tien** pronoun *masc.*, la **tienne** *fem.*,
les **tiens** *masc. plural*,
les **tiennes** *fem. plural*
yours
J'ai un vélo comme le tien. I've got
a bike like yours.
**Ce n'est pas ma balle, c'est la
tienne.** It's not my ball, it's yours.
Voici mes CD. Où sont les tiens?
Here are my CDs. Where are yours?

🗝 **LANGUAGE**
Use **le tien, la tienne, les tiens, les
tiennes** when you're talking to a person
you know well, such as a friend or
somebody in your family, or somebody of
your own age or younger.

tiennent, **tiens**, **tient** verb
SEE **tenir**
**Elles tiennent quelque chose à la
main.** They're holding something
in their hands.
Je tiens la corde. I'm holding the
rope.
Tiens, prends un biscuit! Here,
have a biscuit!
Éric tient mal son stylo. Éric holds
his pen badly.

le **tiers** noun *masc.*
third

le **tiers-monde** noun *masc.*
Third World

le **tigre** noun *masc.*
tiger

le **timbre** noun *masc.*
stamp

timide adjective *masc. & fem.*
shy

la **tirelire** noun *fem.*
moneybox

tirer verb
1 to pull
Elle m'a tiré les cheveux. She
pulled my hair.
Tirez plus fort! Pull harder!
2 to draw
tirer les rideaux to draw the
curtains
tirer au sort to draw lots
3 to shoot
tirer au but to shoot at goal
4 Louise me tire la langue. Louise is
sticking her tongue out at me.

le **tiroir** noun *masc.*
drawer

le **tissu** noun *masc.*
material, fabric

⚠ **FALSE FRIEND**
le tissu = material (*not* a tissue)

le **titre** noun *masc.*
title

🗝 **LANGUAGE**
French = titre
English = title

le **toboggan** noun *masc.*
slide

toi pronoun
1 (*after a preposition, etc.*) **you**
avec toi with you
Je cours plus vite que toi. I run
faster than you.

• *The months of the year and days of the week do not take a capital letter in French.*

toile → tour

Tu vas à la plage? – Non, et toi? Are you going to the beach? – No, are you?

2 yourself
Montre-toi! Show yourself!

3 (no translation)
Lève-toi! Get up!

4 à toi yours
C'est à toi. It's yours.
C'est à toi de jouer. It's your turn to play.

> **LANGUAGE**
> Use **toi** when you're talking to a person you know well, such as a friend or somebody in your family, or somebody of your own age or younger. In other cases, use **vous**.

la **toile** noun fem.
1 cloth
2 web
une toile d'araignée a spider's web

la **toilette** noun fem.
Je fais ma toilette. I'm washing.

les **toilettes** plural noun fem.
toilet
Je peux aller aux toilettes? Can I go to the toilet?

le **toit** noun masc.
roof

la **tomate** noun fem.
tomato

tomber verb ⊘
1 to fall
Attention, tu vas tomber! Careful, you'll fall!
2 to fall over
Ton petit frère est tombé. Your little brother has fallen over.
3 to fall off
Aurélie est tombée de sa chaise. Aurélie has fallen off her chair.

ton adjective masc., **ta** fem., **tes** masc. & fem. plural
your
ton frère your father

⊘ means use être to make the past tense.

ta chemise your shirt
ton épaule your shoulder
tes jouets your toys

> **LANGUAGE**
> Use **ton** Instead of **ta** before a feminine noun starting with a, e, i, o, u, or silent h, for example **ton idée**. Use **ton**, **ta**, and **tes** when you're talking to a person you know well, such as a friend or somebody in your family, or somebody of your own age or younger. In other cases, use **votre** or **vos**.

le **tonnerre** noun masc.
thunder

le **torchon** noun masc.
tea towel

le **tort** noun masc.
Tu as tort. You're wrong.

> **LANGUAGE**
> French = **avoir** tort **J'ai tort.**
> English = **to be** wrong **I'm wrong.**

la **tortue** noun fem.
tortoise

tôt adverb
early

totalement adverb
completely
C'est totalement faux. It's completely wrong.

toucher verb
to touch

toujours adverb
1 always
Je perds toujours! I always lose!
pour toujours for ever
2 still
Katie habite toujours à Londres. Katie still lives in London.

le **tour** noun masc.
1 turn
À qui le tour? Whose turn is it?
C'est au tour de Luc. It's Luc's turn.
C'est mon tour. It's my turn.

185

a
b
c
d
e
f
g
h
i
j
k
l
m
n
o
p
q
r
s
t
u
v
w
x
y
z

2 trick
un tour de magie a magic trick
3 walk
Tu veux faire un tour? Do you want to go for a walk?
4 ride
Tayeb a fait un tour à vélo. Tayeb went for a ride on his bike.

CULTURE
The **Tour de France** cycle race takes place in France every summer. The 4,000 kilometre route changes every year but aways finishes in Paris. The previous day's winner wears a special yellow jersey.

5 Je voudrais faire le tour du monde. I'd like to go round the world.
Nous avons fait le tour de la ville. We went round the town.

la **tour** noun fem.
1 tower
la tour Eiffel the Eiffel Tower
2 tower block
habiter dans une tour to live in a tower block

le **tourisme** noun masc.
faire du tourisme to go sightseeing
l'office du tourisme the tourist office

le or la **touriste** noun masc. & fem.
tourist

tourner verb
to turn
Tournez à droite! Turn right!
Tournez à gauche! Turn left!
Tu dois tourner le bouton. You have to turn the knob.

le **tournesol** noun masc.
sunflower

le **tournoi** noun masc.
tournament

tous plural adjective masc.,
toutes fem. SEE **tout**

la **Toussaint** noun fem.
All Saints' Day (1 November)

• See the centre section for verb tables.

186

les vacances de la Toussaint the autumn half-term

CULTURE
On the day of **la Toussaint**, French people think about relatives who have died and put flowers on their graves. Around this time, French schools break up for **les vacances de la Toussaint**, the autumn half-term holiday.

tousser verb
to cough

tout adjective masc., **toute** fem.,
tous masc. plural,
toutes fem. plural
1 all
tout l'argent all the money
toute la confiture all the jam
tous les garçons all the boys
toutes les filles all the girls
2 every
tous les jours every day
tous les lundis every Monday
toutes les semaines every week
tout le monde everybody
3 tous les deux, toutes les deux both

tout pronoun masc., **toute** fem.,
tous masc. plural, **toutes** fem. plural
1 everything
J'ai tout vu. I saw everything.
2 all
Ne bois pas tout! Don't drink it all!

tout adverb
1 very
tout petit very small
tout près d'ici very close to here
2 all
tout seul all alone
Je suis tout mouillé. I'm all wet.
3 tout droit straight ahead

tout à coup adverb
suddenly

tout à fait adverb
absolutely

tout à l'heure adverb
1 later
Je vais lui parler tout à l'heure.
I'm going to speak to him later.
À tout à l'heure! See you later!
2 a little while ago
Elle est sortie tout à l'heure.
She went out a little while ago.

tout de suite adverb
straight away

tracer verb
to draw
tracer une ligne to draw a line

le **tracteur** noun masc.
tractor

traditionnel adjective masc.,
traditionnelle fem.
traditional

la **traduction** noun fem.
translation

traduire verb
to translate

le **train** noun masc.
1 train
en train by train
le train pour Lille the train to Lille
2 être en train de faire quelque chose
to be doing something
Papa est en train de faire le
ménage. Dad's doing the
housework.

le **traîneau** noun masc. (plural les
traîneaux)
sledge
le traîneau du père Noël Father
Christmas's sledge

le **trait** noun masc.
line
tirer un trait to draw a line
un trait d'union a hyphen

le **tramway** noun masc.
tram

la **tranche** noun fem.
slice

tranquille adjective masc. & fem.
quiet
un endroit tranquille a quiet place
Reste tranquille! Keep quiet!
Laisse-moi tranquille! Leave me
alone!

transformer verb
to change

se **transformer** verb
to change into
Il se transforme en loup-garou.
He changes into a werewolf.

le **transport** noun masc.
un moyen de transport a means of
transport

le **travail** noun masc. (plural les
travaux)
1 work
J'ai trop de travail. I've got too
much work.
Maman est au travail. Mum's at
work.
2 job
C'est un travail très facile. It's a
very easy job.
3 les travaux manuels arts and
crafts

travailler verb
1 to work
Tu as bien travaillé à l'école?
Did you work hard in school?
2 to practise
Je travaille mon anglais tous les
jours. I practise my English every
day.

travailleur adjective masc.,
travailleuse fem.
hard-working

les **travaux** plural noun masc.
roadworks

à **travers** preposition
through

a
b
c
d
e
f
g
h
i
j
k
l
m
n
o
p
q
r
s
t
u
v
w
x
y
z

⊘ *means use* être *to make the past tense.*

Je t'ai vu à travers les rideaux.
I saw you through the curtains.

la **traversée** noun fem.
crossing
la traversée de Calais à Douvres
the crossing from Calais to Dover

traverser verb
1 to cross
Victor a traversé la rue tout seul.
Victor crossed the road by himself.
2 to go through
On traverse la cuisine pour aller au jardin. You go through the kitchen to get to the garden.

le **trèfle** noun masc.
clubs (in cards)

treize number
thirteen
treize huîtres thirteen oysters
Il a treize ans. He's thirteen.
Le train arrive à treize heures.
The train arrives at one o'clock.
le treize juin the thirteenth of June

le **tremblement de terre** noun masc.
earthquake

trembler verb
1 to shiver
Tu trembles de froid. You're shivering.
2 to shake

trempé adjective masc.,
trempée fem.
soaking wet

la **trentaine** noun fem.
une trentaine d'élèves about thirty pupils

trente number
thirty
trente jours thirty days
Mon père a trente ans. My dad is thirty.
le trente novembre the thirtieth of November

très adverb
very
très bien very good
J'ai très faim. I'm very hungry.

le **trésor** noun masc.
treasure

la **tresse** noun fem.
plait

tricher verb
to cheat

le **tricheur** noun masc.,
la **tricheuse** fem.
cheat

tricolore adjective masc. & fem.
le drapeau tricolore the French flag

LANGUAGE
The French flag is also called the 'tricolour' because it is made up of three colours: blue, white, and red.

tricoter verb
to knit

le **trimestre** noun masc.
term

trinidadien adjective masc.,
trinidadienne fem.
Trinidadian

le **Trinidadien** noun masc.,
la **Trinidadienne** fem.
Trinidadian (person)

la **Trinité** noun fem.
l'île de la Trinité Trinidad

triste adjective masc. & fem.
sad
Zac a l'air triste. Zac looks sad.

tristement adverb
sadly

trois number
three
trois petits cochons three little pigs
à trois heures at three

• Use le and un for masculine words and la and une for feminine words.

Hakim a trois ans. Hakim is three.
le trois décembre the third of December

troisième adjective *masc. & fem.*
third

la **troisième** noun *fem.*
Year 10

le **trombone** noun *masc.*
1 **trombone**
2 **paperclip**

la **trompe** noun *fem.*
trunk (*of an elephant*)

se **tromper** verb ⓔ
to be wrong
Tu te trompes, Damien! You're wrong, Damien!
Je me suis trompée de bus. I got on the wrong bus.

la **trompette** noun *fem.*
trumpet

le **tronc** noun *masc.*
trunk
un tronc d'arbre a tree trunk

le **trône** noun *masc.*
throne

trop adverb
1 **too**
C'est trop petit. It's too small.
Tim est trop fatigué pour faire ses devoirs. Tim's too tired to do his homework.
2 **too much**
Paul a trop mangé. Paul has eaten too much.
3 **trop de** too much, too many
Tu as bu trop de café. You've drunk too much coffee.
Il y a trop de voitures. There are too many cars.

la **trottinette** noun *fem.*
scooter

le **trottoir** noun *masc.*
pavement

🔑 **LANGUAGE**
The **trottoir** was once a path for horses to trot along.

le **trou** noun *masc.*
hole

la **trousse** noun *fem.*
pencil case

trouver verb
1 **to find**
Je ne trouve pas mon portable. I can't find my mobile.
2 **to think**
Je trouve que c'est super! I think it's great!

se **trouver** verb ⓔ
to be located
Où se trouve la gare? Where's the station?

le **truc** noun *masc.*
1 **thing**
un petit truc en plastique a little plastic thing
2 **stuff**
Maman a acheté un truc pour nettoyer la cuisine. Mum bought some stuff to clean the kitchen.

tu pronoun
you
Tu as un frère et une sœur. You have a brother and a sister.
Tu viens ou tu restes? Are you coming or staying?

🔑 **LANGUAGE**
Use **tu** when you're talking to a person you know well, such as a friend or somebody in your family, or somebody of your own age or younger. In other cases, use **vous**.

le **tube** noun *masc.*
1 **tube**
un tube de dentifrice a tube of toothpaste

ⓔ *means use* **être** *to make the past tense.*

a
b
c
d
e
f
g
h
i
j
k
l
m
n
o
p
q
r
s
t
u
v
w
x
y
z

French English

a
b
c
d
e
f
g
h
i
j
k
l
m
n
o
p
q
r
s
t
u
v
w
x
y
z

2 hit song
C'est leur dernier tube. It's their latest hit.

tuer verb
to kill

la **Tunisie** noun fem.
Tunisia

tunisien adjective masc.,
tunisienne fem.
Tunisian

le **Tunisien** noun masc.,
la **Tunisienne** fem.
Tunisian (person)

le **tunnel** noun masc.
tunnel
le tunnel sous la Manche the Channel Tunnel

turc adjective masc., **turque** fem.
Turkish

le **Turc** noun masc., la **Turque** fem.
Turk

Uu

un determiner masc., **une** fem.,
des masc. & fem. plural

1 a
un garçon a boy
une fille a girl
2 an
un éléphant an elephant
une pomme an apple

un number masc., **une** fem.
one
Ça coûte un euro ou deux? Does it cost one euro or two?
Il est sorti à une heure. He went out at one.
Ma petite sœur a un an. My little sister is one.

la **Turquie** noun fem.
Turkey

le **tuteur** noun masc., la **tutrice** fem.
(legal) **guardian**

tutoyer verb
tutoyer quelqu'un to say 'tu' to somebody
Je peux tutoyer ton frère? Can I say 'tu' to your brother?
Ne tutoie pas ton prof! Don't say 'tu' to your teacher!

> 🔑 **LANGUAGE**
> You can use either **tu** or **vous** to mean 'you' in French. Use **tu** when you know somebody well, such as a friend or somebody in your family, or somebody of your own age or younger. In other cases, use **vous**.

typique adjective masc. & fem.
typical

un pronoun masc., **une** fem.,
uns masc. plural, **unes** fem. plural
one
un des élèves one of the pupils
l'un d'eux, l'une d'elles one of them
l'un ou l'autre, l'une ou l'autre either of them
l'un et l'autre, l'une et l'autre both of them
les uns et les autres everybody

un **uniforme** noun masc.
uniform
en uniforme in uniform

 CULTURE
In France schoolchildren don't wear uniforms.

• Languages, nationalities, and religions do not take a capital letter in French.

l'**Union européenne** noun fem.
the European Union

unique adjective masc. & fem.
only
Jonathan est fils unique. Jonathan is an only child.
Claire est fille unique. Claire is an only child.

uniquement adverb
only

l'**univers** noun masc.
universe

l'**université** noun fem.
university

l'**urgence** noun fem.
emergency
en cas d'urgence in an emergency

les **USA** plural noun masc.
USA
Ils habitent aux USA. They live in the USA.

une **usine** noun fem.
factory

utile adjective masc. & fem.
useful

utiliser verb
to use

Vv

va verb SEE **aller**
1 Nicolas va chez ses grands-parents tous les dimanches. Nicolas goes to his grandparents every Sunday.
2 Comment ça va? How are you?
3 (used with another verb in the infinitive to talk about the future) Demain on va déménager. Tomorrow we're going to move house.

les **vacances** plural noun fem.
holiday
Tu as passé de bonnes vacances? Did you have a good holiday?
Nous sommes en vacances. We're on holiday.
Nous partons en vacances lundi. We're going on holiday on Monday.
les vacances de Noël the Christmas holidays
les grandes vacances the summer holidays
Bonnes vacances! Have a good holiday!

la **vache** noun fem.
cow

la **vague** noun fem.
wave

le **vainqueur** noun masc.
winner
le vainqueur de la course the winner of the race

vais verb SEE **aller**
1 Je vais à l'école en bus. I go to school by bus.
Je ne vais pas à Paris. I'm not going to Paris.
2 (used with another verb in the infinitive to talk about the future) Je vais jouer dans le jardin. I'm going to play in the garden.

le **vaisseau** noun masc. (plural les **vaisseaux**)
un vaisseau spatial a spaceship

la **vaisselle** noun fem.
washing-up
faire la vaisselle to do the washing-up

la **valise** noun fem.
suitcase

ⓔ means use **être** to make the past tense.

Je fais ma valise. I'm packing my case.

la **vallée** noun fem.
valley

valoir verb
to be worth
Ça vaut combien? How much is it?
Ça ne vaut rien. It isn't worth anything.

la **vanille** noun fem.
vanilla
une glace à la vanille a vanilla ice cream

se **vanter** verb ⊘
to boast
Il est toujours en train de se vanter. He's always boasting.

la **vapeur** noun fem.
steam

la **varicelle** noun fem.
chickenpox

vas verb SEE **aller**
1 **Tu y vas en vélo?** Are you going by bike?
2 (used with another verb in the infinitive to talk about the future) **Tu vas m'aider demain?** Are you going to help me tomorrow?

vaut verb SEE **valoir**
Ça vaut mieux. That's better.
Il vaut mieux rester à la maison. It's better to stay at home.
Ça ne vaut pas la peine. It's not worth the trouble.

le **veau** noun masc. (plural les **veaux**)
1 **calf**
2 (meat) **veal**

vécu verb SEE **vivre**
J'ai vécu aux États-Unis. I've lived in the United States.

la **vedette** noun fem.
star
une vedette de cinéma a film star

végétarien adjective masc.,
végétarienne fem.
vegetarian

le **végétarien** noun masc.,
la **végétarienne** fem.
vegetarian
Emily est végétarienne. Emily is a vegetarian.

le **véhicule** noun masc.
vehicle

la **veille** noun fem.
day before
la veille de mon anniversaire the day before my birthday
la veille de Noël Christmas Eve

le **vélo** noun masc.
bike
Je vais à l'école à vélo. I go to school by bike.
Tu sais faire du vélo? Can you ride a bike?
un vélo tout-terrain a mountain bike

le **vendeur** noun masc.,
la **vendeuse** fem.
shop assistant

vendre verb
to sell
J'ai vendu mon ordinateur. I sold my computer.
maison à vendre house for sale

le **vendredi** noun masc.
1 **Friday**
On est vendredi aujourd'hui. It's Friday today.
vendredi prochain next Friday
vendredi dernier last Friday
tous les vendredis every Friday
2 **on Friday**
On part vendredi soir. We're leaving on Friday evening.
À vendredi! See you on Friday!
3 **on Fridays**
C'est fermé le vendredi. It's closed on Fridays.

• The months of the year and days of the week do not take a capital letter in French.

192

4 le vendredi saint Good Friday

venir verb *ⓔ*

1 to come

Viens chez moi cet après-midi!
Come to my house this afternoon!
Papa va venir nous chercher. Dad
will come to get us.
Pourquoi est-ce que tu n'es pas
venu? Why didn't you come?

2 (venir de *with the infinitive to say you've
done something a short time ago*) venir de
faire quelque chose to have just
done something
Je viens de finir. I've just finished.
Elle vient de partir. She's just left.

le **vent** noun *masc.*
wind
Il y a du vent. It's windy.

le **ventilateur** noun *masc.*
fan

le **ventre** noun *masc.*
stomach
avoir mal au ventre to have a
stomach ache

venu verb *masc.*, **venue** *fem.*
SEE **venir**

le **ver** noun *masc.*
worm

le **verbe** noun *masc.*
verb

le **verglas** noun *masc.*
ice

vérifier verb
to check

véritable adjective *masc. & fem.*
real

la **vérité** noun *fem.*
truth

le **vernis à ongles** noun *masc.*
nail varnish

ⓔ means use être to make the past tense.

verra, **verrai**, **verras** verb
SEE **voir** (voir *in the future tense*)
On verra demain. We'll see
tomorrow.
Il se trompe, tu verras! He's
wrong, you'll see!

le **verre** noun *masc.*
glass
C'est en verre. It's made of glass.
une assiette en verre a glass
plate
un verre d'eau a glass of water

verrez, **verrons**, **verront** verb
SEE **voir** (voir *in the future tense*)
Elle a raison, vous verrez. She's
right, you'll see.
Nous verrons. We'll see.

la **verrue** noun *fem.*
wart

vers preposition
1 towards
Elle a couru vers moi. She ran
towards me.
2 about
Le film finit vers sept heures.
The film finishes about seven.

le **vers** noun *masc.*
line (*of a poem*)
Lis le premier vers du poème! Read
the first line of the poem!

verser verb
to pour
Verse-moi un peu d'eau! Pour me
some water!

vert adjective *masc.*, **verte** *fem.*
green

le **vert** noun *masc.*
green
Le vert te va bien. Green looks good
on you.

verticalement adverb
vertically

la **veste** noun *fem.*
jacket

> ⚠ **FALSE FRIEND**
> **une veste = a jacket** (*not* a vest)

le **vestiaire** noun *masc.*
1 **cloakroom**
2 **changing room**

les **vêtements** plural noun *masc.*
clothes
des vêtements de sport sports gear

le *or* la **vétérinaire** noun *masc. & fem.*
vet
Mon père est vétérinaire. My dad's a vet.

veulent, **veut** verb SEE **vouloir**
Elles ne veulent pas rester. They don't want to stay.
Caroline veut venir avec nous. Caroline wants to come with us.

veux verb SEE **vouloir**
Je veux partir. I want to leave.
Tu veux du pain? Do you want some bread?

la **viande** noun *fem.*
meat

la **victoire** noun *fem.*
victory

vide adjective *masc. & fem.*
empty

vidéo adjective *masc. & fem.*
video
un jeu vidéo a video game
une cassette vidéo a video

> 🔑 **LANGUAGE**
> **Vidéo** is the same in the masculine, feminine, or plural, for example: **des jeux vidéo**.

la **vidéo** noun *fem.*
video
Je regarde une vidéo. I'm watching a video.

• *See the centre section for verb tables.*

le **vidéoclip** noun *masc.*
music video

le **vidéoclub** noun *masc.*
video shop

vider verb
to empty

la **vie** noun *fem.*
life

vieil adjective *masc.* SEE **vieux**
old
un vieil homme an old man
un vieil ami an old friend

> 🔑 **LANGUAGE**
> **Vieil** is used before a masculine singular noun beginning with *a, e, i, o, u,* or *silent h.*

le **vieillard** noun *masc.*
old man

vieille adjective *fem.* SEE **vieux**
old
Ma grand-mère est très vieille. My grandmother is very old.

la **vieille** noun *fem.*
old woman

vieillir verb
to become old

viennent, **viens**, **vient** verb
SEE **venir**
Ils viennent souvent chez moi. They often come to my house.
Viens vite! Come quickly!
Elle vient de Marseille. She comes from Marseilles.

le **vieux** noun *masc.*
old man
les vieux old people

vieux adjective *masc.*, **vieil** *masc.*,
vieille *fem.*, **vieux** *masc. plural*,
vieilles *fem. plural*
old
Tu es plus vieux que moi. You're older than me.
une vieille maison an old house
de vieux arbres old trees

vif adjective *masc.*, **vive** *fem.*
bright
rouge vif bright red

la **vigne** noun *fem.*
vine

le **vignoble** noun *masc.*
vineyard

vilain adjective *masc.*, **vilaine** *fem.*
1 **ugly**
le vilain petit canard the ugly duckling
2 **naughty**
Il est vilain de mentir. It's naughty to tell lies.

🔑 **LANGUAGE**
In English a 'villain' is a very bad person, not just somebody who's being naughty.

le **village** noun *masc.*
village

la **ville** noun *fem.*
1 **town**
Nous allons en ville. We're going into town.
2 **city**
une grande ville a city
la ville de Paris the city of Paris

le **vin** noun *masc.*
wine
le vin blanc white wine
le vin rouge red wine

le **vinaigre** noun *masc.*
vinegar

la **vinaigrette** noun *fem.*
French dressing

vingt number
twenty
vingt questions twenty questions
Ma sœur a vingt ans. My sister is twenty.
Il est trois heures moins vingt.
It's twenty to three.
Il est huit heures vingt. It's twenty past eight.
le vingt avril the twentieth of April

la **vingtaine** noun *fem.*
une vingtaine de leçons about twenty lessons

vingtième adjective *masc. & fem.*
twentieth

violet adjective *masc.*, **violette** *fem.*
purple
des chaussettes violettes purple socks

le **violet** noun *masc.*
purple
Le violet est ma couleur préférée.
Purple is my favourite colour.

le **violon** noun *masc.*
violin
Aurélie joue du violon. Aurélie plays the violin.

le **violoncelle** noun *masc.*
cello

la **vipère** noun *fem.*
adder

la **virgule** noun *fem.*
1 **comma**
2 **point**
trois virgule neuf three point nine

🔑 **LANGUAGE**
In French you use a comma in decimal numbers, for example: 3.9 is **3,9**.

vis verb SEE **vivre**
Je vis à Paris. I live in Paris.

le **visage** noun *masc.*
face

la **visite** noun *fem.*
1 **visit**
une courte visite chez mon oncle
a short visit to my uncle
rendre visite à quelqu'un to visit somebody
2 **tour**
Nous avons fait la visite du château. We went on a tour of the castle.

a
b
c
d
e
f
g
h
i
j
k
l
m
n
o
p
q
r
s
t
u
v
w
x
y
z

➎ *means use* **être** *to make the past tense.*

a
b
c
d
e
f
g
h
i
j
k
l
m
n
o
p
q
r
s
t
u
v
w
x
y
z

visiter verb
to visit
Je vais visiter la tour Eiffel.
I'm going to visit the Eiffel Tower.

vit verb SEE **vivre**
Elle vit en Belgique. She lives in
Belgium.

vite adverb
1 fast
Vous parlez trop vite. You're
speaking too fast.
Marche plus vite! Walk faster!
2 quick
Vite, papa arrive! Quick, dad's
coming!
Fais vite! Be quick!
3 quickly
Venez le plus vite possible! Come
as quickly as possible!
4 soon
Écris-moi vite! Write soon!

la **vitesse** noun fem.
1 speed
en vitesse quickly
2 gear
Mon vélo a six vitesses. My bike
has six gears.

la **vitre** noun fem.
window, window pane
Tu as cassé une vitre! You've
broken a window!

la **vitrine** noun fem.
shop window
faire les vitrines to go
window-shopping

vivant adjective masc.,
vivante fem.
alive
Mon arrière-grand-mère est
encore vivante. My
great-grandmother is still alive.

vive adjective fem. SEE **vif**
bright
des couleurs vives bright colours

vivre verb
to live
Mes cousins vivent à la campagne.
My cousins live in the country.

le **vocabulaire** noun masc.
vocabulary

le **vœu** noun masc. (plural les **vœux**)
wish
faire un vœu to make a wish
Meilleurs Vœux! Best wishes!
(especially in the New Year)

voici preposition
1 here is
Voici mon père! Here's my father!
2 here are
Voici les assiettes! Here are the
plates!

voilà preposition
1 there is
Voilà Rachid! There's Rachid!
2 there are
Voilà mes parents! There are my
parents!

la **voile** noun fem.
sailing
faire de la voile to go sailing

le **voile** noun masc.
veil

le **voilier** noun masc.
sailing boat

voir verb
1 to see
Jérôme ne voit pas sans lunettes.
Jérôme can't see without glasses.
On va voir ma grand-mère demain.
We're going to visit my
grandmother tomorrow.
Tu vois ce que je veux dire? Do you
see what I mean?
Ça n'a rien à voir! That has nothing
to do with it!

• Use **le** and **un** for masculine words and **la** and **une** for feminine words.

2 faire voir to show
Fais voir! Let me see!
Fais-moi voir tes CD! Show me your CDs!

le **voisin** noun *masc.*, la **voisine** *fem.*
neighbour

la **voiture** noun *fem.*
1 car
en voiture by car
une voiture de sport a sports car
2 carriage (*on a train*)

la **voix** noun *fem.*
voice
à voix basse in a low voice
Lis cette phrase à haute voix! Read this sentence aloud!

le **vol** noun *masc.*
1 flight
2 robbery

le **volant** noun *masc.*
steering wheel

le **volcan** noun *masc.*
volcano

voler verb
1 to fly
L'avion vole très haut. The plane is flying very high.
2 to steal
On m'a volé mon portable. Somebody has stolen my mobile.

les **volets** plural noun *masc.*
shutters

 CULTURE
Shutters are a lot more common in France; they are covers that 'shut' over the outside of windows.

le **voleur** noun *masc.*,
la **voleuse** *fem.*
thief

le **volley-ball** noun *masc.*
volleyball

le or la **volontaire** noun *masc. & fem.*
volunteer

vomir verb
to be sick
Il a vomi. He was sick.
J'ai envie de vomir. I'm going to be sick.

vont verb SEE **aller**
1 Où est-ce qu'ils vont? Where are they going?
2 (*used with another verb in the infinitive to talk about the future*) **Elles vont m'aider.** They're going to help me.

vos plural adjective *masc. & fem.*
your
Sortez vos cahiers! Get your exercise books!
Maîtresse, où sont vos kleenex? Please Miss, where are your tissues?

🔑 **LANGUAGE**
Use **vos** when you're talking to an adult who isn't part of your family or when you're talking to two or more people that you would usually call **tu**.

voter verb
to vote

votre adjective *masc. & fem.*
your
Votre portable sonne, maîtresse. Your mobile is ringing, Miss.
Il est dans votre classe? Is he in your class?

🔑 **LANGUAGE**
Use **votre** when you're talking to an adult who isn't part of your family or when you're talking to two or more people that you would usually call **tu**.

voudrais verb SEE **vouloir**
1 Je voudrais ... I would like ...
Je voudrais une glace à la vanille, s'il vous plaît. I would like a vanilla ice cream, please.

ℯ means use **être** *to make the past tense.*

a
b
c
d
e
f
g
h
i
j
k
l
m
n
o
p
q
r
s
t
u
v
w
x
y
z

vouloir verb

1 to want

Tu veux jouer? – Oui, je veux bien. Do you want to play? – Yes, please.

Il ne veut pas de fromage. He doesn't want any cheese.

Qu'est-ce que vous voulez, monsieur? What would you like, sir?

2 vouloir dire to mean

Que veut dire 'ladder'? What does 'ladder' mean?

Qu'est-ce que ça veut dire? What does that mean?

voulu verb SEE **vouloir**

Il n'a pas voulu venir. He didn't want to come.

vous pronoun

1 you

Qui êtes-vous? Who are you?

Alain et Marc, vous voulez venir chez moi? Alain and Marc, do you want to come to my house?

C'est pour vous, M. Roland. It's for you, Mr Roland.

2 to you

Je vous écrirai. I'll write to you.

3 (no translation)

Taisez-vous! Be quiet!

4 yourself

Montrez-vous! Show yourself!

5 yourselves

Regardez-vous, tous les deux! Look at yourselves, both of you!

6 à vous yours

Ce livre est à vous? Is this book yours?

C'est à vous de jouer. It's your turn to play.

> **⚷ LANGUAGE**
> Use **vous** when you're talking to an adult who isn't part of your family or when you're talking to two or more people that you would usually call **tu**.

vouvoyer verb

vouvoyer quelqu'un to say 'vous' to somebody

Le directeur nous vouvoie. The headmaster says 'vous' to us.

> **⚷ LANGUAGE**
> You can use either **tu** or **vous** to mean 'you' in French. Use **tu** when you know somebody well, such as a friend or somebody in your family, or somebody of your own age or younger. Use **vous** when you're talking to an adult who isn't part of your family (such as a teacher or doctor).

le **voyage** noun masc.

1 journey

un long voyage a long journey

2 trip

Nous avons fait un petit voyage en Angleterre. We went on a little trip to England.

Bon voyage! Have a good trip!

voyager verb
to travel

le **voyageur** noun masc.,
la **voyageuse** fem.
passenger

la **voyelle** noun fem.
vowel

vrai adjective masc., **vraie** fem.

1 true

Ce n'est pas vrai! That's not true!

une histoire vraie a true story

2 real

C'est ton vrai nom? Is that your real name?

vraiment adverb
really

le **VTT** noun masc.
mountain bike

vu verb masc., **vue** fem. SEE **voir**

Tu as vu mes lunettes? Have you seen my glasses?

Je l'ai vue hier. I saw her yesterday.

• Languages, nationalities, and religions do not take a capital letter in French.

la **vue** noun *fem.*
1 **eyesight**
2 **view**
   On a une belle vue sur la vallée.
   We have a lovely view over the
   valley.

Ww

le **wagon** noun *masc.*
   railway carriage

les **WC** plural noun *masc.*
   toilet
   aller aux WC to go to the toilet

le **web** noun *masc.*
   web
   une page web a web page
   un site web a website

le **week-end** noun *masc.*
   weekend
   ce week-end this weekend

le week-end prochain next
weekend

Qu'est-ce que tu fais le week-end?
What do you do at weekends?

Luc est parti en week-end.
Luc's gone away for the
weekend.

Bon week-end! Have a nice
weekend!

le **western** noun *masc.*
   western

Yy

y pronoun
1 **there**
   J'y vais ce soir. I'm going there this
   evening.
   Allons-y! Let's go!
   Vas-y, mange! Go ahead and eat!
   Allez-y, les enfants! Go ahead,
   children!
2 **about it**
   J'y pense souvent. I think about it
   a lot.
3 **il y a** there is, there are
   Il y a du pâté en entrée. There's
   pâté as a starter.

Il y a des fraises au dessert.
There are strawberries for
dessert.

le **yaourt** noun *masc.*
   yoghurt
   un yaourt nature a plain yoghurt
   un yaourt à la fraise a strawberry
   yoghurt

les **yeux** plural noun *masc.*
   eyes
   J'ai les yeux verts. I have green
   eyes.

ⓔ *means use* **être** *to make the past tense.*

Zz

le **zèbre** noun *masc.*
zebra

le **zéro** noun *masc.*
1 zero
Il a eu zéro en anglais! He got zero in English!
2 nil
On a gagné quatre à zéro. We won four nil.

la **zone** noun *fem.*
1 zone
2 area
une zone piétonne a pedestrian area

le **zoo** noun *masc.*
zoo
Je voudrais aller au zoo. I'd like to go to the zoo.

a
b
c
d
e
f
g
h
i
j
k
l
m
n
o
p
q
r
s
t
u
v
w
x
y
z

• *The months of the year and days of the week do not take a capital letter in French.*

Animals
Clothes and colours
Calendar

Time
Body
Numbers

In the classroom
Friends
The weather

Shopping
Countries and places
Family

Healthy eating
Jobs
Where are you?

Feelings
A letter, a text, an email
Where I live

Sports
Hobbies
Story time

Les animaux / Animals
As-tu un animal? / Do you have a pet?

Non, je n'ai pas d'animal.
No, I don't have any pets.

Oui, j'ai …
Yes, I have…

un animal / des animaux	an animal / animals
un chat / des chats	a cat / cats
un chien / des chiens	a dog / dogs
un oiseau / des oiseaux	a bird / birds
un cheval / des chevaux	a horse / horses
un poisson / des poissons	a fish / fish
une souris / des souris	a mouse / mice
un hamster / des hamsters	a hamster / hamsters
un cochon d'Inde / des cochons d'Inde	a guinea pig / guinea pigs
un lapin / des lapins	a rabbit / rabbits
un serpent / des serpents	a snake / snakes
un caméléon / des caméléons	a chameleon / chameleons

cui, cui
tweet, tweet

ouah, ouah
woof, woof

**J'ai un chat. Il s'appelle Minou.
Il est noir et blanc.**
I have a cat called Minou.
He is black and white.

J'ai deux chiens.
I have two dogs.

Je n'ai pas de chien.
I don't have a dog.

miaou
miaow

Les vêtements et les couleurs / Clothes and colours

Ma couleur préférée, c'est le bleu.
My favourite colour is blue.

Je déteste le bleu.
I hate blue.

une chemise
shirt

des chaussures
shoes

un tee-shirt
T-shirt

un sweatshirt
sweatshirt

un pantalon
trousers

J'aime le rouge.
I love red.

un jean
jeans

un pull
sweater

une jupe
skirt

un chapeau
hat

des chaussettes
socks

C'est de quelle couleur? / What colour is it?

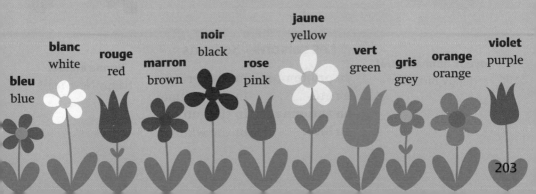

blanc
white

bleu
blue

rouge
red

marron
brown

noir
black

rose
pink

jaune
yellow

vert
green

gris
grey

orange
orange

violet
purple

203

Le calendrier / Calendar

Les jours de la semaine / Days of the week

lundi	Monday
mardi	Tuesday
mercredi	Wednesday
jeudi	Thursday
vendredi	Friday
samedi	Saturday
dimanche	Sunday

On est quel jour?
What day is it?

On est mardi.
It is Tuesday.

Les mois / Months

janvier	January
février	February
mars	March
avril	April
mai	May
juin	June
juillet	July
août	August
septembre	September
octobre	October
novembre	November
décembre	December
Fête Nationale	Bastille Day

C'est quoi la date d'aujourd'hui?
What is today's date?

Le 24 janvier.
24th January.

Days and months don't start with a capital letter in French.

Joyeux Noël!
Merry Christmas!

The first of the month is *le premier* not *le un*.

Les saisons / Seasons

au printemps	in the spring
en été	in the summer
en automne	in the autumn
en hiver	in the winter

Joyeux anniversaire!
Happy Birthday!

Bonne année!
Happy New Year!

L'heure / Time

Quelle heure est-il?
What time is it?

Il est une heure.
It is one o'clock.

Il est trois heures.
It is three o'clock.

Il est cinq heures.
It is five o'clock.

Il est sept heures.
It is seven o'clock.

Il est deux heures.
It is two o'clock.

Il est quatre heures.
It is four o'clock.

Il est six heures.
It is six o'clock.

Il est huit heures.
It is eight o'clock.

Il est dix heures.
It is ten o'clock.

Il est midi.
It is noon / midday.

Il est neuf heures.
It is nine o'clock.

Il est onze heures.
It is eleven o'clock.

Il est minuit.
It is midnight.

Il est midi.	It is midday.	**Il est minuit et demi.**	It is half past midnight.
Il est une heure.	It is one o'clock.	**Il est une heure et demie.**	It is half past one.
Il est une heure et quart.	It is quarter past one.	**Il est une heure moins le quart.**	It is quarter to one.

du matin / in the morning   **de l'après-midi** / in the afternoon   **du soir** / in the evening

C'est à quelle heure?
At what time is it?

L'école commence à 8 h 45.
School starts at 8.45am.

Je me couche à 20 h.
I go to bed at 8 o'clock.

C'est à 1 h 25.
It is at 1.25.

On mange à 18 h 30.
We eat at 6.30pm.

La récréation est à 11 h.
Playtime is at 11am.

Je me lève à 7 h.
I get up at 7am.

L'école finit à 16 h 30.
School finishes at 4.30pm.

Le corps / Body

J'ai mal au genou.
I have a sore knee.

J'ai mal à la tête.
I have a headache.

la tête
head

les yeux / l'œil
eyes / eye

J'ai mal aux oreilles.
I have earache.

le nez
nose

les oreilles
ears

la bouche
mouth

les épaules
shoulders

les bras
arms

le ventre
tummy

la main
hand

les doigts
fingers

les genoux
knees

les jambes
legs

les pieds
feet

les orteils
toes

Les nombres / Numbers

zéro	zero	**onze**	eleven	**trente**	thirty
un	one	**douze**	twelve	**quarante**	forty
deux	two	**treize**	thirteen	**cinquante**	fifty
trois	three	**quatorze**	fourteen	**soixante**	sixty
quatre	four	**quinze**	fifteen		
cinq	five	**seize**	sixteen		
six	six	**dix-sept**	seventeen		
sept	seven	**dix-huit**	eighteen		
huit	eight	**dix-neuf**	nineteen		
neuf	nine	**vingt**	twenty		
dix	ten	**vingt et un**	twenty-one		
		vingt-deux	twenty-two		

plus + add

huit plus deux
eight add two
8 + 2

moins - subtract

huit moins deux
eight subtract two
8 − 2

multiplié par x multiplied by

huit multiplié par deux
eight multiplied by two
8 x 2

divisé par ÷ divided by

huit divisé par deux
eight divided by two
8 ÷ 2

2ᵉ / 2nd
deuxième

1ᵉʳ / 1st
premier/
première

3ᵉ / 3rd
troisième

Dans la classe / In the classroom

Excellent! Bravo!
Excellent! Well done!

Qu'est-ce que c'est?
What is it?

Je peux aller aux toilettes?
May go I to the toilet?

Prenez un crayon.
Take a pencil.

un livre
a book

une gomme
a rubber

une trousse
a pencil case

une table
a table

**le maître /
la maîtresse**
teacher

Silence! / Taisez-vous!
Silence!

Écrivez!
Write!

Levez-vous!
Stand up!

Asseyez-vous!
Sit down!

Montrez-moi!
Show me!

Regardez!
Look!

Donnez-moi ... !
Give me ...!

Répétez!
Repeat!

Écoutez!
Listen!

un crayon
a pencil

un stylo
a pen

J'ai perdu mon crayon.
I've lost my pencil.

un / une élève
a pupil

Présent/e.
Here.

Absent/e.
Absent.

un cahier
an exercise book

une chaise
a chair

un taille-crayon
a pencil sharpener

J'ai fini.
I've finished.

un feutre
a felt-tip pen

un cartable
a schoolbag

une règle
a ruler

209

Des amis / Friends

Bonjour!
Hello!

Salut!
Hi!

Comment t'appelles-tu?
What is your name?

Je m'appelle Philippe.
My name is Philip.

Quel âge as-tu?
How old are you?

J'ai huit ans.
I am eight.

Où habites-tu?
Where do you live?

J'habite à York en Angleterre.
I live in York in England.

Au revoir!
Goodbye!

À bientôt!
See you soon!

Ça va?
How are you?

Ça va bien, merci.
Well, thanks.

Ça ne va pas.
Not good.

Tu parles français?
Do you speak French?

Oui, un peu.
Yes, a little.

Pas très bien.
Not very well.

C'est quand, ton anniversaire?
When is your birthday?

C'est le dix décembre. Et toi?
It's the tenth of December. And you?

Mon anniversaire, c'est le premier avril.
My birthday is the first of April.

Joyeux anniversaire!
Happy Birthday!

Je vais au cinéma samedi.
Tu viens avec moi?
I am going to the cinema on Saturday. Are you coming with me?

Oui, merci.
Yes, thanks.

C'est quoi ton adresse électronique?
What is your email address?

C'est …
It is …

Le temps / weather

Il gèle.
It's freezing.

Il neige.
It's snowing.

Il fait froid.
It's cold.

Il fait beau.
It's beautiful.

Quel temps fait-il?
What is the weather like?

Il y a du soleil.
It's sunny.

Quel temps fait-il à Paris?
What is the weather like in Paris?

Il y a du vent.
It's windy.

Il fait gris.
It's dull.

Il pleut.
It's raining.

Il y a de l'orage.
It's stormy.

Il fait chaud.
It's hot.

Il y a du brouillard.
It's foggy.

213

Les courses / Shopping

un thé
a cup of tea

une glace
an ice cream

un café
a coffee

Je voudrais ...
I would like…

une limonade
a lemonade

un sandwich au fromage
a cheese sandwich

Le chocolat, c'est combien?
Chocolate. How much is that?

... s'il vous plaît
… please

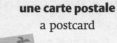

une carte postale
a postcard

un timbre
a stamp

du pain
some bread

un magazine
a magazine

un gâteau
a cake

un croissant
a croissant

une baguette
a baguette

la pharmacie
chemist

la boulangerie
baker

la pâtisserie
cake shop

la maison de la presse
newsagent

215

Les pays / Countries

C'est quel pays?
What country is this?

C'est ...
This is ...

la Grande-Bretagne
Great Britain

le Pays de Galles
Wales

l'Écosse
Scotland

l'Irlande
Ireland

l'Espagne
Spain

la France
France

Où est ...?
Where is...?

C'est ...	**dans le nord.**	**dans le sud.**	**dans l'est.**	**dans l'ouest.**
It is ...	in the north.	in the south.	in the east.	in the west.
	nord-est	**sud-ouest**	**sud-est**	**nord-ouest**
	north-east	south-west	south-east	north-west

Tu es de quelle nationalité?
What nationality are you?

Je suis anglais (boy)**/ anglaise** (girl).   I am English.
Je suis britannique.   I am British.
Je suis gallois/e.   I am Welsh.
Je suis écossais/e.   I am Scottish.
Je suis irlandais/e.   I am Irish.

Quelle langue parles-tu?
What language do you speak?

Je parle anglais.   I speak English.
Je parle français, je suis belge.   I speak French, I am Belgian.
Je parle français, je suis canadien.   I speak French, I am Canadian.
Il parle français, il est suisse.   He speaks French, he is Swiss.
Elle parle français, elle est luxembourgeoise.   She speaks French, she is from Luxembourg.
Il parle français, il est congolais.   He speaks French, he is Congolese.
Je parle français, je suis camerounais.   I speak French, I am Cameroonian.
Il parle français, il est grenadien.   He speaks French, he is Grenadian.
Il parle français, il est dominicain.   He speaks French, he is Dominican.

En famille / Family

Tu as / Est-ce que tu as des frères et sœurs?
Do you have any brothers and sisters?

Je suis fils / fille unique.
I am an only child.

J'ai un grand / petit frère.
I have a big / little brother.

J'ai une grande / petite sœur qui s'appelle …
I have a big / little sister who is called…

J'ai / Je n'ai pas de frère / sœur
I have / don't have a brother / sister.

Qui est-ce?
Who is this?

C'est …
This is …

Voici …
Here is…

ma mère/belle-mère
my mother / step-mother

C'est moi!
This is me!

ma sœur / demi-sœur
my sister / half-sister

mon père / beau-père
my father / stepfather

218

mon grand-père
my grandfather

grand / grande
tall

petit / petite
small

mince
slim

brun / brune
brown

blond / blonde
blonde

ma grand–mère
my grandmother

roux / rousse
red

sympa
nice

pénible
difficult

**J'ai des lunettes /
Il/elle a des lunettes.**
I wear /
he/she wears glasses.

**J'ai un appareil /
il/elle a un appareil.**
I have/
he/she has a brace.

mon frère / demi-frère
my brother / half-brother

219

Manger sain / Healthy eating

Mangez
un peu.
Eat a little.

Mangez avec
modération.
Eat in moderation.

Mangez beaucoup.
Eat a lot.

la carotte
carrot

la pomme
apple

la tomate
tomato

le poulet
chicken

la banane
banana

la salade
lettuce

l'orange
orange

les pommes de terre
potatoes

le riz
rice

l'eau
water

le pain
bread

les spaghettis
spaghetti

l'ail
garlic

le fromage
cheese

la glace
ice cream

le jus de pomme
apple juice

les céréales
cereal

le yaourt
yoghurt

les œufs
eggs

J'aime bien les sucreries.
I like sweets.

Je n'aime pas le café.
I don't like coffee.

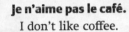
les frites
chips

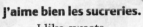

le chocolat
chocolate

le hamburger
burger

la confiture
jam

la boisson
drink

le sucre
sugar

le gâteau
cake

les chips
crisps

Les emplois / Jobs

Un jour, je serai...
One day, I will be...

Mon papa est pilote d'avion.
My Dad is a pilot.

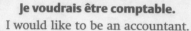

Je voudrais être comptable.
I would like to be an accountant.

un professeur
a teacher

un astronaute
an astronaut

un photographe
a photographer

un pompier
a firefighter

un médecin
a doctor

un électricien
an electrician

un chauffeur d'autobus
a bus driver

un agent de police
a policeman

222

Où êtes-vous? / Where are you?

et and	ou or	mais but	pourtant though
d'abord first	ensuite / puis then	finalement finally	donc so, therefore

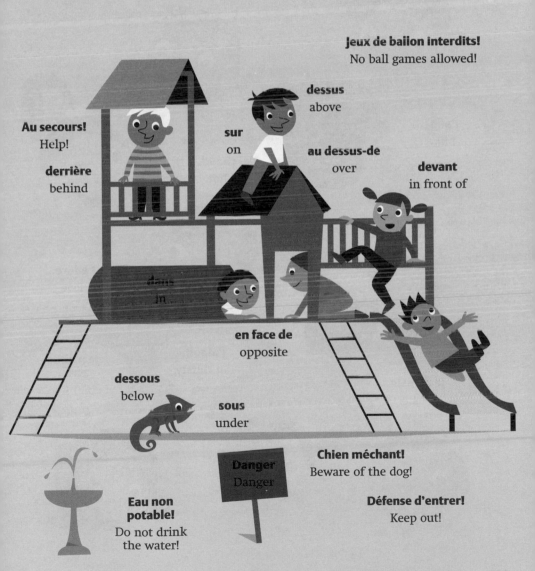

Jeux de baiion interdits!
No ball games allowed!

dessus
above

Au secours!
Help!

sur
on

au dessus-de
over

devant
in front of

derrière
behind

dans
in

en face de
opposite

dessous
below

sous
under

Chien méchant!
Beware of the dog!

Danger
Danger

Eau non potable!
Do not drink the water!

Défense d'entrer!
Keep out!

Sentiments / Feelings

Tu veux…? Do you want…?	**Pardon.** Sorry.	**cool** cool	**Je ne comprends pas.** I don't understand.
Oui, je veux bien. Yes, please.	**Excusez-moi.** Excuse me.	**facile** easy	**Ça m'est égal.** I don't mind.
Non, merci. No, thank you.	**Je suis désolé/e.** I'm sorry.	**difficile** difficult	**D'accord!** OK!
Peut-être. Maybe.	**Merci.** Thank you.	**amusant** funny	**Je n'ai pas envie.** I don't feel like it.

La lettre / A letter

une lettre
a letter

Vitry, le deux mars
Vitry, 2nd March.

Chère Tante Marie
Dear Aunty Mary,

Merci beaucoup pour le joli cadeau.

Thank you very much for the lovely present.

Grosses bises
Lots of love

Amélie

une enveloppe
an envelope

un timbre
a stamp

Un texto / A text

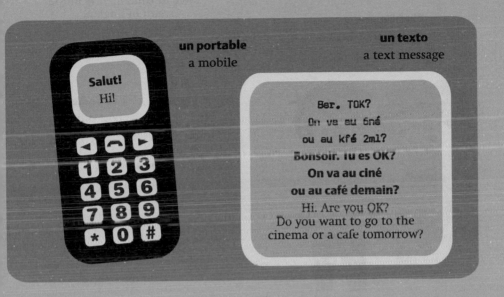

un portable
a mobile

un texto
a text message

Salut!
Hi!

Ber. TOK?
On va au 6né
ou au kfé 2m1?
Bonsoir. Tu es OK?
On va au ciné
ou au café demain?
Hi. Are you OK?
Do you want to go to the
cinema or a café tomorrow?

Un courriel / An email

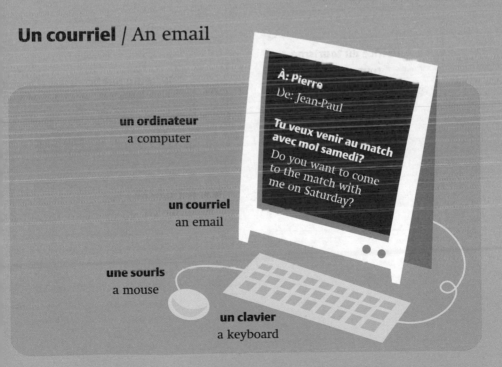

un ordinateur
a computer

À: Pierre
De: Jean-Paul

Tu veux venir au match
avec moi samedi?
Do you want to come
to the match with
me on Saturday?

un courriel
an email

une souris
a mouse

un clavier
a keyboard

Où j'habite / Where I live

J'habite à Londres. C'est dans le sud de l'Angleterre.
I live in London. It is in the south of England.

J'habite ...
I live ...

dans une maison / un appartement.
in a house / a flat.

Il y a ...
There is ...

la poste
post office

le marché
market

l'office du tourisme
tourist office

le jardin public
park

le supermarché
supermarket

À pied, en bus, en train...
By foot, by bus, by train...

à la campagne / en ville
in the country / in the town

la piscine
pool

la mosquée
mosque

l'école
school

la gare
railway station

Excusez-moi, monsieur!
Excuse me, sir!

le cinéma
cinema

Où est ... s'il vous plaît?
Where is .... please?

l'église
church

Allez tout droit!
Go straight ahead!

Prenez la première /
deuxième à droite / à gauche!
Take the first / second right / left!

229

Les sports / Sports

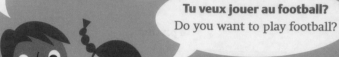

Tu fais du sport?
Do you play sport?

Je fais du rugby.
I play rugby.

Tu veux jouer au football?
Do you want to play football?

Mon sport préféré, c'est le...
My favourite sport is...

le tennis
tennis

l'équitation
horse-riding

la natation
swimming

le football
football

le badminton
badminton

le rugby
rugby

la gymnastique
gymnastics

la danse
dancing

le judo
judo

Les passe-temps / Hobbies

la clarinette
the clarinet

la flûte
the flute

Je joue du piano et de la batterie.
I play the piano and the drums.

Je joue de la guitare.
I play the guitar.

le synthétiseur (du synthé)
the keyboard

Mon passe-temps préféré, c'est ...
My favourite hobby is...

la lecture
reading

la musique
music

la télévision
television

le dessin
drawing

les jeux de société
board games

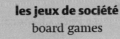

l'ordinateur
computing

les jeux vidéo
computer games

Les contes de fées / Story time

le chapeau
the hat

la méchante sorcière
the big bad witch

le chat
the cat

le manche à balai
the broomstick

La Belle au bois dormant
Sleeping Beauty

Pinocchio
Pinocchio

Cendrillon
Cinderella

Rumpelstiltskin
Rumpelstiltskin

la maison en pain d'épices
the gingerbread house

Il était une fois ...
Once upon a time ...

un heureux dénouement
happy ending

Ils vécurent heureux.
They lived happily ever after.

le conte de fées
fairy tale

la magie
magic

le gentil magicien
the good wizard

Le Petit Chaperon rouge
Little Red Riding Hood

la baguette magique
the magic wand

Le Chat botté
Puss in Boots

Verb tables

In French, there are three main types of verbs, ones that end in -er, -ir, or -re.

On the following page you can see how they change to express the present, the past, and the future tense. Most verbs follow the same patterns.

To make the past tense for some verbs, you have to use the verb être (to be) instead of the usual avoir (to have). These verbs are: aller, arriver, descendre, entrer, monter, mourir, naître, partir, passer, rester, retourner, sortir, tomber, and venir, and other related forms like revenir and rentrer. In the dictionary these verbs are marked with the symbol ⊘ and you'll see there is a footnote in the dictionary to remind you to use être for these verbs.

In French, there are also verbs called reflexive verbs. A reflexive verb is used with a pronoun (like me, te, se) for example: se lever (to get up): Je me lève is 'I get up', tu te lèves is 'you get up', etc. You can think of a reflexive verb as something you do to yourself, rather than somebody else. Reflexive verbs in French always use être. These are also marked with the symbol ⊘.

These verb tables show some typical verbs, in alphabetical order, for you to use as models to express the present, past, and future tenses.

Main verbs

Here are the main verbs ending in:
-er (like **donner**), -ir (like **choisir**),
and -re (like **entendre**).

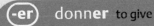

-er donner to give

present tense

je donne	I give
tu donnes	you give
il/elle donne	he/she gives
nous donnons	we give
vous donnez	you give
ils/elles donnent	they give

past tense

j'ai donné	I gave
tu as donné	you gave
il/elle a donné	he/she gave
nous avons donné	we gave
vous avez donné	you gave
ils/elles ont donné	they gave

future tense

je donnerai	I will give
tu donneras	you will give
il/elle donnera	he/she will give
nous donnerons	we will give
vous donnerez	you will give
ils/elles donneront	they will give

-ir choisir to choose

present tense

je choisis	I choose
tu choisis	you choose
il/elle choisit	he/she chooses
nous choisissons	we choose
vous choisissez	you choose
ils/elles choisissent	they choose

past tense

j'ai choisi	I chose
tu as choisi	you chose
il/elle a choisi	he/she chose
nous avons choisi	we chose
vous avez choisi	you chose
ils/elles ont choisi	they chose

future tense

je choisirai	I will choose
tu choisiras	you will choose
il/elle choisira	he/she will choose
nous choisirons	we will choose
vous choisirez	you will choose
ils/elles choisiront	they will choose

-re entendre to hear

present tense

j'entends	I hear
tu entends	you hear
il/elle entend	he/she hears
nous entendons	we hear
vous entendez	you hear
ils/elles entendent	they hear

past tense

j'ai entendu	I heard
tu as entendu	you heard
il/elle a entendu	he/she heard
nous avons entendu	we heard
vous avez entendu	you heard
ils/elles ont entendu	they heard

future tense

j'entendrai	I will hear
tu entendras	you will hear
il/elle entendra	he/she will hear
nous entendrons	we will hear
vous entendrez	you will hear
ils/elles entendront	they will hear

aller to go

present tense

je vais	I go
tu vas	you go
il/elle va	he/she goes
nous allons	we go
vous allez	you go
ils/elles vont	they go

past tense

je suis allé/e	I went
tu es allé/e	you went
il/elle est allé/e	he/she went
nous sommes allé(e)s	we went
vous êtes allé(e)(s)	you went
ils/elles sont allé(e)s	they went

future tense

j'irai	I will go
tu iras	you will go
il/elle ira	he/she will go
nous irons	we will go
vous irez	you will go
ils/elles iront	they will go

avoir to have

present tense

j'ai	I have
tu as	you have
il/elle a	he/she has
nous avons	we have
vous avez	you have
ils/elles ont	they have

past tense

j'ai eu	I had
tu as eu	you had
il/elle a eu	he/she had
nous avons eu	we had
vous avez eu	you had
ils/elles ont eu	they had

future tense

j'aurai	I will have
tu auras	you will have
il/elle aura	he/she will have
nous aurons	we will have
vous aurez	you will have
ils/elles auront	they will have

devoir to have to, must

present tense

je dois	I have to, I must
tu dois	you have to, you must
il/elle doit	he/she has to, he/she must
nous devons	we have to, we must
vous devez	you have to, you must
ils/elles doivent	they have to, they must

past tense

j'ai dû	I had to
tu as dû	you had to
il/elle a dû	he/she had to
nous avons dû	we had to
vous avez dû	you had to
ils/elles ont dû	they had to

future tense

je devrai	I will have to
tu devras	you will have to
il/elle devra	he/she will have to
nous devrons	we will have to
vous devrez	you will have to
ils/elles devront	they will have to

dire to say

present tense

je dis	I say
tu dis	you say
Il/elle dit	he/she says
nous disons	we say
vous dites	you say
ils/elles disent	they say

past tense

j'ai dit	I said
tu as dit	you said
il/elle a dit	he/she said
nous avons dit	we said
vous avez dit	you said
ils/elles ont dit	they said

future tense

je dirai	I will say
tu diras	you will say
il/elle dira	he/she will say
nous dirons	we will say
vous direz	you will say
ils/elles diront	they will say

écrire to write

present tense

j'écris	I write
tu écris	you write
il/elle écrit	he/she writes
nous écrivons	we write
vous écrivez	you write
ils/elles écrivent	they write

past tense

j'ai écrit	I wrote
tu as écrit	you wrote
il/elle a écrit	he/she wrote
nous avons écrit	we wrote
vous avez écrit	you wrote
ils/elles ont écrit	they wrote

future tense

j'écrirai	I will write
tu écriras	you will write
il/elle écrira	he/she will write
nous écrirons	we will write
vous écrirez	you will write
ils/elles écriront	they will write

être to be

present tense

je suis	I am
tu es	you are
Il/elle est	he/she is
nous sommes	we are
vous êtes	you are
ils/elles sont	they are

past tense

j'ai été	I was
tu as été	you were
Il/elle a été	he/she was
nous avons été	we were
vous avez été	you were
ils/elles ont été	they were

future tense

je serai	I will be
tu seras	you will be
il/elle sera	he/she will be
nous serons	we will be
vous serez	you will be
ils/elles seront	they will be

faire to do, to make

present tense

je fais	I do, I make
tu fais	you do, you make
il/elle fait	he/she does, he/she makes
nous faisons	we do, we make
vous faites	you do, you make
ils/elles font	they do, they make

past tense

j'ai fait	I did, I made
tu as fait	you did, you made
il/elle a fait	he/she did, he/she made
nous avons fait	we did, we made
vous avez fait	you did, you made
ils/elles ont fait	they did, they made

future tense

je ferai	I will do, I will make
tu feras	you will do, you will make
il/elle fera	he/she will do, he/she will make
nous ferons	we will do, we will make
vous ferez	you will do, you will make
ils/elles feront	they will do, they will make

lire to read

present tense

je lis	I read
tu lis	you read
il/elle lit	he/she reads
nous lisons	we read
vous lisez	you read
ils/elles lisent	they read

past tense

j'ai lu	I read
tu as lu	you read
il/elle a lu	he/she read
nous avons lu	we read
vous avez lu	you read
ils/elles ont lu	they read

future tense

je lirai	I will read
tu liras	you will read
il/elle lira	he/she will read
nous lirons	we will read
vous lirez	you will read
ils/elles liront	they will read

mettre to put

present tense

je mets	I put
tu mets	you put
il/elle met	he/she puts
nous mettons	we put
vous mettez	you put
ils/elles mettent	they put

past tense

j'ai mis	I put
tu as mis	you put
il/elle a mis	he/she put
nous avons mis	we put
vous avez mis	you put
ils/elles ont mis	they put

future tense

je mettrai	I will put
tu mettras	you will put
il/elle mettra	he/she will put
nous mettrons	we will put
vous mettrez	you will put
ils/elles mettront	they will put

pouvoir can

present tense

je peux	I can
tu peux	you can
il/elle peut	he/she can
nous pouvons	we can
vous pouvez	you can
ils/elles peuvent	they can

past tense

j'ai pu	I could
tu as pu	you could
il/elle a pu	he/she could
nous avons pu	we could
vous avez pu	you could
ils/elles ont pu	they could

future tense

je pourrai	I will be able
tu pourras	you will be able
il/elle pourra	he/she will be able
nous pourrons	we will be able
vous pourrez	you will be able
ils/elles pourront	they will be able

prendre to take

present tense

je prends	I take
tu prends	you take
il/elle prend	he/she takes
nous prenons	we take
vous prenez	you take
ils/elles prennent	they take

past tense

j'ai pris	I took
tu as pris	you took
il/elle a pris	he/she took
nous avons pris	we took
vous avez pris	you took
ils/elles ont pris	they took

future tense

je prendrai	I will take
tu prendras	you will take
il/elle prendra	he/she will take
nous prendrons	we will take
vous prendrez	you will take
ils/elles prendront	they will take

savoir to know

present tense

je sais	I know
tu sais	you know
il/elle sait	he/she knows
nous savons	we know
vous savez	you know
ils/elles savent	they know

past tense

j'ai su	I knew
tu as su	you knew
il/elle a su	he/she knew
nous avons su	we knew
vous avez su	you knew
ils/elles ont su	they knew

future tense

je saurai	I will know
tu sauras	you will know
il/elle saura	he/she will know
nous saurons	we will know
vous saurez	you will know
ils/elles sauront	they will know

venir to come

present tense

je viens	I come
tu viens	you come
il/elle vient	he/she comes
nous venons	we come
vous venez	you come
ils/elles viennent	they come

past tense

je suis venu/e	I came
tu es venu/e	you came
il/elle est venu/e	he/she came
nous sommes venu(e)s	we came
vous êtes venu(e)(s)	you came
ils/elles sont venu(e)s	they came

future tense

je viendrai	I will come
tu viendras	you will come
il/elle viendra	he/she will come
nous viendrons	we will come
vous viendrez	you will come
ils/elles viendront	they will come

voir to see

present tense

je vois	I see
tu vois	you see
il/elle voit	he/she sees
nous voyons	we see
vous voyez	you see
ils/elles voient	they see

past tense

j'ai vu	I saw
tu as vu	you saw
il/elle a vu	he/she saw
nous avons vu	we saw
vous avez vu	you saw
ils/elles ont vu	they saw

future tense

je verrai	I will see
tu verras	you will see
il/elle verra	he/she will see
nous verrons	we will see
vous verrez	you will see
ils/elles verront	they will see

vouloir to want

present tense

je veux	I want
tu veux	you want
il/elle veut	he/she wants
nous voulons	we want
vous voulez	you want
ils/elles veulent	they want

past tense

j'ai voulu	I wanted
tu as voulu	you wanted
il/elle a voulu	he/she wanted
nous avons voulu	we wanted
vous avez voulu	you wanted
ils/elles ont voulu	they wanted

future tense

je voudrai	I will want
tu voudras	you will want
il/elle voudra	he/she will want
nous voudrons	we will want
vous voudrez	you will want
ils/elles voudront	they will want

se réveiller to wake up

present tense

je me réveille	I wake up
tu te réveilles	you wake up
il/elle se réveille	he/she wakes up
nous nous réveillons	we wake up
vous vous réveillez	you wake up
ils/elles se réveillent	they wake up

past tense

je me suis réveillé/e	I woke up
tu t'es réveillé/e	you woke up
il/elle s'est réveillé/e	he/she woke up
nous nous sommes réveillé(e)s	we woke up
vous vous êtes réveillé(e)(s)	you woke up
ils/elles se sont réveillé(e)s	they woke up

future tense

je me réveillerai	I will wake up
tu te réveilleras	you will wake up
il/elle se réveillera	he/she will wake up
nous nous réveillerons	we will wake up
vous vous réveillerez	you will wake up
ils/elles se réveilleront	they will wake up

Aa

a determiner

🔑 **LANGUAGE**
a = *un* + *masc. noun* , *une* + *fem. noun*

1 un *masc.*, **une** *fem.*
a garden un jardin
a school une école
2 (*when saying how many times*) **par**
three times a week trois fois par
semaine
3 (*no translation when saying what someone's job is*)
My dad's a dentist. Mon père est
dentiste.

abbreviation noun
une **abréviation** *fem.*

able adjective
to be able to pouvoir
Annie won't be able to come.
Annie ne pourra pas venir.

about adverb
1 environ
It's about three o'clock. Il est
environ trois heures.
2 (*showing the time when something happens*)
vers
We're leaving at about six. Nous
partons vers six heures.

about preposition
1 au sujet de
It's about your sister. C'est au
sujet de ta sœur.
2 (*with films, books, songs, etc.*) **sur**
a book about animals un livre sur
les animaux
3 (*with talk*) **de**
to talk about something parler de
quelque chose
He's talking about his neighbours.
Il parle de ses voisins.
4 about to sur le point de
I'm about to go out. Je suis sur le
point de sortir.

ⓔ means use **être** *to make the past tense.*

above preposition
au-dessus de
There is a poster above my bed.
Il y a un poster au-dessus de mon lit.

abroad adverb
à l'étranger
I would like to go abroad.
J'aimerais partir à l'étranger.

absent adjective
absent *masc.*, **absente** *fem.*
Paul's absent today. Paul est
absent aujourd'hui.

absolutely adverb
tout à fait
You're absolutely right. Tu as tout
à fait raison.

accent noun
un accent *masc.*
He has a strange accent. Il a un
accent bizarre.

to **accept** verb
accepter

accident noun
un **accident** *masc.*
Jamie had an accident. Jamie a eu
un accident.
a car accident un accident de
voiture

accidentally adverb
accidentellement
**She accidentally knocked over the
cup.** Elle a accidentellement
renversé la tasse.

according to preposition
selon
according to Cathy selon Cathy

to **accuse** verb
accuser

to **ache** verb
My ear aches. J'ai mal à l'oreille.
My back is aching. J'ai mal au dos.
Do your legs ache? Tu as mal aux jambes?

acrobat noun
un or une **acrobate** *masc. & fem.*

across preposition
1 (*going from one side to the other*)
to go across traverser
Mark went across the road. Mark a traversé la rue.
2 (*already on the other side*) **de l'autre côté de**
Our school is across the street. Notre école est de l'autre côté de la rue.

to **act** verb
jouer
Sally wants to act in our play. Sally veut jouer dans notre pièce.

activity noun
une **activité** *fem.*

actor noun
un **acteur** *masc.*

actress noun
une **actrice** *fem.*

actually adverb
en fait
Actually, your friend is right. En fait, ton ami a raison.

AD abbreviation
apr. J.-C.
in 200 AD en 200 apr. J.-C.

to **add** verb
1 (*something extra*) **ajouter**
Add a bit of salt. Ajoutez un peu de sel.
2 (*using numbers*) **additionner**

Paul added up the two numbers. Paul a additionné les deux nombres.

address noun
une **adresse** *fem.*
Here's my address. Voici mon adresse.

adjective noun
un **adjectif** *masc.*

adult noun
un or une **adulte** *masc. & fem.*

advantage noun
un **avantage** *masc.*

adventure noun
une **aventure** *fem.*

adverb noun
un **adverbe** *masc.*

advert noun
1 (*on TV*) la **publicité** *fem.*
2 (*in the newspaper*) une **annonce** *fem.*

advice noun
les **conseils** *masc. plural*

aerial noun
une **antenne** *fem.*

aeroplane noun
un **avion** *masc.*
to travel on an aeroplane voyager en avion

to **afford** verb
avoir l'argent pour acheter
We can't afford a new car. Nous n'avons pas l'argent pour acheter une nouvelle voiture.

• *Languages, nationalities, and religions do not take a capital letter in French.*

afraid *adjective*
1 (*scared*) **to be afraid of something**
avoir peur de quelque chose
I'm afraid of dogs. J'ai peur des chiens.
2 (*sorry*) **désolé** *masc.*, **désolée** *fem.*
I'm afraid it's too late. Je suis désolé mais il est trop tard. (*boy speaking*); Je suis désolée mais il est trop tard. (*girl speaking*)

Africa *noun*
l'**Afrique** *fem.*

African *adjective*
africain *masc.*, **africaine** *fem.*

African *noun*
un **Africain** *masc.*,
une **Africaine** *fem.*

after *preposition*
après
after me après moi
after school après l'école
What are you doing after?
Qu'est-ce que tu fais après?

afternoon *noun*
un or une **après-midi** *masc. & fem.*
this afternoon cet après-midi
at two o'clock in the afternoon
à deux heures de l'après-midi
on Friday afternoons le vendredi après-midi
We play tennis in the afternoon.
On joue au tennis l'après-midi.
the afternoons les après-midi

afterwards *adverb*
après

again *adverb*
1 (*one more time*) **encore une fois**
Can you sing that again? Tu peux chanter ça encore une fois?
2 **encore**
You again! Encore toi!

I've forgotten again. J'ai encore oublié.
3 (*using 're-' in French*)
Can I see it again? Je peux le revoir?

against *preposition*
contre
Manchester United are playing against Chelsea. Manchester United joue contre Chelsea.

age *noun*
l'**âge** *masc.*
my age mon âge
at the age of ten à l'âge de dix ans
Rachel is seven years of age.
Rachel a sept ans.

ago *adverb*
il y a
two days ago il y a deux jours
a long time ago il y a longtemps

to **agree** *verb*
être d'accord
I agree. Je suis d'accord.
Do you agree with me? Tu es d'accord avec moi?

ahead *adverb*
1 **devant**
the road ahead la route devant nous
2 (*in sport*) **d'avance**
We're three points ahead. On a trois points d'avance.

air *noun*
1 l'**air** *masc.*
Throw the ball up into the air.
Lance la balle en l'air.
2 **to travel by air** voyager en avion

English French

a
b
c
d
e
f
g
h
i
j
k
l
m
n
o
p
q
r
s
t
u
v
w
x
y
z

English French

a
b
c
d
e
f
g
h
i
j
k
l
m
n
o
p
q
r
s
t
u
v
w
x
y
z

air-conditioned adjective
climatisé *masc.*, climatisée *fem.*

airmail noun
by airmail par avion

airport noun
un aéroport *masc.*

alarm noun
1 une alarme *fem.*
a fire alarm une alarme d'incendie
2 an alarm clock un réveil

album noun
un album *masc.*
a photo album un album photos

alcohol noun
l'alcool *masc.*

Algeria noun
l'Algérie *fem.*

alien noun
un or une extra-terrestre *masc.* & *fem.*

alike adjective
to look alike se ressembler ⊕
Pauline and Ruth look alike.
Pauline et Ruth se ressemblent.

alive adjective
vivant *masc.*, vivante *fem.*

all adjective
tout *masc.*, toute *fem.*
all the time tout le temps
all week toute la semaine
all the boys tous les garçons
all the girls toutes les filles

all pronoun
1 (*everything*) tout
That's all. C'est tout.
Don't eat it all. Ne mange pas tout.
2 (*everybody*) tous *masc. plural*,
toutes *fem. plural*
They all came. Ils sont tous venus.
(ils = *boys or boys and girls*); Elles sont
toutes venues. (*girls*)
3 Repeat all together! Répétez tous
ensemble!

all adverb
1 tout
all of a sudden tout à coup
2 (*in scores*) partout
It was a draw: two all. Ils ont fait
match nul: deux partout.

allergic adjective
allergique *masc. & fem.*
She's allergic to chocolate. Elle est
allergique au chocolat.

alligator noun
un alligator *masc.*

allowed adjective
1 to be allowed to do something
avoir le droit de faire quelque chose
Ben isn't allowed to play outside.
Ben n'a pas le droit de jouer dehors.
2 That's not allowed. Ce n'est pas
permis.

all right adverb
1 (*saying yes*) d'accord
Can you help me? – All right!
Tu peux m'aider? – D'accord!
2 (*good*) bien
How are you? – All right.
Comment vas-tu? – Bien.
Everything's all right. Tout va
bien.
Are you all right? Ça va?
3 (*not so bad*) pas mal
How did you like the book? – All
right. Comment tu as trouvé le
livre? – Pas mal.

almost adverb
presque
I've almost finished. J'ai presque
terminé.

alone adjective
1 seul *masc.*, seule *fem.*
I am alone. Je suis seul. (*boy
speaking*) Je suis seule. (*girl speaking*)
2 Leave me alone! Laissez-moi
tranquille!
Leave my computer alone!
Ne touchez pas à mon ordinateur!

• *The months of the year and days of the week do not take a capital letter in French.*

along preposition
le long de
all along the street tout le long de la rue

aloud adverb
à haute voix
Read this sentence aloud! Lisez cette phrase à haute voix!

alphabet noun
l'**alphabet** *masc.*

alphabetical adjective
alphabétique *masc. & fem.*
in alphabetical order par ordre alphabétique

already adverb
déjà
David has already left. David est déjà parti.

also adverb
aussi

although conjunction
bien que
although you're my friend bien que tu sois mon ami

altogether adverb
en tout
That's ten euros altogether. Ça fait dix euros en tout.

always adverb
toujours
You always win! Tu gagnes toujours!

am verb SEE **be**

a.m. abbreviation
du matin
at 6 a.m. à six heures du matin

amazing adjective
1 (*really good or unusual*) extraordinaire *masc. & fem.*
She's an amazing singer. C'est une chanteuse extraordinaire.
2 (*really surprising*) incroyable *masc. & fem.*
Amazing! Incroyable!

@ *means use être to make the past tense.*

ambulance noun
une **ambulance** *fem.*

America noun
l'**Amérique** *fem.*
in America en Amérique

American adjective
américain *masc.*, **américaine** *fem.*
an American car une voiture américaine
He's American. Il est américain.
She's American. Elle est américaine.

American noun
un **Américain** *masc.*,
une **Américaine** *fem.*

among preposition
parmi

amount noun
1 (*of money*) la **somme** *fem.*
a large amount of money une grosse somme d'argent
2 (*of different things*) la **quantité** *fem.*
a large amount of apples une grande quantité de pommes

amusement arcade noun
la **salle de jeux électroniques** *fem.*

amusement park noun
le **parc d'attractions** *masc.*

an determiner
un *masc.*, une *fem.*
an egg un œuf
an orange une orange

🔑 **LANGUAGE**
un + *masc. noun*
une + *fem. noun*

and conjunction
et
Mum and dad Maman et papa

angel noun
un **ange** *masc.*

a
b
c
d
e
f
g
h
i
j
k
l
m
n
o
p
q
r
s
t
u
v
w
x
y
z

angry adjective
fâché *masc.*, fâchée *fem.*
I'm angry. Je suis fâché. (*boy speaking*) Je suis fâchée. (*girl speaking*)

animal noun
un **animal** *masc.* (plural des **animaux**)

ankle noun
la **cheville** *fem.*

anniversary noun
un **anniversaire** *masc.*
a wedding anniversary un anniversaire de mariage

to **annoy** verb
énerver
You're annoying me.
Tu m'énerves.

anorak noun
un **anorak** *masc.*

another adjective
1 un autre *masc.*, une autre *fem.*
another day un autre jour
another little girl une autre petite fille
I want another one. J'en veux un autre.
2 **encore**
another two weeks encore deux semaines

answer noun
la **réponse** *fem.*
the right answer la bonne réponse
the wrong answer la mauvaise réponse

to **answer** verb
1 **répondre**
She didn't answer. Elle n'a pas répondu.
2 **répondre à**
Answer my question! Réponds à ma question!

• *See the centre section for verb tables.*

answering machine noun
le **répondeur** *masc.*

ant noun
la **fourmi** *fem.*

anthem noun
the national anthem l'hymne national *masc.*

antibiotic noun
un **antibiotique** *masc.*
He's on antibiotics. Il prend des antibiotiques.

any adjective
1 (*in questions and after 'if'*) du *masc.*, de la *fem.*, de l' *masc. & fem.*, des *masc. & fem. plural*
Do you have any chocolate?
Avez-vous du chocolat?
Tell me if you want any jam.
Dis-moi si tu veux de la confiture.
Do you want any water? Tu veux de l'eau?
Are there any questions? Il y a des questions?
2 (*with negatives*) de, d'
I don't have any bread. Je n'ai pas de pain.
We don't have any pets. On n'a pas d'animaux.

any pronoun
en
Do you want any? Tu en veux?
I don't want any. Je n'en veux pas.

anybody pronoun
1 (*in questions and after 'if'*) quelqu'un
Does anybody want some cake?
Quelqu'un veut du gâteau?
2 (*with negatives*) personne
I don't know anybody. Je ne connais personne.

anyone pronoun SEE **anybody**

anything pronoun
1 (*in questions and after 'if'*) quelque chose

Would you like anything to drink?
Vous voulez quelque chose à boire?
2 (*with negatives*) **rien**
He doesn't do anything. Il ne fait
rien.

anywhere adverb
1 (*in questions and after* **if**) **quelque part**
**Have you seen my glasses
anywhere?** As-tu vu mes lunettes
quelque part?
2 (*with negatives*) **nulle part**
I can't find them anywhere. Je ne
les trouve nulle part.

apart adverb
1 with feet apart les pieds écartés
2 apart from à part
They're all here apart from Stuart.
Ils sont tous là à part Stuart.

to **apologize** verb
s'excuser ⓔ
I apologize. Je m'excuse.

apostrophe noun
une **apostrophe** *fem.*

apple noun
la **pomme** *fem.*
apple juice le jus de pommes
an apple tree un pommier

appointment noun
le **rendez-vous** *masc.*
I have a doctor's appointment.
J'ai rendez-vous chez le médecin.

April noun
1 avril *masc.*
in April en avril
They arrive on the fifth of April. Ils
arrivent le cinq avril.
2 April fool! Poisson d'avril!
April Fools' Day le premier avril

CULTURE
In France there's a tradition of sticking a
paper fish on somebody's back as a joke
on April Fools' Day.

ⓔ *means use* **être** *to make the past tense.*

apron noun
le **tablier** *masc.*

Arab adjective
arabe
the Arab countries les pays arabes

Arab noun
un or une **Arabe** *masc. & fem.*

are verb SEE **be**

area noun
1 (*of a country*) la **région** *fem.*
2 (*of a town*) le **quartier** *masc.*

to **argue** verb
se disputer ⓔ
They're always arguing. Ils se
disputent toujours.

argument noun
la **dispute** *fem.*

arm noun
le **bras** *masc.*

armchair noun
le **fauteuil** *masc.*

army noun
l'**armée** *fem.*
in the army dans l'armée

around preposition
1 (*with time*) **vers**
Asif gets up around seven. Asif se
lève vers sept heures.
2 (*all the way round*) **autour de**
a wall around the garden un mur
autour du jardin

around adverb
(*close by*) **around here** près d'ici

to **arrive** verb
arriver ⓔ
They arrive at 2 o'clock.
Ils arrivent à deux heures.
He has arrived. Il est arrivé.
She has arrived. Elle est arrivée.

arrow noun
la **flèche** *fem.*

247

art noun
1 (*in school*) le **dessin** *masc.*
I like art. J'aime le dessin.
2 **an art gallery** un musée

artist noun
un or une **artiste** *masc. & fem.*

as conjunction
1 **comme**
Do as you like. Fais comme tu veux.
2 (*because*) **puisque**
I'm going to bed as it's late. Je vais me coucher puisqu'il est tard.
3 **as well** aussi
Are you coming as well? Tu viens aussi?

as adverb
(*when comparing*) **as ... as** aussi ... que
I'm as clever as you. Je suis aussi intelligent que toi. (*boy speaking*); Je suis aussi intelligente que toi. (*girl speaking*)

Asia noun
l'**Asie** *fem.*

Asian adjective
1 (*from Asia*) **Asiatique** *masc. & fem.*
2 (*from India or Pakistan*) **indo-pakistanais** *masc.*, **indo-pakistanaise** *fem.*
He's Asian. Il est indo-pakistanais.
She's Asian. Elle est indo-pakistanaise.

Asian noun
1 (*from Asia*) un or une **Asiatique** *masc. & fem.*
2 (*from India or Pakistan*) un **Indo-pakistanais** *masc.*, une **Indo-pakistanaise** *fem.*

to **ask** verb
1 **demander**
I'm going to ask. Je vais demander.
He's asking the way. Il demande son chemin.

2 **to ask somebody** demander à quelqu'un
Ask the teacher. Demande à la maîtresse.
3 **to ask for something** demander quelque chose
Ask for a sandwich. Demande un sandwich.
4 **to ask somebody for something** demander quelque chose à quelqu'un
Zoe asked me for a pen. Zoe m'a demandé un stylo.
5 **to ask a question** poser une question
Can I ask you a question? Je peux te poser une question?
6 (*invite*) **inviter**
Can I ask him to my party? Je peux l'inviter à ma fête?

asleep adjective
to be asleep dormir
He's asleep. Il dort.
to fall asleep s'endormir ℮

assembly noun
la **réunion des élèves** *fem.*

CULTURE
French schools do not have assemblies.

assistant noun
1 (*in a shop*) le **vendeur** *masc.*, la **vendeuse** *fem.*
2 (*in the classroom*) un **aide-éducateur** *masc.*, une **aide-éducatrice** *fem.*
3 (*for languages*) un **assistant** *masc.*, une **assistante** *fem.*

asthma noun
l'**asthme** *masc.*
I've got asthma. J'ai de l'asthme.

astronaut noun
un or une **astronaute** *masc. & fem.*

at preposition
1 à
at eight o'clock à huit heures

• *Use le and un for masculine words and la and une for feminine words.*

at the cinema au cinéma
at home à la maison
at school à l'école
at meetings aux réunions

🔑 **LANGUAGE**
à + le = au
à + les = aux

2 (*at somebody's house*) **chez**
He's at Julie's house. Il est chez Julie.
3 at last enfin

🔑 **LANGUAGE**
In some expressions, à is left out:
at night = la nuit
at the weekend = le weekend

Atlantic noun
l'**Atlantique** *masc.*

atlas noun
un **atlas** *masc.*

to **attack** verb
attaquer

to **attend** verb
to attend school aller @ à l'école

attention noun
l'**attention** *fem.*
Pay attention! Fais attention!

attractive adjective
beau *masc.*,
belle *fem.*, **beaux** *masc. plural*,
belles *fem. plural*

🔑 **LANGUAGE**
Beau becomes **bel** before a vowel or silent 'h'.

audience noun
les **spectateurs** *masc. plural*

August noun
août *masc.*
in August en août
I'm going on holiday in August.
Je pars en vacances en août.
the tenth of August le dix août

@ *means use* **être** *to make the past tense.*

aunt noun
la **tante** *fem.*
She's my aunt. C'est ma tante.

au pair noun
la **jeune fille au pair** *fem.*

Australia noun
l'**Australie** *fem.*
My cousins live in Australia.
Mes cousins habitent en Australie.

Australian adjective
australien *masc.*,
australienne *fem.*
He's Australian. Il est australien.
She's Australian. Elle est australienne.

Australian noun
un **Australien** *masc.*,
une **Australienne** *fem.*

Austria noun
l'**Autriche** *fem.*

author noun
un **auteur** *masc.*

autumn noun
l'**automne** *masc.*
In the autumn en automne

average noun
la **moyenne** *fem.*

average adjective
moyen *masc.*, **moyenne** *fem.*

to **avoid** verb
éviter

away adjective
1 absent *masc.*, **absente** *fem.*
Sarah is away. Sarah est absente.
2 (*in the distance*) **loin**
not very far away pas très loin

awful adjective
affreux *masc.*, **affreuse** *fem.*

awkward adjective
(*situation*) **difficile** *masc. & fem.*
That's a bit awkward. C'est un peu difficile.

Bb

baby noun
le **bébé** *masc.*

to **babysit** verb
faire du baby-sitting

babysitter noun
le or la **baby-sitter** *masc. & fem.*

back noun
1 (*of a person or animal*) le **dos** *masc.*
He's lying on his back. Il est
allongé sur le dos.
2 (*of a house or car*) l'**arrière** *masc.*
in the back of the car à l'arrière de
la voiture
3 (*of a room*) le **fond** *masc.*
at the back of the class au fond de
la classe

back adjective
1 **arrière** *masc. & fem.*
the back seat le siège arrière
the back wheels les roues arrière
2 **de derrière**
the back door (*of a house*) la porte de
derrière

🔑 **LANGUAGE**
Arrière is the same in masculine,
feminine, and plural.

back adverb
1 (*for saying that somebody comes back*) **de
retour**
Dad's back. Papa est de retour.
I'll be back in five minutes. Je
reviens dans cinq minutes.
2 (*meaning backwards*) **en arrière**
Take three steps back! Fais trois
pas en arrière!

backpack noun
le **sac à dos** *masc.*

backside noun
le **derrière** *masc.*

He fell on his backside. Il est tombé
sur le derrière.

backwards adverb
en arrière
Don't lean backwards! Ne te
penche pas en arrière!

bacon noun
le **bacon** *masc.*
bacon and eggs des œufs au bacon

bad adjective
1 **mauvais** *masc.*, **mauvaise** *fem.*
a bad idea une mauvaise idée
Louis is bad at English. Louis est
mauvais en anglais.
2 (*serious*) **grave**
a bad accident un accident grave
3 **gros** *masc.*, **grosse** *fem.*
a bad cold un gros rhume
4 (*evil*) **méchant** *masc.*,
méchante *fem.*
The ogre is bad. L'ogre est
méchant.
5 **That's not bad.** Ce n'est pas mal.
How are you? – Not bad! Comment
ça va? – Pas mal!
Bad luck! Pas de chance!

badge noun
le **badge** *masc.*

badly adverb
1 **mal**
Tom played very badly. Tom a très
mal joué.
2 **badly hurt** gravement blessé

badminton noun
le **badminton** *masc.*
Kelly plays badminton. Kelly joue
au badminton.

bag noun
le **sac** *masc.*
Don't forget your bag! N'oublie
pas ton sac!

• *Languages, nationalities, and religions do not take a capital letter in French.*

a b c d e f g h i j k l m n o p q r s t u v w x y z

bagpipes plural noun
la **cornemuse** *fem.*
Don plays the bagpipes. Don joue de la cornemuse.

the **Bahamas** plural noun
les **Bahamas** *fem. plural*

to **bake** verb
to bake something faire cuire quelque chose au four
a baked potato une pomme de terre cuite au four
to bake a cake faire un gâteau

baked beans plural noun
les **haricots blancs à la sauce tomate** *masc. plural*

CULTURE
French people don't eat tinned baked beans.

baker noun
le **boulanger** *masc.*,
la **boulangère** *fem.*
He's a baker. Il est boulanger.
We're going to the baker's. Nous allons à la boulangerie.

bakery noun
la **boulangerie** *fem.*

balance noun
l'**équilibre** *masc.*
I lost my balance. J'ai perdu l'équilibre.

balcony noun
le **balcon** *masc.*

bald adjective
chauve *masc. & fem.*

ball noun
1 (*for tennis, cricket, or golf*) la **balle** *fem.*
a tennis ball une balle de tennis
2 (*for football, rugby, or basketball*) le **ballon** *masc.*
a rugby ball un ballon de rugby

ballet dancing noun
la **danse classique** *fem.*

She does ballet dancing. Elle fait de la danse classique.

balloon noun
le **ballon** *masc.*
We're blowing up balloons for the party. Nous gonflons des ballons pour la fête.

ballpoint pen noun
le **stylo à bille** *masc.*

banana noun
la **banane** *fem.*

band noun
1 (*playing rock or pop music*) le **groupe** *masc.*
a rock band un groupe de rock
2 **a brass band** une fanfare *fem.*

bandage noun
le **bandage** *masc.*

bang noun
un **boum** *masc.*
a loud bang un grand boum

to **bang** verb
1 (*to knock*) **cogner**
to bang on the door cogner à la porte
2 (*to slam*) **claquer**
Don't bang the door! Ne claque pas la porte!

bank noun
1 (*for money*) la **banque** *fem.*
2 (*at the side of a river*) le **bord** *masc.*
on the river bank au bord de la rivière

bar noun
1 (*made of metal*) la **barre** *fem.*
an iron bar une barre de fer
2 (*selling drinks*) le **bar** *masc.*
3 **a bar of chocolate** une tablette de chocolat
a bar of soap une savonnette

Barbados noun
la **Barbade** *fem.*

a
b
c
d
e
f
g
h
i
j
k
l
m
n
o
p
q
r
s
t
u
v
w
x
y
z

means use être to make the past tense.

barbecue noun
le **barbecue** *masc.*

bare adjective
nu *masc.*, **nue** *fem.*
I've got bare feet. J'ai les pieds nus.

to **bark** verb
aboyer
The dog is barking. Le chien aboie.

baseball noun
le **base-ball** *masc.*
Charlie is playing baseball.
Charlie joue au base-ball.
a baseball cap une casquette de
base-ball

basement noun
le **sous-sol** *masc.*
There's a TV in the basement. Il y a
une télévision au sous-sol.

to **bash** verb
cogner
David bashed his head. David s'est
cogné la tête.

basin noun
le **lavabo** *masc.*

basket noun
le **panier** *masc.*

basketball noun
le **basket** *masc.*
We're playing basketball. On
joue au basket.

bat noun
1 (*for cricket or baseball*) la **batte** *fem.*
2 (*for table tennis*) la **raquette** *fem.*
3 (*flying animal*) la **chauve-souris** *fem.*
(plural les **chauves-souris**)

⚷ **LANGUAGE**
Word for word **chauve-souris** means
'bald mouse'.

bath noun
1 (*wash*) le **bain** *masc.*
I want to have a bath. Je veux
prendre un bain.
2 (*bathtub*) la **baignoire** *fem.*

**There's too much water in the
bath.** Il y a trop d'eau dans la
baignoire.

bathroom noun
la **salle de bains** *fem.* (plural les
salles de bains)

battery noun
(*for a torch, radio, camera, toy*) la **pile** *fem.*

battle noun
la **bataille** *fem.*

battleships noun
la **bataille navale** *fem.* (*game*)

BC abbreviation
av. J.-C.
in 300 BC en 300 av. J.-C.

⚷ **LANGUAGE**
av. J.-C. is short for **avant Jésus-Christ**

to **be** verb
1 **être**
I'm in my room. Je suis dans ma
chambre.
Are you sad? Tu es triste?
He's in London. Il est à Londres.
She's tall. Elle est grande.
It's not a problem. Ce n'est pas un
problème.
It's the tenth of May. C'est le dix
mai.
We're very tired. Nous sommes
très fatigués.
Are you ready? Vous êtes prêts?
The cakes are delicious. Les
gâteaux sont délicieux.
Has your father been ill? Ton père
a été malade?
I don't like being late. Je n'aime
pas être en retard.
2 (*when talking about sensations or states*)
avoir
I'm hot. J'ai chaud.
Ashley is sleepy. Ashley a
sommeil.
We're hungry. Nous avons faim.
They're afraid. Ils ont peur.
3 (*when saying how old somebody is*) **avoir**

• *The months of the year and days of the week do not take a capital letter in French.*

I am eleven. J'ai onze ans.

4 (*when saying how you feel*) **aller** @
How are you? Comment
vas-tu?, Comment ça va?
I'm fine. Je vais bien.
5 (*when talking about the weather*) **faire**
It's hot. Il fait chaud.
It's a lovely day today. Il fait beau
aujourd'hui.
6 (*in maths*) **faire**
Two and two are four. Deux et
deux font quatre.
7 (*to translate questions such as 'isn't it?'*
or 'aren't you?')
It's hard, isn't it? C'est difficile,
non?
You are tired, aren't you? Tu es
fatigué, non?

beach noun
la **plage** *fem.*

beak noun
le **bec** *masc.*

bean noun
le **haricot** *masc.*
green beans les haricots verts
baked beans les haricots blancs à
la sauce tomate

bear noun
un **ours** *masc.*

beard noun
la **barbe** *fem.*

to **beat** verb
battre
I beat my brother. J'ai battu mon
frère.

beautiful adjective
beau *masc.*,
belle *fem.*, **beaux** *masc. plural*,
belles *fem. plural*
a beautiful smile un beau sourire
a beautiful dress une belle robe

@ *means use* **être** *to make the past tense.*

Your pictures are very beautiful.
Tes dessins sont très beaux.

because conjunction
1 parce que
I'm not going out because it's
raining. Je ne sors pas parce qu'il
pleut.
2 because of à cause de
We're late because of Emma.
On est en retard à cause d'Emma.

to **become** verb
devenir @
We've become friends. Nous
sommes devenus amis.

bed noun
1 le **lit** *masc.*
I'm in bed. Je suis au lit.
2 to go to bed se coucher @
Alex goes to bed at nine. Alex se
couche à neuf heures.
3 to make your bed faire son lit

bedroom noun
la **chambre** *fem.*
in my bedroom dans ma chambre

bedtime noun
It's bedtime! Au lit!

bee noun
une **abeille** *fem.*

beef noun
le **bœuf** *masc.*
Do you like beef? Tu aimes le
bœuf?

beefburger noun
le **humburger** *masc.*

been verb SEE **be**

beer noun
la **bière** *fem.*
Do your parents drink beer? Tes
parents boivent de la bière?

beetle noun
le **scarabée** *masc.*

beetroot noun
la **betterave rouge** *fem.*

a b c d e f g h i j k l m n o p q r s t u v w x y z

a
b
c
d
e
f
g
h
i
j
k
l
m
n
o
p
q
r
s
t
u
v
w
x
y
z

before preposition
avant
before this evening avant ce soir

before adverb
1 avant
Before I was in Ms Miller's class.
Avant, j'étais dans la classe de
Madame Miller.
2 (*already*) **déjà**
Have you read this book before?
Tu as déjà lu ce livre?

before conjunction
before doing something avant de
faire quelque chose
Phone me before leaving!
Téléphone-moi avant de partir!

to **begin** verb
commencer
My name begins with a 'd'.
Mon nom commence par un 'd'.
I'm beginning to get hungry.
Je commence à avoir faim.

beginner noun
le **débutant** *masc.*,
la **débutante** *fem.*
I'm a beginner. Je suis débutant.
(*boy speaking*); Je suis débutante. (*girl
speaking*)

beginning noun
le **début** *masc.*
at the beginning au début

to **behave** verb
1 se comporter ⊘
Colin behaves badly. Colin se
comporte mal.
2 (*to have good manners*) **être sage**
Behave yourself! Sois sage!

behind preposition
derrière
behind your back derrière ton dos

being verb SEE **be**

being noun
a human being un être humain
masc.

• *See the centre section for verb tables.*

Belgian adjective
belge
Belgian chocolate le chocolat
belge
He's Belgian. Il est belge.
She's Belgian. Elle est belge.

Belgian noun
le or la **Belge** *masc. & fem.*

Belgium noun
la **Belgique** *fem.*

to **believe** verb
croire
I believe you. Je te crois.
They believe in God. Ils croient en
Dieu.

bell noun
1 (*on a door or bicycle*) la **sonnette** *fem.*
2 (*school bell*) la **sonnerie** *fem.*
It's the bell! C'est la sonnerie!
3 (*of a church*) la **cloche** *fem.*

to **belong** verb
(*to somebody*) **appartenir à**
This bike belongs to Jamie. Ce vélo
appartient à Jamie.
Who does this pen belong to?
À qui appartient ce stylo?
It belongs to me. C'est à moi.

below preposition
au-dessous de
the flat below ours l'appartement
au-dessous du nôtre

belt noun
la **ceinture** *fem.*

bench noun
le **banc** *masc.*

bend noun
(*in the road*) le **virage** *masc.*

to **bend** verb
plier
Try to bend your arm. Essaie de
plier le bras.

beneath preposition
sous

beside preposition
à côté de
beside the window à côté de la fenêtre

best adjective
meilleur *masc.*, **meilleure** *fem.*
my best friend mon meilleur ami (*boy*); ma meilleure amie (*girl*)
the best holiday of my life les meilleures vacances de ma vie
Best wishes! Meilleurs vœux!

best noun
le **meilleur** *masc.*,
la **meilleure** *fem.*
This book is the best. Ce livre est le meilleur.
Jo is the best in French. Jo est le meilleur en français.

best adverb
le mieux
Barbara plays best. C'est Barbara qui joue le mieux.

better adjective
1 **meilleur** *masc.*, **meilleure** *fem.*
Your idea is better than mine. Ton idée est meilleure que la mienne.
2 **mieux**
Yes, that's better. Oui, c'est mieux.
I'm better today. Je vais mieux aujourd'hui.
It's better to tell the truth. Il vaut mieux dire la vérité.

better adverb
mieux
I sing better than you. Je chante mieux que toi.
My cold is getting better. Mon rhume va mieux.
Get better soon! Remets-toi vite!

between preposition
entre
The bakery is between the butcher's and the post office. La boulangerie se trouve entre la boucherie et la poste.

Bible noun
la **Bible** *fem.*

bicycle noun
le **vélo** *masc.*
I go to school by bicycle. Je vais à l'école à vélo.

big adjective
1 **grand** *masc.*, **grande** *fem.*
Our house is big. Notre maison est grande.
a big tree un grand arbre
my big sister ma grande sœur
2 **gros** *masc.*, **grosse** *fem.*
a big dog un gros chien
the biggest piece le plus gros morceau

> 🔑 **LANGUAGE**
> **Grand** and **gros** both mean 'big':
> grand = 'tall', 'older' or 'important'
> gros = 'heavy' or 'fat'

bike noun
le **vélo** *masc.*
by bike à vélo

bikini noun
le **bikini** *masc.*

bilingual adjective
bilingue *masc & fem.*

bill noun
l'**addition** *fem.*
The bill, please! L'addition, s'il vous plaît!

billion noun
le **milliard** *masc.*

bin noun
la **poubelle** *fem.*

bingo noun
le **loto**
Can we play bingo? On peut jouer au loto?

a
b
c
d
e
f
g
h
i
j
k
l
m
n
o
p
q
r
s
t
u
v
w
x
y
z

ⓔ means use **être** *to make the past tense.*

binoculars plural noun
les **jumelles** *fem. plural*

bird noun
un **oiseau** *masc.* (plural les **oiseaux**)

Biro® noun
le **bic**® *masc.*

birth noun
la **naissance** *fem.*
What's your date of birth? Quelle est ta date de naissance?

birthday noun
un **anniversaire** *masc.*
My birthday is the tenth of December. Mon anniversaire, c'est le dix décembre.
When is your birthday? C'est quand, ton anniversaire?, Quelle est la date de ton anniversaire?
a birthday card une carte d'anniversaire
a birthday cake un gâteau d'anniversaire
a birthday party une fête d'anniversaire
Happy birthday! Joyeux anniversaire!

biscuit noun
le **biscuit** *masc.*

bit noun
1 (*a piece*) le **morceau** *masc.* (plural les **morceaux**)
a bit of cheese un morceau de fromage
2 (*not very much*)
a bit un peu
He's a bit tired. Il est un peu fatigué. (*boy speaking*)
Just a bit for me. Juste un peu pour moi.

to **bite** verb
mordre
Does your dog bite? Est-ce que ton chien mord?

black adjective
noir *masc.*, **noire** *fem.*
a black dress une robe noire
He's black. Il est noir.
She's black. Elle est noire.

black noun
le **noir** *masc.*
Sally likes black. Sally aime bien le noir.

blackberry noun
la **mûre** *fem.*

blackboard noun
le **tableau** *masc.* (plural les **tableaux**)
on the blackboard au tableau

blank noun
le **blanc** *masc.*
Fill in the blanks! Remplis les blancs!

blanket noun
la **couverture** *fem.*

blazer noun
le **blazer** *masc.*

to **bleed** verb
saigner
My nose is bleeding. Je saigne du nez.

to **bless** verb
Bless you! À tes souhaits!

CULTURE
Say **À tes souhaits!** (meaning 'To your wishes') when somebody sneezes.

---

blind adjective
aveugle *masc. & fem.*
He's blind. Il est aveugle.

blind noun
(*on a window*) le **store** *masc.*

block noun
a block of flats un immeuble *masc.*

• *Use* le *and* un *for masculine words and* la *and* une *for feminine words.*

blond adjective
blond *masc.*, **blonde** *fem.*
I've got blond hair. J'ai les cheveux
blonds.

blood noun
le sang *masc.*

blouse noun
le chemisier *masc.*

to **blow** verb
1 souffler
The wind is blowing. Le vent
souffle.
Gerry blew out the candle. Gerry a
soufflé la bougie.
2 **to blow a whistle** siffler
The referee blew his whistle.
L'arbitre a sifflé.
3 **to blow your nose** se moucher @
Blow your nose! Mouche-toi!
4 **to blow up a balloon** gonfler un
ballon

blue adjective
bleu *masc.*, bleue *fem.*
a blue shirt une chemise bleue

blue noun
le bleu *masc.*
My favourite colour is blue.
Ma couleur préférée, c'est le bleu.

to **blush** verb
rougir
You're blushing! Tu rougis!

board noun
1 le tableau *masc.* (plural les
tableaux)
**The teacher is writing on the
board.** L'institutrice écrit au
tableau.
2 **a board game** un jeu de société

boarding school noun
un internat *masc.*
She's at boarding school. Elle est
interne.

@ *means use* être *to make the past tense.*

boat noun
le bateau *masc.* (plural les **bateaux**)
by boat en bateau

body noun
le corps *masc.*

to **boil** verb
bouillir
The water is boiling. L'eau bout.
to boil the water faire bouillir
l'eau

boiled egg noun
un œuf à la coque *masc.*

boiling adjective
(*water*) bouillant *masc.*,
bouillante *fem.*

bomb noun
la bombe *fem.*

bone noun
un os *masc.* (plural les **os**)

bonfire noun
le feu *masc.* (plural les **feux**)

> **CULTURE**
> Bonfire Night (5th November) is not
> celebrated in France but on 14th July
> there are fireworks for the French national
> holiday.

book noun
1 le livre *masc.*
I'm reading my book. Je lis mon
livre.
2 (*exercise book*) le cahier *masc.*
3 (*of tickets, stamps, addresses*) le carnet
masc.
an address book un carnet
d'adresses

to **book** verb
réserver
Can we book seats? On peut
réserver des places?

bookcase noun
la bibliothèque *fem.*

English French

a
b
c
d
e
f
g
h
i
j
k
l
m
n
o
p
q
r
s
t
u
v
w
x
y
z

bookshop noun
la **librairie** *fem.*

> ⚠ **FALSE FRIEND**
> Une **librairie** is a shop where you buy
> books, not a **library** where you borrow
> them.

boot noun
1 la **botte** *fem.*
Put your boots on, it's snowing!
Mets tes bottes, il neige!
2 (*for sports*) la **chaussure** *fem.*
football boots des chaussures de
foot
3 le **coffre** *masc.*
the boot of the car le coffre de la
voiture

border noun
la **frontière** *fem.*

bored adjective
to be bored s'ennuyer ⊘
I'm bored. Je m'ennuie.

boring adjective
ennuyeux *masc.*, **ennuyeuse** *fem.*
a boring story une histoire
ennuyeuse

born adjective
né *masc.*, **née** *fem.*
He was born in Ireland. Il est né en
Irlande.
She was born in Bristol. Elle est
née à Bristol.

> **LANGUAGE**
> English = I **was** born
> French = Je **suis** né (*masc.*)
>   Je **suis** née. (*fem.*)

to **borrow** verb
emprunter
Can I borrow your rubber? Je peux
emprunter ta gomme?

boss noun
le **patron** *masc.*, la **patronne** *fem.*

bossy adjective
autoritaire *masc. & fem.*

both pronoun
1 (*when talking about people*) **tous les
deux** *masc. plural*, **toutes les deux**
fem. plural
Ben and Sam are both tired. Ben et
Sam sont tous les deux fatigués.
**Lucy and Mia both want some
cake.** Lucy et Mia veulent toutes les
deux du gâteau.
2 (*when talking about things*) **les deux**
masc. & fem. plural
**Do you like French or English? –
Both.** Tu aimes le français ou
l'anglais? – Les deux.

to **bother** verb
1 (*to disturb somebody*) **déranger**
Sorry to bother you! Désolé de
vous déranger!
2 (*to make somebody angry*) **embêter**
Stop bothering me! Arrête de
m'embêter!
3 **Don't bother!** Ce n'est pas la peine!

bottle noun
la **bouteille** *fem.*

bottom noun
1 (*of a hole, bag, river, etc.*) le **fond** *masc.*
at the bottom of the garden au
fond du jardin
2 (*of a page*) le **bas** *masc.*
at the bottom of the page en bas
de la page
3 (*a part of the body*) le **derrière** *masc.*

to **bounce** verb
rebondir

bow noun
1 (*in a ribbon or shoelaces*) le **nœud** *masc.*
to tie a bow faire un nœud
2 un **arc** *masc.*
a bow and arrow un arc et une
flèche

bowl noun
le **bol** *masc.*
a bowl of cereal un bol de céréales

bowling noun
le **bowling** *masc.*

• *Languages, nationalities, and religions do not take a capital letter in French.*

We're going bowling. On va jouer au bowling.
a bowling alley un bowling

box noun
1 la **boîte** *fem.*
a box of chocolates une boîte de chocolats
a cardboard box un carton
2 (*on forms, worksheets, etc.*) la **case** *fem.*
Tick the box. Coche la case.

boxer shorts plural noun
le **caleçon** *masc.*

> 🔑 **LANGUAGE**
> English = **boxer shorts** is plural
> French = **le caleçon** is singular

boxing noun
la **boxe** *fem.*

Boxing Day noun
le **lendemain de Noël** *masc.*

> 🌍 **CULTURE**
> Boxing Day is not a holiday in France.

boy noun
le **garçon** *masc.*

boyfriend noun
le **copain** *masc.*

bra noun
le **soutien-gorge** *masc.* (plural les **soutiens-gorge**)

brace noun
un **appareil dentaire** *masc.*
I wear a brace. Je porte un appareil dentaire.

bracelet noun
le **bracelet** *masc.*

brain noun
le **cerveau** *masc.* (plural les **cerveaux**)

brainy adjective
intelligent *masc.*,
intelligente *fem.*

brake noun
le **frein** *masc.*
to put on the brakes freiner

branch noun
la **branche** *fem.*

brand-new adjective
tout neuf *masc.*, **toute neuve** *fem.*
a brand-new mobile phone un portable tout neuf

brave adjective
courageux *masc.*,
courageuse *fem.*

bread noun
le **pain** *masc.*
I'm eating some bread. Je mange du pain.
a slice of bread and butter une tartine de pain beurré

break noun
(*in school*) la **récréation** *fem.*
What are you doing at break? Qu'est-ce que tu fais à la récréation?

to **break** verb
1 **to break something** casser quelque chose
Jack has broken a plate. Jack a cassé une assiette.
2 **se casser** ⊘
The glass fell and broke. Le verre est tombé et s'est cassé.
Jenny broke her arm. Jenny s'est cassé le bras.

to **break down** verb
tomber ⊘ **en panne**
The car broke down. La voiture est tombée en panne.

breakfast noun
le **petit déjeuner** *masc.*
We have breakfast at seven. Nous prenons le petit déjeuner à sept heures.

⊘ *means use* **être** *to make the past tense.*

English French

a
b
c
d
e
f
g
h
i
j
k
l
m
n
o
p
q
r
s
t
u
v
w
x
y
z

to **break up** verb
We break up on Thursday. Les cours finissent jeudi.

breath noun
out of breath à bout de souffle

to **breathe** verb
respirer

brick noun
la **brique** fem.

bride noun
la **mariée** fem.

bridegroom noun
le **marié** masc.

bridesmaid noun
la **demoiselle d'honneur** fem.

bridge noun
le **pont** masc.

bright adjective
1 **vif** masc., **vive** fem.
bright colours des couleurs vives
bright red rouge vif
2 (sun, light) **éclatant** masc.,
éclatante fem.
a bright light une lumière éclatante
3 (person) **intelligent** masc.,
intelligente fem.

brilliant adjective
génial masc.,
géniale fem., **géniaux** masc. plural,
géniales fem. plural
The concert was brilliant! Le concert était génial!

to **bring** verb
1 (a thing you can carry) **apporter**
Bring your camera! Apporte ton appareil photo!
2 (a person) **amener**
Bring your friend! Amène ton copain!

to **bring back** verb
rapporter quelque chose
She brought back the key. Elle a rapporté la clé.

to **bring somebody back** ramener quelqu'un

Britain noun
la **Grande-Bretagne** fem.
We live in Britain. Nous habitons en Grande-Bretagne.

British adjective
britannique masc. & fem.
I am British. Je suis britannique.
the British Isles les îles Britanniques fem. plural

British noun
the British les Britanniques masc. plural

Brittany noun
la **Bretagne** fem.

broccoli noun
le **brocoli**
Do you like broccoli? Tu aimes le brocoli?

LANGUAGE
English = broccoli
French = brocoli
---

broken adjective
cassé masc., **cassée** fem.
It's broken. C'est cassé.
a broken window une vitre cassée

bronze noun
le **bronze** masc.
a bronze medal une médaille de bronze

broom noun
le **balai** masc.

brother noun
le **frère** masc.
my little brother mon petit frère
Do you have brothers and sisters? Tu as des frères et sœurs?
I have a brother. J'ai un frère.

brown adjective
1 **marron** masc. & fem.
a brown cardigan un gilet marron

• *The months of the year and days of the week do not take a capital letter in French.*

brown shoes des chaussures marron
brown eyes des yeux marron

> 🔑 **LANGUAGE**
> **Marron** is the same in the masculine, feminine, and plural.

2 (*hair*) **brun** *masc.*, **brune** *fem.*
I've got brown hair. J'ai les cheveux bruns.
3 (*from the sun*) **bronzé** *masc.*, **bronzée** *fem.*

brown noun
le **marron** *masc.*
Brown looks good on you. Le marron te va bien.

brown bread noun
le **pain complet** *masc.*

Brownie noun
la **jeannette** *fem.*
Are you a Brownie? Tu es jeannette?

bruise noun
le **bleu** *masc.*
I have a bruise on my knee. J'ai un bleu au genou.

brush noun
la **brosse** *fem.*
a hairbrush une brosse à cheveux

to **brush** verb
1 **brosser**
He's brushing the dog. Il brosse le chien.
2 **se brosser** ℮
I'm brushing my teeth. Je me brosse les dents.
She brushes her hair. Elle se brosse les cheveux.

Brussels sprouts plural noun
les **choux de Bruxelles** *masc. plural*

bubble noun
la **bulle** *fem.*

bucket noun
le **seau** *masc.* (plural les **seaux**)

a bucket and spade un seau et une pelle

budgie noun
la **perruche** *fem.*

bug noun
1 (*insect*) la **bestiole** *fem.*
2 (*germ*) le **microbe** *masc.*

buggy noun
la **poussette** *fem.*

to **build** verb
construire

> 🔑 **LANGUAGE**
> In English 'construct' is another word for 'build'.

builder noun
le **maçon** *masc.*

building noun
le **bâtiment** *masc.*

bulb noun
une **ampoule** *fem.*
to change a light bulb changer une ampoule

bull noun
le **taureau** *masc.* (plural les **taureaux**)

bully noun
la **terreur** *fem.*
Jack's the class bully. Jack est la terreur de la classe.

bump noun
(*on your head, in the road*) la **bosse** *fem.*

to **bump** verb
(*to knock*) **se cogner** ℮
I bumped my head. Je me suis cogné la tête.

bun noun
1 (*sweet*) le **petit cake** *masc.*
2 (*for a burger*) le **petit pain** *masc.*

bunch noun
1 **a bunch of flowers** un bouquet de fleurs

℮ *means use* **être** *to make the past tense.*

261

English French

a
b
c
d
e
f
g
h
i
j
k
l
m
n
o
p
q
r
s
t
u
v
w
x
y
z

2 a bunch of friends un groupe d'amis

bunk beds plural noun
les **lits superposés** *masc. plural*

burger noun
le **hamburger** *masc.*
burger and chips un hamburger frites

burglar noun
le **cambrioleur** *masc.*
a burglar alarm une sonnerie d'alarme

to **burn** verb
1 brûler
The cake's burning. Le gâteau brûle.
2 se brûler ⊘
Careful, don't burn yourself! Attention, ne te brûle pas!

burnt adjective
brûlé *masc.*, **brûlée** *fem.*

bus noun
1 le **bus** *masc.*
I go to school by bus. Je vais à l'école en bus.
a bus stop un arrêt de bus
2 a school bus un car scolaire
3 the bus station la gare routière

bush noun
le **buisson** *masc.*

business noun
les **affaires** *fem. plural*
a business trip un voyage d'affaires

busy adjective
1 occupé *masc.*, **occupée** *fem.*
Dad's very busy. Papa est très occupé.
2 a busy street une rue animée

but conjunction
mais
Max is small but strong. Max est petit mais fort.

• *See the centre section for verb tables.*

262

butcher noun
le **boucher** *masc.*, la **bouchère** *fem.*
Ian's a butcher. Ian est boucher.
Mum went to the butcher's. Maman est allée à la boucherie.

butter noun
le **beurre** *masc.*

butterfly noun
le **papillon** *masc.*

button noun
le **bouton** *masc.*

to **buy** verb
acheter
We're going to buy a new computer. On va acheter un nouvel ordinateur.
I bought some flowers. J'ai acheté des fleurs.

by preposition
1 par
a poster made by the children une affiche faite par les enfants
by mistake par erreur
by chance par hasard
2 de
a song by Paul McCartney une chanson de Paul McCartney
a book by Roald Dahl un livre de Roald Dahl
3 (*with car, bike, plane, etc.*) **en**
by train en train
by boat en bateau
4 (*near to*) **à côté de**
The supermarket is by the railway station. Le supermarché est à côté de la gare.
5 by myself tout seul *masc.*, toute seule *fem.*
I'm by myself. Je suis tout seul. (*boy speaking*) Je suis toute seule. (*girl speaking*)

bye exclamation
salut
Bye for now! À bientôt!

Cc

cab noun
le **taxi** *masc.*

cabbage noun
le **chou** *masc.* (plural les **choux**)
I don't like cabbage. Je n'aime pas le chou.

cable noun
le **câble** *masc.*
cable television la télévision par câble

cafe noun
le **café** *masc.*

cafeteria noun
la **cafétéria** *fem.*

cage noun
la **cage** *fem.*

cake noun
le **gâteau** *masc.* (plural les **gâteaux**)
Billy's eating some cake. Billy mange du gâteau.

calculator noun
la **calculatrice** *fem.*

calendar noun
le **calendrier** *masc.*

calf noun
le **veau** *masc.* (plural les **veaux**)

call noun
(*phone call*) un **appel** *masc.*
There was a call for you.
Quelqu'un t'a téléphoné.

to **call** verb
1 **appeler**
I'm going to call the doctor. Je vais appeler le médecin.
Call the police! Appelez la police!
to call the register faire l'appel
2 **to be called** s'appeler *ⓔ*
My sister's called Salma. Ma sœur s'appelle Salma.

ⓔ means use être to make the past tense.

What's it called in French?
Comment ça s'appelle en français?
3 **to call back** rappeler
I'll call back later. Je rappellerai plus tard.

calm adjective
calme *masc. & fem.*

to **calm down** verb
se calmer *ⓔ*
Calm down, Rachel! Calme-toi, Rachel!

camcorder noun
le **caméscope®** *masc.*

came verb SEE **come**

camel noun
le **chameau** *masc.* (plural les **chameaux**)

camera noun
1 (*for photos*) un **appareil photo** *masc.*
2 (*television or film camera*) la **caméra** *fem.*

camp noun
le **camp** *masc.*
a holiday camp une colonie de vacances

camping noun
le **camping** *masc.*
to go camping faire du camping
We're going camping in France.
Nous allons faire du camping en France.

campsite noun
le **terrain de camping** *masc.*

can noun
la **boîte** *fem.*
a can of beans une boîte de haricots
a can of Coke® une canette de coca

263

can → cardigan

can verb
1 **pouvoir**
I can help you. Je peux t'aider.
Can you close the door? Tu peux fermer la porte?
He can stay. Il peut rester.
2 (to know how to) **savoir**
Can you read? Tu sais lire?
We can't swim. Nous ne savons pas nager.
3 (sometimes not translated)
Can you hear? Vous entendez?
She can't speak French. Elle ne parle pas français.

Canada noun
le **Canada** masc.
We're going to Canada. Nous allons au Canada.

Canadian adjective
canadien masc., **canadienne** fem.
He's Canadian. Il est canadien.
She's Canadian. Elle est canadienne.

Canadian noun
le **Canadien** masc.,
la **Canadienne** fem.

canal noun
le **canal** masc. (plural les **canaux**)

canary noun
le **canari** masc.

to **cancel** verb
annuler
It's cancelled. C'est annulé.

cancer noun
le **cancer** masc.
She has cancer. Elle a un cancer.

candle noun
la **bougie** fem.

candyfloss noun
la **barbe à papa** fem.

LANGUAGE
Word for word it means 'dad's beard'!

cannot verb SEE **can**

canoe noun
le **canoë** masc.

can-opener noun
un **ouvre-boîtes** masc. (plural les **ouvre-boîtes**)

can't verb SEE **can**

canteen noun
la **cantine** fem.
We eat in the canteen. On mange à la cantine.

cap noun
la **casquette** fem.

capital noun
1 (capital city) la **capitale** fem.
Paris is the capital of France. Paris est la capitale de la France.
2 (capital letter) la **majuscule** fem.
in capitals en majuscules

captain noun
le **capitaine** masc.

caption noun
la **légende** fem.

to **capture** verb
capturer

car noun
la **voiture** fem.
by car en voiture
a car park un parking

caravan noun
la **caravane** fem.

card noun
la **carte** fem.
a birthday card une carte d'anniversaire
to play cards jouer aux cartes

cardboard noun
le **carton** masc.
a cardboard box un carton

cardigan noun
le **cardigan** masc.

• Use le and un for masculine words and la and une for feminine words.

264

care noun
le **soin** masc.
with care avec soin

to **care** verb
I don't care. Ça m'est égal.

careful adjective
prudent masc., **prudente** fem.
Martin is always careful. Martin
est toujours prudent.
Careful! Attention!
Be careful, there's a car! Fais
attention, il y a une voiture!

carefully adverb
1 (gently) **doucement**
Put down the glass carefully! Pose
le verre doucement!
2 (well) **bien**
Listen carefully! Écoutez bien!

caretaker noun
le **gardien** masc., la **gardienne** fem.

the **Caribbean** noun
les **Caraïbes** fem. plural

carnival noun
le **carnaval** masc. (plural les
carnavals)

carol noun
a Christmas carol un chant de Noël

carpenter noun
le **menuisier** masc.

carpet noun
la **moquette** fem.

carriage noun
(on a train) la **voiture** fem.

carrier bag noun
le **sac en plastique** masc.

carrot noun
la **carotte** fem.

> ⚷ **LANGUAGE**
> English = carrot
> French = carotte

to **carry** verb
1 **porter**

Can I carry your case? Je peux
porter ta valise?
2 **to carry on** continuer
Carry on reading! Continue à lire!

carton noun
(of milk or juice) la **brique** fem.

cartoon noun
1 (film) le **dessin animé** masc.
2 (drawings in a comic) la **bande
dessinée** fem.

case noun
(luggage) la **valise** fem.
Your case is heavy. Ta valise est
lourde.

cash noun
l'**argent** masc.
Do you have any cash? Tu as de
l'argent?

cashier noun
le **caissier** masc., la **caissière** fem.

cassava noun
le **manioc** masc.

cassette noun
la **cassette** fem.

castle noun
le **château** masc. (plural les
châteaux)

cat noun
le **chat** masc., la **chatte** fem.
We have a black cat. Nous avons
un chat noir.

to **catch** verb
1 **attraper**
Catch the ball! Attrape la balle!
He's going to catch a fish. Il va
attraper un poisson.
2 (a bus or train) **prendre**
I caught the bus. J'ai pris le bus.

cathedral noun
la **cathédrale** fem.

caterpillar noun
la **chenille** fem.

ℯ *means use **être** to make the past tense.*

Catholic adjective
catholique masc. & fem.

cauliflower noun
le **chou-fleur** masc. (plural les
choux-fleurs)

cave noun
la **grotte** fem.

CD noun
le **CD** masc. (plural les **CD**)
a CD player une platine laser
a CD-ROM un CD-ROM

ceiling noun
le **plafond** masc.

to **celebrate** verb
fêter
We're celebrating my birthday.
On fête mon anniversaire.

celery noun
le **céleri** masc.

cellar noun
la **cave** fem.

cello noun
le **violoncelle** masc.
Matt plays the cello. Matt joue du
violoncelle.

cemetery noun
le **cimetière** masc.

cent noun
le **centime** masc.
**There are a hundred cents in a
euro.** Il y a cent centimes dans un
euro.

centimetre noun
le **centimètre** masc.

centre noun
le **centre** masc.
a shopping centre un centre
commercial
a sports centre un centre sportif

century noun
le **siècle** masc.

in the twenty-first century au
vingt-et-unième siècle

cereal noun
les **céréales** fem. plural
Rajiv has cereal for breakfast.
Rajiv mange des céréales au petit
déjeuner.

> 🔑 **LANGUAGE**
> English = **cereal** is singular
> French = **les céréales** is plural

certain adjective
certain masc., **certaine** fem.

certainly adverb
certainement
Certainly not! Certainement pas!

certificate noun
le **certificat** masc.

chain noun
la **chaîne** fem.

chair noun
1 la **chaise** fem.
2 (armchair) le **fauteuil** masc.

chalk noun
la **craie** fem.

challenge noun
le **défi** masc.

champion noun
le **champion** masc.,
la **championne** fem.
Harry is the champion. Harry est le
champion.
Carol is the champion. Carol est la
championne.

championship noun
le **championnat** masc.

chance noun
1 (opportunity) une **occasion** fem.
I will have a chance to visit Paris.
Je vais avoir l'occasion de visiter
Paris.
2 **You're taking a chance.** Tu prends
un risque.

• Languages, nationalities, and religions do not take a capital letter in French.

to **change** verb

1 changer
They've changed the date. Ils ont changé la date.

2 changer de
I'm going to change my shoes. Je vais changer de chaussures.
Can we change places? On peut changer de place?
I've changed my mind. J'ai changé d'avis.

> ⚿ **LANGUAGE**
> You use **changer de** when you mean to change something for something else.

change noun

1 (money) la **monnaie** fem.
I don't have any change. Je n'ai pas de monnaie.

2 le **changement** masc.
We've made lots of changes. On a fait beaucoup de changements.

changing room noun

1 (for sports) le **vestiaire** masc.

2 (for trying on clothes in shops) la **cabine d'essayage** fem.

channel noun

(on TV) la **chaîne** fem.
Can you change the channel? Tu peux changer de chaîne?

Channel noun

1 la Manche fem.
the Channel Tunnel le tunnel sous la Manche

2 the Channel Islands les îles Anglo-Normandes

chapter noun

le **chapitre** masc.

character noun

1 (in a book, play, or film) le **personnage** masc.
the main character le personnage principal

2 (somebody's personality) le **caractère** masc.

℮ means use être to make the past tense.

charge noun

1 (money)
There's an extra charge. Il y a un supplément à payer.
There's no charge. C'est gratuit.

2 to be in charge of something être responsable de quelque chose
Mary is the person in charge. C'est Mary la responsable.

chart noun

(diagram) le **tableau** masc. (plural les **tableaux**)

to **chase** verb

pourchasser

to **chat** verb

bavarder

cheap adjective

bon marché masc. & fem.
These shoes are cheap. Ces chaussures sont bon marché.

> ⚿ **LANGUAGE**
> Bon marché is the same in masculine, feminine, and plural.

cheat noun

le **tricheur** masc., la **tricheuse** fem.
You're a cheat. Tu es un tricheur.

to **cheat** verb

tricher
He's cheating. Il triche.
Don't cheat! Ne triche pas!

to **check** verb

1 (to make sure) **vérifier**
Check the date. Vérifie la date.

2 (passports or tickets) **contrôler**

3 to check in (luggage at an airport) enregistrer

checkout noun

(at a supermarket) la **caisse** fem.
Dad's at the checkout. Papa est à la caisse.

cheek noun

la **joue** fem.

a
b
c
d
e
f
g
h
i
j
k
l
m
n
o
p
q
r
s
t
u
v
w
x
y
z

cheeky adjective
insolent masc., **insolente** fem.

to **cheer** verb
applaudir

cheerful adjective
gai masc., **gaie** fem.

cheerio exclamation
salut

cheers exclamation
(thanking somebody) **merci**

cheese noun
le **fromage** masc.
some cheese du fromage
a cheese sandwich un sandwich au fromage

chef noun
le **chef cuisinier** masc.

chemist noun
le **pharmacien** masc.,
la **pharmacienne** fem.
She's a chemist. Elle est pharmacienne.
David went to the chemist's. David est allé à la pharmacie.

cheque noun
le **chèque** masc.

cherry noun
la **cerise** fem.

chess noun
les **échecs** masc. plural
I like playing chess. J'aime bien jouer aux échecs.

chest noun
1 la **poitrine** fem.
2 **a chest of drawers** une commode

to **chew** verb
mâcher

chewing gum noun
le **chewing-gum** masc.

chick noun
le **poussin** masc.

chicken noun
le **poulet** masc.
Do you want some chicken?
Tu veux du poulet?

chickenpox noun
la **varicelle** fem.

child noun
un or une **enfant** masc. & fem.

childminder noun
la **nourrice** fem.

children plural noun
les **enfants** masc. & fem. plural

chilly adjective
froid masc., **froide** fem.
It's chilly today. Il fait un peu froid aujourd'hui.

chimney noun
la **cheminée** fem.

chin noun
le **menton** masc.

China noun
la **Chine** fem.

Chinese adjective
chinois masc., **chinoise** fem.
a Chinese man un Chinois
a Chinese woman une Chinoise

Chinese noun
1 (the language) le **chinois** masc.
2 **the Chinese** les Chinois masc. plural

chip noun
la **frite** fem.
burger and chips un hamburger frites

chocolate noun
le **chocolat** masc.
Do you like chocolate? Tu aimes le chocolat?
a chocolate cake un gâteau au chocolat

choice noun
le **choix** masc.

• The months of the year and days of the week do not take a capital letter in French.

I don't have a choice. Je n'ai pas le choix.

choir noun
la **chorale** *fem.*

to **choose** verb
choisir

chop noun
la **côtelette** *fem.*
a lamb chop une côtelette d'agneau

chopsticks plural noun
les **baguettes** *fem. plural*

Christian adjective
chrétien *masc.*, **chrétienne** *fem.*

Christmas noun
Noël *masc.*
at Christmas à Noël
Happy Christmas! Joyeux Noël!
a Christmas card une carte de Noël

🌍 **CULTURE**
French people don't usually send cards at Christmas but they send New Year cards **(les cartes de vœux)** in January instead.

Christmas Day le jour de Noël
Christmas dinner le repas de Noël
Christmas Eve la veille de Noël
a Christmas present un cadeau de Noël
a Christmas tree un sapin de Noël

church noun
une **église** *fem.*
to go to church aller ❷ à l'église

cider noun
le **cidre** *masc.*

cinema noun
le **cinéma** *masc.*
I'm going to the cinema. Je vais au cinéma.

circle noun
le **cercle** *masc.*
Draw a circle. Dessinez un cercle.

Sit down in a circle! Asseyez-vous en cercle!

circus noun
le **cirque** *masc.*

city noun
la **ville** *fem.*
the city of Paris la ville de Paris
We live in a city. Nous habitons dans une grande ville.
the city centre le centre-ville

to **clap** verb
1 (*when you like something*) **applaudir**
2 (*with the music*) **taper des mains**
Listen and clap! Écoutez et tapez des mains!

clarinet noun
la **clarinette** *fem.*
I play the clarinet. Je joue de la clarinette.

class noun
1 (*group*) la **classe** *fem.*
in my class dans ma classe
2 (*lesson*) le **cours** *masc.*
Do you like French classes? Tu aimes les cours de français?

classroom noun
la **salle de classe** *fem.*
a classroom assistant un aide-éducateur *masc.*, une aide-éducatrice *fem.*

clean adjective
propre *masc. & fem.*
My hands are clean. J'ai les mains propres.

to **clean** verb
nettoyer
Clean your room! Nettoie ta chambre!
to clean your teeth se brosser ❷ les dents

cleaning noun
le **ménage** *masc.*

clear adjective
clair *masc.*, **claire** *fem.*

❷ *means use* **être** *to make the past tense.*

to **clear** verb
1 **to clear the table** débarrasser la table
2 **to clear up** ranger
Clear up your toys! Range tes jouets!

clementine noun
la **clémentine** fem.

clever adjective
intelligent masc.,
intelligente fem.

to **click** verb
cliquer
Click on the picture. Cliquez sur l'image.

cliff noun
la **falaise** fem.

climate noun
le **climat** masc.

to **climb** verb
grimper

climbing noun
l'**escalade** fem.
a climbing frame une cage à poules
a climbing wall un mur d'escalade

cloakroom noun
1 (for coats) le **vestiaire** masc.
2 (toilet) les **toilettes** fem. plural

clock noun
1 (small) la **pendule** fem.
2 (big) une **horloge** fem.
the station clock l'horloge de la gare
3 (alarm clock) le **réveil** masc.

to **close** verb
fermer
Close the door! Ferme la porte!
The shops close at seven. Les magasins ferment à sept heures.

close adjective
1 (near) **proche** masc. & fem.

Where is the closest cafe? Où est le café le plus proche?
2 (nearby)
close to près de
The school is close to the station.
L'école est près de la gare.

closed adjective
fermé masc., **fermée** fem.
The supermarket is closed.
Le supermarché est fermé.

cloth noun
1 (for cleaning) le **chiffon** masc.
2 (material) le **tissu** masc.

clothes plural noun
les **vêtements** masc. plural

cloud noun
le **nuage** masc.

cloudy adjective
nuageux masc., **nuageuse** fem.
It's cloudy. Le temps est nuageux.

clown noun
le **clown** masc.

⚷ **LANGUAGE**
The French word **clown** is pronounced 'cloon'.

---

club noun
1 le **club** masc.
a football club un club de foot
2 **clubs** (in cards) le **trèfle**
the king of clubs le roi de trèfle

clue noun
1 un **indice** masc.
Give me a clue! Aide-moi!
2 (for a crossword puzzle) la **définition** fem.

clumsy adjective
maladroit masc., **maladroite** fem.

coach noun
le **car** masc.
by coach en car
a coach trip une excursion en car
the coach station la gare routière

• See the centre section for verb tables.

coal noun
le **charbon** masc.

coast noun
la **côte** fem.
on the south coast sur la côte sud

coat noun
le **manteau** masc. (plural les **manteaux**)

cobweb noun
la **toile d'araignée** fem.

cocoa noun
le **cacao** masc.

coconut noun
la **noix de coco** fem.

coffee noun
le **café** masc.
a black coffee un café
a white coffee un café au lait
a coffee table une table basse

coin noun
la **pièce de monnaie** fem.
a one pound coin une pièce d'une livre

Coke® noun
le **coca** masc.

cold adjective
1 **froid** masc., **froide** fem.
The water is cold. L'eau est froide.
2 **to be cold** avoir froid
I'm cold. J'ai froid.

LANGUAGE
English = to be cold   **I'm cold.**
French = **avoir** froid   **J'ai froid.**
---

3 (when talking about the weather) **It's cold.** Il fait froid.
The weather is very cold. Il fait très froid.

cold noun
1 (the cold weather) le **froid** masc.
I don't like the cold. Je n'aime pas le froid.
2 (illness) le **rhume** masc.
a bad cold un gros rhume

⊘ means use **être** to make the past tense.

I've got a cold. J'ai un rhume.

collar noun
le **col** masc.
my shirt collar le col de ma chemise

to **collect** verb
1 (to pick up) **ramasser**
Collect the exercise books, Tom! Ramasse les cahiers, Tom!
2 (to go and get) **passer prendre**
Can you collect me? Tu peux passer me prendre?
3 (as a hobby) **collectionner**
Do you collect stamps? Tu collectionnes les timbres?

collection noun
la **collection** fem.

college noun
le **lycée** masc.

colour noun
la **couleur** fem.
What colour is it? C'est de quelle couleur?

to **colour** verb
colorier
Colour in the pictures! Coloriez les images!
a colouring book un album à colorier

column noun
la **colonne** fem.

comb noun
le **peigne** masc.

to **comb** verb
to comb your hair se peigner ⊘

to **come** verb
1 **venir** ⊘
Come here! Viens ici!
I want to come with you. Je veux venir avec toi.
Miguel comes from Spain. Miguel vient d'Espagne.
2 **Come on!** Allez!
3 (to get to a place) **arriver** ⊘

a
b
c
d
e
f
g
h
i
j
k
l
m
n
o
p
q
r
s
t
u
v
w
x
y
z

English French

a
b
c
d
e
f
g
h
i
j
k
l
m
n
o
p
q
r
s
t
u
v
w
x
y
z

The bus is coming. Le bus arrive.
I'm coming! J'arrive!

to **come back** verb
revenir ⊘
Come back later. Reviens plus tard.

to **come down** verb
descendre ⊘
Can I come down and watch TV?
Je peux descendre regarder la télé?

to **come in** verb
entrer ⊘
Come in! Entrez!
She came into the kitchen. Elle est entrée dans la cuisine.

to **come out** verb
sortir ⊘
Can you come out? Tu peux sortir?

to **come up** verb
monter ⊘
Come up to bed! Monte te coucher!

comfortable adjective
(chair, shoes, etc.)
confortable masc. & fem.

> ⊶ **LANGUAGE**
> English = comfortable
> French = confortable

comic noun
la **bande dessinée** fem.
Annie loves comics. Annie adore les bandes dessinées.

comma noun
la **virgule** fem.
There is a comma after the noun.
Il y a une virgule après le nom.

comments plural noun
(by teacher on homework etc.)
les **remarques** fem. plural

common adjective
courant masc., **courante** fem.
This word isn't very common.
Ce mot n'est pas très courant.

company noun
la **compagnie** fem.
Can you keep me company?
Tu peux me tenir compagnie?

to **compare** verb
comparer

competition noun
1 le **concours** masc.
2 (for sports) la **compétition** fem.

competitor noun
le **concurrent** masc.,
la **concurrente** fem.

to **complain** verb
se plaindre ⊘
You complain about everything!
Tu te plains de tout!

complete adjective
1 (stop, change, etc.) **complet** masc.,
complète fem.
complete silence un silence complet
2 (finished) **fini** masc., **finie** fem.
It's not quite complete. Ce n'est pas tout à fait fini.

to **complete** verb
1 (to add something missing) **compléter**
Complete this sentence.
Complétez cette phrase.

completely adverb
complètement

complicated adjective
compliqué masc., **compliquée** fem.

comprehension noun
a comprehension test un exercice de compréhension masc.

comprehensive noun
a comprehensive school une école publique secondaire

computer noun
un **ordinateur** masc.
a computer game un jeu électronique

• Use **le** and **un** for masculine words and **la** and **une** for feminine words.

272

a computer program un programme informatique
a computer room une salle d'informatique

to **concentrate** verb
se concentrer ⊘
Concentrate, Liz! Concentre-toi, Liz!

concert noun
le concert *masc.*

conductor noun
(*of an orchestra*) le chef d'orchestre *masc.*

cone noun
le cornet *masc.*
an ice-cream cone un cornet de glace

confused adjective
I'm confused about what's going on. Je ne comprends pas ce qui se passe.

congratulations plural noun
les félicitations *fem. plural*

conjunction noun
la conjonction *fem.*

to **connect** verb
to connect to the Internet se connecter ⊘ à Internet

conservatory noun
la véranda *fem.*

to **consist** verb
to consist of something être composé de quelque chose

console noun
a games console une console de jeux vidéo

consonant noun
la consonne *fem.*

to **contact** verb
contacter

to **contain** verb
contenir

container noun
le récipient *masc.*

contest noun
le concours *masc.*

continent noun
1 le continent *masc.*
2 (*Europe*)
on the Continent en Europe continentale

continental adjective
a continental breakfast un petit déjeuner à la française

to **continue** verb
continuer
Continue reading! Continue à lire!

convenient adjective
(*tool, time, place, etc.*) commode *masc. & fem.*

conversation noun
la conversation *fem.*

to **cook** verb
1 faire la cuisine, cuisiner
I love cooking. J'adore faire la cuisine., J'adore cuisiner.
2 **to cook something** faire cuire quelque chose
Cook the vegetables for twenty minutes. Faites cuire les légumes pendant vingt minutes.

cook noun
le cuisinier *masc.*, la cuisinière *fem.*
Dad's a good cook. Papa est un bon cuisinier.

cookbook noun
le livre de cuisine *masc.*

cooked adjective
cuit *masc.*, cuite *fem.*
It isn't cooked. Ce n'est pas cuit.

cooker noun
la cuisinière *fem.*
a gas cooker une cuisinière à gaz

⊘ *means use* **être** *to make the past tense.*

a
b
c
d
e
f
g
h
i
j
k
l
m
n
o
p
q
r
s
t
u
v
w
x
y
z

cooking noun
la **cuisine** fem.
Who does the cooking? Qui fait la cuisine?

cool adjective
1 **frais** masc., **fraîche** fem.
The weather is cool. Il fait frais.
2 (good or great) **cool** masc. & fem.
She's really cool! Elle est vraiment cool!

copy noun
la **copie** fem.
to make a copy faire une copie

to **copy** verb
copier
Copy these sentences. Copiez ces phrases.

cork noun
(in a bottle) le **bouchon** masc.

corn noun
(wheat) le **blé** masc.

corner noun
le **coin** masc.
in the corner dans le coin

cornflakes plural noun
les **corn-flakes** masc. plural

Cornwall noun
la **Cornouailles** fem.

correct adjective
(answer, order, etc.) **bon** masc.,
bonne fem.
the correct answer la bonne réponse
That's correct. C'est ça.

to **correct** verb
corriger

correction noun
la **correction** fem.

correctly adverb
correctement

corridor noun
le **couloir** masc.

Corsica noun
la **Corse** fem.

to **cost** verb
coûter
How much does it cost? Ça coûte combien?
It costs quite a lot. Ça coûte assez cher.

costume noun
le **costume** masc.

cot noun
le **lit d'enfant** masc.

cottage noun
la **petite maison** fem.

cotton noun
le **coton** masc.
a cotton shirt une chemise en coton
cotton wool le coton hydrophile

⚷ **LANGUAGE**
English = cotton
French = coton

couch noun
le **canapé** masc.

cough noun
la **toux** fem.
cough medicine un sirop contre la toux
I have a cough. Je tousse.

to **cough** verb
tousser

could verb
pouvoir
Could I ... ? Je peux ... ?
Could I ask you a question? Je peux te poser une question?
Could you ... ? Tu peux ... ?
Could you open the window? Tu peux ouvrir la fenêtre?
I couldn't sleep. Je ne pouvais pas dormir.

to **count** verb
compter

• *Languages, nationalities, and religions do not take a capital letter in French.*

Count up to ten! Comptez jusqu'à dix!

counter noun
1 (*in a shop*) le **comptoir** *masc.*
2 (*for board games*) le **jeton** *masc.*

country noun
1 (*Britain, France, etc.*) le **pays** *masc.*
 a foreign country un pays étranger
2 (*not the town*) la **campagne** *fem.*
 I live in the country. J'habite à la campagne.

countryside noun
 la **campagne** *fem.*
 in the countryside à la campagne

couple noun
1 **a couple of** deux ou trois
2 (*two people*) le **couple** *masc.*

courgette noun
 la **courgette** *fem.*

course noun
1 (*lessons*) le **cours** *masc.*
 a French course un cours de français
2 (*part of a meal*) le **plat** *masc.*
 the main course le plat principal
3 **of course** bien sûr
 Can you help me? – Of course I can! Tu peux m'aider? – Bien sûr que oui!

court noun
 le **court** *masc.*
 a tennis court un court de tennis

cousin noun
 le **cousin** *masc.*, la **cousine** *fem.*

cover noun
 la **couverture** *fem.*

to **cover** verb
 couvrir
 You're covered in mud! Tu es couvert de boue!

cow noun
 la **vache** *fem.*

crab noun
 le **crabe** *masc.*

cracker noun
 (*biscuit*) le **cracker** *masc.*

> **CULTURE**
> Christmas crackers do not exist in France.

crash noun
 un **accident** *masc.*
 a car crash un accident de voiture
 a crash helmet un casque

crayon noun
 le **crayon gras** *masc.*

crazy adjective
 fou *masc.*, **folle** *fem.*

cream noun
 la **crème** *fem.*
 cream cake un gâteau à la crème

cress noun
 le **cresson** *masc.*

crew noun
 (*on a plane or ship*) un **équipage** *masc.*

cricket noun
 le **cricket** *masc.*
 Do you play cricket? Tu joues au cricket?
 a cricket bat une batte de cricket

> **CULTURE**
> French people do not play cricket.

crisps plural noun
 les **chips** *fem. plural*
 a bag of crisps un paquet de chips

to **criticize** verb
 critiquer

crocodile noun
 le **crocodile** *masc.*

to **cross** verb
1 **traverser**
 Be careful when you cross the road! Faites attention quand vous traversez la rue!
2 **to cross your legs** croiser les jambes

ⓔ means use être to make the past tense.

a
b
c
d
e
f
g
h
i
j
k
l
m
n
o
p
q
r
s
t
u
v
w
x
y
z

3 to cross something out barrer quelque chose

cross noun
la **croix** fem.

cross adjective
(angry) **fâché** masc., **fâchée** fem.
Are you cross? Tu es fâché?

crossing
1 (safe place to cross the road) le **passage pour piétons** masc.
2 (by boat) la **traversée** fem.
the crossing from Dover to Calais la traversée de Douvres à Calais

crossroads noun
le **carrefour** masc.
at the crossroads au carrefour

crossword noun
les **mots croisés** masc. plural
I like doing crosswords. J'aime faire des mots croisés.

crowd noun
la **foule** fem.

crowded adjective
It's crowded. Il y a du monde.
The shops are crowded. Il y a du monde dans les magasins.

crown noun
la **couronne** fem.

cruel adjective
cruel masc., **cruelle** fem.

crumbs plural noun
les **miettes** fem. plural

to **crush** verb
écraser

crust noun
la **croûte** fem.

to **cry** verb
pleurer
Don't cry! Ne pleure pas!

cub noun
(young lion, bear, etc.) le **petit** masc.

Cub noun
(Scout) le **louveteau** masc. (plural les **louveteaux**)
Are you a Cub? Tu es louveteau?

Cuba noun
Cuba fem.

cube noun
le **cube** masc.

cucumber noun
le **concombre** masc.

cup
1 la **tasse** fem.
a cup of tea une tasse de thé
2 (prize) la **coupe** fem.
the World Cup la Coupe du Monde

cupboard noun
le **placard** masc.

curious adjective
curieux masc., **curieuse** fem.

curly adjective
1 (with loose curls) **bouclé** masc., **bouclée** fem.
2 (with small, tight curls) **frisé** masc., **frisée** fem.

curriculum noun
le **programme** masc.

curry noun
le **curry** masc.
I like chicken curry. J'aime le curry de poulet.

cursor noun
le **curseur** masc.

curtain noun
le **rideau** masc. (plural les **rideaux**)

cushion noun
le **coussin** masc.

custard noun
la **crème anglaise** fem.

customer noun
le **client** masc., la **cliente** fem.

• The months of the year and days of the week do not take a capital letter in French.

to **cut** verb
1 **couper**
  I cut a piece of bread. J'ai coupé un morceau de pain.
2 **se couper** ⓔ
  Don't cut yourself! Ne te coupe pas!
3 **to cut something out** découper ⓔ quelque chose

cutlery noun
  les **couverts** *masc. plural*

Dd

dad noun
1 le **papa** *masc.*
  Where's dad? Où est papa?
2 le **père** *masc.*
  My dad is a carpenter. Mon père est menuisier.

🔑 **LANGUAGE**
You use **papa** when talking about your dad or your dad inside the family.

daddy noun
  le **papa** *masc.*

daily adjective
  (*newspaper, visit, etc.*) **quotidien** *masc.*, **quotidienne** *fem.*

damp adjective
  humide *masc. & fem.*

dance noun
  la **danse** *fem.*

to **dance** verb
  danser
  I love dancing. J'adore danser.
  I go to dancing classes. Je fais de la danse.

dancer noun
  le **danseur** *masc.*, la **danseuse** *fem.*

to **cycle** verb
  aller ⓔ **à vélo**
  Jenny cycles to school. Jenny va à l'école à vélo.
  to go cycling faire du vélo
  a cycle path une piste cyclable

cycling noun
  (*sport*) le **cyclisme** *masc.*

cyclist noun
  le or la **cycliste** *masc. & fem.*

Dane noun
  (*the person*) le **Danois** *masc.*, la **Danoise** *fem.*

danger noun
  le **danger** *masc.*
  We're in danger. Nous sommes en danger.

dangerous adjective
  dangereux *masc.*, **dangereuse** *fem.*

Danish adjective
  danois *masc.*, **danoise** *fem.*

Danish noun
  (*the language*) le **danois** *masc.*

to **dare** verb
  oser
  I dare you! Chiche!

dark adjective
1 (*room, street, etc.*) **sombre** *masc. & fem.*
  It's dark here. C'est sombre ici.
2 (*describing night-time*)
  It's dark. Il fait nuit.
  It's getting dark. Il commence à faire nuit.
3 (*describing colours*) **foncé** *masc.*, **foncée** *fem.*
  dark blue bleu foncé

ⓔ *means use* **être** *to make the past tense.*

English French

a
b
c
d
e
f
g
h
i
j
k
l
m
n
o
p
q
r
s
t
u
v
w
x
y
z

4 (*describing skin or hair*) **brun** *masc.*, **brune** *fem.*
I have dark hair. J'ai les cheveux bruns.

dark noun
le **noir** *masc.*
Are you afraid of the dark? Est-ce que tu as peur du noir?

darling noun
le **chéri** *masc.*, la **chérie** *fem.*

darts plural noun
les **fléchettes** *fem. plural*
to play darts jouer aux fléchettes

date noun
la **date** *fem.*
date of birth date de naissance
What's the date today? Quelle est la date d'aujourd'hui?

daughter noun
la **fille** *fem.*

day noun
1 le **jour** *masc.*
every day tous les jours
What day is it today? Quel jour sommes-nous?
2 la **journée** *fem.*
a day at the beach une journée sur la plage
3 the day before the wedding la veille du mariage
the day after my birthday le lendemain de mon anniversaire

> 🔑 **LANGUAGE**
> French has two words for day:
> **jour** and **journée**.
> **un jour** = a period of twenty-four hours
> **une journée** = from morning till evening (the daytime) when people are awake

daytime noun
la **journée** *fem.*
during the daytime pendant la journée

dead adjective
1 mort *masc.*, **morte** *fem.*

He's dead. Il est mort.
2 a dead end une impasse

deaf adjective
sourd *masc.*, **sourde** *fem.*

deal noun
a great deal of something beaucoup de quelque chose
We don't have a great deal of time. On n'a pas beaucoup de temps.

dear adjective
1 (*person*) **cher** *masc.*, **chère** *fem.*
Dear Anne ... Chère Anne ...
2 (*expensive*) **cher** *masc.*, **chère** *fem.*
That's too dear. C'est trop cher.

dear exclamation
Oh dear! Oh là là!

death noun
la **mort** *fem.*

December noun
décembre *masc.*
in December en décembre
the fifteenth of December le quinze décembre
I was born in December. Je suis né en décembre. (*boy speaking*) Je suis née en décembre. (*girl speaking*)

to **decide** verb
décider
I decided to stay. J'ai décidé de rester.
I can't decide. Je n'arrive pas à me décider.

decimal adjective
the decimal point la virgule

> 🌍 **CULTURE**
> In French maths you use a comma (**une virgule**) instead of a decimal point.

decision noun
la **décision** *fem.*
to make a decision prendre une décision

• *The months of the year and days of the week do not take a capital letter in French.*

deckchair noun
la **chaise longue** fem.

to **decorate** verb
1 (with pictures, balloons, etc.) **décorer**
I want to decorate the Christmas tree. Je veux décorer le sapin de Noël.
2 (to paint) **peindre**
We're going to decorate my bedroom. Nous allons peindre ma chambre.

decorations plural noun
les **décorations** fem. plural
Shall we put up the decorations? On met les décorations?

deep adjective
profond masc., **profonde** fem.
a deep hole un trou profond

deer noun
(red deer) le **cerf** masc.

to **defend** verb
défendre

definite
1 (exact) **précis** masc., **précise** fem.
a definite date une date précise
2 (certain) **sûr** masc., **sûre** fem.
It's not definite yet. Ce n'est pas encore sûr.

definitely adverb
sans aucun doute

degree noun
1 (of temperature) le **degré** masc.
It's twenty-five degrees. Il fait vingt-cinq degrés.
2 (university certificate) la **licence** fem.
a degree in French une licence de français

delay noun
le **retard** masc.

to **delay** verb
retarder
Our flight was delayed. Notre vol a été retardé.

@ means use être to make the past tense.

to **delete** verb
(a file, word, etc.) **effacer**

delicious adjective
délicieux masc., **délicieuse** fem.

to **deliver** verb
1 (milk, newspapers, etc.) **livrer**
2 **to deliver mail** distribuer le courrier

to **demand** verb
exiger

denim noun
le **jean** masc.
a denim shirt une chemise en jean

Denmark noun
le **Danemark** masc.

dentist noun
le or la **dentiste** masc. & fem.
I'm going to the dentist's. Je vais chez le dentiste.

department noun
1 (in a store) le **rayon** masc.
the toy department le rayon des jouets
2 **a department store** un grand magasin

departure noun
le **départ** masc.

to **depend** verb
dépendre
It all depends. Ça dépend.
It depends on the weather. Ça dépend du temps.

deposit noun
un **acompte** masc.

deputy head noun
le **directeur adjoint** masc.,
la **directrice adjointe** fem.

to **describe** verb
décrire
Describe your family. Décris ta famille.

description noun
la **description** *fem.*

desert noun
le **désert** *masc.*

to **deserve** verb
mériter

design noun
le **motif** *masc.*
a flower design un motif à fleurs

to **design** verb
1 (*to produce*) **créer**
2 (*to draw on paper*) **dessiner**

desk noun
1 (*for a pupil*) la **table** *fem.*
2 (*for a teacher, and in an office*) le **bureau** *masc.* (plural les **bureaux**)

dessert noun
le **dessert** *masc.*
What do you want for dessert?
Qu'est-ce que tu veux comme dessert?

destination noun
la **destination** *fem.*

to **destroy** verb
détruire

detail noun
le **détail** *masc.*
in detail en détail

detective noun
1 (*in the police*) un **inspecteur de police** *masc.*
2 (*private*) le **détective** *masc.*
a detective story un roman policier

detention noun
la **retenue** *fem.*
Jamie is in detention. Jamie est en retenue.

determined adjective
décidé *masc.*, **décidée** *fem.*
He's determined to do it. Il est décidé à le faire.

• *See the centre section for verb tables.*

to **develop** verb
développer

diabetes noun
le **diabetes** *masc.*

diagram noun
le **schéma** *masc.*

to **dial** verb
to dial a number faire un numéro

dialogue noun
le **dialogue** *masc.*

diamond noun
1 le **diamant** *masc.*
a diamond ring une bague de diamants
2 (*in cards*) le **carreau** *masc.*
the queen of diamonds la reine de carreau

diary noun
1 (*for writing appointments in*) un **agenda** *masc.*
2 (*for writing private things in*) le **journal** *masc.* (plural les **journaux**)
Do you keep a diary? Tu tiens un journal?

> **LANGUAGE**
> **Un journal** is also the French word for 'a newspaper'.

dice noun
le **dé** *masc.*
Throw the dice! Jette le dé!

dictionary noun
le **dictionnaire** *masc.*

> **LANGUAGE**
> English = dictionary
> French = dictionnaire

did verb SEE **do**

to **die** verb
mourir ⊘
My budgie died yesterday.
Ma perruche est morte hier.

diet noun
1 (food) l'**alimentation** fem.
I have a healthy diet. J'ai une alimentation saine.
2 (for getting thinner) le **régime** masc.
My sister's on a diet. Ma sœur est au régime.

difference noun
la **différence** fem.
What's the difference between the two? Quelle est la différence entre les deux?

different adjective
différent masc., **différente** fem.
I'm very different from my brother. Je suis très différent de mon frère.

difficult adjective
difficile masc. & fem.
This question is difficult. Cette question est difficile.

difficulty noun
la **difficulté** fem.

to **dig** verb
creuser
My dog likes digging holes. Mon chien aime creuser des trous.

digital adjective
(camera, television) **numérique** masc. & fem.

dining room noun
la **salle à manger** fem. (plural les **salles à manger**)

dinner noun
1 (in the evening) le **dîner** masc.
to have dinner dîner
It's dinner time. C'est l'heure du dîner.
2 (at midday) le **déjeuner** masc.
to have dinner déjeuner
It's dinner time. C'est l'heure du déjeuner.
Do you have school dinners? Est-ce que tu manges à la cantine?

a dinner lady une femme de service

dinosaur noun
le **dinosaure** masc.

direct adjective
direct masc., **directe** fem.

direction noun
la **direction** fem.
Are we going in the right direction? On va dans la bonne direction?
Ask for directions to the station. Demandez le chemin pour aller à la gare.

dirty adjective
sale masc. & fem.
a dirty shirt une chemise sale

disabled adjective
handicapé masc., **handicapée** fem.

to **disagree** verb
I disagree. Je ne suis pas d'accord.

to **disappear** verb
disparaître
She has disappeared. Elle a disparu.

disappointed adjective
déçu masc., **déçue** fem.
Gerry is disappointed. Gerry est déçu.

disaster noun
le **désastre** masc.

disc-jockey noun
le **disc-jockey** masc.

disco noun
1 (party where you dance) la **soirée disco** fem.
2 (place where you dance) la **discothèque** fem.

to **discover** verb
découvrir

a
b
c
d
e
f
g
h
i
j
k
l
m
n
o
p
q
r
s
t
u
v
w
x
y
z

❷ means use **être** to make the past tense.

281

English French

a
b
c
d
e
f
g
h
i
j
k
l
m
n
o
p
q
r
s
t
u
v
w
x
y
z

discovery noun
la **découverte** *fem.*

to **discuss** verb
to discuss something discuter de quelque chose

disease noun
la **maladie** *fem.*

disguised adjective
déguisé *masc.*, **déguisée** *fem.*
disguised as a fireman déguisé en pompier

disgusting adjective
dégoûtant *masc.*,
dégoûtante *fem.*

dish noun
le **plat** *masc.*
My favourite dish is curry. Mon plat préféré c'est le curry.
Can I do the dishes? Je peux faire la vaisselle?

dishwasher noun
le **lave-vaisselle** *masc.* (plural les **lave-vaisselle**)

disk noun
le **disque** *masc.*
on disk sur disque

to **dislike** verb
ne pas aimer

distance noun
la **distance** *fem.*
the distance between London and Paris la distance entre Londres et Paris
in the distance au loin

district noun
(*in a town*) le **quartier** *masc.*

to **disturb** verb
déranger
Sorry to disturb you! Excusez-moi de vous déranger!

to **dive** verb
plonger

Steve dived into the swimming pool. Steve a plongé dans la piscine.
to go diving faire de la plongée

to **divide** verb
diviser
Ten divided by two is five. Dix divisé par deux égale cinq.
Divide the cake into six. Divise le gâteau en six.

divorced adjective
divorcé *masc.*, **divorcée** *fem.*
His parents are divorced. Ses parents sont divorcés.

DIY noun
le **bricolage** *masc.*

dizzy adjective
I feel dizzy. J'ai la tête qui tourne.

DJ noun
le **disc-jockey** *masc.*

to **do** verb
1 **faire**
I do my homework. Je fais mes devoirs.
What is dad doing? Que fait papa?
What has she done with my pen? Qu'est-ce qu'elle a fait de mon stylo?
What did you do to the dog? Qu'est-ce que tu as fait au chien?
2 (*when making questions*)
Do you want a glass of water? Est-ce que tu veux un verre d'eau?
How much does it cost? Combien est-ce que ça coûte?
3 (*in negative sentences translate using* ne ... pas)
I don't know. Je ne sais pas.
Lucy doesn't like tomatoes. Lucy n'aime pas les tomates.
4 (*to translate questions such as* **doesn't it?** *or* **don't you?**) **She likes pasta, doesn't she?** Elle aime les pâtes, non?

to **do up** verb
1 (*clothes with buttons*) **boutonner**

• *Use* le *and* un *for masculine words and* la *and* une *for feminine words.*

Do up your jacket! Boutonne ta veste!

2 (*clothes with zips*) **fermer**
I can't do up my anorak. Je n'arrive pas à fermer mon anorak.

3 (*shoes with laces*) **lacer**
You haven't done up your shoes. Tu n'as pas lacé tes chaussures.

doctor noun
le **médecin** *masc.*
She's a doctor. Elle est médecin.
I'm going to the doctor's. Je vais chez le médecin.

> 🔑 **LANGUAGE**
> When you are speaking to the doctor, say **Docteur**, for example: 'Yes, doctor' is **Oui, docteur.**

dog noun
le **chien** *masc.*
I've got a dog. J'ai un chien.

doll noun
la **poupée** *fem.*
a doll's house une maison de poupée

dollar noun
le **dollar** *masc.*

dolphin noun
le **dauphin** *masc.*

Dominican Republic noun
la **République dominicaine** *fem.*

dominoes plural noun
les **dominos** *masc. plural*
We are playing dominoes. On joue aux dominos.

done verb SEE **do**

donkey noun
un **âne** *masc.*

door noun
la **porte** *fem.*
Shut the door, please! Ferme la porte s'il te plaît!

doorbell noun
la **sonnette** *fem.*

dormitory noun
le **dortoir** *masc.*

dot noun
le **point** *masc.*

double adjective
double *masc. & fem.*
a double bed un grand lit
a double room une chambre pour deux personnes

double-decker bus noun
un **autobus à impériale** *masc.*

doubt noun
le **doute** *masc.*
There's no doubt about it. Il n'y a aucun doute.

to **doubt** verb
I doubt it. J'en doute.

dough noun
la **pâte** *fem.*

doughnut noun
le **beignet** *masc.*

Dover noun
Douvres

down adverb
en bas
Down there! Là-bas!

> 🔑 **LANGUAGE**
> 'Down' is most often part of a verb such as 'to go down' (**descendre**) or 'to sit down' (**s'asseoir**), and need not be translated separately.

down preposition
en bas de
I'll wait for you down the street. Je t'attends en bas de la rue.

down adjective
(*not working*) **en panne**
The computers are down. Les ordinateurs sont en panne.

❷ *means use* **être** *to make the past tense.*

to download verb
télécharger

downstairs adverb
en bas
He's downstairs in the kitchen.
Il est en bas dans la cuisine.
Come downstairs! Descends!

dozen noun
la **douzaine** fem.
a dozen eggs une douzaine d'œufs

dragon noun
le **dragon** masc.

drama noun
le **théâtre** masc.
I belong to a drama club. Je suis
membre d'un club de théâtre.

draughts plural noun
les **dames** fem. plural
We are playing draughts. Nous
jouons aux dames.

to draw verb
1 **dessiner**
Draw a cat. Dessinez un chat.
You draw well. Tu dessines bien.
to draw a picture faire un dessin
to draw a line tracer une ligne
2 **to draw the curtains** tirer les
rideaux
3 (in a match) **faire match nul**
We drew two all. Nous avons fait
match nul deux à deux.

draw noun
le **match nul** masc.
It's a draw! Match nul!

drawer noun
le **tiroir** masc.

drawing noun
le **dessin** masc.

drawing pin noun
la **punaise** fem.

dreadful adjective
affreux masc., **affreuse** fem.

dream noun
le **rêve** masc.
I had a funny dream. J'ai fait un
drôle de rêve.

to dream verb
rêver
I dreamt about you! J'ai rêvé de
toi!

dress noun
la **robe** fem.
She's wearing a pretty dress.
Elle porte une jolie robe.

to dress verb
1 **s'habiller**
She's getting dressed. Elle
s'habille.
2 **to dress up** se déguiser
I'm going to dress up as a witch.
Je vais me déguiser en sorcière.

dressed adjective
1 **habillé** masc., **habillée** fem.
Are you dressed? Tu es habillé?
Nicole is dressed in blue. Nicole est
habillée de bleu.
2 **to get dressed** s'habiller
I get dressed at eight o'clock.
Je m'habille à huit heures.

dressing gown noun
la **robe de chambre** fem.

drink noun
la **boisson** fem.
a hot drink une boisson chaude
a cold drink une boisson fraîche

to drink verb
boire
I'd like something to drink.
Je voudrais quelque chose à boire.

drive noun
1 le **tour en voiture** masc.
Can we go for a drive? On peut
faire un tour en voiture?
2 (place in front of the house) une **allée** fem.
Park your car in the drive. Garez
votre voiture dans l'allée.

• Languages, nationalities, and religions do not take a capital letter in French.

284

to drive verb
1 **conduire**
 to drive a car conduire une voiture
 She knows how to drive. Elle sait conduire.
2 **rouler**
 In France they drive on the right. En France on roule à droite.
3 (*to go somewhere by car*) **aller ⊙ en voiture**
 We drove to Scotland. Nous sommes allés en Écosse en voiture.

driver noun
1 (*of a car or bus*) le **conducteur** *masc.*, la **conductrice** *fem.*
 a bus driver un conducteur de bus
2 (*of a bus, truck, or taxi*) le **chauffeur** *masc.*
 a taxi driver un chauffeur de taxi

driving licence noun
 le **permis de conduire** *masc.*

driving school noun
 une **auto-école** *fem.*

drop noun
 la **goutte** *fem.*
 a little drop of milk une petite goutte de lait

to drop verb
 laisser tomber
 Sorry, I dropped a glass. Désolé, j'ai laissé tomber un verre.

to drown verb
 se noyer ⊙

drum noun
1 le **tambour** *masc.*
 She's playing the drum. Elle joue du tambour.
2 **the drums** la batterie
 I play the drums. Je joue de la batterie.

dry adjective
 sec *masc.*, **sèche** *fem.*
 Your jeans are not dry yet. Ton jean n'est pas encore sec.

to dry verb
1 **sécher**
 She's drying her hair. Elle se sèche les cheveux.
2 (*to wipe*) **essuyer**
 Tim is drying the dishes. Tim essuie la vaisselle.

duck noun
 le **canard** *masc.*

due adjective
 The plane is due at ten o'clock. L'avion est attendu à dix heures.

dull adjective
1 (*boring*) **ennuyeux** *masc.*, **ennuyeuse** *fem.*
2 (*weather*)
 It's dull today. Le temps est couvert aujourd'hui.

dumb adjective
 (*stupid*) **idiot** *masc.*, **idiote** *fem.*

dummy noun
 (*for baby*) la **tétine** *fem.*

dump noun
 What a dump! (*room, hotel, etc.*) C'est vraiment minable!

dungarees plural noun
 la **salopette** *fem.*

during preposition
 pendant
 during the holidays pendant les vacances

dust noun
 la **poussière** *fem.*

dustbin noun
 la **poubelle** *fem.*

Dutch adjective
 hollandais *masc.*, **hollandaise** *fem.*
 He's Dutch. Il est hollandais.

Dutch noun
1 (*the language*) le **hollandais** *masc.*
2 **the Dutch** les Hollandais *masc. plural*

⊙ *means use* **être** *to make the past tense.*

a
b
c
d
e
f
g
h
i
j
k
l
m
n
o
p
q
r
s
t
u
v
w
x
y
z

duvet noun
la **couette** fem.

DVD noun
le **DVD** masc. (plural les **DVD**)
a DVD player un lecteur DVD

dwarf noun
le **nain** masc., la **naine** fem.

dyslexic adjective
dyslexique masc. & fem.
I'm dyslexic. Je suis dyslexique.

Ee

each adjective
chaque masc. & fem.
That happens each time. Cela
arrive chaque fois.

each pronoun
chacun masc., **chacune** fem.
The pupils have a computer each.
Les élèves ont chacun un
ordinateur.

each other pronoun
They love each other. Ils s'aiment.
We hate each other! Nous nous
détestons!
Do you know each other? Vous
vous connaissez?

eagle noun
un **aigle** masc.

ear noun
une **oreille** fem.

earache noun
I have earache. J'ai mal aux
oreilles.

early adverb
1 tôt
I get up early. Je me lève tôt.
It's too early to go to bed. Il est
trop tôt pour se coucher.
2 en avance
You're early. Tu es en avance.
She arrived ten minutes early. Elle
est arrivée dix minutes en avance.

to **earn** verb
gagner

**Marie earns a hundred euros a
week.** Marie gagne cent euros par
semaine.

earring noun
la **boucle d'oreille** fem.

earth noun
la **terre** fem.

earthquake noun
le **tremblement de terre** masc.

easily adverb
facilement

east noun
l'**est** masc.
We live in the east of England.
Nous vivons dans l'est de
l'Angleterre.
to the east of London à l'est de
Londres

east adjective
est masc. & fem.
the east coast la côte est

Easter noun
Pâques
at Easter à Pâques
Happy Easter! Joyeuses Pâques!
an Easter egg un œuf de Pâques
during the Easter holidays
pendant les vacances de Pâques

easy adjective
facile masc. & fem.
It's easy to do. C'est facile à faire.

to **eat** verb
manger

• The months of the year and days of the week do not take a capital letter in French.

I eat an apple a day. Je mange une pomme par jour.
What do you want to eat? Qu'est-ce que tu veux manger?

edge noun
le **bord** masc.

Edinburgh noun
Édimbourg

education noun
l'**éducation** fem.

educational adjective
(game, toy, etc.) **éducatif** masc., **éducative** fem.

effort noun
un **effort** masc.
Make an effort! Fais un effort!

e.g. abbreviation
par ex

egg noun
un **œuf** masc.
a boiled egg un œuf à la coque
a hard-boiled egg un œuf dur
scrambled eggs des œufs brouillés
a fried egg un œuf sur le plat
a dozen eggs une douzaine d'œufs

eggcup noun
le **coquetier** masc.

Egypt noun
l'**Égypte** fem.

Eiffel Tower noun
la **tour Eiffel** fem.

eight number
huit
eight girls huit filles
Alistair is eight years old. Alistair a huit ans.
We're leaving at eight. Nous partons à huit heures.

eighteen number
dix-huit
My sister is eighteen. Ma sœur a dix-huit ans.

eighth adjective
huitième masc. & fem.
on the eighth floor au huitième étage
the eighth of May le huit mai

eighty number
quatre-vingts
eighty five quatre-vingt-cinq

Éire noun
la **République d'Irlande** fem.

either adverb
non plus
I don't like sweets and I don't like chocolate either. Je n'aime pas les bonbons et le chocolat non plus.
You're not coming? – Then I'm not either! Tu ne viens pas? – Alors moi non plus!

either pronoun
l'un ou l'autre masc., **l'une ou l'autre** fem.
Choose either! Choisis l'un ou l'autre!
I don't want either of them. Je ne veux ni l'un ni l'autre.

either conjunction
either ... or ou ... ou ...
either Friday or Sunday ou vendredi ou dimanche

elastic band noun
un **élastique** masc.

elbow noun
le **coude** masc.

elderly noun
les **personnes âgées** fem. plural

eldest adjective
aîné masc., **aînée** fem.
my eldest brother mon frère aîné

electric adjective
électrique masc. & fem.

electrician noun
un **électricien** masc., une **électricienne** fem.

a
b
c
d
e
f
g
h
i
j
k
l
m
n
o
p
q
r
s
t
u
v
w
x
y
z

ⓔ *means use* **être** *to make the past tense.*

a
b
c
d
e
f
g
h
i
j
k
l
m
n
o
p
q
r
s
t
u
v
w
x
y
z

electricity noun
l'**électricité** fem.

electronic adjective
électronique masc. & fem.

elephant noun
un **éléphant** masc.

eleven number
onze
eleven players onze joueurs
Jason goes to bed at eleven. Jason se couche à onze heures.
My brother is eleven. Mon frère a onze ans.

eleventh adjective
onzième masc. & fem.
on the eleventh floor au onzième étage
the eleventh of December le onze décembre

else adverb
d'autre
somebody else quelqu'un d'autre
nobody else personne d'autre
nothing else rien d'autre
something else autre chose
I want something else. Je veux autre chose.
everybody else tous les autres
somewhere else ailleurs
I will look somewhere else. Je vais chercher ailleurs.

email noun
1 (*email message*) un **email** masc.
Send me an email. Envoie-moi un email.
an email address une adresse électronique
2 (*way of sending messages*) **le courrier électronique** masc.
by email par courrier électronique

to **email** verb
to email somebody envoyer un email à quelqu'un

embarrassed adjective
gêné masc., **gênée** fem.

embarrassing adjective
gênant masc., **gênante** fem.

emergency noun
l'**urgence** fem.
in an emergency en cas d'urgence
emergency exit sortie de secours

empty adjective
vide masc. & fem.
The classroom is empty. La salle de classe est vide.

to **encourage** verb
encourager

end noun
1 (*the last part*) la **fin** fem.
the end of the book la fin du livre
We're going on holiday at the end of July. On part en vacances fin juillet.
2 (*of a place, table, finger, etc.*) le **bout** masc.
at the end of the garden au bout du jardin

to **end** verb
finir
The film ends in five minutes. Le film finit dans cinq minutes.

ending noun
(*of a book, film, or play*) la **fin** fem.

enemy noun
un **ennemi** masc., une **ennemie** fem.

🔑 **LANGUAGE**
English = enemy
French = ennemi

energy noun
l'**énergie** fem.

engaged adjective
1 (*going to be married*) **fiancé** masc., **fiancée** fem.
My big brother is engaged. Mon grand frère est fiancé.
2 (*phone or toilet*) **occupé** masc., **occupée** fem.

• *See the centre section for verb tables.*

engagement noun
les **fiançailles** *fem. plural*
an engagement ring une bague de
fiançailles

engine noun
1 (*in a car*) le **moteur** *masc.*
2 (*of a train*) la **locomotive** *fem.*

engineer noun
(*who designs things*) un **ingénieur** *masc.*

England noun
l'**Angleterre** *fem.*
I live in England. J'habite en
Angleterre.
When are you coming to England?
Quand est-ce que tu viens en
Angleterre?

English adjective
anglais *masc.*, **anglaise** *fem.*
the English countryside
la campagne anglaise
He's English. Il est anglais.
She's English. Elle est anglaise.
We love English lessons. Nous
adorons les cours d'anglais.

English noun
1 (*the language*) l'**anglais** *masc.*
Do you speak English? Est-ce que
vous parlez anglais?
2 **the English** les Anglais *masc. plural*

Englishman noun
un **Anglais** *masc.*

Englishwoman noun
une **Anglaise** *fem.*

to **enjoy** verb
1 **aimer**
I enjoy playing the guitar. J'aime
jouer de la guitare.
2 **to enjoy yourself** s'amuser ⊘
I enjoyed myself. Je me suis bien
amusé. (*boy speaking*) Je me suis bien
amusée. (*girl speaking*)

⊘ *means use être to make the past tense.*

enjoyable adjective
agréable *masc. & fem.*

enormous adjective
énorme *masc. & fem.*

enough adverb & pronoun
assez
I've had enough! J'en ai assez!
That's enough. Ça suffit.
Have you had enough to eat?
Est-ce que tu as assez mangé?
**My brother is big enough to go out
by himself.** Mon frère est assez
grand pour sortir tout seul.

enough adjective
assez de
I have enough time. J'ai assez de
temps.

🗝 **LANGUAGE**
English = **enough** + noun
French = **assez de** + noun

to **enter** verb
1 **entrer** ⊘ **dans**
to enter the castle entrer dans le
château
2 **s'inscrire** ⊘ **pour**
Are you entering the race? Tu vas
t'inscrire pour la course?

entrance noun
l'**entrée** *fem.*
Wait for me at the entrance.
Attends-moi à l'entrée.
an entrance exam un examen
d'entrée

entry noun
'**No entry**' (*on a door*) 'Défense
d'entrer'

envelope noun
une **enveloppe** *fem.*

🗝 **LANGUAGE**
English = envelope
French = enveloppe

episode noun
un **épisode** *masc.*

a
b
c
d
e
f
g
h
i
j
k
l
m
n
o
p
q
r
s
t
u
v
w
x
y
z

equal adjective
égal masc., **égale** fem.
an equal number of boys and girls
un nombre égal de garçons et de
filles

to **equal** verb
égaler
Four times five equals twenty.
Quatre fois cinq égalent vingt.

to **equalize** verb
égaliser

equator noun
l'**équateur** masc.

error noun
une **erreur** fem.

escalator noun
un **escalier roulant** masc.

to **escape** verb
s'échapper @
The hamster has escaped.
Le hamster s'est échappé.

especially adverb
(most of all) **surtout**
**I like Paris, especially the Eiffel
Tower.** J'aime Paris, surtout la tour
Eiffel.

essay noun
la **rédaction** fem.

estate noun
(housing estate) la **cité** fem.
We live on an estate. Nous
habitons dans une cité.

EU noun
l'**UE** fem.

LANGUAGE
l'UE = l'Union européenne

euro noun
un **euro** masc.
It costs ten euros. Ça coûte dix
euros.

Europe noun
l'**Europe** fem.

European adjective
européen masc., **européenne** fem.
the European Union l'Union
européenne fem.

European noun
un **Européen** masc.,
une **Européenne** fem.

Eve noun
Christmas Eve la veille de Noël
New Year's Eve la Saint-Sylvestre

even adverb
1 **même**
**We're all going to the cinema,
even Katy.** Nous allons tous au
cinéma, même Katy.
2 **encore**
It's even better. C'est encore
mieux.

LANGUAGE
Use **encore** when 'even' is followed by a
word such as 'bigger' or 'better', or by
'more' or 'less'.

even adjective
an even number un nombre pair

evening noun
1 le **soir** masc.
this evening ce soir
tomorrow evening demain soir
yesterday evening hier soir
In the evening we watch TV. Le
soir, nous regardons la télé.
at eight o'clock in the evening à
huit heures du soir
Good evening! Bonsoir!
2 la **soirée** fem.
We watched TV all evening. On a
regardé la télé toute la soirée.

LANGUAGE
French has two words for 'evening': **soir**
and **soirée**.
le soir = the normal period between
afternoon and night
la soirée = the whole time from the
afternoon till you go to bed

• Use **le** and **un** for masculine words and **la** and **une** for feminine words.

event noun
un **événement** *masc.*

ever adverb
1 **jamais**
   Have you ever seen a ghost? As-tu jamais vu un fantôme?
   I hardly ever go by bus. Je ne prends presque jamais le bus.
2 **for ever** pour toujours
3 **ever since** depuis
   It's been raining ever since we arrived. Il pleut depuis que nous sommes arrivés.

every adjective
1 **tous** *masc. plural*,
   toutes *fem. plural*
   every day tous les jours
   every week toutes les semaines
   every Saturday tous les samedis
2 **chaque** *masc. & fem.*
   every time I see you chaque fois que je te vois

everybody pronoun
   tout le monde
   Is everybody ready? Tout le monde est prêt?

everyone pronoun
   tout le monde
   Say hello to everyone. Dis bonjour à tout le monde.

everything pronoun
   tout
   Everything is ready. Tout est prêt.
   Everything is fine. Tout va bien.

everywhere adverb
   partout
   He follows me everywhere. Il me suit partout.

evil adjective
   mauvais *masc.*, **mauvaise** *fem.*

exact adjective
   exact *masc.*, **exacte** *fem.*

⊘ *means use être to make the past tense.*

exactly adverb
   exactement
   These two pictures are exactly the same. Ces deux images sont exactement les mêmes.

to **exaggerate** verb
   exagérer

exam noun
   un **examen** *masc.*
   a French exam un examen de français

example noun
   un **exemple** *masc.*
   for example par exemple

> **LANGUAGE**
> English = example
> French = exemple

excellent adjective
   excellent *masc.*, **excellente** *fem.*

except preposition
   sauf
   Everybody's coming except Sara. Tout le monde vient sauf Sara.

to **exchange** verb
   échanger
   Can I exchange this green T-shirt for a blue one? Je peux échanger ce tee-shirt vert contre un bleu?

excited adjective
   excité *masc.*, **excitée** *fem.*

exciting adjective
   passionnant *masc.*,
   passionnante *fem.*
   an exciting match un match passionnant

exclamation mark noun
   le **point d'exclamation** *masc.*

to **excuse** verb
   Excuse me! Excusez-moi!

exercise noun
un **exercice** masc.
a French exercise un exercice de français
You don't get enough exercise. Tu ne fais pas assez d'exercice.
an exercise book un cahier

🔑 **LANGUAGE**
English = exercise
French = exercice

exhibition noun
une **exposition** fem.

to **exist** verb
exister

exit noun
la **sortie** fem.

to **expect** verb
1 (to wait for) **attendre**
I'm expecting a letter. J'attends une lettre.
She's expecting a baby. Elle attend un bébé.
2 (to suppose) **imaginer**
I expect you want an ice cream! J'imagine que tu veux une glace!

expensive adjective
cher masc., **chère** fem.
It's expensive. C'est cher.

experience noun
l'**expérience** fem.

experiment noun
une **expérience** fem.

expert noun
le or la **spécialiste** masc. & fem.

to **explain** verb
expliquer
Explain to me how it works.
Explique-moi comment ça marche.

explanation noun
une **explication** fem.

to **explode** verb
exploser

to **explore** verb
explorer

explosion noun
une **explosion** fem.

expression noun
(sentence, look) une **expression** fem.

extension noun
(to a house) un **agrandissement** masc.

extra adjective
supplémentaire masc. & fem.
extra homework des devoirs supplémentaires

extra adverb
(in a restaurant etc.) **to pay extra** payer un supplément
The croissants are extra. Il y a un supplément pour les croissants.

extraordinary adjective masc. & fem.
extraordinaire

extraterrestrial noun
un or une **extra-terrestre** masc. & fem.

extremely adverb
extrêmement

eye noun
un **œil** masc. (plural les **yeux**)
I have blue eyes. J'ai les yeux bleus.

eyebrow noun
le **sourcil** masc.

eyelid noun
la **paupière** fem.

eyesight noun
la **vue** fem.

• Languages, nationalities, and religions do not take a capital letter in French.

Ff

fabulous adjective
formidable masc. & fem.

face noun
le **visage** masc.

to **face** verb
Face your partner! Mets-toi en face de ton partenaire!

fact noun
le **fait** masc.
in fact en fait

factory noun
une **usine** fem.
My mother works in a factory. Ma mère travaille dans une usine.

to **fail** verb
rater
My sister failed her driving test. Ma sœur a raté son permis.

to **faint** verb
s'évanouir *ⓔ*
Lisa fainted. Lisa s'est évanouie.

fair adjective
1 (*right*) **juste** masc. & fem.
It's not fair! Ce n'est pas juste!
2 (*hair*) **blond** masc., **blonde** fem.
He has fair hair. Il a les cheveux blonds.

fair noun
la **foire** fem.
to go to the fair aller à la foire.

fair-haired adjective
blond masc., **blonde** fem.
Amy is fair-haired. Amy est blonde.

fairly adverb
assez
That's fairly obvious. C'est assez évident.

fairy noun
la **fée** fem.
a fairy tale un conte de fées

to **fall** verb
tomber
I fell over. Je suis tombé. (*boy speaking*) Je suis tombée. (*girl speaking*)

false adjective
faux masc., **fausse** fem.
True or false? Vrai ou faux?

familiar adjective
(*face, name, etc.*) **familier** masc., **familière** fem.

family noun
la **famille** fem.
the Taylor family la famille Taylor
a big family une famille nombreuse

famous adjective
célèbre masc. & fem.

fan noun
1 (*of a person*) le or la **fan** masc. & fem.
I'm a Harry Potter fan. Je suis un fan de Harry Potter.
2 (*of a team*) le or la **supporter** masc. & fem.
a Manchester United fan
un supporter de Manchester United
3 (*machine for keeping cool*)
le **ventilateur** masc.

to **fancy** verb
avoir envie de
Do you fancy an ice cream? Tu as envie d'une glace?

fancy dress noun
le **déguisement** masc.
She's in fancy dress. Elle est déguisée.

fantastic adjective
fantastique masc. & fem.

*ⓔ means use **être** to make the past tense.*

a
b
c
d
e
f
g
h
i
j
k
l
m
n
o
p
q
r
s
t
u
v
w
x
y
z

far adverb
1 loin
Is it far? C'est loin?
It's not far. Ce n'est pas loin.
far away très loin
How far is it from Glasgow to Edinburgh? Glasgow est à quelle distance d'Édimbourg?
2 as far as jusqu'à
Go as far as the post office and wait for me! Va jusqu'à la poste et attends-moi là!
3 (*much*) **beaucoup**
That's far too much cake! Ça fait beaucoup trop de gâteau!

Far East noun
l'**Extrême-Orient** *masc.*

farm noun
la **ferme** *fem.*
on the farm à la ferme

farmer noun
un **agriculteur** *masc.*,
une **agricultrice** *fem.*

fashion noun
la **mode** *fem.*
a fashion show un défilé de mode

fashion designer noun
le or la **styliste** *masc. & fem.*

fashionable adjective
à la mode
These shoes are fashionable.
Ces chaussures sont à la mode.

fast adverb
1 vite
You're speaking too fast. Tu parles trop vite.
Go faster! Allez plus vite!
2 He's fast asleep. Il dort.

fast adjective
rapide
a fast train un train rapide

fat adjective
gros *masc.*, **grosse** *fem.*

My cat is very fat. Mon chat est très gros.

father noun
le **père** *masc.*
My father works in an office.
Mon père travaille dans un bureau.
Father Christmas le père Noël
Father's Day la fête des Pères

fatty adjective
gras *masc.*, **grasse** *fem.*
fatty food les aliments gras

fault noun
la **faute** *fem.*
It's not my fault! Ce n'est pas ma faute!

favourite adjective
préféré *masc.*, **préférée** *fem.*
My favourite sport is tennis. Mon sport préféré, c'est le tennis.

fear noun
la **peur** *fem.*

feather noun
la **plume** *fem.*

February noun
février *masc.*
in February en février
on the tenth of February le dix février

fed up adjective
I'm fed up! J'en ai marre!

to **feed** verb
donner à manger à
Have you fed the dog? As-tu donné à manger au chien?

to **feel** verb
1 se sentir ⊚
I don't feel well. Je ne me sens pas bien.
2 I feel cold. J'ai froid.
I feel thirsty. J'ai soif.
3 to feel something (*to touch*) **toucher quelque chose**
Feel my hand! Touche ma main!

• *The months of the year and days of the week do not take a capital letter in French.*

4 to feel like something (*to want*) avoir envie de quelque chose
Do you feel like an orange juice? Tu as envie d'un jus d'orange?

feet plural noun
les **pieds** *masc. plural*
My feet are hurting. J'ai mal aux pieds.

felt-tip pen noun
le **feutre** *masc.*

female noun
la **femelle** *fem.*

female adjective
femelle *masc. & fem.*
a female elephant un éléphant femelle

feminine adjective
féminin *masc.*, **féminine** *fem.*

fence noun
la **barrière** *fem.*

fencing noun
(*the sport*) l'**escrime** *fem.*

ferry noun
le **ferry** *masc.*

to **fetch** verb
aller ❷ **chercher**
Fetch my glasses! Va chercher mes lunettes!

few adjective
a few quelques
a few days quelques jours
quite a few problems pas mal de problèmes

few pronoun
a few quelques-uns *masc. plural*, quelques-unes *fem. plural*
a few of the boys quelques-uns des garçons

field noun
1 (*with grass or plants*) le **champ** *masc.*
2 (*for sports*) le **terrain** *masc.*

❷ *means use* **être** *to make the past tense.*

fierce adjective
féroce *masc. & fem.*

fifteen number
quinze
My brother is fifteen. Mon frère a quinze ans.

fifth adjective
cinquième *masc. & fem.*
on the fifth floor au cinquième étage
the fifth of June le cinq juin

fifty number
cinquante
My granddad is fifty. Mon grand-père a cinquante ans.

fight noun
la **bagarre** *fem.*

to **fight** verb
se battre ❷
There are some boys fighting in the corridor. Il y a des garçons qui se battent dans le couloir.

figure noun
(*number*) le **chiffre** *masc.*
Write the amount in figures. Écris la somme en chiffres.

file
1 (*cover for papers*) la **chemise** *fem.*
I keep these papers in a file. Je garde ces papiers dans une chemise.
2 (*on a computer*) le **fichier** *masc.*
I've saved the file. J'ai sauvegardé le fichier.
3 in single file en file indienne

to **fill** verb
remplir
Fill the bottle with water! Remplis la bouteille d'eau!
to fill in a form remplir un formulaire

film noun
1 (*in the cinema or on TV*) le **film** *masc.*
a film star une vedette de cinéma

2 (*in a camera*) la **pellicule** *fem.*

final adjective
(*last*) **dernier** *masc.*, **dernière** *fem.*

final noun
la **finale** *fem.*
When's the final? C'est quand la finale?

to **find** verb
trouver
I can't find my exercise book. Je ne trouve pas mon cahier.

to **find out** verb
1 (*to ask people*) **se renseigner** ⓔ
I don't know – I'll find out. Je ne sais pas – je vais me renseigner.
2 (*to discover what really happened*) **découvrir**
Have you found out why? As-tu découvert pourquoi?

fine adjective
(*good*) **bien**
I'm fine now. Je vais bien maintenant.
The weather's fine. Il fait beau.

fine adverb
bien
It's working fine. Ça marche bien.

finger noun
le **doigt** *masc.*
She has a ring on her finger. Elle a une bague au doigt.

fingerprint noun
une **empreinte digitale** *fem.*

finish noun
(*in a race*) l'**arrivée** *fem.*

to **finish** verb
finir
I've finished. J'ai fini.
Lessons finish at three. Les cours finissent à trois heures.
Have you finished watching TV? Tu as fini de regarder la télé?

• *See the centre section for verb tables.*

Finland noun
la **Finlande** *fem.*

Finnish adjective
finnois *masc.*, **finnoise** *fem.*

Finnish noun
(*the language*) le **finnois** *masc.*

fire noun
1 le **feu** *masc.* (plural les **feux**)
by the fire au coin du feu
to catch fire prendre feu
2 (*fire that destroys things*) un **incendie** *masc.*
The firemen have put out the fire. Les pompiers ont éteint l'incendie.
Fire! Au feu!
a fire alarm une alarme incendie
a fire engine une voiture de pompiers
a fire station une caserne de pompiers

firefighter noun
le **pompier** *masc.*

fireman noun
le **pompier** *masc.*
My uncle's a fireman. Mon oncle est pompier.

fireplace noun
la **cheminée** *fem.*

fireworks plural noun
(*display*) le **feu d'artifice** *masc.*

CULTURE
In France, firework displays are traditionally held nationwide on the 14th of July, the National day.

first adjective
premier *masc.*, **première** *fem.*
the first two lessons les deux premiers cours

first pronoun
(*the first one*) le **premier** *masc.*, la **première** *fem.*
Naomi will be the first. Naomi sera la première.

on the first of March le premier mars

first *adverb*
1 **le premier** *fem.*, **la première** *fem.*
Peter came first. (*in a race*) Peter est arrivé le premier.
Can I go first? (*start first*) Je peux commencer?
2 **d'abord**
First, I'm going to wash my hands. D'abord, je vais me laver les mains.
first of all tout d'abord
3 **at first** au début

first aid *noun*
les **premiers secours** *masc. plural*

first name *noun*
le **prénom** *masc.*

fish *noun*
le **poisson** *masc.*
Some more fish? Encore du poisson?
fish fingers les bâtonnets de poisson *masc. plural*
fish shop la poissonnerie *fem.*
fish tank l'aquarium *masc.*

fisherman *noun*
le **pêcheur** *masc.*

fishing *noun*
la **pêche** *fem.*
We're going fishing. On va aller à la pêche.
a fishing rod une canne à pêche

fist *noun*
le **poing** *masc.*

fit *adjective*
en forme
Josh is fit. Josh est en forme.

to **fit** *verb*
to fit somebody être à la taille de quelqu'un
This T-shirt doesn't fit me. Ce tee-shirt n'est pas à ma taille.

five *number*
cinq

five fingers cinq doigts
I'm five. J'ai cinq ans.
at five à cinq heures
It's five to nine. Il est neuf heures moins cinq.
It's five past ten. Il est dix heures cinq.

to **fix** *verb*
(*to repair*) **réparer**
Dad fixed the computer. Papa a réparé l'ordinateur.

fizzy *adjective*
gazeux *masc.*, **gazeuse** *fem.*
a fizzy drink une boisson gazeuse

flag *noun*
le **drapeau** *masc.* (plural les **drapeaux**)

flame *noun*
la **flamme** *fem.*

flan *noun*
la **tarte** *fem.*

flannel *noun*
le **gant de toilette** *masc.*

🌍 **CULTURE**
Un gant de toilette is worn on the hand like a glove.

flash *noun*
a flash of lightning un éclair

flask *noun*
le or la **thermos** *masc. & fem.*

flat *adjective*
1 **plat** *masc.*, **plate** *fem.*
a flat surface une surface plate
2 **a flat tyre** un pneu crevé

flat *noun*
un **appartement** *masc.*

flavour *noun*
(*when choosing an ice cream etc.*)
le **parfum** *masc.*
What flavour do you want? Quel parfum veux-tu?

a b c d e **f** g h i j k l m n o p q r s t u v w x y z

ⓔ *means use* **être** *to make the past tense.*

English French

a b c d e **f** g h i j k l m n o p q r s t u v w x y z

fleece noun
la **polaire** fem.
It's chilly, I'm going to wear my fleece. Il fait frais, je vais mettre ma polaire.

flight noun
le **vol** masc.
a seven-hour flight un vol de sept heures

to **float** verb
flotter

flood noun
une **inondation** fem.

floor noun
1 (made of wood) le **plancher** masc.
2 (made of stone etc.) le **sol** masc.
3 **on the floor** par terre
You've left your toys on the floor. Tu as laissé tes jouets par terre.
4 (a level in a building) un **étage** masc.
on the second floor au deuxième étage
the ground floor le rez-de-chaussée

florist noun
le or la **fleuriste** masc. & fem.

flour noun
la **farine** fem.

flower noun
la **fleur** fem.

flu noun
la **grippe** fem.
I have flu. J'ai la grippe.

fluently adverb
couramment
James speaks French fluently. James parle couramment français.

flute noun
la **flûte** fem.
Jackie plays the flute. Jackie joue de la flûte.

to **fly** verb
1 (talking about birds, planes, balloons, etc.) **voler**
2 (to go somewhere by plane) **aller** ⊘ **en avion**
We flew to Nice. Nous sommes allés à Nice en avion.

fly noun
la **mouche** fem.
I hate flies. J'ai horreur des mouches.

flying saucer noun
la **soucoupe volante** fem.

fog noun
le **brouillard** masc.

foggy adjective
It's foggy. Il y a du brouillard.

to **fold** verb
1 **plier**
to fold something in half plier quelque chose en deux
2 **to fold your arms** croiser les bras

folder noun
1 (for papers) la **chemise** fem.
2 (on a computer) le **dossier** masc.

to **follow** verb
suivre
Follow me, children! Suivez-moi, les enfants!

following adjective
suivant masc., **suivante** fem.
the following week la semaine suivante

food noun
1 la **nourriture** fem.
We like healthy food. Nous aimons la nourriture saine.
We have no food. On n'a rien à manger.
2 (cooking) **English food** la cuisine anglaise

fool noun
un **idiot** masc., une **idiote** fem.

• Use **le** and **un** for masculine words and **la** and **une** for feminine words.

foot noun
le **pied** masc.
My foot hurts. J'ai mal au pied.
on foot à pied
I'm five foot tall. Je mesure un
mètre cinquante.

CULTURE
A foot is about 30 centimetres.

football noun
1 (game) le **football** masc., le **foot**
masc.
to play football jouer au
football, jouer au foot
football boots des chaussures de
football fem. plural
football shirt le maillot de
football masc.
2 (ball) le **ballon de football** masc.

footballer noun
le **footballeur** masc.,
la **footballeuse** fem.

for preposition
1 **pour**
a letter for you une lettre pour toi
I'm going to Paris for Christmas. Je
vais à Paris pour Noël.
What's this for? Ça sert à quoi?
2 (for something still going on) **depuis**
I've been waiting for an hour.
J'attends depuis une heure.
3 (for something that happened in the past)
pendant
I lived in Leeds for six months. J'ai
vécu à Leeds pendant six mois.

to **forbid** verb
défendre
That's forbidden! C'est défendu!

forecast noun
(weather forecast) la **météo** fem.

forehead noun
le **front** masc.

foreign adjective
étranger masc., **étrangère** fem.
a foreign country un pays étranger

foreigner noun
un **étranger** masc.,
une **étrangère** fem.

forest noun
la **forêt** fem.

LANGUAGE
English = forest
French = forêt

to **forget** verb
oublier
Don't forget to come! N'oublie pas
de venir!

to **forgive** verb
pardonner
Forgive me! Pardonne-moi!

fork noun
la **fourchette** fem.

form noun
1 (paper) le **formulaire** masc.
to fill in a form remplir un
formulaire
2 (in school) la **classe** fem.

to **form** verb
former
Form a circle! Formez un cercle!

fortnight noun
quinze jours masc. plural
In a fortnight it's my birthday.
Dans quinze jours c'est mon
anniversaire.

LANGUAGE
Word for word **quinze jours** is fifteen days
although a fortnight is fourteen days.

fortunately adverb
heureusement

forty number
quarante
My mum is forty. Ma mère a
quarante ans.

forward adverb
en avant

@ means use être to make the past tense.

English French

a b c d e **f** g h i j k l m n o p q r s t u v w x y z

Take two steps forward. Faites deux pas en avant.
to move forward avancer
We're moving forward faster now. On avance plus vite maintenant.

fountain noun
la **fontaine** fem.

four number
quatre
four apples quatre pommes
The party starts at four. La fête commence à quatre heures.
Mark is four. Mark a quatre ans.

fourteen number
quatorze
fourteen days quatorze jours
My sister is fourteen. Ma sœur a quatorze ans.

fourth adjective
quatrième masc. & fem.
on the fourth floor au quatrième étage
the fourth of February le quatre février

fox noun
le **renard** masc.

France noun
la **France** fem.
Fabrice lives in France. Fabrice habite en France.
I'm going to France. Je vais en France.

freckles plural noun
les **taches de rousseur** fem. plural

free adjective
1 (when you don't pay) **gratuit** masc., **gratuite** fem.
a free ticket un billet gratuit
It's free of charge. C'est gratuit.
2 (not occupied) **libre** masc. & fem.
Are you free tomorrow? Tu es libre demain?
This seat is free. Cette place est libre.

freedom noun
la **liberté** fem.

to freeze verb
1 (in the cold weather) **geler**
It's freezing today. Il gèle aujourd'hui.
You're freezing! Tu es gelé!
2 (in a freezer) **congeler**

freezer noun
le **congélateur** masc.

French adjective
français masc., **française** fem.
French cooking la cuisine française
He's French. Il est français.
She's French. Elle est française.
a French lesson un cours de français
French fries les frites fem. plural

French noun
1 (the language) le **français** masc.
Do you speak French? Est-ce que vous parlez français?
2 **the French** les Français masc. plural

Frenchman noun
le **Français** masc.

Frenchwoman noun
la **Française** fem.

fresh adjective
frais masc., **fraîche** fem.
fresh eggs des œufs frais

Friday noun
vendredi masc.
It's Friday today. C'est vendredi aujourd'hui.
on Friday vendredi
next Friday vendredi prochain
last Friday vendredi dernier
every Friday tous les vendredis
I'm coming back on Friday. Je reviens vendredi.
on Fridays le vendredi

fridge noun
le **frigo** masc.

• Languages, nationalities, and religions do not take a capital letter in French.

fried adjective
frit masc., **frite** fem.
fried fish le poisson frit
a fried egg un œuf sur le plat

friend noun
un **ami** masc., une **amie** fem.
She's my best friend. C'est ma
meilleure amie.
Are you friends with him? Tu es
ami avec lui?

friendly adjective
sympathique masc. & fem.

fries plural noun
les **frites** fem. plural

to **frighten** verb
to frighten somebody faire peur à
quelqu'un
I'm frightened. J'ai peur.
Lorraine is frightened of dogs.
Lorraine a peur des chiens.

> 🔑 **LANGUAGE**
> English = **to be frightened**
> **I'm frightened.**
> French = **avoir** peur
> **J'ai peur.**

fringe noun
la **frange** fem.

frisbee® noun
le **frisbee**® masc.

frog noun
la **grenouille** fem.
frogs' legs les cuisses de grenouille

> 🌍 **CULTURE**
> On French restaurant menus, you will
> sometimes see **des cuisses de**
> **grenouille.** They are a delicacy, even
> French people don't eat them very often.

from preposition
de
It's a letter from my penfriend.
C'est une lettre de mon
correspondant.

I come from Manchester. Je viens
de Manchester.
from four to six o'clock de quatre à
six heures

front noun
1 (of a house, box, shirt, etc.) le **devant**
masc.
The front of your jacket is dirty.
Le devant de ta veste est sale.
2 (of a car) l'**avant** masc.
Ben is sitting in the front. Ben est
assis à l'avant.
3 (of a classroom, theatre, etc.) le **premier**
rang masc.
I always sit at the front. Je
m'assois toujours au premier
rang.
4 **in front of** devant
in front of the school devant
l'école

front adjective
1 (garden, wall, leg, etc.) **de devant**
its front legs ses pattes de
devant
the front door la porte d'entrée
2 **avant** masc. & fem.
the front seat le siège avant

> 🔑 **LANGUAGE**
> **Avant** is the same in the masculine,
> feminine, and plural.

frost noun
le **gel** masc.

frosty adjective
It's frosty. Il gèle.

frozen adjective
1 **I'm frozen.** Je suis gelé.
2 (vegetables, etc.) **surgelé** masc.,
surgelée fem.

fruit noun
les **fruits** masc. plural
Do you want some fruit? Tu veux
un fruit?
Do you like fruit? Tu aimes les
fruits?
a fruit juice un jus de fruits

*ℯ means use **être** to make the past tense.*

a
b
c
d
e
f
g
h
i
j
k
l
m
n
o
p
q
r
s
t
u
v
w
x
y
z

a **fruit salad** une salade de fruits

🔑 **LANGUAGE**
Use **fruit** in French in the singular when you mean one piece of fruit, and **fruits** in the plural when you mean more than one.

frying pan noun
la **poêle** *fem.*

full adjective
1 **plein** *masc.*, **pleine** *fem.*
My room is full of books. Ma chambre est pleine de livres.
I'm full. J'ai assez mangé., Je n'ai plus faim.
2 (*hotel, flight, etc.*) **complet** *masc.*, **complète** *fem.*
The hotel is full. L'hôtel est complet.
3 **a full stop** un point

fun noun
to have fun s'amuser ⊘
Have fun! Amusez-vous bien!

It's fun! C'est amusant!

funfair noun
la **fête foraine** *fem.*

funny adjective
1 (*making you laugh*) **drôle** *masc. & fem.*
2 (*strange*) **bizarre** *masc. & fem.*

fur noun
1 (*of an animal*) le **poil** *masc.*
2 (*for a coat*) la **fourrure** *fem.*

furious adjective
furieux *masc.*, **furieuse** *fem.*

furniture noun
les **meubles** *masc. plural*
a piece of furniture un meuble

further adverb
plus loin

future noun
l'**avenir** *masc.*
in the future à l'avenir

Gg

game noun
1 le **jeu** *masc.* (plural les **jeux**)
a computer game un jeu électronique
Do you want to play a game? Tu veux jouer à un jeu?
the Olympic Games les Jeux Olympiques
2 (*of chess, hide-and-seek, cards, tennis, etc.*) la **partie** *fem.*
a game of hide-and-seek une partie de cache-cache
3 (*match*) le **match** *masc.*
We're going to a football game. On va à un match de foot.
4 (*in school*) **games** le sport *masc.*
We have games on Thursday. On a sport le jeudi.

gang noun
la **bande** *fem.*
He's one of our gang. Il fait partie de notre bande.

gap noun
(*in a fence or wall*) le **trou** *masc.*

garage noun
le **garage** *masc.*

garden noun
le **jardin** *masc.*

gardener noun
le **jardinier** *masc.*, la **jardinière** *fem.*

gardening noun
le **jardinage** *masc.*

garlic noun
l'**ail** *masc.*

• *The months of the year and days of the week do not take a capital letter in French.*

gas noun
le **gaz** *masc.*
a gas cooker une cuisinière à gaz

gate noun
1 (*metal gate, to a garden*) la **grille** *fem.*
2 (*big gate, at school*) le **portail** *masc.*
3 (*wooden gate, to a field*) la **barrière** *fem.*

GCSE noun
le **certificat d'études secondaires** *masc.*
My brother is doing his GCSEs. Mon frère passe son brevet.

> 🌍 **CULTURE**
>
> In France **le brevet des collèges** (word for word 'schools' certificate') is an exam children take at the age of fifteen when they leave the **collège**: It is the closest equivalent to the GCSE.

geese plural noun
les **oies** *fem. plural*

gender noun
le **genre** *masc.*
What gender is 'fenêtre'? Quel est le genre de 'fenêtre'?

general adjective
général *masc.*,
générale *fem.*, **généraux** *masc,* *plural*, **générales** *fem. plural*

generally adverb
généralement

generous adjective
généreux *masc.*, **généreuse** *fem.*

genius noun
le **génie** *masc.*
You're a genius! Tu es un génie!

gentle adjective
doux *masc.*, **douce** *fem.*

gently adverb
doucement

gents noun
les **toilettes pour hommes** *fem.* *plural*

ℯ *means use* **être** *to make the past tense.*

geography noun
la **géographie** *fem.*

gerbil noun
la **gerbille** *fem.*

German adjective
allemand *masc.*, **allemande** *fem.*
He's German. Il est allemand.
She's German. Elle est allemande.

German noun
1 (*the language*) l'**allemand** *masc.*
Can you speak German? Est-ce que vous parlez allemand?
2 (*the person*) un **Allemand** *masc.*, une **Allemande** *fem.*

Germany noun
l'**Allemagne** *fem.*

germs plural noun
les **microbes** *masc. plural*

to **get** verb

> 🔑 **LANGUAGE**
>
> When choosing the correct translation of 'get', look at the English signpost words until you find the meaning you want.

1 (*to have or be given*) **avoir**
I got a computer for my birthday. J'ai eu un ordinateur pour mon anniversaire.
I get money at Christmas. J'ai de l'argent à Noël.
2 (*to receive*) **recevoir**
I got your message. J'ai reçu ton message.
3 (*when translating 'have got' or 'has got'*) **avoir**
I've got long hair. J'ai les cheveux longs.
Have you got a bike? Est-ce que tu as un vélo?
4 (*to find*) **trouver**
Where did you get that? Où as-tu trouvé ça?
5 (*to buy*) **acheter**
Dad's getting me a present. Papa va m'acheter un cadeau.

a
b
c
d
e
f
g
h
i
j
k
l
m
n
o
p
q
r
s
t
u
v
w
x
y
z

6 (*to catch*) **attraper**
John got the flu. John a attrapé la grippe.
7 (*a bus or train*) **prendre**
You get the bus here. On prend le bus ici.
8 (*to fetch*) **aller** ⊕ **chercher**
Get some bread from the kitchen. Va chercher du pain dans la cuisine.
9 (*to arrive somewhere*) **arriver**
We get to York at three o'clock. On arrive à York à trois heures.
10 (*when translating* **have got** *or* **has got to do something**) **devoir**
I've got to go to the doctor's. Je dois aller chez le médecin.
You've got to help me. Tu dois m'aider.
11 to get better **aller** ⊕ **mieux**
She's been ill but she's getting better. Elle a été malade mais elle va mieux.
Get better soon! Remets-toi vite!

to **get away** verb
s'échapper ⊕
Careful, he's getting away! Attention, il s'échappe!

to **get back** verb
rentrer ⊕
Dad gets back at eight. Papa rentre à huit heures.

to **get down** verb
descendre ⊕
Get down, Sally! Descends, Sally!

to **get in** verb
monter ⊕
Get in the car! Monte dans la voiture!

to **get off** verb
descendre ⊕
He got off the bus at Chelsea. Il est descendu du bus à Chelsea.

to **get on** verb
1 monter ⊕

• *See the centre section for verb tables.*

304

We got on the bus. Nous sommes montés dans le bus.
Get on your bicycle! Monte sur ton vélo!
2 How are you getting on? Comment ça va?

to **get out** verb
sortir ⊕
Let's get out of here! Sortons d'ici!
Get your exercise books out! Sortez vos cahiers!

to **get up** verb
se lever ⊕
I get up at six. Je me lève à six heures.

ghost noun
le **fantôme** *masc.*

giant noun
le **géant** *masc.*, la **géante** *fem.*

gift noun
le **cadeau** *masc.* (plural les **cadeaux**)

gigantic adjective
gigantesque *masc. & fem.*

ginger adjective
roux *masc.*, **rousse** *fem.*
He has ginger hair. Il est roux.

giraffe noun
la **girafe** *fem.*

🔑 **LANGUAGE**
English = gira**ff**e
French = gira**f**e

girl noun
la **fille** *fem.*
a little girl une petite fille
There are ten girls in the class. Il y a dix filles dans la classe.

girlfriend noun
la **copine** *fem.*

to **give** verb
donner
Give me a pen! Donne-moi un stylo!

to **give back** verb
rendre
Give me back my sweets!
Rends-moi mes bonbons!

to **give in** verb
rendre
Give in your exercise books!
Rendez vos cahiers!

to **give out** verb
distribuer
Rachel gave out the books. Rachel
a distribué les livres.

to **give up** verb
abandonner
I'm not going to give up. Je ne vais
pas abandonner.

glad adjective
content masc., contente fem.
I'm glad to see you again. Je suis
content de te revoir. (boy speaking) Je
suis contente de te revoir. (girl
speaking)

glass noun
le verre masc.
It's made of glass. C'est en verre.
a glass bottle une bouteille en
verre
a glass of water un verre d'eau

glasses plural noun
les lunettes fem. plural
I wear glasses. Je porte des
lunettes.

globe noun
le globe masc.

glove noun
le gant masc.

glue noun
la colle fem.

go noun
le tour masc.
It's your go. C'est ton tour.
Whose go is it? C'est à qui le tour?

to **go** verb
1 aller @
I'm going to school. Je vais à
l'école.
Do you like going to the park?
Tu aimes aller au parc?
Where are you going? Où vas-tu?
Where has he gone? Où est-il allé?
Let's go! Allons-y!
2 (used with another verb when talking about
the future) aller @
What are you going to do?
Qu'est-ce que tu vas faire?
I'm going to stay. Je vais rester.
3 (to leave) partir
Don't go! Ne pars pas!
Harry has already gone. Harry est
déjà parti.
4 (to become) devenir
Have you gone mad? Tu es devenu
fou?
5 (to do an activity) faire
to go cycling faire du vélo
to go riding faire du cheval

to **go away** verb
s'en aller @
Go away, Chris! Va-t'en, Chris!
Go away, boys! Allez-vous-en, les
garçons!

to **go back** verb
1 (to return somewhere) retourner
Go back to your seats! Retournez à
vos places!
2 (to move backwards) reculer
Go back one step! Reculez d'un pas!

to **go down** verb
descendre
Liam went down to the basement.
Liam est descendu au sous-sol.
She went down the stairs. Elle a
descendu l'escalier.

to **go in** verb
entrer @
Let's go in! Entrons!

@ *means use* être *to make the past tense.*

a
b
c
d
e
f
g
h
i
j
k
l
m
n
o
p
q
r
s
t
u
v
w
x
y
z

to **go on** verb
continuer
Go on reading. Continue à lire.
What's going on? Qu'est-ce qui se passe?

to **go out** verb
sortir Ⓔ
Go out of the kitchen! Sortez de la cuisine!
Ben's going out with Jan. Ben sort avec Jan.

to **go up** verb
monter Ⓔ
I went up to my room. Je suis monté dans ma chambre. (*boy speaking*) Je suis montée dans ma chambre. (*girl speaking*)

goal noun
le **but** *masc.*
Anne scored a goal. Anne a marqué un but.

goalkeeper noun
le **gardien de but** *masc.*

goat noun
la **chèvre** *fem.*

god noun
le **dieu** *masc.*

goddaughter noun
la **filleule** *fem.*

godfather noun
le **parrain** *masc.*

godmother noun
la **marraine** *fem.*

godson noun
le **filleul** *masc.*

goggles plural noun
(*for swimming*) les **lunettes de plongée** *fem. plural*

gold noun
l'**or** *masc.*
a gold bracelet un bracelet en or

goldfish noun
le **poisson rouge** *masc.*

> 🔑 **LANGUAGE**
> English = **gold**fish
> French = le poisson **rouge**

golf noun
le **golf** *masc.*
Andy plays golf. Andy joue au golf.
a golf course un terrain de golf

gone verb SEE **go**

good adjective
1 **bon** *masc.*, **bonne** *fem.*
a good example un bon exemple
a good idea une bonne idée
Chloe is good at French. Chloe est bonne en français.
Peas are good for you. Les petits pois sont bons pour la santé.
2 (*behaving right*) **sage** *masc. & fem.*
Be good! Soyez sages!
3 (*when wishing somebody something*)
Good morning! Bonjour!
Good afternoon! Bonjour!
Good evening! Bonsoir!
Good night! Bonne nuit!
Have a good trip! Bon voyage!

goodbye exclamation
au revoir

Good Friday noun
le **vendredi saint** *masc.*

good-looking adjective
beau *masc.*,
belle *fem.*, **beaux** *masc. plural*,
belles *fem. plural*
He's very good-looking. Il est très beau.

goose noun
une **oie** *fem.*
goose pimples le chair de poules

gorilla noun
le **gorille** *masc.*

got verb SEE **get**

• *Use* **le** *and* **un** *for masculine words and* **la** *and* **une** *for feminine words.*

grade noun
(*in school subjects*) la **note** *fem.*
I always get good grades.
J'ai toujours de bonnes notes.

gradually adverb
peu à peu

graffiti noun
les **graffiti** *masc. plural*

gram noun
le **gramme** *masc.*

grammar noun
la **grammaire** *fem.*

grandchildren plural noun
les **petits-enfants** *masc. plural*

granddad noun
le **papi** *masc.*

granddaughter noun
la **petite-fille** *fem.* (plural les
petites-filles)

grandfather noun
le **grand-père** *masc.* (plural les
grands-pères)

grandma noun
la **mamie** *fem.*

grandmother noun
la **grand-mère** *fem.* (plural les
grands-mères)

grandpa noun
le **papi** *masc.*

grandparents plural noun
les **grands-parents** *masc. plural*

grandson noun
le **petit-fils** *masc.* (plural les
petits-fils)

granny noun
la **mamie** *fem.*

grapefruit noun
le **pamplemousse** *masc.*
grapefruit juice le jus de
pamplemousse

grapes plural noun
le **raisin** *masc.*
I love grapes. J'adore le raisin.
a grape un grain de raisin

> **LANGUAGE**
> English = **grapes** is plural
> French = **le raisin** is singular

grass noun
l'**herbe** *fem.*
They're sitting on the grass.
Ils sont assis sur l'herbe.

to **grate** verb
râper
grated cheese le fromage râpé

gravy noun
la **sauce** *fem.*
Do you want some gravy? Tu veux
de la sauce?

greasy adjective
gras *masc.*, **grasse** *fem.*
greasy food la nourriture grasse

great adjective
génial *masc.*,
géniale *fem.*, **géniaux** *masc. plural*,
géniales *fem. plural*
That's great! C'est génial!

Great Britain noun
la **Grande-Bretagne** *fem.*
I live in Great Britain. J'habite en
Grande-Bretagne.

Greece noun
la **Grèce** *fem.*

greedy adjective
gourmand *masc.*,
gourmande *fem.*
Don't be greedy! Ne sois pas
gourmand!

Greek adjective
grec *masc.*, **grecque** *fem.*
She's Greek. Elle est grecque.

Greek noun
1 (*the language*) le **grec** *masc.*

*❷ means use **être** to make the past tense.*

a
b
c
d
e
f
g
h
i
j
k
l
m
n
o
p
q
r
s
t
u
v
w
x
y
z

2 (*the person*) le **Grec** *masc.*, la **Grecque** *fem.*

green adjective
vert *masc.*, **verte** *fem.*
a green dress une robe verte

green noun
1 le **vert** *masc.*
I like green. J'aime le vert.
2 greens les légumes verts *masc. plural*
Eat your greens! Mange tes légumes!

greengrocer noun
le **marchand de fruits et légumes** *masc.*

greetings card noun
la **carte de vœux** *fem.*

grey adjective
gris *masc.*, **grise** *fem.*
My dad has grey hair. Mon père a les cheveux gris.

grey noun
le **gris** *masc.*
Is grey your favourite colour? Ta couleur préférée, c'est le gris?

to **grill** verb
faire griller
grilled sausages des saucisses grillées

to **grin** verb
sourire

grocer noun
un **épicier** *masc.*, une **épicière** *fem.*
We're going to the grocer's. Nous allons à l'épicerie.

groom noun
le **marié** *masc.*
the bride and groom les mariés *masc. plural*

ground noun
1 la **terre** *fem.*
Sit on the ground! Asseyez-vous par terre!
2 (*for football etc.*) le **terrain** *masc.*
a sports ground un terrain de sport

ground floor noun
le **rez-de-chaussée** *masc.*
We live on the ground floor. Nous habitons au rez-de-chaussée.

group noun
le **groupe** *masc.*

to **grow** verb
1 (*talking about plants or hair*) **pousser**
Your hair grows fast. Tes cheveux poussent vite.
2 (*talking about people, body, town, etc.*) **grandir**
You've grown! Tu as grandi!
when I grow up quand je serai grand (*boy speaking*) quand je serai grande (*girl speaking*)

to **growl** verb
(*talking about dogs*) **grogner**

grown-up noun
la **grande personne** *fem.*

grumpy adjective
grincheux *masc.*, **grincheuse** *fem.*

guava noun
la **goyave** *fem.*

to **guess** verb
deviner
Guess what happened! Devine ce qui s'est passé!

guest noun
un **invité** *masc.*, une **invitée** *fem.*

guide noun
(*person or book*) le **guide** *masc.*

Guide noun
une **éclaireuse** *fem.*
I'm a Guide. Je suis éclaireuse.

guidebook noun
le **guide** *masc.*

guilty adjective
coupable *masc. & fem.*

• *Languages, nationalities, and religions do not take a capital letter in French.*

guinea pig noun
le **cochon d'Inde** *masc.*

> **LANGUAGE**
> Word for word **cochon d'Inde** = 'pig from India'.

guitar noun
la **guitare** *fem.*

> **LANGUAGE**
> English = guitar
> French = guitare

guitarist noun
le or la **guitariste** *masc. & fem.*

gun noun
le **revolver** *masc.*

guy noun
(*man*) le **type** *masc.*
He's a nice guy. C'est un type sympa.
Hi guys! Salut les gars!

gym noun
1 (*PE*) la **gym** *fem.*
We have gym on Mondays. On a gym le lundi.
2 (*room in a school*) le **gymnase** *masc.*

gymnastics noun
la **gymnastique** *fem.*
Maria does gymnastics. Maria fait de la gymnastique.

Hh

habit noun
l'**habitude** *fem.*
a bad habit une mauvaise habitude

had verb SEE **have**

hail noun
la **grêle** *fem.*

to **hail** verb
grêler
It's hailing. Il grêle.

hair noun
1 les **cheveux** *masc. plural*
I've got long hair. J'ai les cheveux longs.
I'm going to have my hair cut. Je vais me faire couper les cheveux.
2 (*an animal's fur*) le **poil** *masc.*
Our dog has short hair. Notre chien a le poil court.

> **LANGUAGE**
> English = **hair** is singular
> French = **les cheveux** is plural

hairbrush noun
la **brosse à cheveux** *fem.*

hairdresser noun
le **coiffeur** *masc.*, la **coiffeuse** *fem.*
Mum went to the hairdresser's. Maman est allée chez le coiffeur.

hairdrier noun
le **sèche-cheveux** *masc.* (plural les **sèche-cheveux**)

hairstyle noun
la **coiffure** *fem.*

hairy adjective
poilu *masc.*, **poilue** *fem.*

half noun
la **moitié** *fem.*
half the boys la moitié des garçons
Zev cut the paper in half. Zev a coupé la feuille en deux.

half adjective
demi *masc.*, **demie** *fem.*
six and a half six et demi
half an hour une demi-heure

@ *means use **être** to make the past tense.*

half a litre un demi-litre
half a dozen eggs une demi-douzaine d'œufs
3 (*when telling the time*)
It's half past five. Il est cinq heures et demie.

half adverb
à moitié
My glass is half empty. Mon verre est à moitié vide.

half-brother noun
le **demi-frère** *masc.* (plural les **demi-frères**)

half-sister noun
la **demi-sœur** *fem.* (plural les **demi-sœurs**)

half-term noun
les **vacances de demi-trimestre** *fem. plural*

CULTURE
French children have two half-term holidays: at the end of October (**les vacances de la Toussaint**), and in February (**les vacances d'hiver** or **les vacances de février**).

half-time noun
la **mi-temps** *fem.*
at half-time à la mi-temps

halfway adverb
à mi-chemin
It's halfway between London and Oxford. C'est à mi-chemin entre Londres et Oxford.

hall noun
1 (*big room*) la **salle** *fem.*
a concert hall une salle de concert
2 (*in a school*) la **grande salle** *fem.*
3 (*in a house*) l'**entrée** *fem.*

Hallowe'en noun
Halloween

ham noun
le **jambon** *masc.*

a ham sandwich un sandwich au jambon

hamburger noun
le **hamburger** *masc.*

hammer noun
le **marteau** *masc.* (plural les **marteaux**)

hamster noun
le **hamster** *masc.*

hand noun
1 la **main** *fem.*
I've got my mobile in my hand. J'ai mon portable à la main.
Put your hand up! Levez la main!
Give me a hand! Donne-moi un coup de main!
2 (*on a clock or watch*) l'**aiguille** *fem.*
the big and the little hand la grande et la petite aiguille

to **hand** verb
1 passer
2 to hand something in rendre quelque chose
Hand in your homework! Rendez vos devoirs!
3 to hand something out distribuer quelque chose
Ahmed handed out the books. Ahmed a distribué les livres.

handbag noun
le **sac à main** *masc.*

handkerchief noun
le **mouchoir** *masc.*

handle noun
1 (*on a door*) la **poignée** *fem.*
2 (*on a knife, broom, etc.*) le **manche** *masc.*

handlebars plural noun
le **guidon** *masc.*

LANGUAGE
English = **handlebars** is plural
French = **le guidon** is singular

• *The months of the year and days of the week do not take a capital letter in French.*

handsome adjective
beau masc.,
belle fem., **beaux** masc. plural,
belles fem. plural
Serge is handsome. Serge est beau.

handwriting noun
l'**écriture** fem.
What lovely handwriting! Quelle belle écriture!

handy adjective
(useful) **pratique** masc. & fem.
A mobile phone is very handy.
Un portable, c'est très pratique.

to hang verb
1 (with a hook) **accrocher**
2 **Hang on!** Attendez!

hangman noun
le **pendu** masc.
We're playing hangman. On joue au pendu.

to happen verb
se passer ❷
What's happening? Qu'est-ce qui se passe?

happy adjective
1 **heureux** masc., **heureuse** fem.
Samir is happy. Samir est heureux.
2 (when wishing somebody something)
Happy birthday! Bon anniversaire!
Happy Christmas! Joyeux Noël!
Happy New Year! Bonne année!

Happy Families noun
les **sept familles** fem. plural (card game)
Let's play Happy Families! On joue aux sept familles?

harbour noun
le **port** masc.

hard adjective
1 (not soft) **dur** masc., **dure** fem.
This bread is hard. Ce pain est dur.
a hard-boiled egg un œuf dur
2 (not easy) **difficile** masc. & fem.

This exercise is too hard. Cet exercice est trop difficile.

hard adverb
(to hit, push, etc.) **fort**
Push harder! Poussez plus fort!
I work hard. Je travaille dur.

hard-working adjective
travailleur masc.,
travailleuse fem.

has verb SEE have

hat noun
1 le **chapeau** masc. (plural les **chapeaux**)
2 (woolly hat) le **bonnet** masc.

to hate verb
détester
I hate soup. Je déteste la soupe.
I hate getting up early. Je déteste me lever tôt.

to have verb
1 **avoir**
I have two sisters. J'ai deux sœurs.
Have you got a computer? Est-ce que tu as un ordinateur?
He had a lot of homework. Il a eu beaucoup de devoirs.
She has got short hair. Elle a les cheveux courts.
They have a problem. Ils ont un problème.

> 🔑 **LANGUAGE**
> 'Have' and 'have got' often mean the same, and have the same translation in French.

2 (to eat) **prendre**
I'm having cereal. Je prends des céréales.
3 (to do an activity) **faire**
to have a walk faire une promenade
4 (used for making past tenses) **avoir**
I have finished. J'ai fini.
She hasn't read the book. Elle n'a pas lu le livre.

❷ means use **être** to make the past tense.

5 (when translating 'have to do something' or 'have got to do something') **devoir**
I have to go to the dentist. Je dois aller chez le dentiste.
You've got to make an effort. Vous devez faire un effort.
They've got to leave. Ils doivent partir.

6 (to translate questions such as 'hasn't he?' or 'haven't you?') **He's gone, hasn't he?** Il est parti, non?
You've finished, haven't you? Tu as fini, non?

hay noun
le **foin** masc.
hay fever le rhume des foins

he pronoun
il
He's tired. Il est fatigué.

head
1 la **tête** fem.
I turned my head. J'ai tourné la tête.
2 (headteacher) le **directeur** masc., la **directrice** fem.
3 (when throwing a coin) **Heads!** Face!
Heads or tails? Pile ou face?

headache noun
I have a headache. J'ai mal à la tête.

headmaster noun
le **directeur** masc.

headmistress noun
la **directrice** fem.

headphones noun
le **casque** masc.

headteacher noun
le **directeur** masc., la **directrice** fem.

health noun
la **santé** fem.

healthy adjective
1 (person) **en bonne santé**
2 (food, life, etc.) **sain** masc., **saine** fem.

to **hear** verb
entendre
I can hear you. Je t'entends.
Can you hear a noise? Tu entends un bruit?

heart noun
1 le **cœur** masc.
She knows the song by heart. Elle connaît la chanson par cœur.
2 **hearts** (in cards) le cœur
the nine of hearts le neuf de cœur

heater noun
le **radiateur** masc.

heating noun
le **chauffage** masc.

heavy adjective
lourd masc., **lourde** fem.

hedgehog noun
le **hérisson** masc.

heel noun
le **talon** masc.

height noun
1 (of a person) la **taille** fem.
2 (of a wall, building, etc.) la **hauteur** fem.

helicopter noun
l'**hélicoptère** masc.

hello exclamation
1 **bonjour**
2 (when answering the phone) **allô**

helmet noun
le **casque** masc.

help noun
l'**aide** fem.
I need help. J'ai besoin d'aide.

to **help** verb
1 **aider**
Help me! Aide-moi!
Help! Au secours!
2 **Help yourself!** Sers-toi!

• See the centre section for verb tables.

English French

a
b
c
d
e
f
g
h
i
j
k
l
m
n
o
p
q
r
s
t
u
v
w
x
y
z

hen noun
la **poule** *fem.*

her pronoun
1 (*after a verb*) **la**
I can see her. Je la vois.
Help her! Aide-la!
I've forgotten her. Je l'ai oubliée.

> 🔑 **LANGUAGE**
> la = l' before a vowel sound

2 (*to her*) **lui**
Give her the pencil! Donne-lui le crayon!
I'm going to speak to her. Je vais lui parler.
3 (*after a preposition, after* it's) **elle**
with her avec elle
It's her. C'est elle.

her adjective
1 (*before a masculine noun*) **son**
her bike son vélo
2 (*before a feminine noun*) **sa**
her dress sa robe
3 (*before a plural noun*) **ses**
her parents ses parents

> 🔑 **LANGUAGE**
> Use **son** instead of **sa** when a feminine noun starts with a, e, i, o, u, or silent h, for example: 'her plate' is **son assiette**.

here adverb
1 **ici**
Is it far from here? C'est loin d'ici?
2 **là**
She isn't here. Elle n'est pas là.
3 **here is** voici
Here's my question. Voici ma question.
4 **here are** voici
Here are the photos. Voici les photos.

hero noun
le **héros** *masc.*

> 🔑 **LANGUAGE**
> English = hero
> French = héros

heroine noun
l'**héroïne** *fem.*

hers pronoun
à elle
It's hers. C'est à elle.

herself pronoun
1 **elle-même**
She's doing it herself. Elle le fait elle-même.
2 **se**
She's going to hurt herself. Elle va se faire mal.

> 🔑 **LANGUAGE**
> se = s' before a vowel or silent 'h'

3 **by herself** toute seule
She goes out by herself. Elle sort toute seule.

hi exclamation
salut!

hiccups plural noun
to have hiccups avoir le hoquet

hide
1 **se cacher** ⊘
He's hiding behind a tree. Il se cache derrière un arbre.
2 **to hide something** cacher quelque chose
Hide his bike! Cache son vélo!

hide-and-seek noun
to play hide-and-seek jouer à cache-cache

high adjective
haut *masc.*, **haute** *fem.*
Jump higher! Sautez plus haut!
high jump le saut en hauteur

high school noun
1 (*for children from 11 to 15*) le **collège** *masc.*
2 (*for children from 15 to 18*) le **lycée** *masc.*

⊘ *means use* être *to make the past tense.*

a
b
c
d
e
f
g
h
i
j
k
l
m
n
o
p
q
r
s
t
u
v
w
x
y
z

hill noun
la **colline** *fem.*

him pronoun
1 *(after a verb)* **le**
I know him. Je le connais.
Call him! Appelle-le!

> 🔑 **LANGUAGE**
> **le** = **l'** before a vowel or silent 'h'

I've forgotten him. Je l'ai
oublié.
2 *(to him)* **lui**
Give him the guitar. Donne-lui la
guitare.
I'm going to speak to him. Je vais
lui parler.
3 *(after a preposition, after 'it's')* **lui**
with him avec lui
It's him. C'est lui.

himself pronoun
1 **lui-même**
He's doing it himself. Il le fait
lui-même.
2 **se**
He's going to burn himself. Il va se
brûler.

> 🔑 **LANGUAGE**
> **se** = **s'** before a vowel or silent 'h'

3 **by himself** tout seul
He goes out by himself. Il sort tout
seul.

Hindu adjective
hindou *masc.*, **hindoue** *fem.*

hip hip hurrah exclamation
hip hip hip hourra

hippopotamus noun
un **hippopotame** *masc.*

to **hire** verb
(a DVD, video, bike, etc.) **louer**

his adjective
1 *(before a masculine noun)* **son**
his dog son chien
2 *(before a feminine noun)* **sa**
his shirt sa chemise

3 *(before a plural noun)* **ses**
his parents ses parents

> 🔑 **LANGUAGE**
> Use **son** instead of **sa** when a feminine
> noun starts with *a, e, i, o, u,* or *silent h,* for
> example: 'his plate' is **son assiette**.

his pronoun
à **lui**
This DVD is his. Ce DVD est à lui.

history noun
l'**histoire** *fem.*

hit noun
(song) le **tube** *masc.*

to **hit** verb
frapper
He hit me! Il m'a frappé!

hobby noun
le **passe-temps** *masc.* (plural les
passe-temps)

hockey noun
le **hockey** *masc.*
Do you play hockey? Tu joues au
hockey?

to **hold** verb
tenir
**What are you holding in your
hand?** Qu'est-ce que tu tiens à la
main?

to **hold on** verb
(to wait) **attendre**
Hold on, I'm coming! Attendez,
j'arrive!

to **hold up** verb
(to lift up) **lever**

hold-up noun
(traffic jam) le **bouchon** *masc.*

hole noun
le **trou** *masc.*

holiday noun
1 les **vacances** *fem. plural*
We're on holiday. Nous sommes
en vacances.

• *Use* **le** *and* **un** *for masculine words and* **la** *and* **une** *for feminine words.*

Did you have a good holiday?
Tu as passé de bonnes vacances?
Have a good holiday! Bonnes
vacances!
to go on holiday partir en
vacances
the Christmas holidays les
vacances de Noël
the school holidays les vacances
scolaires
2 (*from work*) le **congé** *masc.*
My mum's on holiday this week.
Ma mère est en congé cette
semaine.
3 (*public holiday*) le **jour férié** *masc.*

Holland noun
la **Hollande** *fem.*

holly noun
le **houx** *masc.*

holy adjective
saint *masc.*, **sainte** *fem.*

home noun
1 la **maison** *fem.*
I want to stay at home. Je veux
rester à la maison.
Come to my home. Viens chez moi.
2 (*on web page*) l'**accueil** *masc.*
the home page la page d'accueil

home adverb
à la maison
Do you want to go home? Tu veux
rentrer à la maison?
I'm going home. Je rentre chez
moi.
Dad gets home at seven. Papa
rentre à sept heures.

homeless adjective
a homeless person un *or* une
sans-abri *masc. & fem.* (plural les
sans-abri)

homework noun
les **devoirs** *masc. plural*
my French homework mes devoirs
de français

a homework diary un cahier de
textes

honest adjective
(*telling the truth*) **franc** *masc.*,
franche *fem.*
Be honest! Sois franc!

honey noun
le **miel** *masc.*

hood noun
(*on a coat*) le **capuchon** *masc.*

hook noun
(*for a picture or clothes*) le **crochet** *masc.*

hooray exclamation
hourra

hoover® noun
un **aspirateur** *masc.*

to **hoover** verb
passer l'aspirateur
I hoover my room. Je passe
l'aspirateur dans ma chambre.

to **hop** verb
(*on one leg*) **sauter à cloche-pied**

to **hope** verb
espérer
I hope you can come. J'espère que
tu peux venir.
We are hoping to win. Nous
espérons gagner.
I hope so! Je l'espère bien!
I hope not! J'espère que non!

hopeless adjective
nul *masc.*, **nulle** *fem.*
I'm hopeless at dancing! Je suis
nul en danse! (*boy speaking*) Je suis
nulle en danse! (*girl speaking*)

hopscotch noun
la **marelle** *fem.*

horrible adjective
horrible *masc. & fem.*

horror film noun
le **film d'horreur** *masc.*

a
b
c
d
e
f
g
h
i
j
k
l
m
n
o
p
q
r
s
t
u
v
w
x
y
z

*◉ means use **être** to make the past tense.*

horse noun
le **cheval** *masc.* (plural les **chevaux**)

hospital noun
l'**hôpital** *masc.* (plural les **hôpitaux**)
My aunt's in hospital. Ma tante est
à l'hôpital.

LANGUAGE
English = hospital
French = hôpital

---

hot adjective
1 **chaud** *masc.*, **chaude** *fem.*
The water is hot. L'eau est
chaude.
a hot chocolate un chocolat
chaud
2 **to be hot** avoir chaud
I'm hot. J'ai chaud.

LANGUAGE
English = **to be** hot   **I'm hot.**
French = **avoir** chaud   **J'ai chaud.**

---

3 (*when talking about the weather*) **It's hot.**
Il fait chaud.
The weather is very hot. Il fait très
chaud.

hot dog noun
le **hot-dog** *masc.*

hotel noun
l'**hôtel** *masc.*

hour noun
l'**heure** *fem.*
The film lasts two hours. Le film
dure deux heures.
half an hour une demi-heure
a quarter of an hour un quart
d'heure
three and a half hours trois heures
et demie
thirty miles an hour cinquante
kilomètres à l'heure

house noun
1 la **maison** *fem.*
I live in a little house. J'habite dans
une petite maison.

2 (*when using* **at** *or* **to**) **chez**
at my house chez moi
**We're going to play at Karl's
house.** On va jouer chez Karl.
**Can I come to your house
tomorrow?** Je peux venir chez toi
demain?

housework noun
le **ménage** *masc.*
to do the housework faire le
ménage

how adverb
1 **comment**
How are you? Comment vas-tu?
**How do you say 'always' in
French?** Comment dit-on 'always'
en français?
How did you do it? Comment as-tu
fait ça?
2 **how much?** combien?
How much is it? C'est combien?
3 **how many?** combien?
**How many boys are there in your
class?** Il y a combien de garçons
dans ta classe?
4 **how old?** quel âge?
How old are you? Quel âge
as-tu?

huge adjective
énorme *masc. & fem.*

human adjective
humain *masc.*, **humaine** *fem.*
a human being un être humain

humour noun
to have a sense of humour avoir le
sens de l'humour

hundred number
cent
a hundred cent
two hundred deux cents
two hundred euros deux cents
euros
two hundred and twenty deux
cent vingt

• *Languages, nationalities, and religions do not take a capital letter in French.*

hundreds of cars des centaines de voitures

> 🔑 **LANGUAGE**
> Add **s** to make **cent** plural, for example: **deux cents**, except when **cent** is followed by another number, for example: **deux cent vingt** (220).

Hungary noun
la **Hongrie** *fem.*

hungry adjective
I'm hungry. J'ai faim.
She isn't hungry. Elle n'a pas faim.

> 🔑 **LANGUAGE**
> English = **to be** hungry **I'm hungry.**
> French = **avoir** faim **J'ai faim.**

to **hunt** verb
chasser
We don't like hunting. Nous n'aimons pas la chasse.

Ii

I pronoun
1 je
I'm tired. Je suis fatigué. (*boy speaking*); Je suis fatiguée. (*girl speaking*)

> 🔑 **LANGUAGE**
> **je** = **j'** before a vowel or silent 'h'

I have green eyes. J'ai les yeux verts.
2 moi
Jo and I play together. Jo et moi jouons ensemble.

ice noun
la **glace** *fem.*
There's ice on the window. Il y a de la glace sur la fenêtre.

ice-cold adjective
(*hands, water, etc.*) **glacé** *masc.*, **glacée** *fem.*

to **hurry up** verb
se dépêcher ⊘
Hurry up! Dépêche-toi!

to **hurt** verb
1 My back hurts. J'ai mal au dos.
It hurts. Ça fait mal.
2 to hurt somebody faire mal à quelqu'un
You're hurting me! Tu me fais mal!
3 to hurt yourself se faire ⊘ mal
Have you hurt yourself? Tu t'es fait mal?

husband noun
le **mari** *masc.*

hymn noun
le **cantique** *masc.*

hyphen noun
le **trait d'union** *masc.*

ice cream noun
la **glace** *fem.*
a chocolate ice cream une glace au chocolat

ice cube noun
le **glaçon** *masc.*

ice lolly noun
la **glace à l'eau** *fem.*

ice rink noun
la **patinoire** *fem.*

ice-skating noun
le **patin à glace** *masc.*
Do you go ice-skating? Tu fais du patin à glace?

icon noun
une **icône** *fem.*
Click on the icon. Cliquez sur l'icône.

a b c d e f g h i j k l m n o p q r s t u v w x y z

⊘ *means use* **être** *to make the past tense.*

ICT noun
les **TIC** *fem. plural*

> **LANGUAGE**
> TIC = Technologies de l'Information et de la Communication

icy adjective
1 (*wind, hands, etc.*) **glacé** *masc.*, **glacée** *fem.*
2 **The roads are icy.** Il y a du verglas sur les routes.

idea noun
une **idée** *fem.*
I have an idea. J'ai une idée.

identical adjective
identique *masc. & fem.*

idiot noun
un **idiot** *masc.*, une **idiote** *fem.*

if conjunction
si
Help me if you can. Aide-moi si tu peux.
I don't know if he wants to come. Je ne sais pas s'il veut venir.
if not sinon

> **LANGUAGE**
> si = s' before **il** or **ils**

ill adjective
malade *masc. & fem.*

illness noun
la **maladie** *fem.*

imagination noun
l'**imagination** *fem.*

to **imagine** verb
imaginer
Imagine you win the lottery! Imagine que tu gagnes à la loterie!

to **imitate** verb
imiter

immediately adverb
immédiatement

important adjective
important *masc.*, **importante** *fem.*

impossible adjective
impossible *masc. & fem.*

to **improve** verb
améliorer
I want to improve my French. Je veux améliorer mon français.

in preposition
1 **dans**
in my classroom dans ma classse
Write the word in your notebook! Écris le mot dans ton cahier!
I'm coming back in two days. Je reviens dans deux jours.
2 **à**
in school à l'école
in Paris à Paris
in Portugal au Portugal
in the United States aux États-Unis

> **LANGUAGE**
> Use **à** with towns, **au** with countries that are masculine, and **aux** with countries that are masculine and plural.

3 **en**
in winter en hiver
in January en janvier
in 2006 en 2006
in French en français
in France en France

> **LANGUAGE**
> Use **en** with countries that are feminine.

4 **de**
He's the tallest one in the class. C'est le plus grand de la classe.
at six o'clock in the evening à six heures du soir
5 (*during*) **pendant**
What are you doing in the holidays? Qu'est-ce que tu fais pendant les vacances?

in adverb
(*at home*) **là**
Is Juan in? Est-ce que Juan est là?
He's not in. Il n'est pas là.

• *The months of the year and days of the week do not take a capital letter in French.*

inch noun
She's two inches taller than you.
Elle est plus grande que toi de cinq
centimètres.

 CULTURE
An inch is about 2.5 centimetres.

included adjective
compris *masc.*, **comprise** *fem.*
The service is included. Le service
est compris.

to **increase** verb
augmenter

incredible adjective
incroyable *masc. & fem.*

indeed adverb
vraiment
very good indeed vraiment très
bon
Thanks very much indeed! Merci
beaucoup!

indefinite adjective
the indefinite article l'article
indéfini

independent adjective
indépendant *masc.*,
indépendante *fem.*

⚿ **LANGUAGE**
English = independent
French = indépendant

India noun
l'**Inde** *fem.*

Indian adjective
indien *masc.*, **indienne** *fem.*
an Indian town une ville indienne

Indian noun
un **Indien** *masc.*, une **Indienne** *fem.*

indoor adjective
(*swimming pool, tennis court, etc.*)
couvert *masc.*, **couverte** *fem.*
an indoor pool une piscine
couverte

indoors adverb
à l'intérieur
I'm indoors. Je suis à l'intérieur.
Go indoors! Rentre!

infant school noun
l'**école maternelle** *fem.*

 CULTURE
L'école maternelle is for children aged
3 to 6.

infinitive noun
l'**infinitif** *masc.*

information noun
les **renseignements** *masc. plural*
information about France des
renseignements sur la France
**I need one more piece of
information.** J'ai besoin d'un
renseignement de plus.

ingredient noun
l'**ingrédient** *masc.*

inhabitant noun
l'**habitant** *masc.*, l'**habitante** *fem.*

injection noun
la **piqûre** *fem.*

to **injure** verb
blesser
Nobody's injured. Il n'y a pas de
blessés.

injury noun
la **blessure** *fem.*

ink noun
l'**encre** *fem.*

insect noun
un **insecte** *masc.*

in-service day noun
la **journée de formation** *fem.*

inside adverb
à l'intérieur
Look inside! Regardez à l'intérieur!
Your sweater is inside out. Ton
pull est à l'envers.

𝒆 *means use* **être** *to make the past tense.*

a
b
c
d
e
f
g
h
i
j
k
l
m
n
o
p
q
r
s
t
u
v
w
x
y
z

inside preposition
à l'intérieur de
They're inside the house. Ils sont à l'intérieur de la maison.

inspector noun
(*school inspector*) un **inspecteur** *masc.*, une **inspectrice** *fem.*

instance noun
for instance par exemple

instant noun
Come here this instant! Viens ici tout de suite!

instead adverb
1 (*instead of somebody*) **à sa place**
Holly's not well. Can I go instead? Holly est malade. Je peux aller à sa place?
2 (*instead of something*) **à la place**
There are no more crisps. Have a biscuit instead. Il n'y a plus de chips. Prends un biscuit à la place.
3 instead of au lieu de
Help me instead of watching TV. Aide-moi au lieu de regarder la télé.

instructions plural noun
les **instructions** *fem. plural*
Follow the instructions! Suivez les instructions!

instructor noun
le **moniteur** *masc.*, la **monitrice** *fem.*
a skiing instructor un moniteur de ski

instrument noun
un **instrument** *masc.*
She plays an instrument. Elle joue d'un instrument.

intelligent adjective
intelligent *masc.*, **intelligente** *fem.*

interest noun
Football is his only interest. Le foot est la seule chose qui l'intéresse.

to **interest** verb
intéresser
I'm not interested. Ça ne m'intéresse pas.
to be interested in something s'intéresser ⊘ à quelque chose
I'm interested in music. Je m'intéresse à la musique.

interesting adjective
intéressant *masc.*, **intéressante** *fem.*
an interesting book un livre intéressant

international adjective
international *masc.*, **internationale** *fem.*, **internationaux** *masc. plural*, **internationales** *fem. plural*

Internet noun
l'**Internet** *masc.*
on the Internet sur Internet
an Internet cafe un cybercafé

to **interrupt** verb
interrompre
Don't interrupt! Ne m'interromps pas!

interval noun
(*at cinema or theatre*) un **entracte** *masc.*

interview noun
(*by a journalist*) une **interview** *fem.*

interviewer noun
un **intervieweur** *masc.*, une **intervieweuse** *fem.*

into preposition
1 dans
We went into the classroom. Nous sommes entrés dans la classe.
2 en
Translate the sentence into French. Traduis la phrase en français.
Split into groups of four! Répartissez-vous en groupes de quatre!

• *See the centre section for verb tables.*

to **introduce** verb
présenter
Can I introduce myself? Je me présente.
Can I introduce you to my mother? Je te présente ma mère.

to **invent** verb
inventer

invention noun
une **invention** fem.

inventor noun
un **inventeur** masc.,
une **inventrice** fem.

invisible adjective
invisible masc. & fem.

invitation noun
une **invitation** fem.

to **invite** verb
inviter
Max has invited me to his party. Max m'a invité à sa fête.

Iran noun
l'**Iran** masc.

Iraq noun
l'**Irak** masc.

Ireland noun
l'**Irlande** fem.
I live in Ireland. J'habite en Irlande.

Irish adjective
irlandais masc., **irlandaise** fem.
He's Irish. Il est irlandais.
She's Irish. Elle est irlandaise.

Irish noun
1 (the language) l'**irlandais** masc.
2 **the Irish** les Irlandais masc. plural

Irishman noun
un **Irlandais** masc.

Irishwoman noun
une **Irlandaise** fem.

iron noun
1 (metal) le **fer** masc.

2 (for clothes) le **fer à repasser** masc.

to **iron** verb
repasser
Dad's ironing his trousers. Papa repasse son pantalon.

irritating adjective
irritant masc., **irritante** fem.

is verb SEE **be**

Islamic adjective
islamique masc. & fem.

island noun
une **île** fem.

isle noun
une **île** fem.
the Isle of Man l'île de Man
the Isle of Wight l'île de Wight

Israel noun
Israël masc.

it pronoun

○— **LANGUAGE**
Remember: you need to know if the word that 'it' stands for is masculine or feminine.

1 (standing for a masculine noun) **il**
Have you seen my picture? – Yes, it's great! Tu as vu mon dessin? – Oui, il est formidable!
2 (standing for a feminine noun) **elle**
Look at my shirt. It's dirty. Regarde ma chemise. Elle est sale.
3 (after a verb, standing for a masculine noun) **le**
Where's my bag? – I can't see it. Où est mon sac? – Je ne le vois pas.
4 (after a verb, standing for a feminine noun) **la**
Here's Elia's letter. You can read it. Voici la lettre d'Elia. Tu peux la lire.
What's your address? I've forgotten it. Quelle est ton adresse? Je l'ai oubliée.

○— **LANGUAGE**
le or **la** = **l'** before a vowel or silent 'h'

❷ means use **être** to make the past tense.

a
b
c
d
e
f
g
h
i
j
k
l
m
n
o
p
q
r
s
t
u
v
w
x
y
z

a
b
c
d
e
f
g
h
i
j
k
l
m
n
o
p
q
r
s
t
u
v
w
x
y
z

5 (*to it*) **lui**
The dog's hungry. Give it a bone.
Le chien a faim. Donne-lui un os.
6 ce
Who is it? Qui est-ce?
It's good. C'est bon.
It's me. C'est moi.

> **LANGUAGE**
> **ce = c'** before an 'e'

7 ça
It doesn't matter. Ça ne fait rien.
How's it going? Comment ça va?
That's it! It's finished. Ça y est!
C'est fini.
8 (*talking about the weather*) **il**
It's hot. Il fait chaud.
It's a nice day. Il fait beau.
It's raining. Il pleut.
9 (*talking about the time*) **il**
It's four o'clock. Il est quatre
heures.

IT noun
l'**informatique** *fem.*

Italian adjective
italien *masc.*, **italienne** *fem.*
She's Italian. Elle est italienne.

Italian noun
1 (*the language*) l'**italien** *masc.*
I speak Italian. Je parle italien.
2 (*the person*) un **Italien** *masc.*,
une **Italienne** *fem.*

Jj

jab noun
la **piqûre** *fem.*
The doctor will give you a jab. Le
médecin va te faire une piqûre.

jacket noun
1 la **veste** *fem.*
2 a jacket potato une pomme de
terre cuite au four

Italy noun
l'**Italie** *fem.*

its adjective
1 (*before a masculine noun*) **son**
What's its name? Quel est son
nom?
2 (*before a feminine noun*) **sa**
The dog's in its kennel. Le chien est
dans sa niche.
3 (*before a plural noun*) **ses**
Its wings are blue. Ses ailes sont
bleues.

> **LANGUAGE**
> Remember: the three words for 'its' are
> **son, sa**, and **ses**.

itself pronoun
1 (*standing for a masculine noun*)
lui-même
the book itself le livre lui-même
2 (*standing for a feminine noun*)
elle-même
the school itself l'école elle-même
3 se
The cat hurt itself. Le chat s'est
blessé.

> **LANGUAGE**
> **se = s'** before a vowel or silent 'h'

4 by itself tout seul *masc.*, tout seule
fem.

jail noun
la **prison** *fem.*
in jail en prison

jam noun
1 la **confiture** *fem.*
raspberry jam la confiture de
framboises
2 a traffic jam un embouteillage
masc.

• *Use le and un for masculine words and la and une for feminine words.*

Jamaica noun
la Jamaïque *fem.*

Jamaican adjective
jamaïquain *masc.*,
jamaïquaine *fem.*

Jamaican noun
le Jamaïquain *masc.*,
la Jamaïquaine *fem.*

jammed adjective
(*drawer, door, etc.*) coincé *masc.*,
coincée *fem.*

January noun
janvier *masc.*
in January en janvier
at the beginning of January début
janvier
It's Friday the ninth of January.
Nous sommes le vendredi neuf
janvier.

Japan noun
le Japon *masc.*

Japanese adjective
japonais *masc.*, japonaise *fem.*
Japanese food la cuisine japonaise

Japanese noun
(*the language*) le japonais *masc.*
Do you speak Japanese? Vous
parlez japonais?

jar noun
le pot *masc.*
a jar of jam un pot de confiture

jealous adjective
jaloux *masc.*, jalouse *fem.*
Are you jealous of me? Tu es
jalouse de moi?

jeans plural noun
le jean *masc.*
I'm wearing jeans. Je porte un
jean.
a pair of jeans un jean

🔑 **LANGUAGE**
English = **jeans** is plural
French = **le jean** is singular

---

jelly noun
la gelée *fem.*

jersey noun
1 le pull *masc.*
2 (*for football*) le maillot *masc.*

jewel noun
le bijou *masc.* (plural les **bijoux**)

jewellery noun
les bijoux *masc. plural*
a jewellery shop une bijouterie
fem.

Jewish adjective
juif *masc.*, juive *fem.*

jigsaw puzzle noun
le puzzle *masc.*
I'm doing a jigsaw puzzle. Je suis
un puzzle.

job noun
(*in an office, factory, etc.*)
un emploi *masc.*
My brother has found a job.
Mon frère a trouvé un emploi.

jogging noun
le jogging *masc.*
to go jogging faire du jogging

to **join** verb
faire partie de
I want to join your group. Je veux
faire partie de votre groupe.

to **join in** verb
to join in participer
Can I join in your game? Je peux
participer à votre jeu?

joke noun
la plaisanterie *fem.*

to **joke** verb
plaisanter
I'm joking! Je plaisante!

jotter noun
le cahier *masc.*

journey noun
le voyage *masc.*
a long journey un long voyage

a b c d e f g h i j k l m n o p q r s t u v w x y z

🄮 *means use* **être** *to make the past tense.*

joystick noun
(for computer games) la **manette** fem.

judge noun
le **juge** masc.

to **judge** verb
juger

judo noun
le **judo** masc.
Do you do judo? Tu fais du judo?

jug noun
(for water or wine) la **carafe** fem.

to **juggle** verb
jongler

juice noun
le **jus** masc.
Do you want an orange juice?
Tu veux un jus d'orange?

July noun
juillet masc.
in July en juillet
It's the twentieth of July. On est le
vingt juillet.

to **jump** verb
sauter
Jump! Sautez!
Ryan jumped over the hedge.
Ryan a sauté par-dessus la haie.

Kk

kangaroo noun
le **kangourou** masc.

karate noun
le **karaté** masc.
She does karate. Elle fait du
karaté.

keen adjective
enthousiaste masc. & fem.

jumper noun
le **pull** masc.

June noun
juin masc.
in June en juin
**His birthday is at the beginning of
June.** Son anniversaire est début
juin.
It's Thursday the fifth of June. On
est jeudi cinq juin.

junior school noun
l'**école primaire** fem.

> **CULTURE**
> French children go to the **école primaire**
> from age 6 to 11.

just adverb
1 **juste**
just before my birthday juste
avant mon anniversaire
just in time juste à temps
2 **seulement**
How many? Just one! Combien?
Un seulement!
3 (no translation)
I'm just coming! J'arrive!
Wait just a moment! Attends un
instant!
4 **She's just gone out.** Elle vient de
sortir.

Connor is always very keen.
Connor est toujours très
enthousiaste.

to **keep** verb
1 (to have) **garder**
Keep the CD! Garde le CD!
2 (to carry on) **continuer**
Keep working! Continue à
travailler!

• *Languages, nationalities, and religions do not take a capital letter in French.*

Keep going as far as the station.
Continuez jusqu'à la gare.
3 (*to stay*) **rester** @
Keep calm! Restez calmes!

keep fit noun
la **gymnastique** *fem.*
to do keep fit faire de la
gymnastique

kettle noun
la **bouilloire** *fem.*

key noun
la **clé** *fem.*

keyboard noun
(*for a computer, electric piano*) le **clavier**
masc.

kick noun
le **coup de pied** *masc.*

to **kick** verb
to kick somebody donner un coup
de pied à quelqu'un
She kicked me. Elle m'a donné un
coup de pied.
to kick the ball donner un coup de
pied dans le ballon

kid noun
le or la **gosse** *masc. & fem.*
Where have the kids gone? Où
sont passés les gosses?

to **kill** verb
tuer

kilo noun
le **kilo** *masc.*
three euros a kilo trois euros le kilo

kilogramme noun
le **kilogramme** *masc.*

kilometre noun
le **kilomètre** *masc.*
fifty kilometres an hour cinquante
kilomètres à l'heure

kind noun
la **sorte** *fem.*

**What kind of computer do you
have?** Quelle sorte d'ordinateur tu
as?
all kinds of people toutes sortes de
gens

kind adjective
gentil *masc.*, **gentille** *fem.*
Liz is always kind to me. Liz est
toujours gentille avec moi.

king noun
le **roi** *masc.*

kingdom noun
le **royaume** *masc.*
the United Kingdom
le Royaume-Uni

kiss noun
la **bise** *fem.*
Give me a kiss! Fais-moi une bise!

to **kiss** verb
1 **embrasser**
She kissed me. Elle m'a embrassé.
2 (*to kiss each other*) **s'embrasser** @
Anna and Jake are kissing. Anna et
Jake s'embrassent.

CULTURE
In France girls kiss their friends (girls and
boys) on each cheek when they say hello
or goodbye. Boys shake hands.

kit noun
(*clothes*) les **affaires** *fem. plural*
my football kit mes affaires de
foot

kitchen noun
la **cuisine** *fem.*

kite noun
le **cerf-volant** *masc.*
to fly a kite faire voler un
cerf-volant

kitten noun
le **chaton** *masc.*

knee noun
le **genou** *masc.* (plural les **genoux**)

@ *means use* **être** *to make the past tense.*

to **kneel** verb
se mettre à genoux
Kneel down! Mettez-vous à genoux!

knickers noun
la culotte *fem.*

🔑 **LANGUAGE**
English = **knickers** is plural
French = **la culotte** is singular

knife noun
le couteau *masc.* (plural les couteaux)

to **knit** verb
tricoter
I like knitting. J'aime tricoter.

knock noun
le coup *masc.*
I got a knock on my head. J'ai reçu un coup sur la tête.

to **knock** verb
frapper
Somebody's knocking at the door. On frappe à la porte.

to **knock over** verb

to **knock something or somebody over** renverser quelque chose ou quelqu'un

knot noun
le nœud *masc.*
to tie a knot faire un nœud

to **know** verb
1 savoir
Do you know where mum is? Tu sais où est maman?
to know how to do something savoir faire quelque chose
Do you know how to knit? Tu sais tricoter?
I don't know. Je ne sais pas.
2 connaître
Do you know my brother? Tu connais mon frère?
I don't know her. Je ne la connais pas.
You know the rules. Tu connais le règlement.

knowledge noun
la connaissance *fem.*

Koran noun
le Coran *masc.*

Ll

label noun
une étiquette *fem.*

lace noun
(*for a shoe*) le lacet *masc.*
Tie your laces! Attache tes lacets!

ladder noun
une échelle *fem.*
to climb a ladder grimper à une échelle

ladies noun
1 les toilettes pour dames *fem. plural*
Where's the ladies? Où sont les toilettes pour dames?

2 **Ladies and Gentlemen** Mesdames, Mesdemoiselles, Messieurs

lady noun
la dame *fem.*
a young lady une jeune fille

ladybird noun
la coccinelle *fem.*

lake noun
le lac *masc.*

lamb noun
un agneau *masc.* (plural les agneaux)

• *The months of the year and days of the week do not take a capital letter in French.*

a lamb chop une côtelette d'agneau

lamp noun
la **lampe** fem.

land noun
1 (*not the sea*) la **terre** fem.
2 (*a piece of land*) le **terrain** masc.

to **land** verb
atterrir
Our plane lands in an hour. Notre avion atterrit dans une heure.

lane noun
1 (*in the countryside*) le **chemin** masc.
2 (*on a main road*) la **voie** fem.

language noun
la **langue** fem.
We're learning a foreign language. Nous apprenons une langue étrangère.

lap noun
les **genoux** masc. plural
on my lap sur mes genoux

laptop noun
un **ordinateur portable** masc.

large adjective
1 **grand** masc., **grande** fem.
a large garden un grand jardin
a large number un grand nombre
2 **gros** masc., **grosse** fem.
a large dog un gros chien
a large packet un gros paquet
the largest piece le plus gros morceau

last adjective
dernier masc., **dernière** fem.
last month le mois dernier
last year l'année dernière
last Saturday samedi dernier
last night (*yesterday evening*) hier soir
the last two months les deux derniers mois

last adverb
1 (*last of all*) **en dernier**

Fabien came last. (*in the race*) Fabien est arrivé en dernier.
2 **at last** enfin

to **last** verb
durer
The holidays last two weeks. Les vacances durent deux semaines.

late adjective
(*not on time*) **en retard**
I'm late. Je suis en retard.
Sorry, I'm late. Désolé d'être en retard!
I'm going to be late for school. Je vais être en retard à l'école.
to have a late night se coucher ⓔ tard

late adverb
(*late in the day*) **tard**
Claire gets up late. Claire se lève tard.
It's too late to go out. Il est trop tard pour sortir.
He arrived five minutes late. Il est arrivé avec cinq minutes de retard.

later adverb
plus tard
later than usual plus tard que d'habitude
See you later! À tout à l'heure!

latest adjective
dernier masc., **dernière** fem.
the latest Disney film le dernier film de Disney

to **laugh** verb
rire
She makes me laugh. Elle me fait rire.
Don't laugh! Ne ris pas!

law noun
la **loi** fem.
It's against the law! C'est interdit!

lawn noun
la **pelouse** fem.

ⓔ *means use* **être** *to make the past tense.*

a
b
c
d
e
f
g
h
i
j
k
l
m
n
o
p
q
r
s
t
u
v
w
x
y
z

lawnmower noun
la **tondeuse à gazon** fem.

lawyer noun
un **avocat** masc., une **avocate** fem.

to **lay** verb
to lay the table mettre la table

lazy adjective
paresseux masc., **paresseuse** fem.

lead noun
to be in the lead (in a race or game) être en tête

to **lead** verb
mener
This path leads to our school.
Ce chemin mène à notre école.
Our team is leading by three goals to two. Notre équipe mène par trois buts à deux.

leader noun
(of a group or gang) le **chef** masc.

leaf noun
la **feuille** fem.

to **lean out** verb
se pencher ⊚
Don't lean out of the window! Ne te penche pas par la fenêtre!

to **learn** verb
apprendre
I'm learning French. J'apprends le français.
Joël is learning to play the guitar. Joël apprend à jouer de la guitare.

least adverb
1 (when an adjective follows) le **moins** masc., la **moins** fem. (plural les **moins**)
the least interesting book le livre le moins intéressant
the least intelligent person la personne la moins intelligente
the least expensive CDs les CD les moins chers
2 **at least** au moins

I've read at least three books. J'ai lu au moins trois livres.

least adjective
le **moins de**
the least cake le moins de gâteau

leather noun
le **cuir** masc.
a leather bag un sac en cuir

to **leave** verb
1 (to go away) **partir** ⊚
What time do we leave? On part à quelle heure?
2 (to go away from) **quitter**
to leave the house quitter la maison
3 **laisser**
I left my mobile phone at your house. J'ai laissé mon portable chez toi.
Leave me alone! Laissez-moi tranquille!

left adjective
1 **gauche** masc. & fem.
Show me your left hand! Montre-moi ta main gauche!
2 (left over)
to be left rester ⊚
There are three chocolates left. Il reste trois chocolats.
I have twenty euros left. Il me reste vingt euros.
There's nothing left. Il ne reste plus rien.

left adverb
à gauche
Turn left! Tournez à gauche!

left noun
la **gauche** fem.
on the left à gauche
We drive on the left. Nous roulons à gauche.
the first street on your left la première rue sur votre gauche

• See the centre section for verb tables.

left-hand adjective
It's on the left-hand side. C'est à gauche.

left-handed adjective
gaucher masc., **gauchère** fem.
Daniel is left-handed. Daniel est gaucher.

left-luggage office noun
la **consigne** fem.

leg noun
(of a person) la **jambe** fem.
to break your leg se casser ◉ la jambe
Leah broke her leg. Leah s'est cassé la jambe.

leisure centre noun
le **centre de loisirs** masc.

lemon noun
le **citron** masc.

⚷ **LANGUAGE**
Citron is related to 'citrus' in English: 'citrus fruits' include lemons and oranges.

lemonade noun
la **limonade** fem.

to **lend** verb
prêter
to lend something to somebody prêter quelque chose à quelqu'un
Can you lend me your bike? Tu peux me prêter ton vélo?

less adjective
moins de
We have less money. Nous avons moins de d'argent.

less pronoun
1 **moins**
I've got less than you. J'en ai moins que toi.
2 **less than** (with numbers) **moins de**
It costs less than thirty euros. Ça coûte moins de trente euros.

◉ means use **être** to make the past tense.

lesson noun
1 (one lesson as part of a course) la **leçon** fem.
an interesting lesson une leçon intéressante
2 (class) le **cours** masc.
I enjoy French lessons. J'aime bien les cours de français.

to **let** verb
1 **laisser**
to let somebody do something laisser quelqu'un faire quelque chose
Let me watch TV! Laisse-moi regarder la télé!
Can you let me in? Tu peux me laisser entrer?
Let go of me! Lâche-moi!
2 (making suggestions)
Let's go! Allons-y!
Let's leave now! Partons maintenant!

letter noun
la **lettre** fem.
the letter P la lettre P
I'm writing a letter. J'écris une lettre.
a letter box une boîte aux lettres

lettuce noun
la **laitue** fem.

liar noun
le **menteur** masc., la **menteuse** fem.
He's a liar. C'est un menteur.

library noun
la **bibliothèque** fem.

licence noun
le **permis** masc.
a driving licence un permis de conduire

to **lick** verb
lécher

lid noun
le **couvercle** masc.

lie noun
le **mensonge** masc.

You're telling me lies! Tu me dis des mensonges!

to **lie** verb
1 (*to tell lies*) **mentir**
You're lying! Tu mens!
2 (*to be flat*) **s'allonger** ⊘
I'm going to lie down on the grass.
Je vais m'allonger sur l'herbe.

life noun
la **vie** *fem.*
all my life toute ma vie

lifebelt noun
la **bouée de sauvetage** *fem.*

lift noun
un **ascenseur** *masc.*

to **lift** verb
(*something heavy*) **soulever**
I can't lift your suitcase. Je ne peux pas soulever ta valise.

light noun
la **lumière** *fem.*
Turn on the light! Allume la lumière!
Turn off the light! Éteins la lumière!

light adjective
1 (*not heavy*) **léger** *masc.*, **légère** *fem.*
My bag is quite light. Mon sac est assez léger.
2 (*describing colours*) **clair** *masc.*, **claire** *fem.*
light blue bleu clair
3 (*talking about daylight*)
It's light. Il fait jour.

to **light** verb
(*the oven, the gas, a candle, etc.*) **allumer**
to light a fire allumer un feu

light bulb noun
une **ampoule** *fem.*
to change a light bulb changer une ampoule

lighthouse noun
le **phare** *masc.*

lightning noun
les **éclairs** *masc. plural*
a flash of lightning un éclair

to **like** verb
1 **aimer**
I like oranges. J'aime les oranges.
I like Théo. J'aime bien Théo.
She likes singing. Elle aime bien chanter.
2 **I would like ...** Je voudrais ...
I'd like a lemonade. Je voudrais une limonade.
I would like to go to bed. Je voudrais aller me coucher.
Stay if you like! Reste si tu veux!
3 (*in questions*)
Would you like ...?
Tu veux ...?, Vous voulez ...?
What dessert would you like, sir?
Qu'est-ce que vous désirez comme dessert, monsieur?
Would you like some cake, dad?
Tu veux du gâteau, papa?

like preposition
1 **comme**
like me comme moi
Write like this! Écris comme ça!
2 **What's your house like?** Comment est ta maison?
What's the weather like? Quel temps fait-il?

likely adjective
probable *masc. & fem.*

line noun
1 la **ligne** *fem.*
a straight line une ligne droite
to draw a line tracer une ligne
2 la **file** *fem.*
a line of people une file de gens

to **line up** verb
(*in school*) **se mettre** ⊘ **en rang**

lion noun
le **lion** *masc.*

lip noun
la **lèvre** *fem.*

• *Use* **le** *and* **un** *for masculine words and* **la** *and* **une** *for feminine words.*

lipstick noun
le **rouge à lèvres** masc.

list noun
la **liste** fem.
shopping list la liste des courses

to **listen** verb
écouter
Listen! Écoutez!
I'm listening to some music.
J'écoute de la musique.
Listen to me, Jo! Écoute-moi, Jo!

litre noun
le **litre** masc.

litter noun
les **détritus** masc. plural
a litter bin une poubelle

little adjective
1 (not big) **petit** masc., **petite** fem.
a little boy un petit garçon
2 (not much of something)
very little très peu de
I have very little money. J'ai très
peu d'argent.

little pronoun
1 **a little** un peu
**Do you speak French? – Just a
little.** Vous parlez français? – Juste
un peu.
A little more? Un peu plus?
2 **very little** très peu
She eats very little. Elle mange
très peu.

to **live** verb
1 (talking about where your home is)
habiter
I live in Glasgow. J'habite à
Glasgow.
Where do you live? Tu habites où?
2 (to have a life or to be alive) **vivre**
I want to live to be a hundred.
Je veux vivre jusqu'à cent ans.
**'The prince and the princess lived
happily ever after.'** (in stories) 'Le
prince et la princesse vécurent
heureux.'

liver noun
le **foie** masc.

living room noun
le **salon** masc.

load noun
le **tas** masc.
loads of un tas de
loads of money un tas d'argent
I have loads of things to do. J'ai un
tas de choses à faire.

loaf noun
le **pain** masc.
a loaf of bread un pain

lock noun
la **serrure** fem.

to **lock** verb
fermer à clé
Don't forget to lock the door!
N'oublie pas de fermer la porte à
clé!

locker noun
le **casier** masc.

loft noun
le **grenier** masc.

log noun
la **bûche** fem.

to **log off** verb
(when using a computer)
se déconnecter ⊜

to **log on** verb
(when using a computer) **se connecter** ⊜

lollipop noun
la **sucette** fem.
the lollipop lady la dame qui aide
les enfants à traverser la rue
the lollipop man le monsieur qui
aide les enfants à traverser la rue

lolly noun
la **sucette** fem.

London noun
Londres
I am in London. Je suis à Londres.

a
b
c
d
e
f
g
h
i
j
k
l
m
n
o
p
q
r
s
t
u
v
w
x
y
z

⊜ means use **être** to make the past tense.

I'm going to London. Je vais à Londres.

lonely adjective
seul masc., **seule** fem.
He feels lonely. Il se sent seul.

long adjective
1 **long** masc., **longue** fem.
a long journey un long voyage
a long dress une robe longue
He has long hair. Il a les cheveux longs.
2 **a long time** longtemps
It lasts a long time. Ça dure longtemps.
3 **a long way** loin
Is it a long way? C'est loin?
4 **how long** combien de temps
How long is the journey? Le voyage dure combien de temps?

long adverb
longtemps
We didn't wait long. Nous n'avons pas attendu longtemps.

loo noun
les **toilettes** fem. plural
Where's the loo? Où sont les toilettes?

look noun
to have a look regarder
Have a look at my new bike! Regarde mon nouveau vélo!

to **look** verb
1 **regarder**
Look! Regarde!
Look at me! Regarde-moi!
I'm looking at the photos. Je regarde les photos.
2 (followed by an adjective) **avoir l'air**
You look sad. Tu as l'air triste.
That pizza looks delicious. Cette pizza a l'air délicieuse.
3 **to look like** ressembler à

to **look after** verb
s'occuper ℮ **de**

Dad's going to look after the children. Papa va s'occuper des enfants.

to **look for** verb
chercher
I'm looking for my glasses. Je cherche mes lunettes.

to **look out** verb
faire attention
Look out! Attention!

to **look up** verb
chercher
Look up 'earring' in the dictionary. Cherche 'earring' dans le dictionnaire.

loose adjective
1 (clothes) **large** masc. & fem.
2 **I have a loose tooth.** J'ai une dent qui bouge.

lorry noun
le **camion** masc.
a lorry driver un routier

to **lose** verb
perdre
I've lost my watch. J'ai perdu ma montre.
We don't want to lose the match. Nous ne voulons pas perdre le match.

lost adjective
perdu masc., **perdue** fem.
to get lost se perdre ℮
I got lost. Je me suis perdu. (boy speaking) Je me suis perdue. (girl speaking)
lost property les objets trouvés

🗝 **LANGUAGE**
Word for word **les objets trouvés** means 'found objects'.

lot noun
1 **a lot** beaucoup
a lot of beaucoup de
Kate reads a lot. Kate lit beaucoup.

• Languages, nationalities, and religions do not take a capital letter in French.

I have a lot of books. J'ai beaucoup de livres.
lots of people beaucoup de gens
2 **quite a lot** pas mal
I have quite a lot of friends. J'ai pas mal d'amis.

lottery noun
la **loterie** fem.
to win the lottery gagner à la loterie

loud adjective
fort masc., **forte** fem.
The music is too loud. La musique est trop forte.
Not so loud! Pas si fort!
A bit louder! Un peu plus fort!
out loud à haute voix

lounge noun
le **salon** masc.

love noun
l'**amour** masc.
a love story une histoire d'amour
in love with somebody amoureux de quelqu'un masc., amoureuse de quelqu'un fem.
She's in love with Mark. Elle est amoureuse de Mark.
They're in love. Ils s'aiment.
Love, Steve. (in a letter) Grosses bises, Steve.

to **love** verb
1 **aimer**
He loves her. Il l'aime.
2 (to like a person or place a lot) **aimer beaucoup**
My sister loves school. Ma sœur aime beaucoup l'école.
3 (to like something very very much) **adorer**
I love sweets. J'adore les bonbons.
Ted loves skiing. Ted adore le ski.

lovely adjective
1 (beautiful) **beau** masc., **belle** fem., **beaux** masc. plural, **belles** fem. plural
a lovely dress une belle robe

It's a lovely day. C'est une belle journée., Il fait beau.
2 (wonderful) **formidable** masc. & fem.
a lovely meal un repas formidable

low adjective
bas masc., **basse** fem.

luck noun
la **chance** fem.
Good luck! Bonne chance!
Bad luck! Pas de chance!
to bring somebody luck porter bonheur à quelqu'un

lucky adjective
1 (talking about people)
to be lucky avoir de la chance
You're always lucky. Tu as toujours de la chance.
2 (talking about things or numbers)
to be lucky porter bonheur
The number seven is lucky. Le chiffre sept porte bonheur.
a lucky number un chiffre porte-bonheur

luggage noun
les **bagages** masc. plural
My luggage is here. Mes bagages sont ici.

> **LANGUAGE**
> English = **luggage** is singular
> French = **bagages** is plural

lunch noun
le **déjeuner** masc.
What's for lunch? Qu'est-ce qu'on mange au déjeuner?
to have lunch déjeuner
a lunch box une boîte à sandwichs

lunchtime noun
l'**heure du déjeuner** fem.

lung noun
le **poumon** masc.

Luxembourg noun
le **Luxembourg** masc.

*means use **être** to make the past tense.*

a
b
c
d
e
f
g
h
i
j
k
l
m
n
o
p
q
r
s
t
u
v
w
x
y
z

Mm

mac noun
un **imper** *masc.*

macaroni noun
les **macaronis** *masc. plural*

machine noun
la **machine** *fem.*

mad adjective
1 (*crazy*) **fou** *masc.*, **folle** *fem.*
He's mad! Il est fou!
2 (*angry*) **en colère**
She's mad at you. Elle est en colère
contre toi.
3 **to be mad about something** adorer
quelque chose
He's mad about animals. Il adore
les animaux.

madam noun
madame *fem.*
Yes, madam! Oui, madame!

made verb SEE **make**

magazine noun
le **magazine** *masc.*

magic adjective
magique *masc. & fem.*
a magic wand une baguette
magique
a magic trick un tour de magie

magic noun
la **magie** *fem.*
by magic par magie

magician noun
le **magicien** *masc.*,
la **magicienne** *fem.*

magnifying glass noun
la **loupe** *fem.*

mail noun
le **courrier** *masc.*
Is there any mail? Il y a du
courrier?

to mail verb
poster
to mail a letter poster une lettre

mailbox noun
(*for getting email*) la **boîte aux lettres**
fem.

main adjective
principal *masc.*,
principale *fem.*, **principaux** *masc.*
plural, **principales** *fem. plural*
the main road la route principale
**He's not hurt – that's the main
thing.** Il n'est pas blessé – c'est
l'essentiel.

mainly adverb
surtout
There are mainly girls in our class.
Il y a surtout des filles dans notre
classe.

make noun
la **marque** *fem.*
What make is your computer? De
quelle marque est ton ordinateur?

to make verb
1 **faire**
I'm making a cup of tea. Je fais une
tasse de thé.
Dad's making the bed. Papa fait le
lit.
They make me laugh. Ils me font
rire.
Three and four make seven. Trois
et quatre font sept.
2 (*to build*) **fabriquer**
to make cars fabriquer des voitures
Made in China Fabriqué en Chine
3 (*to get ready*) **préparer**
I'm making breakfast. Je prépare
le petit déjeuner.
4 (*to earn*) **gagner**
How much money does he make?
Il gagne combien d'argent?

• *The months of the year and days of the week do not take a capital letter in French.*

a
b
c
d
e
f
g
h
i
j
k
l
m
n
o
p
q
r
s
t
u
v
w
x
y
z

5 (*to force*) **obliger**
We're not going to make you play!
On ne va pas t'obliger à jouer!

6 (*with adjectives*) **rendre**
It makes me sad. Ça me rend triste.

7 (*with* **hungry** *and* **thirsty**) **donner**
It makes me hungry. Ça me donne faim.

to **make up** verb
(*a story*) **inventer**
You're making it up! Tu inventes!

make-up noun
le **maquillage** *masc.*
She's putting her make-up on. Elle se maquille.

male noun
le **mâle** *masc.*

male adjective
mâle *masc. & fem.*
a male rabbit un lapin mâle

man noun
l' **homme** *masc.*
a man and a woman un homme et une femme

> 🔑 **LANGUAGE**
> Use **un monsieur** for talking about a stranger and to be polite, for example: 'Ask the man' is **Demande au monsieur.**

to **manage** verb
(*to get on okay*) **se débrouiller** ⓔ
I can manage. Je me débrouille.

manager noun
1 (*of a company*) le **directeur** *masc.*,
la **directrice** *fem.*
2 (*of a shop or restaurant*) le **gérant** *masc.*,
la **gérante** *fem.*

manners plural noun
les **manières** *fem. plural*
to teach somebody good manners
apprendre les bonnes manières à quelqu'un
He has good manners. Il est bien élevé.
That's bad manners! Ce n'est pas poli!

many adjective and pronoun
1 **beaucoup de**
many young people beaucoup de jeunes
2 **how many?** combien de?
How many times? Combien de fois?
How many girls are there? Il y a combien de filles?
3 **so many** tant de
Natasha has so many friends!
Natasha a tant d'amies!
4 **as many** autant de
Jason has as many CDs as me.
Jason a autant de CD que moi.
5 **too many** trop de
That's too many. C'est trop.
I have too many. J'en ai trop.
I've got too many things to do.
J'ai trop de choses à faire.
6 **not many** pas beaucoup
I don't have many. Je n'en ai pas beaucoup.

> 🔑 **LANGUAGE**
> English = **many** + noun
> French = **beaucoup de** + noun

map noun
1 (*of a country*) la **carte** *fem.*
a map of France une carte de France
2 (*of a town*) le **plan** *masc.*
a map of Dieppe un plan de Dieppe

marathon noun
le **marathon** *masc.*
to run in a marathon courir un marathon

marble noun
la **bille** *fem.*
Do you like playing marbles?
Tu aimes jouer aux billes?

March noun
mars *masc.*
in March en mars
at the end of March fin mars

a b c d e f g h i j k l **m** n o p q r s t u v w x y z

ⓔ *means use* **être** *to make the past tense.*

My birthday is the eighth of March.
Mon anniversaire est le huit mars.

margarine noun
la **margarine** *fem.*

margin noun
la **marge** *fem.*
Put down the date in the margin.
Écrivez la date dans la marge.

mark noun
(*in school subjects*) la **note** *fem.*
Julie always gets good marks.
Julie a toujours de bonnes notes.

to **mark** verb
1 (*homework etc.*) **corriger**
I will mark the exercises tomorrow. Je vais corriger les exercices demain.
2 (*to show*) **marquer**
It's marked with a cross. C'est marqué d'une croix.

market noun
le **marché** *masc.*

marmalade noun
la **confiture d'oranges** *fem.*

marriage noun
le **mariage** *masc.*

> **LANGUAGE**
> English = marriage
> French = mariage

married adjective
marié *masc.*, **mariée** *fem.*
Are they married? Sont-ils mariés?
to get married se marier @

to **marry** verb
épouser

masculine adjective
masculin *masc.*, **masculine** *fem.*

mashed potatoes plural noun
la **purée de pommes de terre** *fem.*

> **LANGUAGE**
> English = **mashed potatoes** is plural
> French = **purée** is singular

mask noun
le **masque** *masc.*

mass noun
1 (*church service*) la **messe** *fem.*
They go to mass. Ils vont à la messe.
2 **masses of** beaucoup de
She has masses of DVDs. Elle a beaucoup de DVD.

massive adjective
énorme *masc. & fem.*

masterpiece noun
le **chef-d'œuvre** *masc.* (plural les **chefs-d'œuvre**)

mat noun
(*for wiping your feet*) le **paillasson** *masc.*

match noun
1 une **allumette** *fem.*
a box of matches une boîte d'allumettes
2 (*a team game*) le **match** *masc.*
a football match un match de football

to **match** verb
1 (*talking about clothes, etc.*) **aller @ avec**
Your top doesn't match your skirt.
Ton haut ne va pas avec ta jupe.
2 (*to find similar things*)
Match the words and the pictures!
Trouvez les mots qui correspondent aux images!

matching adjective
assorti *masc.*, **assortie** *fem.*
a hat with matching scarf and gloves un chapeau avec une écharpe et des gants assortis

mate noun
le **copain** *masc.*, la **copine** *fem.*

material noun
(*cloth*) le **tissu** *masc.*

mathematics noun
les **mathématiques** *fem. plural*

• *The months of the year and days of the week do not take a capital letter in French.*

maths noun
les **maths** *fem. plural*
I enjoy maths. J'aime bien les maths.

matter noun
What's the matter? Qu'est-ce qu'il y a?
What's the matter with you? Qu'est-ce que tu as?

to **matter** verb
It doesn't matter. Ça n'a pas d'importance., Ça ne fait rien.

mattress noun
le **matelas** *masc.*

maximum noun
le **maximum** *masc.*

may verb
(*asking for permission*) **May I go?** Je peux partir?

May noun
mai *masc.*
in May en mai
Come to my house on the fifth of May. Viens chez moi cinq mai.
May Day le Premier Mai

CULTURE
In France the **Premier Mai** is a holiday when people give each other small bunches of **muguet** (lily of the valley) for good luck.

maybe adverb
peut-être
Maybe it's too late. C'est peut-être trop tard.
Maybe not! Peut-être pas!

mayonnaise noun
la **mayonnaise** *fem.*

mayor noun
le **maire** *masc.*

maze noun
le **labyrinthe** *masc.*

means use être to make the past tense.

me pronoun
1 (*after a verb*) **me**
She knows me. Elle me connaît.
Is he looking for me? Est-ce qu'il me cherche?
Mum's calling me. Maman m'appelle.

LANGUAGE
me = m' before a vowel or silent 'h'

2 (*to me*) **me**
Can you give me that CD? Tu peux me donner ce CD?
3 (*when telling somebody to do something*) **moi**
Help me! Aide-moi!
Give me the keys! Donne-moi les clés!
4 (*after a preposition, after* **it's**) **moi**
with me avec moi
It's me. C'est moi.

meal noun
le **repas** *masc.*
We had a good meal. Nous avons fait un bon repas.

to **mean** verb
vouloir dire
What does 'sourire' mean? Que veut dire 'sourire'?
What do you mean? Qu'est-ce que tu veux dire?
It doesn't mean anything. Ça ne veut rien dire.

mean adjective
1 (*with money*) **radin** *masc.*, **radine** *fem.*
2 (*nasty*) **méchant** *masc.*, **méchante** *fem.*
He's always mean to me. Il est toujours méchant avec moi.

meaning noun
le **sens** *masc.*
the meaning of a word le sens d'un mot

measles noun
la **rougeole** *fem.*

a
b
c
d
e
f
g
h
i
j
k
l
m
n
o
p
q
r
s
t
u
v
w
x
y
z

a
b
c
d
e
f
g
h
i
j
k
l
m
n
o
p
q
r
s
t
u
v
w
x
y
z

to **measure** verb
mesurer

meat noun
la **viande** fem.
Do you eat meat? Tu manges de la viande?

mechanic noun
le **mécanicien** masc.,
la **mécanicienne** fem.

medal noun
la **médaille** fem.
a gold medal une médaille d'or

medicine noun
le **médicament** masc.
Take some medicine! Prends un médicament!

Mediterranean noun
the Mediterranean
la **Méditerranée** fem.

medium adjective
moyen masc., **moyenne** fem.
Small, medium or large? Petit, moyen ou grand?

to **meet** verb
1 (to meet somebody by chance) **rencontrer**
I met him in the supermarket. Je l'ai rencontré au supermarché.
We met by chance. Nous nous sommes recontrés par hasard.
2 (to plan to meet somebody) **retrouver**
I'll meet you in front of the library. Je te retrouve devant la bibliothèque.
3 (to go and get somebody) **aller** ⓔ **chercher**
We're going to meet Tom at the airport. On va chercher Tom à l'aéroport.

meeting noun
(in an office, club, etc.) la **réunion** fem.

melon noun
le **melon** masc.

to **melt** verb
fondre
Your ice cream it will melt. Ta glace va fondre.

member noun
le **membre** masc.

memory noun
la **mémoire** fem.
I have a very good memory. J'ai une très bonne mémoire.

men plural noun
les **hommes** masc. plural

to **mend** verb
réparer

to **mention** verb
to mention something parler de quelque chose

menu noun
le **menu** masc.

mermaid noun
la **sirène** fem.

merry adjective
Merry Christmas! Joyeux Noël!

merry-go-round noun
le **manège** masc.

mess noun
le **désordre** masc.
My room's in a mess. Ma chambre est en désordre.

to **mess up** verb
(papers, books, hair, etc.) **déranger**
You've messed up my toys! Tu as dérangé mes jouets!

message noun
le **message** masc.

messy adjective
(room, house, etc.) **en désordre**

metal noun
le **métal** masc. (plural les **métaux**)

metre noun
le **mètre** masc.

• See the centre section for verb tables.

mice plural noun
les **souris** *fem. plural*

microphone noun
le **micro** *masc.*

microwave noun
le **micro-ondes** *masc.*

midday noun
midi *masc.*
at midday à midi
It's midday. Il est midi.

middle noun
le **milieu** *masc.*
in the middle of au milieu de
the middle drawer le tiroir du milieu
a middle name un deuxième prénom

Middle East noun
le **Moyen-Orient** *masc.*

midnight noun
minuit *masc.*
at midnight à minuit
It's midnight. Il est minuit.

might verb
She might be ill. Elle est peut-être malade.
Are you coming? – I might.
Tu viens? Peut-être.

mild adjective
doux *masc.*, **douce** *fem.*
The weather's mild. Il fait doux.

mile noun
The school is three miles away.
L'école est à cinq kilomètres d'ici.

CULTURE
In France they use kilometres for distances: one mile is just over one and a half kilometres.

milk noun
le **lait** *masc.*
Would you like some milk?
Tu veux du lait?
a milk shake un milk-shake

million noun
le **million** *masc.*
two million deux millions
a million people un million de personnes

LANGUAGE
English = **a million** + noun
French = **un million de** + noun

millionaire noun
le or la **millionnaire** *masc. & fem.*

LANGUAGE
English = millionaire
French = millionnaire

mince noun
la **viande hachée** *fem.*

mind noun
I've changed my mind. J'ai changé d'avis.
to make up your mind se décider ⊕

to **mind** verb
1 (*to look after*) **garder**
Can you mind the baby? Tu peux garder le bébé?
2 **do you mind ...?** ça vous dérange ...?
Do you mind if I close the window?
Ça vous dérange si je ferme la fenêtre?
I don't mind. Ça ne me dérange pas.
3 (*when you don't care*)
Do you want some orange juice or some water? I don't mind. Tu veux du jus d'orange ou de l'eau? Ça m'est égal.
Never mind! Tant pis!
4 (*to watch out*)
Mind the step! Attention à la marche!

mine pronoun
à moi
This CD is mine. Ce CD est à moi.
It's mine. C'est à moi.

⊕ *means use* **être** *to make the past tense.*

a
b
c
d
e
f
g
h
i
j
k
l
m
n
o
p
q
r
s
t
u
v
w
x
y
z

mine noun
la **mine** fem.
a gold mine une mine d'or

mineral water noun
l'**eau minérale** fem.

minibus noun
le **minibus** masc.

minimum noun
le **minimum** masc.

mint noun
1 (sweet) le **bonbon à la menthe** masc.
2 (plant) la **menthe** fem.

minus preposition
moins
Eleven minus six is five. Onze moins six font cinq.

minute noun
la **minute** fem.

mirror noun
la **glace** fem.

to **misbehave** verb
se **conduire** ⊚ **mal**
Katie misbehaves in class. Katie se conduit mal en classe.

mischief noun
les **bêtises** fem. plural
He's getting up to mischief. Il fait des bêtises.

miserable adjective
1 (sad) **malheureux** masc., **malheureuse** fem.
She looks miserable. Elle a l'air malheureuse.
2 **The weather's miserable.** Il fait mauvais.

miss noun
1 (talking to your teacher)
Please, miss! S'il vous plaît, maîtresse!
2 (in front of a name)
Miss Mademoiselle

Miss Kelly Mademoiselle Kelly

⚷ **LANGUAGE**
Mademoiselle is often written down as **Mlle**.

to **miss** verb
1 (the bus, film, etc.) **rater**
We missed the train. On a raté le train.
2 (to feel sad)
I miss my parents. Mes parents me manquent.

missing adjective
1 (lost)
to be missing avoir disparu
Two people are missing. Deux personnes ont disparu.
2 (not in the usual place)
There's a page missing from my book. Il manque une page à mon livre.

mist noun
la **brume** fem.

mistake noun
1 (in your writing, spelling, or typing)
la **faute** fem.
to make a spelling mistake faire une faute d'orthographe
2 (wrong idea or thing to do) une **erreur** fem.
You've taken my coat by mistake. Tu as pris mon manteau par erreur.

misty adjective
brumeux masc., **brumeuse** fem.
a misty morning un matin brumeux
It's misty. Il y a de la brume.

to **mix** verb
1 **mélanger**
Mix these two colours together. Mélangez ces deux couleurs.
You've mixed up all my CDs! Tu as mélangé tous mes CD!

• Use **le** and **un** for masculine words and **la** and **une** for feminine words.

2 to get something mixed up with something confondre quelque chose avec quelque chose
I get her and her friend mixed up. Je la confonds avec sa copine.

mixture noun
le **mélange** masc.

mix-up noun
la **confusion** fem.

to **moan** verb
(to complain) **râler**

mobile, **mobile phone** noun
le **portable** masc.
I've lost my mobile. J'ai perdu mon portable.

model noun
1 (a copy of a bigger thing) le **modèle réduit** masc.
a model plane un modèle réduit d'avion
2 (a type of thing) le **modèle** masc.
It's the latest model. C'est le dernier modèle.
3 (a person) le **mannequin** masc.
She's a model. Elle est mannequin.

modern adjective
moderne masc. & fem.

moment noun
1 un **instant** masc.
Wait a moment! Attendez un instant!
I'll be back in a moment. Je reviens dans un instant.
2 le **moment** masc.
the right moment le bon moment
at the moment en ce moment

Monday noun
lundi masc.
It's Monday today. Aujourd'hui, c'est lundi.
on Monday lundi
Come to my house on Monday! Viens chez moi lundi!
next Monday lundi prochain
last Monday lundi dernier

every Monday tous les lundis
on Mondays le lundi
We have games on Mondays. On a sport le lundi.

money noun
l'**argent** masc.
I haven't got enough money. Je n'ai pas assez d'argent.

money box noun
la **tirelire** fem.

monitor noun
(computer screen) le **moniteur** masc.

monkey noun
le **singe** masc.

monster noun
le **monstre** masc.

month noun
le **mois** masc.
at the beginning of the month au début du mois
at the end of the month à la fin du mois
this month ce mois-ci
last month le mois dernier
next month le mois prochain

mood noun
l'**humeur** fem.
Are you in a good or bad mood? Tu es de bonne ou de mauvaise humeur?

moon noun
la **lune** fem.

more adverb
plus
more interesting plus intéressant
more and more de plus en plus
I read more than you. Je lis plus que toi.

more adjective
1 plus de
My brother has more homework than me. Mon frère a plus de devoirs que moi.

a
b
c
d
e
f
g
h
i
j
k
l
m
n
o
p
q
r
s
t
u
v
w
x
y
z

⊙ means use **être** to make the past tense.

2 (*talking about extra things or things you ask for*) **encore de**
Would you like some more bread?
Tu veux encore du pain?
some more apples encore des pommes
six more days encore six jours

more pronoun
1 plus
You have more than me. Tu en as plus que moi.
Are you having a bit more? Tu en prends un peu plus?
I don't want any more. Je n'en veux plus.
2 (*asking for something extra*) **encore**
I would like some more, please.
J'en voudrais encore, s'il vous plaît.
3 more than (*with numbers and weights*) plus de
more than a kilo plus d'un kilo

morning noun
1 le **matin** *masc.*
In the morning, I go to school.
Le matin, je vais à l'école.
at six o'clock in the morning à six heures du matin
this morning ce matin
tomorrow morning demain matin
yesterday morning hier matin
Good morning! Bonjour!
2 la **matinée** *fem.*
They watched TV all morning.
Ils ont regardé la télé toute la matinée.

🔑 **LANGUAGE**
French has two words for 'morning': **matin** and **matinée**. Use **matinée** when you mean the whole time from when you get up until the afternoon.

Morocco noun
le **Maroc** *masc.*

mosque noun
la **mosquée** *fem.*

mosquito noun
le **moustique** *masc.*
a mosquito bite une piqûre de moustique

most adverb
1 (*with verbs*) **le plus**
I like Harry Potter the most. C'est Harry Potter que j'aime le plus.
2 (*when an adjective follows*) **le plus** *masc.*, **la plus** *fem.* (plural les **plus**)
the most interesting book le livre le plus intéressant
the most intelligent girl la fille la plus intelligente
the most expensive shoes les chaussures les plus chères

most adjective
1 (*over half*) **la plupart des**
most people la plupart des gens
2 (*more than all the others*) **le plus de**
I have the most money. J'ai le plus d'argent.

most pronoun
1 (*over half*) **la plupart**
most of my friends la plupart de mes amis
2 (*when a singular noun follows*) **presque tout** *masc.*, **presque toute** *fem.*
most of the water presque toute l'eau
3 most of all surtout

moth noun
le **papillon de nuit** *masc.*

mother noun
la **mère** *fem.*
My mother is a teacher. Ma mère est professeur.
Mother's Day la fête des Mères
Happy Mother's Day! Bonne Fête maman!

 CULTURE
In France, Mother's Day is the last Sunday in May.

• *Languages, nationalities, and religions do not take a capital letter in French.*

motorbike noun
la **moto** fem.

motorcycle noun
la **moto** fem.

motorcyclist noun
le or la **motocycliste** masc. & fem.

motorist noun
un or une **automobiliste** masc. & fem.

motorway noun
l'**autoroute** fem.

mountain noun
la **montagne** fem.
We're going to the mountains.
On va à la montagne.
a mountain bike un VTT (= vélo tout-terrain)

mouse noun
la **souris** fem.
a mouse mat un tapis de souris

moustache noun
la **moustache** fem.

mouth noun
la **bouche** fem.
Open your mouth! Ouvre la bouche!

move noun
(in a game) le **tour** masc.
It's my move. C'est mon tour.

to **move** verb
1 **bouger**
Don't move! Ne bouge pas!
2 (to put out of the way) **pousser**
Can you move your bag? Vous pouvez pousser votre sac?
3 (to move house) **déménager**
When are you moving? Vous déménagez quand?

to **move back** verb
reculer

to **move forward** verb
avancer

❷ means use être to make the past tense.

movement noun
le **mouvement** masc.

movie noun
le **film** masc.
We're going to the movies. On va au cinéma.

to **mow** verb
to mow the lawn tondre la pelouse

Mr noun
Monsieur masc.
Mr Lewis Monsieur Lewis

> **LANGUAGE**
> **Monsieur** is sometimes written down as **M.**

Mrs noun
Madame fem.
Mrs Singh Madame Singh

> **LANGUAGE**
> **Madame** is sometimes written down as **Mme.**

Ms noun
Madame fem.
Ms Mitchell Madame Mitchell

> **CULTURE**
> In French, there is no exact equivalent to **Ms.** Use **Madame.**

much adverb
1 **beaucoup**
I don't read much. Je ne lis pas beaucoup.
much bigger beaucoup plus grand
very much beaucoup
Thank you very much! Merci beaucoup!
2 **too much** trop
Dad's working too much. Papa travaille trop.

much adjective
1 **beaucoup de**
I don't have much time. Je n'ai pas beaucoup de temps.
2 **how much?** combien de?

343

How much time is left? Il reste combien de temps?

3 as much autant de
Lucy has as much work as me. Lucy a autant de travail que moi.

4 too much trop de
too much noise trop de bruit

🔑 **LANGUAGE**
English = **much** + noun
French = **beaucoup de** + noun

much pronoun
1 beaucoup
not much pas beaucoup
2 how much? combien?
How much is it? C'est combien?
How much do you have? Tu en as combien?
3 too much trop
That's too much. C'est trop.

mud noun
la **boue** fem.

muddy adjective
(hands, car, etc.) **plein de boue** masc.,
pleine de boue fem.

mug noun
(of tea or coffee) la **grande tasse** fem.

to **multiply** verb
multiplier
Five multiplied by four is twenty. Cinq multiplié par quatre égale vingt.

mum noun
1 la **maman** fem.
Yes, mum! Oui, maman!
Where's mum? Où est maman?
2 la **mère** fem.
My mum is a doctor. Ma mère est médecin.

🔑 **LANGUAGE**
You use **maman** when talking to your mum or about your mum inside the family.

mummy noun
la **maman** fem.
Bye, mummy! Au revoir, maman!

mumps noun
les **oreillons** masc. plural

murder noun
le **meurtre** masc.

to **murder** verb
assassiner

🔑 **LANGUAGE**
The English word 'assassinate' is like **assassiner** and means 'to murder somebody important or famous'.

murderer noun
un **assassin** masc.

muscle noun
le **muscle** masc.

museum noun
le **musée** masc.

mushroom noun
le **champignon** masc.

music noun
la **musique** fem.
I'm listening to music. J'écoute de la musique.

musical adjective
a musical instrument un instrument de musique

musician noun
le **musicien** masc.,
la **musicienne** fem.

Muslim adjective
musulman masc.,
musulmane fem.

mussels plural noun
les **moules** fem. plural

must verb
devoir
I must go. Je dois partir.
You mustn't touch! Tu ne dois pas toucher!

• The months of the year and days of the week do not take a capital letter in French.

You must be hungry, boys. Vous devez avoir faim, les garçons.
It must be late. Il doit être tard.

mustard noun
　la **moutarde** *fem.*

my adjective
1 (*before a masculine noun*) **mon**
　my bike mon vélo
2 (*before a feminine noun*) **ma**
　my house ma maison
3 (*before a plural noun*) **mes**
　my shoes mes chaussures

⚷ **LANGUAGE**
Use **mon** instead of **ma** for a feminine noun starting with a vowel or a silent 'h', for example: 'my idea' is **mon idée**.

myself pronoun
1 **moi-même**

I can do it myself. Je peux le faire moi-même.
2 **me**
　I've cut myself. Je me suis coupé.
　(*boy speaking*) Je me suis coupée. (*girl speaking*)
　I'm enjoying myself. Je m'amuse.

⚷ **LANGUAGE**
me = **m'** before a vowel or silent 'h'

3 **by myself** tout seul *masc.*, toute seule *fem.*
　My parents let me go out by myself. Mes parents me laissent sortir toute seule.

mysterious adjective
　mystérieux *masc.*,
　mystérieuse *fem.*

mystery noun
　le **mystère** *masc.*

Nn

nail noun
1 (*on fingers and toes*) un **ongle** *masc.*
　nail varnish le vernis à ongles
2 (*for woodwork*) le **clou** *masc.*
　Dad bought some nails. Papa a acheté des clous.

naked adjective
　nu *masc.*, **nue** *fem.*

name noun
　le **nom** *masc.*
　How do you spell your name? Comment écris-tu ton nom?
　What's your name? Comment tu t'appelles?
　My name's Luke. Je m'appelle Luke.
　What's his name? Comment s'appelle-t-il?

Their names are Megan and Shazia. Elles s'appellent Megan et Shazia.

⚷ **LANGUAGE**
There are several ways to ask somebody their name: **Comment tu t'appelles?**; **Tu t'appelles comment?**; **Comment t'appelles-tu?**

nanny noun
1 (*who looks after children*) la **nourrice** *fem.*
2 (*grandmother*) la **mamie** *fem.*

nap noun
　la **sieste** *fem.*
　to have a nap faire la sieste

napkin noun
　la **serviette** *fem.*

narrow adjective
　étroit *masc.*, **étroite** *fem.*

ⓔ *means use* **être** *to make the past tense.*

English French

a
b
c
d
e
f
g
h
i
j
k
l
m
n
o
p
q
r
s
t
u
v
w
x
y
z

nasty adjective
1 (*bad*) **mauvais** *masc.*,
   mauvaise *fem.*
   a nasty taste un mauvais goût
2 (*wicked*) **méchant** *masc.*,
   méchante *fem.*
   She's nasty to her brother. Elle est
   méchante avec son frère.

national adjective
   national *masc.*,
   nationale *fem.*, **nationaux** *masc.*
   plural, **nationales** *fem. plural*
   the national anthem l'hymne
   national

nationality noun
   la **nationalité** *fem.*
   What nationality are you? Tu es
   de quelle nationalité?

natural adjective
   naturel *masc.*, **naturelle** *fem.*

nature noun
   la **nature** *fem.*

naughty adjective
   vilain *masc.*, **vilaine** *fem.*
   He's a naughty boy. C'est un vilain
   garçon.

navy blue adjective
   bleu marine *masc. & fem.*
   navy blue socks des chaussettes
   bleu marine

🔑 **LANGUAGE**
Bleu marine is the same in the masculine,
feminine, and plural.

near adjective
   proche *masc. & fem.*
   It's very near. C'est tout proche.
   Where's the nearest cafe? Où est le
   café le plus proche?

neck adverb
   près
   too near trop près

near preposition
   près de
   I live very near here. J'habite tout
   près d'ici.
   The school is near the park. L'école
   est près du parc.
   Is there a tourist office near here?
   Est-ce qu'il y a un office du tourisme
   près d'ici?

near adverb
   près
   too near tout près

nearly adverb
   presque
   I've nearly finished. J'ai presque
   fini.
   It's nearly four o'clock. Il est
   presque quatre heures.

neat adjective
1 (*work, clothes, etc.*) **soigné** *masc.*,
   soignée *fem.*
   neat handwriting une écriture
   soignée
2 (*room, house*) **neat and tidy** bien
   rangé *masc.*, bien rangée *fem.*

necessary adjective
   nécessaire *masc. & fem.*

neck noun
   le **cou** *masc.*

necklace noun
   le **collier** *masc.*

to **need** verb
   avoir besoin de
   I need a pencil sharpener.
   J'ai besoin d'un taille-crayon.

needle noun
   une **aiguille** *fem.*

negative noun
   (*in grammar*) la **forme négative** *fem.*

neighbour noun
   le **voisin** *masc.*, la **voisine** *fem.*

• *See the centre section for verb tables.*

346

neither conjunction
1 **neither ... nor** ni ... ni
neither Rachel nor Adam ni Rachel
ni Adam
2 (*in replies*)
He's not coming! – Neither am I!
Il ne vient pas! – Moi non plus!

neither pronoun
ni l'un ni l'autre *masc.*, **ni l'une ni**
l'autre *fem.*
The red one or the blue one? –
Neither. Le rouge ou le bleu? – Ni
l'un ni l'autre.

nephew noun
le **neveu** *masc.* (plural les **neveux**)

nerve noun
le **nerf** *masc.*
He gets on my nerves. Il me tape
sur les nerfs.

nervous adjective
nerveux *masc.*, **nerveuse** *fem.*

nest noun
le **nid** *masc.*

net noun
le **filet** *masc.*

Net noun
le **Net** *masc.*
to look something up on the Net
chercher quelque chose sur le Net

netball noun
le **netball** *masc.*

 CULTURE
Girls do not play **netball** in France;
instead they can play basketball or
handball.

Netherlands noun
the Netherlands les Pays-Bas *masc.*
plural

never adverb
1 **ne ... jamais**
I never eat meat. Je ne mange
jamais de viande.

ⓔ *means use* **être** *to make the past tense.*

2 **jamais**
When do you do the washing-up? –
Never! Quand est-ce que tu fais la
vaisselle? – Jamais!

new adjective
1 **nouveau** *masc.*,
nouvelle *fem.*, **nouveaux** *masc.*
plural, **nouvelles** *fem. plural*
Come and see my new bike! Venez
voir mon nouveau vélo!
My brother has a new girlfriend.
Mon frère a une nouvelle copine.

> **LANGUAGE**
> Use **nouvel** with a masculine singular
> noun beginning with *a, e, i, o, u*, or a *silent h*,
> for example: **un nouvel ordinateur** is 'a
> new computer'.

2 (*never been used*) **neuf** *masc.*,
neuve *fem.*
I've got new shoes. J'ai des
chaussures neuves.
3 **the New Year** le nouvel an
New Year's Day le jour de l'an
New Year's Eve la Saint-Sylvestre

news noun
1 les **nouvelles** *fem. plural*
good news de bonnes nouvelles
I have some news for you. J'ai une
nouvelle pour toi.

> **LANGUAGE**
> **une nouvelle** = one piece of news

2 (*on TV or the radio*) les **informations**
fem. plural
I saw it on the news. Je l'ai vu aux
informations.

newsagent noun
le **marchand de journaux** *masc.*

newspaper noun
le **journal** *masc.* (plural les
journaux)

New Zealand noun
la **Nouvelle-Zélande** *fem.*

a
b
c
d
e
f
g
h
i
j
k
l
m
n
o
p
q
r
s
t
u
v
w
x
y
z

next adjective
1 (*in time*) **prochain** *masc.*,
prochaine *fem.*
next week la semaine prochaine
next Tuesday mardi prochain
next time la prochaine fois
2 (*following after something*)
suivant *masc.*, **suivante** *fem.*
It's on the next page. C'est à la
page suivante.
the next customer le client suivant
They arrived the next day. Ils sont
arrivés le lendemain.
I'm next. (*in a queue or game*) C'est à
moi.
Who's next? C'est à qui?

next adverb
1 (*after this*) **ensuite**
What did you do next? Qu'est-ce
que tu as fait ensuite?
2 (*now*) **maintenant**
What shall we do next? Qu'est-ce
qu'on va faire maintenant?
3 **next door** à côté
She lives next door. Elle habite à
côté.
4 **next to** à côté de
Can I sit next to you? Je peux
m'asseoir à côté de toi?

nice adjective
1 (*good*) **bon** *masc.*, **bonne** *fem.*
Have a nice day! Bonne journée!
2 (*pretty*) **joli** *masc.*, **jolie** *fem.*
It's nice here. C'est joli ici.
3 (*kind*) **gentil** *masc.*, **gentille** *fem.*
The headmistress is very nice.
La directrice est très gentille.
4 (*talking about the weather*)
It's a nice day. Il fait beau.

nicely adverb
(*in a friendly way*) **gentiment**
Ask nicely. Demande gentiment.

nickname noun
le **surnom** *masc.*

niece noun
la **nièce** *fem.*

night noun
1 la **nuit** *fem.*
during the night pendant la nuit
2 (*evening*) le **soir** *masc.*
at seven o'clock at night à sept
heures du soir
last night hier soir

nightdress , **nightie** noun
la **chemise de nuit** *fem.*

> 🔑 **LANGUAGE**
> Word for word **chemise de nuit** means
> 'night shirt'.

nightmare noun
le **cauchemar** *masc.*
to have nightmares faire des
cauchemars

nil noun
le **zéro** *masc.*
We won two nil. Nous avons
gagné deux à zéro.

nine number
neuf
nine girls neuf filles
I'm nine. J'ai neuf ans.
Dad goes to work at nine. Papa va
au travail à neuf heures.

nineteen number
dix-neuf

ninety number
quatre-vingt-dix

ninth adjective
neuvième *masc. & fem.*
on the ninth floor au neuvième
étage
the ninth of October le neuf
octobre

no adverb
non
Do you like broccoli? – No!
Tu aimes le brocoli? – Non!
No thanks! Non merci!

• Use **le** and **un** for masculine words and **la** and **une** for feminine words.

no adjective
1 (*not any*) **pas de**
We have no pets. Nous n'avons pas d'animaux de compagnie.
No problem! Pas de problème!
2 (*on signs*)
'No smoking' 'Défense de fumer'

nobody pronoun
1 **ne … personne**
There's nobody at home. Il n'y a personne à la maison.
2 **personne**
Who's there? – Nobody! Qui est là? – Personne!

🔑 **LANGUAGE**
ne + *verb* + **personne**, for example: Je **ne** vois **personne**.

noise noun
le **bruit** *masc.*
You're making too much noise. Tu fais trop de bruit.

noisy adjective
bruyant *masc.*, **bruyante** *fem.*

none pronoun
1 **aucun** *masc.*, **aucune** *fem.*
How many? – None! Combien? – Aucun!
None of these boys know me. Aucun de ces garçons ne me connaît.
2 (*with amounts*)
There are none left. Il n'y en a plus.

nonsense noun
les **bêtises** *fem. plural*
You're talking nonsense! Tu dis des bêtises!

🔑 **LANGUAGE**
English = **nonsense** is singular
French = **les bêtises** is plural

noodles plural noun
les **nouilles** *fem. plural*

noon noun
midi *masc.*

at noon à midi
It's noon. Il est midi.

no-one pronoun
1 **ne … personne**
There's no-one at home. Il n'y a personne à la maison.
2 **personne**
Who's there? – No-one! Qui est là? – Personne!

🔑 **LANGUAGE**
ne + *verb* + **personne**, for example: Je **ne** vois **personne**.

nor conjunction
neither … nor ni … ni
neither you nor I ni toi ni moi
I don't like meat. – Nor do I. Je n'aime pas la viande. – Moi moi non plus.

normal adjective
1 **normal** *masc.*, **normale** *fem.*, **normaux** *masc. plural*, **normales** *fem. plural*
2 (*time or place*) **habituel** *masc.*, **habituelle** *fem.*
at the normal time à l'heure habituelle

normally adverb
normalement

north noun
le **nord** *masc.*
They live in the north. Ils habitent dans le nord.

north adjective
1 **nord** *masc. & fem.*
the north coast la côte nord
2 **the North Pole** le pôle Nord

North America noun
l'**Amérique du Nord** *fem.*

Northern Ireland noun
l'**Irlande du Nord** *fem.*
I live in Northern Ireland. J'habite en Irlande du Nord.

🔹 *means use* **être** *to make the past tense.*

a
b
c
d
e
f
g
h
i
j
k
l
m
n
o
p
q
r
s
t
u
v
w
x
y
z

English French

Norway noun
la **Norvège** *fem.*

nose noun
le **nez** *masc.*

not adverb
1 pas
Why not? Pourquoi pas?
Do you want some or not? Tu en
veux ou pas?
not bad pas mal
not much pas beaucoup
not now pas maintenant
not yet pas encore
2 ne ... pas
I'm not in your class. Je ne suis pas
dans ta classe.
It isn't late. Il n'est pas tard.

🔑 **LANGUAGE**
ne + *verb* + **pas**, for example: Je **ne** sais **pas**

note noun
1 (*message for somebody*) le **mot** *masc.*
Dad has left a note for you. Papa
t'a laissé un mot.
2 (*paper money*) le **billet** *masc.*
a five-pound note un billet de cinq
livres

notebook noun
le **carnet** *masc.*

notepad noun
le **bloc-notes** *masc.* (plural les
blocs-notes)

nothing adverb
1 ne ... rien
It's nothing. Ce n'est rien.
Nothing has changed. Rien n'a
changé.
2 rien
What do you want? – Nothing.
Qu'est-ce que tu veux? – Rien.

🔑 **LANGUAGE**
ne + *verb* + **rien**, for example: Je **ne**
comprends **rien**

notice noun
(*on a wall, door, etc*) une **affiche** *fem.*
a notice board un panneau
d'affichage

to **notice** verb
remarquer
I didn't notice anything. Je n'ai
rien remarqué.

noun noun
le **nom** *masc.*
Is it a noun or a verb? C'est un nom
ou un verbe?

novel noun
le **roman** *masc.*

November noun
novembre *masc.*
in November en novembre
**It's my birthday at the beginning
of November.** C'est mon
anniversaire début novembre.
on the third of November le trois
novembre

now adverb
maintenant
I'm going now. Je pars
maintenant.

nowhere adverb
nulle part

number noun
1 (*of a phone, house, bus, page, etc.*)
le **numéro** *masc.*
My phone number is ... Mon
numéro de téléphone, c'est le ...
I live at number twenty-five.
J'habite au numéro vingt-cinq.
2 (*figure or amount*) le **nombre** *masc.*
an even number un nombre pair
an odd number un nombre impair
a large number of un grand
nombre de
3 (*written figure*) le **chiffre** *masc.*
the number after the decimal point
le chiffre après la virgule

• *Languages, nationalities, and religions do not take a capital letter in French.*

nun noun
la **religieuse** *fem.*

nurse noun
un **infirmier** *masc.*,
une **infirmière** *fem.*
Kay's a nurse. Kay est infirmière.

nursery noun
la **crèche** *fem.*
He goes to a nursery. Il va à la crèche.
a nursery rhyme une comptine *fem.*

Oo

oats plural noun
l'**avoine** *fem.*

to **obey** verb
1 to obey somebody obéir à quelqu'un
2 to obey the rules (*in a game*) respecter les règles

object noun
un **objet** *masc.*

obvious adjective
évident *masc.*, **évidente** *fem.*
That's obvious. C'est évident.

obviously adverb
évidemment

occasion noun
1 une **occasion** *fem.*
It's a very special occasion. C'est une occasion très spéciale.
2 on this occasion cette fois-ci

occasionally adverb
de temps en temps

nursery school noun
l'**école maternelle** *fem.*

CULTURE
L'école maternelle is for children from 3 to 6.

nut noun
1 (*walnut*) la **noix** *fem.*
2 (*peanut*) la **cacahuète** *fem.*
3 (*hazelnut*) la **noisette** *fem.*

LANGUAGE
There are different words in French for nut: you have to decide what sort you mean.

occupation noun
(*job*) la **profession** *fem.*

ocean noun
un **océan** *masc.*

o'clock adverb
at seven o'clock à sept heures
It's eight o'clock. Il est huit heures.

October noun
octobre *masc.*
in October en octobre
at the end of October fin octobre
It's my birthday on the eighth of October. C'est mon anniversaire le huit octobre.

octopus noun
la **pieuvre** *fem.*

odd adjective
1 (*strange*) **bizarre** *masc. & fem.*
2 an odd number un nombre impair

of preposition
1 de
a cup of tea une tasse de thé
a child of eight une enfant de huit ans

*❷ means use **être** to make the past tense.*

the end of the holidays la fin des vacances

the corner of the street le coin de la rue

the title of the book le titre du livre

the colours of the rainbow les couleurs de l'arc-en-ciel

> **LANGUAGE**
> de + la = de la
> de + le = du
> de + les = des
> de + le or la + a, e, i, o, u, or silent h = de l'
> de + a, e, i, o, u, y or silent h = d'

2 of it, of them en

Would you like some of it? Tu en veux?

I have two of them. J'en ai deux.

> **LANGUAGE**
> En goes before the verb.

of course adverb
bien sûr

off adjective

1 (light, TV, radio, etc.) **éteint** masc., **éteinte** fem.

The TV is off. La télé est éteinte.

2 (tap, gas) **fermé** masc., **fermée** fem.

The tap is off. Le robinet est fermé.

3 (away from school or work) **absent** masc., **absente** fem.

Paul is off today. Paul est absent aujourd'hui.

a day off un jour de congé

We have a week off. On a une semaine de congé.

4 (cancelled) **annulé** masc., **annulée** fem.

Is the match off? Est-ce que le match est annulé?

off preposition

(from) **de**

I fell off the bike. Je suis tombé de vélo.

off adverb

1 (going somewhere)

to be off partir

We're going off on holiday. On part en vacances.

> **LANGUAGE**
> 'Off' is often translated as part of a verb, for example: 'to switch off' (**éteindre**) or 'to take something off' (**enlever**).

to **offer** verb
offrir

to offer somebody something offrir quelque chose à quelqu'un

office noun

le **bureau** masc. (plural les **bureaux**)

She works in an office. Elle travaille dans un bureau.

often adverb
souvent

We often go to France. On va souvent en France.

not often pas souvent

ogre noun
un **ogre** masc.

oil noun
l'**huile** fem.

okay adverb

1 (saying yes) **d'accord**

Can you help me? – Okay! Tu peux m'aider? – D'accord!

2 (good) **bien**

How are you? – Okay. Comment vas-tu? – Bien.

Everything's okay here. Tout va bien ici.

Are you all okay? Ça va?

3 (not so bad) **pas mal**

Do you like the book? – It's okay. Tu aimes le livre? – Il n'est pas mal.

old adjective

1 **vieux** masc.,
vieille fem., **vieux** masc. plural,
vieilles fem. plural

• The months of the year and days of the week do not take a capital letter in French.

an old bike un vieux vélo
an old lady une vieille dame
old toys des vieux jouets
my old socks mes vieilles chaussettes

⚷ **LANGUAGE**
Use **vieil** with a masculine singular noun beginning with *a, e, i, o, u,* or *silent h,* for example: **un vieil homme** is 'an old man'.

2 (*when you want to be polite*) **âgé** *masc.,* **âgée** *fem.*
old people les personnes âgées
3 (*talking about ages*)
How old are you? Quel âge as-tu?
I'm ten years old. J'ai dix ans.

older adjective
(*talking about ages*) **plus âgé** *masc.,* **plus âgée** *fem.*
He's older than you. Il est plus âgé que toi.

oldest adjective
1 (*talking about ages*) **le plus âgé** *masc.,* **la plus âgée** *fem.*
the oldest boy in the class le garçon le plus âgé de la classe
2 (*talking about brothers and sisters*) **aîné** *masc.,* **aînée** *fem.*
my oldest sister ma sœur aînée

old-fashioned adjective
(*clothes, music, etc.*) **démodé** *masc.,* **démodée** *fem.*

Olympic adjective
the Olympic Games les Jeux Olympiques *masc. plural*

omelette noun
une **omelette** *fem.*

on preposition
1 sur
sitting on a chair assis sur une chaise
a book on dinosaurs un livre sur les dinosaures
on DVD sur DVD

ⓔ *means use* **être** *to make the past tense.*

2 à
Write your name on the board! Écris ton nom au tableau!
on foot à pied
to play a tune on the guitar jouer un air à la guitare
on TV à la télé
on page ten à la page dix
3 (*talking about buses, trains, etc.*) **dans**
on the bus dans le bus
4 en
on holiday en vacances
on video en vidéo
5 (*no translation with days and dates*)
on Sunday dimanche
on Sundays le dimanche
on the sixth of January le six janvier
on my birthday le jour de mon anniversaire
on Christmas Day le jour de Noël

on adjective
1 (*light, TV, computer, oven, etc.*) **allumé** *masc.,* **allumée** *fem.*
The TV is on. La télé est allumée.
2 (*tap, gas*) **ouvert** *masc.,* **ouverte** *fem.*
The tap is on. Le robinet est ouvert.

⚷ **LANGUAGE**
'On' is often translated as part of a verb, for example: 'to switch on' (**allumer**) or 'to put on' (**mettre**), and need not be translated separately.

once adverb
1 une fois
once a day une fois par jour
once again encore une fois
2 at once tout de suite
3 (*a long time ago*) **autrefois**
'Once upon a time ...' (*in stories*) 'Il était une fois ...'

one number
un *masc.,* **une** *fem.*
one euro un euro
It's one o'clock. Il est une heure.
I have one brother and one sister. J'ai un frère et une sœur.

a
b
c
d
e
f
g
h
i
j
k
l
m
n
o
p
q
r
s
t
u
v
w
x
y
z

onion noun
un **oignon** masc.

online adjective
en ligne
online games des jeux en ligne

only adjective
1 **seul** masc., **seule** fem.
the only boy le seul garçon
It's the only thing to do. C'est la seule chose à faire.
2 **unique** masc. & fem.
Andrew is an only child. Andrew est fils unique.
Jessica is an only child. Jessica est fille unique.

only adverb
1 **seulement**
only two people deux personnes seulement
2 (with verbs) **ne ... que**
I only have four CDs. Je n'ai que quatre CD.
She only speaks French. Elle ne parle que le français.

🔑 **LANGUAGE**
ne + verb + que, for example:
Je n'ai que ...

onto preposition
sur

open adjective
ouvert masc., **ouverte** fem.
The library is open. La bibliothèque est ouverte.

to **open** verb
ouvrir
Open the door! Ouvre la porte!
The post office opens at nine. La poste ouvre à neuf heures.

operation noun
to have an operation se faire ℗ opérer
Joël had an operation on his leg. Joël s'est fait opérer de la jambe.

opinion noun
un **avis** masc.
in my opinion à mon avis

opponent noun
un or une **adversaire** masc. & fem.

opportunity noun
une **occasion** fem.

opposite noun
le **contraire** masc.
What's the opposite of 'big'? Quel est le contraire de 'grand'?

opposite adjective
opposé masc., **opposée** fem.
in the opposite direction dans la direction opposée
on the opposite side of the road de l'autre côté de la rue

opposite preposition
en face de
Abdul is sitting opposite me. Abdul est assis en face de moi.

optician noun
un **opticien** masc.,
une **opticienne** fem.

optimistic adjective
optimiste masc. & fem.

or conjunction
1 **ou**
small or big petit ou grand
2 (in sentences with **not**, **never**, etc.) **ni ... ni**
I don't have a brother or sister. Je n'ai ni frère ni sœur.
3 (otherwise) **sinon**
I'm going now or I'll be late. Je pars tout de suite, sinon je vais être en retard.

orange noun
1 (fruit) une **orange** fem.
Do you want an orange? Tu veux une orange?
orange juice le jus d'orange
2 (colour) l'**orange** masc.
My favourite colour is orange. Ma couleur préférée, c'est l'orange.

• See the centre section for verb tables.

orange adjective
orange *masc. & fem.*
orange shirts des chemises orange

🔑 **LANGUAGE**
Orange is the same in the masculine, feminine, and plural.

orchestra noun
un **orchestre** *masc.*

order noun
1 l'**ordre** *masc.*
to put words in alphabetical order ranger des mots par ordre alphabétique
in the correct order dans le bon ordre
2 **out of order** (*machine, lift*) en panne

to **order** verb
(*in a restaurant*) **commander**

ordinary adjective
ordinaire *masc. & fem.*

to **organize** verb
organiser

original adjective
(*idea, version, etc.*) **original** *masc.*, **originale** *fem.*, **originaux** *masc. plural*, **originales** *fem. plural*

orphan noun
un **orphelin** *masc.*,
une **orpheline** *fem.*

other adjective
autre *masc. & fem.*
the other day l'autre jour
Where's the other sock? Où est l'autre chaussette?

other pronoun
l'**autre** *masc. & fem.*
The others are going to watch TV. Les autres vont regarder la télé.

otherwise conjunction
sinon
Don't shout, otherwise I can't hear the music. Ne criez pas, sinon je n'entends pas la musique.

ouch exclamation
aïe

ought verb
devoir
You ought to come. Tu devrais venir.

our adjective
1 (*before a singular noun*) **notre**
our school notre école
2 (*before a plural noun*) **nos**
our parents nos parents

ours pronoun
à nous
This tent is ours. Cette tente est à nous.
It's ours. C'est à nous.

ourselves pronoun
1 **nous-mêmes**
We can do it ourselves. Nous pouvons le faire nous-mêmes.
2 **nous**
We're enjoying ourselves. Nous nous amusons.
3 **by ourselves** tout seuls *masc. plural*, toutes seules *fem. plural*

out adverb
1 (*outside*) **dehors**
It's cold out. Il fait froid dehors.
2 (*not here*) **sorti** *masc.*, **sortie** *fem.*
Manuel is out. Manuel est sorti.
3 (*from*)
It's made out of glass. C'est en verre.
Take the money out of my bag. Prends l'argent dans mon sac.

ⓔ means use **être** *to make the past tense.*

a b c d e f g h i j k l m n **o** p q r s t u v w x y z

a
b
c
d
e
f
g
h
i
j
k
l
m
n
o
p
q
r
s
t
u
v
w
x
y
z

out adjective
1 (*light, fire*) **éteint** *masc.*, **éteinte** *fem.*
The lights are out. Les lumières sont éteintes.
2 (*in games*) **éliminé** *masc.*, **éliminée** *fem.*
You're out! Tu es éliminé!

> **LANGUAGE**
> 'Out' is often part of a verb, for example: 'to go out' (**sortir**), and need not be translated separately.

outdoor adjective
(*swimming pool, restaurant, etc.*) **en plein air**
outdoor sports les sports de plein air

outdoors adverb
dehors

outer space noun
l'**espace** *masc.*

outing noun
la **sortie** *fem.*
to go on a school outing faire une sortie avec l'école

outside adverb
dehors
Wait for me outside! Attends-moi dehors!

outside preposition
(*in front of*) **devant**
Wait for me outside the school! Attends-moi devant l'école!

outside noun
l'**extérieur** *masc.*
It's dirty on the outside. C'est sale à l'extérieur.

oven noun
le **four** *masc.*

over adjective
fini *masc.*, **finie** *fem.*
The holidays are over. Les vacances sont finies.

over preposition
1 (*above*) **au-dessus de**
the mirror over the washbasin le miroir au-dessus du lavabo
2 **par-dessus**
to jump over something sauter par-dessus quelque chose
3 (*more than*) **plus de**
You can see the film if you are over 12. Tu peux voir le film si tu as plus de 12 ans.
4 (*during*) **pendant**
over the summer pendant l'été
5 (*across*)
over the road de l'autre côté de la rue

> **LANGUAGE**
> 'Over' is often part of a verb, for example: 'to be left over' (**rester**), and need not be translated separately.

over adverb
over here ici
over there là-bas
all over partout

to **owe** verb
devoir
I owe my brother five euros. Je dois cinq euros à mon frère.

owl noun
le **hibou** *masc.* (plural les **hiboux**)

own adjective
propre *masc. & fem.*
Do you have your own computer? Tu as ton propre ordinateur?

own pronoun
on your own tout seul *masc.*, toute seule *fem.*
He goes out on his own. Il sort tout seul.

owner noun
le or la **propriétaire** *masc. & fem.*

• *Use* **le** *and* **un** *for masculine words and* **la** *and* **une** *for feminine words.*

Pp

Pacific noun
le **Pacifique** masc.

to **pack** verb
1 **faire ses valises**
I'm packing. Je fais mes valises.
2 **a packed lunch** un casse-croûte masc.
Do you take a packed lunch? Tu apportes un casse-croûte pour le déjeuner?

CULTURE
In France children do not have packed lunches in school; **casse-croûte** is the French word for 'snack'.

pack noun
a pack of cards un jeu de cartes masc.

packet noun
(of crisps, biscuits, etc.) le **paquet** masc.

page noun
la **page** fem.
on page eleven à la page onze

pain noun
la **douleur** fem.
I have a pain in my ear. J'ai mal à l'oreille.

painful adjective
(leg, burn, etc.) **douloureux** masc., **douloureuse** fem.

paint noun
la **peinture** fem.
a tin of paint un pot de peinture

to **paint** verb
peindre
Can we paint it blue? On peut le peindre en bleu?

paintbrush noun
le **pinceau** masc. (plural les **pinceaux**)

painter noun
le **peintre** masc.

painting noun
1 (picture) le **tableau** masc. (plural les **tableaux**)
a painting by Matisse un tableau de Matisse
2 la **peinture** fem.
I like painting. J'aime faire de la peinture.

pair noun
1 **la paire** fem.
a pair of socks une paire de chaussettes
We're working in pairs On travaille en groupes de deux.
2 **a pair of jeans** un jean
a pair of trousers un pantalon

Pakistan noun
le **Pakistan** masc.

Pakistani adjective
pakistanais masc., **pakistanaise** fem.

Pakistani noun
le **Pakistanais** masc., la **Pakistanaise** fem.

pal noun
le **copain** masc., la **copine** fem.
She's my best pal. C'est ma meilleure copine.

palace noun
le **palais** masc.

pale adjective
pâle masc. & fem.
You look very pale, Charlotte. Tu es toute pâle, Charlotte.

palm tree noun
le **palmier** masc.

a
b
c
d
e
f
g
h
i
j
k
l
m
n
o
p
q
r
s
t
u
v
w
x
y
z

*means use **être** to make the past tense.*

English French

a
b
c
d
e
f
g
h
i
j
k
l
m
n
o
p
q
r
s
t
u
v
w
x
y
z

pan noun
1 (*saucepan*) la **casserole** *fem.*
2 (*frying pan*) la **poêle** *fem.*

pancake noun
la **crêpe** *fem.*
Pancake Day mardi gras

 CULTURE
Mardi gras is Shrove Tuesday, when children in France as well as in Britain eat pancakes.

panda noun
le **panda** *masc.*

panic noun
la **panique** *fem.*

pantomime noun
le **spectacle pour enfants** *masc.*

 CULTURE
There are no Christmas pantomimes in France.

pants plural noun
le **slip** *masc.*
a pair of pants un slip

 LANGUAGE
English = **pants** is plural
French = **le slip** is singular

paper noun
1 le **papier** *masc.*
I've got some paper. J'ai du papier.
a sheet of paper une feuille de papier
a paper bag un sac en papier
2 (*newspaper*) le **journal** *masc.* (plural les **journaux**)

paperback noun
le **livre de poche** *masc.*

paperclip noun
le **trombone** *masc.*

parachute noun
le **parachute** *masc.*

parade noun
le **défilé** *masc.*

paragraph noun
le **paragraphe** *masc.*

parcel noun
le **colis** *masc.*

pardon noun
Pardon? Pardon?

parents plural noun
les **parents** *masc. plural*
my parents mes parents

Paris noun
Paris
in Paris à Paris
We're going to Paris. Nous allons à Paris.

park noun
1 le **parc** *masc.*
Let's go to the park! Allons au parc!
2 **a car park** un parking

to **park** verb
to park the car garer la voiture

parking noun
le **stationnement** *masc.*
'no parking' 'stationnement interdit'

parrot noun
le **perroquet** *masc.*

part noun
1 la **partie** *fem.*
the last part of the book la dernière partie du livre
2 (*in a play or show*) le **rôle** *masc.*

parting noun
(*in hair*) la **raie** *fem.*
He has a parting on the side. Il se fait la raie sur le côté.

partly adverb
en partie

• *Languages, nationalities, and religions do not take a capital letter in French.*

partner noun
(*in a game etc.*) le or la **partenaire**
masc. & fem.

party noun
1 la **fête** *fem.*
**I'm having a party for my
birthday.** Je fais une fête pour mon
anniversaire.
a Christmas party une fête de Noël
party games des jeux de société
2 (*children's afternoon party*) le **goûter**
masc.
a children's birthday party un
goûter d'anniversaire

to **pass** verb
1 (*to go past*) **passer ⊘ devant**
We passed the school. Nous
sommes passés devant l'école.
2 (*to give*) **passer**
Pass me the chocolates, please!
Passe-moi les chocolats, s'il te plaît!
3 **to pass an exam** être reçu à un
examen

passenger noun
1 (*in a car, boat, or plane*)
le **passager** *masc.*,
la **passagère** *fem.*
2 (*in a bus or train*) le **voyageur** *masc.*,
la **voyageuse** *fem.*

passport noun
le **passeport** *masc.*

password noun
le **mot de passe** *masc.*

past preposition
1 (*after*) **après**
It's just past the supermarket.
C'est juste après le supermarché.
2 (*talking about the time*)
It's five past seven. Il est sept
heures cinq.
It's a quarter past eleven. Il est
onze heures et quart.
It's half past five. Il est cinq heures
et demie.

past noun
le **passé** *masc.*
in the past dans le passé

pasta noun
les **pâtes** *fem. plural*
Do you like pasta? Tu aimes les
pâtes?

LANGUAGE
English = **pasta** is singular
French = **les pâtes** is plural

path noun
1 (*in fields etc.*) le **chemin** *masc.*
2 (*in a park or garden*) une **allée** *fem.*

patient adjective
patient *masc.*, **patiente** *fem.*

patient noun
(*of a doctor*) le **patient** *masc.*,
la **patiente** *fem.*

pattern noun
le **motif** *masc.*

pavement noun
le **trottoir** *masc.*

paw noun
la **patte** *fem.*

pawpaw noun
la **papaye** *fem.*

pay noun
le **salaire** *masc.*

to **pay** verb
1 **payer**
I'll pay. Je vais payer.
to pay the bill payer l'addition
to pay for something payer
quelque chose
My sister paid twenty euros for it.
Ma sœur l'a payé vingt euros.
2 **Pay attention!** Faites attention!

PC noun
le **PC** *masc.*

⊘ *means use* être *to make the past tense.*

PE noun
l'**EPS** fem.

🔑 **LANGUAGE**
EPS = éducation physique et sportive
(physical and sports education)

pea noun
le **petit pois** masc.
Do you like peas? Tu aimes les
petits pois?

peace noun
la **paix** fem.
I want some peace. Je veux avoir la
paix.
We need peace and quiet. Nous
avons besoin de calme.

peaceful adjective
tranquille masc. & fem.
It's peaceful here. C'est tranquille
ici.

peach noun
la **pêche** fem.

peanut noun
la **cacahuète** fem.
peanut butter le beurre de
cacahuètes

pear noun
la **poire** fem.

pearl noun
la **perle** fem.

pebble noun
(on the beach) le **galet** masc.

pedal noun
la **pédale** fem.

pedestrian noun
le **piéton** masc., la **piétonne** fem.

to **peel** verb
éplucher

peg noun
(hook for coats) le **portemanteau**
masc. (plural les **portemanteaux**)

pen noun
le **stylo** masc.
a felt-tip pen un feutre

pencil noun
le **crayon** masc.
in pencil au crayon
a coloured pencil un crayon de
couleur
a pencil case une trousse
a pencil sharpener un
taille-crayon

penfriend noun
le **correspondant** masc.,
la **correspondante** fem.
**My French penfriend lives in
Poitiers.** Ma correspondante
française habite à Poitiers.

penguin noun
le **pingouin** masc.

pensioner noun
le **retraité** masc., la **retraitée** fem.

people plural noun
1 les **gens** masc. plural
a lot of people beaucoup de gens
most people la plupart des gens
2 (talking about numbers of people)
les **personnes** fem. plural
ten people dix personnes
a few people quelques personnes
3 **young people** les jeunes
English people les Anglais
French people les Français

pepper noun
1 le **poivre** masc.
Would you like some pepper?
Tu veux du poivre?
2 (vegetable) le **poivron** masc.
a green pepper un poivron vert

per cent adverb
pour cent
ten per cent dix pour cent

• The months of the year and days of the week do not take a capital letter in French.

perfect adjective
parfait masc., **parfaite** fem.
His French is perfect. Son français est parfait.

perfectly adverb
parfaitement

performance noun
(of a play, film, etc.) le **spectacle** masc.

perfume noun
le **parfum** masc.

perhaps adverb
peut-être
Perhaps it's true. C'est peut-être vrai.

period noun
la **période** fem.
the Christmas period la période de Noël

permission noun
la **permission** fem.
Do you have permission? Tu as la permission?

person noun
la **personne** fem.
an old person une personne âgée

⚷ LANGUAGE
English = person
French = personne

personality noun
la **personnalité** fem.

personal stereo noun
le **baladeur** masc.

pessimistic adjective
pessimiste masc. & fem.

pest noun
He's a pest! Il est casse-pieds!

pet noun
un **animal de compagnie** masc.
(plural les **animaux de compagnie**)
Do you have a pet at home? Tu as un animal chez toi?

petrol noun
l'**essence** fem.
a petrol station une station-service

phone noun
1 le **téléphone** masc.
He's on the phone to his friend.
Il est au téléphone avec son copain.
2 **the phone book** l'annuaire masc.
a phone call un appel
to make a phone call téléphoner
a phone number un numéro de téléphone

to **phone** verb
1 **téléphoner**
Can I phone my parents? Je peux téléphoner à mes parents?
2 **to phone somebody** appeler quelqu'un

photo noun
la **photo** fem.
Can I take a photo of you? Je peux te prendre en photo?
That's my dog in the photo. C'est mon chien sur la photo.

photocopier noun
la **photocopieuse** fem.

photocopy noun
la **photocopie** fem.

to **photocopy** verb
photocopier

photograph noun
la **photo** fem.

photographer noun
le or la **photographe** masc. & fem.

phrase noun
une **expression** fem.
a phrase book un guide de conversation

physical adjective
physique masc. & fem.
physical education l'éducation physique

a
b
c
d
e
f
g
h
i
j
k
l
m
n
o
p
q
r
s
t
u
v
w
x
y
z

ⓔ means use **être** to make the past tense.

English French

a
b
c
d
e
f
g
h
i
j
k
l
m
n
o
p
q
r
s
t
u
v
w
x
y
z

pianist noun
le or la **pianiste** *masc. & fem.*

piano noun
le **piano** *masc.*
I play the piano. Je joue du piano.

pick noun
Take your pick! Choisis!

to **pick** verb
1 (*to choose*) **choisir**
I picked the red one. J'ai choisi le rouge.
2 (*flowers or fruit*) **cueillir**
She's picking some flowers. Elle cueille des fleurs.

to **pick up** verb
1 (*from the floor etc.*) **ramasser**
Pick up your toys! Ramasse tes jouets!
2 (*to come to get*) **venir** ⊚ **chercher**
Can you pick me up at school? Tu peux venir me chercher à l'école?

picnic noun
le **pique-nique** *masc.*
to have a picnic pique-niquer

picture noun
1 (*drawing*) le **dessin** *masc.*
Ambika drew a nice picture. Ambika a fait un joli dessin.
Draw a picture of your house. Dessinez votre maison.
2 (*in a book or on TV*) une **image** *fem.*
Look at all the pictures! Regardez toutes les images!
3 (*by a painter*) le **tableau** *masc.* (plural les **tableaux**)
a picture by Van Gogh un tableau de Van Gogh
4 (*photo*) la **photo** *fem.*
Do you have a picture of your family? Tu as une photo de ta famille?

pie noun
la **tarte** *fem.*
an apple pie une tarte aux pommes

• *See the centre section for verb tables.*

piece noun
(*bit of something*) le **morceau** *masc.*
(plural les **morceaux**)
a piece of bread un morceau de pain

pierced adjective
percé *masc.*, **percée** *fem.*
I have pierced ears. J'ai les oreilles percées.

pig noun
le **cochon** *masc.*

pigeon noun
le **pigeon** *masc.*

piggy bank noun
la **tirelire** *fem.*

pigtails plural noun
les **nattes** *fem. plural*
She has pigtails. Elle a des nattes.

pile noun
le **tas** *masc.*

pill noun
la **pilule** *fem.*

pillow noun
un **oreiller** *masc.*

🔑 **LANGUAGE**
Oreiller comes from **oreille** (ear) – you put your ear on the pillow.

pilot noun
le **pilote** *masc.*

pin noun
(*for sewing*) une **épingle** *fem.*

pinball noun
le **flipper** *masc.*
to play pinball jouer au flipper

pineapple noun
un **ananas** *masc.*

pink adjective
rose *masc. & fem.*
pink flowers des fleurs roses

pink noun
le **rose** *masc.*
Do you like pink? Tu aimes le rose?

> **LANGUAGE**
> le rose = **pink** *(the colour)*
> la rose = **the rose** *(the flower)*

pint noun
a pint of milk un demi-litre de lait

 CULTURE
In France litres and centilitres are used rather than pints. A pint is just over half a litre.

pirate noun
le **pirate** *masc.*

pitch noun
le **terrain** *masc.*
a football pitch un terrain de football

pity noun
What a pity! Quel dommage!

pizza noun
la **pizza** *fem.*

place noun
1 un **endroit** *masc.*
a nice place un endroit agréable
2 *(position or seat)* la **place** *fem.*
Do you want to change places with me? Tu veux changer de place avec moi?
Liam finished in third place. Liam a terminé à la troisième place.

plain adjective
1 **simple** *masc. & fem.*
a very plain dress une robe toute simple
2 *(with no special flavour)* **nature** *masc. & fem.*
Do you like plain yoghurts? Tu aimes les yaourts nature?

> **LANGUAGE**
> Nature is the same in the plural, for example: **des yaourts nature**.

plait noun
la **natte** *fem.*
Debbie has plaits. Debbie a des nattes.

plan noun
1 le **projet** *masc.*
Do you have any plans for the summer? As-tu des projets pour l'été?
2 *(map of a building)* le **plan** *masc.*
the plan of a town le plan d'une ville

to **plan** verb
(a journey, surprise, etc.) **préparer**
My parents are planning a trip. Mes parents préparent un voyage.

plane noun
un **avion** *masc.*
to travel by plane voyager en avion

planet noun
la **planète** *fem.*

plant noun
la **plante** *fem.*

plaster noun
(for a cut, burn, etc.) le **pansement** *masc.*
I put a plaster on my knee. J'ai mis un pansement sur mon genou.

plastic noun
le **plastique** *masc.*
a plastic bottle une bouteille en plastique

Plasticine® noun
la **pâte à modeler** *fem.*

plate noun
une **assiette** *fem.*

platform noun
(at a train station) le **quai** *masc.*

play noun
(for acting in) la **pièce** *fem.*
We're putting on a play. On monte une pièce.

e means use être to make the past tense.

a b c d e f g h i j k l m n o p q r s t u v w x y z

a b c d e f g h i j k l m n o p q r s t u v w x y z

to play verb
1 **jouer**
Jamal is playing with his friends. Jamal joue avec ses amis.
Sophie is going to play a tune. Sophie va jouer un air.
2 (games and sports) **jouer à**
Do you play tennis? Tu joues au tennis?
They're playing chess. Ils jouent aux échecs.
3 (an instrument) **jouer de**
Daniel plays the guitar and violin. Daniel joue de la guitare et du violon.
4 (a CD, DVD, or tape) **mettre**
I'm going to play my new CD. Je vais mettre mon nouveau CD.

player noun
1 le **joueur** masc., la **joueuse** fem.
a football player un joueur de football
2 **a CD player** une platine laser

playground noun
1 (in school) la **cour de récréation** fem.
2 (in the park) le **terrain de jeux** masc.

playgroup noun
la **garderie** fem.

playing field noun
le **terrain de sport** masc.

playtime noun
la **récréation** fem.

please adverb
1 **s'il vous plaît**
A kilo of apples, please! Un kilo de pommes, s'il vous plaît!
2 (to family or friends) **s'il te plaît**
Please close the door, dad! Ferme la porte, papa, s'il te plaît!

pleased adjective
content masc., **contente** fem.

plenty pronoun
1 (a lot)
plenty of beaucoup de
You have plenty of books. Tu as beaucoup de livres.
2 (enough)
I've got plenty of time. J'ai largement le temps.
That's plenty, thanks. Ça suffit, merci.

to plug in verb
brancher
Is the TV plugged in? Est-ce que la télé est branchée?

plum noun
la **prune** fem.

LANGUAGE
English = **a prune** is a dried plum
French = **une prune** is a fresh plum

plumber noun
le **plombier** masc.

plural noun
le **pluriel** masc.
in the plural au pluriel

plus preposition
plus
Nine plus three is twelve. Neuf plus trois font douze.

p.m. abbreviation
1 (from midday until evening) **de l'après-midi**
at 2 p.m. à deux heures de l'après-midi
2 (from evening until midnight) **du soir**
at 8 p.m. à huit heures du soir

pocket noun
la **poche** fem.
in my pocket dans ma poche
pocket money l'argent de poche
I get 5 euros pocket money. Je reçois 5 euros d'argent de poche.

• Use **le** and **un** for masculine words and **la** and **une** for feminine words.

poem noun
le **poème** masc.

point noun
1 (in a game) le **point** masc.
Tina has scored three points. Tina
a marqué trois points.
2 (of a pencil, knife, etc.) la **pointe** fem.
3 (decimal point) la **virgule** fem.
four point six quatre virgule six

> 🔑 **LANGUAGE**
> In French you use a comma (**virgule**) in
> decimal numbers, e.g. 4.6 is **4,6**.

4 (the reason for something)
There's no point waiting. Ça ne
sert à rien d'attendre.

to **point** verb
(with your finger) **montrer (du doigt)**
Point to the right picture!
Montre-moi la bonne image!

to **point out** verb
montrer
**The taxi driver pointed out the
Eiffel Tower.** Le chauffeur de taxi
nous a montré la tour Eiffel.

poison noun
le **poison** masc.

poisonous adjective
1 (snake or insect) **venimeux** masc.,
venimeuse fem.
a poisonous snake un serpent
venimeux
2 (mushroom or plant) **vénéneux** masc.,
vénéneuse fem.
a poisonous mushroom un
champignon vénéneux

Poland noun
la **Pologne** fem.

polar bear noun
un **ours polaire** masc.

police noun
la **police** fem.
The police are coming. La police
arrive.

Ⓔ means use **être** to make the past tense.

a police car une voiture de
police
a police station un commissariat
de police

> 🔑 **LANGUAGE**
> English = **the police** + verb in the plural
> French = **la police** + singular verb

policeman noun
un **agent de police** masc.

policewoman noun
la **femme policier** fem.

polite adjective
poli masc., **polie** fem.

politely adverb
poliment

polluted adjective
pollué masc., **polluée** fem.

pollution noun
la **pollution** fem.

pond noun
1 un **étang** masc.
2 (a small pond in a garden) le **bassin** masc.

pony noun
le **poney** masc.

> 🔑 **LANGUAGE**
> English = pony
> French = poney

ponytail noun
la **queue de cheval** fem.

poodle noun
le **caniche** masc.

pool noun
la **piscine** fem.
an indoor swimming pool une
piscine couverte

poor adjective
pauvre masc. & fem.
a poor country un pays pauvre

pop noun
(*music*) le **pop** *masc.*
My brother likes pop. Mon frère
aime bien le pop.
pop music la musique pop
a pop singer un chanteur de pop

popcorn noun
le **pop-corn** *masc.*

poppy noun
le **coquelicot** *masc.*

popular adjective
populaire *masc. & fem.*

pork noun
le **porc** *masc.*
a pork chop une côtelette de porc

porridge noun
le **porridge** *masc.*

port noun
le **port** *masc.*
the port of Dover le port de
Douvres

portable adjective
(*television, computer, etc.*) **portable**
masc. & fem.

portion noun
(*of food*) la **portion** *fem.*

Portugal noun
le **Portugal** *masc.*

posh adjective
(*hotel, place, etc.*) **chic** *masc. & fem.*
posh shops des magasins chic

⚿ **LANGUAGE**
Chic is the same in the masculine,
feminine, and plural.

position noun
la **position** *fem.*

positive adjective
(*certain*) **sûr** *masc.*, **sûre** *fem.*
Are you positive? Tu es sûr?

possible adjective
possible *masc. & fem.*

as quickly as possible le plus vite
possible

possibly adverb
(*maybe*) **peut-être**

post noun
(*letters*) le **courrier** *masc.*
There's some post for you. Il y a du
courrier pour toi.

to **post** verb
poster
Can you post my letter? Tu peux
poster ma lettre?

postbox noun
la **boîte aux lettres** *fem.*

🌍 **CULTURE**
In France **postboxes** are yellow, not red.

postcard noun
la **carte postale** *fem.*

postcode noun
le **code postal** *masc.*

poster noun
le **poster** *masc.*

postman noun
le **facteur** *masc.*

post office noun
la **poste** *fem.*
Mum has to go to the post office.
Maman doit aller à la poste.

pot noun
1 (*teapot*) la **théière** *fem.*
A pot of tea for two, please.
Deux thés, s'il vous plaît.
2 (*for flowers*) le **pot** *masc.*

potato noun
la **pomme de terre** *fem.*
baked potatoes des pommes de
terre cuites au four
boiled potatoes des pommes de
terre à l'eau
potato salad la salade de pommes
de terre

• *Languages, nationalities, and religions do not take a capital letter in French.*

pound noun
(*money and weight*) la **livre** *fem.*
It costs eight pounds. Ça coûte huit livres.
I bought a pound of cherries. J'ai acheté une livre de cerises.

to **pour** verb
1 **verser**
Pour the milk into a bowl. Verse le lait dans un bol.
2 (*to rain*) **pleuvoir à verse**
It's pouring. Il pleut à verse.

powerful adjective
puissant *masc.*, **puissante** *fem.*

practically adverb
(*almost*) **pratiquement**

practice noun
1 (*sports training*) l'**entraînement** *masc.*
We have football practice tomorrow. Nous avons un entraînement de football demain.
2 (*on an instrument*)
He's doing his guitar practice. Il travaille sa guitare.

to **practise** verb
1 (*a language or instrument*) **travailler**
I need to practise my French. Je dois travailler mon français.
2 (*to do a sport*) **s'entraîner** ◉
We practise every day. On s'entraîne tous les jours.

prawn noun
la **crevette** *fem.*

to **pray** verb
prier

to **prefer** verb
préférer
I prefer broccoli to cabbage. Je préfère le brocoli au chou.
She prefers to stay at home. Elle préfère rester à la maison.

prehistoric adjective
préhistorique *masc. & fem.*

prep noun
(*homework*) les **devoirs** *masc. plural*

to **prepare** verb
préparer
Dad's preparing dinner. Papa prépare le dîner.

preposition noun
la **préposition** *fem.*

prep school noun
une **école primaire privée** *fem.*

present adjective
1 **présent** *masc.*, **présente** *fem.*
All the children are present. Tous les enfants sont présents.
2 **the present tense** le présent

present noun
1 (*gift*) le **cadeau** *masc.* (plural les **cadeaux**)
My brother gave me a lovely present. Mon frère m'a offert un beau cadeau.
a birthday present un cadeau d'anniversaire
2 (*the time now*) le **présent** *masc.*
the past and the present le passé et le présent

president noun
le **président** *masc.*, la **présidente** *fem.*

to **press** verb
appuyer
Press the button. Appuie sur le bouton.

to **pretend** verb
faire semblant
He's pretending to be asleep. Il fait semblant de dormir.

a
b
c
d
e
f
g
h
i
j
k
l
m
n
o
p
q
r
s
t
u
v
w
x
y
z

◉ *means use* être *to make the past tense.*

English French

a b c d e f g h i j k l m n o **P** q r s t u v w x y z

pretty adjective
joli *masc.*, **jolie** *fem.*
a very pretty girl une très jolie fille

pretty adverb
(*fairly*) **assez**
Estelle's pretty tired. Estelle est assez fatiguée.

to **prevent** verb
(*an accident, illness, etc.*) **éviter**
It's to prevent accidents. C'est pour éviter les accidents.

price noun
le **prix** *masc.*
a price list une liste des prix

priest noun
le **prêtre** *masc.*

primary school noun
une **école primaire** *fem.*

CULTURE
L'école primaire is for children between 6 and 11: **le CP (cours préparatoire)** for children from 6 to 7; **le CE1** and **le CE2 (cours élémentaire)** for ages 7 to 9; **le CM1** and **le CM2 (cours moyen)** for ages 9 to 11.

Prime Minister noun
le **Premier ministre** *masc.*

prince noun
le **prince** *masc.*
Prince Harry le prince Harry

princess noun
la **princesse** *fem.*
Princess Anne la princesse Anne

to **print** verb
1 (*on a computer etc.*) **imprimer**
Can you print out my story? Tu peux imprimer mon histoire?
2 (*to write in big letters*) **écrire en majuscules**
Print your name. Écrivez votre nom en majuscules.

printer noun
une **imprimante** *fem.*
Turn on the printer! Allume l'imprimante!

prison noun
la **prison** *fem.*
He's in prison. Il est en prison.

prisoner noun
le **prisonnier** *masc.*, la **prisonnière** *fem.*

private adjective
privé *masc.*, **privée** *fem.*
a private school une école privée
I have private lessons. Je prends des cours particuliers.

prize noun
le **prix** *masc.*
You've won a prize! Tu as gagné un prix!
the prize-giving la distribution des prix

prizewinner noun
le **gagnant** *masc.*, la **gagnante** *fem.*

probably adverb
probablement
probably not probablement pas

problem noun
le **problème** *masc.*
No problem! Pas de problème!

professor noun
le **professeur d'université** *masc.*

program noun
(*on a computer*) le **programme** *masc.*
a computer program un programme informatique

programme noun
1 (*on TV or radio*) une **émission** *fem.*
a TV programme une émission de télévision
2 (*timetable, details of a show, etc.*)
le **programme** *masc.*
How much is the programme? Combien coûte le programme?

• *The months of the year and days of the week do not take a capital letter in French.*

progress noun
les **progrès** *masc. plural*
Karl is making progress. Karl fait des progrès.

🔑 **LANGUAGE**
English = **progress** is singular
French = **les progrès** is plural

promise noun
la **promesse** *fem.*
You made a promise! Tu m'as fait une promesse!
Will you keep your promise or not? Tu vas tenir ta promesse ou pas?
That's a promise. C'est promis.

to **promise** verb
promettre
I promise to come. Je te promets de venir.
I promise! Je te le promets!

pronoun noun
le **pronom** *masc.*

to **pronounce** verb
prononcer
How do you pronounce this word in French? Comment est ce qu'on prononce ce mot en français?

pronunciation noun
la **prononciation** *fem.*

proper adjective
(*real*) **vrai** *masc.*, **vraie** *fem.*
Kevin isn't my proper name. Kevin n'est pas mon vrai prénom.

properly adverb
comme il faut
Sit properly! Assieds-toi comme il faut!

to **protect** verb
protéger

Protestant adjective
protestant *masc.*,
protestante *fem.*

proud adjective
fier *masc.*, **fière** *fem.*
We're proud of you. Nous sommes fiers de toi.

prune noun
le **pruneau** *masc.* (plural les **pruneaux**)

⚠ **FALSE FRIEND**
a prune = **un pruneau** (*not* une prune)

pub noun
le **pub** *masc.*

public noun
le **public** *masc.*
Is it open to the public? C'est ouvert au public?

public adjective
1 (*for everybody*) **public** *masc.*, **publique** *fem.*
a public meeting une réunion publique
2 **a public library** une bibliothèque municipale
a public swimming pool une piscine municipale
3 **a public holiday** un jour férié
4 **public transport** les transports en commun *masc. plural*
5 **a public school** une école privée

pudding noun
1 le **pudding** *masc.*
a chocolate pudding un pudding au chocolat
rice pudding le riz au lait
2 (*part of a meal*) le **dessert** *masc.*

puddle noun
la **flaque d'eau** *fem.*

Puerto Rican adjective
portoricain *masc.*,
portoricaine *fem.*

ⓔ means use être to make the past tense.

a b c d e f g h i j k l m n o p q r s t u v w x y z

Puerto Rican noun
le **Portoricain** *masc.*,
la **Portoricaine** *fem.*

Puerto Rico noun
Porto Rico *fem.*

to **pull** verb
tirer

pullover noun
le **pull** *masc.*

pump noun
la **pompe** *fem.*
a bicycle pump une pompe à vélo

to **pump** verb
pomper
to pump water pomper de l'eau
to pump up a tyre gonfler un pneu

pumpkin noun
la **citrouille** *fem.*

punch noun
le **coup de poing** *masc.*

to **punch** verb
to punch somebody donner un
coup de poing à quelqu'un
He punched me. Il m'a donné un
coup de poing.

punctual adjective
to be punctual être à l'heure
Be punctual, boys! Soyez à l'heure,
les garçons!

punctuation noun
la **ponctuation** *fem.*

⚷ **LANGUAGE**
English = pu**n**ctuation
French = po**n**ctuation

to **punish** verb
punir

punishment noun
la **punition** *fem.*

pupil noun
un or une **élève** *masc. & fem.*
**There are twenty-five pupils in my
class.** Il y a vingt-cinq élèves dans
ma classe.

puppet noun
la **marionnette** *fem.*

puppy noun
le **chiot** *masc.*

pure adjective
pur *masc.*, **pure** *fem.*

purple adjective
violet *masc.*, **violette** *fem.*
purple curtains des rideaux violets

purple noun
le **violet** *masc.*
My favourite colour is purple.
Ma couleur préférée est le violet.

purpose noun
on purpose exprès
I didn't do it on purpose. Je ne l'ai
pas fait exprès.

purse noun
le **porte-monnaie** *masc.* (plural les
porte-monnaie)
I've lost my purse. J'ai perdu mon
porte-monnaie.

to **push** verb
1 **pousser**
Push! Pousse!
2 (*a button, pedal, etc.*) **appuyer sur**
I pushed the button. J'ai appuyé
sur le bouton.

pushchair noun
la **poussette** *fem.*

to **put** verb
mettre
**Put your exercise books on the
table!** Mettez vos cahiers sur la
table!
Where did you put it, Craig?
Où l'as-tu mis, Craig?

• *See the centre section for verb tables.*

to **put away** verb
ranger
Put your books away! Rangez vos livres!

to **put down** verb
poser
Put your bag down and come here! Pose ton sac et viens ici!
Put your hand down! Baisse ta main!

to **put off** verb
1 (*a party, lesson, etc.*) **remettre à plus tard**
They've put off the school outing. Ils ont remis la sortie scolaire à plus tard.
2 (*a TV, light, etc.*) **éteindre**
Put the light off! Éteins la lumière!

to **put on** verb
(*clothes, music, a CD, etc*) **mettre**
Put your gloves on! Mets tes gants!
Can I put the radio on? Je peux mettre la radio?

to **put out** verb
(*a fire, light, etc.*) **éteindre**

to **put up** verb
1 (*a poster, photo, etc.*) **mettre**
Lee put up some posters on the wall. Lee a mis des posters au mur.
2 to put your hand up lever la main
Put your hands up! Levez la main!
3 to put up the price augmenter le prix

puzzle noun
1 le **puzzle** *masc.*
Do you want to do a jigsaw puzzle? Tu veux faire un puzzle?
2 a crossword puzzle des mots croisés *masc. plural*

puzzled adjective
perplexe *masc. & fem.*

pyjamas noun
le **pyjama** *masc.*
I'm in my pyjamas. Je suis en pyjama.
a pair of pyjamas un pyjama

> **LANGUAGE**
> English = **pyjamas** is plural
> French = **pyjama** is singular

Qq

quality noun
la **qualité** *fem.*

quantity noun
la **quantité** *fem.*

to **quarrel** verb
se disputer ⊘

quarter noun
1 le **quart** *masc.*
Three is a quarter of twelve. Trois est le quart de douze.
three quarters of the girls les trois quarts des filles
2 (*with time*)
a quarter of an hour un quart d'heure

three quarters of an hour trois quarts d'heure
It's a quarter past nine. Il est neuf heures et quart.
at a quarter to nine à neuf heures moins le quart

queen noun
la **reine** *fem.*
Queen Elizabeth la reine Élizabeth

question noun
la **question** *fem.*
to ask somebody a question poser une question à quelqu'un
I'd like to ask you a question. Je voudrais te poser une question.

⊘ *means use être to make the past tense.*

a question mark un point d'interrogation

queue noun
la **queue** fem.
We're standing in the queue. On fait la queue.

🔑 **LANGUAGE**
The French word **queue** also means a tail.

to **queue** verb
faire la queue
I don't want to queue up. Je ne veux pas faire la queue.

quick adjective
rapide masc. & fem.
You were quick! Tu as été rapide!
Take your bike, it's quicker. Prends ton vélo, c'est plus rapide.
Get your books and be quick! Allez chercher vos cahiers et faites vite!

quickly adverb
vite
Come quickly! Viens vite!

quiet adjective
1 (calm or peaceful) **tranquille** masc. & fem.
a quiet corner un coin tranquille

2 (not noisy) **silencieux** masc., **silencieuse** fem.
You're quiet today, Sean! Tu es bien silencieux aujourd'hui, Sean!
3 **to keep quiet** (to stop talking) se taire ⓔ
Be quiet! Tais-toi!

quietly adverb
doucement
He closed the door quietly. Il a fermé la porte doucement.
Speak quietly! Parle doucement!

quite adverb
1 (fairly) **assez**
It's quite late. Il est assez tard.
quite often assez souvent
2 (completely) **tout à fait**
It's not quite finished. Ce n'est pas tout à fait fini.
3 **quite a lot** pas mal
He's read quite a lot of books. Il a lu pas mal de livres.

quiz noun
1 (a game) le **jeu de questions-réponses** masc.
2 (on TV) le **jeu télévisé** masc.
3 (in books) le **jeu-test** masc.

Rr

rabbi noun
le **rabbin** masc.

rabbit noun
le **lapin** masc.

race noun
la **course** fem.
Shall we have a race? On fait la course?
a horse race une course de chevaux

racing car noun
la **voiture de course** fem.

racket noun
la **raquette** fem.
a tennis racket une raquette de tennis

radiator noun
le **radiateur** masc.

radio noun
la **radio** fem.
Turn off the radio! Éteins la radio!
Did you hear it on the radio? Tu l'as entendu à la radio?

• Use **le** and **un** for masculine words and **la** and **une** for feminine words.

a radio station une station de radio

rail noun
to travel by rail voyager par le train

railway noun
le **chemin de fer** masc.

railway station noun
la **gare** fem.

rain noun
la **pluie** fem.
Don't go out in the rain! Ne sors pas sous la pluie!
a rain forest une forêt tropicale

to **rain** verb
pleuvoir
It's raining. Il pleut.
Is it going to rain? Est-ce qu'il va pleuvoir?

rainbow noun
un **arc-en-ciel** masc. (plural les **arcs-en-ciel**)

raincoat noun
un **imperméable** masc.

rainy adjective
a rainy day un jour de pluie

to **raise** verb
lever

raisin noun
le **raisin sec** masc.

ramp noun
(for a wheelchair) la **rampe d'accès** fem.

range noun
(of colours, sizes, objects, etc.) le **choix** masc.
a wide range of CDs un grand choix de CD

rap noun
le **rap** masc.
a rap singer un chanteur de rap

rare adjective
rare masc. & fem.

rash noun
les **rougeurs** fem. plural
You have a rash on your legs. Tu as des rougeurs sur les jambes.

raspberry noun
la **framboise** fem.
raspberry jam la confiture de framboises
raspberry yoghurt le yaourt à la framboise

rat noun
le **rat** masc.

rather adverb
1 (talking about preferring something)
I would rather wait. Je préfère attendre.
What would you rather do? Qu'est-ce que tu préfères faire?
2 (instead)
rather than plutôt que
Choose Leah rather than Sam! Choisis Leah plutôt que Sam!
3 (quite) **plutôt**
My book's rather boring. Mon livre est plutôt ennuyeux.
4 **rather a lot** pas mal
rather a lot of CDs pas mal de CD

raw adjective
cru masc., **crue** fem.
a raw carrot une carotte crue

razor noun
le **rasoir** masc.

to **reach** verb
1 (to get to) **arriver** ⊘ à
When do we reach London? Quand est-ce que nous arrivons à Londres?
2 (by stretching your arm) **atteindre**
I can't reach the books on that shelf. Je n'arrive pas à atteindre les livres sur cette étagère.

⊘ *means use* être *to make the past tense.*

a
b
c
d
e
f
g
h
i
j
k
l
m
n
o
p
q
r
s
t
u
v
w
x
y
z

a
b
c
d
e
f
g
h
i
j
k
l
m
n
o
p
q
r
s
t
u
v
w
x
y
z

to **read** verb
lire
Lisa can't read yet. Lisa ne sait pas encore lire.
Go away! I'm reading. Va-t'en! Je lis.
Have you read this magazine? As-tu lu ce magazine?

reading noun
la **lecture** *fem.*
I like reading. J'aime la lecture.

⚠️ **FALSE FRIEND**
la lecture = reading (*not* lecture)

ready adjective
1 prêt *masc.*, **prête** *fem.*
Jo is ready. Jo est prête.
Nearly ready? Presque prêt?
We're ready to leave. Nous sommes prêts à partir.
Ready, steady, go! À vos marques, prêts, partez!
2 to get ready se préparer ⊘
She's getting ready to go out. Elle se prépare à sortir.
to get something ready préparer quelque chose

real adjective
vrai *masc.*, **vraie** *fem.*
It's a real problem. C'est un vrai problème.

really adverb
vraiment
I really like that music. J'aime vraiment cette musique.
Are you hungry? – Not really. Est-ce que tu as faim? – Pas vraiment.

reason noun
la **raison** *fem.*
For what reason? Pour quelle raison?
the reason for the crash la raison de l'accident

reasonable adjective
(*person, idea, distance, etc.*)
raisonnable *masc. & fem.*

🔑 **LANGUAGE**
English = re**a**sonable
French = r**ai**sonnable

to **receive** verb
recevoir
Have you received my letter? Tu as reçu ma lettre?

recent adjective
récent *masc.*, **récente** *fem.*

recently adverb
récemment

reception noun
1 (*desk in hotel*) la **réception** *fem.*
Wait for me at reception! Attends-moi à la réception!
2 reception class la première année d'école primaire

🌍 **CULTURE**
Children in reception class in Britain are 4 and 5 years old; at this age French children are in nursery school (**l'école maternelle**).

receptionist noun
le or la **réceptionniste** *masc. & fem.*

recipe noun
la **recette** *fem.*

to **reckon** verb
penser

to **recognize** verb
reconnaître
Do you recognize me? Tu me reconnais?

to **recommend** verb
conseiller
I recommend the latest Disney film. Je te conseille le dernier film de Disney.

• *Languages, nationalities, and religions do not take a capital letter in French.*

record noun
1 (*in sport*) le **record** *masc.*
We're going to beat the record!
On va battre le record!
2 (*for music*) le **disque** *masc.*
an old record un vieux disque

to **record** verb
enregistrer
Don't forget to record the film! N'oublie pas d'enregistrer le film!
The video's recording. Le magnétoscope est en train d'enregistrer.

recorder noun
la **flûte à bec** *fem.*
I play the recorder. Je joue de la flûte à bec.

rectangle noun
le **rectangle** *masc.*

red adjective
1 **rouge** *masc. & fem.*
a red car une voiture rouge
a red light (*for stopping at*) un feu rouge
You're going red! (*blushing*) Tu rougis!
2 (*hair*) **roux** *masc.*, **rousse** *fem.*
I have red hair. J'ai les cheveux roux.

red noun
le **rouge** *masc.*
I prefer red. Je préfère le rouge.

to **redo** verb
refaire
I have to redo my drawing. Je dois refaire mon dessin.

to **reduce** verb
(*price, speed, etc.*) **réduire**

referee noun
un **arbitre** *masc.*
The referee has blown the whistle.
L'arbitre a sifflé.

ⓔ *means use* **être** *to make the past tense.*

reflexive adjective
(*in grammar*) **réfléchi** *masc.*, **réfléchie** *fem.*
a reflexive verb un verbe pronominal réfléchi

> 🔑 **LANGUAGE**
> In French a reflexive verb is a verb that is used with a pronoun (like **me**, **te**, **se**), for example: **se lever** (to get up), **je me lève** is 'I get up', **tu te lèves** is 'you get up', etc. You can think of a reflexive verb as something you do to yourself, rather than somebody else. There are more reflexive verbs in French than in English.

refrigerator noun
le **réfrigérateur** *masc.*

to **refuse** verb
refuser
I refuse to lend you my bike. Je refuse de te prêter mon vélo.

region noun
la **région** *fem.*

register noun
(*in school*) le **cahier d'appel** *masc.*
The teacher takes the register.
La maîtresse fait l'appel.

registration noun
(*in school*) l'**appel** *masc.*
I missed registration. J'ai raté l'appel.

regular adjective
régulier *masc.*, **régulière** *fem.*

regularly adverb
régulièrement

rehearsal noun
la **répétition** *fem.*

reindeer noun
le **renne** *masc.*

related adjective
1 (*people, words*) **de la même famille**
'Go' and 'went' are related. 'Go' et 'went' sont de la même famille.
2 (*ideas, problems*) **lié** *masc.*, **liée** *fem.*

a
b
c
d
e
f
g
h
i
j
k
l
m
n
o
p
q
r
s
t
u
v
w
x
y
z

relation noun
I have relations in Leeds. J'ai de la famille à Leeds.
all my relations toute ma famille

relative noun
le **membre de la famille** *masc.*
I have relatives in Paris. J'ai de la famille à Paris.

to **relax** verb
se **détendre** ⊘
I watch TV to relax. Je regarde la télé pour me détendre.

relaxed adjective
détendu *masc.*, **détendue** *fem.*
You look relaxed. Tu as l'air détendu.

religion noun
la **religion** *fem.*

religious adjective
religieux *masc.*, **religieuse** *fem.*

to **remain** verb
rester ⊘

to **remember** verb
1 se souvenir ⊘
I don't remember. Je ne me souviens pas.
Do you remember? Tu te souviens?
to remember something se souvenir de quelque chose
Can you remember your email address? Tu te souviens de ton adresse électronique?
to remember somebody se souvenir de quelqu'un
I don't remember Jason. Je ne me souviens pas de Jason.
2 (*talking about not forgetting something you have to do*) **ne pas oublier**
Remember to close the door! N'oublie pas de fermer la porte!

> ⚷ **LANGUAGE**
> In English a souvenir is something you buy to remember a place.

to **remind** verb
rappeler
Remind Dad to take his umbrella! Rappelle à papa de prendre son parapluie!

remote adjective
1 isolé *masc.*, **isolée** *fem.*
a remote farm une ferme isolée
2 the remote control la télécommande

to **remove** verb
enlever
Remove all your things! Enlève toutes tes affaires!

to **rent** verb
louer
I'm going to rent a bike. Je vais louer un vélo.

to **repair** verb
réparer

to **repeat** verb
répéter
Repeat these words after me! Répétez ces mots après moi!

to **replace** verb
remplacer

reply noun
la **réponse** *fem.*
We didn't get a reply. Nous n'avons pas eu de réponse.

to **reply** verb
répondre
Have they replied? Ont-ils répondu?

report noun
le **bulletin scolaire** *masc.*
Leah got a good school report. Leah a eu un bon bulletin scolaire.

to **rescue** verb
sauver
The firemen rescued him from the fire. Les pompiers l'ont sauvé de l'incendie.

• *The months of the year and days of the week do not take a capital letter in French.*

reserve noun
(*football player etc.*) le **remplaçant**
masc., la **remplaçante** *fem.*

to **reserve** verb
réserver
This seat is reserved. Cette place
est réservée.

resort noun
1 (*for holidays at the seaside*) la **station**
balnéaire *fem.*
2 a ski resort une station de ski

to **respect** verb
respecter

responsible adjective
responsable *masc. & fem.*
I'm not responsible for the
accident. Je ne suis pas
responsable de l'accident.

> ⚷ **LANGUAGE**
> English = responsible
> French = responsable

rest noun
1 (*talking about something left over*) **the rest**
le reste *masc.*
I've eaten the rest of the cake. J'ai
mangé le reste du gâteau.
2 (*talking about other people*) **the rest** les
autres *masc. & fem. plural*
Where are the rest of the boys? Où
sont les autres garçons?
3 (*time to relax*) le repos *masc.*
I need some rest. J'ai besoin de
repos.

to **rest** verb
se reposer ⊘
After school I like to rest. Après
l'école j'aime me reposer.

restaurant noun
le **restaurant** *masc.*
We're going to a restaurant. On va
au restaurant.

⊘ *means use* être *to make the past tense.*

result noun
le **résultat** *masc.*

return noun
1 le **retour** *masc.*
the return journey le voyage de
retour
2 (*ticket*) un **aller retour** *masc.*
She bought a return to Bristol. Elle
a acheté un aller retour pour
Bristol.
a return ticket un aller retour
3 Many happy returns! Bon
anniversaire!

to **return** verb
1 (*to come back*) **revenir** ⊘
I'll return in five minutes. Je
reviens dans cinq minutes.
2 (*to go back*) **retourner** ⊘
Carlos has returned to Spain.
Carlos est retourné en Espagne.
3 (*to give back*) **rendre**
I returned my book to the library.
J'ai rendu mon livre à la
bibliothèque.

to **revise** verb
réviser
You have to revise your French. Tu
dois réviser ton français.

revision noun
les **révisions** *fem. plural*
My sister has done a lot of revision.
Ma sœur a fait beaucoup de
révisions.

> ⚷ **LANGUAGE**
> English = revision is singular
> French = révisions is plural

revolting adjective
infect *masc.*, **infecte** *fem.*

reward noun
la **récompense** *fem.*
a fifty euro reward une
récompense de cinquante euros

English French

rhinoceros noun
le **rhinocéros** masc.

LANGUAGE
The English word rhino has the same translation; there is no abbreviation in French.

rhubarb noun
la **rhubarbe** fem.

rhyme noun
la **rime** fem.

to **rhyme** verb
rimer
'Tall' rhymes with 'fall'. 'Tall' rime avec 'fall'.

rhythm noun
le **rythme** masc.

LANGUAGE
English = rhythm
French = rythme

rib noun
la **côte** fem.

ribbon noun
le **ruban** masc.

rice noun
le **riz** masc.
Would you like some rice? Tu veux du riz?

rich adjective
riche masc. & fem.

rid adjective
to get rid of something se débarrasser de quelque chose
Get rid of your old trainers! Débarrasse-toi de tes vieilles baskets!

ride noun
la **promenade** fem.
I went for a ride on my bike. J'ai fait une promenade à vélo.
She's going for a ride on her horse. Elle va faire une promenade à cheval.

Let's go for a ride in the car! Faisons un tour en voiture!

to **ride** verb
1 **to ride a bike** faire du vélo
Can you ride a bike? Tu sais faire du vélo?
to ride a horse monter à cheval
2 (to travel somewhere on a bicycle, horse, etc.) **aller**
I ride my bike to school. Je vais à l'école à vélo.

rider noun
(on a horse) le **cavalier** masc., la **cavalière** fem.

ridiculous adjective
ridicule masc. & fem.

riding noun
l'**équitation** fem.
I go riding. Je fais de l'équitation.

right adjective
1 (correct) **bon** masc., **bonne** fem.
the right answer la bonne réponse
Is this the right house? C'est la bonne maison?
Right! I'm leaving. Bon! Je m'en vais.
2 (time on the clock)
the right time l'heure exacte
Do you have the right time? Tu as l'heure exacte?
3 (true)
Is that right? C'est vrai?
4 (the opposite of left) **droit** masc., **droite** fem.
Show me your right hand! Montre-moi ta main droite!
5 (talking about people) **to be right** avoir raison
You're right. Tu as raison.

LANGUAGE
English = to be right I'm right.
French = avoir raison J'ai raison.

• The months of the year and days of the week do not take a capital letter in French.

right adverb
1 (*correctly*) **correctement**
Am I doing it right? Est-ce que je le fais correctement?
2 (*completely*) **tout**
right at the beginning tout au début
3 (*straight*) **juste**
right in front of you juste devant toi
right away tout de suite
4 **à droite**
Turn right! Tournez à droite!

right noun
la **droite** *fem.*
on the right à droite
In France they drive on the right. En France on roule à droite.
the second street on your right la deuxième rue sur votre droite

right-hand adjective
It's on the right-hand side. C'est à droite.

right-handed adjective
droitier *masc.*, **droitière** *fem.*
Amber is right-handed. Amber est droitière.

ring noun
1 (*for your finger*) la **bague** *fem.*
a gold ring une bague en or
2 (*phone call*)
to give somebody a ring donner un coup de fil à quelqu'un
3 (*circle*) le **cercle** *masc.*
Stand in a ring, children! Formez un cercle, les enfants!

to **ring** verb
1 (*to phone*) **appeler**
Ring me tomorrow! Appelle-moi demain!
2 (*talking about a phone, alarm clock, church bell, etc.*) **sonner**
The phone's ringing. Le téléphone sonne.
Somebody rang the doorbell. On a sonné à la porte.

ⓔ means use être to make the past tense.

The bell's ringing! (*in school*) C'est la sonnerie!

rink noun
an ice rink une patinoire *fem.*

ripe adjective
mûr *masc.*, **mûre** *fem.*

risk noun
le **risque** *masc.*

river noun
1 la **rivière** *fem.*
2 le **fleuve** *masc.*

> 🔑 **LANGUAGE**
> There are two words for 'river' in French: **un fleuve** flows into the sea, and a **une rivière** is smaller and usually flows into a **fleuve.**

Riviera noun
the French Riviera la Côte d'Azur *fem.*

road noun
1 (*between places*) la **route** *fem.*
the road to Manchester la route de Manchester
a road accident un accident de la route
a road sign un panneau
2 (*a street in a town or village*) la **rue** *fem.*
I live across the road. J'habite de l'autre côté de la rue.

roadworks plural noun
les **travaux** *masc. plural*

to **roar** verb
rugir
The lion roared. Le lion a rugi.

roast adjective
rôti *masc.*, **rôtie** *fem.*
roast beef le rôti de bœuf
Do you want some roast chicken? Tu veux du poulet rôti?

to **rob** verb
(*a person*) **voler**
We've been robbed. On nous a volés.

a b c d e f g h i j k l m n o p q r s t u v w x y z

379

robber noun
le **voleur** masc., la **voleuse** fem.

robbery noun
le **vol** masc.

robot noun
le **robot** masc.

rock noun
1 (big stone) le **rocher** masc.
2 (music) le **rock** masc.
rock music la musique rock
a rock singer un chanteur de rock

rocket noun
la **fusée** fem.

rocking horse noun
le **cheval à bascule** masc.

rod noun
a fishing rod une canne à pêche fem.

role-play noun
le **jeu de rôles** masc.

roll noun
(bread roll) le **petit pain** masc.

to **roll** verb
rouler
The ball has rolled under the bed.
La balle a roulé sous le lit.
Roll the dice! Lance le dé!

rollerblades plural noun
les **rollers** masc. plural

roller coaster noun
les **montagnes russes** fem. plural

roller skates plural noun
les **patins à roulettes** masc. plural

roller-skating noun
le **patin à roulettes** masc.
to go roller-skating faire du patin à roulettes

Roman noun
the Romans les Romains masc. plural

Roman Catholic adjective
catholique masc. & fem.

roof noun
le **toit** masc.

room noun
1 (in a house) la **pièce** fem.
There are six rooms in my house.
Il y a six pièces dans ma maison.
2 (bedroom) la **chambre** fem.
I'm in my room. Je suis dans ma chambre.
a hotel room une chambre d'hôtel
3 (in school) la **salle** fem.
the computer room la salle d'informatique
4 (space) la **place** fem.
There isn't enough room. Il n'y a pas assez de place.

rope noun
la **corde** fem.

rose noun
la **rose** fem.
a red rose une rose rouge

rotten adjective
(apple, pear, etc.) **pourri** masc., **pourrie** fem.
It's rotten weather. Il fait un temps pourri.

rough adjective
1 (scratchy) **rugueux** masc., **rugueuse** fem.
2 (person, game) **brutal** masc., **brutale** fem., **brutaux** masc. plural, **brutales** fem. plural
3 **a rough copy** un brouillon
a rough book un cahier de brouillon

roughly adverb
à peu près
We waited roughly an hour. On a attendu à peu près une heure.

round adjective
rond masc., **ronde** fem.
She has a round face. Elle a le visage rond.

• See the centre section for verb tables.

round preposition
1 **autour de**
   a wall round the school un mur autour de l'école
   We're sitting round the table. Nous sommes assis autour de la table.

round adverb
   Can I come round to your house? Je peux venir chez toi?
   round here (*close by*) près d'ici

roundabout noun
1 (*merry-go-round*) le **manège** *masc.*
2 (*for traffic*) le **rond-point** *masc.* (plural les **ronds-points**)

rounders noun
   un jeu un peu comme le base-ball

 CULTURE
French children do not play rounders.

row noun
1 (*of people in the cinema, etc.*) le **rang** *masc.*
   in the front row au premier rang
2 (*of houses, trees, chairs, etc.*) la **rangée** *fem.*
   a row of little houses une rangée de petites maisons

to **row** verb
   (*in a boat*) **ramer**

rowing boat noun
   la **barque** *fem.*

royal adjective
   royal *masc.*,
   royale *fem.*, **royaux** *masc. plural*,
   royales *fem. plural*
   the royal family la famille royale

rubber noun
1 (*for rubbing out*) la **gomme** *fem.*
   I've lost my rubber. J'ai perdu ma gomme.
2 **rubber gloves** des gants en caoutchouc
   a rubber band un élastique

rubbish noun
1 (*food, papers, etc. thrown out*) les **ordures** *fem. plural*
   a rubbish bin une poubelle
2 (*nonsense*) les **bêtises** *fem. plural*
   She's talking rubbish! Elle dit des bêtises!

rubbish adjective
   (*very bad*) **nul** *masc.*, **nulle** *fem.*
   This book is rubbish. Ce livre est nul.

to **rub out** verb
   effacer

rude adjective
   impoli *masc.*, **impolie** *fem.*
   Don't be rude! Ne sois pas impoli!
   a rude word un gros mot

⚠ **FALSE FRIEND**
un gros mot = a rude word (*not* a big word)

rug noun
   le **tapis** *masc.*

rugby noun
   le **rugby** *masc.*
   My brother plays rugby. Mon frère joue au rugby.

to **ruin** verb
1 (*a dress, shoes, a toy, etc.*) **abîmer**
   He has ruined his shoes. Il a abîmé ses chaussures.
2 (*the holidays, trip, etc.*) **gâcher**
   She ruined my party. Elle a gâché ma fête.

ruin noun
   la **ruine** *fem.*
   the ruins of the church les ruines de l'église

rule noun
1 (*of a game, grammar, etc.*) la **règle** *fem.*
   You're not obeying the rules of the game. Tu ne respectes pas les règles du jeu.
2 (*in a school, club, group*)

⊘ *means use* être *to make the past tense.*

a b c d e f g h i j k l m n o p q r s t u v w x y z

the rules le règlement

the school rules le règlement de l'école

It's against the rules. C'est interdit par le règlement.

ruler noun
la **règle** *fem.*

run noun
to go for a run courir
Cathy's going for a three-mile run. Cathy va courir cinq kilomètres.

to **run** verb
1 **courir**
I ran to the bus stop. J'ai couru jusqu'à l'arrêt de bus.
2 (*to organize*) **organiser**
to run a competition organiser un concours
3 **My nose is running.** Mon nez coule.

runner noun
le **coureur** *masc.*, la **coureuse** *fem.*

runner-up noun
le **deuxième** *masc.*,
la **deuxième** *fem.*

running noun
la **course à pied** *fem.*
I like running. J'aime la course à pied.

rush noun
1 **Are you in a rush?** Tu es pressé?
2 **the rush hour** les heures de pointe *fem. plural*

to **rush** verb
se dépêcher ⊘
We have to rush. Il faut se dépêcher.

Russia noun
la **Russie** *fem.*

Russian adjective
russe *masc. & fem.*
He's Russian. Il est russe.

Russian noun
1 (*the language*) le **russe** *masc.*
2 (*the person*) le or la **Russe** *masc. & fem.*

Ss

sack noun
le **sac** *masc.*

sad adjective
triste *masc. & fem.*
You look sad. Tu as l'air triste.

saddle noun
la **selle** *fem.*

sadly adverb
tristement

safe adjective
1 (*not dangerous*) **pas dangereux** *masc.*,
pas dangereuse *fem.*
The path is safe. Ce sentier n'est pas dangereux.
2 (*away from danger*) **en sécurité**

You're safe here. Vous êtes en sécurité ici.
3 (*not hurt*) **sain et sauf** *masc.*, **saine et sauve** *fem.*
Dad came back safe. Papa est revenu sain et sauf.

safe noun
(*for money*) le **coffre-fort** *masc.*
(plural les **coffres-forts**)

safety noun
la **sécurité** *fem.*

sailing noun
la **voile** *fem.*
to go sailing faire de la voile
a sailing boat un voilier

• *Use* **le** *and* **un** *for masculine words and* **la** *and* **une** *for feminine words.*

sailor noun
le **marin** masc.

saint noun
le **saint** masc., la **sainte** fem.

salad noun
la **salade** fem.
a cheese salad une salade au fromage

sale noun
1 la **vente** fem.
for sale à vendre
2 **the sales** les soldes masc. plural
The sales start in January. Les soldes commencent en janvier.

salmon noun
le **saumon** masc.

salt noun
le **sel** masc.
Do you want some salt? Tu veux du sel?

salty adjective
salé masc., **salée** fem.
It's too salty. C'est trop salé.

same adjective
1 **même** masc. & fem.
the same thing la même chose
We arrived at the same time. Nous sommes arrivés en même temps.
I have the same one. J'ai le même.
2 (talking about things that look the same) **pareil** masc., **pareille** fem.
Our bikes are the same. Nos vélos sont pareils.

sand noun
le **sable** masc.
a sand castle un château de sable

sandal noun
la **sandale** fem.
a pair of sandals une paire de sandales

sandwich noun
le **sandwich** masc.
a cheese sandwich un sandwich au fromage

Santa Claus noun
le **père Noël** masc.

satellite noun
le **satellite** masc.
satellite television la télévision par satellite
a satellite dish un parabole

Saturday noun
samedi masc.
It's Saturday today. C'est samedi aujourd'hui.
on Saturday samedi
I'm leaving on Saturday. Je pars samedi.
next Saturday samedi prochain
last Saturday samedi dernier
every Saturday tous les samedis
on Saturdays le samedi
Is it open on Saturdays? C'est ouvert le samedi?

sauce noun
la **sauce** fem.

saucepan noun
la **casserole** fem.

saucer noun
la **soucoupe** fem.
a flying saucer une soucoupe volante

sausage noun
la **saucisse** fem.

to **save** verb
1 (to rescue) **sauver**
He saved the cat from the fire. Il a sauvé le chat de l'incendie.
2 (money to buy something) **mettre de côté**
I've saved fifty euros. J'ai mis cinquante euros de côté.

ⓔ means use être to make the past tense.

a
b
c
d
e
f
g
h
i
j
k
l
m
n
o
p
q
r
s
t
u
v
w
x
y
z

I'm saving up for a guitar. Je mets de l'argent de côté pour m'acheter une guitare.

3 (to keep) **garder**
I've saved you some cake. Je t'ai gardé du gâteau.

4 **to save time** gagner du temps

5 (on a computer) **sauvegarder**
to save a file on to a CD sauvegarder un fichier sur un CD

saxophone noun
le **saxophone** masc.
Molly plays the saxophone. Molly joue du saxophone.

to **say** verb
1 **dire**
What are you saying? Qu'est-ce que tu dis?
I didn't say anything. Je n'ai rien dit.
How do you say 'garden' in French? Comment dit-on 'garden' en français?
2 (to repeat) **répéter**
Could you say it again? Tu peux répéter?

scales noun
1 (for food) la **balance** fem.
2 (for people) le **pèse-personne** masc.

Scandinavia noun
la **Scandinavie** fem.

scanner noun
le **scanner** masc.

scar noun
la **cicatrice** fem.

scared adjective
to be scared avoir peur
I'm scared. J'ai peur.
Peter is scared of the dark. Peter a peur du noir.

🔑 **LANGUAGE**
English = to be scared   I'm scared.
French = **avoir** peur   J'ai peur.

scarf noun
1 (long and warm scarf) une **écharpe** fem.
a woolly scarf une écharpe en laine
2 (thin square scarf) le **foulard** masc.
a silk scarf un foulard en soie

scary adjective
That's scary. Ça fait peur.
a scary monster un monstre qui fait peur

scenery noun
le **paysage** masc.
Look at this lovely scenery! Regarde ce beau paysage!

school noun
une **école** fem.
Do you like school? Tu aimes l'école?
at school à l'école
I go to school with my mum. Je vais à l'école avec ma mère.
a schoolbag un cartable
a schoolbook un livre scolaire
a school bus un car scolaire
the school holidays les vacances scolaires
the school library la bibliothèque de l'école
the school year l'année scolaire

schoolboy noun
un **écolier** masc.

schoolchildren noun
les **écoliers** masc. plural

schoolgirl noun
une **écolière** fem.

science noun
1 la **science** fem.
2 (as a school subject) les **sciences** fem. plural

scientist noun
le or la **scientifique** masc. & fem.

• Languages, nationalities, and religions do not take a capital letter in French.

scissors plural noun
les **ciseaux** masc. plural
a pair of scissors une paire de
ciseaux

scooter noun
1 (for children) la **trottinette** fem.
2 (motorcycle) le **scooter** masc.

score noun
le **score** masc.
The score is two nil. Le score est de
deux à zéro.

to **score** verb
(a goal or point) **marquer**
Sean scored a goal. Sean a marqué
un but.

Scot noun
un **Écossais** masc.,
une **Écossaise** fem.

Scotland noun
l'**Écosse** fem.
I live in Scotland. J'habite en
Écosse.

Scotsman noun
un **Écossais** masc.

Scotswoman noun
une **Écossaise** fem.

Scottish adjective
écossais masc., **écossaise** fem.
a Scottish football player
un joueur de football écossais
He's Scottish. Il est écossais.
She's Scottish. Elle est écossaise.

Scout noun
le **scout** masc.
I'm a Scout. Je suis scout.

CULTURE
There are more Scouts in Britain than in
France.

scrambled eggs plural noun
les **œufs brouillés** masc. plural

scrapbook noun
un **album** masc.

to **scratch** verb
(of an itch) **se gratter** ⊜
Don't scratch! Ne te gratte pas!

to **scream** verb
hurler

screen noun
un **écran** masc.

sea noun
la **mer** fem.
Hastings is by the sea. Hastings est
au bord de la mer.
to travel by sea voyager en bateau

seafood noun
les **fruits de mer** masc. plural

seal noun
le **phoque** masc.

to **search** verb
chercher
I've searched everywhere.
J'ai cherché partout.

seashore noun
la **plage** fem.

seasick adjective
I'm seasick. J'ai le mal de mer.

seaside noun
le **bord de la mer** masc.
We're going to the seaside. Nous
allons au bord de la mer.

season noun
la **saison** fem.

seat noun
1 le **siège** masc.
the back seat of the car le siège
arrière de la voiture
2 la **place** fem.
Can you keep my seat? Tu peux
garder ma place?

seatbelt noun
la **ceinture de sécurité** fem.

a b c d e f g h i j k l m n o p q r **s** t u v w x y z

⊜ means use **être** to make the past tense.

385

second adjective
deuxième *masc. & fem.*
This is the second time. C'est la deuxième fois.
Beth came second. (*in the race*) Beth est arrivée deuxième.
on the second of December le deux décembre

second noun
la **seconde** *fem.*
one minute and ten seconds une minute et dix secondes
Wait a second! Attends une seconde!

secondary school noun
1 (*for children from 11 to 15*) le **collège** *masc.*
2 (*for children from 15 to 18*) le **lycée** *masc.*

CULTURE
French children go to the **collège** from the ages of 11 to 15, and then go on to the **lycée** until they are 18.

secret noun
le **secret** *masc.*
Can you keep a secret? Sais-tu garder un secret?

secret adjective
secret *masc.*, **secrète** *fem.*
a secret place un endroit secret

secretary noun
le or la **secrétaire** *masc. & fem.*

to **see** verb
1 **voir**
Come and see me! Viens me voir!
Can you see that man? Tu vois ce monsieur?
I haven't seen the latest Disney. Je n'ai pas vu le dernier Disney.
Let me see your new bike! Montre-moi ton nouveau vélo!
2 **See you!** Salut!
See you later! À tout à l'heure!
See you tomorrow! À demain!

seed noun
la **graine** *fem.*

to **seem** verb
sembler
He seems tired. Il a l'air fatigué.

seesaw noun
la **balançoire** *fem.*

selfish adjective
égoïste *masc. & fem.*

to **sell** verb
vendre
I'm selling my computer. Je vends mon ordinateur.
I sold my bike to my cousin. J'ai vendu mon vélo à mon cousin.
The tickets are sold out. Tous les billets sont vendus.

Sellotape® noun
le **scotch®** *masc.*

semicircle noun
le **demi-cercle** *masc.*
in a semicircle en demi-cercle

semifinal noun
la **demi-finale** *fem.*

to **send** verb
envoyer
Send me a photo! Envoie-moi une photo!
I sent my grandparents a letter. J'ai envoyé une lettre à mes grands-parents.

to **send back** verb
renvoyer

senior citizen noun
la **personne âgée** *fem.*

sense noun
le **sens** *masc.*
It doesn't make sense. Ça n'a pas de sens.
Emma has a sense of humour. Emma a le sens de l'humour.

• *The months of the year and days of the week do not take a capital letter in French.*

sensible adjective
raisonnable *masc. & fem.*
Charlotte is very sensible.
Charlotte est très raisonnable.

⚠ **FALSE FRIEND**
sensible = raisonnable (*not* sensible)

sensitive adjective
sensible *masc. & fem.*
Claire is very sensitive. Claire est
très sensible.

sentence noun
la **phrase** *fem.*
Write a few short sentences!
Écrivez quelques phrases courtes!

separate adjective
1 (*different*) **autre** *masc. & fem.*
They were put in a separate class.
On les a mis dans une autre classe.
2 (*own*) **The children have separate
rooms.** Les enfants ont chacun leur
chambre.

to **separate** verb
séparer
**Separate the blue cards from the
red!** Séparez les cartes bleues des
rouges!

separated adjective
séparé *masc.,* **séparée** *fem.*
My parents are separated. Mes
parents sont séparés.

September noun
septembre *masc.*
In September en septembre
at the beginning of September
début septembre
**It's my birthday on the third of
September.** C'est mon
anniversaire le trois septembre.

series noun
la **série** *fem.*
a TV series une série télévisée

serious adjective
1 (*illness, accident, mistake*) **grave** *masc. &
fem.*
a serious illness une maladie grave
2 **sérieux** *masc.,* **sérieuse** *fem.*
Liam looks serious. Liam a l'air
sérieux.

seriously adverb
gravement
seriously injured gravement blessé

servant noun
le or la **domestique** *masc. & fem.*

to **serve** verb
1 **servir**
2 **It serves him right.** C'est bien fait
pour lui.

serviette noun
la **serviette** *fem.*

set noun
1 **a chess set** un jeu d'échecs *masc.*
2 **a TV set** une télé *fem.*
Switch off the TV set! Éteins la télé!

to **set** verb
1 **mettre**
to set the table mettre la table
I've set the alarm for eight. J'ai
mis le réveil à huit heures.
2 **The sun is setting.** Le soleil se
couche.

to **set off** verb
partir ⓔ
They set off at noon. Ils sont partis
à midi.

settee noun
le **canapé** *masc.*

to **settle down** verb
(*to calm down*) **se calmer** ⓔ
Settle down, boys! Calmez-vous,
les garçons!

seven number
sept
seven days sept jours
I'm seven. J'ai sept ans.

ⓔ *means use* être *to make the past tense.*

a
b
c
d
e
f
g
h
i
j
k
l
m
n
o
p
q
r
s
t
u
v
w
x
y
z

English French

Come to my house at seven! Viens chez moi à sept heures!

seventeen number
dix-sept
My sister is seventeen. Ma sœur a dix-sept ans.

seventh adjective
septième masc. & fem.
on the seventh floor au septième étage
the seventh of February le sept février

seventy number
soixante-dix

several adjective
plusieurs masc. & fem. plural
several books plusieurs livres
several times plusieurs fois

to **sew** verb
coudre
I can sew. Je sais coudre.

sewing noun
la couture fem.
Do you like sewing? Tu aimes la couture?

shh exclamation
chut

shade noun
l'ombre fem.
in the shade à l'ombre

shadow noun
une **ombre** fem.

to **shake** verb
1 secouer
You shake the bottle before you open it. Tu secoues la bouteille avant de l'ouvrir.
2 to shake hands with somebody serrer la main à quelqu'un
3 trembler
You're shaking! Tu trembles!

• *See the centre section for verb tables.*

shall verb
Shall I turn off the TV? J'éteins la télé?
Shall we go for a swim? On va nager?

shallow adjective
peu profond masc.,
peu profonde fem.

shame noun
What a shame! Quel dommage!

shampoo noun
le **shampooing** masc.

shape noun
la **forme** fem.
a cake in the shape of a star un gâteau en forme d'étoile

to **share** verb
partager
I share a room with my sister. Je partage une chambre avec ma sœur.

shark noun
le **requin** masc.

sharp adjective
(*knife, scissors*) **bien aiguisé** masc.,
bien aiguisée fem.
sharp scissors des ciseaux bien aiguisés
Be careful, it's sharp! Attention, ça coupe!

to **sharpen** verb
tailler
to sharpen a pencil tailler un crayon

she pronoun
elle
She's hungry. Elle a faim.

sheep noun
le **mouton** masc.

sheet noun
1 le **drap** masc.
The sheets are clean. Les draps sont propres.

388

2 a sheet of paper une feuille de papier

shelf noun
une **étagère** fem.

shell noun
1 (of an egg, snail, or nut) la **coquille** fem.
2 (a seashell) le **coquillage** masc.

shepherd noun
le **berger** masc.

to **shine** verb
briller
The sun is shining. Le soleil brille.

shiny adjective
(metal, hair, etc.) **brillant** masc.,
brillante fem.

ship noun
le **bateau** masc. (plural les **bateaux**)
by ship en bateau

shirt noun
1 la **chemise** fem.
a clean shirt une chemise propre
2 (for football) le **maillot** masc.

to **shiver** verb
trembler de froid

shoe noun
la **chaussure** fem.
a pair of shoes une paire de chaussures
a shoe shop un magasin de chaussures

shoelace noun
le **lacet** masc.
Do your shoelaces up! Attache tes lacets!

shop noun
le **magasin** masc.
The shops are closed. Les magasins sont fermés.

shop assistant noun
le **vendeur** masc., la **vendeuse** fem.

shopkeeper noun
le **commerçant** masc.,
la **commerçante** fem.

shopping noun
1 (for food) les **courses** fem. plural
to go shopping in the supermarket
faire les courses au supermarché
a shopping centre un centre commercial
a shopping list une liste de courses
a shopping bag un sac à provisions
2 (for clothes, books, CDs, gifts)
to go shopping aller ⊘ faire du shopping
Nick hates going shopping. Nick déteste faire du shopping.

short adjective
1 **court** masc., **courte** fem.
short hair les cheveux courts
a short dress une robe courte
2 **petit**
a short walk une petite promenade
Ned is short for his age. Ned est petit pour son âge.
a short cut un raccourci

shorts plural noun
le **short** masc.
I wear shorts for PE. Je mets un short pour la gym.
a pair of shorts un short

🗝 **LANGUAGE**
English = **shorts** is plural
French = **un short** is singular

---

short-sighted adjective
myope masc. & fem.

should verb
devoir
You should listen. Tu devrais écouter.
You shouldn't tell lies. Tu ne devrais pas mentir.

shoulder noun
une **épaule** fem.

⊘ *means use **être** to make the past tense.*

a
b
c
d
e
f
g
h
i
j
k
l
m
n
o
p
q
r
s
t
u
v
w
x
y
z

to **shout** verb
crier
Stop shouting! Arrête de crier!

to **show** verb
montrer
Show me how to do it! Montre-moi comment faire!
I showed my new video game to Jamie. J'ai montré mon nouveau jeu vidéo à Jamie.

show noun
(*with actors, musicians, etc.*)
le spectacle *masc.*
a Christmas show un spectacle de Noël

shower noun
la douche *fem.*
I'd like to have a shower. Je voudrais prendre une douche.

show-off noun
le frimeur *masc.*, la frimeuse *fem.*

Shrove Tuesday noun
Mardi gras *masc.*

🌍 **CULTURE**
Children in France and in Britain eat pancakes on this day (also called Pancake Day).

to **shuffle** verb
to shuffle the cards battre les cartes

to **shut** verb
1 fermer
Shut your eyes! Ferme les yeux!
The shops shut at eight. Les magasins ferment à huit heures.
2 (*to be quiet*)
to shut up se taire ⓔ
Shut up! Tais-toi!

shut adjective
fermé *masc.*, fermée *fem.*
Is the window shut? Est-ce que la fenêtre est fermée?

shuttle noun
la navette *fem.*
the space shuttle la navette spatiale

shy adjective
timide *masc. & fem.*

sick adjective
1 (*ill*) malade *masc. & fem.*
I'm sick. Je suis malade.
2 **to feel sick** avoir envie de vomir
I'm going to be sick. Je vais vomir.

side noun
1 le côté *masc.*
on this side of the road de ce côté de la rue
on the other side de l'autre côté
2 (*team*) une équipe *fem.*
Our side won. Notre équipe a gagné.

sightseeing noun
le tourisme *masc.*
to go sightseeing faire du tourisme

sign noun
le panneau *masc.* (plural les **panneaux**)
a road sign un panneau
Follow the signs! Suivez les panneaux!

to **sign** verb
signer
Sign here. Signez ici.

signal noun
le signal *masc.* (plural les **signaux**)

signature noun
la signature *fem.*

sign language noun
le langage des signes *masc.*

Sikh adjective
sikh *masc. & fem.*

silence noun
le silence *masc.*

silent adjective
silencieux *masc.*, silencieuse *fem.*

• *Use* le *and* un *for masculine words and* la *and* une *for feminine words.*

silk noun
la **soie** fem.
a silk blouse un chemisier en soie

silly adjective
bête masc. & fem.
Don't be silly! Ne soyez pas bêtes!

silver noun
l'**argent** masc.
a silver medal une médaille
d'argent
silver earrings des boucles
d'oreille en argent

SIM card noun
la **carte SIM** masc.

similar adjective
semblable masc. & fem.

Simon says phrase
Jacques a dit
Let's play Simon says! Jouons à
Jacques a dit!

simple adjective
simple masc. & fem.

since preposition
depuis
since then depuis ce moment-là
**I've been waiting since this
morning.** J'attends depuis ce
matin.

to **sing** verb
chanter
I sing in the shower. Je chante sous
la douche.
singing lessons des cours de chant

singer noun
le **chanteur** masc.,
la **chanteuse** fem.

single adjective
1 **seul** masc., **seule** fem.
We didn't score a single goal.
Nous n'avons pas marqué un seul
but.
2 **in single file** en file indienne

3 **a single room** une chambre pour
une personne
4 **a single ticket** un aller simple

single noun
(*ticket*) un **aller** masc.
Mum bought a single to Oxford.
Maman a acheté un aller pour
Oxford.

single-parent family noun
la **famille mono-parentale** fem.

singular noun
le **singulier** masc.
in the singular au singulier

sink noun
1 (*in the kitchen*) un **évier** masc.
2 (*in the bathroom*) un **lavabo** masc.

to **sink** verb
couler

sir noun
1 **monsieur** masc.
2 (*in a letter*) **Dear Sir ...** Monsieur ...

sister noun
la **sœur** fem.
my big sister ma grande sœur

to **sit** verb
1 **s'asseoir** ⊘
Come and sit next to me! Viens
t'asseoir a côté de moi!
to be sitting être assis
She's sitting on the sofa. Elle est
assise sur le canapé.
2 **to sit down** s'asseoir ⊘
I sat down on the floor. Je me suis
assis par terre.
Sit down, Jack! Assieds-toi, Jack!
Sit down, girls! Asseyez-vous, les
filles!

site noun
1 (*website*) le **site** masc.
Did you go to their site? Tu as visité
leur site?
2 **a camping site** un terrain de
camping masc.

⊘ *means use* **être** *to make the past tense.*

a
b
c
d
e
f
g
h
i
j
k
l
m
n
o
p
q
r
s
t
u
v
w
x
y
z

a
b
c
d
e
f
g
h
i
j
k
l
m
n
o
p
q
r
s
t
u
v
w
x
y
z

sitting room noun
le **salon** *masc.*

situation noun
la **situation** *fem.*

six number
six
six pencils six crayons
We went out at six. Nous sommes
sortis à six heures.

sixteen number
seize

sixth adjective
sixième *masc. & fem.*
on the sixth floor au sixième étage
the sixth of April le six avril

sixty number
soixante

size noun
la **taille** *fem.*
What size are you? Vous faites
quelle taille?
It's the wrong size. Ce n'est pas la
bonne taille.

to **skate** verb
1 (*on ice*) **faire du patin à glace**
2 (*on rollerskates*) **faire du patin à
roulettes**

skateboard noun
le **skateboard** *masc.*

skateboarding noun
le **skateboard** *masc.*
I go skateboarding. Je fais du
skateboard.

skating noun
(*on ice*) le **patin à glace** *masc.*
We go skating. On fait du patin à
glace.
a skating rink une patinoire

skeleton noun
le **squelette** *masc.*

ski noun
le **ski** *masc.*
a pair of skis une paire de skis

ski boots les chaussures de ski *fem.*
plural
a ski slope une piste de ski

to **ski** verb
skier
I'm learning to ski. J'apprends à
skier.

skiing noun
le **ski** *masc.*
Do you go skiing? Tu fais du ski?
They're going on a skiing holiday.
Ils vont aux sports d'hiver.

skin noun
la **peau** *fem.*

skinny adjective
maigre *masc. & fem.*

to **skip** verb
(*with a rope*) **sauter à la corde**
a skipping rope une corde à sauter

skirt noun
la **jupe** *fem.*

sky noun
le **ciel** *masc.*

skyscraper noun
le **gratte-ciel** *masc.* (plural les
gratte-ciel)

to **slam** verb
claquer
She slammed the door. Elle a
claqué la porte.

sledge noun
la **luge** *fem.*

to **sleep** verb
dormir
He's sleeping. Il dort.
Did you sleep well? Tu as bien
dormi?
a sleeping bag un sac de couchage

⚷ LANGUAGE
Dormir is related to the English word
'dormitory' (a place where people sleep).

• *Languages, nationalities, and religions do not take a capital letter in French.*

sleepover noun
Kate's coming for a sleepover.
Kate vient dormir chez moi.

sleepy adjective
to be sleepy avoir sommeil
I'm sleepy. J'ai sommeil.

🔑 **LANGUAGE**
English = **to be** sleepy **I'm sleepy**
French = **avoir** sommeil **J'ai sommeil**

sleeve noun
la **manche** fem.
I prefer shirts with short sleeves.
Je préfère les chemises à manches
courtes.

slice noun
la **tranche** fem.
a slice of bread une tranche de
pain

slide noun
(in a playground) le **toboggan** masc.

to **slide** verb
glisser
The children are sliding on the ice.
Les enfants glissent sur la glace.

slight adjective
(difference, accent, etc.) **léger** masc.,
légère fem.

slightly adverb
légèrement

slim adjective
mince masc. & fem.

to **slip** verb
glisser
I slipped on the floor. J'ai glissé sur
le sol.

slipper noun
la **pantoufle** fem.
a pair of slippers une paire de
pantoufles

slow adjective
lent masc., **lente** fem.

slowly adverb
lentement
Speak more slowly! Parle plus
lentement!

smack noun
la **claque** fem.

small adjective
petit masc., **petite** fem.

smart adjective
1 (clothes, shop, etc.) **chic** masc. & fem.
You're very smart! Tu es très chic!

🔑 **LANGUAGE**
Chic is the same in the masculine,
feminine, and plural.

2 (clever) **intelligent** masc.,
intelligente fem.

to **smash** verb
casser

to **smell** verb
sentir
This smells nice. Ça sent bon.

smell noun
une **odeur** fem.
a nasty smell une mauvaise odeur

to **smile** verb
sourire
Smile! Souriez!
The baby smiled at me. Le bébé
m'a souri.

smile noun
le **sourire** masc.
a nice smile un beau sourire

snack noun
le **casse-croûte** masc. (plural les
casse-croûte)
a snack bar un snack-bar

snail noun
un **escargot** masc.

🌍 **CULTURE**
French people eat snails, but only
occasionally: they are expensive! They
are most often served with garlic butter.

ⓔ *means use* **être** *to make the past tense.*

a
b
c
d
e
f
g
h
i
j
k
l
m
n
o
p
q
r
s
t
u
v
w
x
y
z

snake noun
le **serpent** *masc.*
snakes and ladders (*board game*)
le joue de l'oie

to **sneeze** verb
éternuer

to **snore** verb
ronfler

snow noun
la **neige** *fem.*

to **snow** verb
neiger
It's snowing. Il neige.

snowball noun
la **boule de neige** *fem.*

snowflakes plural noun
les **flocons de neige** *masc. plural*

snowman noun
le **bonhomme de neige** *masc.*

so adverb
1 (*very much*) **si**
It's so far away! C'est si loin!
2 (*also*) **aussi**
Joël has two brothers and so do I.
Joël a deux frères et moi aussi.
3 (*after think, hope, etc.*)
I think so.
Je pense.
I hope so. Je l'espère.
4 **so much, so many** tellement de
You have so much work! Tu as
tellement de travail!
You have so many friends! Tu as
tellement d'amis!

so conjunction
alors
He's ill, so he isn't coming. Il est
malade, alors il ne vient pas.
So what? Et alors?

soaking wet adjective
trempé *masc.*, **trempée** *fem.*

soap noun
1 le **savon** *masc.*
2 (*TV programme*) le **feuilleton** *masc.*

soccer noun
le **football** *masc.*

sock noun
la **chaussette** *fem.*

sofa noun
le **canapé** *masc.*

soft adjective
1 (*cushion, butter, ball, etc.*) **mou** *masc.*,
molle *fem.*
a soft mattress un matelas mou
2 (*hands, music, voice, etc.*) **doux** *masc.*,
douce *fem.*
soft skin la peau douce
3 **a soft drink** une boisson non
alcoolisée

software noun
le **logiciel** *masc.*

solar adjective
solaire *masc. & fem.*
the solar system le système solaire

sold adjective
vendu *masc.*, **vendue** *fem.*

soldier noun
le **soldat** *masc.*
He's a soldier. Il est soldat.

to **solve** verb
résoudre

some adjective
1 (*before a masculine singular noun*) **du**
some orange juice du jus d'orange
2 (*before a feminine singular noun*) **de la**
some salad de la salade
**Do you want to listen to some
music?** Tu veux écouter de la
musique?
3 (*before a singular word starting with a, e, i, o,
u, or silent h.*) **de l'**
some money de l'argent
4 (*before a plural noun*) **des**
some DVDs des DVD

• *The months of the year and days of the week do not take a capital letter in French.*

I'm going to buy some books.
Je vais acheter des livres.

some pronoun

1 (*compared to others*) **certains** *masc. plural*, **certaines** *fem. plural*
Some are too expensive. Certains sont trop chers.

2 (*when* **some** *means* **some of it** *or* **some of them**) **en**
Mum bought a cake. Do you want some? Maman a acheté un gâteau. Tu en veux?
Take some chocolates. – No, thanks, I have some. Prends des chocolats. – Non merci, j'en ai déjà.

somebody pronoun
quelqu'un
Somebody wants to see you. Quelqu'un veut te voir.
somebody else quelqu'un d'autre

someone pronoun SEE **somebody**

something pronoun
quelque chose
Do you want something to eat? Tu veux quelque chose à manger?
something else autre chose

sometimes adverb
quelquefois

somewhere adverb
quelque part
He's somewhere in the house. Il est quelque part dans la maison.

son noun
le **fils** *masc.*

song noun
la **chanson** *fem.*
to sing a song chanter une chanson

soon adverb
1 **bientôt**
We're leaving soon. On part bientôt.
See you soon! À bientôt!
as soon as possible aussitôt que possible

2 (*quickly*) **vite**
Write soon! Écris-moi vite!

sore adjective
It's sore. Ça fait mal.
I have a sore throat. J'ai mal à la gorge.

sorry adjective
1 **désolé** *masc.*, **désolée** *fem.*
I'm very sorry. Je suis vraiment désolé. (*boy speaking*) Je suis vraiment désolée. (*girl speaking*)
Sorry I'm late! Désolé d'être en retard!

2 (*meaning* **excuse me!** *when being polite or not hearing*)
Sorry! Pardon!
Sorry? What did you say? Pardon? Qu'est-ce que vous avez dit?

sort noun
la **sorte** *fem.*
What sort of film is it? C'est quelle sorte de film?

to **sort** verb
(*to tidy up*)
to sort out ranger
Sort out your toys! Range tes jouets!

sound noun
1 (*noise*) le **bruit** *masc.*
Can you hear a sound? Tu entends un bruit?
2 (*of the TV etc.*) le **son** *masc.*
Turn down the sound! Baisse le son!

to **sound** verb
1 (*to seem*) **sembler**
It sounds a good idea to me. Il me semble que c'est une bonne idée.
2 (*followed by an adjective*) **avoir l'air**
That sounds dangerous. Ça a l'air dangereux.

soup noun
la **soupe** *fem.*
vegetable soup la soupe de légumes

ⓔ *means use* **être** *to make the past tense.*

a
b
c
d
e
f
g
h
i
j
k
l
m
n
o
p
q
r
s
t
u
v
w
x
y
z

sour adjective
aigre *masc. & fem.*

south noun
le sud *masc.*
They live in the south. Ils habitent
dans le sud.
to the south of Cambridge au sud
de Cambridge
the South of France le sud de la
France

south adjective
1 sud *masc. & fem.*
the south coast la côte sud
2 **the South Pole** le pôle Sud

South America noun
l'Amérique du Sud *fem.*

souvenir noun
le souvenir *masc.*
a souvenir shop une boutique de
souvenirs

space noun
1 (*between words or objects*) un espace
masc.
Leave a space for your name.
Laissez un espace pour votre nom.
2 (*room*) la place *fem.*
**The computer takes up a lot of
space.** L'ordinateur prend
beaucoup de place.
3 (*outer space*) l'espace *masc.*
a journey into space un voyage
dans l'espace
the space shuttle la navette
spatiale
4 (*square in board games*) la case *fem.*

spaceship noun
le vaisseau spatial *masc.*

spade noun
1 la pelle *fem.*
a bucket and spade un seau et une
pelle
2 **spades** (*in cards*) le pique
the jack of spades le valet de pique

• *See the centre section for verb tables.*

spaghetti noun
les spaghettis *masc. plural*

🔑 **LANGUAGE**
English = **spaghetti** is singular
French = **spaghettis** is plural

Spain noun
l'Espagne *fem.*

Spanish adjective
espagnol *masc.*, espagnole *fem.*
He's Spanish. Il est espagnol.

Spanish noun
1 (*the language*) l'espagnol *masc.*
Can you speak Spanish? Vous
parlez espagnol?
2 **the Spanish** les Espagnols *masc.
plural*

spare adjective
a spare room une chambre d'amis
spare time le temps libre
**What do you do in your spare
time?** Que fais-tu pendant ton
temps libre?

to **speak** verb
parler
I speak French. Je parle français.
Do you speak French? Vous parlez
français?

special adjective
spécial *masc.*,
spéciale *fem.*, spéciaux *masc.
plural*, spéciales *fem. plural*

specially adverb
(*most of all*) surtout
**I like London, specially the
museums.** J'aime Londres, surtout
les musées.

speech noun
le discours *masc.*
to make a speech faire un discours
parts of speech les parties du
discours

speed noun
la vitesse *fem.*

What speed is dad doing? Papa roule à quelle vitesse?

to **speed up** verb
aller ❷ plus vite

to **spell** verb
1 (*to write*) écrire
How do you spell that? Comment ça s'écrit?
Do you know how to spell 'enough'? Sais-tu comment on écrit 'enough'?
2 (*to say out loud*) épeler
Can you spell your name? Pouvez-vous épeler votre nom?

spell noun
a magic spell (*words*) une formule magique *fem.*

spelling noun
l'orthographe *fem.*
a spelling mistake une faute d'orthographe

to **spend** verb
1 (*money*) dépenser
I spent a lot of money. J'ai dépensé beaucoup d'argent.
2 (*time*) passer
We spent a week in Nice. Nous avons passé une semaine à Nice.

spicy adjective
épicé *masc.*, épicée *fem.*
a very spicy curry un curry très épicé

spider noun
une araignée *fem.*

to **spill** verb
renverser

spinach noun
les épinards *masc. plural*
Do you like spinach? Tu aimes les épinards

⚷ **LANGUAGE**
English = spinach is singular
French = épinards is plural

❷ *means use être to make the past tense.*

spite noun
in spite of malgré

to **split** verb
1 (*to divide*) diviser
They're going to split the class into two. On va diviser la classe en deux.
2 (*to share out*) partager
Split the chocolates among yourselves. Partagez les chocolats entre vous.

spoilsport noun
le or la trouble-fête *masc. & fem.* (plural les **trouble-fête**)

spoilt adjective
gâté *masc.*, gâtée *fem.*
He's a spoilt child. C'est un enfant gâté.

sponge noun
une éponge *fem.*

to **sponsor** verb
parrainer
Will you sponsor me? Voulez-vous me parrainer?

spooky adjective
(*place, house, etc.*) sinistre *masc. & fem.*
It's spooky! Ça fait peur!

spoon noun
la cuillère *fem.*

sport noun
le sport *masc.*
My favourite sport is football. Mon sport préféré, c'est le football.
a sports bag un sac de sport
a sports car une voiture de sport
a sports club un club sportif
sports day la fête des sports
a sports ground un terrain de sport

sporty adjective
sportif *masc.*, sportive *fem.*

to **spot** verb
(*to find*) trouver
Spot the mistakes! Trouvez les erreurs!

397

a
b
c
d
e
f
g
h
i
j
k
l
m
n
o
p
q
r
s
t
u
v
w
x
y
z

spot noun
1 (*pimple*) le **bouton** *masc.*
covered in spots couvert de
boutons
2 (*dot*) le **pois** *masc.*
a green blouse with black spots
un chemisier vert à pois noirs
3 (*place*) un **endroit** *masc.*
He's looking for a quiet spot.
Il cherche un endroit calme.

to **sprain** verb
I've sprained my ankle. Je me suis
fait une entorse à la cheville.

to **spread** verb
(*glue, butter, etc.*) **étaler**

spring noun
le **printemps** *masc.*
in the spring au printemps

sprouts plural noun
les **choux de Bruxelles** *masc. plural*

spy noun
un **espion** *masc.*, une **espionne** *fem.*

square adjective
carré *masc.*, **carrée** *fem.*
Is it round or square? C'est rond ou
carré?

square noun
1 (*shape*) le **carré** *masc.*
a circle and a square un cercle et
un carré
2 (*in a town or village*) la **place** *fem.*
the village square la place du
village

squash noun
1 (*sport*) le **squash** *masc.*
They're playing squash. Ils jouent
au squash.
2 (*drink*) le **sirop** *masc.*
an orange squash un sirop
d'orange

squirrel noun
un **écureuil** *masc.*

stable noun
une **écurie** *fem.*

stack noun
la **pile** *fem.*
a stack of CDs une pile de CD

stadium noun
le **stade** *masc.*

staff noun
(*in a school*) les **instituteurs** *masc.*
plural

staff room noun
la **salle des maîtres** *fem.*

stage noun
la **scène** *fem.*

staircase noun
un **escalier** *masc.*

stairs plural noun
un **escalier** *masc.*
Louis fell down the stairs. Louis est
tombé dans l'escalier.

stamp noun
le **timbre** *masc.*
How much is a stamp for England?
C'est combien un timbre pour
l'Angleterre?
a stamp album un album de
timbres
a stamp collection une collection
de timbres

to **stamp** verb
to stamp your feet taper des pieds

to **stand** verb
1 (*with legs straight*) **être debout**
He's sitting and I'm standing. Il est
assis et je suis debout.
2 (*to go and stand somewhere*) **se mettre** ⊘
Stand by me! Mets-toi à côté de
moi!
Stand in line, children!
Mettez-vous en rang, les enfants!
3 (*to hate something*)
I can't stand that music. Je ne peux
pas supporter cette musique.

• *Use **le** and **un** for masculine words and **la** and **une** for feminine words.*

to **stand up** verb
se lever @
Stand up, everyone! Levez-vous, tout le monde!

star noun
1 (*in the sky etc.*) une **étoile** *fem.*
2 (*person*) la **vedette** *fem.*
a film star une vedette de cinéma

start noun
1 le **début** *masc.*
at the start of the year au début de l'année
to make a start commencer
Have you made a start on your book? Tu as commencé ton livre?
2 (*of a race*) le **départ** *masc.*

to **start** verb
1 **commencer**
You start! À toi de commencer!
This word starts with a 't'. Ce mot commence par un 't'.
It's starting at three. Ça commence à trois heures.
Let's start again! On recommence.
I've started learning French. J'ai commencé à apprendre le français.
2 (*a club, group, etc.*) **créer**

starter noun
une **entrée** *fem.*

to **starve** verb
I'm starving, mum! Je meurs de faim, maman!

States plural noun
the States les États-Unis *masc. plural*
We're going to the States. Nous allons aux États-Unis.

station noun
1 (*for trains*) la **gare** *fem.*
at the station à la gare
the coach station la gare routière
2 (*for underground trains, radio, TV*) la **station** *fem.*
a tube station une station de métro
3 **a police station** un commissariat de police *masc.*

stationery noun
(*for school*) les **fournitures scolaires** *fem. plural*
the stationery cupboard le placard à fournitures

statue noun
la **statue** *fem.*

stay noun
le **séjour** *masc.*
Enjoy your stay! Bon séjour!

to **stay** verb
1 **rester** @
Stay in your room! Reste dans ta chambre!
Stay calm, Julien! Reste calme, Julien!
Stay still! Ne bouge pas!
2 (*to spend the night*) **loger**
Are you going to stay in a hotel? Vous allez loger à l'hôtel?

to **stay in** verb
rester @ **à la maison**

to **stay up** verb
(*until it's late*) **se coucher** @ **tard**
We're going to stay up until ten. Nous allons nous coucher à dix heures.

steak noun
le **steak** *masc.*

to **steal** verb
voler
Somebody has stolen my bike. On m'a volé mon vélo.

steering wheel noun
le **volant** *masc.*

step noun
1 (*with your foot*) le **pas** *masc.*
Take two steps backwards! Faites deux pas en arrière!
one step forward un pas en avant
2 (*of stairs*) la **marche** *fem.*
Mind the step! Attention à la marche!

@ *means use* **être** *to make the past tense.*

a
b
c
d
e
f
g
h
i
j
k
l
m
n
o
p
q
r
s
t
u
v
w
x
y
z

399

a
b
c
d
e
f
g
h
i
j
k
l
m
n
o
p
q
r
s
t
u
v
w
x
y
z

stepbrother noun
le **demi-frère** masc. (plural les **demi-frères**)

stepdaughter noun
la **belle-fille** fem. (plural les **belles-filles**)

stepfather noun
le **beau-père** masc. (plural les **beaux-pères**)

stepmother noun
la **belle-mère** fem. (plural les **belles-mères**)

stepsister noun
la **demi-sœur** fem. (plural les **demi-sœurs**)

stepson noun
le **beau-fils** masc. (plural les **beaux-fils**)

stereo noun
la **chaîne stéréo** fem. (plural les **chaînes stéréo**)

stew noun
le **ragoût** masc.

stick noun
le **bâton** masc.

to **stick** verb
(with glue) **coller**

sticker noun
un **autocollant** masc.

still adverb
1 **encore**
better still encore mieux
2 **toujours**
I still don't like cheese. Je n'aime toujours pas le fromage.

still adjective
Keep still! Reste tranquille!

to **sting** verb
piquer
I was stung by a wasp. Je me suis fait piquer par une guêpe.

sting noun
la **piqûre** fem.
a wasp sting une piqûre de guêpe

stitch noun
le **point de suture** masc.
Did you have any stitches? On t'a fait des points de suture?

stomach noun
l'**estomac** masc.

stomach ache noun
I've got stomach ache. J'ai mal au ventre.

stone noun
1 (large stone) la **pierre** fem.
Jason threw a stone. Jason a lancé une pierre.
2 (small stone) le **cailleau** masc. (plural les **cailleux**)
3 (of a fruit) le **noyau** masc. (plural les **noyeaux**)
4 (when weighing people)
She weighs four stone. Elle pèse environ vingt-cinq kilos.

🌍 **CULTURE**
1 stone = 6.3 kilos

stool noun
le **tabouret** masc.

stop noun
un **arrêt** masc.
a bus stop un arrêt de bus
Get off at the next stop. Descendez au prochain arrêt.

to **stop** verb
1 **arrêter**
Stop! Arrête!
Stop talking, boys! Arrêtez de parler, les garçons!
2 **s'arrêter** @
The bus stops here. Le bus s'arrête ici.
The music stopped. La musique s'est arrêtée.

• Languages, nationalities, and religions do not take a capital letter in French.

store noun
(*department store*) le **grand magasin** *masc.*

storey noun
un **étage** *masc.*
a three-storey house une maison à trois étages

storm noun
1 (*with wind, rain, or snow*) la **tempête** *fem.*
2 (*with thunder*) un **orage** *masc.*

stormy adjective
orageux *masc.*, **orageuse** *fem.*

story noun
l' **histoire** *fem.*
Tell us a story! Raconte-nous une histoire!

straight adjective
1 **droit** *masc.*, **droite** *fem.*
a straight line une ligne droite
2 **to have straight hair** avoir les cheveux raides

straight adverb
1 **directement**
He came straight home. Il est rentré directement à la maison.
2 **straight ahead** tout droit
Go straight ahead! Continuez tout droit!
3 **straight away** tout de suite

strange adjective
bizarre *masc. & fem.*

stranger noun
un **inconnu** *masc.*,
une **inconnue** *fem.*
Don't talk to strangers! Ne parlez pas à des inconnus!

strap noun
1 (*on a watch*) le **bracelet** *masc.*
2 (*on a dress, swimsuit, etc.*) la **bretelle** *fem.*

straw noun
la **paille** *fem.*

strawberry noun
la **fraise** *fem.*
strawberry jam la confiture de fraises
strawberry yoghurt le yaourt à la fraise

stream noun
le **ruisseau** *masc.* (plural les **ruisseaux**)

street noun
la **rue** *fem.*
I live in Charles street. J'habite rue Charles.

to **stretch** verb
(*arm, neck, etc.*) **tendre**
Stretch out your hand! Tends la main!

strict adjective
strict *masc.*, **stricte** *fem.*

strike noun
la **grève** *fem.*
They're on strike. Ils sont en grève.

string noun
1 (*for tying*) la **ficelle** *fem.*
Do you have any string? Tu as de la ficelle?
2 (*for a guitar, violin, etc.*) la **corde** *fem.*

stripe noun
la **rayure** *fem.*

striped adjective
rayé *masc.*, **rayée** *fem.*

to **stroke** verb
(*a cat, dog, etc.*) **caresser**

strong adjective
fort *masc.*, **forte** *fem.*

student noun
un **étudiant** *masc.*,
une **étudiante** *fem.*
My sister's a student. Ma sœur est étudiante.

a b c d e f g h i j k l m n o p q r s t u v w x y z

⊘ *means use* **être** *to make the past tense.*

a
b
c
d
e
f
g
h
i
j
k
l
m
n
o
p
q
r
s
t
u
v
w
x
y
z

to **study** verb
1 (*to revise*) **réviser**
2 (*to be a student*) **faire des études**
   David is studying French. David fait des études de français.

stuff noun
1 (*thing or things*) le **truc** *masc.*, les **trucs** *masc. plural*
   Put all that stuff in your bag! Mets tous ces trucs dans ton sac!
2 (*things that belong to you*) les **affaires** *fem. plural*
   Don't forget your stuff! N'oublie pas tes affaires!

stupid adjective
stupide *masc. & fem.*

subject noun
1 (*in school*) la **matière** *fem.*
   French is my favourite subject. Le français est ma matière préférée.
2 (*of a book etc.*) le **sujet** *masc.*

to **subtract** verb
soustraire

suburb noun
a suburb une banlieue *fem.*
the suburbs la banlieue
We live in the suburbs. Nous habitons en banlieue.

success noun
le **succès** *masc.*
a great success un grand succès

successful adjective
(*show, party, etc.*) **réussi** *masc.*, **réussie** *fem.*

such adverb
1 **tellement**
   such a clever girl une fille tellement intelligente
   such clever girls des filles tellement intelligentes
   It's such a long way away. C'est tellement loin.

You've got such a lot of CDs! Tu as tellement de CD!
2 **such as** comme
   animals such as cats and dogs des animaux comme les chats et les chiens

sudden adjective
(*pain, shower, etc.*) **soudain** *masc.*, **soudaine** *fem.*
all of a sudden tout à coup

suddenly adverb
tout à coup

to **suffer** verb
souffrir

sugar noun
le **sucre** *masc.*
Do you want some sugar? Tu veux du sucre?

suggestion noun
la **suggestion** *fem.*

suit noun
1 (*for a man*) le **costume** *masc.*
2 (*for a woman*) le **tailleur** *masc.*

to **suit** verb
(*when talking about clothes etc.*)
to suit somebody aller bien à quelqu'un
That jacket suits you, Tom. Cette veste te va bien, Tom.

suitcase noun
la **valise** *fem.*

summer noun
l'**été** *masc.*
in the summer en été
this summer cet été
the summer holidays les vacances d'été

summertime noun
l'**été** *masc.*
in the summertime en été

• *The months of the year and days of the week do not take a capital letter in French.*

sums plural noun
le **calcul** masc.
Are you good at sums? Tu es bon en calcul?

🔑 **LANGUAGE**
English = sums is plural
French = calcul is singular

sun noun
le **soleil** masc.
In the sun au soleil
The sun's out. Il y a du soleil.

to **sunbathe** verb
se faire ⓔ bronzer

sunburnt adjective
You're sunburnt. Tu as pris un coup de soleil.

Sunday noun
dimanche masc.
It's Sunday today. C'est dimanche aujourd'hui.
on Sunday dimanche
last Sunday dimanche dernier
next Sunday dimanche prochain
every Sunday tous les dimanches
on Sundays le dimanche

sunflower noun
le **tournesol** masc.

sunglasses plural noun
les **lunettes de soleil** fem. plural

sunny adjective
ensoleillé masc., **ensoleillée** fem.
a sunny day une journée ensoleillée
It's sunny. Il y a du soleil.

sunset noun
le **coucher du soleil** masc.

sunshine noun
le **soleil** masc.
There isn't much sunshine. Il n'y a pas beaucoup de soleil.

suntan noun
le **bronzage** masc.
to get a suntan se faire ⓔ bronzer

super adjective
super masc. & fem.
That's a super idea! C'est une idée super!

🔑 **LANGUAGE**
Super is the same in the masculine, feminine, and plural.

supermarket noun
le **supermarché** masc.

supper noun
le **dîner** masc.
to have supper dîner

to **support** verb
(a team) **être supporter de**
Which team do you support? Tu es supporter de quelle équipe?
I support Manchester United. Je suis supporter de Manchester United.

to **suppose** verb
supposer
I suppose you're right. Je suppose que tu as raison.
I suppose so. Probablement.

sure adjective
sûr masc., **sûre** fem.
Are you sure, Tom? Tu es sûr, Tom?

to **surf** verb
to surf the Internet surfer sur Internet

surface noun
la **surface** fem.

surname noun
le **nom de famille** masc.

surprise noun
la **surprise** fem.
What a surprise! Quelle surprise!

ⓔ *means use* **être** *to make the past tense.*

a
b
c
d
e
f
g
h
i
j
k
l
m
n
o
p
q
r
s
t
u
v
w
x
y
z

surprised adjective
surpris masc., **surprise** fem.
He's surprised to see you. Il est surpris de te voir.

survey noun
le **sondage** masc.

to **swallow** verb
avaler

swan noun
le **cygne** masc.

to **swap** verb
échanger
I want to swap this CD. Je veux échanger ce CD.
Do you want to swap places? Tu veux changer de place?

to **swear** verb
dire des gros mots
Don't swear! Ne dis pas de gros mots!

swearword noun
le **gros mot** masc.

sweater noun
le **pull** masc.

sweatshirt noun
le **sweatshirt** masc.,
le **sweat** masc.

Sweden noun
la **Suède** fem.

to **sweep** verb
balayer

sweet noun
1 le **bonbon** masc.
Do you want a bag of sweets? Tu veux un paquet de bonbons?
a sweet shop une confiserie
2 (part of a meal) le **dessert** masc.

sweet adjective
1 (like sugar) **sucré** masc., **sucrée** fem.
It's too sweet. C'est trop sucré.
2 (cute) **mignon** masc., **mignonne** fem.

Your baby's so sweet! Il est mignon, ton bébé!
3 (kind) **gentil** masc., **gentille** fem.
She's very sweet. Elle est très gentille.

sweetcorn noun
le **maïs** masc.

to **swim** verb
nager
I can swim. Je sais nager.

swimmer noun
le **nageur** masc., la **nageuse** fem.
He's a good swimmer. C'est un bon nageur.

swimming noun
la **natation** fem.
I love swimming. J'adore la natation.
I go swimming a lot. (in the pool) Je vais souvent à la piscine.
a swimming costume un maillot de bain
a swimming pool une piscine
swimming trunks un maillot de bain

swimsuit noun
le **maillot de bain** masc.

swing noun
la **balançoire** fem.

Swiss adjective
suisse masc. & fem.

switch noun
1 (for turning or pressing) le **bouton** masc.
2 (up-down type) un **interrupteur** masc.

to **switch** verb
(to exchange) **échanger**
Let's switch places! Changeons de place!

• See the centre section for verb tables.

to **switch off** verb
(*a light, radio, computer, etc.*) **éteindre**
Switch the TV off! Éteins la télé!

to **switch on** verb
(*a light, TV, computer, etc.*) **allumer**
Switch the radio on! Allume la radio!

Switzerland noun
la **Suisse** *fem.*

to **swop** verb SEE **to swap**

Tt

table noun
1 la **table** *fem.*
The keys are on the table. Les clés sont sur la table.
2 **the times tables** les tables de multiplication
the five-times table la table de cinq

tablespoon noun
la **cuillère à soupe** *fem.*

table tennis noun
le **ping-pong** *masc.*
They're playing table tennis. Ils jouent au ping-pong.

tadpole noun
le **têtard** *masc.*

tail noun
1 (*of an animal*) la **queue** *fem.*
2 (*when throwing a coin*) **Tails!** Pile!
Heads or tails? Pile ou face?

to **take** verb
1 **prendre**
Take a book each! Prenez un livre chacun!
I take the bus. Je prends le bus.
Who's taken my pen? Qui a pris mon stylo?

@ *means use* être *to make the past tense.*

syllable noun
la **syllabe** *fem.*

🔑 **LANGUAGE**
English = syllable
French = syllabe

symbol noun
le **symbole** *masc.*

synagogue noun
la **synagogue** *fem.*

system noun
le **système** *masc.*

It takes two hours. Ça prend deux heures.
2 (*a person*) **emmener**
My dad takes me to school. Mon père m'emmène à l'école.
3 **to take an exam** passer un examen

to **take away** verb
1 (*fast food*) **emporter**
a Chinese meal to take away un repas chinois à emporter
2 (*in sums*) **Twenty, take away ten.** Vingt moins dix.

takeaway noun
(*meal*) le **repas à emporter** *masc.*

to **take back** verb
rapporter
Mum took my shoes back to the shop. Maman a rapporté mes chaussures au magasin.

to **take off** verb
1 (*to remove*) **enlever**
Take your coat off! Enlève ton manteau!
2 (*for a plane*) **décoller**
The plane takes off at two. L'avion décolle à deux heures.

a
b
c
d
e
f
g
h
i
j
k
l
m
n
o
p
q
r
s
t
u
v
w
x
y
z

a
b
c
d
e
f
g
h
i
j
k
l
m
n
o
p
q
r
s
t
u
v
w
x
y
z

take-off noun
(*of a plane*) le **décollage** *masc.*

to **take out** verb
sortir
Take your hands out of your pockets! Sors les mains de tes poches!

tale noun
le **conte** *masc.*
a fairy tale un conte de fées

to **talk** verb
parler
Let's talk about French food! On va parler de la cuisine française.
He's talking to his brother. Il parle à son frère.

talkative adjective
bavard *masc.*, **bavarde** *fem.*

tall adjective
1 (*big*) **grand** *masc.*, **grande** *fem.*
Alice is tall. Alice est grande.
How tall are you? Tu mesures combien?
I'm five foot tall. Je mesure un mètre cinquante.
a tall tree un grand arbre
2 (*high*) **haut** *masc.*, **haute** *fem.*
This building is very tall. Ce bâtiment est très haut.

tan noun
le **bronzage** *masc.*
to get a tan se faire @ bronzer

tank noun
1 (*used in war*) le **char** *masc.*
2 **a fish tank** un aquarium

tap noun
le **robinet** *masc.*
Turn off the tap! Ferme le robinet!
Turn on the tap! Ouvre le robinet!

tape noun
1 la **cassette** *fem.*
a tape recorder un magnétophone
2 (*sticky tape*) le **ruban adhésif** *masc.*

to **tape** verb
enregistrer
Remember to tape the film! N'oublie pas d'enregistrer le film!

tart noun
la **tarte** *fem.*
an apple tart une tarte aux pommes

tartan adjective
écossais *masc.*, **écossaise** *fem.*
a tartan skirt une jupe écossaise

taste noun
le **goût** *masc.*
It has a funny taste. Ça a un goût bizarre.

to **taste** verb
(*to eat or drink*) **goûter**
Taste this, it's delicious! Goûte ça, c'est délicieux!

tasty adjective
délicieux *masc.*, **délicieuse** *fem.*

tattoo noun
le **tatouage** *masc.*
He's got a tattoo on his arm. Il a un tatouage sur le bras.

taxi noun
le **taxi** *masc.*
by taxi en taxi
a taxi driver un chauffeur de taxi

tea noun
1 le **thé** *masc.*
tea with milk le thé au lait
lemon tea le thé au citron

CULTURE
In France people usually have lemon rather than milk in their tea.

2 (*evening meal for a family*) le **repas du soir** *masc.*

teabag noun
le **sachet de thé** *masc.*

to **teach** verb
1 (*in a school etc.*) **enseigner**

• Use **le** and **un** for masculine words and **la** and **une** for feminine words.

Madame Perrier teaches French. Madame Perrier enseigne le français.

2 to teach somebody something apprendre quelque chose à quelqu'un

Mum's teaching me to play the piano. Maman m'apprend à jouer du piano.

teacher noun

1 (*in a primary or nursery school*) un **instituteur** *masc.*, une **institutrice** *fem.*

My dad's a teacher. Mon père est instituteur.

2 (*in a secondary school*) le **professeur** *masc.*

a French teacher un professeur de français

> **LANGUAGE**
> **Professeur** is masculine even if it refers to a female teacher.

team noun
une **équipe** *fem.*

a football team une équipe de football

teapot noun
la **théière** *fem.*

to tear verb
déchirer

She tore up the letter. Elle a déchiré la lettre.

teaspoon noun
la **petite cuillère** *fem.*

teatime noun
(*evening meal*) l'**heure du dîner** *fem.*

technology noun
la **technologie** *fem.*

teddy bear noun
un **ours en peluche** *masc.*

teenager noun
un **adolescent** *masc.*, une **adolescente** *fem.*

⊘ means use être to make the past tense.

teens plural noun
She's in her teens. Elle est adolescente.

teeth plural noun
les **dents** *fem. plural*

I clean my teeth. Je me brosse les dents.

> **LANGUAGE**
> **Dents** is related to the English word 'dentist' (somebody who looks after teeth).

telephone noun
le **téléphone** *masc.*

She's on the telephone. Elle est au téléphone.

a telephone number un numéro de téléphone

a telephone call un appel

to make a telephone call téléphoner

television noun
la **télévision** *fem.*

on television à la télévision

a television programme une émission de télévision

I watch television every day. Je regarde la télévision tous les jours.

to tell verb

1 **dire**

Tell the truth! Dis la vérité!

to tell somebody something dire quelque chose à quelqu'un

Tell me where you're going, children! Dites-moi où vous allez, les enfants!

I told you to be quiet. Je vous ai dit de vous taire.

2 (*to talk about*) **parler**

Tell me about your family! Parle-moi de ta famille!

3 (*to tell about what happens*) **raconter**

Tell us a story! Raconte-nous une histoire!

to tell off verb
gronder

The teacher is going to tell Joshua off. Le professeur va gronder Joshua.

telly noun
la **télé** *fem.*
on telly à la télé

temper noun
to lose your temper se mettre @ en colère

temperature noun
la **température** *fem.*
The temperature is 20°. La température est de 20°.
I've got a temperature. J'ai de la fièvre.

ten number
dix
ten pounds dix livres
I'm ten. J'ai dix ans.
The film starts at ten. Le film commence à dix heures.
It's ten to eight. Il est huit heures moins dix.
It's ten past five. Il est cinq heures dix.

tennis noun
le **tennis** *masc.*
Ambika plays tennis. Ambika joue au tennis.
a tennis ball une balle de tennis
a tennis court un court de tennis
a tennis racket une raquette de tennis

tense noun
the present tense le présent
the past tense le passé
the future tense le futur

tent noun
la **tente** *fem.*
to put up a tent monter une tente

tenth adjective
dixième *masc. & fem.*
on the tenth floor au dixième étage
the tenth of April le dix avril

term noun
le **trimestre** *masc.*
It's the last day of term. C'est le dernier jour du trimestre.

terrible adjective
affreux *masc.*, **affreuse** *fem.*
The weather's terrible. Le temps est affreux.
I'm terrible at drawing. Je suis nul en dessin. (*boy speaking*); Je suis nulle en dessin. (*girl speaking*)

terrified adjective
terrifié *masc.*, **terrifiée** *fem.*
I was terrified! J'étais terrifié! (*boy speaking*)
I'm terrified of spiders. J'ai très peur des araignées.

test noun
(*in school*) le **contrôle** *masc.*
a French test un contrôle de français

text noun
1 (*of a book*) le **texte** *masc.*
2 (*by mobile*) le **texto®** *masc.*

to **text** verb
to text somebody envoyer un texto à quelqu'un
Text me! Envoie-moi un texto!

textbook noun
le **manuel** *masc.*

than conjunction
1 **que**
I'm younger than you. Je suis plus jeune que toi.
You run faster than her. Tu cours plus vite qu'elle.

LANGUAGE
que = qu' before *a, e, i, o, u,* or *silent h*

---

2 (*with numbers*) **de**
It costs more than twenty euros. Ça coûte plus de vingt euros.

thanks exclamation
merci!
No thanks! Non merci!

• *Languages, nationalities, and religions do not take a capital letter in French.*

a b c d e f g h i j k l m n o p q r s t u v w x y z

thank you exclamation
merci
Thank you very much! Merci beaucoup!
Thank you for the present! Merci pour le cadeau!

that adjective
1 **ce** *masc.*, **cet** *masc.*, **cette** *fem.*
that book ce livre
that house cette maison
that computer cet ordinateur

> **⚷ LANGUAGE**
> Use **cet** before masculine nouns beginning with a vowel or a silent 'h'.

2 (*when pointing to 'that one', not 'this one'*)
that book ce livre-là
that house cette maison-là
that computer cet ordinateur-là
3 **that one** celui-là *masc.*, celle-là *fem.*
Which CD? – That one. Quel CD? – Celui-là.
This key? – No, that one. Cette clé-ci? – Non, celle-là.

that pronoun
1 **ça**
I don't like that. Je n'aime pas ça.
2 (*before verb 'to be'*) **ce**
Who's that? Qui est-ce?
That's not me. Ce n'est pas moi.
That's my mum. C'est ma mère.
What's that? Qu'est-ce que c'est?
That's good. C'est bon.

> **⚷ LANGUAGE**
> ce = c' before an 'e'

that conjunction
que
I think that it's great. Je pense que c'est génial.
She says that she can't come. Elle dit qu'elle ne peut pas venir.

> **⚷ LANGUAGE**
> que = qu' before a vowel or a silent 'h'

θ *means use* **être** *to make the past tense.*

the determiner
1 (*with masculine singular noun*) **le** *masc.*
the bag le sac
2 (*with feminine singular nouns*) **la** *fem.*
the window la fenêtre
3 (*with singular nouns starting with a, e, i, o, u, or silent h*) **l'**
the computer l'ordinateur
4 (*with plural nouns*) **les** *masc. & fem. plural*
the bikes les vélos
the elephants les éléphants

theatre noun
le **théâtre** *masc.*

their adjective
1 (*before a singular noun*) **leur**
their teacher leur prof
their school leur école
2 (*before a plural noun*) **leurs**
their trainers leurs baskets

theirs pronoun
à eux *masc. plural*, **à elles** *fem. plural*
This bike is theirs. Ce vélo est à eux.

them pronoun
1 (*after a verb*) **les**
I can see them. Je les vois.
Call them! Appelle-les!
2 (*to them*) **leur**
He's going to speak to them. Il va leur parler.
3 (*after a preposition*) **eux** *masc. plural*, **elles** *fem. plural*
with them avec eux, avec elles

theme park noun
le **parc d'attractions** *masc.*

themselves pronoun
1 **eux-mêmes** *masc. plural*, **elles-mêmes** *fem. plural*
They made it themelves. Ils l'ont fait eux-mêmes.
2 **se**
The children are enjoying themselves. Les enfants s'amusent.

> **⚷ LANGUAGE**
> se = s' before a vowel or a silent 'h'

a
b
c
d
e
f
g
h
i
j
k
l
m
n
o
p
q
r
s
t
u
v
w
x
y
z

then adverb
1 (next) **ensuite**
I went to the cinema and then to a cafe. Je suis allé au cinéma et ensuite au café.
2 (at that time) **à ce moment-là**

there adverb
1 **là**
Sit there! Assieds-toi là!
He isn't there. Il n'est pas là.
down there là-bas
over there là-bas
up there là-haut
2 (to or in a place) **y**
Paris? I'm going there next week. Paris? J'y vais la semaine prochaine.
3 **there is** il y a
There's a TV in my bedroom. Il y a une télévision dans ma chambre.
4 **there are** il y a
There are thirty children in my class. Il y a trente élèves dans ma classe.
There aren't any chocolates. Il n'y a pas de chocolats.

> **⚷ LANGUAGE**
> **Il y a** is used for both 'there is' and 'there are'.

5 (when shouting, or pointing to something)
There is...! Voilà...!
There's Zack! Voilà Zack!
There he is! Le voilà!
There she is! La voilà!
6 **There are...!** Voilà...!
There are mum and dad! Voilà maman et papa!
There they are! Les voilà!

> **⚷ LANGUAGE**
> **Voilà!** is used for both 'there is!' and 'there are!'

these adjective
1 **ces** masc. & fem. plural
these pages ces pages
2 (when you mean **these just here**)
these books ces livres-ci

these pronoun
ceux-ci masc. plural,
celles-ci fem. plural
Which boys? – These. Quels garçons? – Ceux-ci.
Those cards? – No, these. Ces cartes-là? – Non, celles-ci.

they pronoun
1 (standing for a masculine noun in French) **ils**
Do you know my parents? – Yes, they're nice. Tu connais mes parents? – Oui, ils sont gentils.
2 (standing for a feminine noun) **elles**
What colour are your shoes? – They're brown. Tes chaussures sont de quelle couleur? – Elles sont marron.

thick adjective
épais masc., **épaisse** fem.

thief noun
le **voleur** masc., la **voleuse** fem.

thin adjective
1 (not fat) **mince** masc. & fem.
I'm quite thin. Je suis assez mince.
2 (skinny) **maigre** masc. & fem.
I've got thin arms. J'ai les bras maigres.

thing noun
1 la **chose** fem.
two or three things deux ou trois choses
There are lots of things to do. Il y a beaucoup de choses à faire.
2 (things that belong to you)
my things mes affaires fem. plural
Put your things in your room! Mets tes affaires dans ta chambre!

to **think** verb
1 (to believe) **penser**
I think she's hungry. Je pense qu'elle a faim.
I think so. Je pense.
I don't think so. Je ne pense pas.
2 (to spend time going over ideas carefully)
réfléchir

• The months of the year and days of the week do not take a capital letter in French.

Think carefully! Réfléchissez bien!
My dad's thinking about it.
Mon père y réfléchit.

third adjective
troisième *masc. & fem.*
on the third floor au troisième étage
William came third. (*in the race*) William est arrivé troisième.
the third of September le trois septembre

third noun
le **tiers** *masc.*
a third of the class un tiers de la classe

thirsty adjective
I'm thirsty. J'ai soif.
He isn't thirsty. Il n'a pas soif.

> **LANGUAGE**
> English = **to be thirsty**   **I'm thirsty.**
> French = **avoir soif**   **J'ai soif.**

thirteen number
treize
My cousin is thirteen. Mon cousin a treize ans.

thirty number
trente

this adjective
1 **ce** *masc.*, **cet** *masc.*, **cette** *fem.*
this morning ce matin
this school cette école
this money cet argent

> **LANGUAGE**
> Use **cet** with masculine nouns beginning with *a, e, i, o, u,* or *silent h.*

2 (*when pointing to* **this one,** *not that one*)
this DVD ce DVD-ci
this box cette boîte-ci
this man cet homme-ci
3 **this one** celui-ci *masc.*, celle-ci *fem.*
Which drawing? – This one.
Quel dessin? – Celui-ci.
That page? – No, this one.
Cette page-là? – Non, celle-ci.

ⓔ means use **être** *to make the past tense.*

this pronoun
1 **ça**
I don't lile this. Je n'aime pas ça.
2 (*before verb 'to be'*) **ce**
Who's this? Qui est-ce?
This is my friend. C'est mon ami.
What's this? Qu'est-ce que c'est?
This is very good. C'est très bon.

> **LANGUAGE**
> **ce** = **c'** before an 'e'

those adjective
1 **ces** *masc. & fem. plural*
those trees ces arbres
2 (*when you mean* **those over there**)
those children ces enfants-là

those pronoun
ceux-là *masc. plural,*
celles-là *fem. plural*
These books? – No, those.
Ces livres-ci? – Non, ceux-là.
Which girls? – Those. Quelles filles? – Celles-là.

though adverb
pourtant
It's a good idea, though. Pourtant, c'est une bonne idée.

thousand number
1 **mille**
a thousand mille
two thousand euros deux mille euros
2 **about a thousand people** un millier de personnes
thousands of euros des milliers d'euros

to **threaten** verb
menacer

three number
trois
I went home at three. Je suis rentré chez moi à trois heures.
My brother is three. Mon frère a trois ans.

a
b
c
d
e
f
g
h
i
j
k
l
m
n
o
p
q
r
s
t
u
v
w
x
y
z

a
b
c
d
e
f
g
h
i
j
k
l
m
n
o
p
q
r
s
t
u
v
w
x
y
z

three-D noun
in three-D en trois dimensions
a three-D film un film en trois
dimensions

throat noun
la **gorge** fem.
I have a sore throat. J'ai mal à la
gorge.

throne noun
le **trône** masc.

through preposition
par
I'm looking through the window.
Je regarde par la fenêtre.

through adverb
to get through passer @
Go through! Passez!

to **throw** verb
lancer
Throw the ball to me! Lance-moi le
ballon!

to **throw away** verb
jeter
Throw these old magazines away!
Jette ces vieux magazines!

thumb noun
le **pouce** masc.

thunder noun
le **tonnerre** masc.

thunderstorm noun
un **orage** masc.

Thursday noun
jeudi masc.
It's Thursday today. C'est jeudi
aujourd'hui.
on Thursday jeudi
next Thursday jeudi prochain
last Thursday jeudi dernier
every Thursday tous les jeudis
on Thursdays le jeudi

to **tick** verb
(*an answer, name, etc.*) **cocher**
Tick the box. Cochez la case.

ticket noun
1 (*for train, plane, cinema, etc.*) le **billet**
masc.
a plane ticket un billet d'avion
2 (*for bus or underground*) le **ticket** masc.
a bus ticket un ticket de bus
3 **a ticket office** un guichet masc.

tidy adjective
(*room or house*) **bien rangé** masc.,
bien rangée fem.
My bedroom is tidy. Ma chambre
est bien rangée.

to **tidy** verb
ranger
Remember to tidy your room!
N'oublie pas de ranger ta chambre!

tie noun
1 la **cravate** fem.
to wear a tie porter une cravate
2 (*in a match*) le **match nul** masc.
It's a tie! Match nul!
3 (*in a race*) **It's a tie for the second
place.** Il y a deux ex æquo pour la
deuxième place.

to **tie** verb
1 (*with string etc.*) **attacher**
She tied the package with string.
Elle a attaché le paquet avec une
ficelle.
2 (*to make a knot in shoelaces, a scarf, etc.*)
nouer
Tie your laces! Noue tes lacets!
to tie a knot faire un nœud

tiger noun
le **tigre** masc.

tight adjective
1 (*talking about uncomfortable clothes*)
juste masc. & fem.
This skirt's a bit tight. Cette jupe
est un peu juste.
2 (*close to the body*) **moulant** masc.,
moulante fem.
a tight pair of jeans un jean
moulant

• *See the centre section for verb tables.*

tights plural noun
le **collant** masc.
She's wearing tights. Elle porte un collant.
a pair of tights un collant

🔑 **LANGUAGE**
English = **tights** is plural
French = **le collant** is singular

till noun
la **caisse** fem.
Pay at the till. Payez à la caisse.

till preposition
1 (until) **jusqu'à**
Wait till Friday. Attends jusqu'à vendredi.
2 **not till** pas avant
You can't open your present till Christmas! Tu ne peux pas ouvrir ton cadeau avant Noël!

time noun
1 le **temps** masc.
Do you have enough time? Tu as assez de temps?
at the same time en même temps
It's time to leave. Il est temps de partir.
free time le temps libre
Have a nice time! Amuse-toi bien!
a long time longtemps
2 (on the clock) l'**heure** fem.
What time is it? Quelle heure est-il?
What's the time? Il est quelle heure?
At what time? À quelle heure?
What time do you go to school? À quelle heure tu vas à l'école?
to be on time être à l'heure
3 (a point in time) le **moment** masc.
Is this the right time? C'est le bon moment?
4 (an occasion) la **fois** fem.
How many times? Combien de fois?
four times quatre fois
many times de nombreuses fois

the first time la première fois
this time cette fois-ci
Three times four is twelve. Trois fois quatre font douze.

timetable noun
1 (in school) un **emploi du temps** masc.
2 (for buses and trains) l'**horaire** masc.

tin noun
la **boîte** fem.
a tin of beans une boîte de haricots

tinfoil noun
le **papier alu** masc.

🔑 **LANGUAGE**
Alu is short for **aluminium**.

tin opener noun
un **ouvre-boîtes** fem. (plural les **ouvre-boîtes**)

tinsel noun
(for Christmas tree) les **guirlandes** fem. plural

tiny adjective
minuscule masc. & fem.

tip noun
1 (end) le **bout** masc.
the tip of my nose le bout de mon nez
2 (money) le **pourboire** masc.
Dad gave the waitress a tip. Papa a donné un pourboire à la serveuse.
3 (advice) le **conseil** masc.

tiptoe noun
on tiptoe sur la pointe des pieds

tired adjective
fatigué masc., **fatiguée** fem.
Are you tired? Tu es fatigué?

tiring adjective
fatigant masc., **fatigante** fem.

tissue noun
le **kleenex**® masc.
I need a tissue. J'ai besoin d'un kleenex.

ⓔ means use **être** to make the past tense.

a
b
c
d
e
f
g
h
i
j
k
l
m
n
o
p
q
r
s
t
u
v
w
x
y
z

a
b
c
d
e
f
g
h
i
j
k
l
m
n
o
p
q
r
s
t
u
v
w
x
y
z

title noun
le **titre** *masc.*

🔑 **LANGUAGE**
English = title
French = titre

to preposition
1 *(to a town, a person)* à
to Paris à Paris
Give it to Julien. Donne-le à Julien.
2 *(with a feminine singular noun)* à
I'm going to the canteen. Je vais à la cantine.
3 *(with a masculine singular noun)* **au**
from Monday to Friday du lundi au vendredi
Give some milk to the cat! Donne du lait au chat!
4 *(with a plural noun)* **aux**
I'm going to the toilet. Je vais aux toilettes.
5 *(to somebody's house, shop, etc.)* **chez**
I'm going to Yasmina's house. Je vais chez Yasmina.
6 *(with feminine country names)* **en**
I'm going to France. Je vais en France.
7 *(with masculine country names)* **au**
We're going to Japan. Nous allons au Japon.
8 *(with plural country names)* **aux**
She's going to the United States. Elle va aux États-Unis.
9 *(with 'train', 'plane', etc.)* **pour**
the train to Cambridge le train pour Cambridge
10 *(talking about the time)*
It's ten to seven. Il est sept heures moins dix.

toad noun
le **crapaud** *masc.*

toast noun
le **pain grillé** *masc.*
a slice of toast une tranche de pain grillé

today adverb
aujourd'hui
It's Thursday today. Aujourd'hui c'est jeudi.
What day is it today? Quel jour sommes-nous aujourd'hui?
Today's date is the fifth of June. Nous sommes le cinq juin.

toe noun
le **doigt de pied** *masc.*

🔑 **LANGUAGE**
Word for word **doigt de pied** means 'finger of the foot'.

toffee noun
le **caramel** *masc.*

together adverb
ensemble
Keep together! Restez ensemble!

toilet noun
les **toilettes** *fem. plural*
Can I go to the toilet? Je peux aller aux toilettes?
toilet paper le papier toilette

tomato noun
la **tomate** *fem.*
tomato sauce la sauce tomate
tomato soup la soupe à la tomate

tomorrow adverb
demain
Come to my house tomorrow! Viens chez moi demain!
See you tomorrow! À demain!
tomorrow morning demain matin
tomorrow night demain soir
the day after tomorrow après-demain

tongue noun
la **langue** *fem.*

🔑 **LANGUAGE**
Langue also means 'language' in French: you speak a language using your tongue.

tonight adverb
1 *(talking about the evening)* **ce soir**

• Use **le** and **un** for masculine words and **la** and **une** for feminine words.

Are you watching TV tonight? Tu regardes la télé ce soir?
2 (*talking about the night-time*) **cette nuit**

tonsillitis noun
une **angine** *fem.*
I've got tonsillitis. J'ai une angine.

too adverb
1 (*as well*) **aussi**
Me too! Moi aussi!
2 (*more than something*) **trop**
It's too late. Il est trop tard.
3 too much trop
There's too much sugar. Il y a trop de sucre.
4 too many trop
That's too many. C'est trop.
I have too many things to do. J'ai trop de choses à faire.

> **⚷ LANGUAGE**
> English = **too much** or **too many** + noun
> French = **trop de** + noun

tooth noun
la **dent** *fem.*
the tooth fairy la petite souris

> **🐾 CULTURE**
> When French children lose a tooth, they put it under their pillow at bedtime. In the morning, they find some money there instead. A little mouse (**petite souris**) comes to take the tooth away, instead of a tooth fairy.

toothache noun
I have a toothache. J'ai mal aux dents.

toothbrush noun
la **brosse à dents** *fem.*

toothpaste noun
le **dentifrice** *masc.*

top noun
1 (*of a mountain, hill, tree, etc.*) le **sommet** *masc.*
at the top of the mountain au sommet de la montagne

2 (*of a wall, page, swimsuit, etc.*) le **haut** *masc.*
at the top of the page en haut de la page
3 on top of sur
Don't put that on top of the computer! Ne mets pas ça sur l'ordinateur!

top adjective
1 (*shelf, drawer, etc.*) **du haut**
the top drawer le tiroir du haut
2 the top floor le dernier étage
3 to get top marks avoir la meilleure note

topic noun
le **sujet** *masc.*

torch noun
la **lampe de poche** *fem.*

torn adjective
déchiré *masc.*, **déchirée** *fem.*

tortoise noun
la **tortue** *fem.*

total noun
le **total** *masc.* (plural les **totaux**)

to **touch** verb
toucher
Don't touch my CDs! Ne touche pas à mes CD!

tough adjective
(*hard*) **dur** *masc.*, **dure** *fem.*

tour noun
1 (*of a town, museum, etc.*) la **visite** *fem.*
We went on a tour of the castle. On a fait la visite du château.
2 (*of a country*) le **voyage** *masc.*

tourist noun
le or la **touriste** *masc. & fem.*
the tourist office l'office du tourisme

towards preposition
vers

a
b
c
d
e
f
g
h
i
j
k
l
m
n
o
p
q
r
s
t
u
v
w
x
y
z

*❷ means use **être** to make the past tense.*

a
b
c
d
e
f
g
h
i
j
k
l
m
n
o
p
q
r
s
t
u
v
w
x
y
z

towel noun
la **serviette** *fem.*

tower noun
la **tour** *fem.*
a tower block une tour
the Eiffel Tower la tour Eiffel

town noun
la **ville** *fem.*
We're going into town. On va en ville.
the town centre le centre-ville

toy noun
le **jouet** *masc.*
a toy shop un magasin de jouets

⚷ **LANGUAGE**
Un jouet comes from the verb **jouer** (to play).

to **trace** verb
(*with tracing paper*) **décalquer**
Trace this picture! Décalquez ce dessin!
tracing paper le papier-calque

track noun
(*for races*) la **piste** *fem.*

tracksuit noun
le **survêtement** *masc.*

tractor noun
le **tracteur** *masc.*

traffic noun
la **circulation** *fem.*
There's too much traffic. Il y a trop de circulation.
a traffic jam un embouteillage
traffic lights les feux *masc. plural*

train noun
le **train** *masc.*
by train en train
the train to Edinburgh le train pour Édimbourg
a train set un train électrique

trainers plural noun
les **baskets** *fem. plural*
I like your trainers. J'aime bien tes baskets.

training noun
(*for football etc.*) l'**entraînement** *masc.*

tram noun
le **tramway** *masc.*

trampoline noun
le **trampoline** *masc.*

to **translate** verb
traduire
Can you translate this sentence into English? Tu sais traduire cette phrase en anglais?

translation noun
la **traduction** *fem.*

transport noun
public transport les transports en commun *masc. plural*

to **travel** verb
voyager
I like travelling. J'aime bien voyager.

travel noun
les **voyages** *masc. plural*
a travel agency une agence de voyages

treasure noun
le **trésor** *masc.*
treasure hunt le chasse au trésor

treat noun
(*food*) la **gâterie** *fem.*
Here's a little treat. Tiens, une petite gâterie.

tree noun
un **arbre** *masc.*

triangle noun
le **triangle** *masc.*

trick noun
le **tour** *masc.*

• *Languages, nationalities, and religions do not take a capital letter in French.*

to do a magic trick faire un tour de magie

to play a trick on somebody jouer un tour à quelqu'un

tricky adjective
(*difficult*) **difficile** *masc. & fem.*
That's a bit tricky! C'est un peu difficile!

Trinidad noun
l'**île de la Trinité** *fem.*

Trinidadian adjective
trinidadien *masc.*,
trinidadienne *fem.*

Trinidadian noun
le **Trinidadien** *masc.*,
la **Trinidadienne** *fem.*

trip noun
1 le **voyage** *masc.*
We're going on a trip to Spain.
Nous faisons un voyage en Espagne.
Have a good trip! Bon voyage!
2 (*short trip by bus etc.*) une **excursion** *fem.*
We went on a trip to the seaside.
On a fait une excursion au bord de la mer.

trolley noun
(*for shopping*) le **chariot** *masc.*

trouble noun
(*problems*) **les problèmes** *masc. plural*
We're having trouble with the computer. On a des problèmes avec l'ordinateur.

trousers plural noun
le **pantalon** *masc.*
I wear trousers in winter. Je porte un pantalon en hiver.
a pair of trousers un pantalon

> **LANGUAGE**
> English = **trousers** is plural
> French = **le pantalon** is singular

truck noun
le **camion** *masc.*
a truck driver un routier
He's a truck driver. Il est routier.

> **LANGUAGE**
> **Routier** comes from **la route**, which means 'the road'.

true adjective
vrai *masc.*, **vraie** *fem.*
a true story une histoire vraie
That's true. C'est vrai.
True or false? Vrai ou faux?

trumpet noun
la **trompette** *fem.*
Keith plays the trumpet. Keith joue de la trompette.

trunk noun
1 le **tronc** *masc.*
a tree trunk un tronc d'arbre
2 la **trompe** *fem.*
the elephant's trunk la trompe de l'éléphant

trunks plural noun
le **maillot de bain** *masc.*
Bring your swimming trunks.
Apporte ton maillot de bain.
a pair of trunks un maillot de bain

> **LANGUAGE**
> English = **trunks** is plural
> French = **le maillot** is singular

truth noun
la **vérité** *fem.*
It's the truth! C'est la vérité!

to **try** verb
1 **essayer**
Can I try this bike? Je peux essayer ce vélo?
I tried to turn on the computer. J'ai essayé d'allumer l'ordinateur.
Try again! Essaie encore!
2 (*to taste*) **goûter**

ⓔ means use **être** *to make the past tense.*

Try this, it's delicious! Goûte ça, c'est délicieux!

to **try on** verb
essayer
Try these trousers on! Essaie ce pantalon!

try noun
I'll have a try. Je vais essayer.

T-shirt noun
le **tee-shirt** masc.

tube noun
1 le **tube** masc.
a tube of toothpaste un tube de dentifrice
2 (underground) le **métro** masc.
Let's go by tube! Prenons le métro!

Tuesday noun
mardi masc.
It's Tuesday today. C'est mardi aujourd'hui.
on Tuesday mardi
Come on Tuesday! Viens mardi!
next Tuesday mardi prochain
last Tuesday mardi dernier
every Tuesday tous les mardis
on Tuesdays le mardi
It's not open on Tuesdays. Ce n'est pas ouvert le mardi.

tummy noun
le **ventre** masc.

tummy ache noun
I have a tummy ache. J'ai mal au ventre.

tuna noun
le **thon** masc.
a tuna sandwich un sandwich au thon

tune noun
l'**air** masc.
to sing a tune chanter un air

tunnel noun
le **tunnel** masc.
the Channel Tunnel le tunnel sous la Manche

Tunisia noun
la **Tunisie** fem.

turkey noun
1 (food) la **dinde** fem.
2 (the bird) le **dindon** masc.

Turkey noun
la **Turquie** fem.

Turkish adjective
turc masc., **turque** fem.

Turkish noun
(the language) le **turc**

turn noun
le **tour** masc.
Whose turn is it? C'est à qui le tour?
It's my turn. C'est mon tour.
Miss a turn! Passe un tour!
It's Adam's turn to sing. C'est à Adam de chanter.

to **turn** verb
tourner
Turn left! Tournez à gauche!

to **turn down** verb
(the heating, a radio, etc.) baisser
Turn down the sound! Baisse le son!

turning noun
le **virage** masc.
Take the next turning on the left. Prenez la prochaine rue à gauche.

to **turn into** verb
se changer ⊘ **en**
The prince turned into a frog! Le prince s'est changé en grenouille!

to **turn off** verb
(a TV, radio, computer, etc.) éteindre
Turn the light off! Éteins la lumière!

• *The months of the year and days of the week do not take a capital letter in French.*

to **turn on** verb
(*a light, radio, computer, etc.*) allumer
Turn the TV on! Allume la télé!

to **turn out** verb
(*a light, the gas*) **éteindre**

to **turn over** verb
(*a card, piece of paper, etc.*) retourner
Turn the card over! Retourne la
carte!

to **turn round** verb
se retourner ⊘
Everybody turned round. Tout le
monde s'est retourné.

to **turn up** verb
(*a TV, radio, etc.*) mettre plus fort
Can I turn the music up? Je peux
mettre la musique plus fort?

TV noun
la **télé** *fem.*
on TV à la télé
a TV set une télé

twelfth adjective
douzième *masc. & fem.*
on the twelfth floor au douzième
étage
the twelfth of January le douze
janvier

twelve number
douze
twelve children douze enfants
I'm twelve. J'ai douze ans.
We eat at twelve. Nous déjeunons
à midi.
On Saturdays I go to bed at twelve!
Le samedi, je me couche à minuit!

twentieth adjective
vingtième *masc. & fem.*
on the twentieth floor au
vingtième étage
the twentieth of July le vingt
juillet

twenty number
vingt

It's twenty past nine. Il est neuf
heures vingt.

twice adverb
deux fois
twice a week deux fois par
semaine

twin noun
le **jumeau** *masc.*, la **jumelle** *fem.*,
les **jumeaux** *masc. plural*,
les **jumelles** *fem. plural*
They're twins. Ils sont jumeaux.
identical twins de vrais jumeaux
my twin brother mon frère
jumeau
my twin sister ma sœur jumelle
twin beds les lits jumeaux

twinned adjective
jumelé *masc.*, jumelée *fem.*
Our town is twinned with Poitiers.
Notre ville est jumelée avec Poitiers.

to **twist** verb
tordre
I twisted my ankle. Je me suis
tordu la cheville.

two number
deux
two pizzas deux pizzas
The plane takes off at two. L'avion
décolle à deux heures.
Line up in twos! Rangez-vous deux
par deux!

type noun
le **type** *masc.*
What type of guitar is it? C'est quel
type de guitare?

tyre noun
le **pneu** *masc.*
to pump up the tyres gonfler les
pneus

⊘ *means use* **être** *to make the past tense.*

a
b
c
d
e
f
g
h
i
j
k
l
m
n
o
p
q
r
s
t
u
v
w
x
y
z

Uu

UFO noun
un **OVNI** *masc.*

🔑 **LANGUAGE**
OVNI = **objet volant non identifié**
matching the English 'unidentified flying
object'.

ugly adjective
laid *masc.*, **laide** *fem.*

UK noun
(= *United Kingdom*) le **Royaume-Uni**
masc.
I live in the UK. J'habite au
Royaume-Uni.

Ulster noun
l'**Irlande du Nord** *fem.*
I live in Ulster. J'habite en Irlande
du Nord.

umbrella noun
le **parapluie** *masc.*

umpire noun
(*in cricket, tennis*) un **arbitre** *masc.*

unbelievable adjective
incroyable *masc. & fem.*

uncle noun
un **oncle** *masc.*

uncomfortable adjective
(*chair, shoes, etc.*) **pas confortable**
masc. & fem.
This chair is uncomfortable. Cette
chaise n'est pas confortable.

under preposition
1 sous
under the table sous la table
2 (*less than*) **moins de**
**Children under twelve are not
allowed.** C'est interdit aux enfants
de moins de douze ans.
under twenty euros moins de
vingt euros

• *See the centre section for verb tables.*

underground noun
le **métro** *masc.*
to go by underground aller @ en
métro

underground adjective
souterrain *masc.*,
souterraine *fem.*
an underground car park un
parking souterrain

to **underline** verb
souligner

underneath preposition
sous
underneath the box sous la boîte

underneath adverb
en dessous
Have you looked underneath?
As-tu regardé en dessous?

to **understand** verb
comprendre
I don't understand. Je ne
comprends pas.
I don't understand that sentence.
Je ne comprends pas cette phrase.
Do you understand, Jo? Tu
comprends, Jo?
Do you understand, boys? Vous
comprenez, les garçons?
Did you understand everything?
Avez-vous tout compris?

underwear noun
les **sous-vêtements** *masc. plural*

to **undo** verb
défaire
to undo a knot défaire un nœud
Your laces are undone. Tes lacets
sont défaits.

to **undress** verb
se déshabiller @
to get undressed se déshabiller

a b c d e f g h i j k l m n o p q r s t u v w x y z

I'll get undressed in the bedroom. Je vais me déshabiller dans la chambre.

unemployed adjective
au chômage
My dad's unemployed. Mon père est au chômage.

unexpected adjective
inattendu masc., inattendue fem.

unfair adjective
injuste masc. & fem.
That's unfair! C'est injuste!

unfortunately adverb
malheureusement

unfriendly adjective
pas sympathique masc. & fem.
She's unfriendly. Elle n'est pas sympathique.

unhappy adjective
malheureux masc., malheureuse fem.
Claire is unhappy. Claire est malheureuse.

unhealthy adjective
mauvais pour la santé masc., mauvaise pour la santé fem.

uni noun
l'université fem.
at uni à l'université

uniform noun
un uniforme masc.
I wear a school uniform. Je porte un uniforme à l'école.

 CULTURE
In France schoolchildren don't wear uniforms.

Union Jack noun
the Union Jack le drapeau du Royaume-Uni masc.

United Kingdom noun
le Royaume-Uni masc.
I live in the United Kingdom. J'habite au Royaume-Uni.

United States plural noun
les États-Unis masc. plural
We're going to the United States. Nous allons aux États-Unis.

universe noun
l'univers masc.

university noun
l'université fem.
I want to go to university. Je veux aller à l'université.

unless conjunction
sauf si
We'll go out unless it rains. On va sortir sauf s'il pleut.

unlikely adjective
pas très probable

unlucky adjective
1 (talking about people)
to be unlucky ne pas avoir de chance
He's really unlucky. Il n'a vraiment pas de chance.
2 (talking about things or numbers)
to be unlucky porter malheur
The number thirteen is unlucky. Le numéro treize porte malheur.
an unlucky number un numéro qui porte malheur

to **unpack** verb
défaire ses valises
I've unpacked my case. J'ai défait ma valise.

unpleasant adjective
désagréable masc. & fem.

untidy adjective
(room or house) en désordre
My bedroom's untidy. Ma chambre est en désordre.

@ means use être to make the past tense.

a
b
c
d
e
f
g
h
i
j
k
l
m
n
o
p
q
r
s
t
u
v
w
x
y
z

a
b
c
d
e
f
g
h
i
j
k
l
m
n
o
p
q
r
s
t
u
v
w
x
y
z

to **untie** verb
défaire
to untie a knot défaire un nœud

until preposition
1 **jusqu'à**
until now jusqu'à maintenant
Wait until two o'clock! Attends jusqu'à deux heures!
2 **not until** pas avant
Not until your birthday! Pas avant ton anniversaire!

unusual adjective
peu commun *masc.*, **peu commune** *fem.*

to **unwrap** verb
(*presents etc.*) **ouvrir**

up adverb
en haut
Up there! Là-haut!

⚷ **LANGUAGE**
'Up' is most often translated as part of a verb such as 'to go up' (**monter**) or 'to tidy up' (**ranger**).

up preposition
1 **en haut de**
up the ladder en haut de l'échelle
2 **up to** jusqu'à
Count up to twenty! Comptez jusqu'à vingt!
up to now jusqu'à maintenant
3 **That's up to you.** Ça dépend de toi.
What are you up to? Qu'est-ce que tu fais?

upset adjective
1 (*sad*) **triste** *masc. & fem.*
2 (*angry*) **fâché** *masc.*, **fâchée** *fem.*
3 **to have an upset stomach** avoir l'estomac dérangé

to **upset** verb
faire de la peine
That's really upset me. Ça m'a vraiment fait de la peine.

upside down adjective
à l'envers
The picture is upside down. Le tableau est à l'envers.

upstairs adverb
en haut
I left my bag upstairs. J'ai laissé mon sac en haut.
Go upstairs! Monte!

up-to-date adjective
(*computer, camcorder, etc.*) **moderne** *masc. & fem.*

urgent adjective
urgent *masc.*, **urgente** *fem.*

us pronoun
1 (*after a verb*) **nous**
They know us. Ils nous connaissent.
Help us! Aidez-nous!
They've forgotten us. Ils nous ont oubliés.
2 (*to us*) **nous**
Tell us a story! Racontez-nous une histoire!
She's going to speak to us. Elle va nous parler.
3 (*after a preposition*) **nous**
with us avec nous

US, **USA** noun
les **USA** *masc. plural*
We're going to the US. On va aux USA.

to **use** verb
to use something utiliser quelque chose
I use a computer. J'utilise un ordinateur.
Can I use your rubber? Je peux utiliser ta gomme?
Do you want to use the toilet? Tu veux aller aux toilettes?
What's it used for? Ça sert à quoi?

• *Use* **le** *and* **un** *for masculine words and* **la** *and* **une** *for feminine words.*

use noun
 It's no use. Ça ne sert à rien.
 It's no use crying. Ça ne sert à rien de pleurer.

used adjective
 to be used to doing something avoir l'habitude de faire quelque chose
 I'm used to watching TV every evening. J'ai l'habitude de regarder la télé tous les soirs.
 I'm used to it. J'ai l'habitude.

useful adjective
 utile masc. & fem.
 That's useful. C'est utile.

useless adjective
 (really bad) **nul** masc., **nulle** fem.
 She's useless at karate! Elle est nulle en karaté!

usual adjective
 habituel masc., **habituelle** fem.
 at the usual time à l'heure habituelle
 as usual comme d'habitude

usually adverb
 d'habitude
 I usually get up at seven. D'habitude, je me lève à sept heures.

Vv

vacuum cleaner noun
 un **aspirateur** masc.

valentine card noun
 la **carte de la Saint-Valentin** fem.

Valentine's Day noun
 la **Saint-Valentin** fem.

valley noun
 la **vallée** fem.

valuable adjective
 de valeur
 a valuable watch une montre de valeur
 Is it valuable? Ça a de la valeur?

van noun
 la **camionnette** fem.

vanilla noun
 la **vanille** fem.
 a vanilla ice cream une glace à la vanille

to **vanish** verb
 disparaître
 He vanished. Il a disparu.

various adjective
 plusieurs masc. & fem. plural
 There are various answers. Il y a plusieurs réponses.

vase noun
 le **vase** masc.

vegetable noun
 le **légume** masc.
 vegetable soup la soupe aux légumes

vegetarian adjective
 végétarien masc., **végétarienne** fem.
 a vegetarian meal un repas végétarien

vegetarian noun
 le **végétarien** masc., la **végétarienne** fem.
 Emily is a vegetarian. Emily est végétarienne.

verb noun
 le **verbe** masc.

Ø means use être to make the past tense.

a
b
c
d
e
f
g
h
i
j
k
l
m
n
o
p
q
r
s
t
u
v
w
x
y
z

a
b
c
d
e
f
g
h
i
j
k
l
m
n
o
p
q
r
s
t
u
v
w
x
y
z

very adverb
très
very young très jeune
not very easily pas très facilement
very much beaucoup

vest noun
le **maillot de corps** masc.

vet noun
le or la **vétérinaire** masc. & fem.
My mum's a vet. Ma mère est
vétérinaire.

vicar noun
le **pasteur** masc.

victory noun
la **victoire** fem.

video noun
1 (film) la **vidéo** fem.
Shall we watch a video?
On regarde une vidéo?
on video en vidéo
a video game un jeu vidéo
2 (cassette) la **cassette vidéo** fem.
I've got the video in my bag. J'ai la
cassette dans mon sac.
3 (machine) le **magnétoscope** masc.
The video isn't working.
Le magnétoscope ne marche
pas.
a video recorder un magnétoscope
4 (music video) le **clip** masc.
their latest video leur dernier
clip

view noun
la **vue** fem.
What a lovely view! Quelle belle
vue!

village noun
le **village** masc.

vinegar noun
le **vinaigre** masc.

violent adjective
violent masc., **violente** fem.

violin noun
le **violon** masc.
I play the violin. Je joue du violon.

virus noun
le **virus** masc.
a computer virus un virus
informatique

visit noun
1 (to a person, museum, etc.) la **visite** fem.
I'm on a visit to my grandparents.
Je suis en visite chez mes
grands-parents.
2 (to a country) le **séjour** masc.
We went on a visit to France.
Nous avons fait un séjour en
France.

to **visit** verb
1 (a place) **visiter**
**We're going to visit the Eiffel
Tower.** Nous allons visiter la tour
Eiffel.
2 (a person) **rendre visite à**
I want to visit granny. Je veux
rendre visite à mamie.

visitor noun
un **invité** masc., une **invitée** fem.
We have visitors. Nous avons des
invités.

vitamin noun
la **vitamine** fem.

vocabulary noun
le **vocabulaire** masc.

voice noun
la **voix** fem.

volcano noun
le **volcan** masc.

volleyball noun
le **volley-ball** masc.
I play volleyball. Je joue au
volley-ball.

• Languages, nationalities, and religions do not take a capital letter in French.

volume noun
le **volume** *masc.*
Turn down the volume! Baisse le volume!

volunteer noun
le or la **volontaire** *masc. & fem.*

Ww

waist noun
la **taille** *fem.*

to **wait** verb
attendre
Wait a minute! Attends une minute!
I'll wait for you downstairs. Je t'attends en bas.
Wait for the bus here, children! Attendez le bus ici, les enfants!
a waiting room une salle d'attente

waiter noun
le **serveur** *masc.*

> **LANGUAGE**
> To call a waiter in a cafe or restaurant, say **monsieur!** or **s'il vous plaît!**

waitress noun
la **serveuse** *fem.*

> **LANGUAGE**
> To call a waitress in a cafe or restaurant, say **mademoiselle!** or **madame!** or **s'il vous plaît!**

to **wake up** verb
1 **se réveiller** ⊘
Wake up! Réveille-toi!
I wake up at six. Je me réveille à six heures.
2 **réveiller**
Wake me up at nine. Réveille-moi à neuf heures.

⊘ *means use être to make the past tense.*

to **vote** verb
voter

voucher noun
a gift voucher un chèque-cadeau *masc.* (plural les **chèques-cadeaux**)

vowel noun
la **voyelle** *fem.*

Wales noun
le **pays de Galles** *masc.*
Cardiff is in Wales. Cardiff est au pays de Galles.
the prince of Wales le prince de Galles

walk noun
la **promenade** *fem.*
We're going for a walk in the park. On va faire une promenade dans le parc.
to take the dog for a walk promener le chien

to **walk** verb
1 **marcher**
You're walking too slowly. Tu marches trop lentement.
2 (*on foot, not by bike or car or bus*) **aller** ⊘ **à pied**
I walk to school. Je vais à l'école à pied.
We walk two kilometres every day. Nous faisons deux kilomètres à pied tous les jours.

walking noun
la **marche à pied** *fem.*
My brother loves walking. Mon frère adore la marche à pied.

walkman® noun
le **walkman®** *masc.*

wall noun
le **mur** *masc.*

wallet noun
le **portefeuille** *masc.*

wallpaper noun
le **papier peint** *masc.*

> **⚷ LANGUAGE**
> Word for word, **papier peint** means 'painted paper'.

wand noun
la **baguette** *fem.*
a magic wand une baguette magique

to **want** verb
vouloir
I want some orange juice. Je veux du jus d'orange.
Amy doesn't want any ice cream. Amy ne veut pas de glace.
Do you want to watch TV, dad? Tu veux regarder la télé, papa?
What do you want to do, children? Qu'est-ce que vous voulez faire, les enfants?

war noun
la **guerre** *fem.*

wardrobe noun
une **armoire** *fem.*

warm adjective
1 **chaud** *masc.*, **chaude** *fem.*
warm water l'eau chaude
warm clothes des vêtements chauds
The weather is very warm. Il fait très chaud.
It's warm. Il fait chaud.
I'm warm. J'ai chaud.

> **⚷ LANGUAGE**
> English = to be warm **I'm warm.**
> French = avoir chaud **J'ai chaud.**

to **warn** verb
prévenir
I'm warning you! Je te préviens!

was verb SEE **be**
I was tired. J'étais fatigué. (*boy speaking*) J'étais fatiguée. (*girl speaking*)
She was happy. Elle était heureuse.

to **wash** verb
1 (*clothes, floor, car, etc.*) **laver**
Have you washed the vegetables? As-tu lavé les légumes?
2 (*yourself*) **se laver**
I'm washing my hands. Je me lave les mains.
She's washing her face. Elle se lave le visage.
Are you washing your hair? Est-ce que tu te laves les cheveux?
Have you washed today? Est-ce que tu t'es lavé aujourd'hui?
3 **to wash the dishes** faire la vaisselle

washbasin noun
le **lavabo** *masc.*

washing noun
1 (*clothes*) le **linge** *masc.*
the dirty washing le linge sale
2 **to do the washing** faire la lessive
a washing machine une machine à laver
washing powder la lessive

washing-up noun
la **vaisselle** *fem.*
to do the washing-up faire la vaisselle

to **wash up** verb
faire la vaisselle
I don't like washing up. Je n'aime pas faire la vaisselle.

wasp noun
la **guêpe** *fem.*

waste noun
a waste of time une perte de temps

wastepaper basket noun
la **corbeille à papiers** *fem.*

• *The months of the year and days of the week do not take a capital letter in French.*

watch noun
la **montre** *fem.*
Do you have a watch? Est-ce que tu as une montre?

to **watch** verb
(*to look at*) **regarder**
We're watching TV. Nous regardons la télé.

to **watch out** verb
faire attention
Watch out, children! Faites attention, les enfants!

water noun
l'**eau** *fem.*
Do you want some water? Tu veux de l'eau?
a glass of water un verre d'eau

wave noun
la **vague** *fem.*
a big wave une grosse vague

to **wave** verb
1 (*with your hand*) **faire un signe de la main**
Alex waved to me. Alex m'a fait un signe de la main.
2 (*arms, flag, etc.*) **agiter**
She's waving a flag. Elle agite un drapeau.

wavy adjective
to have wavy hair avoir les cheveux ondulés

way noun
1 (*to a place*) le **chemin** *masc.*
Ask the way! Demande le chemin!
I asked the way to the station. J'ai demandé le chemin pour aller à la gare.
Can you tell us the way to the Eiffel Tower? Pour aller à la tour Eiffel, s'il vous plaît?
on the way en route
It's a long way to Paris. Paris est loin.
You're in my way! Tu m'empêches de passer!

the way in l'entrée *fem.*
the way out la sortie *fem.*
2 (*direction*)
Is this the right way? C'est la bonne direction?
Which way is it? C'est par où?
this way par ici
that way par là
3 (*a way of doing something*) la **façon** *fem.*
This is the only way to do it. C'est la seule façon de le faire.
Open it this way. Ouvre-le comme ça.
You're doing it the wrong way. Ce n'est pas comme ça qu'on fait.

we pronoun
1 **nous**
We're late. Nous sommes en retard.
2 **on**
Shall we play football? On joue au foot?

LANGUAGE
'We' is normally translated by **nous**, but in everyday language most children use **on**.

weak adjective
faible *masc. & fem.*

weapon noun
une **arme** *fem.*

to **wear** verb
1 (*to have on*) **porter**
I wear glasses. Je porte des lunettes.
2 (*to put on*) **mettre**
What shall I wear? Qu'est-ce que je vais mettre?

weather noun
1 le **temps** *masc.*
What's the weather like? Quel temps fait-il?
The weather's nice. Il fait beau.
The weather's awful. Il fait un temps affreux.
2 **the weather forecast** la météo *fem.*

a b c d e f g h i j k l m n o p q r s t u v w x y z

*ⓔ means use **être** to make the past tense.*

a
b
c
d
e
f
g
h
i
j
k
l
m
n
o
p
q
r
s
t
u
v
w
x
y
z

What's the weather forecast?
Que dit la météo?

web noun
1 la **toile** fem.
a spider's web une toile d'araignée
2 (the Internet) le **web** masc.
a web page une page web

website noun
le **site web** masc.
Did you go to their website? Tu as
visité leur site web?

wedding noun
le **mariage** masc.
a wedding anniversary un
anniversaire de mariage

Wednesday noun
mercredi masc.
It's Wednesday today. C'est
mercredi aujourd'hui.
on Wednesday mercredi
I'm leaving on Wednesday. Je pars
mercredi.
on Wednesdays le mercredi
I visit my aunt on Wednesdays. Je
rends visite à ma tante le mercredi.
last Wednesday mercredi dernier
next Wednesday mercredi
prochain
every Wednesday tous les
mercredis

weed noun
la **mauvaise herbe** fem.

🔑 **LANGUAGE**
Word for word **la mauvaise herbe** means
'bad grass'.

week noun
la **semaine** fem.
at the beginning of the week au
début de la semaine
at the end of the week à la fin de la
semaine
this week cette semaine
last week la semaine dernière
next week la semaine prochaine
every week toutes les semaines

• See the centre section for verb tables.

in two weeks' time dans deux
semaines

weekday noun
on weekdays en semaine

weekend noun
le **week-end** masc.
Come to my house at the weekend!
Viens chez moi ce week-end!
At the weekend I stay at home.
Le week-end, je reste chez moi.
this weekend ce week-end
last weekend le week-end dernier
next weekend le week-end
prochain

to **weigh** verb
peser
I weigh thirty-five kilos. Je pèse
trente-cinq kilos.

welcome exclamation
bienvenue!
Welcome to Liverpool! Bienvenue
à Liverpool!

welcome adjective
bienvenu masc., **bienvenue** fem.
Children are welcome. Les enfants
sont les bienvenus.
Thank you! – You're welcome!
Merci! – De rien!

well adverb
1 **bien**
You dance well. Tu danses bien.
It's well cooked. C'est bien cuit.
Well done! Bravo!
2 **as well** aussi
Are you coming as well? Tu viens
aussi?

well adjective
(in good health)
to be well aller ⊘ bien
I'm not very well. Je ne vais pas
très bien.
Get well soon! Remets-toi vite!

well exclamation
eh bien
Well, it's true! Eh bien, c'est vrai!

well-behaved adjective
sage masc. & fem.

wellingtons plural noun
les **bottes en caoutchouc** fem.
plural

well-known adjective
célèbre masc. & fem.

🔑 **LANGUAGE**
Célèbre is like the English word 'celebrity'
(a well-known person).

Welsh adjective
gallois masc., **galloise** fem.
He's Welsh. Il est gallois.
She's Welsh. Elle est galloise.

Welsh noun
1 (language) le **gallois** masc.
I speak Welsh. Je parle gallois.
2 the Welsh les Gallois masc. plural

Welshman noun
le **Gallois** masc.

Welshwoman noun
la **Galloise** fem.

went verb SEE **go**

were verb SEE **be**
We were at home. On était chez
nous.
You were my friend. Tu étais mon
ami.
You were my friends. Vous étiez
mes amis.
They were sad. Ils étaient tristes.

west noun
l'**ouest** masc.
in the west dans l'ouest
to the west of Oxford à l'ouest
d'Oxford

west adjective
ouest masc. & fem.
the west coast la côte ouest

western noun
le **western** masc.

ⓔ means use être to make the past tense.

West Indian adjective
antillais masc., **antillaise** fem.

West Indian noun
un **Antillais** masc.,
une **Antillaise** fem.

West Indies plural noun
les **Antilles** fem. plural

wet adjective
1 **mouillé** masc., **mouillée** fem.
The towel is wet. La serviette est
mouillée.
to get wet se mouiller ⓔ
2 (rainy)
It's wet today. Il pleut
aujourd'hui.

whale noun
la **baleine** fem.

what pronoun
1 **qu'est-ce que**
What is it? Qu'est-ce que c'est?
What do you want? Qu'est-ce que
tu veux?
What have you done, children?
Qu'est-ce vous avez fait, les
enfants?
What's the matter? Qu'est-ce qu'il
y a?

🔑 **LANGUAGE**
Use qu'est-ce qu' before a vowel.

2 **qu'est-ce qui**
What's happening? Qu'est-ce qui
se passe?
3 **quoi**
What are you talking about?
De quoi tu parles?
What? (when you didn't hear)
Comment?
What for? (why) Pourquoi?
What about me? Et moi alors?
4 **ce que**, **ce qui**
Tell me what you've got! Dis-moi
ce que tu as!
Tell me what happened. Dis-moi
ce qui c'est passé.

a b c d e f g h i j k l m n o p q r s t u v w x y z

429

a
b
c
d
e
f
g
h
i
j
k
l
m
n
o
p
q
r
s
t
u
v
w
x
y
z

what adjective
1 **quel** *masc.*,
quelle *fem.*, **quels** *masc. plural*,
quelles *fem. plural*
What day is it today? Quel jour
sommes-nous?
What time is it? Quelle heure
est-il?
What's your address? Quelle est
ton adresse?
What's the French for 'computer'?
Comment dit-on 'computer' en
français?
2 (*in exclamations*)
What luck! Quelle chance!
What a pity! Quel dommage!

wheel noun
la **roue** *fem.*

wheelchair noun
le **fauteuil roulant** *masc.*

LANGUAGE
Word for word, **le fauteuil roulant**
means 'rolling armchair'.

when adverb
quand
When are you leaving? Tu pars
quand?

where adverb
où
Where are you? Où es-tu?
Tell me where it is! Dis-moi où
c'est!

whether adverb
si
**I don't know whether she wants to
play.** Je ne sais pas si elle veut
jouer.

LANGUAGE
si = s' before il or ils

which adjective
1 **quel** *masc.*,
quelle *fem.*, **quels** *masc. plural*,
quelles *fem. plural*

Which house is it? C'est quelle
maison?
Which book have you chosen?
Tu as choisi quel livre?
2 **which one?** lequel? *masc.*,
laquelle? *fem.*
**I have two CDs. Which one do you
want?** J'ai deux CD. Lequel tu
veux?
which ones? lesquels? *masc. plural*,
lesquelles? *fem. plural*
**Do you like the photos? Which
ones do you want?** Tu aimes les
photos? Lesquelles tu veux?

which pronoun
1 **qui**
the knife which is on the table
le couteau qui est sur la table
2 **que**
the pen which I lent you le stylo
que je t'ai prêté

while conjunction
pendant que
**I'm staying here while dad goes
shopping.** Je reste ici pendant que
papa fait les courses.

whiskers plural noun
les **moustaches** *fem. plural*

to **whisper** verb
chuchoter

whistle noun
le **sifflet** *masc.*
The referee has blown his whistle.
L'arbitre a sifflé.

to **whistle** verb
siffler

white adjective
blanc *masc.*, **blanche** *fem.*
a white dress une robe blanche
a white coffee un café au lait

white noun
le **blanc** *masc.*
I prefer white. Je préfère le blanc.

• Use **le** and **un** for masculine words and **la** and **une** for feminine words.

whiteboard noun
le **tableau blanc** masc.
on the whiteboard au tableau

who pronoun
qui
Who's that? Qui est-ce?, Qui c'est?
Who wants to come? Qui veut
venir?
my uncle who lives in York mon
oncle qui habite à York

whole adjective
tout masc., **toute** fem.
the whole village tout le village
the whole class toute la classe
the whole world le monde entier

whose pronoun
à qui
Whose is it? C'est à qui?
Whose exercise book is this? À qui
est ce cahier?

why adverb
pourquoi
Why did you do that? Pourquoi tu
as fait ça?
Why is he tired? Pourquoi il est
fatigué?
Why not? Pourquoi pas?

wicked adjective
1 (evil) **méchant** masc.,
méchante fem.
a wicked boy un garçon méchant
2 (very good) **génial** masc.,
géniale fem., **géniaux** masc. plural,
géniales fem. plural
Wicked! Génial!

wide adjective
large masc. & fem.
Our road is very wide. Notre rue
est très large.
wide awake complètement
réveillé

wife noun
la **femme** fem.

wild adjective
sauvage masc. & fem.
wild animals les animaux
sauvages

will verb
1 (for talking about the future) **I will do it
soon.** Je vais le faire bientôt.
She'll be back in five minutes.
Elle va revenir dans cinq minutes.
I will be in France next week.
Je serai en France la semaine
prochaine.
2 (when asking or telling what you want)
vouloir
Will you have a Coke®? Tu veux un
coca?
Will you listen to me, children!
Voulez-vous m'écouter, les enfants!
She won't help me. Elle ne veut
pas m'aider.

to **win** verb
gagner
I've won. J'ai gagné.
Who won? Qui a gagné?

wind noun
le **vent** masc.

window noun
la **fenêtre** fem.

windy adjective
It's windy. Il y a du vent.

wine noun
le **vin** masc.
a bottle of wine une bouteille de
vin
red wine le vin rouge
white wine le vin blanc

wing noun
une **aile** fem.

winner noun
le **gagnant** masc.,
la **gagnante** fem.

winter noun
l'**hiver** masc.
in the winter en hiver

a
b
c
d
e
f
g
h
i
j
k
l
m
n
o
p
q
r
s
t
u
v
w
x
y
z

② means use **être** to make the past tense.

wintertime noun
l'**hiver** *masc.*
in the wintertime en hiver

to **wipe** verb
essuyer

wise adjective
sage *masc. & fem.*

wish noun
le **vœu** *masc.* (plural les **vœux**)
to make a wish faire un vœu
Best wishes! Meilleurs vœux!

to **wish** verb
1 **souhaiter**
I wish you a happy birthday. Je te
souhaite un joyeux anniversaire.
2 **I wish that ...!** si seulement ...!
I wish I had a bike! Si seulement
j'avais un vélo!

witch noun
la **sorcière** *fem.*

with preposition
1 **avec**
Can I come with you? Je peux venir
avec toi?
2 (*at somebody's house*) **chez**
I'm staying the night with Ben.
Je vais passer la nuit chez Ben.

without preposition
sans
Don't go without me! Ne pars pas
sans moi!
without a jacket sans veste
without looking sans regarder

wizard noun
le **sorcier** *masc.*

wolf noun
le **loup** *masc.*

woman noun
la **femme** *fem.*
men and women les hommes et les
femmes

to **wonder** verb
se demander ⊘
I wonder why she's not coming.
Je me demande pourquoi elle ne
vient pas.

wonderful adjective
merveilleux *masc.*,
merveilleuse *fem.*

wood noun
1 le **bois** *masc.*
It's made of wood. C'est en bois.
2 (*little forest*)
the woods les bois *masc. plural*

wooden adjective
en bois
a wooden chair une chaise en bois

wool noun
la **laine** *fem.*

word noun
1 le **mot** *masc.*
What does this word mean? Que
veut dire ce mot?
What's the French word for 'tired'?
Comment est-ce qu'on dit 'tired' en
français?
2 (*of a song*) **the words** les paroles *fem.*
plural
**I don't know the words of the
song.** Je ne connais pas les paroles
de la chanson.

work noun
le **travail** *masc.*
We have lots of work. On a
beaucoup de travail.
She's at work. Elle est au travail.

to **work** verb
1 **travailler**
He works in a factory. Il travaille
dans une usine.
2 (*talking about machines, TVs, radios, etc.*)
marcher
My watch isn't working.
Ma montre ne marche pas.

• *Languages, nationalities, and religions do not take a capital letter in French.*

432

worker noun
1 (*in a factory etc.*) un **ouvrier** *masc.*, une **ouvrière** *fem.*
2 **an office worker** un employé de bureau *masc.*, une employée de bureau *fem.*

to **work out** verb
(*to calculate*) calculer
Can you work out how much it is? Tu peux calculer combien ça fait?

worksheet noun
la **feuille d'exercices** *fem.*

world noun
le **monde** *masc.*
the whole world le monde entier
to travel all over the world voyager dans le monde entier

worried adjective
inquiet *masc.*, **inquiète** *fem.*
Mum's very worried. Maman est très inquiète.

to **worry** verb
s'inquiéter
Don't worry! Ne t'inquiète pas!

worse adjective
pire *masc. & fem.*
It's worse than last time. C'est pire que la dernière fois.

worse adverb
moins bien, **plus mal**
I feel worse. Je me sens plus mal.

worst adjective
plus mauvais *masc.*, **plus mauvaise** *fem.*
the worst book of all le plus mauvais livre de tous
my worst mark ma plus mauvaise note

worst noun
le or la **pire** *masc. & fem.*
He's the worst. C'est lui le pire.

worth adjective
It's worth a lot of money. Ça vaut beaucoup d'argent.

would verb
1 (*when asking for something*)
I would like ... Je voudrais ...
I'd like a glass of water. Je voudrais un verre d'eau.
I would like to go to bed. Je voudrais me coucher.
2 (*in questions*)
Would you like ...? Vous voulez ...?, Tu veux ...?
What would you like? Qu'est-ce que tu veux?
3 (*when telling somebody politely*)
Would you wait here, please? Pouvez-vous attendre ici, s'il vous plaît?

to **wrap** verb
envelopper
The sandwiches are wrapped in paper. Les sandwichs sont enveloppés dans du papier.
wrapping paper du papier cadeau

wrist noun
le **poignet** *masc.*

to **write** verb
écrire
Write your name! Écris ton nom!
I'm writing a letter to my penfriend! J'écris une lettre à mon correspondant!

to **write back** verb
répondre
Write back soon! Réponds-moi vite!

to **write down** verb
noter
Write down the date. Notez la date.

a b c d e f g h i j k l m n o p q r s t u v **w** x y z

➍ *means use* **être** *to make the past tense.*

writer noun
un **écrivain** masc.

writing noun
une **écriture** fem.
You have nice writing. Tu as une belle écriture.
a writing pad un bloc-notes (plural les **blocs-notes**)

wrong adjective
1 (not correct) **mauvais** masc., **mauvaise** fem.
the wrong answer la mauvaise réponse
2 (number, calculation, etc.) **faux** masc., **fausse** fem.

Xx

Xmas noun SEE **Christmas**
Noël masc.

X-ray noun
la **radio** fem.
I need to have an X-ray. Je dois passer une radio.

Yy

yacht noun
le **voilier** masc.

yard noun
It's a few yards away. C'est à quelques mètres de là.

CULTURE
French measurements are in metres and centimetres; a yard is about 90 centimetres.

That's wrong! C'est faux!
3 (talking about people) **to be wrong**
se tromper @
You're wrong, Samir. Tu te trompes, Samir.
4 **What's wrong?** Qu'est-ce qu'il y a?
What's wrong with you? Qu'est-ce que tu as?
There's something wrong with the TV. La télé ne marche pas bien.

wrong adverb
(not correctly) **mal**
You're pronouncing it wrong, Emma. Tu le prononces mal, Emma.

to **X-ray** verb
(somebody's arm, lungs, etc.) **faire une radio de**
They've X-rayed my knee. Ils ont fait une radio de mon genou.

xylophone noun
le **xylophone** masc.
Angela plays the xylophone. Angela joue du xylophone.

to **yawn** verb
bâiller

year noun
1 une **année** fem.
this year cette année
last year l'année dernière
next year l'année prochaine
Happy New Year! Bonne année!
2 un **an** masc.
I'm eleven years old J'ai onze ans.
the New Year le nouvel an

• *The months of the year and days of the week do not take a capital letter in French.*

434

3 (*in primary schools*)
I'm in Year 4. Je suis au CE2.
He's in Year 5. Il est au CM1.
She's in Year 6. Elle est au CM2.

CULTURE
L'école primaire is for children between 6 and 11; **le CP** (**cours préparatoire**) for children from 6 to 7; **le CE1** and **le CE2** (**cours élémentaire**) for ages 7 to 9; **le CM1** and **le CM2** (**cours moyen**) for ages 9 to 11.

yellow adjective
jaune *masc. & fem.*
a yellow T-shirt un tee-shirt jaune

yellow noun
le **jaune** *masc.*
Yellow suits you. Le jaune te va bien.

yes adverb
oui
Are you hungry? – Yes! Tu as faim? – Oui!

yesterday adverb
hier
She came back yesterday. Elle est revenue hier.
yesterday morning hier matin
yesterday evening hier soir
the day before yesterday avant-hier

yet adverb
1 not yet pas encore
I haven't seen him yet. Je ne l'ai pas encore vu.
2 (*not translated in questions*)
Are you ready yet? Tu es prêt?

yoga noun
le **yoga** *masc.*
to do yoga faire du yoga

yoghurt noun
le **yaourt** *masc.*
a plain yoghurt un yaourt nature

yolk noun
le **jaune d'œuf** *masc.*

you pronoun

🔑 **LANGUAGE**
Use **tu**, **te**, and **toi** when you're talking to one person you know well, such as a friend or someone in your family, or someone of your own age or younger. Use **vous** to talk to more than one person (such as two friends). Use **vous** also to be polite to a grown-up who is not a family member.

1 (*to a friend, a relative*) **tu**
You're late. Tu es en retard.
Where are you going? Où est-ce que tu vas?
2 (*after a verb*) **te**
I can't see you Je ne te vois pas.
I'll phone you tomorrow. Je vais t'appeler demain.
Can I speak to you? Est-ce que je peux te parler?

🔑 **LANGUAGE**
te = t' before a vowel sound

3 (*after a preposition etc.*) **toi**
with you avec toi
I'm younger than you. Je suis plus jeune que toi.
Is that you, mum? C'est toi, maman?
4 (*talking to several people or using the polite form*) **vous**
Have you finished, girls? Avez-vous fini, les filles?
Could you tell me the way to the station? Vous pouvez me dire comment aller à la gare?
I have something to say to you. J'ai quelque chose à vous dire.
with you avec vous
I sing better than all of you. Je chante mieux que vous tous.
5 (*when 'you' means 'people'*) **on**
Can you get to Glasgow by bus? Est-ce qu'on peut aller à Glasgow en autobus?

*❷ means use **être** to make the past tense.*

a b c d e f g h i j k l m n o p q r s t u v w x **y** z

a
b
c
d
e
f
g
h
i
j
k
l
m
n
o
p
q
r
s
t
u
v
w
x
y
z

young adjective
jeune *masc. & fem.*
I'm too young. Je suis trop jeune.
a young man un jeune homme
a young woman une jeune femme
young people les jeunes *masc. plural*

younger adjective
plus jeune *masc. & fem.*
I'm younger than you. Je suis plus jeune que toi.
Shana is a year younger than me. Shana a un an de moins que moi.

youngest adjective
le or la **plus jeune** *masc. & fem.*
the youngest girl in the class la fille la plus jeune de la classe

youngest noun
le or la **plus jeune** *masc. & fem.*
Ross is the youngest in the class. Ross est le plus jeune de la classe.

your adjective
1 (*when talking to somebody you call tu: before a masculine noun*) **ton**
your bike ton vélo
2 (*when talking to somebody you call tu: before a feminine noun*) **ta**
your house ta maison
3 (*when talking to somebody you call tu: before a plural noun*) **tes**
your parents tes parents

> 🔑 **LANGUAGE**
> Use **ton** instead of **ta** for a feminine noun starting with *a, e, i, o, u*, or *silent h*, for example **ton idée**.

4 (*when talking to people you call vous: before a singular noun*) **votre**
Mark and Tom, here's your new teacher! Mark et Tom, voici votre nouveau prof!
Is your house far away, sir? Votre maison est loin, monsieur?

• *See the centre section for verb tables.*

5 (*when talking to people you call vous: before a plural noun*) **vos**
Put your books away, children! Rangez vos livres, les enfants!

yours pronoun
1 (*when talking to people you call tu*) **à toi**
It's yours, Yasmin. C'est à toi, Yasmin.
2 (*when talking to people you call vous*) **à vous**
Are these bags yours, boys? Ces cartables sont à vous, les garçons?

yourself pronoun
1 (*when talking to somebody you call tu*) **toi-même**
Can you do it yourself, Jack? Tu peux le faire toi-même, Jack?
2 (*when talking to somebody you call tu*) **te**
Are you enjoying yourself? Tu t'amuses bien?
3 by yourself tout seul *masc.*, toute seule *fem.*
Do you go out by yourself, Marie? Tu sors toute seule, Marie?
4 (*when talking to somebody you call vous*) **vous-même**
You told me yourself, Mrs Grant. Vous me l'avez dit vous-même, Madame Grant.
5 vous
Have you hurt yourself, Miss? Vous vous êtes fait mal, mademoiselle?

yourselves pronoun
1 vous-mêmes
Can you do it yourselves? Vous pouvez le faire vous-mêmes?
2 vous
Are you enjoying yourselves? Vous vous amusez bien?
3 by yourselves tout seuls *masc. plural*, toutes seules *fem. plural*

youth hostel noun
une **auberge de jeunesse** *fem.*

Zz

zebra noun
le **zèbre** *masc.*
zebra crossing le passage pour
piétons

zero noun
le **zéro** *masc.*

zip noun
la **fermeture éclair**® *fem.*

My zip is stuck. Ma fermeture est
coincée.

zoo noun
le **zoo** *masc.*
We're going to the zoo. On va au
zoo.

a
b
c
d
e
f
g
h
i
j
k
l
m
n
o
p
q
r
s
t
u
v
w
x
y
z

*ℯ means use **être** to make the past tense.*

Oxford Children's Dictionaries
Think Dictionaries. Think Oxford.
www.oup.com